ENCLOSURE

Enclosure
A Trappist Tale

Jerry Buzyniski

Copyright © 2011 by Jerry Buzyniski.

Library of Congress Control Number:		2011917475
ISBN:	Hardcover	978-1-4653-7213-0
	Softcover	978-1-4653-7212-3
	Ebook	978-1-4653-7214-7

All rights reserved. No part of this book may be reproduced or transmitted in any form or by any means, electronic or mechanical, including photocopying, recording, or by any information storage and retrieval system, without permission in writing from the copyright owner.

This is a work of fiction. Names, characters, places and incidents either are the product of the author's imagination or are used fictitiously, and any resemblance to any actual persons, living or dead, events, or locales is entirely coincidental.

This book was printed in the United States of America.

To order additional copies of this book, contact:
Xlibris Corporation
1-888-795-4274
www.Xlibris.com
Orders@Xlibris.com

Contents

Chapter One	The Observer	9
Chapter Two	Transgressions	32
Chapter Three	Murmurs	44
Chapter Four	Duplicity	51
Chapter Five	Sibling Symmetry	67
Chapter Six	Etched Trauma	82
Chapter Seven	Recovery	92
Chapter Eight	The Retreat	100
Chapter Nine	The Meeting	179
Chapter Ten	Seeds of Discontent	197
Chapter Eleven	The Foot	225
Chapter Twelve	The Confession	243
Chapter Thirteen	The Red Baron	252
Chapter Fourteen	Joshua's Intervention	266
Chapter Fifteen	The Moreland Mesa	278
Chapter Sixteen	Father Gerald's Disclosure	300
Chapter Seventeen	The Proving Ground	308
Chapter Eighteen	Emerging Symptoms	316
Chapter Nineteen	Vacation by Raft	328

Chapter Twenty	The Mountie	373
Chapter Twenty-One	Shrink Time	382
Chapter Twenty-Two	Another Loss	387
Chapter Twenty-Three	Talk Therapy	390
Chapter Twenty-Four	Another Christmas Eve	403
Chapter Twenty-Five	The Breakthrough	416
Chapter Twenty-Six	Disintegration	419
Chapter Twenty-Seven	An Unexpected Exit	435
Chapter Twenty-Eight	The Return	454
Chapter Twenty-Nine	Imminent Decompensation	471
Chapter Thirty	Halsen Encore	493
Chapter Thirty-One	A Changed Moral Viewpoint	550
Chapter Thirty-Two	Adirondack Farewells	581
Chapter Thirty-Three	Only Atheists Go to Heaven	601
Chapter Thirty-Four	A Proper Prodigal Welcome	609
Chapter Thirty-Five	The Third Man	618
Chapter Thirty-Six	Presenting with Symptoms	626
Chapter Thirty-Seven	Unexpected Assault	645
Chapter Thirty-Eight	The Cleansing	655
Chapter Thirty-Nine	Hell Materialized	660
Chapter Forty	Matthew's Return and Resolution	663

Epilogue...675

Chapter One

The Observer

Father Martin's head was cleaved nearly in half when the benign-looking clump of sandstone fell from the canyon, crashed through the windshield of the truck, and exploded out the rear window. There was no time to scream, to dodge, or to know what had just happened. It was simply an accident yet a sobering introduction for Andrew to monastic life at St. Anthony's—a life that began with the unexpected funeral of an encouraging mentor, whom he was just beginning to know.

Still quite naïve at the age of twenty-four, Andrew came to the monastery reasonably humbled, ready to experience an ascetic lifestyle and eager to be spiritually mended. Often conflicted and, at times, distracted, he welcomed the rigorous schedule—rising early for vigils, the 3:00 a.m. prayers, and meditating for hours in the cold stone church, with his robe pulled warmly around him and his hood obscuring his face. Solitude became a healing refuge, allowing him to breathe freely and slowly in the sandalwood-scented chapel. He was soon aware that he had found a new home—an environment filled with adventure, mystery, and a sense of spiritual awe. Life, as he once knew it, seemed to be upside down; success and the accumulation of material goods were cast to the wind, along with excessive ego. It was, he discovered, a newfound sense of freedom.

* * *

Grey September skies, heavy with threatening clouds, erased the mountain peaks and filtered a translucent haze on the landscape. The alpine land was ringed with foothills, which then gave way to a jagged spinal column of mountains. The monastery sat silently in the center, a sprawling complex of stone and brick arches with worn ceramic floors and heavy oak doors that led to wide staircases and long echoing cloisters.

The refectory, with its vaulted ceiling, contained heavy wooden tables, set end to end, in a row of six; the opposite wall was similarly configured so that the monks faced each other across the room when eating. Near the main entrance, a brick staircase led to a reader's pulpit, which overlooked the entire refectory. From that elevated vantage point, assigned monks would read spiritual literature while the rest of the community ate in silence.

On this particular day, Andrew had been asked to read from a book about St. Bernard. It was acceptable for the reader to leave his work chores one-half hour early to have an opportunity to preread the passages and feel comfortable with pronunciation. The words of St. Bernard were clear and meaningful and offered Andrew silent affirmation of his decision to be a monk. Bernard spoke eloquently of humility, voluntary poverty, and obedience to an abbot, all within the framework of silence. He also spoke of the necessity of fasting, vigils, manual labor and charity, and the need to progress and persevere daily until death inevitably released the soul.

The wood-burning stove in the refectory crackled and hissed, comfortably warming the raised pulpit area. Andrew looked away from the book through the expanse of windows to the distant peaks. Autumn had drained all colors with a faded sepia wash, while the few leaves that remained on the aspens seemed afraid to let go as they danced out of step in the strong breeze. Just as he was about to continue with his silent reading, he heard the door below him open with a groan and then close. When he looked down, he saw Brother Adrian, the monastery's principal chef, stop at the first table and slowly survey the room. He was unable to see Andrew, high in the reader's pulpit, and seemed satisfied that he was alone. Unexpectedly, Brother Adrian lifted his robe slightly, climbed onto the bench, and then stood on top of the first table. Very quickly, he skipped its entire length, hopped lightly to the next, and continued across all six tables to the other end of the room. He then carefully jumped down, made an awkward bow to an imaginary audience, and disappeared into the kitchen. Bewildered, Andrew smiled, quietly closed the book (remembering to replace the worn brass bookmark), and returned to his cell.

Once inside, he closed the door and sat on his bed, surveying his small private world, an eight-feet-by-ten-feet room, large enough for a small desk, a twin bed, and a squat three-shelf bookcase. The fairly spacious closet contained an upper shelf where Andrew had placed some of his personal clothing, including underwear and socks. The entire outer wall consisted of a sliding glass door, complete with a screen, and a heavy drape for privacy. Andrew noticed the mattress, a standard six-inch-thick dormitory item, and remembered thinking that he might be sleeping on a straw pad, an ascetic notion he was happy to forgo.

The view through the glass door allowed him to see a large part of the monastery's garth, an uncluttered garden area surrounded on three sides by arched cloisters, where Japanese laceleaf maples and several spruce trees coexisted in quiet harmony. In the distance, the mountain ridge cut into the horizon with connected peaks of jagged slate against a pewter sky. Andrew got up from his bed and glanced at the worn surface of the desk that was illuminated by an old gooseneck lamp. He ran his fingers through the dust and wondered who may have used this chair, this desk, this bed, this cell before. Was he still a monk? Did he leave the monastery? The thoughts snowballed through his brain, and he soon found himself smiling. He thought of *Goldilocks and the Three Bears:* Who has been sleeping in my bed?

* * *

Each day, after the morning mass, the monks gathered in the library to wait for Father Luke and learn of their work assignments. It was an awkward time as some of the monks would go off by themselves to read or slowly scan the bookshelves for an interesting title, doing so with tilted heads and, in their habits, resembling curious penguins.

Father Luke, the prior, was second in command at the monastery, one step short of being abbot. He was responsible for daily work assignments and a litany of administrative tasks. Andrew had no idea of what was involved in running a monastery and found it difficult to imagine budgets, profits and deficits, and other fiscal matters relating to a spiritual environment. Nevertheless, he realized that, somehow, there must be bills, and they had to be paid. He noticed that Father Luke would, at times, appear to be exhausted; his smile was less evident, and his eyes appeared dull, yet he continued to project a warm gentleness, regardless of his enormous responsibilities.

Andrew settled in one of the more comfortable fabric chairs, knowing if he closed his eyes, he would probably fall asleep. Brother Mark and Brother Scott were leaning against one of the mahogany tables, with arms folded and vacuous stares, a typical monastic still life. Andrew decided to remove his habit, an arbitrary task, to help him stay awake. He stood up, untied the cloth cincture, and placed it on the chair. Next, he slid the oyster-colored scapular over his head and draped it over the table. All that remained was the floor-length Nehru-collared robe. With a third of it pulled over his head, Andrew gazed up through the opening to see Brother Mark staring at him, rigid and wide-eyed.

"What are you doing?" Brother Mark asked. His whispered attempt at silence resulted in aspirated astonishment, which caused all of the monks to focus on Andrew, who looked like the headless horseman.

"I'm removing my habit," he said quietly and slowly pulled the rest of the robe over his head.

Brother Mark looked relieved yet flustered. "I wasn't sure if you were wearing jeans underneath, and I thought . . ." Brother Mark smiled as he left the sentence unfinished.

Andrew watched as Brother Mark's face flushed slightly.

"Oh, I know," Andrew ventured. "You were thinking I was St. Francis and that I had suddenly decided to strip myself of all my worldly possessions."

Their laughter was barely controlled as they walked in different directions in an attempt to regain composure.

* * *

Andrew was assigned to help Brother Mark irrigate the Cutter fields, an area named after the previous owner of the property who still had a few relatives in the valley. In silence, he followed the monks out of the library, through the dimly lit cloister to the top of the stairwell that led to the basement. He was suddenly aware of a strong smell of garlic, herbs, and tomatoes being cooked; and a smile briefly crossed his face. He knew that Brother Adrian was making his signature spaghetti sauce.

A flurry of insects erupted before them and flew away with a soft crackling sound as Andrew walked with Brother Mark through the knee-high grass, a sign of remaining life, he thought, prior to the inevitable snowfall. Andrew hesitated to initiate a conversation, even though it was acceptable during work hours, as long as the discussion was more than just idle chatter. He respected Brother Mark as a sincere and seasoned monk who, although only in his early thirties, was already solemnly professed and had been a member of the community for ten years.

"How are you finding the life so far?" Brother Mark asked in his usual soft voice.

Andrew's delayed response was tenuous. "It's sort of difficult . . . yet beautiful and, at times, sometimes sad." He quickly wondered if his reply was too honest or, at least, too personal.

Brother Mark continued walking in silence and then suddenly stopped and smiled. "If you don't mind me saying, you sound very much like a veteran monk. It's an answer that I might have given after being here all these years, yet you've been here for only one month."

Andrew smiled and felt relieved. He looked at Brother Mark and felt unexpected warmth spread quickly through his body and color his face and ears more deeply than the chill of the mountain air.

Two red-tailed hawks, riding the updrafts, circled slowly over the ridge. Their whistling screech pierced the air, causing both monks to look skyward.

Brother Mark squinted his eyes. "I have to say, there are times when I wonder why I do this," he said pensively.

"You mean you don't know?" The question shot out of Andrew's mouth before he had time to think.

Brother Mark seemed to take it in stride. "Well, I do and I don't. I know what all the books say, but that doesn't necessarily make it any easier."

"Then, how have you managed to stay here this long?" Andrew asked.

Brother Mark smiled broadly, revealing small unblemished teeth. "With trust in the Lord and a good sense of humor."

Andrew smiled. "Yeah, you're probably right."

"Well, judging from your comment in the library, it sounds as though it's a quality you're not lacking, and believe me, that's good. It will make your transition easier."

A pale light reflected off the irrigation ditch as the small canvas dam was removed, allowing the water to surge down the dry channel to other parts of the field. The canvas, along with three rocks that held the dam in place, was carried approximately fifty feet where Brother Mark and Andrew constructed another dam. Once the canvas was set and secured by the heavy rocks, they used their shovels to make small cutouts in the low side of the ditch, which let the water flow out, across the parched hillside.

"It's such an amazing system," Andrew said, leaning slightly on his shovel. "I never knew how flood irrigation worked, that the water comes from so far away and is picked up by the lower ditches and used again."

"Wait until you see the main gates that divert the water from Empire Creek, just below Greystone Mountain. It's quite impressive." Brother Mark was pointing toward the water's source, a bald peak, appearing only two dimensional in the fading light. "We'll probably go up there soon to shut down the system before the snow comes in."

"I'd like to see that," Andrew said.

From the fields, the roofs and spires of the monastery resembled a small lonely village with curls of smoke rising like incense in the windless dusk. Here and there, lights barely illuminated the arched cloisters and refectory windows as Brother Mark and Andrew began their walk back to the monastery.

Andrew smiled. "Before I entered, I wondered if monks wore their robes while working and thought how cumbersome that would be."

"Sort of like playing soccer in a dress," Brother Mark said with a laugh.

Andrew too laughed heartily and realized that Brother Mark's healthy sense of humor seemed to cement a bond of friendship between them, yet he felt a compelling need to know more.

"Do you mind if I ask you something personal . . . like, why you decided to enter the monastery?"

There was a short silence. Brother Mark grinned from ear to ear. "Couldn't get any women!" he said.

Again, their laughter echoed off the surrounding mountains as deer, feeding in the shadows, jerked upright and remained stationary.

"Being here is really important to me, but there is just so much that I'm unsure of," Andrew said, somewhat solemnly. He looked away.

"Hey, that's to be expected," Brother Mark said.

"Speaking of women . . ." Andrew paused, quickly drew a breath, and continued. "How do you do it? I mean, seriously, I came here with the realization that I would lead a celibate life, but I don't know how much longer I can go on without . . ." He stopped and shrugged his shoulders.

"Without masturbating?" Brother Mark asked bluntly.

"You got it," Andrew admitted. "It's on my mind more than ever, and I keep thinking, this is what it must take to enter the kingdom of heaven, but it's wrecking my prayer life and God only knows what it's doing to my prostate."

Attempting to imitate Groucho Marx, Brother Mark raised and lowered his eyebrows while pretending to smoke a cigar and said, "Look, kid. There are some things you gotta do or you'll pop your buttons. Now, I can't tell you what to do, but what I do is—I do it—sometimes twice!"

Andrew grew wide-eyed. "You serious?"

Brother Mark, still in the Groucho mode, said, "Yes, you bet your life."

Andrew exhaled slowly. "Well, I think you just *saved* my life."

* * *

Because of the lengthy distance from his home, Andrew was given special consideration to remain at the monastery for an extended stay rather than involuntarily depart after the usual one-month visit. As a postulant, he was about to receive his full habit at the formal clothing ceremony where he had to prostrate himself before the abbot in the presence of the entire monastic community.

Father Jude began. "Brother Andrew, what do you ask?"

Andrew responded clearly to the cold floor. He feared that he might forget his practiced answer. "The mercy of God and of the Order." Heat from his breath briefly condensed and evaporated from the tiles.

Father Jude continued. "Are you willing to accept the burdens?"

"Yes, Reverend Father, with the help of God's grace and the assistance of your prayers."

Father Jude then asked Andrew to be seated. He proceeded to talk graciously about Andrew's qualities and, finally, welcomed him into the community amid abundant applause.

Andrew could feel the heat in his face, as the excitement of acceptance became a reality for him. Monks who were more familiar with him offered short encouraging remarks. When there was a sufficient pause, Andrew knew that he had to express his thanks to his brothers for their consent. "Thanks," he said, "to all of you who spoke in my favor, and for those who remained silent, I'd like to extend extra special thanks for keeping this very appreciated ceremony as short as possible!"

Loud, hiccupping laughter from Brother Adrian boomed above the rest.

Andrew closed the door to his cell and removed his habit. Sitting at his desk, he picked up a worn book he had been reading, *The Way of a Pilgrim*, and reread the following: "Sit silently in your cell and it will teach you everything." The room was quite cold. 'Perhaps,' he thought, 'this cell is telling me to climb under my blankets to stay warm.' He removed his shoes and pulled the heavy covers up to his neck. As his eyes grew heavy, Andrew read a final sentence before falling soundly asleep: "Save and help your servant. Take this desire of mine as a cry of love, which you have commanded."

* * *

The sound of the monastery bell, clanging away at a firehouse pace, caused Andrew to bolt upright. He immediately thought he had missed Vespers, the evening service; however, his alarm clock showed that it was only 5:00 p.m., and Vespers did not begin until seven. He quickly put on his shoes and walked through the cloister where he saw Brother Matthew, a fellow postulant, tugging firmly on the thick bell rope.

"What's going on?" Andrew whispered.

Brother Matthew looked pale and continued to pull on the rope. "Father Martin is dead." The quiver in his voice was obvious.

Andrew drew a sharp breath and continued walking toward the refectory where he saw Brother Mark speaking with Father Luke.

"Excuse me, Father Luke, but is it true about Father Martin?" Andrew asked.

Father Luke was visibly shaken. "Yes," he said, softly.

Brother Mark spoke quietly to Andrew. "We'll be meeting in the Community Room in twenty minutes to talk about the circumstances. In the meantime, please keep him in your prayers."

Andrew immediately went into the chapel where several of his brothers were already praying. It was strange, he realized, to be kneeling in the vanishing light without wearing his habit; he felt naked and more vulnerable to the cold. The tabernacle candle's golden flame cast flickering geometric patterns high on the wooden ceiling. Andrew closed his eyes to concentrate and pray for Father Martin; he remembered him as he was—a simple prayerful man, in his early fifties, with a good sense of humor, who smiled easily and made Andrew feel very welcomed in the community. It was not long before he sensed a familiar tightness in his throat as his eyes blurred with tears.

With most of the monks gathered in the Community Room, Father Luke cleared his throat and addressed his audience. "You may have already heard the tragic news of Father Martin's death. It was a sudden accident on the interstate. Fortunately, the two companions with whom he was traveling were not badly injured. I expect that we will be receiving his body from the funeral home within two days. It is a tremendous loss, unexpected . . . and very, very sad, even though I am sure that Father Martin is now home and at peace."

His hand trembled slightly as he blessed the monks, and then he quickly exited the room.

Somberly, Andrew returned to his cell.

* * *

His alarm clock beeped progressively louder until Andrew found its green glow and pushed down on the snooze button. It was just after 2:00 a.m. when he suddenly realized that it was his turn to light both woodstoves so that his brothers would have a warm room for vigils, the 3:00 a.m. prayer service, and a warm refectory for breakfast.

On his way to the washroom, Andrew noticed Brother Mark near the end of the cloister.

When Andrew approached, Brother Mark looked up and motioned for him to enter the library.

"I still can't believe he's dead," Brother Mark whispered, as he leaned against a bookshelf. "All this talk about Father Martin being at peace is fine, but the loss is tough to deal with."

Andrew remained silent, surprised at seeing Brother Mark's pain and his willingness to disclose it. He rubbed his eyes with the thumb and middle finger of one hand, a habit he often resorted to when feeling unsettled. "Does anyone know what happened?"

Brother Mark flinched. "Apparently, a large rock fell from the canyon, came through the windshield of the truck, and severed the back of his head."

Andrew gasped and felt his stomach tighten; it was more than he needed to hear.

Brother Mark continued. "The two priests he was with were only slightly injured, but were hospitalized for shock. They said the rock fell from one of the canyons on Rt. 60. At first, they thought it was only a clump of dirt until it crashed through the windshield on the passenger side and continued through the rear window. Somehow, they were able to control the truck and stop it on the grassy median."

At 2:00 a.m. on an empty stomach, Andrew blanched and felt as though he might vomit. "I'm really sorry this happened," Brother Andrew said abruptly. He left the library as quickly as possible and walked toward the small entrance room. The cloister air against his face cooled his sweaty forehead. In the darkness, he was barely able to discern a hooded black figure gliding toward him on a collision course. Andrew quickly stepped to the right, hugging the cloister wall, as Brother Cyril, an elder member of the community, brushed past—all two hundred and fifty pounds of him—in silence.

The woodstove in the entrance room was Andrew's favorite. Lapis blue porcelain embossed with raised woodland grouse and a bare Maple tree decorated both sides, with a variety of Dutch hex designs for the air vents. Even the stovepipe, ascending through the ceiling, was the same lapis porcelain. It was a quick-starting efficient source of heat, which could easily heat the room to an uncomfortable temperature, if allowed too much air.

Andrew twisted three pages of the Wall Street Journal and placed them inside. On top of the paper, he scattered five pieces of thin kindling, followed by three chunks of firewood, which had been properly cut to fit into the stove. He opened the vents and, after three tries, he managed to strike a match and set the paper on fire. He quickly closed the door, and the interior ignited with a whoosh. Peering through the vents, Andrew saw that the firewood had caught. He adjusted the vents, hurried back into the cloister and walked toward the refectory to repeat the process on the old black stove in the corner.

When he opened the door to the refectory, Andrew immediately smelled the fresh brewed coffee that Brother Adrian made each morning in the large urn. It was difficult to concentrate on lighting the stove; he could think only of the coffee and the feel of the double-handled ceramic mug. When he was sure that the wood had caught fire, Andrew rushed into the kitchen.

Brother Adrian was barely visible behind the counter. He appeared to be whispering to the floor, bent over and pouring milk, when Andrew realized he was feeding the monastery's cat, Buddha, a large Calico who clearly had not missed many meals. Brother Adrian stood up and smiled at Andrew.

Andrew returned the smile and then crouched to rub Buddha's head. Buddha paused and stretched her neck, turning her head to the right and then slowly to the left, until her head nearly pivoted in a circle, as she looked at Andrew with obvious pleasure.

He quickly poured himself a mug of coffee. Seeing his reflection on the dark liquid surface, he was reminded of his admitted caffeine addiction, trying to live as a monk, but wondering if he could ever make it through the morning without his daily fix—'some monk,' he thought.

Brother Adrian had already gathered supplies for the noonday meal, which was almost always a surprise and almost always delicious. With limited selections as vegetarians, Brother Adrian learned over the years to be creative and earned solid respect for his innovative culinary skills, which included his famous pizza, French bread, and delicious sauces and casseroles. But Andrew dreaded his "boiled birdseed with minced carrots," otherwise known as millet. He looked at his watch and realized it was time for vigils.

The hooded monks filed, one by one, into the comfortably warm and dimly lit room. Andrew began to recognize them individually in the darkness by the sound of their gait and other idiosyncrasies. Brother Adrian wore the same squeaky oxfords and had a slight limp; Father Cyril stomped; Father Robert always smelled of garlic.

As the wind began to strengthen, small branches scraped against the windowpanes with a nails-on-chalkboard pitch. A single yelp in the distance soon turned into a chorus of howling coyotes, sending shivers up Andrew's spine. Candles flickered, as though on cue, and soon, the room seemed to chill. Andrew's meditation became a montage of unrelated stills. He saw Father Martin, frozen in terror, as the back of his head exploded through the window of the truck; Sara lay naked, half smiling, with both hands pressed firmly against her inner thighs; Nick, outlined by the ocean sun, stood above him, shaking his wet head, after being tossed by the waves at Surfside. Andrew tried to concentrate on his breathing, which had quickened considerably. 'Just let them go,' he thought, 'let them go,' yet Sara drifted back, close-up this time, her face contorted in pleasure. Nick also returned, sleeping soundly, his naked body barely covered in twisted sheets. Father Martin slumped in the truck, drenched in blood.

Andrew barely managed to hear the last reading of the service. Together, the community rose and bowed deeply. Several monks chose to leave while others continued with their meditation. Aware of his erection, Andrew settled back in his chair and gazed out the window into the empty darkness.

* * *

Working alone in the bright midmorning sun, Andrew heard the crunching of gravel as the hearse slowly made its way toward the monastery from the main road. The grey Mercedes motored effortlessly, scattering stones, ignoring potholes, and looking strangely appropriate within an elegant landscape of aspen-lined roads and buildings of distinguished architecture. Andrew thought of its contents—the corpse—and immediately began to hum to distract himself from his earlier thoughts while meditating during vigils. In the monastery's private cemetery, Brother Cyril had already begun to dig the grave with the old yellow backhoe.

The hearse continued through the monastic enclosure and stopped at the service entrance. Two men, not much older than Andrew, got out and walked to the back of the vehicle. Both wore black pants and colorful sweaters, attire that surprised Andrew. They slid Father Martin's body, which was covered with a white shroud, onto a gurney and then wheeled him inside.

Andrew was willingly distracted by the distant drone of exhaust fans that maintained the proper temperature for ten thousand hens in the eggery. He viewed the eggery as the "testing ground" for unwary Observers, or newcomers; a pit of stench and disease, intentionally designed to weed out the "faint of heart" from those with "true vocations."

Experiencing it for the first time, Andrew remembered saying to Brother Mark, "Why didn't I choose a place that makes fruitcakes?" The ammonia smell from the poultry urine burned Andrew's eyes; the excrement that collected in the troughs under the cages was infinitely more offensive than his high school locker room after a football game. And the dense dust of chicken dander diminished the glow of the tin-shaded bulbs; he wondered whether he should continue to breathe. Collectively, the effect was overwhelming.

The heat from thousands of hens required several large fans to exhaust the inner air and maintain the correct temperature to prevent the birds from dying. Andrew felt the stifling warmth contribute to his anxiety as perspiration beaded on his forehead.

"Even on the coldest days, the hens maintain their own heat," Brother Mark said. "Neither house has a heat source."

Andrew did not appear to be impressed. He looked at Brother Mark. "How healthy is this place?"

Brother Mark smiled. "It's a good question. When we're in here collecting the eggs, we all wear dust masks to reduce breathing in the fine particles floating around in the air. It also helps with the smell a bit."

Looking closely at the putrid dung heap under one row of suspended cages, Andrew thought he saw something moving. As he drew closer for a better view, he could see a mound of maggots, pulsating like a bowl of animated rice.

He wheeled quickly. "Let's get out of here," he gasped. "I can't breathe."

Once outside, Andrew inhaled the fresh mountain air, which quickly chilled his sweaty forehead.

Brother Mark tried to offer him some comfort by sharing his own thoughts. "I guess I felt the same about this place when I first saw it," he said. "It's an ungodly mix of shit and disease, but it gets easier as you get used to it."

Andrew wrinkled his nose. "How is that possible . . .," he said.

The sound of the door closing on the hearse startled Andrew out of his daydream. The two undertakers waved to someone inside the service entrance and then drove off toward the main road. Andrew slowly waved back at the departing hearse. The sun was nearly directly overhead when he looked at his watch; he realized it was time to return to the monastery to wash for lunch and prepare for the reading.

He descended the outside stairs to a small room filled with outerwear and foul weather gear where hip-length rubber irrigation boots, some still caked with mud, filled the far corner. It reminded Andrew of a Salvation Army store with worn and unwanted clothing, yet a plaid hunting jacket caught his eye. He lifted it from the hanger and was surprised by the quality and condition of the coat. The stitched label read Lord & Taylor.

The far door led into the main shower and toilet area where a row of six toilets were separated by six-feet-high walls of glazed ceramic blocks. Each stall was equipped with an exhaust fan and a cloth privacy curtain.

Andrew routinely chose the third toilet, closed the curtain and sat down; out of habit, he turned on the fan. He noticed that the tips of his work boots stuck out past the bottom of the curtain, so he quickly drew them back. He casually grabbed a handful of toilet paper to wipe two drops of clear fluid from the front edge of the seat.

Five tiled showers sat in back of the toilets, each with its own dressing area and double white curtains. Country club showerheads dispersed generous quantities of hot water, depending on the amount of heat absorbed that day by the solar panels and the amount of water already used.

Opposite the showers, a row of ten sinks, with mirrors above each, lined the rear wall. Andrew washed his hands with the small bar of soap, which he had heard was collected from the local motels, after being used by their guests and then donated to the monastery. The thought of it made him uncomfortable.

Perched in the reader's pulpit, high above the refectory, Andrew was prepared for the reading; he waited for the monks to get settled before beginning. Looking down, he observed the community—a room filled with young, old, hairy, bald, and definitely hungry men. Homemade vegetable soup rapidly disappeared along with grilled cheese and tomato sandwiches and the recommended glass of wine. Reading from 1 Corinthians 13, Andrew continued with the following:

> "When I was a child, I used to speak as a child, think as a child, reason as a child; when I became a man, I did away with childish things. For now we see in a mirror dimly, but then face to face; now I know in part, but then I shall now fully just as I also have been fully known."

Andrew paused at that point as lunch was nearly over. He saw Father Jude look up at him as a signal that he was about to ring the prayer bell for thanksgiving.

The entire community helped with the cleanup of the kitchen. Most often, Father Jude would wash the dishes in the large stainless steel sink while the others would dry dishes, put away food, and do miscellaneous chores—all completed in silence, with occasional monastic sign language and gestures as needed. Andrew was progressively learning what was expected from him during this cleanup, which became easier as he grasped the familiar. When the work was completed, most of the monks returned to their cells for the customary noonday nap.

Alone in the kitchen, wiping the countertops, Andrew suddenly heard a hissing sound. He looked up to see Brother Adrian gesturing from the pantry. He left his sponge on the counter and approached Brother Adrian, who motioned for him to enter the long narrow room. Once they were inside, Brother Adrian quickly shut the wooden door.

"I know that we are not supposed to be talking, but I don't think Jesus would mind," he said. He smiled broadly, displaying gaps and teeth in need of attention, yet Andrew felt it was a look congruent with Adrian's asceticism.

"How are you doing?" Brother Adrian asked.

Andrew smiled. "I guess I'm doing all right, thanks."

Brother Adrian climbed up a small wooden ladder, reached behind several juice cans, and brought forth a thin rectangular box, which Andrew immediately recognized as chocolates. Brother Adrian removed the cover and offered them to Andrew.

"Is it okay to eat these?" Andrew asked innocently, knowing fully that Brother Adrian's offer was sincere.

"Well, I don't think Jesus would mind; he might even have some with us."

Andrew enjoyed chocolates, particularly the dark ones, and he wasted no time finding a raspberry cream.

Brother Adrian did not discriminate; he arbitrarily grabbed three and ate them all at once.

He moved closer to Andrew and whispered, "Father Martin is in the chapel. Have you ever seen a dead body?" His wide-eyed stare bordered on the theatrical.

Andrew might have been offended if he had not been aware of Brother Adrian's nearly childlike qualities.

"I have, actually," Andrew said. "My uncle died of a heart attack two years ago—very unexpectedly."

Brother Adrian frowned in disbelief. "How old was he?"

"He was only forty-two," Andrew explained.

"Much too young to die," Brother Adrian said.

After a pause, Brother Adrian took four more chocolates and shoved the box toward Andrew, who willingly ate another.

"Would you like me to go with you to view Father Martin's body?" Brother Adrian asked.

Andrew smiled. "Yes, I'd like that," he said softly, "and thank you for the chocolates."

"What chocolates?" Brother Adrian asked sarcastically.

The cloister was silent except for the squeak of Brother Adrian's oxfords. Timid sunlight cast vague shadows over the brick and tile floors while gently illuminating a large pot of multicolored nasturtiums, which scented the air like perfume. Andrew was reminded of the Sunday mass and the chapel, redolent with cologne, candle wax, and incense that lingered long after the guests had left.

And suddenly, there it was—Father Martin's body, lying on a draped frame, dressed in the traditional black-and-white habit. Andrew felt a slight shiver; he had forgotten that monks were buried without coffins, and Father Martin appeared excessively exposed. He thought about the accident and hesitated to raise his eyes past Father Martin's folded hands, which were clutching jellybean-sized black rosary beads. Timidly, his eyes reached Father Martin's chin, and as Andrew relaxed his squint, his intentionally blurred vision cleared. The face was colorless, perhaps grey, yet intact. Father Martin's hood was pulled over his forehead and gathered close to his face so that Andrew could see nothing beyond the cheekbones. An unexpected look of serenity on Father Martin's face softened Andrew's apprehension.

Brother Adrian knelt in silent prayer, with closed eyes, while Andrew knelt beside him. He decided that the Lord's Prayer would help him focus on Father Martin's death, his absence from the community, and his new journey beyond the monastic realm. Halfway through his third prayer, Andrew looked down again at Father Martin's peaceful yet unnaturally waxy face. Suddenly, he heard a sharp exhaling sound as Father Martin's lips parted slightly, and a thin white fluid began to ooze from the corner of his mouth.

Andrew heard himself moan as he jumped back, nearly knocking Brother Adrian to the floor.

"Oh my god!" he shouted. He ran out of the church into the safety of the open air.

Honeybees flew busily around several of the hummingbird feeders, crawling in and out of the red plastic openings that dispensed the sought after sugar water. Andrew watched as two female hummingbirds hovered effortlessly then darted quickly to an available opening. He knew that the male birds could not be far away since the females almost always arrived first to determine the safety of the area.

Hearing footsteps, Andrew turned to see Father Luke and Brother Adrian approaching.

"Andrew, I'm so sorry you had to see that." Father Luke opened his arms to hug him, a common gesture, which Andrew welcomed. They sat on the wooden benches near the feeders.

"I've called the funeral home," Father Luke explained. "They are coming up immediately."

"What the heck happened?" Andrew asked.

Father Luke smiled a half smile. "Apparently, the church is too warm and caused the special sealing wax on his lips to melt, allowing them to separate."

Andrew felt relieved but embarrassed. "I've never seen anything like that before," he said.

"No, I'm sure you haven't," Father Luke said, rubbing his hands together. "It's getting chilly out here. Why don't we all go back inside?"

Andrew nodded and followed Father Luke and Brother Adrian into the monastery.

* * *

The darkness came suddenly as the sun dropped behind the peaks. Andrew walked alone on the access road in the brisk air; he zipped up his old parka as far as it would go and pulled up his collar. Smoke from a neighbor's ranch rose, vaguely visible above the mesa, in a broken stream, bantered by a gentle breeze.

"What am I doing?" he said unexpectedly. He stopped walking, surprised to hear his own voice, as loneliness rushed over him like a black wave—a cork, bobbing helplessly in a murky sea, with no land in sight. Andrew suddenly succumbed to the consequences of his self-imposed exile. He realized fully that the word "monk" truly translated into "one who is alone" and, even though he was often surrounded by his brothers, the absence of another's physical touch, no matter how benign and loving, overwhelmed him. He felt his chest grow heavy; he could not breathe. He inhaled quickly and exhaled just as quickly, again, and again, and again until finally, light-headed, he slumped to the ground and lay there on his side.

Feeling someone shaking him, Andrew opened his eyes and looked up into Brother Matthew's face, which, even in the darkness, was wide-eyed with fear.

"Are you all right?" Brother Matthew asked.

Andrew continued to gaze at Brother Matthew. He said the first thing that came into his mind. "Tell me I'm in heaven and you're an angel."

Brother Matthew smiled and laughed. "Well, I'm no angel, but we still might be in heaven," he said.

Andrew sat up and brushed the dirt from his face. "You really think so?" he said.

Brother Matthew locked his eyes on Andrew and smiled. It was a look that Andrew seemed to recognize from the past.

Back on his feet, Andrew and Brother Matthew walked slowly toward the monastery.

"I wasn't too far behind you," Brother Matthew said. "Then I saw you fall to the ground like a sack of potatoes. What happened?"

Andrew hesitated. "I'm not sure," he said. "I felt as though I couldn't breathe and the next thing I felt was you shaking me. Maybe I'm not used to the vegetarian diet."

"Maybe you should get checked out at the infirmary," Brother Matthew suggested.

"Maybe . . . although I think I'm okay."

The gravel under their shoes crunched loudly in the darkness. Andrew surveyed the sky, which was filled with stars and a thin fingernail moon.

"So am I the only one who thinks that this is a lonely life?" Brother Matthew said suddenly.

Andrew shook his head. "Hardly," he said. "There are times when I really wonder if I can do this."

"Yeah, me too," Brother Matthew said. He glanced at Andrew.

Andrew quickly looked back at Brother Matthew. "If you don't mind, I have to tell you something. When I first saw you I thought, 'What is this guy doing here?'"

Matthew smiled. "I know; you don't have to say it," he admitted. "I look like the typical California surfer—twenty-something, dirty blond hair, with a head full of air."

Andrew laughed. "No, don't be so tough on yourself . . . but you got the look right."

Matthew's smile faded. He stopped walking and faced Andrew. "I wanted to talk with you before. I'm glad we finally had the chance."

"Me too," Andrew said. "I guess we'll have plenty of time from now on."

Matthew hugged Andrew with a powerful grip, which seemed to intensify with his breathing. Just when the embrace became almost painful, Brother Matthew released him and disappeared into the darkness.

* * *

The monastery bells reminded Andrew that he had ten minutes before the start of Compline, the last prayer service of the day. He hurried to his cell, hastily pulled his robe over his T-shirt and jeans and rushed to the Entrance room. Once inside, he bowed reverently toward the crucifix and found a vacant seat. He thought, 'We end as we begin . . . the candles, the incense, and the emptiness.' He closed his eyes; the solitude and deep breathing soothed his mind and relaxed him.

Father Paul, the primary cantor, stood and began singing. The community rose and responded in practiced, Gregorian chant, sung in English rather than Latin. Andrew often felt goose bumps during the singing, as if an internal chord had been struck. He sang easily and well, a quality that did not go unheeded by his elders.

The second reading was nearly completed when Andrew looked around the dimly lit room. Some of the monks stood with bowed heads; others looked straight ahead, yet Brother Matthew was obviously absent, an unusual occurrence for a novice. Just then, he heard the door groan open and shut. Brother Matthew entered, bowed, and found a seat almost directly opposite Andrew who immediately dropped his gaze to the floor.

During the final reading, Andrew slowly looked up and found Brother Matthew's familiar black sneakers. Andrew's gaze continued, up the torso to the chin, the nose, until both monks found themselves looking unabashedly at each other for what seemed to be an eternity. A smile emerged on Brother Matthew's face, and Andrew felt himself return the same.

After Compline, Andrew stood, bowed, and returned to his cell, which felt much colder than usual. He knew that the thermostat in Brother Edward's cell, the cell next to his, controlled the heat for three of the units.

Brother Edward was in his late fifties, yet Andrew felt that he was much older because of his haggard appearance—a scraggly grey beard with a pasty pallor to match. Andrew often watched in disbelief as Brother Edward consumed between ten and thirty vitamins and minerals with each meal, followed by additional supplements throughout the day. He wondered if the vitamins were killing him; however, Brother Edward was well trained in monastic asceticism, which, for him, included sleeping in a very cold room.

Andrew tapped quietly on the door to Brother Edward's cell, but when there was no answer, he boldly turned the doorknob, which opened readily; yet Brother Edward was not there. Andrew pushed the light switch, expecting the overhead light to go on; instead, a floodlight, sitting on the floor, illuminated a large icon of the Blessed Virgin, two feet by three feet, painted in gold and blue, with outstretched hands and a face radiant with compassion. Andrew was awed by the unexpected and moved by the beauty of the painting. After a slight pause, he found the thermostat and turned the dial to increase the heat to sixty-four degrees—'still fairly ascetic,' he thought. Facing the icon, Andrew bowed. "Forgive me," he said, in a barely audible whisper. He returned to his cell unseen.

Getting undressed, he heard the baffles in the heater stammer as they expanded with warmth. 'I'll have some heat tonight, at last,' he thought.

Comfortably tucked in, he reached behind him and found his copy of the New Testament. He closed his eyes, opened to an arbitrary page and, with his eyes still closed he ran his finger down the page and stopped. He saw that he was in Acts 20, and he read the following:

> "And there was a certain young man named Eutychus sitting on the windowsill sinking into a deep sleep; and as Paul kept on talking, he was overcome by sleep and fell down from the third floor and was picked up dead.
> But Paul went down and fell upon him and after embracing him he said, "Do not be troubled for his life is in him"

Andrew closed the book, turned off his light and listened to the Grand Silence—the particular time of night that followed Compline and ended in the morning with the celebration of the mass. It was a time of strict observance, when talking was prohibited, except for emergencies. Andrew often observed the elder monks communicating in monastic sign language like deaf mutes, hands flying, and faces full of expression, and thought, 'I need to learn a few words.'

With the silence, he thought he heard footsteps softly pass his cell and stop. They approached again and suddenly seemed to stop directly in front of his door. Andrew quickly turned and looked at the space between the bottom of the door and the carpet where he could see a definite shadow blocking the yellow glow of the corridor nightlights. He felt his breathing quicken and suddenly heard a barely audible tapping, three times, finger nails against varnish. 'Oh, no,' he thought. 'Somebody died.' He jumped out of bed in the dark and slowly opened the door.

Standing in the hall with his flaxen hair illuminated like gold was Brother Matthew. His face wore a serious expression; he was still wearing his habit.

"Can I talk with you for a second?" he whispered. "I know it's late."

He quickly glanced down at Andrew, who was wearing only shorts and a T-shirt.

"It's okay. Sure, come in." Andrew said quietly.

Brother Matthew entered the room, and Andrew closed the door. They faced each other in the darkness.

"I just wanted to say that I feel like a jerk about what happened outside this evening—that I may be misunderstood or . . . that you might not like me," Matthew stammered. "If I've offended you, I apologize."

"What a relief!" Andrew whispered.

"What do you mean?" Matthew asked, somewhat surprised.

"I thought you were going to tell me that I had a phone call and a relative had died."

Matthew smiled. There was a noticeable pause.

"Look," Andrew said. "I understand completely. The loneliness in this place is really difficult to deal with. I feel it all the time so you know you're not alone. Besides, I do like you, even if you do look like a light-headed surfer!"

Brother Matthew laughed nervously yet seemed relieved after Andrew's joking.

The door to Brother Edward's adjacent cell opened and closed, followed immediately by the staccato sounds of Brother Edward's flatulence, a sound familiar to Andrew.

"Reality check," Andrew said with a grin. "He does this every night."

Matthew smiled. "I guess I'd better go," he said.

"Yeah, before we get struck by lightning for violating the Grand Silence."

"Well, thanks," Matthew said. He turned, walked to the door and started to open it when Andrew quietly pushed the door shut.

"I think it's my turn," he said, as he reached out to hug Matthew in an effort of genuine friendship.

As soon as Matthew left, Andrew shut the door, placed his forehead against its cold surface and, momentarily, stood there with closed eyes.

Chapter Two

Transgressions

Friends and relatives of Father Martin filled the church for his funeral mass and burial where his body lay in front of the altar like an exhausted guest with lips carefully sealed. Andrew was one of six pallbearers responsible for the daunting task of carrying Father Martin out of the church, across the lawn and up to the monastery's private cemetery.

Once the mass ended, Andrew took his position near the middle of the body. He was pleased that he could not see Father Martin's face, just his polished black oxfords sticking up from the bottom of his robe. The crude rope handles attached to the wooden pall were thick and abrasive; Andrew was sure they were cutting into his hand, a welcomed pain which distracted him from the tears he felt washing down his face.

Andrew noticed that Brother Mark, the pallbearer opposite him, was crying openly, as were most of the guests they passed on the way out of the church.

Once outside, Andrew inhaled the crisp, morning air of a day incongruously bright and seemingly inappropriate for a funeral. Sparse thickets of golden aspens highlighted the otherwise barren surroundings, while an eggplant-colored Lear jet made its smooth descent to the Bitter Creek airport. The pallbearers approached the gravesite and carefully set the wooden pall onto thick leather straps, which would be used to lower Father Martin into the grave.

Following the final benediction, the six brothers commenced lowering the body, slowly, with the use of agricultural block and tackles. Standing at the grave's edge, Andrew watched as Father Martin descended almost to the bottom. It was only then that he fully realized there was no coffin to protect or separate his body from the elements.

Suddenly, one of the pulleys jammed, causing the body to twist and rock. Andrew watched as Father Martin rolled on his side, exposing a gaping area in the back of his head, which appeared to be stuffed with waxy gauze, as an audible gasp erupted from those close enough to witness the unfortunate indignity. The stuck pulley then freed itself and quickly dropped the raised corner level with the others. As if by request, the body rolled in the opposite direction and settled on its back. Andrew watched in disbelief—frozen to the spot—until Father Luke handed him a small shovel. He knew that he and the other pallbearers were to throw a symbolic shovel full of earth on the body. He saw Brother Mark reluctantly lob a small amount of dirt into the hole, which fell mostly on Father Martin's chest. Andrew watched the golf ball-size rocks bounced feebly off Father Martin's black scapular and robe. He angrily thrust his shovel deep into the loose soil, picked up a handful, and scattered it over Father Martin's oxfords. He then turned and walked quickly through the crowd toward the monastery.

Back in his cell, Andrew removed his habit and put on an old sweater and jacket; he felt the need to walk, think, and be alone. Before leaving, he grabbed a paperback from his desk and stuffed it into his pocket. He knew it would be better to go through the refectory and out the back door to avoid the guests who were invited to share food and refreshments after the funeral.

Brother Adrian had placed two large tables in the refectory, which were covered with pastries, cakes, rolls, and some fancy desserts that Andrew could not identify. At one end of the table, Andrew saw his favorite brownies, made with macadamia nuts—one of Brother Adrian's specialties. He lifted the plastic wrap and carefully selected the least obvious. Some of the food had been sent by guests and delivered earlier. Black forest cake, petit fours, and cream puffs would soon be devoured with perfect coffee and, for those who wished, cordials of B and B or sherry. Andrew finished the brownie before he was through the door.

The familiar sight of frolicking red-tail hawks made Andrew smile as he headed for his special place, which overlooked the monastery and much of the valley. Worn rock outcrops jutted from the hillside like crude seats, providing a panoramic view of the valley and the jagged mountain range beyond. Sagebrush grew easily and plentiful in the barren earth, protecting the site from observation and excessive wind. Andrew could see that only a few guests remained near the gravesite while the others had either gone inside or left.

As the sun began to dull, Andrew sat quietly, listening to the wind and looking at the distant peaks, which were constantly transformed by shadow and light. The sporadic muffled buzz of a chain saw in the distance gently prompted Andrew to focus on the present. He learned that mental drift appeared to be both a luxury and an adversary yet a mainstay of the vocation; meditation could easily be friend or foe.

Unexpectedly, Andrew heard the scurry of what sounded like a small animal coming directly toward him. Stopping just inches from his elbow, a weasel stared at him with frightened beady eyes, its nose twitching in the air and its fur bristling. As quickly as it approached, the creature suddenly bolted away. Andrew laughed out loud at the welcomed intrusion.

He settled back and opened his paperback to the tattered bookmark. It was one of Andrew's favorite books, *New Seeds of Contemplation*, by Thomas Merton. He underlined the following passage:

> "But in all that happens, my one desire and my one joy should be to know: here is the thing that God has willed for me. In this His love is found and, in accepting this, I can give back His love to Him and give myself with it to Him. For in giving Myself I shall find Him and He is life everlasting."

The distinct sound of the abbot's Peugeot caused Andrew to glance toward the monastery. The blue car circled out of the lot, around the building toward the main road and then stopped at a small pull-off where a large white sedan was parked. Andrew had not noticed the car earlier; however, he saw what appeared to be, a fairly young woman, get out of the car, fumble with the door locks and get into the Peugeot with the abbot. The car then continued toward the main road and out of sight.

"I thought I might find you here." Brother Mark's casual greeting startled Andrew as he jumped up to see his new intruder.

"Oh, it's you! I thought my recent visitor had returned with his big brother!" Andrew smiled and offered a hand to Brother Mark.

"I don't know about this," Brother Mark said. "You sound as though you've been in the sun too long. Is it safe to come up there?"

Andrew laughed. "Don't worry, it's just another of my mystical experiences with an errant weasel."

Brother Mark smiled his "yeah, right" grin and then settled on the stone outcrop. "I hope you don't mind me being here, but I knew that you were upset at the funeral, and when you left quickly and didn't return, I decided to go looking for you to see how you were doing."

Andrew rubbed his eyes with the thumb and middle finger of one hand. "Actually, I'm glad you're here. It's nice to have some company. It was sort of difficult for me to experience the burial, especially when it came time to shovel dirt on Father Martin."

"I know," Brother Mark said. "A symbolic gesture, yet it's very difficult when there isn't a coffin."

The sound of the backhoe's diesel engine drew their attention toward the gravesite where Brother Cyril continued the task of burying Father Martin. Andrew looked away. In the fading light, the air began to chill. Andrew blew into his hands and rubbed them together. He looked at Brother Mark, who sat silently with his eyes closed. His face appeared angular and strong with high cheekbones and a proportional nose. The wind tossed his hair in a careless maze across his forehead.

"Maybe we should start back," Andrew suggested. "The weather is turning cold."

"Good idea," Brother Mark said.

They walked in silence toward the Gothic structure they called home; two twentieth century figures who might have fallen from an updated canvas of Hieronymus Bosch.

Brother Mark sensed Andrew's sullen mood. "I may be closing the main gates to the irrigation system soon, up on Empire Creek. If you're interested, I'm sure it would be O.K. if you wanted to see it."

Andrew squinted at Greystone Mountain, massive and airbrushed in the distance. "I'd like that," he said.

Brother Mark suddenly pointed to a low-slung furry creature several yards ahead of them. Both stopped.

"We had better avoid this guy. They have nasty reputations."

An adult badger searching for food returned to his half-circle burrow, which was located near the center of the dirt road.

"Is that what made that strange shaped opening?" Andrew asked. "I've probably hit it a dozen times with my dirt bike."

Brother Mark laughed. "I've seen him come out of the hole and run down the road a ways, as though he were going to eat me when I rode by. You've got to be careful."

They left the road and made a wide detour through the field.

Having completed his work, Brother Cyril was returning the backhoe to the barn on the far side of the property. The diesel engine faded slowly with soft dissolving clots of sound.

"The holidays will be here pretty soon," Brother Mark said. "Have you been away from your relatives and friends before?"

It was an unexpected question.

"Oh, yeah," Andrew replied. "I haven't been back home for the holidays in quite a while, mostly because of the distance. Upstate New York is quite a haul." He glanced at Brother Mark. "How about you?"

Brother Mark smiled. "Well, as you know, we're not given the opportunity but my parents have visited a few times in the summer." He hesitated. "It's funny . . . I enjoy their company, yet I'm almost glad to see them leave."

Andrew was surprised by Brother Mark's candor. "So does this mean you're another product of a dysfunctional family?"

Brother Mark smiled. "Aren't we all, more or less," he said, once again, mimicking, Groucho Marx. "I mean, look around you, kid."

Andrew laughed. "Yeah, I guess you're right." His smile slowly faded to a vacant stare.

"When I was younger, my mother would always yell at me because I would tell people that my father was in the V-8 hospital, rather than the VA hospital—where he still is. He's been there for quite a while due to a stress disorder of sorts. He's never really recovered and, as I grew older, I kept thinking, maybe I wasn't all that wrong. You know, V-8; it's the place they keep the vegetables. Well, it's one of the few times my mom ever hit me."

Brother Mark exhaled loudly. "I never knew that about your father. I'm really sorry."

Squinting, Andrew pointed toward the ridge. Two crows were engaged in an aerial battle with one of the local red-tail hawks, who appeared awkward under pursuit. As the birds flew nearer, the hawk appeared to be clutching something black, which may have explained its clumsy maneuvers. The crows attacked relentlessly until the hawk released its prey and then disappeared out of sight.

When they reached the back of the monastery, Andrew left Brother Mark and continued his walk toward the front of the property, past the tall firs and through the open fields. With his hand in his pocket, he felt the worn shape of his old rosary beads, always tangled and, for some, personally controversial. His lips silently shaped a familiar Hail, Mary.

Dust from an approaching vehicle caught Andrew's attention; he watched as the blue car pulled in alongside of the white car he had noticed earlier. A woman got out, unlocked her car, and, once inside, quickly drove away. The blue car was easily identified as the abbot's Peugeot, which was fast approaching Andrew. The abbot appeared to be absorbed by something above the windshield, and just as the car was about to pass, the abbot pushed down the visor. Andrew waved; however, the car continued on past him without notice.

By the time he had completed nearly four decades of the rosary, Andrew reached the main road, where he turned around immediately, as though an invisible shield prevented him from going one step farther. The small wooden sign, with faded blue letters, read, "St. Anthony's Monastery—Private—Enclosure." It was in need of repair and appeared to Andrew as innocuous as a Yield sign on the entrance ramp of a highway.

The view toward the monastery, however, always caused him to catch his breath—it was definitely not in need of repair, even in the fading light. Standing alone on the edge of the road, Andrew felt quite privileged to experience such a spectacular view and to live in such an environment; the natural beauty of his surroundings often, unexpectedly, overshadowed the hard work, the loneliness, and the struggle to live simply. Once again, he felt a genuine oneness with world, as if he were transparent, and the wind, the light, and his very being were blended in subtle harmony with the universe.

Bales of hay stacked neatly under the open-sided barn provided a private respite for Andrew. This particular moment in time begged for complete absorption, and Andrew took full advantage of the feeling. He opened his book to the inside of the back cover. In his somewhat cryptic handwriting, he had copied a line from another of Merton's books, *The Monastic Journey*, which read,

> "In looking at the postulant, the monastic community will no longer assume that he comes to the monastery with ideas and aspirations that are all wrong, but that some of the deepest needs of his heart, even though they may not be explicitly religious needs, are genuinely human and specifically contemporary needs which the monastic life is called upon to fulfill."

He leaned back against the hay, feeling it crunch against his jacket. It was not long before his eyes grew heavy, and he fell asleep.

He awoke in the dark and cold, looked at his watch and realized he was about to miss the evening supper. He collected his book and was about to leave when he saw headlights and heard the approach of a car. As it neared the hay barn, the lights of the car shone directly at Andrew who, feeling compromised in this situation, decided to duck behind the bales. He could see that it was the same bulky white car that had been parked in the pull-off earlier that day. The driver stopped the car in the same spot, turned off the ignition and remained seated in the vehicle. Andrew watched intently, waiting for some activity, yet nothing moved except his rosary beads, settling in his pocket. Inside the car, a small red glow flashed briefly and faded as the driver lit a cigarette.

'Now what,' he thought. 'Should I walk past and return to monastery, or sit here and wait?' He felt uneasy and decided that he would rather wait for a while before getting bold, however, the late autumn air seemed to penetrate his clothing, and his urge to urinate was growing stronger.

Headlights from the direction of the monastery grew brighter as they approached. Before he could see the car, he recognized the sound of the abbot's Peugeot, which pulled in alongside of the white car. Andrew could see a woman get out of the parked car and open the passenger side door of the Peugeot.

"I thought you had forgotten, Jude," she said in a casual voice. This was followed by laughter and a response from Father Jude, but Andrew could not hear what he said. She got into the car, and they drove past him toward the main road.

Andrew hastily urinated and headed for the refectory.

* * *

Andrew sat at his desk as the Grand Silence, which followed Vespers, permeated the walls and filled every inch of space in his cell like an invisible gas. He knew that he should meditate prior to sleeping, so he dimmed the overhead light, positioned himself on a squat two-legged Zen stool and then pulled the blanket off his bed and wrapped it around himself until he felt snug and squawlike. Hoping to clear his thoughts, he began breathing deeply and slowly, letting all mental images drift in and out, neither clinging nor forcing them away. He began to focus on his particular mantra, "omnes," which was silently repeated with each exhalation of breath. He could feel his entire body relax and his breathing slow considerably. He continued to meditate and repeat his mantra, over and over, until he was not sure of his actual state; without verbal questioning, he felt a mild concern, pleasant yet unsure as to whether he was awake or sleeping.

A faint knock on his door caused him to bolt immediately into the present—he sat in the darkness waiting to confirm what he had just heard. Again, the tapping on his door was clear. He jumped up, tipping the Zen stool, and opened the door.

"You look like Sitting Bull," Brother Matthew whispered.

Andrew had forgotten that he was still wrapped in his blanket and was confused by Brother Matthew's untimely visit.

"May I come in?"

Andrew hesitated slightly. "Sure, come in," he said. "I was just trying to do some meditating before I hit the sack." He closed the door.

Brother Matthew sat in Andrew's desk chair so Andrew decided to sit on the edge of his bed.

"So what's up?" Andrew said, quietly.

Matthew leaned forward slightly and looked at his hands. "Oh, I don't know. I think the funeral got me down, or something." He looked at Andrew. "I thought we could talk for a while but . . . maybe it's a bad time. I'd better let you get back to your meditation." Matthew began to get up.

"Hang on; it's all right," Andrew said, as he stood up quickly. Suddenly, he winced with pain, a stabbing sensation in his lower back, and he grabbed the corner of the desk.

"Are you okay?" Matthew asked.

Andrew attempted to stand upright. "Damn!" he said. "I must have pulled a muscle in my back again."

"What can I do?" Matthew asked with genuine concern in his voice.

"Well, maybe you can help me lay on the floor. That sometimes eases the pain."

Matthew threw Andrew's blanket on the carpet and carefully helped lower Andrew to the floor.

With a suppressed groan, Andrew sat slowly and then stretched out on his back.

Matthew kneeled beside him. "You're not going to die, are you?" he said with a smile. "I don't think I could handle two funerals in one day."

"Humor in the face of adversity; I like that in a man."

Andrew explained that he had pulled back muscles before, probably an old injury from a fall while skiing. He asked Matthew to get his medication from the shelf in the closet where he kept a supply of pain relievers and muscle relaxants, which were prescribed by his doctor, just for such an occurrence.

Matthew filled Andrew's mug with water and gave him the medication.

"It's a good thing you're here," Andrew said. "I don't think I would have been able to reach my pills."

Matthew continued to kneel over Andrew. "Perhaps if I weren't here, this wouldn't have happened."

Andrew laughed. "It's God's will," he said. "Or . . . someone has one of those Voodoo dolls and they just stuck a pin in it."

Matthew grimaced. "Ouch! What a thought," he said, as he sat down, cross-legged, next to Andrew.

Once again, silence filled the cell. Andrew focused on the ceiling and began to feel more relaxed as the medication flooded his system. The wind stirred the brittle leaves in the garth, blowing them against the screen, yet the hollow feeling Andrew usually experienced on such a night was gone. He was not alone—and he felt happy. He looked at Matthew and smiled. "I feel good," he said with a slight slur.

"Me too," Matthew said, "and I haven't had any drugs." He returned to a kneeling position, close to Andrew. "Do you think you could roll over, or would you be too uncomfortable?" he asked.

Hindered by the acute pain, Andrew slowly turned on his side and then onto his stomach.

Matthew carefully began to massage Andrew's lower back, applying gentle pressure to the sore muscles. "Let me know if anything hurts," he said.

Andrew's response was barely audible. "Feels great," he whispered.

Matthew's fingers worked diligently, searching for knotted muscles, up and down the spinal area. He continued onto the shoulders, neck, and back of the head, with unexpected practiced skill.

Andrew remained silent; he closed his eyes and felt his entire body yield to Matthew's touch.

Matthew lifted Andrew's hand and applied strong pressure, in a small circular motion, to his palm and fingers, including the fleshy areas between them.

Andrew turned his head slightly to look at Matthew. He never had his hand massaged before and never expected that it would be done in a monastery—by a fellow monk—and that it could possibly feel so therapeutic. He closed his eyes as Brother Matthew continued with the opposite shoulder, arm, and hand.

Matthew carefully threw his leg over Andrew, straddling his back, and then resumed the massage, pushing gently, yet deeply, on Andrew's lower spine.

Andrew could feel the pressure, exactly where the muscles were knotted—a feeling of both pain and relief, and he acknowledged, silently, of physical contact, a feeling almost totally absent in this ascetic setting.

As Brother Matthew worked his way upward, toward the middle of Andrew's back, he gradually increased the pressure; Andrew sensed the intensity, which was still pleasurable yet increasingly powerful. He briefly opened his eyes to see Matthew completely absorbed in the process: his head was stretched forward; his eyes closed, while his body alternately swayed and arched over Andrew. Matthew's breathing increased, and when his grasp tightened on Andrew's shoulders, his body appeared to shudder momentarily, followed by a quick inhalation and relaxation of his grip.

Silence surrounded them in the semidarkness as Matthew settled alongside Andrew who appeared to be sleeping.

"I guess I'd better be going," he said. "Can I help you get back into bed?"

Andrew opened his eyes. "I'll be okay right here on the floor," he said quietly. He reached out and placed his hand on Matthew's. "Thanks," he said. "The massage was incredible."

Matthew squeezed Andrew's hand, pulled the pillow from his bed and tucked it under Andrew's head.

* * *

The following day began cold and sunny, the type of day that would have invigorated Andrew, however, he could still feel residual pain in his back, and he knew he would have to stay off his feet as much as possible.

Brother Matthew looked in on him early and offered to get him breakfast. He returned a short time later with hot coffee, rye toast, orange juice, and cereal. "How's the invalid?" he teased.

Andrew smiled. "Nice talk," he admonished, "but much better after your professional therapy. Where did you learn how to do that?"

"Well," Matthew admitted, "I flunked out of massage school in California."

"Are you serious?"

"Yes. I guess I wasn't fast enough—too much time with each person."

Andrew laughed and quickly winced when he felt the sharp lower back pain.

"Hey, I've got to go," Matthew said. "Get some rest—orders from the prior!" He was gone before Andrew could thank him for breakfast.

Andrew spent most of the day in bed, reading, sleeping, and thinking about the night before; about Matthew, himself, and what, if anything, it all meant. He felt some confusion as to whether a growing familiarity should, as Monastic Rule would imply, be discouraged or, was he misreading an innocent gesture of friendship—an atmosphere which the abbot, Aelred of Rievaulx, an early Cistercian Father, encouraged within his community, where it was not uncommon to see monks holding hands as they walked through the cloister. Andrew smiled at the thought. He reached for his copy of the writings of Aelred and found the following, worn passage:

> It is such a joy to have the consolation of someone's affection—someone to whom we are deeply united by the bonds of love, someone in whom our weary spirit may find rest, and to whom we may pour out our soul . . . someone whose conversation is as sweet as a song in the tedium of our daily life. He is someone whose soul will be to us a refuge to creep into when the world is altogether too much for us, someone to whom we can confide our thoughts. His spirit will give us the comforting kiss that heals all the sickness of our preoccupied heart. He will weep with us when we are troubled, and rejoice with us when we are in doubt. We will be so deeply bound to him in our heart that even when he is far away we will find him together with us in the spirit, together and alone. The world will fall asleep around us, we will find, and our souls will be at rest, embraced in absolute peace. Our two hearts will be quiet together, united as if they were one, as the grace of the Holy Spirit flows over both of us.

Andrew closed the book and gazed into the garth where sunlight and shadow played freely over the arched cloisters.

Chapter Three

Murmurs

A silent early snow signaled the beginning of the winter season. It fell gently through the pines and gathered overnight on the sparse aspens, bleaching the landscape with a monochromatic tint. Andrew was elated to awake to such a surprise; his world was suddenly new and fresh, a metamorphosis that lifted his spirits like a child staring at a Christmas tree. The snow dusted the slate roofs white and united the very ground and sky at a seamless horizon. All was perfectly one.

Brother Mark reminded Andrew that he would be closing the sluice gates on Empire Creek later that morning. Andrew looked forward to the task, as he was curious about the irrigation system and eager to learn more about it.

As the two monks bounced along in the four-wheel drive truck through the silver morning, Mrs. Oakley, a neighbor who was severely afflicted with osteoporosis and nearly bent in half, managed to sweep the feathery snow from her sidewalk. She slowly waved her bare hand and smiled as the truck approached. Brother Mark beeped the horn and returned the wave. "What a trooper," he said. "You know, she's probably in her late eighties."

Andrew turned to look again at the withered figure who resumed her sweeping.

Brother Mark pulled off the main road onto a small cart path, which lead into the woods. The truck rocked and yawed on the rutted road as the large tires threw snow, up over the side panels. Andrew unexpectedly felt his head bounce off the window. He looked at Brother Mark in disbelief, and both laughed spontaneously. "I hate when that happens," Andrew said.

"Me too," Brother Mark teased.

The road came to an end in a small clearing where Brother Mark stopped the truck and walked with Andrew to the floodgates. Water rushed into the opened sluice and filled the main ditch, the source of the monastery's water for irrigation. Wafers of ice in the quiet backwater shattered into small shards as they were caught by the current and sent along their way. Pieces of wood, tree branches, and other debris had collected in the corners of the metal gates, which prevented them from being closed. Brother Mark retrieved a long-handled rake from the truck and pulled several pieces at a time onto the slippery bank. Andrew helped remove the wet and frozen wood before it was caught in the current and sent back into the monastery's ditches.

"Well, I guess we're ready," Brother Mark said. "I hope we're able to get them to close."

Andrew and Brother Mark grabbed opposite sides of the large wheel. They pulled in unison against what appeared to be a metal monster, however, the wheel refused to budge. Andrew kicked a foothold in the rocky soil and Brother Mark did the same.

"Okay, Andrew," Brother Mark snorted. "One, two, three!"

Both monks strained until the rusted wheel finally groaned, and the gate slowly inched its way against the roiled current.

"All right!" Andrew shouted. "We did it."

"Yes!" Brother Mark said. "Now let's try to free the other one."

The wheel for the second gate proved less obstinate than the first. It also resisted, yet it released with another groan and moved slowly inward.

"Let's see if we can close both at the same time," Brother Mark suggested. "There may be less resistance that way."

The gates grew closer and closer until they finally joined and locked. The water level in the ditch dropped quickly, exposing a worn rocky bottom.

"Another job well done," Brother Mark said. "How about some coffee?"

"Sure," Andrew replied.

Once inside the truck, Brother Mark brought out a chrome thermos and extra paper cups. He started the engine and adjusted the heater until the temperature in the cab grew comfortable.

Andrew used both hands to hold his coffee and enjoy its warmth and flavor. "I can see why this stuff is addicting," he said, carefully sipping the hot liquid.

"Yeah, I'd probably kill for it," Brother Mark joked.

Andrew looked at him and laughed. He watched as the new fallen snow melted quickly on the truck's hood, leaving an "x" pattern over the insulation.

"I'd like to ask you something, but I want you to tell me if it's an area we shouldn't be talking about," Andrew said.

"Sure, what is it?" Brother Mark said.

Andrew paused for a while. "How well do you know Father Jude?"

Brother Mark took a long sip of his coffee. "Why? Did you see him with a small woman driving a big white car?"

Andrew choked on his coffee, spilling some on his parka.

Brother Mark reached behind the seat and handed him a roll of paper towels.

Andrew blotted the wet spots and then used a fresh sheet to wipe his face. "How did you know I was going to ask that?"

"Just a hunch," Brother Mark said. He looked directly at Andrew. "Besides, you appear to be an observant person; two plus two generally adds up to four."

Andrew inhaled deeply and slowly exhaled through his nose. He rubbed his eyes, his characteristic gesture of bewilderment, unconsciously reserved for momentary reflection and composure. "Am I to assume, then, that the abbot is having an affair with this petite woman?"

"Well, we can't assume anything," Brother Mark said, "yet it's an issue that has been raised among some of the brothers—at the risk of breaking the Rule by murmuring."

"Murmuring?"

"You know, talking about one of the brothers in a less-than-charitable way."

Andrew unzipped his parka as the heat in the truck increased. "Sort of like *'remove the log from your own eye before you remove the splinter from the eye of your brother.'*"

"That's it," Brother Mark said.

"Then, perhaps I'm guilty of murmuring," Andrew said. "I shouldn't have asked you about Father Jude."

Brother Mark poured more coffee. "Heck, no," he said. "I brought the issue into the open because somehow, I knew you were aware of whatever it is that's happening, and because it's been a troubling and painful issue for me personally. I've talked with Father Luke about this and he doesn't see it as an issue. Apparently, he's convinced that Jude's relationship with this woman is based on pastoral counseling and is completely platonic."

"Well," Andrew said. "I wonder why he meets her at night by the hay barn and they drive off together in his car."

"You've seen this?"

"Yes, but only once," Andrew said.

Brother Mark's face grew even more concerned. "I'm curious to know how you happened to see them."

Andrew hesitated. "I fell asleep in the hay barn late one day and, when I woke up, both met at the turn off and drove away. I was sort of embarrassed to be there so I hid behind a hay bale until they left." Andrew paused and then added, "That's actually not the first time I've seen Father Jude with her, now that I think of it. He was also with her after Father Martin's funeral."

Brother Mark laughed quietly and slowly shook his head, as though he were the only one in the truck. After finishing his coffee, he stored the thermos and looked at Andrew. "I don't know what this is all about, Andrew—and it may be nothing—but you might be better off not mentioning this to the other members of the community, particularly the other novices."

"I understand," Andrew said.

"Besides," Brother Mark said with a smile, "neither of us wants to be guilty of the "m" word."

"No, not the "m" word," Andrew mimicked.

* * *

When he returned to his cell, Andrew reflected on Brother Mark's conversation. He knew that the topic was a genuine concern for Brother

Mark, yet Andrew felt less consumed by the issue and simply more accepted as a peer by an elder monk who would openly share his thoughts on such grave matters.

He pulled his habit over his jeans and arrived early for Vespers. After choosing a seat in the back of the darkened church where he could meditate quietly, he closed his eyes and began to breathe deeply and slowly, repeating his mantra with each exhalation. He was vaguely aware of occasional footsteps passing in the cloister or, even a brief laugh or a bit of conversation in the distance; however, he let the distractions come and go until he had reached a deep, meditative state, marked by decreased breathing and minimal disruptive thought. He was awake yet he felt as though he was transparent, empty, as if he no longer inhabited his own body. A remote feeling of concern, mixed with contentment, inundated his senses and then subsided into a subtle numbness. Footsteps grew less abrasive and echoed softly in the semidarkness; an errant word became simply a blurred sound with no message. Time became irrelevant.

At one point, Andrew sensed a presence, someone on his right, shoulder-to-shoulder, arm-to-arm. He felt something graze his ear, slowly, up and down, and then he heard a whisper: "proud" and "love," echoed, haunting words, barely discernable. As quickly as it happened, it was over. The obscure incident dissolved into the darkness.

The clanging of the bells being rung by Brother Edward caused Andrew to focus sharply on the present. The church was still dark. He looked around, but saw no one in the immediate area, and wondered if he had dreamed the occurrence or had it, in fact, been real. He recalled the two words, "proud" and "love" and tried to make some sense of their meaning, however, nothing came to mind and there was no connection. Suddenly, the lights in the church illuminated the interior and confirmed Andrew's suspicion—no one else was present.

One by one, the monks entered the church and took their assigned seats, which were arranged in two separate rows, facing each other from opposite walls. Andrew was positioned directly across from Brother Conrad, a small balding man in his early forties, who wore a leg brace as a result of a birth defect. Brother Conrad appeared to Andrew as loud and, at times, supercilious; he spoke rapidly, with constant hand movements flailing the air, however, prolonged standing proved difficult for him, so he was given special permission to sit as needed during services. Andrew noticed that Brother Conrad had an unusual behavior when standing: he would bend forward slightly and rotate his hips in a wide circle, as though he were using an invisible Hula-Hoop. His habit would sway accordingly, and afterward, Brother Conrad would simply stare widely at Andrew with an occasional frog-eyed blink.

Observing Brother Conrad, Andrew was suddenly overcome with laughter, which he attempted to conceal. He could feel the urgency growing within his chest, as barely perceptible giggles escaped unnoticed. He told himself, 'Take control, take control,' as he focused his gaze on the floor. He felt his face grow warm as the giggles grew louder, and tears flowed down his cheeks. He slowly raised his eyes to see if he had been noticed, however, Brother Conrad appeared, once again, to be staring directly at him. Just as Andrew began to lower his gaze, Brother Conrad, once again, executed his Hula-Hoop movement. This time, Andrew had no choice. He bolted for the door and exited. With the door closed and, in the safety of the cloister, Andrew laughed hysterically into the gathered folds of his robe.

After returning to his cell, he retrieved his Zen stool from the top of his closet and, still in his habit, he attempted to resume his meditation. Each time he tried to dismiss his thoughts, he would see Brother Conrad, gyrating like a frog in a Hula-Hoop, while an unstoppable smile on Andrew's face disrupted his meditation. He removed the Zen stool and his habit and settled for some reading.

This time, rather than Brother Conrad's image, Andrew began to think about Sara. He remembered the intensity of their two-year relationship, the heady glow of being in love and having that love returned. He saw her face, small with soft angles, framed by dark shiny hair. He remembered the intoxicating smell of her skin, like a field of wildflowers in sunlight, the softness of her supple body—as though she were present—and as he continued to lower his hand, he recalled the silky texture and the warmth of her genitals.

Andrew closed the book and switched off the desk lamp. He undressed in the dark and climbed naked into bed as thoughts of Sara continued to consume him. He kissed her open mouth, her neck, and firm breasts, as she willingly opened her legs and guided him into her. The rhythmic thrusts increased and then abated in a pattern determined by Sara. Andrew kissed her face with exhilaration while looking at her closed eyes and watching as she arched her neck and softly uttered sounds of pleasure. Unexpectedly, Sara's face appeared to blur; her hair grew shorter, and her face appeared even more angular. Andrew felt the unexplained roughness of her cheeks and the increased muscle mass below him; he raised his head and was suddenly looking into Nick's eyes.

"It's okay," Nick said, as he reached for Andrew's head with both hands and pulled Andrew's mouth over his.

Andrew did not resist. He kissed him eagerly, at times biting and exploring, until he could hold back no longer. The pent-up release appeared to be infinite and was followed by deep exhaustion and sedation.

Andrew removed the damp top sheet, pulled two blankets over himself, and slept soundly.

* * *

Chapter Four

Duplicity

Christmas energized the monastery both externally, with sumptuous decorations and culinary delights, and internally, with anticipation of the Virgin birth and a renewed sense of community and fraternal charity. Brother Adrian, childlike in his simplicity, attempted to outdo himself each season by baking cakes and cookies of confectionary delight, filling the cloisters with mouthwatering aromas and stomachs with satisfying sustenance that exceeded expectations. Nature often cooperated with copious amounts of snow, sometimes gentle yet frequently ruthless storms that deposited three to four feet of powder in the valley, accompanied by howling winds, which obscured the cry of the coyote and buried the hibernating bears even deeper in their dens. Andrew often imagined that the mountains somehow spoke to each other, on the darkest nights, with indecipherable utterances.

The joyous season also underlined the isolation of each monk from his natural family by dredging up earlier memories and good times with loved ones. Christmas, particularly, reinforced friendships within the community as each monk internalized the blunt realization that the community was his immediate family, even though he chose a life of seclusion and solitude. It was not uncommon to see their brothers, young and old alike, quietly shedding tears of joy or, more often, sorrow, for no apparent reason, within the darkened church.

Andrew knew that Brother Matthew was quite excited this Christmas since he was given permission by the abbot, Father Jude, to have his family visit for a week and stay in the large guesthouse, which was located just off the public road on the turn-off to the monastery.

The guesthouse, originally built by the first monks who established the community, prior to the construction of the main buildings, was an old two-story brick and fieldstone dwelling with several bedrooms, which had been converted from larger dormitory rooms. Renovations included updated bathrooms and a practical country kitchen. Victorian touches graced the worn but still functional wraparound porches, which were in need of constant repair. The rear of the house was open to the otherwise fenced pasture and, in the summer months, cattle would rub against the rough brick and stone in an attempt to alleviate a particular itch; from the inside of the house, their rubbing sounded like an eerie monster, attempting to bore through the wall.

Andrew enjoyed the spacious guesthouse for its authentic, lived-in look. There were nooks and crannies to disappear in, and corners where he could curl up with a secular book and feel no serious transgression; something he seldom experienced in his cell.

He had helped clean the house several times, after various guests completed their visits, and he soon became familiar with the subtle idiosyncrasies that often appeared on the repair list and reappeared months later, including the leaky faucet in the upstairs bathroom, the window that would not open, and the bed that easily collapsed because of its broken leg.

With a dusting of new snow on the ground, Andrew decided to walk the one-mile trek to the guesthouse, which he was assigned to clean. He found the key in the usual place, above the window, and went inside. Weak sunlight illuminated the interior, which appeared to be quite orderly and clean except for a soiled glass, partially filled with brown liquid, near the sink. Andrew was about to empty the glass when he thought he smelled whiskey. He sniffed the liquid and, indeed, a strong odor of alcohol confirmed his suspicions. He poured the contents into the sink and rinsed the glass, intending to wash it later.

He removed his jacket, put it on the worn couch in the study, and began his usual ritual of cleaning by starting from the second floor and working his way down to the first. Beds needed changing so Andrew looked into the small bedroom, however, the room had not been used. The beds were neatly made; and clean towels remained folded on the old, second-hand bureau, which, he noticed, needed dusting.

The door to the larger, second bedroom across the hall was partially closed. Andrew felt that this was not unusual since the previous guests most likely used this room. He pushed open the door and froze, temporarily, with fear. In the farthest bed, near the corner of the room, he saw a body, partially covered, lying face down. He could also see what appeared to be the arm of a man. He was not sure whether he should slowly back out of the room and call the monastery or loudly demand an explanation if, in fact, the person were able to respond. He could only think of one thing, 'I don't want to be here,' and he began to very slowly back out of the room when the person in bed rolled to the other side, exposing his face.

"Matthew!" Andrew shouted. "What the heck are you doing here? You scared the crap out of me!"

Matthew slowly raised his head and looked at Andrew. "Oh shit!" he said hoarsely. "Thank God it's you and not the Inquisition. I'd be dead." He dropped his head back on the pillow.

As Andrew approached the bed, Matthew continued to lay face down and shirtless, facing Andrew, with the blanket pulled up to his waist; his left arm hung off the bed, and his hand was touching the floor.

"I don't get it," Andrew said, "what's going on?"

Matthew blinked at Andrew, attempting to make some sense of the situation. "I can't explain it all," he said with a yawn. "Last night, I had to get out of the monastery, went for a walk, and decided to stop in here for a while, just to think or be away . . . or whatever."

Andrew felt a sense of empathy, tinged with mild disbelief. He saw what could have been a fallen angel with blond hair, half wrapped in white sheets, fighting the ever-present Christian dichotomy of good and evil, right and wrong, a familiar and very personal struggle—in many ways, he saw himself.

"And the nearly empty glass of whiskey that I found, sitting near the sink downstairs . . . was that part of the 'whatever'?"

"Damn," Matthew said. "I really left it there?"

"Yup," Andrew said with a slight smile.

Reminded of his evening, Matthew rubbed his head and face. "I think I have a hangover. When I was looking for some munchies, I opened the cabinet under the sink and there were two bottles of Jack Daniel's, so I decided to have just a bit—but I think it turned into more than that."

"Well, you're going to have more than a hangover if you don't get out of here and get back to the monastery. Father Jude would, most likely, throw you out, and with your family coming up for a visit in two weeks, the timing could be better."

"Yeah, I hear you," Matthew said. "Hmm . . . Father Jude," he replied somewhat sarcastically.

"I have to get cleaning," Andrew said, and he turned to leave.

"Wait," Matthew said suddenly. "How about a favor?"

"What?" Andrew asked.

"I feel like I've been through a wringer. Do you think you could spare ten minutes to loosen up my neck and shoulders?"

Andrew hesitated, surprised by the request. "Okay," he said. "I think I owe you one after the incident with my back."

Kneeling alongside the bed, Andrew slowly began to knead Matthew's neck and solid shoulders.

"That feels so incredible," Matthew acknowledged, as Andrew continued to apply pressure.

Unexpectedly, in one swift movement, Matthew raised his feet and purposely kicked off the sheets, exposing his nude body, except for a pair of white crew socks, which he was still wearing.

Andrew was momentarily speechless and clearly uncomfortable.

"You don't mind doing my legs, do you?" Matthew asked nonchalantly.

"N-No," Andrew stammered, feeling nearly overwhelmed. He was acutely aware that he was touching someone with the qualities of a classical sculpture, yet the fair marble skin was warm, pliant, and lightly tanned except for his white athletic buttocks.

Andrew moved to Matthew's calves, massaging slowly and firmly, trying to concentrate on the task. He could feel his body temperature increase, while his heart felt as though it was about to burst through his chest. Completing the work on both calves, Andrew continued up the leg and began to work on Matthew's thighs.

The silence in the room only heightened Andrew's self-consciousness while Matthew sprawled indulgently on the rumpled sheets with his eyes closed and his breathing slow and deep. Andrew noticed a pair of briefs mingled with the wrinkles next to Matthew. He also saw what appeared to be an altar candle partially visible under Matthew's pillow.

"So you had Jack Daniel's by candlelight last night?" Andrew joked, yet as soon as the words left his lips, the entire question and its intended humor somehow lost its effect.

"By candlelight?" Matthew asked with a recurrent yawn.

"Yeah," Andrew continued, "the candle under your pillow."

"Oh, that candle," Matthew replied. He slowly moved his right hand up to the candle and leisurely pushed it completely under the pillow. "I didn't want to turn on the lights up here last night when I was meditating."

Andrew moved on to Matthew's upper thigh; as he did so, Matthew subtly moved his opposite leg apart, which allowed more room for Andrew's hands and, consciously or not, allowed Andrew an unrestricted view of dense reddish-blond pubic hair and scrotum. He cautiously attempted to remain within the area of the thigh, just below the buttocks, realizing that he was very much a part of an occurrence that both tempted and tormented him.

Matthew drew deeper and deeper breaths. He looked at Andrew and then closed his eyes again. "I like being with you . . . you know that," he said quietly.

Andrew remained silent for a minute trying to think of a response as much from the heart as from the head. "Well, that's reassuring," he said, "because I think I feel the same. He continued to knead Matthew's upper thigh, occasionally brushing his hands against his buttocks.

Matthew lifted his head slightly and looked back at Andrew. "They could use a rubdown too" he said, " . . . if that's okay with you."

Andrew felt as though his body was attempting to turn itself inside out; his heart was racing, and he felt flushed. He was incapable of verbally responding to Matthew, so he pushed even more strongly on his thighs, trying to get himself under control. This seemed to give Matthew increased enjoyment as Andrew thought he could hear him whisper "feels great."

Knowing that he could not quit, Andrew gently placed his hands on Matthew's buttocks and slowly traced the curves and crevices of this exquisitely sculpted figure. He felt the smoothness and, more deeply, the strength beneath the surface.

Matthew reached out and placed his hand on Andrew's calf. This time, he moved even closer to the edge of the bed, closer to Andrew, who continued to massage him gently.

Nevertheless, Andrew knew that he had to get out the room. He leaned over Matthew's ear and whispered. "You are truly handsome, but . . . I definitely have to go." Andrew hastily pulled the sheet over Matthew, stood up and quickly exited.

Within seconds, he found himself downstairs, racing for the door to get some air. He stood on the open porch and inhaled the cold comforting wind, which, by now, had grown even stronger, along with the steady snowfall that had already covered his footsteps. He knew that a fierce winter storm was about to descend on the monastery. And it was just such an environment that rekindled Andrew's ongoing love affair with snow, not only for what it was but also for what it did. He was inspired by its beauty, its ability to unify the landscape by erasing flaws and errors and creating common ground; the world in white was simplified, easier to understand. Standing alone on the porch steps, he could feel the calming effect of icy absolution as the flakes melted on his heated face and collected quickly on his shirt.

In the distance, lights from an approaching car caught his attention. The dark-colored car moved very slowly on the unplowed road toward the monastery entrance. Andrew could not be sure, but it looked like the abbot's blue Peugeot, and he did not want to be seen standing on the porch of the guesthouse. He quickly went inside and decided to resume his cleaning, from the bottom up, rather than encounter Matthew who was apparently still upstairs.

He had nearly finished cleaning the downstairs when Matthew appeared in the study, his hair still damp from the shower, and his clothes somewhat disheveled.

"Good morning, again," Andrew said with a smile. "It's nice to see you among the living."

Matthew smiled, stretched, and yawned. "What's for breakfast," he joked.

"How about some Jack Daniel's and nachos?" Andrew replied.

"Don't remind me," Matthew said with a frown. "I don't know what came over me."

"I think I saw the abbot's car drive in a while ago—just to let you know that he's at the monastery."

Matthew paused. "You know," he said, "just between you and me, I wouldn't care if he were sitting in the upstairs bedroom an hour ago." He shifted his weight and glanced at the ceiling. "Pretend I didn't say that."

"Anyway," Andrew said, "you'd better get the heck out of here before they send out the troops for you."

"I know," Matthew replied. "You're right . . . you are always right, Andrew."

"Hey, give me a break, Matt," Andrew pleaded. "I admit, I generally try to do the right thing, whatever that is."

"I know, I know," Matthew said honestly, "and I love you for it." He walked toward Andrew, put his arms around him, and hugged him. Andrew returned the hug as Matthew whispered in his ear: "You make me feel proud to be with you," he said. He turned, walked out the kitchen door and disappeared into the blowing snow.

Andrew was amazed that this particular sentence seemed so familiar. There was silence, yet his mind raced. Words flew through his head like a computer searching for a specific file, half remembered, as though from a dream long ago. He repeated Matthew's words, again and again, until two particular words surfaced clearly in his memory: "proud" and "love." He remembered meditating in the church, after vigils, and recalled that those were the two words he thought he heard.

Embracing the notion, he decided to look out the window in an attempt to see Matthew, however, the snow had intensified and he could barely discern the wooden fence that enclosed the side yard. Instead, Andrew observed a pensive young man with dark hair staring back at him in the window; it was his own reflection, and he was smiling.

* * *

Although it was nearly noon, the light was flat and visibility was limited. The world became a swirl of white and grey as the blizzard whipped across the upper valley and slowly began to bury everything in its path. Andrew's work boots were lost in feathery powder as he trudged toward the monastery, following the dark outline of the pasture fence that ran alongside the road. He could feel the snow melting above his ankles and water soaking his socks, but he never felt happier. It seemed as though the world had nearly disappeared, held hostage by the ravages of nature, while Andrew relished his insignificance by gulping mouthfuls of flakes and becoming one with the storm.

The steps leading to the front entrance of the monastery softened into a gentle white slope. Hesitant to disturb the effect, Andrew attempted to jump the first two steps, slipped and fell face first on the snow covered lawn. He lay there, uninjured and smiling, thinking that this was what he really felt like doing—lying in the snow and observing how quickly he was being erased by the white-out. He rolled onto his back and watched as the incessant flakes landed on his eyelids and quickly melted. There was no focus, no benchmark, just white, sometimes stinging, flakes blurring his vision and increasing his feeling of total oneness with the environment. He briefly wondered how it might feel to freeze to death—'does it hurt? do you get warm before the end?'—and then promptly decided to get up, shake himself off, and go inside.

The smell of pine and the wood-burning stove inundated Andrew, even before he had a chance to observe the newly decorated entrance room where handmade wreaths and spruce roping hung from the brick walls like medals of honor on a worn uniform. Purple ribbons of Advent combined richly with the fragrant dark greenery, a complementary mix, which Andrew preferred over the traditional red and green Christmas colors. On the floor, an antique oriental rug, approximately nine by twelve feet, warmed the room with sumptuous hues of port, cream, and navy. A crèche had been arranged on the carpet with carved wooden figures of the holy family, including a resting baby Jesus in his straw-filled crib.

Andrew felt overwhelmed by the beauty and comfort the room exuded. A sense of security and peace permeated the air, along with subdued joy and anticipation of spending his first Christmas at the monastery. He sat in one of the wingback chairs, wishing that the moment would never end; the day seemed almost too perfect, yet unexpected, as the snow continued to fall and quickly coat the arched windows and nearby pines.

Remembering that he had, again, been assigned to read during lunch, he hurried to his cell, put on dry socks, and continued through the cloister to the refectory. He climbed the steep stairs to the pulpit and searched for the brass bookmark and follow-up note, to see where he had left off. He had been reading from Merton's *New Seeds of Contemplation*, the same book he enjoyed so much when reading in his cell.

On cue, the doors below opened, and the community filed in behind the abbot who led them in song. Once they were seated, Andrew continued with his reading:

> *"Hell is where no one has anything in common with anybody else except the fact that they all hate one another and cannot get away from one another and themselves."*

Andrew managed to momentarily look down at the gathering while he continued to read. He suddenly felt as though his words were practically meaningless as his fellow monks hunched over their plates and ate voraciously; in fact, he wondered if they were even listening. Feeling reckless, he decided to substitute a totally senseless word into the sentence to see if anyone would notice and look up at him. At first, he felt that he could not do it, yet as he read on, he decided to give in. He could feel himself getting tense but continued:

"*Then man is reconstituted in the image of the Holy broccoli,*" he read nonchalantly, substituting "broccoli" for "family." However, it did not seem to matter. No one looked up—everyone continued to eat contentedly.

*   *   *

Given the work-free afternoon, Andrew settled into his cell like a contented cat, ready to curl up into his warm nest with his books, while his lover, the snow, teased at his window and erased the world outside. He diligently attempted to practice the expected monastic ideal for the study of religious works, known as "lectio," or the opening of one's mind and heart to receive God's message. Andrew decided to concentrate on the writing of the early Fathers of monasticism including Anthony, Pachomius, and Benedict, author of *The Rule of St. Benedict*. It was clear to Andrew that the life demanded great sacrifice, and he knew that he was experiencing extensive adversity with certain parts of his calling, particularly purity of heart and the need to empty from his heart his earthly attachments. The early Fathers clearly echoed the need to create a receptive place to hear God's word, a place of solitude, and the ability to constantly pray. The powerful words invigorated Andrew and, in silence, he again asked for God's blessing and forgiveness and a chance to receive his grace.

Andrew was particularly struck by an encounter between two of the early fathers, Abbot Paul and Abbot Basil. Paul told Basil that he was doing his best to be receptive to God's word, yet he wanted to know if Basil could suggest something more for him. Basil raised his hands toward heaven when his fingers suddenly ignited into flames. He then told Paul that he could not truly become a monk unless he was to become like a consuming fire.

The image burned into Andrew's memory. He felt that the passion of Basil, as difficult as his message was, had to be reignited in his soul and allowed to cauterize his hemorrhaging impurities.

As the afternoon wore on, he grew restless to be outside, once more, before the early dusk dimmed the beauty of the storm. He decided to dress warmly and, with the help of a pair of old snowshoes and some ski poles, go for a walk through the lower mesa toward the west end of the property. He was amazed at how easily he was able to walk up steep snowy inclines and still maintain his balance. As if in a postcard, he was suddenly aware that he was walking through a veritable winter wonderland. The snow had eased somewhat, affording him a greater vision of the world around him. He could see the entire monastery, settled in white in the distance, while peaks of the nearby mountains were barely visible above the horizon.

He trudged between sparse bushes of withered sage, capped in white, over small washes and up gentle foothills, enjoying the alpine air and the emptiness of his environment. He continued until he was confronted by a barbed-wire pasture fence, which he could not climb over without removing his snowshoes. He leaned against the low-fence post, released the binding and stepped out of the snowshoe into hip-deep snow. Surprised and laughing, he struggled with the other binding, threw both snowshoes over the fence and carefully climbed up and over to the other side.

Back on his snowshoes, Andrew continued his meandering journey until he found himself overlooking the Morgan cabin, a handsome chalet, owned by a wealthy businessman who was CEO of several construction companies in the state. The Morgans built their vacation home on the edge of the monastic enclosure and, out of gratitude, they allowed the community to use their home for holiday get-togethers and retreats, when they were not planning to be there.

Andrew had been in the cabin only once, with Brother Mark, when they were asked to bring mail and groceries to a visiting abbot who was spending his retreat there. Abbot Edward, visiting from a monastery in New York State, was very gracious and allowed Mark and Andrew to tour the chalet and share a simple meal of fruit, cheese, bread, and dry red wine.

Andrew remembered the beauty of the place with its well-appointed comforts, including a cedar sauna and large sunken hot tub. The massive stone fireplace and expansive glass vistas of the mesa and lower valley were breathtaking, but not totally in keeping with Andrew's concept of the monastic life; nevertheless, he felt relaxed with Abbot Edward, who seemed to enjoy the company of the two young and energetic monks.

Just as he was about to return to the monastery, Andrew heard a vehicle in the distance approaching from the main road. He saw a truck plowing through the snow and coming directly up the driveway toward the back of the cabin. As the truck drew nearer, Andrew thought it looked like the four-wheel-drive pickup owned by the monastery. He quickly stepped behind some bushes and squatted. The truck pulled up to the side deck and stopped. Andrew was sure it was the monastery's grey pickup, and when Father Jude got out from the driver's side, Andrew's suspicions were confirmed.

Father Jude carefully made his way up the steps, unlocked the cabin door and came out with a broom to sweep a path from the door, down the steps to the truck. He then reached into the truck and assisted a petite young woman, dressed in a pastel-colored ski parka, down from the cab and into the cabin.

At first, Andrew had difficulty with the entire concept. 'It's probably just a nun,' he thought and then quietly laughed at his own denial. He felt a flood of emotions—anger and, even fear—and decided that he needed to quickly get away from the area unseen. He slid down a small knoll and, in the receding light, headed for the monastery.

It was nearly dark by the time he returned. The lights within the monastery softly illuminated the snow outside, creating an unusual effect, as if the monastery were floating above the surface like a silent spaceship. Andrew went to his cell, collected clean underwear and walked down to the bathroom to shower.

Ordinarily, he would shower hurriedly, since he was aware that long showers somehow seemed too luxurious for the lifestyle and were silently frowned upon; however, on this particular evening, he felt inwardly defiant. He let the steamy water flood over his chilled and tired body, relishing every moment as it relaxed his tense neck and soothed the muscles of his lower back. 'This feels too good,' he thought, yet he made no effort to leave. With closed eyes, he stood, immobilized, as the water therapeutically melted away the stress of the hike and the mental mishmash at the Morgan cabin.

The sound of water being turned on in the shower next to his interrupted his enjoyment. He heard someone open the inner curtain, get into the shower and then close the curtain. Andrew reluctantly decided to terminate his stay, in the event that he was identified as being somewhat excessive in his personal care. He dried himself vigorously, got dressed and proceeded to comb his hair and brush his teeth. In the mirror, Andrew noticed that Brother Mark's square-toed boots were protruding from under the curtain of the shower that was being used. He was reminded of the conversation Brother Mark and he had and wondered if he should share with him what he experienced earlier in the day.

Andrew went to a small room adjacent to the bathroom where hundreds of CDs and cassettes, mostly liturgical and Gregorian, were stacked haphazardly on shelves that lined the walls. He found a small notepad and pencil and wrote a brief note to Brother Mark. It read, *"Please see me in my room when you're through. Thanks, Andrew."*

He opened the outer curtain of Brother Mark's shower just enough to carefully place the note on top of his clean folded clothes and quietly returned to his cell.

Within twenty minutes, Brother Mark appeared, scrubbed and still damp, at Andrew's door.

"I got your note," Brother Mark said softly.

"I was hoping you wouldn't miss it," Andrew replied. "Come on in."

Brother Mark flopped on Andrew's bed like a college student waiting for a delivery of pizza and beer. He crunched up Andrew's pillow for a bed rest and tucked his feet beneath him.

"It's murmur time," Andrew whispered. "I feel like I need to tell you."

Andrew sat at his desk, facing Brother Mark, and related the afternoon's events. Brother Mark listened intently. He never lost eye contact with Andrew and blinked only occasionally, which seemed to signal to Andrew the gravity of the news he was reporting. When Andrew finished, Brother Mark remained silent. His eyes narrowed as he looked into the darkness of the garth. He then looked at Andrew.

"Holy shit," he exclaimed with a whisper. "This is not good. This is really not good."

Andrew was hesitant to respond, not knowing whether Brother Mark would think badly of him for telling the story or if he did the "right" thing. "You're not going to kill the messenger, are you?" Andrew asked sheepishly.

"No . . . no," Mark said. "I just can't believe this is really happening even though I suspect it has been going on for a while." Brother Mark leaned forward and looked directly at Andrew. "I'm also concerned about how all of this affects you, being relatively new here."

Andrew was genuinely moved by his remark. "It's funny . . . but when I saw her get out of the truck and go inside with Father Jude, I remember feeling angry and later, disappointed . . . sort of."

"I can understand why," Brother Mark said, "even though we're not really sure of anything specific, it's not the expected behavior of an abbot."

After a brief paused, Andrew spoke up. "So what do you think?" he ventured. "Is he screwing her or what?"

Brother Mark appeared unfretted by the coarseness of the question. He sat up slowly and began to mimic his Groucho character. "Does a bear shit in the woods?" he asked, holding an imaginary cigar.

"That's what I thought," Andrew said.

Brother Mark dropped the comedy and looked at Andrew. "Well, this is still serious stuff. I hope it doesn't have an overall negative impact on your vocation."

Andrew was appreciative of Brother Mark's concern for him. "If I can speak openly, there are certain things about Father Jude that just don't seem to fit, yet I've never mentioned what I felt to anyone before, including my novice master, Father Luke." Andrew shifted in his chair and continued. "I guess it's not something a novice should be talking about."

Brother Mark leaned forward, once again. "I used to feel exactly the same way you do when I first came here, and I will admit, there are those times when I feel it now, yet I learned that talking things out is often much better than letting something inside fume and fester out of control." Brother Mark glanced at the floor and then settled back against the pillow. "Perhaps it's easier said than done," he said.

"I'm sure you're right," Andrew said, "especially about the 'easier said than done' part. He got up from the chair and slowly paced the narrow floor.

"You look like a caged tiger," Brother Mark joked.

Andrew flashed a half smile. "Have you ever seen Father Jude meditate after vigils?" Andrew asked abruptly.

"Probably," Brother Mark said, "but I don't remember anything specific."

"It's no big deal," Andrew said, "but one particular morning, I was walking past the church entrance, and before I got there, I saw this bright light reflecting out into the cloister—I thought the place was on fire. As I approached, I saw candles, probably six or seven votives on the floor in a large circle and, in the middle of the circle, was Father Jude. I was really surprised, and for some reason, I felt embarrassed, almost like I felt this afternoon at the Morgan place."

Andrew sat down with a thud at his desk. He rubbed his eyes in his customary way. "I feel as though the 'remove the log from your own eye' message is screaming at me, and yet I just haven't been able to let the feelings go."

Brother Mark got up and placed his hand on Andrew's shoulder. "It's all right . . . I know how you feel and that's okay. It's not easy to understand."

Andrew looked up at Brother Mark and smiled. "Thanks," he said. "I could go on but I'll spare you—for now."

Brother Mark sat on the bed. "For me, it came down to 'how badly do I want this life?' I suppose it's like having anywhere from sixteen to twenty wives or husbands, all at the same time, and attempting to cope with their individual idiosyncrasies. Everyone grows, at least I hope, more forgiving, but that doesn't necessarily make the vocation any easier."

"Yeah, I hear you," Andrew replied softly. He stared into the darkness. "I guess it's that growing awareness that I need to work on . . . I don't know. Like you said earlier, I see in Father Jude weird behaviors that just don't seem to fit with his role as abbot. At times, I feel like I'd like to smack him—not that I would—but, then I wonder if I'm the only one in this place who feels this way." Anticipating a response, Andrew turned to look at Brother Mark who remained cross-legged on the bed.

"Well, I can assure you that you're not the only one who feels this way," Brother Mark said, "but I would prefer that this part of the conversation stays between you and me."

"I understand," Andrew replied.

"You've got to realize, Andrew, that even in the monastery, hierarchy and power, of sorts, are not absent; neither are all the other vices we attempt to conquer like pride and—how can I forget—lust."

"Yeah," Andrew said with a smile. "That's a tough one. Somebody once told me it finally goes away five hours after you're dead."

"It would be my luck that it would raise its ugly head right in the middle of my funeral," Brother Mark said with a laugh. "The difficult part is that the old-timers, who have been here together for most of their lives, are sometimes genuinely naïve or aren't comfortable rocking the boat, so to speak. I know for a fact that Father Luke and Father Jude have been friends since Day One and, Father Luke, as objective and sincere as he is, will not hear clearly any negatives about Father Jude unless the gravity of the situation offers him no choice. And right now,

I'm thinking about the Morgan cabin." Brother Mark paused to shift his position on the bed. "My point is that nothing's perfect until we get to that final resting place we call heaven, and there are times I've had my doubts about even that. But you should feel comfortable talking with Father Luke. My suggestion would be to discretely omit the part about the woman . . . if you're sincerely interested in staying on at St. Anthony's."

Andrew slowly shook his head. "I guess I never expected to be having this conversation in the monastery."

There was a brief pause as the two monks appeared to be digesting the dialogue.

"Can I ask you what you did expect?" Brother Mark queried.

Andrew briefly remained silent. "I'm not exactly sure," he replied thoughtfully. "Mostly solitude and prayer, and, of course, work. I don't expect to bury my head in the sand or simply watch the world go by, but I guess I don't feel a need to be 'out there' either if I really believe in the power of prayer."

"That sounds fairly solid," Brother Mark said, "yet living in community is demanding, as you've experienced. All of our humanness gets exposed for the entire community to see, even if we think they haven't noticed."

Brother Mark stretched and yawned as the door to Brother Edward's adjacent cell opened and closed, followed by the usual rumble of flatulence.

"Right on time," Brother Andrew whispered.

"You've noticed," Brother Mark replied. He stood up and stretched again. "It's getting late. I'd better be going or I won't get up for vigils."

Andrew walked with him to the door. "Thanks for listening and for the advice," Andrew said. "It feels good to be able to talk with someone."

"I know," Brother Mark said. "Now, sleep well."

Andrew quietly closed the door behind him.

Chapter Five

Sibling Symmetry

Brother Matthew's family arrived at the large guesthouse in a minicaravan—three sedans and a rusty old jeep filled to the top with clothes and packages. Matthew was the second youngest in a family of seven siblings, three brothers and three sisters, who were equally graced with good looks and charm, so much so that the standard family joke was deciding whether or not the men were more beautiful than the women. Matthew had no difficulty with that; he would simply admit in front of everyone that he was the best looking one in the family, and most would agree that he was right—not to mention boastful.

Once the family was settled, they invited the monastic community to spend the afternoon with them to eat, socialize, and experience a renewed sense of family and sharing. Family visits were a special time for the monks and often looked forward to. The meals were usually gala affairs with homemade food, a chance to make new acquaintances, and a time for relating stories.

Andrew mixed easily with Matthew's brothers and sisters, who were not much older than he. One exceptional sister, Ellen, the youngest member of the family, was often referred to as the Black Sheep. Surrounded by blondes, Ellen had beautiful jet-black hair, high cheekbones, and the poise and detachment of a European model, yet she was very cordial and relaxed with Andrew, who enjoyed her companionship. He sensed that she appeared, at times, much older than seventeen, as though she had experienced life beyond her years, and very little would astonish her.

Ellen found Andrew sitting alone on a lumpy couch in the living room.

"May I join you?" she asked confidently, leaning forward slightly and offering Andrew her hand. "I'm Matthew's sister, Ellen."

Andrew made an attempt to get up, but Ellen put her other hand on his shoulder and prevented him from doing so.

"Of course," Andrew replied. "I know . . . I mean, yes, please sit down, and I know who you are."

Ellen smiled faintly, amused by Andrew's fumbled greeting.

"I have to say," Andrew said with a smile, "you're every bit as pretty as Matthew said you were."

"And you're every bit as handsome as Matthew said *you* were," Ellen responded.

Andrew could feel some color rise in his cheeks. He smiled and looked at her. "Perhaps it's fair to say that your brother has a keen eye."

"I would agree," Ellen replied.

As a result of that initial conversation, Andrew felt very close to Ellen, as though they had no difficulty understanding each other and, at times, words were not necessary. She seemed to know more about him than Andrew knew about himself, yet she always remained genuine and comfortable to be with. As the afternoon lengthened, Andrew needed to return to the monastery. He looked for Ellen to say goodbye. She was also looking for him.

She hugged Andrew and unexpectedly kissed him on the cheek. "I hope we have a chance to talk again before the week is over," she said.

"Me too," Andrew said. "I really enjoyed our time together."

"And thanks for being so good to Matthew," she added.

Andrew walked back to the monastery, alone in the fading light, thinking about Ellen's last comment about Matthew. He wondered what Matthew may have told her, yet he was not feeling upset about it; in fact, for some reason, he felt good.

The setting sun barely colored the tips of the western peaks with a salmon wash against the indigo sky, as one red-tailed hawk circled high above the ridge, searching for a meal of unwary mice or ground squirrels. Still somewhat euphoric, Andrew imagined that somewhere in the distance, he could probably see a small vapor of steam escaping from the cave of a hibernating bear.

* * *

It was only three days before the celebration of Christmas, and the community was visibly joyful. Carols could be heard at various times throughout the day as the musical schola practiced diligently for the midnight mass—an event filled with incense, memories, and most of all, joy. Neighbors, for miles around, would arrive early to be sure of getting a seat; otherwise, it would mean standing for approximately an hour and a half in an overheated church. And it was not uncommon for a visitor to faint during the lengthy service, either from being overly tired or drinking one too many cocktails before leaving home. Andrew had heard about an older woman from the nearby town of Bitter Creek, an affluent vacation spot, who drove her car off the monastery road after mass and was not discovered until morning, barely alive, by a visiting priest.

On the day before the big celebration, Andrew had been asked to cut more pine boughs to help decorate the church. He was assigned to work with Brother Morgan, who had entered the monastery one year earlier than Andrew, yet both were the same age. Andrew enjoyed Brother Morgan's company because he was almost always humorous or almost always dead serious; and Andrew had difficulty distinguishing between the two, so when Brother Morgan would make a lengthy statement, which he usually did, Andrew was never sure how to react, which, if choosing incorrectly, resulted in total confusion.

They attached the old wooden flatbed to the John Deere tractor and drove toward the Pine Grove at the far end of the property. The snow was deep, but not deep enough to hang up the tractor, which chugged along valiantly through the crisp morning air. Brother Morgan insisted on driving because, as he said, "Machines are my thing." Andrew stood carefully on the power auger housing, in back of Brother Morgan, and hung onto one of the roof supports.

"What a day!" Brother Morgan shouted, even though Andrew was very close to him.

"Yes," Andrew said, "it's a beauty."

"You say you need to do your duty?" Brother Morgan shouted back.

Andrew laughed loudly. "Yes, I need to do my duty," he shouted.

Brother Morgan hit both brakes on the tractor, which started to skid first one way and then the other and finally straightened out and stopped. Andrew jumped off the auger, found a stick, and with the stick in his hand he pretended to be urinating in the field.

"What the heck are you doing?" Brother Morgan asked.

"My duty," Andrew replied. "Isn't it a beauty?"

Brother Morgan laughed heartily knowing that Andrew called him on his humor. He started the tractor, and the two continued into the woods. When they found some suitable trees that were accessible, they began the process of selection and sawing.

"You crack me up," Andrew said as they were both piling pine boughs onto the flatbed.

"Yeah," Brother Morgan said, "I crack myself up. I think that's why I'm here."

"Me too," Andrew responded.

Brother Morgan continued to work in silence. Finally, he asked Andrew, "Why are you here?"

Andrew scratched his head. "I thought we were all here for the same reason," Andrew said sincerely.

"Well, what's that?" Brother Morgan asked.

"Couldn't get any women!" Andrew blurted, stealing a line from Brother Mark. Both men laughed until Brother Morgan fell on the ground.

"You've never heard that one before?" Andrew asked. "It's an old monastic standard."

Brother Morgan looked seriously puzzled. "But," he said with a straight face, "that's why I *am* here!" This time it was Andrew who fell, laughing, to the ground.

Both men continued to work in relative silence until Andrew spoke up.

"You know, Morgan, I've seen the other side of you, so to speak; the more serious Morgan.'"

"And?" Brother Morgan replied.

"And," Andrew continued, "you're fortunate that you have a good grasp of humor and know how to use it because I've heard it's particularly helpful in this life."

"Probably so," Brother Morgan replied. He continued to saw a large bough as snow and sawdust scattered over his head. "There are things, at times, that I just don't understand yet, I'm hoping that with some humor and the grace of God, I can stay the course and become Mr. Monk."

"Well said," Andrew replied with a smile. "I think you're doing just fine."

"You think so?" Brother Morgan shouted. Feigning a lunatic out of control, he pretended to saw off his arm, both legs, and finally, his head before he dropped, motionless in the snow, with his tongue hanging out of his mouth.

When they recovered, they returned to the monastery with a wagon full of pine boughs. This time, Andrew was driving.

* * *

Christmas Eve arrived perfectly with frosty air and clear starry skies, decorating the surrounding mountains with pinpoint lights. The monastery was aglow with warmth and color and wonderful scents—balsam, wood smoke, and sandalwood incense, all mingling with a potpourri of cologne and perfume from the growing number of visiting guests who braved the late hour to attend the midnight mass.

Andrew had difficulty containing his excitement as he pulled his freshly laundered habit over his T-shirt and jeans. Although he never felt totally comfortable in the midst of a crowd, he was looking forward to the experience of his first monastic Christmas. He left his cell and entered the main cloister on his way to the church, just as Brother Matthew's family arrived, rosy-cheeked and filled with holiday spirit. They all whispered, "Merry Christmas," while the men shook Andrew's hand. Ellen waited until Andrew was about to leave, then she quickly moved alongside of him, smiled, and said, "Merry Christmas, Andrew."

Andrew was suddenly aware of Ellen's lips lightly kissing his cheek and her shining eyes looking directly at him. Her perfume, her softness, and her genuine affection momentarily disoriented him as he stood, motionless, in a sea of people, unaware of their presence.

"Merry Christmas, Ellen," he said with a smile. "You look wonderful." He turned quickly and continued into the church, regaining his composure as he walked.

Several monks had already arrived and were seated in a half circle behind the altar, which stood near the far wall of the church. Candles and pine boughs were thoughtfully placed on the clean altar linens, matching the decorations throughout the monastery. Andrew knew that Brother Matthew had been appointed sacristan and was responsible for much of the hard work, which showed so beautifully. In front of the altar, sitting on the polished brick floor, were fifteen gigantic pots of poinsettias in traditional red, white, and soft pinks with contrasting bows. Andrew felt as if he were part of a regal coronation in a medieval castle, awaiting the arrival of the king and queen. Instead, it was Brother Matthew who entered the church, lights reflecting in his golden hair, as he confidently made his way to his assigned seat across from Andrew. He made a deep yet genuine bow to the altar and sat down. Andrew was not sure, but when he glanced at Matthew, he thought he saw him wink and smile. Andrew smiled back, somewhat bashfully, and then lowered his gaze to the floor.

Once the monks were seated, Father Paul led the schola in a medley of sacred Christmas carols. Their rendition of "Silent Night," sung flawlessly, was nearly overwhelming for Andrew, who found it necessary to bite the inside of his cheek so he would not be overcome emotionally at such a public event. Far from shy, Father Paul then spoke directly to the audience and asked them to join in with the monks to sing "Chestnuts Roasting on an Open Fire" because, as he explained, it was always his favorite secular carol. Andrew was more than surprised by Father Paul's choice of songs, yet it was clear that, halfway through the first verse, the audience was enjoying itself, smiling and singing strongly.

Just before the song ended, Father Jude entered the church and took his place in front of the abbatial chair. He was also singing, smiling, and clearly relishing the festive mood of a responsive crowd. When the singing ended he walked to the altar and addressed the gathering. "I know that you've all made Father Paul very happy by singing his favorite Christmas carol . . . and you sang very well." The audience laughed and relaxed. "Before we begin," he continued, "we want to thank you for taking the time to share this special night with us and for sharing your lives with our community throughout the year. We continue to value your friendship. So on behalf of all of us at St. Anthony's, we want to wish you and your family a blessed and peaceful holiday season. May God bless you." Father Jude then bowed over the altar and began the mass.

There were several chairs for the visitors to sit on, however, most of the audience stood for the entire service; some were clearly weary, yawning and shifting from one foot to the other.

Once the communion service was over, Andrew knew that the final procession out of the church was not far behind. He was enjoying the tremendous spiritual essence of the evening, which was, perhaps, overshadowed by his awareness of a sizable crowd and a feeling of being on stage. At times, he felt self-conscious: where should he rest his gaze; should he acknowledge the audience? He would often get preoccupied with deeper personal thoughts, specifically image issues, such as "Do they think I look like a monk?" and "Do people feel that I am genuine?" Yet with time, these questions became less of a concern for him until he was, once again, faced with a large crowd, like those at the midnight mass.

Once Brother Paul began the recessional with "Hark the Herald Angels Sing," Andrew was happy to be leaving the beautiful yet congested environment of the church and walking toward the solitude of his cell. At the end of the cloister, the monks stopped and wished each other a Merry Christmas with hugs and handshakes. Brother Matthew approached Andrew, excited and smiling. He grabbed Andrew and pulled him toward him, hugging him strongly.

"Merry Christmas, Andrew," Brother Matthew said with a glowing smile. His blond hair and white teeth reflected the soft golden light of the wall sconces.

"Merry Christmas, Matt," Andrew replied, smiling and feeling very happy. "It's such an incredible night!"

"You're right," Brother Matthew replied, "and it can only get better." Brother Matthew backed away. "I'll see you in the refectory," he said, moving quickly toward the church.

* * *

Andrew opened the door to his cell and walked in the dark toward his closet. In a somewhat melancholy mood, he began thinking about his own parents, particularly his mom, who would, most likely, spend

Christmas alone. He switched on the small light inside the closet and began to remove his habit.

"Hello, Andrew," she said.

Sparks of light flew through Andrew's brain as fear and adrenaline prepared his body for battle with an unseen spirit. He turned quickly to see Ellen sitting casually, legs crossed, at his desk, smiling in the shadows.

"You scared the crap out of me!" he said. "How did you get in here?"

Ellen stood up and slowly walked toward him. "Well, you guys never lock your doors and I simply walked in." She stood in front of Andrew with her arms crossed; a Mona Lisa smile on her beautifully shaped lips.

Andrew went to the door and locked it. "You know, if they found you in here, I'd be thrown out of the monastery, and God only knows what would happen to you."

"I suppose they'd make me join a nunnery," she said glibly.

Andrew slipped his robe over his head and carefully hung it in the closet.

"I've often wondered what monks wear under those habits," Ellen teased. She then stood behind Andrew who was reaching for his Zen stool on the upper shelf. She gently put her arms around him and nuzzled her face into the back of his neck. "Your hair smells really nice, like you just washed it," she whispered, brushing her lips against his ear. Andrew stood motionless, his arms hanging by his side. "I can't do this, Ellen," he said anxiously.

Ellen continued to nuzzle his neck and ear.

"I'm not asking you to do anything," she said. "Just be with me for a while." She skillfully located the light switch and turned it off.

Andrew slowly turned around to face her. "What do you want?" he asked, as though he were being held hopelessly hostage by an overpowering force.

Ellen looked directly at him. "I want to be with you on this wonderful Christmas Eve." She closed her eyes and placed her head on his shoulder. "You must get very lonely, at times."

Andrew could smell her perfume and feel the softness of her skin. He slowly reached out and put his arms around her. "You have no idea," he whispered.

The wind in the garth gently stirred the trees and cast shadows over the glass slider. Andrew too moved gently, immune to his environment and aspirations.

Ellen then put her hand on his and led him to the bed, and they both sat down. Andrew leaned against the wall as Ellen moved alongside of him. Again, she nuzzled his neck and ear and brushed her lips over his cheek.

Andrew felt his breathing increase as excitement intensified throughout his entire body. "Ellen, I like you very much, but this is wrong for me."

Ellen spoke softly into his ear. "It can't be wrong when the moment is right and two people care about each other." She tenderly kissed his eyes, nose, and cheek and then placed her lips against his. Andrew hesitated, suddenly remembering the long-forgotten taste of lipstick. Ellen then kissed him aggressively, and Andrew could not resist. He kissed her more and more intensely, feeling an uncontrollable desire for her. She ran her mouth down the side of his neck while quickly unbuttoning his shirt. She kissed his chest, quickly making her way to his stomach, unbuttoned Andrew's jeans, slowly slid them down, and, with no hesitation, buried her face in his shorts. Through the cloth, she licked Andrew's erection until he could feel her saliva soaking through to his skin. She then slid his shorts down, past his knees, and continued to provide such oral stimulation that Andrew had no choice but to forcefully release the intention of her desire.

Afterwards, Andrew remained silently immovable, in a satiated yet conflicted state. He watched as Ellen put on her coat and quietly pushed open the glass slider that led outside to the garth. She turned before exiting, and even though Andrew could not clearly see her face, he was sure that she was smiling.

"It's a beautiful night, Andrew," she whispered. "Merry Christmas." She then stepped out into the frigid December air and closed the door behind her.

Andrew stared into the darkness at nothing. He tried to focus, to move, to think, yet it was as if his mind had short-circuited and messages to his brain were derailed. He continued to lie on his bed, half naked, aborting any further thoughts of movement, until he finally closed his eyes and fell asleep.

* * *

Two hours later, Andrew was abruptly awakened by a knock on his door. He tried to stand up but tripped over his jeans which were still around his ankles. In a flash, he remembered what had happened, and a familiar rush of confusion and guilt quickly combined with his apprehension over another visitor, so much so that Andrew felt faint and arrived at the door disoriented. He opened the door as Brother Matthew, who had apparently been leaning against it, fell into the room and onto the floor in front of him.

'Damn . . . where am I?' Andrew thought as he quietly closed the door.

Brother Matthew rolled over and attempted to stifle his laughter. He sat up and looked at Andrew like a puppy that had just had an accident on the carpet.

"Where were you, Andrew?" he asked sheepishly. "I thought you were going to celebrate with us in the refectory."

"I'm not sure where I was," Andrew said softly, and then, in an even softer voice, he added, "I'm not sure where I am now." He turned on his desk lamp and sat in his chair.

Brother Matthew winced and covered his eyes. "Can I turn on a different light?" Without waiting for an answer, he switched on the shaded closet light, turned off the desk lamp, and sat, Indian style, at Andrew's feet.

Andrew stared at the wall. "What time is it?" he asked.

"It's a little after three," Brother Matthew replied.

Andrew looked at Matthew, who appeared childlike on the floor. "I guess I fell asleep," he said.

Brother Matthew got up and stood behind Andrew's chair. He slowly massaged the muscles in Andrew's neck and shoulders and continued up the back of his head and over Andrew's temples.

Andrew could feel the warmth and strength of Brother Matthew's hands therapeutically dissolving the stress and tightness in that area.

He closed his eyes and lowered his head toward his chest. Andrew was mildly surprised as Brother Matthew gently and skillfully massaged his ears and then his eyes. In the midst of this silence, Andrew was keenly aware that a message was being sent to him—a message, perhaps, more genuine than he cared to examine, at a time and place he had never anticipated. And he had no idea of how it should be resolved.

Unlike Andrew, Brother Matthew did not analyze; he simply acted, tempered by a modicum of the environment and, at times, shaped by it. As their friendship grew, Andrew would remember listening with questionable pathos and disbelief as Brother Matthew described his meditative sittings, where he was focused on Jesus, loving him reverentially as the son of God and, physically, as a man by masturbating to the point of orgasm. Matthew seldom expressed guilt; if it was love, he felt it was perfectly acceptable, and he had no difficulty describing the clinical details.

And so it was instinctive for Brother Matthew to express his affection to someone he truly cared about. He brushed his lips against Andrew's ear and barely kissed his cheek.

Andrew remained silent yet, emotionally torn, welcoming a growing bond while, at the same time, fearing the ironic entanglement at this particular point in his life.

"You must know how much I care about you," Brother Matthew whispered.

Andrew said nothing, however, he was aware of a strong smell of alcohol coming from Brother Matthew—a smell familiar to Andrew but not offensive. He turned slightly to observe Brother Matthew, who continued to look like a sad puppy dog, waiting for his master's approval.

"You've been drinking," Andrew said.

"You're right," Brother Matthew replied honestly. "You know how it is . . . the bottles of scotch and B & B magically appear in this place on special occasions. I probably had more than my share." With an awkward grin, Matthew asked, "Is my breath that obvious?"

"Yes," Andrew said with a smile. "It actually smells quite nice; sort of orangey . . . must be the brandy."

Brother Matthew appeared more deliberate as he moved even closer to Andrew and looked directly into his eyes.

"Then maybe we should share it," he said softly, as he lightly touched his lips against Andrew's.

Brother Matthew pulled him closer, with no resistance from Andrew, who suddenly felt his entire body reignite and relish a longing which he had subconsciously anticipated but had tried from the beginning to suppress. Feelings of perpetual loneliness dissolved instantly once the barriers came crashing down, following their physical contact and mutual consent.

Yet for Andrew, all was not right with the world. He moved his head next to Brother Matthew's and held him firmly. Christmas Eve had become a panoply of emotional highs and lows, underscoring a polarity of right and wrong, good and evil, the sacred and the profane. He grew tired of being good yet suffered immeasurably when he faltered, and Andrew knew, that as right as it felt being with Brother Matthew, he could not reconcile nor justify his current behavior with his vocation.

"It's late, Matt," Andrew said. "I think I'll hit the sack." As soon as he said it, Andrew sensed that Brother Matthew knew he was not totally truthful.

Brother Matthew stood up and faced Andrew. "I'll leave, Andrew, but . . . I'd like you to tell me what you *really* feel before I go."

Andrew felt pressured, confused, and unsure of himself. "I don't know where to begin . . . I think I need to sleep so I can think clearly."

Matthew spoke softly. "I know that I'm not exactly sober, but tonight is not something I'll blame on the alcohol in the morning. I hope you'll feel the same way."

"I don't know what I feel anymore," Andrew replied. "Maybe . . . maybe we're not the same—whatever that is."

Brother Matthew felt as though someone had punched him solidly in the stomach; he stared at Andrew and said nothing. He then walked toward the door and stopped. "I'm sorry you feel that way, Andrew," he said. "I'd better go." He left quickly, closing the door behind him.

Andrew sat alone in the silence listening to his heartbeat; the pounding raged within his head as he tried to get undressed. He removed his jeans, turned off the light and fell into bed, hoping that sleep would come quickly and in the morning, he could face the world anew. Rolling from one side of the bed to the other, he struggled with his thoughts, knowing he had lied to Matthew and, even now, that he was lying to himself. With increasing anger, he punched his mattress repeatedly until he could no longer remain in bed; he sat up and knew what he had to do. He grabbed his old flannel robe from the closet and quietly opened the door. Barefooted, he walked softly, through the empty hallway, toward Brother Matthew's cell, which was the very last room in the dormitory.

Afraid that someone would hear him, Andrew hesitated to knock on Brother Matthew's door. Instead, he turned the doorknob slowly, silently. Fortunately, it was unlocked. He quickly entered the room, which, although it was illuminated only by Matthew's gooseneck lamp, was bright enough for Andrew to see what was happening.

"What the . . . !" Brother Matthew half whispered and half shouted.

Before Matthew managed to find the sheet and cover himself, Andrew saw him, lying naked on his bed, with an altar candle in his hand—Andrew felt frozen to the floor.

Brother Matthew raised himself on his elbows. "Shut the damn door!"

Andrew slowly turned and closed the door. With his back to Matthew he spoke softly. "I'm really sorry, Matt. I should have knocked . . . I'll see you in the morning."

"No, wait!" Matthew pleaded. "I'm really upset that this happened, but you're here, and we need to talk, okay?"

Bewildered and embarrassed, Andrew stood, facing the door in silence. "It's not a good time," he said quietly.

"Please, come over here, Andrew, and talk to me," Matthew begged. "Please, don't walk out right now."

Andrew turned to face Brother Matthew, who remained propped up on his elbows. "I don't know what to say anymore, except that this night has been something I never expected."

Matthew shifted from one arm to the other. "I apologize, Andrew, for this and for anything I might have said or done, which caused you to doubt yourself or your life here. And you're right . . . I guess we're not the same." He carefully reached for the desk lamp and turned off the light. "I feel less embarrassed with it off."

In the darkness, Matthew's silhouette was still visible against the moonlit drape. Andrew slowly moved toward him and then knelt beside his bed.

"I came here for a reason," Andrew whispered. "Earlier, when you were with me in my room—I lied. I've often thought about you, about us. I just never expected that these thoughts would ever really happen, at least, not here. I can't deny what I feel anymore, Matt."

Matthew put his hand on Andrew's arm. "You're not just saying this to make me feel like I'm less of a fool," Matthew asked, "especially with the candle and all?"

"No," Andrew whispered. "I mean it. We're really no different in the way we feel. I guess you've always been more open and honest about it while I've usually repressed it. The candle though is . . . peculiar—no big deal—but I have to ask."

"Go ahead," Matthew said.

"Doesn't it hurt?"

"Only if I sit up," Matthew said.

Andrew knew that Matthew was smiling his big sheepish grin.

"You had better lie down then," Andrew said, as he gently pushed on Matthew's chest. He ran his fingers lightly over his shoulders, neck, and forehead, which was damp with perspiration.

"That feels good," Matthew whispered.

Andrew slowly moved his hand down Matthew's chest, over his stomach, barely allowing his fingertips to touch his skin. When his hand reached the thin sheet, Andrew lifted it slightly and drew it back, beyond Matthew's feet, until it fell silently to the floor.

He could feel Matthew tremble, ever so slightly, as he continued down his hip, across his thigh to his lower leg and then onto his foot where Andrew traced with two fingers the outline of his arch, toes, and ankle. He then moved his hands slowly up his calf toward his inner thigh, knowing that his own hand had begun to shake.

Matthew's breathing intensified; his body shuddered involuntarily, as if the room had abruptly been cooled.

Andrew gently moved his hand over Matthew's erection, lightly tracing its shape with his fingers. He could feel his own breathing increase and his trembling became more obvious.

Suddenly, Matthew reached up and forcefully pressed his face against Andrew's.

Andrew could hear him emit intermittent groans of pleasure. He raised his head and spoke into Matthew's ear. "I want you to finish what you started when I walked in here," he said quietly. "I want to be with you."

Matthew turned to look directly at him. "You don't have to do this, Andrew."

"I know, but it's what I want," Andrew admitted.

Andrew smiled. He leaned over Matthew and kissed him, gently at first, and then more and more fiercely. He could feel Matthew's movement beneath him until, suddenly, Matthew's neck and back arched upward, off the bed, and his body stiffened. Andrew held him tight, feeling his body convulse repeatedly. When it was over, Andrew realized that he had also shared in Matthew's release, wetting his flannel robe and Matthew's sheets.

Chapter Six

Etched Trauma

With the passing of the Christmas holidays, the monastery settled in for the long winter season. Work focused primarily on internal projects, which maintained the facilities, while all those nonemergency repairs over the short summer months were finally considered for assignment by the prior.

Andrew realized he had more time for meditation and spiritual reading; he often meditated, three times a day, for longer and longer intervals, either in the small heated entrance room or his cell. The more he practiced, the easier it became for him to sit silently in the darkness as his body gradually relaxed and his thoughts diminished. On several occasions, he could only remember sitting on the Zen stool and later, standing up to end the session. He had no idea how long he had been there or what, if anything, had transpired. On other occasions, he was tormented by continuous rapid thoughts, filled with dark imagery and carnal desires. An overwhelming sense of hopelessness invaded his personal privacy, distracting his purpose and searing his conscience with silent words such as "sinner" and "hypocrite." It was then that Andrew fought to continue his commitment by surrendering himself to God.

He recalled the writings of St. Ammonas, an early Desert Father, who wrote that God would not bring temptation upon you if he did not love you. St. Ammonas felt that temptation was necessary for the faithful because all who were free of temptation were not among the elect. Such wisdom offered Andrew only mild consolation during difficult times.

In addition to his rigorous schedule of meditation and Lexio, Andrew had decided to increase his dietary fasting. At first, he would go without breakfast twice a week and abstain from the evening meal on weekends.

In time, he learned to place less emphasis on food, and this allowed him more time for his spiritual pursuits.

It was Brother Adrian who spoke with Father Luke about asking Andrew to assist with the meal preparations. Initially, Andrew felt extremely anxious about cooking for the entire community, yet he knew that he could not decline a work request from the prior. With his crooked smile, Brother Adrian generously offered to work with Andrew until both felt he was comfortable in the large airy kitchen.

Above the double sink, windows stretched upward to meet the twelve-foot ceiling, bathing the room with copious amounts of natural light while providing a scenic view of the distant peaks. On the remaining three walls were cupboards filled with innumerable spices; their doors were removed at the insistence of Brother Adrian who felt that they "got in his way." Two commercial-sized gas stoves with ovens stood in the center of the room, with a variety of simmering pots on their polished stainless steel surface. The large white refrigerators and freezer were barely noticeable in the spacious spotless kitchen.

Andrew was no stranger to cooking, having worked on and off in food service for several years, yet he was not accustomed to the meatless cuisine and the various methods of food preparation required by the monastery. With Brother Adrian's gentle yet somewhat unorthodox instruction, it was not long before Andrew developed sufficient culinary skills to independently prepare the monastery's meals. At first, he cooked an evening supper, which was the smaller of the two meals and generally a simple dish. Andrew agonized over several vegetarian cookbooks, hoping to find something modest, yet tasty, made with eggs. After much deliberation, he decided on a creamed egg and asparagus cockaigne that would need to be baked in the oven; yet he was unsure about how the oven operated, whether it was an automatic pilot or needed a match, so he decided to look for Brother Adrian who was, rather conveniently, sitting in the refectory, next to the woodstove, reading a large print book.

"Excuse me, Brother Adrian," Andrew said, "but I was wondering if you could help me with the oven."

Brother Adrian's face lit up immediately with a gigantic smile. "Follow me," he intoned slyly, as though a character from a murder mystery.

In the kitchen, Brother Adrian opened the oven door with a flourish. "Is this your oven of choice?" he asked with an exaggerated grin.

Andrew nodded his head, not understanding the frivolity of the situation.

"Yes," he said.

"I am a professional," Brother Adrian said dramatically. "Do not try this at home." He took a large wooden match from a tin box above the stove, closed the oven door and turned on the gas. He then paced back and forth, several times, struck the match and looked at Andrew. "Stand back!" he said. He then opened the oven door and, much to Andrew's disbelief, tossed the lit match into the gas-filled oven, which ignited with a flash and a loud "whoosh." Andrew jumped back, expecting to be completely blown up, however, the flame disappeared and the oven was now on.

Still grinning, Brother Adrian whispered, "I don't show this to everyone, so it would be nice if we can just keep it between us, okay?"

Andrew was thankful that he was still alive. "Okay," he said, somewhat dazed.

He spent most of the afternoon methodically setting out the necessary ingredients and searching for the proper pans and mixers, trying to forget his anxiety and hoping that the end result would be satisfactory to his brothers.

He stood over the stove, oblivious to the world, stirring a basic white sauce with a large metal whisk. He removed the mixture from the flame, waiting for it to thicken a little before adding the eggs and asparagus, when he was startled by a loud cough coming from the direction of the window. Andrew looked up to see Matthew, standing outside, his nose pressed against the glass, a smile on his lips.

Andrew quickly walked over and opened the lower section.

"How is the chef?" Matthew asked softly.

Andrew was happy to see Matthew, even though he was still somewhat uncomfortable since it had been nearly two weeks since they spoke. He knew, at various times, someone had lightly knocked on his locked door, but he decided to pretend he was sleeping.

"I'm not sure," Andrew said, "but I think I'd rather be skiing."

"Don't worry about it; it'll be fine," Matthew said.

"I hope so," Andrew replied. He looked at Matthew whose face was ruddy and wholesome-looking from the cold and snow. "Have you been collecting eggs?"

"Of course." He laughed. "I spent a hot afternoon with the girls."

Andrew laughed quietly.

Matthew shifted back and forth. "Well, I'd better let you get back to your cooking." He looked at Andrew. "I'd like to talk sometime—when you get a chance," he said.

"Sure," Andrew said tentatively.

Matthew started to leave and then abruptly stuck his head back in the window.

"I forgot to ask," he said. "What are you making?"

Andrew borrowed Brother Mark's Groucho imitation, fake cigar and all. "It's a surprise, kid," he mimicked. "I could tell ya, but then I'd have to kill ya." With that, he closed the window on Matthew's smiling face.

* * *

The refectory was dark and vacant when Andrew returned to clean the supper dishes. Barely after six, everyone had either eaten or chosen not to. Andrew slowly walked toward the steamy warming table, fearful of what he might see; he knew that a large quantity of leftover food meant that the community did not like it. He nervously lifted the stainless steel cover and was relieved to see that the largest serving pan was practically scraped clean. He bowed his head in the dim light and silently offered thanks to God and to the *Joy of Cooking* cookbook.

Inside the kitchen, a hastily scratched note was taped to the back of the sink: "It was delicious. I'd better watch out for my job!" The note was signed by Brother Adrian.

Scrubbing the remaining pots, Andrew saw his reflection in the pitch-black windows: rolled up sleeves, exposed arms covered with soapsuds, a torn grey sweatshirt, and baggy blue jeans—darkened across the front from spilled water. A large ball of fur glided effortlessly toward him and rubbed against his shins. Andrew looked down to see what he felt was the fattest cat in the world, Buddha, playfully marking him as her own. She curled her tail halfway up his leg as she weaved in and out, leaving her scent wherever she could.

Andrew had nearly finished the dishes when he heard a truck drive up to the back door. It was difficult to see who it was until the person pressed his laughing face against the frozen glass. Eric Holtz, the only hired hand who helped at the monastery, waved his signature wave at Andrew—a folded fist with the thumb and small finger extended out straight. Andrew knew that this was the California surfer sign language "greeting," and he returned the wave back to Eric who disappeared down the back steps into the basement.

Andrew admired Eric for his overall philosophy of life, which emphasized a low-keyed, relaxed, yet responsible way of living. He lived with his wife and two children in a converted barn, architecturally contemporized with skylights, lofts, and Scandinavian furnishings, an influence introduced by his Swedish wife, Kathleen, whom Eric met when he was in the Navy.

After working for nearly fifteen years for the monks, Eric had experienced an insider's perspective of monastic life. He saw many prospective candidates join the community and, for various reasons, leave; some by their own choice and others who were asked to do so. And when speaking with the monks, particularly the younger postulants, Eric had learned to be gracefully diplomatic, never taking sides and never losing his sense of humor. Andrew found him refreshing and easily likable.

Hearing the bells announce Compline, Andrew hastily left the kitchen and returned to his cell.

* * *

The following day began extraordinarily sunny, with a dramatic contrast of brilliant blue skies and white landscape, jutting upward and forming the numerous peaks that enveloped the vast monastic enclosure. Inside the church, rays of sunshine burned through the large stained glass window behind the altar, casting mixed colors over the white altar linens and then subtly changing into different hues upon the dark red-tiled floor.

Andrew noticed that several people had joined the monks for the morning mass, some whom he recognized as neighbors and guests. Quite often, he had observed new male retreatants, who were staying at the guesthouse, while in the process of discernment, as they attempted to hear the call of God to a solitary life. He thought of his own journey, up to the present, remembering the raw anxiety of attending mass with the entire community and the joy of successful acceptance.

Most often, only a few retreatants would return to begin the practice of monastic life, a vocation which severed them from a familiar lifestyle and quickly required them to sacrifice and reorder priorities.

Andrew's assigned chores for the morning were to clean the bathroom in the upper and lower dormitories and then proceed with the morning egg collection. He knew that he would have to make short work of the cleaning, since he was not given a partner to help him in the eggery, and collecting all of the eggs alone would easily take him till noon.

The half-mile walk from the monastery to the eggery proved invigorating and radiant. Steller's jays squawked their raucous cries, searching for breakfast within the mounds of chicken dung which was cleaned out of the henhouse and piled behind it. Even in the middle of winter, the smell of the dung could turn the strongest stomachs. Andrew was thankful that a cooperative breeze was blowing the odor away from him.

Hidden in a large fuse box, near the entrance of the eggery, was the key that opened the front door. Unable to locate it, Andrew searched every nook inside the dusty metal housing but found nothing. He considered returning to the monastery, but then he remembered seeing footprints in the snow, which came from the main road, joined his at the back of the monastery and ended directly in front of the eggery; he wondered if someone had already begun collecting the eggs. He turned the doorknob and, as anticipated, the door opened quietly and fully, as if it were welcoming him to one of his favorite chores. He stepped inside and closed the door. "Anybody here?" Andrew called, but there was no response. He knew that he could not be heard if someone were collecting, since the room he had entered was separated from the chickens and used for processing the eggs for packing and shipping. The entrance to the henhouse was still two doors away.

Andrew tossed his parka on top of an empty egg box. He found a container of paper face masks and pulled the elastic over his head while adjusting the pliable nosepiece which would help decrease the amount of airborne particles he might inhale. Although he found the mask uncomfortable, Andrew felt that it also made the task more bearable by reducing the acrid stench of five thousand hens enclosed in one place.

He put on a denim apron and looked inside the large walk-in cooler for an egg cart. He expected to see one of the two carts missing, if it were being used, however, both carts were still there. He rolled one of them out to the processing room and slammed the heavy cooler door shut. Suddenly, he was overcome with an inexplicable, eerie feeling, as though something was wrong or, even worse, that he was not alone. He stood motionless in the silence, surveying the room like a child who has to look under his bed before he can go to sleep. The machinery somehow looked unfriendly, almost sinister, in the darkened room. The conveyor, which carried the washed eggs, continued through a candling booth—a small canvas-enclosed area where the eggs would pass over intense lights so that a person sitting in the booth could remove any cracked or dirty eggs and, more significantly, eggs with blood or feed inside of them. Andrew had worked in the candling booth many times and was familiar with the process. He knew that there was a high stool inside the booth where the candler would sit to better observe the eggs as they twisted back and forth over the lights.

Just below the canvas, Andrew noticed what appeared to be the tips of two black rubber boots. His earlier visceral thoughts escalated into full-blown fear; he could feel the hair on the back of his neck and arms stand up—his mouth grew even drier.

He pulled his mask up to his forehead and tried to think clearly and calmly. "Anybody there?" he asked timidly. Again, there was no response, only the distant cackling of the hens and intermittent fans. He realized that he had to end the standoff by satisfying his suspicions. He saw a large broom leaning against a row of egg cartons and decided to use it as a probe and, if necessary, a weapon.

With the broom elevated like a javelin, Andrew attacked the canvas, pushing it aside, and shouted, "Come out, you son of a bitch!" The old green canvas swung open, scattering dust and knocking over egg cartons that had been stacked inside. Much to Andrew's surprise, the booth was empty except for a worn plaid jacket hanging from a nail and the rubber irrigation boots, which someone had removed when they were working.

Relieved, yet somewhat embarrassed, Andrew laughed out loud at his foolish antics. He picked up the cartons, straightened the canvas, and went into the henhouse to finish his chores.

He pushed the cumbersome egg cart through the entrance of the lower henhouse and was immediately inundated with oppressive heat, the smell of ammonia-saturated urine, feces, and chicken dander, floating abundantly in the air. The noise of the cart and the closing doors silenced the hens, as if on cue. This provided Andrew his customary opportunity to announce himself. "Hello, girls," he leered. "I'm here to collect your fruit." With that, the hens resumed their low-grade cackling, and Andrew began to harvest the eggs.

Some of the eggs were still warm with moist shiny shells. Even though the slanted cage bottom forced each egg to gently roll forward and out of reach of the hens, occasionally, a protective chicken would peck Andrew's hand as he picked them up, filling him with a slight twinge of guilt. Eggs that were visibly cracked or leaking were tossed into a bucket attached to the cart and later fed to the monastery's resident pigs that lived, conveniently, next to the upper henhouse. Andrew had never seen an egg without a shell until his work in the eggery; the eggs were nearly perfectly shaped, covered by a modest membrane, and able to be handled. To Andrew, they felt like old Jell-O, strange, yet interesting—hence their nickname—"jellies."

Nearly half way through collecting, Andrew heard several birds squawking, louder and louder, on the other side of the house. Within minutes, all the hens took up the cry, sensing an unseen danger and feeling vulnerable in their cages. Andrew knew that a high state of agitation for the hens could be potentially lethal, so he quickly walked in the direction from which he had originally heard the first noises. Staccato screeches reverberated above the other sounds providing Andrew with an audible beacon and good direction. He quickly studied each cage but saw nothing unusual until suddenly, the problem became obvious. One of the hens had somehow managed to get injured and was bleeding, and like sharks around a swimmer, the blood initiated a frenzied behavior among the four other birds in the cage as they began to viciously peck at the victim in an attempt to kill it. By the time Andrew arrived, the injured chicken was bleeding profusely, her eyes had been gouged out, and her white feathers were covered with red. She frantically flapped her wings, spraying blood on the other hens in the cage.

Andrew lifted the wire door and reached inside to retrieve the injured bird, yet with all the commotion, it was difficult to grab her as she pecked blindly at anything near her, including Andrew, who was also quickly spattered with blood. He finally grabbed both of her legs, quickly pulled her out, and placed her in an empty cage, hoping that she could stand on a perch; however, she was unable to do so and fell to the bottom, where she stayed, panting and dying.

The remaining four hens began to attack each other since each was covered with blood. One by one, Andrew removed the hens and placed each one in a separate cage. By then, the cacophony had subsided and the familiar, more tolerable, cackling resumed.

It was difficult for Andrew to tell whether it was his blood he saw on his arms and hands or blood from the chickens. He could feel a coagulated stickiness on his face and in his hair; his mask was also spattered. Tired and overheated, he decided to return to the processing room to wash in the large utility tub.

After adjusting the water, he began to scrub his hands and arms with an old bar of Lava soap, which foamed into pink suds and stained the plastic sink. He splashed the cool water over his face and hair until he no longer felt the sticky residue, and the water ran clear. From the shelf above the sink, he reached for a clean towel and thoroughly dried himself.

Leaning pensively against the sink, Andrew focused on the candling booth that had concerned him earlier; the rubber boots still protruded from the bottom with ominous detachment, as though waiting for Andrew's inspection to see if someone might now be in them. 'This is ridiculous,' he thought, as he forced himself to look elsewhere. He gazed out the window at the bright snow and blue sky, wishing that his task were completed and then realized that he needed to use the bathroom before he returned to the henhouse.

The lavatory was located next to the small office where orders for deliveries and other eggery-related business were conducted. Although it was not as large as the office, the lavatory had room for a toilet, a small sink, and a paper towel dispenser.

Andrew had used the facility many times and had no reason to expect anything unusual; however, he noticed that the door was completely closed, rather than ajar, an indication that the lavatory might be in use. He felt silly knocking, yet he tapped lightly on the door. "Hello," he said softly, but he got no response. He opened the door and, in the darkness, he searched for the switch box on the left wall, which, when turned on, completely illuminated the room and burned into Andrew's mind an unforgettable tragic sight.

The body hung, suspended, from a large overhead water pipe, by a thick hemp rope which was used for securing egg cases during transit. It twisted, slowly, with its grey contorted face, gaping mouth and open eyes.

Andrew recoiled in horror, wanting to scream, but not being able to breathe. He gasped for air, doubled over, and fell to his knees. He then forced himself to get up, crashed through the office door and picked up the telephone. Frantically, he dialed the kitchen extension and finally heard Brother Adrian's voice.

"Hello," Brother Adrian said.

Andrew tried to talk but only garbled gasps of sound were emitted.

"Hello!" Brother Adrian said, only louder this time.

"The eggery," Andrew whispered. "He's dead." Andrew dropped the phone and collapsed on top of the desk.

Chapter Seven

Recovery

Andrew woke, bleary eyed and disoriented in a world of unusual whiteness. The bed linens, blankets, walls, curtains, and even the floor were extremely white and glaring. He squinted in an attempt to identify its location and his reason for being in bed.

"Good afternoon, Andrew," he said.

Somewhat startled, Andrew looked toward the source of the voice and recognized Father Gerald, the monastery's infirmarian—a distinguished-looking man who quit practicing medicine after his wife died and then decided to join the monastery at the age of fifty-two. "How are you feeling?" he asked.

Andrew tried to sit up, but Father Gerald quickly admonished him.

"You'll be better off to lie flat for a while. You've been through quite an experience."

Andrew gratefully returned his head to the pillow. He felt as though someone had placed a heavy weight on him, sapping his energy, and making him feel somewhat dizzy. He discovered that his feet had been elevated, and he was covered with two or three layers of blankets. "What happened?" he mumbled.

Father Gerald moved close to his side and placed his hand on his forehead. "You fainted at the eggery earlier this morning," Father Gerald explained. "The paramedics found you sprawled across the office desk, suffering from shock. You've been through an awful lot, Andrew, so please, try to get some rest."

Suddenly, Andrew recalled the scene in the lavatory, experiencing it once again, as if it had just happened. He began to thrash hysterically, throwing his blankets and shouting, "No! No!"

Father Gerald held him firmly while managing to press a buzzer above the bed. Within seconds, Brother Nathan rushed in to assist him.

"Hold him down, Brother Nathan," Father Gerald said calmly. "I'm going to give him a sedative."

The request was an easy task for Brother Nathan, who was a recent graduate of Annapolis and a varsity linebacker for their football team.

Father Gerald proceeded to inject Andrew with a strong dose of Valium. "This should help you to relax, Andrew," he said. "Try to take some deep breaths."

Andrew began to breathe deeply and, within a short time, could feel his body settle down.

Brother Nathan relaxed his grip and then took Andrew's pulse. "Should I pull up the side rails?" he asked, looking at Father Gerald.

"Yes, just as a precaution," he replied.

Once the medication took hold, Andrew decided that his muscles had been disconnected, as if his body were in segments and floating, lightly above the bed. He closed his eyes, enjoying a wonderful sensation of weightlessness, while dreaming briefly of billowy gauze drapes dancing in a gentle breeze.

Brother Nathan took Andrew's pulse once again. "Much better," he said with a smile. "That ought to hold him for a while."

The following day, after extensive discussions and further evaluation, Father Gerald felt that Andrew had recovered sufficiently and was ready to return to his cell. "If you have any problems, especially difficulty sleeping, particularly disturbing dreams, please come see me," he cautioned.

"I will . . . thanks," Andrew said. He shook Father Gerald's hand and left.

* * *

The familiar scent of nasturtiums filled the cloister with their fragrance. Andrew stopped to admire the beauty of their petals and to inhale more deeply their exceptional aroma. He carefully removed several dead blossoms, placed them beneath the plant to serve as compost, and then plucked a large healthy leaf from the top of the plant, put it in his mouth, and savored its peppery tangy flavor.

As he was about to turn the corner in the cloister, Andrew stopped abruptly. A deer was lying outside, next to the arched windows, which extended down to the floor, enjoying the protection of the garth and, perhaps, the warmth emanating from the heated ceramic floors. Andrew slowly moved closer, not believing his eyes, until he was sure that he saw the deer blink and reposition her head.

He moved even closer hoping that the animal would not bolt away. When he was able to get a full view of the animal, he was amazed to find that she was not alone; lying alongside of her was a spotted fawn, nestled close, and oblivious to any observation. Both animals remained immobile as Andrew continued to stare through the double thick window at such an incredible spectacle.

* * *

When he returned to his cell, a note, written in pencil, had been stuck to the door. It read, *"Andrew, please see me today at 4 PM. Signed: Father Luke."* He looked at his watch and realized he had approximately one hour before the appointment. Andrew sat at his desk, lightly tapping his fingers against the wooden surface as the flat light reflected off the snow and filled his cell with soft grey tints. Andrew stood up and then sat on his bed. He quickly returned to his feet and began to anxiously pace, from the door to the window and back again. The room felt small after being in the spacious infirmary; too small to remain in—besides, he needed to talk to someone; he needed to see Brother Matthew.

Andrew knocked softly on Matthew's door. He looked at the doorknob, vowing never again to enter without acknowledgment. The door opened suddenly.

"Andrew! Welcome back," Matthew said with a smile, offering Andrew his hand. "Come on in."

Andrew entered the room and stood alongside of Matthew's desk, which was cluttered with books, letters, and a small charcoal sketch pad where the face of a man, roughly yet skillfully sketched, remained unfinished.

"I never knew you were an artist," Andrew said.

Matthew responded with a laugh. "I guess I just needed a decent subject," he said, picking up the pad. "So what do you think? Does it look like you?"

Andrew squinted at the drawing, studying it intently, realizing that the resemblance was quite authentic. "Well, I thought I was better looking than that," he teased.

"You are, but for an amateur, I thought it came out fairly well. I'll let you know after it's finished," Matthew replied with a smile.

Matthew sat on his bed which was covered with a heavy woolen blanket. "Have a seat and stay for a while," he said, gesturing to the empty space alongside of him.

Andrew complied, somewhat cautiously. "I have to see Father Luke at 4:00 p.m.," he said, leaning his back against the wall. "I guess he'll want to talk about what happened at the eggery."

Matthew stared at his own hands. "I don't know how you can ever cope with that," he said thoughtfully. "I'm really sorry you had to go through it."

Andrew placed his head against the wall and closed his eyes. "Me too," he said quietly.

Matthew silently studied Andrew's face knowing that it would be impossible to do him justice through a simple charcoal sketch. "You're right, you know," he said.

"About what?" Andrew asked, with his eyes still closed.

"You are way too handsome for me to ever capture with charcoal," Matthew said.

Andrew could feel himself blush. He said nothing. Then he slowly turned his head toward Matthew, opened one eye, smiled and said, "You know, there are hospitals for guys like you."

"Oh, yeah?" Matthew said, feigning indignation. He jumped up, picked up his pillow and began to beat Andrew who retreated, laughing, into a ball on the floor.

"You'd better stop," Andrew managed to say between the laughter, "before we are both arrested."

The two monks sat on the floor facing each other, each waiting for the other to break the silence.

"Tell me the truth," Matthew ventured. "Do you really think I'm crazy?"

Andrew gazed pensively past Matthew's shoulder. "Absolutely!" he replied somberly. "In fact, I think you should be checked into a clinic for drugs, sex, and rock-'n'-roll rehabilitation."

Instead of finding humor in the situation, Matthew stared silently at the floor. "Maybe I should," he said quietly.

Andrew leaned forward and put his hand on Matthew's shoulder. "I'm only joking, Matt," he said. "And who knows; you may be the most authentic person in the place."

Matthew looked up at Andrew and smiled. "Yeah, right," he said sarcastically.

"If you ever decide to check into that clinic," Andrew continued, "be sure to save the bed next to you for me."

Matthew's face lit up with his characteristic phenomenal smile as he put his hand over Andrew's. "Thanks, I needed that," he said.

The sound of heavy footsteps could be heard, quickly approaching Matthew's room. Matthew and Andrew sat silently, expecting to hear an assertive knock; however, there was none. Instead, the footsteps stopped in front of the door, paused, and then could be heard walking in the opposite direction.

"I wonder what that was all about," Matthew whispered.

"I don't know, but I've got to keep my appointment with the prior," Andrew said as he stood up.

Matthew stood with him. "Well, I'm glad that you decided to stop by . . . I was beginning to think you wouldn't."

"I would have been by earlier, Matt, but it's been an emotional avalanche for me."

I know," Matthew said.

"Besides," Andrew offered, "I now know that I need to spend more time with you."

Matthew hugged Andrew in the genuine monastic tradition, with warmth and respect. He then opened his door quietly and peered down the corridor. "The coast is clear," he whispered.

Andrew got halfway through the door and quickly turned around. Unexpectedly, he reached out, cradling Matthew's face with one hand while he slowly ran his thumb over Matthew's lips.

Matthew closed his eyes. Very slowly, a smile spread across his face. He opened his eyes, looked at Andrew and whispered, "You know, there are hospitals for guys like you."

Andrew smiled. "I think you mean for guys like *us*." He squeezed Matthew's nose and hurried down the corridor.

* * *

Father Luke was not one who felt comfortable doing one-on-one counseling sessions from behind the desk. He usually asked Andrew, and others, if they would like to go for a walk or sit in the office. Andrew sensed that Father Luke would prefer to get out in the open air where even the most difficult issues were mollified and put in perspective by the fresh environment and brilliant alpine scenery that surrounded the monastery.

Andrew quickly learned that silences within a conversation were not always to be considered awkward moments. He used to feel that he needed to say anything just to keep the dialogue flowing; but now, he knew that silence, like meditation, allowed for meaningful thought and proper expression. At times, he wondered if his stillness made Father Luke uneasy, judging by Father Luke's tendency to digress from the topic by pointing out tracks of various animals in the snow or the possibility of imminent bad weather as evidenced by puffy "sheep's back" clouds gathering high above the mountains.

Father Luke enjoyed walking briskly while talking, gesturing, and maintaining adequate eye contact by leaning forward so that he could look nearly directly at Andrew. He was a tall lean man of Scottish descent who spoke with a slight brogue and smiled easily. Andrew guessed that he might be in his late forties.

It was not long before the conversation turned to the recent tragedy at the eggery, a subject which Andrew expected.

"How are you dealing with John's death?" Father Luke asked cautiously. It was the first time Andrew heard a name connected with the person he saw hanging in the lavatory.

"I guess I try not to think of it," he said. "I am hoping that it will eventually become less vivid for me."

"With time, I think that it will probably fade, but I'm afraid it's something that you'll always remember," Father Luke said.

Their pace had slowed somewhat. Andrew felt curious about John but was hesitant to ask.

"You are the first person who mentioned John's name," Andrew said. He stopped and looked at Father Luke. "I feel as though I shouldn't be asking about him, yet . . . I don't know. It's almost as though I need to know something about him."

I understand," Father Luke said. "What would you like to know?"

Andrew looked directly into Father Luke's eyes. "Everything," he said firmly.

Father Luke rubbed his chin. "That's what I was afraid you'd say." He began to walk again, slowly, looking pensively at the road before him. "I can tell you most of what I know and, I hope, Andrew, that it will ease your mind and help you to get beyond what has happened."

Andrew did not respond. He took advantage of the silence, waiting for Father Luke's details.

"There's really not a lot to tell," Father Luke replied. "John was about twenty-seven years old, lived with his mother in Montana and had decided a year ago to seek admission to a contemplative community. He left a Trappist house in Virginia for various reasons; tried a community in New York State and, again, left. He wrote us several months ago and asked to be considered. We had him visit three times and the senior professed brothers decided, after much deliberation, that this particular community would not be mutually compatible. That's about it, in a nutshell."

Andrew stopped. "So John killed himself after he was told that he wouldn't be allowed to enter the community?"

Father Luke frowned and cleared his throat. "I know it looks that way, and, except for God and John, who knows. Do you realize how devastating this has been to the community after making such a decision? If we had known, I'm sure we would have gladly offered him the opportunity to at least try community life at St. Anthony's."

Andrew felt deeply troubled by this disclosure. He walked ahead of Father Luke, wishing that he were alone.

Father Luke quickly caught up with him and matched his stride. Both men walked in silence over the crusty gravel road, digesting the moment and awkwardly tolerating a significant impasse.

Father Luke spoke first. "I can understand how you feel, Andrew, but please try to understand that we are clearly not infallible. I wish that you were never a part of this and I'm sorry that you, and all of us, experienced such a tragedy."

Andrew rubbed his eyes. "I guess I'm feeling anger, confusion . . . whatever, and I apologize."

Father Luke smiled, held out his arms and hugged Andrew.

"This life can be tough enough without such irreversible insults," Father Luke said. "I only wish I could make them go away."

"Thanks," Andrew said.

Father Luke paused, somewhat bewildered. "You know, I hesitate to offer this for fear that it may be misinterpreted, but I want you to know that I already spoke with Father Gerald and he said that I should feel comfortable letting you know that you are free to see our consulting psychiatrist, Dr. Klein, in Bitter Creek, just to help you cope with all of this . . . if you feel the need."

Andrew was surprised by the offer. "I appreciate your concern and Father Gerald's," he said. "Let's see how things go and, if I feel it might be necessary, I'll let you know."

"Sounds good," Father Luke replied.

Chapter Eight

The Retreat

Brother Mark helped Andrew pack for his first solitary retreat at the Cole cabin, a small log structure located approximately two miles from the monastery on the edge of a creek. The Coles spent much of the winter with relatives in Bitter Creek, so they agreed to allow the monks to use their home in exchange for the use of the monastery's land on which they built the cabin. Andrew felt somewhat anxious about whether he had packed enough food and other necessities to make it through this week, yet it really did not matter. He was looking forward to being alone.

"Well, is the adventurous hermit ready?" Brother Mark asked.

"I hope so," Andrew replied cautiously. "Can you think of anything I forgot?"

Brother Mark searched through all three of Andrew's boxes, mumbling softly to himself. "As long as you have plenty of energy bars, you'll be fine," he said with a smile. "I hate to cook."

"I don't mind," Andrew said, "as long as it can be cooked in one pot."

Brother Mark laughed. "Oh, did you pack your skis?" he asked. "You will want to get out on the good days—otherwise you'll go stir crazy."

"Yup," Andrew replied. "They are out back and my ski boots are in my pack."

Brother Mark and Andrew began to load the four-wheel-drive pickup. Andrew put the cross-country skis alongside the boxes, covered the load with canvas and secured the tie-downs.

"Looks like we are ready to hit it," Brother Mark said.

The truck easily made its way through several inches of new fallen snow, past the occasional homes of friends and neighbors and continued up the increasingly barren road until they spotted the red metal gate which identified the entrance to the Cole property. Brother Mark unlocked the gate and drove down the bumpy road to the cabin.

The one-story log structure sat several yards from the bubbling waters of a small creek which had been bridged with thick wooden planks to allow access to the mesa above the cabin.

Three small wooden structures hugged the outer perimeters of the cleared land. They housed an outdoor lavatory, a simple workshop and, a modest greenhouse all built by Art and Linda Cole, with the help of friends, including the assistance of several monks.

Brother Mark showed Andrew where the key was kept, opened the door and began to unload the boxes. "Art comes by every morning when no one is here to set the fire in the woodstove. Then he drives back again in the early evening to rekindle it," he said, rubbing his hands together to warm them. The embers were still glowing while only a small part of a skinny charred log remained.

"It looks like I'd better get this thing going if I want to stay warm tonight," Andrew said. He took some kindling and three large pieces of wood and carefully set them on the coals. He closed the door and adjusted the circular vents to provide maximum airflow which helped ignite the logs. Within seconds, the fire began to hiss and crackle as Andrew readjusted the vents.

"You're pretty good at that," Brother Mark said, warming his hands above the stove.

"I've had a lot of practice," Andrew replied.

Both monks placed chairs near the stove and sat among the unpacked boxes and backpacks. "I've always liked this place," Brother Mark said quietly, staring at the fire through the glass door. "I guess I wish I were staying here with you for the week, but then it wouldn't be quite the same for you."

Andrew sensed a certain longing by Brother Mark to be away from the monastic community. "It's funny," he began, "how we live isolated lives in the monastery yet we still feel the need to get away from it all on retreats."

Brother Mark shifted in his chair, removed his parka, and tossed it over the top of one of the boxes. "I can't tell you how much I look forward to this," he said, gesturing with both hands and leaning back in his chair. "The community life is fine, but every so often, I am climbing the walls and counting the days till my next retreat."

"I never realized how important they are to you," Andrew said.

"Yeah, well, give it some time—you'll feel the same."

By now the woodstove was generating sufficient comfortable heat. Andrew adjusted the vents to minimize the rate of burn while maintaining the current level of warmth.

Brother Mark slouched comfortably with outstretched legs, his hands folded across his chest.

It was clear to Andrew that Brother Mark relished the moment and had no immediate intention of returning to the monastery, judging by his closed eyes and a tranquil manner that seemed to define the mood. All could wait; it was time to "just be" in the present.

Andrew also savored the silence, sitting and watching the fire; however, a sense of "being the host," with Brother Mark "being the guest," prompted Andrew to disrupt the quiet. "How about some coffee?" he asked suddenly.

Brother Mark opened one eye and turned toward Andrew. "Sounds great but . . . maybe I should get going so you can get settled."

Andrew got up to emphasize his point. "No, I've got a whole week to get settled, and besides, I'm enjoying your company," he said.

Brother Mark did his usual Groucho imitation. "Well, I'm glad you said that, kid, because I feel the same. Now . . . put on the pot."

The old aluminum coffeepot sat on top of the gas stove. Andrew removed the metal basket and held the pot under the hand pump in the kitchen sink. The pump groaned and hissed and finally produced a surge of water which soon turned into a well-defined stream.

"Better let her run for a while," Brother Mark admonished. "Art and Linda have been spending a lot of time in town."

Andrew continued to pump until the water ran clear and icy cold. He filled the pot, put coffee into the metal-strainer basket and returned the pot to the stove. He found wooden matches in a tin box and lit one of the burners. Smiling and nearly chuckling aloud, Andrew was reminded of Brother Adrian and his method of lighting the oven. He turned toward Brother Mark, who appeared to be sleeping. "I shouldn't be saying this, but have you ever seen Brother Adrian light the ovens?" he asked.

Brother Mark suddenly squealed with laughter, acknowledging Andrew's question. "I can't believe he's already demonstrated that for you. He must like you."

"Could have fooled me," Andrew replied. "I thought he was trying to kill us."

Brother Mark settled back in his chair. "He's quite a character," he said.

Andrew returned to his seat, listening to the sounds of the fire and the gas flame under the coffeepot. He studied the interior of the cabin and envied the simplicity and self-reliance of its owners. There was no electricity and no telephone. And next to the gas stove stood a gas refrigerator, which baffled and amazed Andrew. 'How could there be a small flame at the bottom,' he thought, 'while, at the very top, there was a spacious freezer filled with frost and ice cream?'

Although the outhouse was a challenge on a cold night, the cabin had a full-sized bathtub in a small room behind the kitchen. A gas-powered water heater allowed for a welcomed, if abbreviated, soak or sponge bath. Gas-powered lamps were conveniently located on opposite walls in the main area while handsome oil lamps hung, suspended from beams, over a small teak dining table and, above one corner of the worn, overstuffed couch.

The loft bedroom was accessible by a sturdy simple ladder, which could be detached if necessary. Covering about one third of the main area, the loft had its own window and a comfortable mattress.

Brother Mark remained silent, unchanged from his last position. Melted snow from his boots left a dark spot on the faded painted floor, which had nearly been worn down to the bare wood.

Andrew decided that the coffee was ready, judging from the deep brown color of the liquid being percolated into the hollow glass knob on top of the pot. He found two ceramic mugs, rinsed them out under the hand pump and filled each of them with the rich aromatic brew. "How do you like your coffee?" Andrew asked. "And please don't say 'like my women.'"

Brother Mark stretched and yawned. He removed his glasses and rubbed his eyes. "What's a woman?" he said with a big grin. "I've forgotten."

Andrew laughed. "I guess it's been a long time," he said.

"Yeah, too long," Brother Mark replied, stressing the word "too."

Andrew removed a plastic container of sugar and a jar of Coffee-Mate from one of the boxes while he pondered Brother Mark's disclosure. "Now what's that supposed to mean?" he asked.

Brother Mark put some sugar in his coffee and stirred it slowly and quietly, making sure that the metal spoon did not clang against the cup. He sipped the coffee. "Now—that's how I like my women—bittersweet," he said, grinning at Andrew.

Andrew slowly shook his head. "Thanks a lot," he said, feigning indignation, "but I think this is a damn good cup of coffee. Nothing beats these old aluminum pots."

Brother Mark returned to his chair, in front of the fire, while Andrew found his highly guarded package of Twinkies and offered one to Brother Mark.

"Twinkies!" Brother Mark exclaimed. "How the heck did you ever get these?"

"I could tell you . . .," Andrew whispered, but Brother Mark finished the sentence for him.

"I know . . . but then you'd have to kill me," Brother Mark said with an imitated whisper.

"That's right," Andrew replied dryly, sitting down next to him. He set his cup on top of the woodstove and proceeded to eat his "forbidden" dessert. "I'll tell you what," Andrew said between mouthfuls. "You enlighten me regarding your comment about being too long without a woman and I'll tell you where I got the Twinkies."

Brother Mark snorted. "Why do I get the feeling that I haven't a choice?" he said laughing.

"Because you don't," Andrew quipped, "and this may be the perfect place and time to enlighten me."

"Is that right?" Brother Mark replied.

"Yes," Andrew said. He picked up his coffee and sat back in his chair. "The Twinkies were given to me by . . .," but before he finished his sentence, once again, Brother Mark chimed in and both, in unison, said, "Brother Adrian!"

"You sure have made an impression on him," Brother Mark said. "He doesn't take easily to some people."

Andrew sipped his coffee. "How does the saying go . . . after God made Adrian, he broke the mold?"

"You got it," Brother Mark replied.

"I heard him talking to Father Gerald after Sunday mass," Andrew said. "He was talking about one of Mrs. Phillip's bad habits and said, 'that woman smokes like a fish'!"

Once again, Brother Mark squealed with laughter. "And I'll bet Father Gerald was as gracious as ever and simply let it go by," Brother Mark said with a grin.

"Yup," Andrew said. He put more wood on the fire and warmed both cups with fresh coffee. "So tell me about this relationship business," he said, attempting to return the conversation back to his original concern.

"What is there to say?" Brother Mark said.

"I don't know but you seemed to imply something earlier," Andrew said.

Brother Mark shuffled his feet while looking reflectively at the ceiling. "Okay," he stammered. "It's difficult to express, but I would like a level of intimacy which, in reality, I can't have. I guess that means some sort of relationship."

Andrew was surprised by Brother Mark's candor. He hesitated, unsure of what to say. "It is a solitary life," he said quietly, and awkwardly, hoping that Brother Mark would continue with his thoughts.

"And painful," Brother Mark disclosed unexpectedly. "The thought of being companionless, human and alone, is unsettling, yet I think it's something I have to simply accept. I know that it's not possible to have a similar relationship as married people have, yet it's necessary that we be loving people, and I'm wondering if that's possible to express in this environment . . . I don't know."

Andrew never expected such blatant honesty. He closed his eyes and rested his head against the back of the chair. "You have the ability to identify a problem with a few words," he said. "Why is it I thought I was the only one who felt that way?"

Brother Mark laughed. "I'd be surprised if 2 percent of the guys felt any different."

"So what's the solution to this apparently endemic problem?" Andrew asked.

"I'm not sure if there is one, but I feel as if I'm dying a slow death," Brother Mark replied. "I shouldn't even be telling you this."

Andrew got up and walked toward the large double-hung window that overlooked a small yard where a combination sundial and birdfeeder, covered with snow and scattered seeds, offered its humble fare to the brave winter birds that were often in competition with the feisty squirrels. Beyond the yard, a forest of hemlock, spruce, and red pines stretched upward, their branches dusted white, as if raised in supplication. Andrew watched as a lone finch nervously picked through the seeds, hopping lightly from place to place and craning its neck to heed potential threats.

"If it's any help, you are telling me something I already know or, at least feel, and I've been trying to deal with the same pain," Andrew said. "Most of all, it's comforting to have someone to talk with who can understand what I'm saying."

"So I guess this is something you wouldn't easily discuss with Father Luke?" Brother Mark asked.

"I don't think I could," Andrew said. "He's a sympathetic man, but I feel like he's part of 'the old guard.'"

"I know what you mean," Brother Mark said. He finished his coffee and placed the mug on top of the stove. He then picked up the coffee pot and drained a few drops into his cup. "I guess we killed that one," he said with a grin.

Andrew quickly began to make more. "We may as well get a caffeine high," he said.

Both monks returned to their chairs in front of the fire, after Andrew put more wood in the stove, feeling as though the discussion was far from over.

Andrew explored the topic more carefully. "We've talked about love and relationships, but neither one of us had mentioned the 'S' word," he said.

"You must mean 'secular,'" Brother Mark said, laughing.

"Almost," Andrew replied sarcastically.

Brother Mark shifted in his chair to a more upright position. "That starts with an 'a,'" he said glibly. "You must be referring to 'sex.'"

"Well done, Watson," Andrew said, with his best attempt at a British accent.

Brother Mark once again settled back. "It's something I think about a lot," he said honestly. "I hope that doesn't surprise you."

Andrew slowly shook his head sideways, "Not really, because I'd say 95 percent of my meditations either begin or end with these bizarre, lascivious, Technicolor visions so . . . I just assume that I'm either a total pervert or God is simply continuing to test me."

Brother Mark laughed. "You really are funny." He got up to pour himself more coffee and held the pot about Andrew's cup.

"Thanks," Andrew said as Brother Mark filled his cup.

Brother Mark pulled his chair closer to the woodstove and sat down. "Sex—the eternal mystery," he began, "or, as someone said—much ado about nothing." He paused, sipped his coffee and continued. "I guess outsiders seldom think of the words 'sex' and 'monasticism' in the same sentence. They probably assume that monks, by virtue of their vocation, are given special graces, which allow them to rise above their human natures and live a life of flawless purity."

Andrew smirked. "It's crazy, but I think those were my *exact* thoughts when I walked through the door . . . well, maybe not exactly but I was beginning to wonder if I was the only one jerking off, at least until the day we talked, when we were working, about my dilemma."

"If the monastery were on springs, you'd probably hear the squeaking ten miles away," Brother Mark replied.

Andrew doubled up with laughter, spilling some coffee on the floor. He retrieved a fat yellow sponge from the sink and cleaned up his mess.

"I've never talked to anyone like this," Brother Mark said. "It must be the coffee."

"Either that or you've been hitting the Jack Daniel's," Andrew said.

"You know, I could really go for some right now," Brother Mark said thoughtfully. He swirled the remaining coffee in his cup as if holding a snifter of fine brandy, observing the color and inhaling the bouquet.

"Why do I get the idea that you're serious about this?" Andrew said.

Brother Mark looked up at Andrew; his face, solemn yet mischievous, answered the question. "I am," he said softly.

Andrew hesitated. " . . . Well, I might be able to help you out, that is, if you feel like driving back to the main guesthouse, and if the Jack Daniel's is still where I last saw it."

"Enlighten me," Brother Mark pleaded.

"The left cabinet beneath the sink."

In a flash, Brother Mark was out of his chair, grabbed his parka and was heading for the door. "Keep my coffee warm," he shouted over his shoulder.

Andrew followed him out the door into the snowy afternoon light. "Did anyone ever tell you you're crazy?" he shouted, squinting against the glare.

Brother Mark jumped into the pickup and was about to close the door. He looked back at Andrew. "Haven't you figured it out yet?" he said smiling. "We all are."

Andrew watched as the truck bounced up the driveway and disappeared when it rounded the turn through the gate.

Inside the cabin, Andrew checked the fire in the woodstove. He opened the door and added another piece of split wood to the glowing coals. He noticed Brother Mark's cup which sat, almost empty, on top of the metal surface near the edge. Touching the outside of the ceramic mug, Andrew decided it was sufficiently warm, as Brother Mark requested.

Suddenly, he remembered that he had not yet refrigerated several perishable items and quickly searched through the boxes for frozen orange juice, waffles, and a variety of fruits and vegetables, which he found and put in the mysterious gas powered refrigerator and freezer. Andrew stowed the dry goods into metal mouse-proof cabinets, complete with doors and secure latches.

He grabbed his rolled-up sleeping bag, raised it above his head and carefully launched it up, into the loft. He then climbed the ladder and found himself surrounded by wood: the closeness of the stained ceiling, the ever present log walls, and the highly polished wide plank floor. He squatted against his sleeping bag, inhaled the smoky scent of the loft, and realized that the cocoonlike space offered warmth and a sense of autonomy, unlike the ascetic environment of his cell. Andrew savored that hint of freedom, a realization that he would not have to wake every morning at 2:30 a.m. for vigils, or spend a large part of his day working at the monastery, either collecting the eggs, irrigating, or cooking. He knew that he could devote even more time to meditation, reading, and perhaps, some writing. He unrolled his sleeping bag and placed it on top of the quilted comforter which covered the mattress. After carefully unzipping the bag, he decided to test the comfort level of his sleeping quarters by crawling on his hands and knees to the center of the bed. He then fell face forward into a delightfully soft yet supportive mattress—a feeling he had not experienced for many months. Behind his head, the partially frosted window framed the tops of two bare aspens, contrasted by a lead-colored sky, which was filled with darting snowflakes. He smiled as he said softly, "I think I'm going to like this."

* * *

The crunch of the wheels against the gravel driveway signaled Brother Mark's return. Andrew heard the truck stop, its door opened and then closed.

Brother Mark barreled into the cabin, shaking snow from his head and wiping his boots on the fiber mat. "Where are you?" he asked, as he removed his parka and draped it over a wooden chair near the door.

Andrew looked down from the loft and smiled. "There are not many places to hide."

Brother Mark stood in the middle of the floor, grinning from ear to ear and holding what appeared to be a half-full bottle of Jack Daniel's. "Eureka!" he shouted. "Let the games begin."

Andrew hurried down from the loft to inspect Brother Mark's treasure. "That's it. That's the one I remember," he said.

Brother Mark found two water glasses and poured nearly three fingers worth into each. "Would you like it straight, with ice, or with water?" he asked as he recapped the bottle.

Andrew was not overly fond of whiskey ever since he remembered drinking Canadian Club and ginger ale as a teen at his parents' house one Christmas and vomiting pieces of pizza. It took several years before he could tolerate pizza without feeling nauseous and remembering the smell of the whiskey. "I think I'll try it with both water and ice," he said. "Let me see if there is any." He opened the freezer and was surprised to find two plastic ice trays tucked into a small aluminum compartment. "Yes!" he said. "There is ice. Would you like some?"

Brother Mark slid, once again, into his Groucho mode. "No thanks, kid," he said. "I like my whiskey like my women—strong and intoxicating."

Andrew put his hand over his eye. "I should've seen that one coming."

"Too late," Brother Mark said as he returned to his chair in front of the fire. He reached for his coffee mug and gingerly finished the contents. "Thanks for keeping it warm. I may need more later."

Andrew put two ice cubes in his glass and filled it half full with water. He then sat down to taste his drink. "Not bad," he said, swallowing the surprisingly smooth concoction.

Brother Mark quickly sat up. "A toast," he said, extending his glass toward Andrew, who reciprocated similarly.

"Yes, a toast," Andrew said, anticipating Brother Mark's comments.

"To perseverance in this baffling life, to friendship and peace." Brother Mark clinked his glass against Andrew's.

"Cheers," Andrew responded.

Both men took a hearty drink and sat back to relish the soothing warmth of the alcohol. "Now, that's quality booze," Brother Mark said, wiping his mouth with the back of his hand. "It's been a while since I've had any."

"It's been a while for a lot of things," Andrew said.

Brother Mark laughed. "Don't remind me," he said.

The warmth from the woodstove kept the cabin at a comfortable temperature while illuminating the immediate area. Outside, the snow fell steadily as the afternoon light began to fade. Andrew decided to light one of the gas lamps since the interior of the cabin had grown quite dim.

"Now that's a little better," Brother Mark said, as he got up to pour himself another drink. "I wasn't sure if I'd find the bottle."

"I'll bet you would have been able to sniff it out in the dark," Andrew joked.

"You're probably right," Brother Mark said, laughing. He then frowned and looked at Andrew. "You making fun of my nose?"

Andrew turned to face Brother Mark. "Now, would I do a thing like that to a friend?"

Brother Mark smiled. "Depends."

"On what?" Andrew replied.

"If you were drunk or sober," Brother Mark said.

"Well relax, Brother. I'm sober." Andrew returned to his chair. "But now I'm curious. Do you think you have a big one?"

As soon as Andrew finished the question, Brother Mark squealed with laughter, nearly falling on the floor and spilling his drink. The laughter was contagious, causing Andrew to respond likewise, yet he was not exactly sure what the joke was. Between gasps of air, with tears streaming down his cheeks, Andrew managed to squeak out, "What's so . . . funny?"

But the question only resulted in more convulsive responses from Brother Mark who was fighting for breath, rolling on the floor. He finally sat up, looked at Andrew and somberly said, "I don't know." Once again, Brother Mark doubled up with hysterical laughter while trying to talk. Words came out in short high-pitched bursts. "Do . . . I . . . have," he rolled on his back, "a . . . big one?" He continued to shake and rolled over to his side.

Andrew finally grasped the implication and both monks laughed uncontrollably until neither one of them had the energy to go on. Brother Mark regained composure, dusted himself off and sat down. Noticing that his drink was empty, he got up, refilled his glass and, instead of returning to his chair, he walked to the window and stood, staring into the grey light beyond the window.

"What do you see out there?" Andrew asked casually.

Brother Mark sipped his drink and continued to look out the window. "Once I get past my own reflection, I can just barely tell that it's still snowing."

Andrew joined him at the window. He shielded the light from his eyes with his free hand to get a better view of the weather. "It looks like it's coming down pretty hard," he said, immediately fogging the glass in front of him. He then returned to his seat, stared into the fire and sensed the salient mood change in Brother Mark—a swing to a darker, quieter, introspective nature, and very different from his earlier behavior. He sipped his drink, waiting for some movement or response from Brother Mark, who continued to face the window.

"How can we not have physical feelings in the community, when people are invited to share on more intimate levels?" Brother Mark said suddenly. "It's like saying 'get close to each other but don't react'! Don't feel anything." He turned to face Andrew. "I say it's unrealistic, but nobody knows where to go from there." He walked toward his chair and sat down heavily. He took a large swallow of his drink and continued. "If we are fortunate enough to share a smile or even verbalize our feelings, it's often in vain—we go our separate ways; I want a commitment to someone on another level, to demonstrate our feeling good about each other. I would like to say to someone 'I love you,' yet what happens after that? It can't be simply 'see ya later' or mutual exclusivity, but something in between which recognizes and expresses our physical needs and desires." He finished his drink and stood up. "Why is it that it all sounds impossible?" He slowly walked toward the kitchen area, poured himself another drink and swallowed it all in one gulp. He then turned to face Andrew who remained slumped in his chair, contemplating the dancing tangerine flames in the woodstove.

"So there you have it," Brother Mark said, his words vaguely slurred, "the updated life and times of Brother Mark, a lonely and often horny monk."

Andrew looked up from the fire. "One of the many," he said softly. He shifted in his chair to an upright position. "You know," he continued, "I haven't been here as long as you but, once again, I feel those feelings, the longings, the incredible loneliness and, like you, I don't know what the answer is." He slowly got up from the chair to refresh his drink.

Brother Mark remained propped up against the kitchen cabinets, holding his empty glass. "Are you sure?" he asked.

The question clobbered Andrew unexpectedly. He took a deep breath and forced a laugh. "When I find out, I'll call you." He splashed the whiskey over the remaining ice cubes and gestured with the bottle toward Brother Mark.

"What the hell—give me another."

Andrew obliged by pouring the remainder of the bottle into Brother Mark's glass.

"We killed that one," Andrew said, surprised at the amount of alcohol they had consumed.

Brother Mark laughed. "Yeah, but what a way to go."

Andrew was totally absorbed by the content of Brother Mark's comments, yet he feared that the Jack Daniel's might make him a little too talkative, too open about his relationship with Brother Matthew—a relationship which Andrew, himself, had not yet defined or entirely understood. He returned to his chair in front of the fire and sat down with a thump.

"So where does this all come down," Andrew said softly, looking toward Brother Mark, who appeared ghostlike in the shadows. "Is it wrong or abnormal to love someone in the community and, if not, how do two people who care about each other respond to their sexual feelings?"

Brother Mark suddenly became animated. "That's it! That's the real question!" He quickly took his place in the chair next to Andrew. "I can see the lightbulbs exploding all over your head." He sat back in his chair and took some deep breaths. "I may be wrong but, I have the feeling that you have been dealing with this question for some time now," Brother Mark said quietly.

Andrew sensed a tightening in his chest, as anxiety rapidly inundated his body. 'He knows,' he thought. 'I knew it.' He remained silent and took a sip of his drink.

Brother Mark did not pressure him to speak.

Andrew cautiously thought about his response and decided that he should be evasive or, at least, vague.

"Maybe I have and maybe I haven't," he said casually. "Why do you ask?"

"Just a hunch," Brother Mark said, using the same casual tone.

"How about you?" Andrew asked, turning the question around.

Brother Mark laughed. "A million times," he said, smiling.

"So," Andrew said, "you've been there many times—what's the answer?"

Brother Mark held his nearly empty glass up to one eye and looked through it, like a kaleidoscope, at the fire. "I'm really not sure," he said softly, "but somewhere in the relationship there is an invisible line, and when it's crossed, you'll both know it." He put his glass on the floor next to his chair and looked at Andrew. "I guess it's important to know that when love makes itself known, you'd be a fool not to cultivate its growth before it withers and dies. Unfortunately, I've never been a very good gardener."

Both men sat in silence until Andrew decided to put another log in the woodstove. He used a long poker to turn the wood in the stove on its side and then added the seasoned wood to the top of the burning coals. It ignited instantly, crackling and flaming, while throwing intense heat and light into the cabin. Andrew shut the door and readjusted the air vents. He turned to sit in his chair and noticed that Brother Mark sat slumped in his seat with his eyes closed. "It looks like someone is pretty tired," he said quietly.

Brother Mark opened his eyes. "And probably pretty drunk," he responded. "Besides," he added, "I have to use the outhouse." He got up to put on his parka and boots.

"How about some fresh coffee?" Andrew asked.

"Good idea," Brother Mark said, over his shoulder, as he opened the cabin door and found several inches of feathery snow outside. "I'll probably need a flashlight."

"Right next to the door," Andrew said.

Brother Mark took the light and disappeared into the darkness, while Andrew quickly made a fresh pot of coffee.

Brother Mark returned covered with a dusting of snow. "That toilet seat is damn cold," he shuddered.

Andrew laughed. "Well, warm yourself by the fire," he said.

They returned to their seats with a fresh mug of coffee.

"I can't believe I stayed this late," Brother Mark said. "I hope I haven't wrecked your first day on retreat."

"No, of course not," Andrew replied. "I really enjoyed our conversation and your company, so stay as long as you want."

"Thanks," Brother Mark replied, "I feel the same, but if I don't get back there fairly soon Father Jude will probably call the highway department to see if there have been any accidents."

Andrew hesitated and then spoke up. "Speaking of Father Jude, where do you think he fits in, if at all, to our conversation?"

Brother Mark took his time before answering. "I'm not completely sure, but if I were a betting man, I'd say he's probably crossed that invisible line—more than once."

"If that's the case," Andrew said, "he may not be anywhere near the monastery."

"Who knows," Brother Mark said with a hint of sadness.

The wind had increased noticeably, howling about the cabin like an invisible predator, searching for any cranny that would allow it to enter and deposit an occasional snowflake or two. From a distance, the cabin glowed warmly in the dark, a reasonably snug sanctuary from the fierce winter storm.

Brother Mark finished his coffee, stretched and stood up. "I guess I'd better be hitting the road," he said with a yawn, "before I fall asleep."

"You're welcome to spend the night here, if you want," Andrew offered quickly. "Are you okay to drive?"

Brother Mark smiled a big lazy grin. "It's a tempting invitation, but . . . I can see all the eyebrows being raised already. Thanks, Andrew." He extended his hand toward him.

Andrew responded with an outstretched hand which Mark grasped solidly, "Yes," he said. "I'm okay to drive."

Brother Mark sat down to put on his boots. "And I'll call you as soon as I get home," he said, laughing, knowing that the cabin had no telephone. He put on his parka and stood by the door. "We'll have to do this again, sometime," he said.

"Any time," Andrew said. "I really enjoyed this."

"Me too," Brother Mark said as he turned to go out the door. He suddenly stopped and turned toward Andrew. "Is there anything you want me to say to Brother Matthew?"

Andrew was completely caught off guard, speechless, at the unexpected request. "No, not really," he said, faltering and confused.

Brother Mark was smiling. "It's all right," he said. "I'll just tell him you said hi." He turned and got into the truck. "Enjoy the retreat!" He slammed the truck door shut with a bang, started the engine and let it idle while he attempted to switch the transfer case into four-wheel drive. With a slow grind and a lunge, the truck effortlessly cut through the deepening snow, up the driveway and onto the unplowed road.

Andrew closed the door, locked the deadbolt and returned to the woodstove to get warm. 'That's that,' he thought. 'He knows about Matthew and me . . .' He smiled faintly, sat down in front of the woodstove and stared at the dancing flames. The heat from the stove, combined with the Jack Daniel's, produced a comfortable numbness which Andrew welcomed. He rested his head on the back of the chair, closed his eyes, and quickly fell asleep.

It was the cold that caused him to wake up; the fire had nearly died, leaving only a glowing bed of embers in the dark. Shivering, Andrew found his parka, retrieved several pieces of wood and put them in the stove where they slowly caught fire and provided some heat to the chilled cabin. He knew that he would have to load extra wood into the stove before going to bed, and wondered how long the fire would last into the night. There was plenty of firewood stacked outside the door, under the protective porch, but rather than have to search for it in the dark, Andrew piled several armfuls inside the cabin next to the door. Before long, the temperature in the cabin was, once again, very comfortable.

After a light meal of packaged vegetable soup, Andrew located his Zen stool and placed it on a thick black pad. He dimmed the gas lantern, pulled a cotton throw from the couch and wrapped it around himself, as he positioned himself on the stool. Once he felt perfectly aligned, with his back straight and his hands comfortably cupped on his lap, Andrew continued with his meditation, breathing deeply at first, and slowly, allowing thoughts to filter through his conscious mind until they were eventually distilled into nothing. He heard but did not acknowledge the sound of the crackling fire, the howling wind and snow blowing against the sides of the cabin, and the occasional gurgle of his dinner as it settled in his stomach. He felt his entire body relax; his breathing slowed significantly. He was awake yet he felt strangely detached from his physical being, as though he were observing himself from the loft, looking down upon an Indian-like figure fixed in front of the fire, while a smoky haze drifted lazily in the dancing light.

Gradually, through the dimness, Sara's pensive face appeared, smiling yet melancholic, as she stared at Andrew with wistful eyes. Andrew recognized her familiar look, a precursor of too many things gone wrong, and too few words, often too late, to heal the wounds of a relationship in major distress. Although her lips never moved, Andrew heard her say, "We miss you very much." In the distance, a figure moved closer until Andrew recognized Nick's face. He appeared concerned, yet comfortable with Sara at his side, staring at Andrew for what seemed to be an eternity. Finally, he spoke. "Come home," he said softly. "Please . . ." Like Sara, his lips were motionless—his expression remained the same. Both figures then faded and dissolved in the smoky haze, curling into wisps and layered vapors.

Andrew's meditation returned to the welcomed silence of quiet emptiness where he sank deeper and deeper into its internal process. Once again, he had successfully attained a level of decreased brain activity and slowed heartbeat; his breathing was barely perceptible, yet he was subconsciously aware of his surroundings, the flicker of firelight, and the shadows on the cabin walls. He remained in this meditative state for approximately one hour until his thoughts, once again, began to form pictures, to take shape, and cause him to become focused on the images. He tried to dismiss them by simply concentrating on his breathing, which had increased considerably; however, the images grew even more defined and three-dimensional.

Suddenly, Matthew appeared, lying on his side, his head propped up by one arm. He was watching Andrew intently, a slight smile on his lips. Andrew heard himself inhale sharply; he was unable to look away, even though Matthew said nothing.

As Matthew began to push away the sheets, Andrew forced himself to stop the visual sequence. He immediately opened his eyes and found himself staring at the fire. Sweat covered his forehead, and his heart was pounding. He threw off his blanket, removed the Zen stool and stretched his legs. Thirsty and overheated, he made his way to the sink to pump a glass of ice cold water.

It was time, he decided, to get some sleep. He filled the stove with as much firewood as it would hold, found his flashlight, turned off the gas lamps, and climbed the steep ladder to the loft. Once he was inside of his sleeping bag, Andrew switched off the flashlight and watched as the flames from the woodstove cast a reassuring glow, illuminating the ceiling with shimmering brightness and shadows. Within minutes, he surrendered himself to a welcomed slumber, as he recalled his favorite thoughts about bears, hibernating in snug dens, while the mountains resumed their dialogue with each other in the darkness.

* * *

It was just after 4:00 a.m. when Andrew woke, shivering in his sleeping bag, to find that the fire in the woodstove had almost gone out. The room was in total darkness. The howling wind continued its assault on the cabin, successfully finding its way inside and creating a slight yet definite air movement within the loft. He knew that he had no choice but to go downstairs, rekindle the fire, or risk freezing to death in the loft. He unzipped his sleeping bag, pulled on jeans and a sweatshirt, and carefully backed down the ladder with his flashlight.

Inside the stove, a faint bed of embers glittered sparsely around the charred leftover logs. Andrew quickly gathered several pieces of kindling, stirred the ashes and set three pieces on the sparks, hoping that they would ignite. He carefully blew over them, trying not to disturb the embers; however, he was rewarded with only a thin wisp of smoke. He then collected an old newspaper, balled up several sheets and placed them inside the stove. Once the paper caught fire, the increased draft was just enough to cause the kindling to ignite. Andrew waited until the kindling was burning well and added three smaller logs and then two large logs to the fire. He closed the door and listened as the air was sucked through the vents with a loud "whooshing" sound and then regulated the vents to ensure a proper burn rate.

Just as he was about to sit down, Andrew realized that he needed to urinate. He thought about having to go out in the cold to the outhouse and dreaded it. 'I need a makeshift urinal,' he thought, as he looked around the room, and then he spied the empty Jack Daniel's bottle. 'Perfect!' he thought. He unscrewed the cap and gratefully relieved himself. He put the cap back on the bottle and left it on the counter, intending to empty it in the morning.

Armed with a mug of tepid, somewhat stale, coffee and wrapped comfortably in his blanket, Andrew resumed his position in front of the fire, enjoying the utter solitude and the freedom from the obligatory monastic horarium. It was a needed change of pace since the rigorous schedule allowed very little room for leisure. With the fire blazing, Andrew luxuriated in the serenity of the moment. He looked at his watch and saw that it was now 4:30 a.m.; early morning was not an unfamiliar time for him, and he wondered what he would be doing if he were back at the monastery. 'I probably would have just finished my meditation and would be on my way to the refectory for breakfast,' he thought. 'I know the coffee would be warmer.' He decided to dump the leftover brew and make a fresh pot to help celebrate his newly acquired venture.

As he stood next to the stove, Andrew thought he heard movement outside the cabin; he cautiously looked out the small window near the door but could see only darkness. He walked away, but once again, he heard a thumping sound, almost as if someone were stomping heavily on the wooden walkway, which was buried in snow. The tightness in his chest was evident as fear increased its grip on him; goose bumps covered his arms and the hair on the back of his neck felt as if it were electrified. He slowly returned to the window and peered into the darkness, however, the moon was clouded and there was no light. Unexpectedly, he saw a face outside the window, staring back at him, and he knew it was not his reflection. Andrew felt as if his heart would explode as he gasped for breath and backed away from the window in horror.

"Andrew, it's me, Matthew! Open the door."

It seemed like an eternity before Andrew was able to grasp where the voice came from and who was outside the cabin. He took several deep breaths and went to the door.

"Is that you, Matt?" he asked nervously, refusing to unlatch the door.

"Of course!" Matthew retorted. "Who the heck else would be here at this hour?"

Andrew reluctantly slid back the deadbolt and slowly pulled open the door.

Matthew's face was scarcely illuminated by the firelight yet his ear-to-ear smile was unmistakably recognizable. The fur-lined parka which covered his head was caked with snow and ice. He stood there with his cross-country skis in one hand and bamboo ski poles in the other.

"Aren't you going to ask me in?" he said, still grinning, and shaking the snow from his ski boots.

Andrew stepped aside and gestured with one arm. "Of course," he said. "Come in."

Matthew brushed past Andrew with his skis and leaned them against the wall, along with his poles.

As he passed, Andrew was aware of the fresh smell of the outdoors, mixed with Matthew's body heat and, quite possibly, the scent of clothes recently laundered.

Matthew removed his parka and hung it on one of the wall hooks. He shook his head like a wet puppy, rubbed his face, and blew into his cupped hands. "It is cold out there," he said as he walked over to the woodstove. He looked at Andrew who remained in the same position—next to the open door. "It's going to get even colder in here if you don't shut the door," he said softly.

Bewildered, Andrew pushed the wooden door closed and slid the deadbolt to its locked position. He noticed that the coffee was percolating rapidly so he removed the pot from the stove where he stood quietly, unsure of what to say. Suddenly, he vented. "You scared the shit out of me!" He sat down in front of the fire and waited for a response.

Matthew squatted in front of him with one hand on the arm of Andrew's chair. "I know," he said, "and I'm sorry. I didn't see you when I looked in and we must have both looked through the window at the same time."

Andrew continued to stare at the fire in silence. He refused to make eye contact with Matthew, who remained crouched in front of him.

"I know you're upset," Matthew said, "but I thought you'd be happy to see me."

Andrew looked at him. "I'm happy to see you—you know that; it's just that I never expected to see you here at . . . God knows what time it is . . . when I'm supposed to be on retreat." He abruptly got up from the chair and stood by the large window, which reflected the softly lit room. He watched as Matthew walked toward him, stopped behind him, and gently began to massage his neck and upper back. Andrew closed his eyes and allowed himself to experience, once again, the exhilaration of compassionate physical contact. Before long, he reached up, over his shoulders, grabbed Matthew's hands, and pulled them down around his waist.

Matthew buried his head in Andrew's hair, nuzzling his neck and ears as Andrew willingly dropped his head, back on Matthew's shoulder.

He looked at Matthew who pressed his cheek against his. Andrew could feel the stubble of his blond beard. "Do you have any idea how dangerous this is?" Andrew whispered, as he allowed Matthew to continue.

Matthew moved his mouth over Andrew's ear. "Yes," he said, gently biting his earlobe, "but I feel powerless to stop it."

Andrew smiled and kissed him on the forehead, and then he quickly stepped to one side. "How about some coffee? You must be frozen."

Matthew let his arms drop to his side. "Not anymore," he said, with his signature smile.

Andrew poured himself some coffee and reached for another mug. "You want some?" he asked, holding the mug in one hand.

Matthew sat in front of the fire. "Sure," he said. "Just black."

Andrew handed Matthew his coffee. "I can't believe you skied all the way over here in the dark," he said, as he sat down next to him. "You must be pretty tired."

"Actually, I feel sort of energized," Matthew said. "I knew that I wanted to see you." He looked at Andrew, who kept his gaze on the fire.

"Well, I appreciate it, even if you did scare the crap out of me," he said. Andrew leaned back in his chair, knowing that he needed to talk with Matthew about the sensitive nature of their relationship. He sipped his coffee, wondering where to start; however, to his surprise, it was Matthew who initiated the conversation.

"Look," he said somewhat hesitantly, "I know what you're thinking so . . . maybe we should talk about it." He shifted in his chair and continued. "I know that I shouldn't be here; I respect the fact that you are on retreat and need to spend this time alone, yet I was thinking about you during vigils, knowing that you were up here by yourself, and I guess I just got crazy and decided that I had to see you."

Andrew smiled at Matthew's honesty. "I'm surprised you didn't just hop into the pickup and drive across the mesa!"

"I thought about it," Matthew said, "but I think the abbot beat me to the truck."

The remark surprised Andrew, but he simply let it pass. He put down his mug and looked directly at Matthew. "I'm in a tough spot, Matt. I'm beginning to have strong feelings for you, and I don't know what to do about it, or how it fits in with my, or should I say, *our* vocations." He rubbed his eyes with the thumb and index finger of his left hand. "I mean, I think about you a lot; I could recognize your sweater by its own particular scent; I can't get the moments we spent together out of my mind. And I can't pretend that our relationship is purely platonic because it hasn't been."

Matthew turned toward Andrew and put his hand on his arm. "Hell, I've been in love with you from the moment I first saw you in the refectory, when I arrived as an Observer. I can tell you what you were wearing, what you were eating, and anything else you would like to know about that day."

"What did I have for dessert?" Andrew asked cavalierly.

Matthew hesitated for a second. "Rice pudding—no whipped cream!" he exclaimed.

Andrew laughed, not knowing if Matthew was right or wrong, but appreciating his chutzpah. His ephemeral smile faded as he returned his gaze to the fire and sat quietly. "I never expected this to happen," he said, breaking the silence in the cabin and reintroducing a more somber mood. "Is this some sort of spiritual test from God, checking to see whether I have the right stuff to make it here? The life is tough enough, and I don't know how capable I am to fight all of this." Andrew closed his eyes and rested his head on the back of the chair.

Outside, the early-morning light began to streak across the sky in vivid orange and salmon. The highest peaks glowed golden white as the lower half of the valley remained in darkness. Birds sang tentatively, at first, searching for their breakfast of thistle and sunflower seeds.

Matthew knelt in front of Andrew. He put his arms around his waist and placed his head on his chest. "It's a challenge we'll face together," Matthew said quietly, "and the outcome will be just fine."

Andrew gently wrapped his arms around him and pushed his face into his hair, inhaling his familiar scent, a scent redolent with earthy freshness, like a field after a summer rain. "God, you smell so good . . . I could devour you!" Andrew said affectionately.

"Go ahead," Matthew replied, "you are welcome to eat me up."

Andrew smiled and squeezed Matthew tighter. "When do you have to be back?" he asked.

Matthew shrugged his shoulders. "Never," he said. "I'm moving in."

Andrew gently turned Matthew's head so he could look at him. "Wrong," he said, laughing. "You had better be back by eight so . . . that gives us about forty-five minutes, assuming that it'll take you close to an hour to get back." Andrew slowly stood, disrupting Matthew who appeared completely comfortable. He walked to the ladder which led to the loft, waiting for Matthew to follow. "Let's get warm," he said as he carefully began his ascent.

Matthew wasted no time making his way to the loft.

Andrew unzipped the sleeping bag and spread it open. He then removed the down quilt from its shelf, threw it over the bed and crawled beneath it. He held up the cover while Matthew followed suit and settled in alongside of him.

Andrew snuggled up to Matthew's back, wrapped his arm around him and placed his hand over his.

"I feel so good . . . I could explode," Matthew stammered, as he moved even closer to Andrew, allowing him to completely envelop him.

Andrew lost himself in Matthew's hair as he explored with his nose and mouth the contours of Matthew's head, neck, and ears.

"I wish this moment could go on forever," Matthew whispered, as if he were intoxicated and giddy with elation.

Andrew agreed. "It's nice just to be with you—here, away from everyone, everything."

Matthew simply squeezed his hand; words were not essential.

The wind continued its relentless assault on the cabin, howling and spraying snow against the window above their heads. Andrew remained silently enthralled as he held Matthew and continued to breathe into the back of his neck and hair. Within minutes he became aware that Matthew had fallen asleep, breathing slowly and deeply, and looking totally content, after rising early for vigils and then skiing the arduous distance in the dark. He carefully lifted his arm to see if his watch was visible in the semidarkness. Matthew shifted, rolling into Andrew and onto his back. Andrew decided to let him sleep for another fifteen minutes before he needed to wake him.

As he watched Matthew sleep, Andrew was reminded of the familiar fallen angel with locks of blond hair across his forehead. He could not resist gently grazing his lips against Matthew's, studying his face and reflecting on the shape of his ears, which appeared somewhat small yet full-lobed. A slight barely noticeable scar, above his upper lip, accented a corner of his mouth and caused Andrew to wonder how it got there: was it a fight during his adolescence; a fall as a child, perhaps, hitting his face on the handlebars of his bicycle? He felt as if he now needed to know everything about Matthew, realizing, after all, he knew very little. 'Who is he, why is he here?' he thought. Without explanation, the questions grew more complicated by thinking about Matthew's sister, Ellen. He wondered if Matthew knew about her visit to his room, and how he would react if he knew the truth.

Matthew trembled slightly and then opened his eyes. He looked up at Andrew who was staring off in the distance. "So what are you thinking about?" he whispered, moving closer to Andrew.

The unexpected questions startled him. He smiled and ran his fingers through Matthew's hair, knowing that this was not a good time to raise critical issues. "I was thinking how lucky I am right now and . . . how crazy we both must be."

Matthew laughed, reached up and pulled Andrew close to him. "I'm the lucky one," he said, "because I thought I'd never see my dreams come true."

"Yeah, right," Andrew said, mockingly, with a smile. "You probably paid off the Pope to get in here, just so you could snag me."

Matthew scoffed. "No, but you're almost right," he teased. "Someday, I'll tell you about it."

Andrew looked at his watch. "You'd better get going or you won't make it back in time for community mass."

"Do I have to?" Matthew implored, squeezing Andrew tightly.

"I'd say so." Andrew replied. "Besides, after my conversation with Brother Mark last night, I got the feeling that he knows about us—not sure what, exactly."

Matthew jumped up suddenly. "That's okay with me," he said. "Let them think what they want."

Andrew followed Matthew downstairs where he put on his ski boots and parka in preparation for his return trip. He looked up just in time to see Matthew place the bottle of Jack Daniel's against his lips. "Don't drink that!" he shouted. He quickly jumped up and grabbed the bottle away from Matthew.

"Why not?" Matthew asked innocently.

"It's urine . . . my urine. I pissed in the bottle rather than go out to the outhouse!"

Matthew wiped his face on his sleeve. "Well, after this, I can say that I definitely know you more intimately!" He grabbed his skis and poles and stood by the door.

"You look like Nanook from the north," Andrew joked.

"Yes, but a handsome one," Matthew replied.

"Very handsome," Andrew said, "and modest."

Matthew swung the door open, exposing a dimly lit world filled with snow and cold. He turned to face Andrew, who stood shoeless, shivering, with folded arms. "Do I have to wait until you come back to the monastery before I can see you again?" he asked.

Andrew shifted from one foot to the other. "Can you come up Friday night for dinner, around five thirty? You'd probably have to skip Compline."

"I thought you'd never ask," Matthew said, smiling. He reached forward with one arm and pulled Andrew toward him, hugging him hard. "Enjoy the week," he said softly. "I'll be thinking about you."

"Me too," Andrew replied.

Matthew walked outside and closed the door behind him. He was adjusting his skis when Andrew opened the door.

"Be careful going back," Andrew said.

"Always," Matthew replied, as he scooped up some snow and threw it at Andrew who tried unsuccessfully to jump out of the way.

"You dog!" Andrew shouted, laughing and brushing the snow away.

Matthew smiled and quickly skied toward the mesa and the monastery.

* * *

From the opposite window, Andrew could see the jays and finches on the feeder as they thrust their heads through the snow, searching for grains of millet, thistle, and corn. The larger birds would flap their wings, scattering the powdery snow, to expose the sought-after seeds. High above them, grey squirrels released white puffs from the pines as they jumped from branch to branch in the thin mountain air.

Andrew finished his breakfast and quickly cleaned his dishes. He dressed warmly, laced up his cross-country boots, and put on his old ski parka. Before leaving the cabin, he made a stop at the outhouse where the toilet seat was cold as ice. 'I've got to wrap that with Styrofoam,' he thought. 'This will never do.'

Tattered copies of *Esquire* and *Vanity Fair* magazine encouraged him to linger; however, the temperature inside the outhouse was less than kind to his exposed buttocks, so he quickly completed his task, zipped up his jeans and parka, and returned to the cabin to make sure that the woodstove was burning properly and the gas stove had been turned off. Once he was convinced that all was in order, Andrew locked the heavy wooden door behind him.

He clamped the lightweight skis to his boots and gingerly made his way toward the plank bridge which forded the narrowest part of the stream. He glided toward the mesa until he came to a sharp incline, the only access to the open fields above. In the snow, Matthew's softened herringbone pattern already marked the way from his earlier departure that morning. Andrew noticed that his climb appeared flawless, a perfect "V formation," evenly spaced, with strategic, supportive pole plants, indicative of one gifted with substantial strength. He forced himself to continue. "Get a grip," he said quietly, "and get up this hill."

Grey and green mountains, draped in white, spanned the horizon and soared toward the azure sky. Andrew felt as if he were standing on Wall Street, looking up at the towering monoliths, mesmerized by their imminence. Across the mesa, rolling foothills expanded upward until they quickly disappeared and dropped into a steep rift near the mountains. The mesa sloped gently and afforded Andrew enough of a descent to practice telemark turns, or to simply enjoy a swift downhill run to the very lowest part of the field, which then dropped sharply into irregular rolling washes. Standing near the lower edge of the field, Andrew could see Matthew's tracks proceed through one of the washes and continue toward the monastery, and over a slight rise, where they disappeared. He knew that it was a fairly strenuous trip for anyone to make, especially in the dark, and again, it made him even more appreciative of his visit.

The sun was intense and warmer than Andrew expected, and he soon found himself sweating through a significant aerobic workout. He unzipped his parka, unbuttoned his shirt and tied a blue handkerchief on his head to absorb perspiration. Most of the afternoon was spent practicing his turns and trying to remember all of the instructions he received from Eric Holtze, who agreed to help him improve, as they skied one afternoon on the slopes in the back of the monastery. He remembered Eric saying, "Pretend you are squeezing an orange with your knees. On every turn you make orange juice." Andrew diligently carved graceful s-curves down the mesa, occasionally punctuating some of them with indents where he floundered and fell. He would pick himself up, brush the snow from his face and glasses, and persist in his efforts to better his form. Before long, Andrew demonstrated considerable improvement—his balance grew stronger and his turns became symmetrical linked patterns that decorated the mesa like entwined figure eights. From the bottom of the mesa, Andrew proudly looked up at the artwork he had carved in the snow and decided that the turns were nicely rounded, connected, and overall—good quality.

A small rocky outcrop to the left of the mesa caught Andrew's attention. He was getting hungry and decided he needed to rest, so he skied to the lichen covered rocks, took off his skis and found a comfortable place to sit. He removed a chocolate energy bar from his pocket and devoured it immediately, when he realized that he forgot to bring a canteen of water. He scooped up some fresh snow and let it melt in his mouth. It disappeared quickly; he had to scoop several more mouthfuls before he felt even remotely satiated. He leaned back against the warmed rocks, closed his eyes and enjoyed the high-mountain environment. With the sun burning into his skin, he felt as if he were lying on a beach in the middle of summer. He searched inside his parka, found a small tube of sunscreen and rubbed it on his face and neck.

The smell of the cream evoked images of summers gone by, of lazy days spent on crystal Adirondack lakes, sailing the J-boat, or daydreaming on the old raft, as classic Chris Craft woodies cut handsomely through the waves, snubbing their bows at the latest v-hulled monsters that prowled the waters like floating dragsters. Suddenly, he felt a slight shiver as a melancholy feeling momentarily enveloped him; he decided it was time to return to the cabin.

Andrew paused on top of the steep descent which led to the creek near the cabin. The double set of herringbone tracks were still visible in the shadows, their distinct patterns too perfectly created to be bisected and marred, yet Andrew had no choice. He leaned forward and quickly picked up speed until the ground flattened near the plank bridge. As he was crossing the creek, he heard someone shout.

"Hello, there!"

Andrew looked up to see Eric Holtze and his children standing by his truck. "Hey, Eric," Andrew called. "Good to see you!" He skied up to the truck and shook Eric's hand.

"I didn't know if anyone was here," Eric said, "so I thought I'd come by and check on the place. You are looking pretty good on those things."

Andrew smiled. "Well, I've had a good teacher. You should see some of the turns I've decorated the mesa with—I think you'd be proud of them."

"I'm sure I would be," Eric said. "You learn fast."

Andrew watched as Eric's children, Tyler and Caleb, threw twigs into the gentle stream, pretending they were boats filled with daredevil riders, who were racing in the whitewater. They would run alongside of the creek, stand on the bridge and cheer as the winning boat passed under the planks.

"I see that the munchkins are looking good," Andrew said, somewhat wistfully.

"Yeah," Eric said. "I can remember, way back, when life was that simple."

"Me too," Andrew replied, kicking his boot in the snow.

Eric started to chuckle. "Now, come on. You guys don't have it all that bad, do you?"

Andrew leaned against the warm hood of the truck. "If anyone knows, I'd say it should be you. I think you've seen more of what goes on here that the abbot himself."

Eric laughed. "Well, I wouldn't go that far but I guess I have seen quite a bit . . . and I know that the life can be pretty radical."

"I guess it goes with the job," Andrew said with a smile. "How about some coffee?"

Eric hesitated. "You're on retreat and I don't want to bother you."

"It's no bother, believe me. In fact, I was going to make some for myself to satisfy my addiction." He playfully punched Eric on the shoulder. "Come on."

"Well, I can't stay long; besides, Father Jude would probably blow a fuse if he knew I was here."

"He'll get over it," Andrew replied.

Eric spoke briefly with Caleb and Tyler, admonishing them not to get wet, and to come into the cabin when they felt cold.

Once inside, Andrew proceeded to make coffee while Eric checked the fire and then made himself comfortable in one of the chairs.

"So why do we do this?" Andrew asked cavalierly, as he put the coffee pot on the stove.

"Beats me," Eric said. "I don't think I could."

Andrew laughed. "I'm beginning to wonder about myself."

Eric slouched in the chair and placed his boots close to the stove. "Here we go," he said. "Why is it I get the feeling I've heard this story before?"

Andrew sat next to him. "Yeah, I'm sure you have . . . sorry about that," he said.

Eric sat up. "No offense," he said. He wiped his shaggy mustache with the back of his hand. "It's just that I have a hard time watching guys I've gotten to know pretty well walk out the door after a couple of years. Once they're gone, you seldom hear from them."

Andrew sensed real regret emanating from someone who generally remained quite guarded when personal issues concerning individual monks arose. Eric seldom took a stand and was very careful not to criticize the monastery's policies and procedures, not only because he valued his job, but also because he knew that many of the men who chose monastic life were often in a formative stage, struggling with the enormous difficulties of the life.

"I guess it's hard for everyone when someone leaves the community," Andrew said. "Another piece of the fabric begins to unravel."

"Ain't that the truth," Eric said. "It's like the family falling apart."

Andrew got up to pour the coffee. "Cream and sugar?" he asked, as he returned the pot to the stove.

"Just some cream," Eric answered.

Andrew brought the coffee to Eric and sat down. "I don't want you to think that life here is all bad because it isn't; in fact, I really like it, yet it's far from easy."

"I'm sure that's true," Eric said. "You guys work pretty hard with the ranching, fencing, eggery, and so on."

"And that's the easy part," Andrew said. "If you don't mind me being honest, I guess it's the overall emptiness, the never-ending loneliness that starts to get to you after a while. I like being alone, but the loneliness thing is sometimes overwhelming."

Tyler and Caleb's laughter, as they raced their twig boats, pierced the ensuing silence with abrasive screeches, prompting Andrew to focus on the benefits of children, marriage, and a caring spouse. He rubbed his eyes in his customary way, wishing that he had omitted the last part of his conversation.

As if he had read his mind, Eric continued. "I don't know if this is any consolation, but marriage is no piece of cake either."

Andrew was surprised by his admission. "No, I'm sure it isn't," he offered. "I guess we should abide by Brother Adrian's famous words: 'Thank God you got a job, Brother.'"

The remark caused both men to laugh and lightened the conversation.

Feeling somewhat venturesome, Andrew decided to quiz Eric for information, which he doubted would be revealed to him. "I know you've been around the monastery for a long time—what's the worst you've seen happen?"

The inquiry clearly took him by surprise. "What kind of question is that?" he said, leaning forward, and placing his coffee on the woodstove.

"I know you can't disclose anything too personal; I guess I don't expect you to, but there must be something you can tell me that won't jeopardize your chances of getting into heaven."

"Now, come on, Andrew. Why would you want to know something like that?"

"I don't know. Perhaps, so I can feel more human."

Eric laughed. "You guys are all alike," he said. "I can't say anything. You know that."

Andrew pleaded. "Well, make something up, then," he said. "Humor me."

Eric appeared to be considering the idea. "Well, I can tell you one thing, not too specific, but if it comes back to me, I'll have to deny that I ever said it."

Andrew feigned indifference. "Never mind, then," he said solemnly.

Eric threw up his hands. "After all that . . . I think I'm going to kill you!"

Andrew laughed. "Okay," he said. "I'm just kidding."

"Okay," Eric said. "It was in the middle of July. I was working in the back of the monastery, moving hoses to irrigate the shrubs. The window was open in the abbot's office so it wasn't unusual to hear things—like the phone and pieces of conversation. I remember hearing people talking, the abbot and a novice. It wasn't long before the talking grew heated—I mean nasty. The novice called the abbot some names; the abbot jumped up and I heard furniture crashing and things falling to the floor. I ran around the front to get to the office but, by the time I got there, Father Luke and Brother Cyril had already arrived and separated the two. They thanked me, but quickly insisted that everything was all right, and they wouldn't need me so I left. That's about it."

Andrew was moved by this story yet unsure of its validity. "You made that up, right?" he asked with a grin.

Eric raised his right hand. "Scouts honor," he said. "It's the truth."

"Whatever happened to the novice?"

"That much I do know. When I came to work the following day, I heard that Brother Xavier had left the monastery; word is that he was thrown out."

Andrew sat silently, digesting the bizarre tale, thinking that he would have enjoyed meeting Brother Xavier to compare notes and, perhaps, verify or dispel some of the myths he internalized and anguished over, yet he knew that his relationship with Brother Matthew did not exactly represent a paragon of monastic virtue, which, in some ways, would be similar to the pot calling the kettle black.

"What do you think of Father Jude?" Andrew asked bluntly.

Eric faltered, shifted in his seat and sipped his coffee. "I guess I never thought much about it . . . he's always been pretty good to me. I've never had much to do with him because Father Luke is the one I report to regarding work duties. Why do you ask?"

Andrew sensed Eric's diplomatic response. "I was just wondering," he said.

Squeals of laughter could be heard approaching the cabin door. The latch clicked open and Tyler and Caleb entered, somewhat sheepishly. Caleb, the younger of the two, stood dripping wet, his hair matted to his forehead and his clothing soaked, as if he had just gotten out of the shower.

Eric jumped up. "You fell in, didn't you?" he said sternly.

Caleb remained silent and closed his eyes, thinking that, if he could not see his father, his father could not see him.

With one quick swoop, Eric picked up Caleb, stood him in front of the fire and began removing his clothes.

Andrew found some clean towels in the bathroom and gave them to Eric who rubbed Caleb dry and wrapped him in a fresh towel.

"I knew I shouldn't have left you two alone out there," Eric said. "It's a wonder you didn't float away to the monastery. Your momma's going to kill me."

Andrew put additional wood on the fire. "How's that feel, Caleb?" he asked.

Caleb smiled shyly.

"I guess that means okay," Andrew said with a big smile. He looked at Eric. "I've got some plastic bags back here," he said, as he walked toward the bathroom. "You can throw the wet clothes in them."

"Thanks," Eric said. "I'll wrap him in my parka to get him home."

"Take the towel with you. He'll feel more comfortable that way."

Eric put his parka around Caleb and picked him up. "Well," he said, "I better get these little rug rats home and into a hot bath." He shook Andrew's hand. "Thanks, again, for your help."

"No problem. Thanks for coming by," Andrew replied. "I'll probably see you at the monastery on Sunday. And good luck with Kathy; tell her I said hello."

Eric stowed both boys in the truck, started the engine and rolled down the window, just enough to speak to Andrew who stood in the doorway watching them leave. "You know that story I told you?" Eric shouted.

Andrew nodded.

"Well, I made it up—all of it!"

Andrew laughed, covered his eyes with one hand and shook his head as the truck disappeared up the driveway.

* * *

The afternoon sun was still strong and warm as Andrew spread the birdseed on the feeder in the back of the cabin. He remembered that he was asked to move the hanging suet gradually nearer to the window so that the birds would feel more comfortable feeding close to the cabin. He pulled the wooden pole out of the snow and carried it half the distance toward the window where he, once again, stuck the poll deep into the snow.

Between two of the small outbuildings, Linda and Arthur had constructed a modest deck which they used for fair-weather relaxation. Andrew climbed up the stairs onto the deck and noticed that summer furniture had been neatly stacked in the workshop. He removed a comfortable looking chaise lounge and strategically placed it in a sunny spot, away from the wind.

He found the warmth, luxury, and beauty of the moment nearly intoxicating, as he settled back and observed the magnificent setting, inhaled the fresh mountain air, scented with balsam, and listened to the sound of the bird's cries mixed with the gentle tumbling of the water in the creek. A sense of guilt temporarily dampened his euphoria but not for long. He quickly dispelled the negatives and told himself that he deserved the respite—a time to truly be alone as his vocation implied, a time to simply be and pay homage to the wonders of God's creation. Today, his meditation would be with open eyes, in the present, mindful of every visible nuance that nature chose to flaunt. He was thankful for his monastic journey, the joy and the pain, the uncertainty, which he faced daily, the awareness of the dignity of man, and his quest to do God's will.

Andrew napped briefly in the warm sun, while squirrels scattered from tree to tree and grey mice with large ears looked out from their home in the workshop at the silent stranger dozing on their deck.

* * *

Within the solitude of the cabin, Andrew read voraciously, reflecting on the printed words and striving to absorb their meaning. He would, at times, become nearly overwhelmed with particular passages that seemed to speak to him directly—to encourage his relationship with God and strengthen his monastic resolve, which, he knew, had been, and would continue to be, tested. He would often forget to eat until the growling in his stomach disrupted his thoughts and reminded him that his physical body also needed attention.

Even his meditations grew more comfortable, more natural, with less distraction and darkness; they also became extensive. Andrew was surprised, one afternoon, to learn that he had been meditating for nearly two hours before he was interrupted by the screech of a low-flying jet, an unusual event since all approaching aircraft in the vicinity were informed by the Bitter Creek tower, at the request of the abbot, that they should minimize engine noise when flying over the monastery. Andrew found himself smiling; he imagined Father Jude calling the airport and complaining politely about the infraction while the tower apologized profusely and then crudely described the caller to coworkers.

By the middle of the week, Andrew had become quite proficient with housekeeping, cooking, and maintaining a proper fire in the woodstove. It reminded him of his earlier years, living mostly alone, and being completely responsible for himself. The monastery, he realized, removed many of the day-to-day obligations, which allowed him to foster his vocational growth and conversion, yet with that freedom came the inevitable inner journey and its inescapable study of oneself, as if standing naked in front of a full-length mirror. There was no place to hide. His dialogue of self-examination grew daily as bits of guilt mingled with a positive self-image. He found himself thinking, 'I'm not so bad . . . I'm okay . . . my love for God is real and solid . . . so why should I be guilty for loving what he has created?'

Andrew bolted out of his chair. He decided to turn up the thermostat on the gas water heater and take a hot bath before going to sleep. The water from the handheld sprayer was gravity fed, yet Andrew enjoyed every drop of its steamy warmth as he soaked comfortably in the tub. After shampooing and rinsing his hair, Andrew slowly moved the sprayer over his body until the tub contained about four inches of water, a conservative level, which would prevent draining the small tank.

As much as he fought it, he could not help thinking about Matthew's impending visit on Friday night; he decided that he would cook something simple, spaghetti sauce with vermicelli and have a small salad. Even though he was looking forward to the visit, he was also anxious about it; he didn't know what to expect, particularly regarding the physical aspect of their relationship and his conflicted feelings.

The silence in the cabin magnified the slightest noise; Andrew heard what sounded like someone walking slowly on the crusted snow. He sat up and reached for the towel to dry his hair and listened again for the footsteps, but he heard nothing. His skin tightened as goose bumps covered his arms and legs. After putting on his robe, he stood motionless waiting to hear more footsteps; however, once again, all was silent. Just as he finished with his hair, he heard the same soft footsteps outside the large window in the living room. He slowly reached up to the gas lamp above the table and extinguished its light. In the dark, he got down on the floor, crawled to the window, and carefully raised his head to the level of the sill. With his heart racing, he peered over it; at first, he saw nothing, however, as his eyes adjusted to the dark, Andrew could see a large furry shape, topped with antlers—an elk had wandered onto the property to scavenge for food. Andrew stood up and was quickly spotted by the animal who immediately bound away into the darkness. With obvious relief, he relit the lantern, drained the tub and restocked the stove for the night.

And for the first time that week, Andrew experienced a growing sense of anxiety at the cabin, once nightfall arrived. It was more than just the elk incident; he felt edgy prior to taking his bath. He was unable to concentrate on his reading or complete his meditation. He wondered, seriously, about his life at the monastery; whether he would have the ability to persevere, to live truly alone, and maintain some sense of happiness or even sanity. Although the thoughts were not new, their intensity and his need to confront them were overpowering and stark. His mind raced with prolific imagery, hurdles with no solutions. 'That's it,' he thought. 'Time for bed.'

He climbed the ladder to the loft with a flashlight in one hand and a small metal urinal tucked under his arm to prevent a midnight trip to the outhouse. He undressed, pulled on fleece sweatpants and a T-shirt and climbed into his sleeping bag.

Unexpectedly, sleep came quickly yet not deeply. Andrew tossed and turned as he continued his earlier struggle, except, in sleep, everything became more visceral and more disturbing. At one point, he found himself back in the eggery bathroom, as John's body twisted slowly on its rope. Once again, Andrew stared in horror, yet this time, he did not run. Instead, he remained, riveted to the floor, as John opened his eyes, looked at Andrew and spoke: "It's not so bad . . . there is nothing." John then held out his lifeless hand to Andrew. "Come with me," he whispered.

Andrew sat up in bed, hyperventilating and covered with sweat. He wiped his head with his T-shirt, searched for the urinal and, in a kneeling position, emptied his bladder. He looked down at the woodstove, which was still glowing brightly and casting familiar shadows on the ceiling. There was no need to go downstairs, so he climbed back into his sleeping bag and lay there with his eyes wide open, listening to the wind, trying to forget his dreams. He reached for the flashlight to check his watch; it was nearly 3:00 a.m. He knew that the monks would be starting vigils, beginning their day with sleepy yawns, prayers, and meditation. He thought of Matthew, barely awake, sitting in the darkened church and fighting sleep. Andrew remembered watching him once as his head dropped onto his chest, and he almost fell out of his chair. He began to smile, in his solitary loft, as previous troublesome thoughts slowly faded.

Yet these thoughts were replaced by others, thoughts about Matthew in a less than spiritual sense. Andrew experienced his closeness, the feeling of his skin, the strength of his touch. This desire was exacerbated by Andrew's awareness of his own physical arousal which made sleep impossible. He felt driven, knowing that he needed to release that yearning. He removed his T-shirt and while continuing to think about Matthew, he did what he needed to do—compassionately, without guilt.

* * *

Andrew spent much of the following day skiing on the mesa and enjoying the brilliant sun. He explored various washes and ravines behind the steep side of the field where he found old cookware, rusty bedsprings, and other remnants related to primitive housekeeping. 'Probably some old backwoods man,' he thought, 'trying to eke out a living.'

As the afternoon wore on, he realized that he had skied quite a distance from the cabin through a maze of turns, valleys, and hills. The sun remained strong and the warm temperatures caused him to perspire easily through his clothing. He climbed a steep wash to help get a better fix on his location. When he reached the top, he was surprised to learn that the mesa was farther away than he expected, and there was no direct route back since several deep rifts stood between him and his destination. He decided to ski the high land, down the valley, and then traverse up and over to the base of the mesa where he could access the cabin. 'At least,' he thought, 'I won't have much climbing to do.'

With more than half of the return trip completed, Andrew began the long gradual traverse which would eventually put him on the lower end of the mesa. He had never skied this part of the land and was enjoying the variety of the terrain and the different scenery as he took the time to observe the beauty around him. He climbed a gentle knoll which provided an expansive view of the property, sixty or seventy yards below him, where he unexpectedly looked down upon a familiar sight. Andrew recognized the Morgan cabin, which he had never seen before from the surrounding hill. His position provided a clear view of the back of the house with its wraparound deck and abundant windows.

Andrew stood silently, looking off in the distance. He then skied, somberly, back toward his cabin, forgetting to look at the streaks of salmon-colored sky or the perpetually gliding red-tail hawks.

He had not been in the cabin for more than ten minutes when he saw the black Volkswagen Rabbit, one of the three cars owned by the monastery, pull up to the front door and stop. Andrew was startled to see the bulky frame of Brother Nathan, the assistant infirmarian, exit the incongruously small vehicle. Andrew immediately opened the cabin door to greet him.

"To what do I owe this honor?" he said. "Wait . . . you drove over here to remind me to take my vitamins, right?"

Brother Nathan laughed. "Not exactly," he said, shaking Andrew's hand. "How are you?"

"I guess I'm doing okay," Andrew said. "I think I could really get used to this eremitic lifestyle."

"I know what you mean. It's nice to get away for a while," Brother Nathan admitted.

Andrew gently guided Brother Nathan into the cabin with his hand on his shoulder. "Come in and sit down." He closed the door, took Brother Nathan's jacket and hung it on a peg. "You've arrived at a good time; I just made some coffee."

Brother Nathan hesitated. "I don't want to disturb you by staying too long. I thought I'd just drop by to see how you're doing."

Andrew dismissed his words with a cursory wave of his hand. "Don't even think about it," he said. "I'm glad to have some company." He filled the two mugs with fresh coffee and handed one to Brother Nathan, who remained standing near the window. "Cream or sugar?"

"No, thanks. Black is fine."

Andrew sat down, and Brother Nathan joined him. He sipped his coffee, placed the mug on the table, and looked at Brother Nathan, who appeared somewhat uncomfortable. "Is everything okay at the monastery?" he asked, with growing apprehension.

Brother Nathan quickly moved the mug away from his lips. "This stuff's hot!"

"Right out of the pot," Andrew said, sensing Brother Nathan's oblique response, which was followed by silence. He shifted in his chair and rubbed his eyes, wondering if Brother Nathan was about to tell him some horrendous news. "Okay, did my mother die?"

Brother Nathan sat upright. "What?"

"I can handle it," Andrew said calmly. "I'm pretty sure you wouldn't just drop in for a casual chat." He ran his fingers through his hair and picked up his mug. "What's going on?"

Brother Nathan smiled. "Relax. This is just about one step above the casual chat."

"So . . . no one died?"

"No one died," Brother Nathan explained. "I'm here because Father Gerald had concerns about you being on retreat—alone—so quickly after the tragedy you witnessed in the eggery."

Andrew exhaled loudly. "Well, that's a relief." He smiled at Brother Nathan. "I'm sorry for being so abrupt, but I just kept thinking that you were the bearer of bad news."

"Not today," Brother Nathan replied.

Andrew raised one eyebrow in response to Brother Nathan's cryptic remark. "Hopefully, not anytime soon. I don't want to associate you with the messenger."

"Well, I wouldn't want that either," Brother Nathan said. He sipped his coffee and settled back in his chair. Even though he was wearing loose-fitting clothing, he exuded an aura of physical strength, perhaps by his very size—over six feet three inches—with a thick neck and a rugged face, characterized by a square jaw, high cheekbones, and an ever-present five o'clock shadow. He sat very erect, probably out of necessity, to properly carry his muscled frame. Andrew imagined it was the result of his training at Annapolis. And yet Brother Nathan also evoked a sense of gentleness and restraint. His voice was unexpectedly soft, his movements seemingly choreographed and graceful; somehow, the entire composite worked for him. His smile could easily disarm the anxious and make anyone in his presence feel genuinely accepted.

"We haven't had the opportunity to talk very much," Andrew said, as he got up to add a piece of wood to the fire.

"That could be my fault," Brother Nathan said quickly. "I guess I tend to keep to myself . . . maybe too much."

Andrew was captivated by his self-effacement. "Oh, I don't know. I think it's one of the traits of the job, an unexpected one, and, quite frankly, one to be admired." He returned to his chair with the coffeepot in one hand. "More?" he asked.

"Just about half," Brother Nathan said, holding out his mug. "Thanks."

"I tend to be a curious George, wondering all sorts of things and wishing that I didn't," Andrew offered.

"You're not alone. I found out, after while, that it generally gets me in trouble."

"I know what you mean," Andrew said.

A silence followed, during which Brother Nathan chose not to pursue the topic. He returned to the nature of his visit. "Father Gerald was at a medical conference when you left for the retreat. He asked me if I thought you would be all right out here, and I told him I wasn't sure. How have you been sleeping?"

Andrew reflected on the question which appeared to catch him off guard. "I guess I've been doing okay . . . maybe sleeping too late in the morning."

"How about the night hours? Are you sleeping through the night?"

"It's funny, but just the other night, I had a dream—a nightmare, I guess—and it was difficult getting back to sleep."

Brother Nathan's interest seemed to peak. "Was the dream about anything in particular that you can remember and feel comfortable talking about?"

Andrew sensed the underlying psychological aspect of the questioning. "It was about John . . . from the eggery. He spoke to me."

Brother Nathan continued. "Can you tell me what he said?"

Andrew had no difficulty recalling the dream, particularly John's words, yet he could feel a growing apprehension over having to actually say them. "He said, 'There is nothing,' and then he held out his hand and said, 'Come with me.'"

Brother Nathan sipped his coffee while staring pensively into the distance. He then turned to look at Andrew. "Was anything else said?"

"No, that was it," Andrew said. "I woke up sweating and I could feel my heart pounding like crazy."

"I'm not surprised," Brother Nathan said. "You've experienced quite a trauma."

"Sometimes, it's not a dream at all—I just start thinking about what happened and I feel . . . jumpy. It may happen when I'm meditating, or just sitting here, reading."

Brother Nathan got up from his chair and walked toward the door. "I'll be right back," he said.

Through the window, Andrew watched Brother Nathan open the car door and retrieve a small black case from the backseat. He returned to the house looking somewhat like a country doctor, carrying his leather satchel.

"You're not going to operate, are you?" Andrew asked jokingly.

Brother Nathan laughed. "I can't," he said, setting the case on the table. "I never completed my residency."

Andrew looked surprised. "I didn't know that you were studying to be a doctor."

"Well, I was torn between football and medicine but I like to think that the Big Guy had different plans for me."

"So you decided to come to the monastery instead."

"It wasn't an easy decision but . . . here I am."

Andrew watched Brother Nathan open the case and remove an amber vial, which he placed on the table.

"Father Gerald decided that you might need some medication to help you relax and get some sleep. He said that I should offer it to you if you seem to be having any problems or flashbacks dealing with John's death. It's a mild anti-anxiety medication which, if necessary, can be taken three times a day, however, you might feel drowsy, so you need to be careful about operating machinery or driving." He handed the container to Andrew who removed the cover and looked inside. Approximately thirty, almond-shaped pills covered the bottom of the vial.

"I've never used anything like this before," Andrew said.

"Understand, there is no obligation; it's up to you, and only if you need them."

Andrew replaced the cap and set the medicine back on the table. "I'll give them a try if I continue to be bothered by this. Tell Father Gerald that I appreciate his concern—and yours—for taking the time to come by."

Brother Nathan smiled. "Well, I'd better be going so you can enjoy your retreat in peace." He got up and walked toward the door. Then he stopped and faced Andrew. "One other thing. Father Gerald asked me to remind you that Dr. Klein's services are available, if you feel you would like some counseling on this—something for you to think about." He did not wait for an answer, but quickly turned, opened the door and left.

Andrew waved goodbye as Brother Nathan backed up the VW and then drove off.

* * *

The evening proved to be productive yet emotionally inconsequential. Andrew ate a late-evening meal, read, meditated, and decided that he needed to get some rest. There were times when he found himself absorbed with the earlier incidents, yet he successfully forced himself to let the thoughts go. Comfortably tucked into his sleeping bag, Andrew switched off his flashlight as sleep slowly seduced his conscious mind.

It was nearly 4:00 a.m. when it happened. From a deep sleep, Andrew suddenly opened his eyes and stared, panic-stricken, into the darkness. A black hooded figure knelt over him, motionless, with no salient facial features other than two glowing red eyes. Andrew felt as if his heart were about to explode into a million pieces, as his body froze against the mattress. A scream stuck in his throat like a garbled moan, which only intensified his horror. Like a choking victim who finally dislodges and spits out the obstruction, Andrew heard himself inhale sharply and then speak in a deep voice, which he knew was not his. The sentence started loudly and ended with a violent shout. "What do you want?" he screamed into the face of the intruder. Immediately, the hooded figure appeared to float backwards, grow smaller, and then completely disappeared.

Perspiration stung Andrew's eyes, yet he was powerless to wipe the sweat away. His heart continued to pound in his ears and chest, as he searched in the darkness for any indication that the black figure might still be present. He tried to move his head from side to side; however, it felt as though it was bolted to the mattress; he scanned the room as best he could with his eyes—nothing glowed. 'Relax,' he thought. 'I've got to relax.' He began to take slow deep breaths, until he could feel the grip of fear gradually abate. Finally, he was able to move his head, arms, and legs; he supported himself on his elbows to get a better view of his surroundings while his right hand searched for the flashlight, which he always placed near the mattress. Armed with the light, Andrew illuminated every nook and cranny of the loft. He then crawled to the edge, overlooking the floor below him, and scanned the interior until he was satisfied that nothing appeared suspicious.

With his courage renewed, Andrew wrapped himself in his bathrobe and climbed down the ladder. He lit one of the gas lamps and proceeded to inspect the cabin for anything that looked unusual or less than natural, however, everything seemed to be in order.

He added two pieces of firewood to the stove, dimmed the gas lamp and sat, curled up with a blanket, on the overstuffed couch. As the wood ignited in the stove, shadows and light increased their intensity against the cabin walls and ceiling. Figures danced ominously, swaying back and forth, as their shapes writhed and expanded, reminding Andrew of nothing less than demons. He pulled the blanket even tighter and closed his eyes, yet the images danced relentlessly inside his eyelids until he could no longer tolerate them. He quickly jumped up and brightened the gas lamp, which promptly washed the shadows from the room.

As he was about to sit back down, Andrew remembered the medication that Brother Nathan had offered him; the vial sat on the table where he had left it. With some reservation, he reached for the bottle and read the instructions on the side of the container: *"For difficulty sleeping—do not exceed two per night."* Andrew removed two pills and put the container back on the table. He swallowed the pills with orange juice, which he drank directly from the carton, realizing, only afterwards, that this was the first time he had done that since he entered the monastery.

Not knowing what to expect, Andrew settled back on the couch in anticipation of the drug's effect. He looked at his watch and saw that it was nearly 5:00 a.m., a time when the first rays of the sun would color the mountain peaks salmon or pink and allow the braver birds to utter their initially feckless chirps. Through the window, Andrew glimpsed a pale blue streak brushed across the indigo sky. Morning, he thought, could not be far away.

When he awoke, Andrew found himself curled up on the couch, under his blanket, which was covered with sunshine, wondering what had happened to him. He quickly glanced at his watch and saw that it was exactly eleven o'clock. The brilliant blue sky confronted his initial skepticism, until he realized that he had taken medication and spent the rest of the night, and most of the morning, sleeping in a dazed state on a lumpy makeshift bed.

He sat up and suddenly remembered why his head felt so fuzzy. 'That had to be a dream,' he thought. 'Otherwise, I am either crazy, or facing some creature from hell.' Looking out on a perfectly sparkling day, Andrew could easily dismiss the latter. He increased the temperature of the water heater, in preparation for his bath, and made himself some breakfast. He quickly realized, with both excitement and trepidation, that it was Friday, the day that Brother Matthew would be coming over for dinner. While he looked forward to the visit, Andrew did not know what to expect: would Matthew interpret this as a less-than-subtle assignation, or simply as a gesture of genuine friendship? Andrew, however, had to ask himself the same question, yet rather than dwell on the answer he allowed denial to take the form of a warm bath.

* * *

Whatever ingredients he was missing, Andrew was fortunate enough to find in the cupboards in the cabin. The Coles had copious supplies of garlic and other spices, which Andrew used to concoct his spaghetti sauce, a task which absorbed much of the afternoon and caused the cabin to smell like a savory Italian kitchen. He let the sauce simmer for several hours to thoroughly blend the flavors, yet he wished, instead of being vegetarians, he could have made meatballs. Just the thought of it made his mouth water.

Andrew quickly made a salad with two types of lettuce, cucumber, peppers, and tomatoes. He then mixed a dressing of olive oil with vinegar, lemon, and a touch of tarragon and set them aside in the refrigerator.

And then, he thought about dessert. 'I've got to have something.' He looked in the small freezer, behind several packages whose contents were a mystery and saw a container of frozen strawberries. 'Shortcake!' he thought. Within minutes, he had the berries defrosting in a bowl while he gathered the necessary ingredients to bake the biscuits.

Once the biscuits were out of the oven and cooling, Andrew decided it was time to get outside, to go for a walk and enjoy the remainder of the afternoon.

* * *

As anticipated, Brother Matthew arrived on skis, at five thirty, while Andrew, anxious yet happy, welcomed him at the door. "You made it!" Andrew said with open arms, waiting for a hug.

Brother Matthew smiled and kicked off his skis. "Of course, I wouldn't have missed this for anything." He dropped his poles in the snow and reached out to pull Andrew firmly into his embrace. "I feel as though I haven't seen you in years."

Andrew laughed and inhaled the familiar laundered scent of his heated body. "And if you don't stop squeezing me, this may be the last time you'll ever see me again."

The remark prompted Brother Matthew to squeeze him even harder as he lifted Andrew into the air.

Andrew gasped. "Okay! Okay! You've been taking way too many vitamins," he said slowly, as he regained his breath. "Are you getting lessons from Brother Edward?"

Matthew raised his eyebrows slightly. "I guess it's just being with you."

"Yeah, right," Andrew said mockingly. "But it's a remark like that which can get you a free dinner so—let's go in." He picked up Matthew's poles and carried them into the cabin.

Matthew leaned his skis against the wall near the door, removed his backpack and hung his parka on one of the wooden pegs. "This place smells great!" he said as he unlaced his ski boots and walked with bare feet toward the woodstove where he slumped into a comfortable chair.

"Thanks," Andrew said. "I hope you like Italian food because there is no second choice."

"Other than the fact that it happens to be my favorite . . . I guess it will do."

Andrew placed two halves of garlic bread under the gas broiler until it turned golden brown and the Parmesan cheese began to bubble. He cut the bread into thick chunks, put them into a wooden bowl and brought them over to Matthew.

"It's not exactly the antipasto platter I'd have preferred," he said, as he set the bowl on the small table between the chairs, "but like you said, it'll have to do."

"It smells terrific," Matthew said. He quickly reached into the bowl, unable to wait any longer. "I'm so hungry I could eat a horse." He was finishing his third piece of bread when he suddenly bolted out of his chair and walked toward the door. "I nearly forgot," he said, as he reached into his backpack and retrieved a three-liter bottle of soft red altar wine, which he held out in front of him, grinning as he stood there. "What's dinner without the wine?"

Andrew smiled and slowly shook his head. "I don't even want to know where that came from," he said quietly.

Matthew stood in the middle of the room looking bewildered yet apologetic. "Is it okay that I brought this?" he asked, as if a negative response would simply make the bottle disappear and resolve the matter.

Andrew smiled. "Of course, in fact, I would probably have been disappointed if you didn't."

Matthew exhaled a sigh of relief, peeled the foil from the top of the bottle and slowly removed the mushroom-shaped cork, which opened with a gentle hissing sound. Searching through the cupboards, Andrew found two champagne flutes, rinsed them, and gave them to Matthew who was eager to pour.

"None of this 'two-thirds full' stuff," he said as he filled the glasses to the brim. "I know we'll want more."

"Why do I get the feeling that you've done this before?" Andrew asked derisively.

"Because I have," Matthew said. "You know how lonely it can get at the monastery."

Andrew nodded slowly and smiled. "Yup. I do."

"So what shall we drink to?" Matthew asked, carefully handing a glass to Andrew.

He looked directly at Matthew. "I should probably say something profound, but I won't. How about something simple, something real, like . . . 'to us.'" He raised his glass as Matthew raised his, carefully touching them together with a faint crystal timbre.

"To us," Matthew said.

Both tilted their glasses and drank deeply.

Matthew set his glass on the table and held out his arms. "Come here," he said as he pulled Andrew toward him and buried his face inside his shirt collar. "You have no idea how much I've missed being with you. Every night, I think about you being up here, alone, and it practically drives me crazy." He slowly ran his mouth up Andrew's neck and under his chin, feeling the rough stubble of his beard and tasting the faint salinity of his skin.

With closed eyes, Andrew was unable to respond verbally, as the physical contact devastated his ability to focus until, suddenly, he was aware of bright lights shining directly at him through the window. He quickly opened his eyes and saw a vehicle coming down the driveway toward the cabin.

"Oh shit!" he said, pushing Matthew toward the floor. "This time, I think it really is the fucking Inquisition."

Brother Matthew crawled into the bathroom area behind the large porcelain tub where he hid quietly in the dark. He then thought about the bottle of wine sitting on the table.

"Hide the wine," he said with a whisper.

Andrew barely had time to grab the bottle and place it between the couch and the wall before he heard the anticipated, yet dreaded, knock.

He unlatched the door and swung it open. "Brother Mark," he said calmly. "This is an unexpected surprise. Come on in."

Brother Mark entered the cabin, shaking his boots and removing his gloves. He extended his hand to Andrew, which he grabbed and shook firmly.

"I hope you're not going to tell me that someone died," Andrew said with forced apprehension.

"No," Brother Mark said. "Nothing quite so serious, but I do want to apologize for disturbing you on the last night of your retreat." He unzipped his parka and wiped his steamed glasses with his handkerchief. "It smells like you are about to have some Italian food."

"You are welcome to stay," Andrew gambled, knowing that his response would be negative.

"Well, I'd like to but I can't. Thanks anyway."

Andrew shifted from one foot to the other. "So what's up?" he asked, hoping that the discussion would be insignificant yet fearing that Brother Mark's visit was more than casual.

"Father Jude saw Brother Matthew this afternoon, skiing across the basin, and since he hasn't returned yet, he was thinking that perhaps you might have seen him, since he appeared to be heading in this direction."

Andrew hesitated slightly as he instantly grasped the reason for this unlikely interrogation. "I hope that he hasn't fallen and injured himself," he said, with as much empathy as he could engender.

"We are concerned about the same possibility," Brother Mark responded. "I know that he's a capable skier, but I fear that he sometimes takes chances."

Andrew nodded in agreement. "That's for sure," he said. "I've seen him ski some pretty nasty stuff and come out smelling like a rose."

"That's true," Brother Mark agreed, "but it only takes one accident."

Brother Mark appeared to scan the room without moving his head. "So," he said, "you haven't, by chance, seen him today, have you?"

Andrew realized that he was being forced to either tell the truth or lie; neither of which was a viable option. Looking over Brother Mark's shoulder, he could see Matthew's parka hanging on a peg near the door. He looked directly at Brother Mark. "I don't really have to answer that, do I?" he said quietly, wishing that he could simply disappear.

"No, you don't," Brother Matthew said, as he stepped forward from the shadows into the light, "because I will."

Andrew's knees grew weak, and he slowly slid down the wall to the floor in a sitting position.

"Hello Matthew," Brother Mark said, holding out his hand, which Matthew boldly refused to shake. "I have to say, I guess I'm not surprised to see you here."

Matthew responded sternly. "You know, I guess I'm not surprised to see you here either," he said, moving slightly closer to Brother Mark, who sensed his growing opposition.

"Well, I'd rather see you here than find you lying in a wash somewhere with a broken leg," he said cordially.

The seemingly genuine remark appeared to defuse Matthew's anger. He relaxed his rigid stance and stepped backwards slightly. He then reached down to Andrew and pulled him to a standing position.

"Yet," Brother Mark continued, "you both realize that this is a serious violation of monastic rule and expectations. When a Brother is on retreat, social visits are prohibited."

"I know," Matthew said peacefully, "and it's my fault. When I saw Andrew skiing on the mesa earlier in the week, I invited myself to dinner on Friday; he didn't have much of a choice. Besides, I thought by then he would appreciate some company."

Andrew attempted to respond, but Matthew quickly nudged him with his elbow.

"Well," Brother Mark replied. "This is exactly the reason why I'm here."

"What do you mean?" Andrew asked.

Brother Mark removed his parka. "Would you mind if we sit down?"

"No, not at all," Andrew said, leading them toward the dinner table where two half-full glasses of wine sat precariously close to the edge.

Brother Mark acknowledged the wine. "You wouldn't happen to have any extra, would you?"

"Sure," Andrew said. He retrieved the bottle from alongside the couch, remembering, only then, that the wine had been taken from the monastery's sacristy. "Don't look—don't ask," Andrew blurted out, as he set the bottle on the table.

Brother Mark ran his hand over his face and slowly shook his head.

Andrew returned with a water glass since he was unable to find anything resembling a wineglass.

Brother Mark filled it three-quarters full and took a long swallow. "Thanks," he said, wiping his mouth with the back of his hand. "I'm going to tell you both something which I shouldn't, but I care about the both of you, and I hope it's something that can be resolved."

Andrew could feel his stomach tighten. "Oh no," he said quietly.

Brother Mark took another swallow of wine. "There are elders at the monastery who feel that your friendship . . . is more than fraternal," he said.

"What?" Andrew responded with disbelief. He refilled his glass and immediately drank half of it. "Look," he said. "We're good friends and we enjoy being in each other's company."

"That's right," Matthew added. "Besides, why do I feel as though this reminds me of the pot calling the kettle you know what." He finished his wine and reached for the bottle.

Brother Mark disregarded his comment. "Like I said, I like the both of you and I don't want to see either one of you make a bad decision and leave the monastery because, on a more selfish level, it's very difficult for me to see people I care about walk out the door."

"I'm sorry, but this is bullshit," Matthew said frankly, setting the wine bottle down with a thud.

Brother Mark stood up and turned toward the window. "Bullshit or not, I feel it's in your best interest to know."

Silence filled the room as Brother Mark continued to stare through the window into the darkness. He placed both palms firmly against the cold panes and watched as condensation slowly traced the outline of his hand onto the glass. "I think I can help resolve this matter by talking with Father Luke."

"What do you mean?" Andrew asked.

"Well, I will simply encourage him to view your friendship as fraternal and remind him of the 'needs' of the younger members of the community." He sat back down at the table.

"Sounds easier said than done," Brother Matthew added quickly.

"Maybe," Brother Mark replied. "I need to think about this." He got up, put his hands on Andrew's shoulders, and gently squeezed him.

"Don't worry about it," he said softly. "It will be all right." Zipping his parka, he walked toward the door. "I guess we'd better be going," he said, as he turned to look at Brother Matthew.

Brother Matthew did not respond immediately. Instead, he made direct eye contact with Andrew, and without looking at Brother Mark, he said, "I'm not leaving."

"What?" Brother Mark asked incredulously.

"I'm fine where I am," he said. "I'm not leaving. Besides, we haven't had dinner yet."

Brother Mark unzipped his parka and walked slowly toward the table. "How can you expect me to help you if you don't understand the gravity of the situation?"

"I hear you," Brother Matthew said, "but you need to understand that I am going to have dinner with Andrew, and then I'll ski back to the monastery."

Brother Mark threw his hands into the air. "Forgive me, but you know you're crazy."

"Maybe," Matthew said, as he refilled his wineglass.

Brother Mark anguished over a response. "What am I going to say to Father Luke?"

"Tell him you haven't seen me. When he questions me tomorrow, which I'm sure he will, I'll tell him that I skied all the way to Greystone Mountain, fell, broke a ski tip, and had to walk back through deep snow, in the dark."

Brother Mark paced between the wall and the stove, painfully aware that he was being asked to lie. "You're putting me in a tremendously difficult position which, nevertheless, I'll consider if you can compromise."

"How's that?" Matthew asked.

"I don't want you skiing back in the dark. I'll pick you up at midnight. That should give us enough time to get you safely back before the community gets up for vigils."

Brother Matthew smiled and hugged Brother Mark. "Thanks," he said. "I really appreciate this. I'll see you at twelve."

Andrew watched as the truck drove up the driveway. As soon as the taillights disappeared into the darkness, he immediately closed the heavy drapes on the large window and then did the same to the other two windows while Matthew observed in silence. "I don't trust them," he said, as he poured himself more wine and sat by the fire. "Maybe the walls have ears."

Brother Matthew refilled his own glass, took a deep drink and sat next to Andrew. "Honestly," he said. "I don't care if the place is bugged which, when you think about it, would be pretty hard to do."

This brought a slight smile to Andrew's face; however, Matthew noticed that it quickly vanished. He placed his hand on Andrew's arm knowing, that Brother Mark's visit had a devastating effect on him, as he struggled tremendously with the polarity of his vocation.

"I'm sorry this happened, Andrew," Matthew admitted, "but as much as you may not think so right now, things *will* be all right."

Andrew finished his wine, got up and poured himself another. He stood, looking at the fire. "That's what I love about you, Matt. You're such an optimist."

"It's true," he said, getting up to face Andrew. "It'll be okay. We're not going before a firing squad—or anything. More than likely, I'll be called in to talk with Father Luke, and he may do the same with you."

"And what will you say to him?" Andrew asked, finally making eye contact with Matthew.

"I'll simply say that I am hopelessly in love with this handsome hunk of a monk and that he can martyr me at the stake."

Andrew was caught off guard by the unexpected response and his own unexpected laughter. He put down his drink, grabbed Matthew in a headlock and wrestled him to the floor. "If you say that, you won't have to worry about a firing squad or martyrdom!"

"Okay, okay," Matthew pleaded. "I promise, I won't say that."

Andrew released him, and both sat on the floor.

"You are wickedly strong!" Matthew said, stretching his neck back and forth.

"Yeah?" Andrew teased. "Maybe you just bring out the beast in me."

"I hope not too often," Matthew joked.

Andrew lay on his back, with his hands behind his head, while familiar shadows from the fire danced less menacingly on the ceiling, thanks to Matthew's presence.

"Do you really think everything is going to be okay?" he asked, as he continued to stare at the images whirling above him.

Matthew lay on his side next to Andrew, supporting his head with his hand. "Yes, I really do," he said softly. "Besides, I think they like us and wouldn't want to see us leave." He ran his free hand through Andrew's hair, massaging his temples with his thumb and middle finger.

"I'm not so sure about that," Andrew replied. "We're not exactly indispensable."

"No, but we're young." Matthew's response seemed baffling.

Andrew sat up and looked at him. "What the heck does that mean?"

"Look around you. Most of the guys here are over thirty and they would probably like to see some of the younger guys stay on and take over whatever needs to be done when the older brothers get . . . old."

"It's a nice thought," Andrew said, "but not powerful enough to prevent us from being thrown out."

Matthew got up into a kneeling position. "You've got to stop thinking like this. We are not going to be thrown out." He grabbed Andrew by the shoulders. "Okay?"

Andrew smiled. "Okay," he said.

Matthew jumped up and walked toward the door, where he put on his boots and parka.

Andrew was startled by his sudden move. "Where are you going?" he asked as he stood up next to the stove.

"I am going out to Art's workshop, put my ski in a vice, and break off the tip. And when I come back, I know I'm going to be really hungry."

"Holy mackerel," Andrew said. "I forgot that we haven't eaten yet." He immediately put a pot of water on the stove as Matthew left the cabin.

By the time Matthew returned, Andrew was pouring the steamy pasta into a colander and shaking it to remove the excess water. "It's al dente," he said. "I hate when it gets too soft."

"That's fine with me," Matthew replied. Holding up his broken ski, he showed it to Andrew. "So what do you think? Does it look like I crashed and burned in the mountains?"

"It looks kind of nasty," Andrew said, "but won't they expect you to look at a little bruise?"

Matthew smiled lasciviously. "That's your job . . . after dinner."

Andrew dismissed the remark with raised eyebrows and rolled his eyes. "Sit down and eat," he said with a grin. He refilled the wineglasses and noticed that the bottle was nearly empty. "It didn't take long for us to kill that bottle," he said, holding it up to the light to estimate the remainder. "That Brother Mark is a fish."

The last comment struck Matthew as humorous and ironic. He doubled up with laughter and pushed away from the table to regain some control.

Andrew sat down, surprised, yet happy with Matthew's reaction. "Come on . . . it wasn't that funny, was it?" he said with a giggle. "Besides, I have to attribute it to Br. Adrian."

"Maybe not to you," Matthew replied, "but I think I'm a little under the weather and, I'm not sure, but you may be right behind me."

"Great," Andrew said sarcastically. "Two drunk monks on the eve of destruction."

"I think it's my turn to tell you to shut up and eat," Matthew said, as he navigated a fork full of pasta into his mouth.

Andrew waited a while, thinking that Brother Matthew would say something, good or bad, about his cooking, however, he continued to consume large quantities of pasta with occasional slurps and sucking sounds.

"So how's the sauce?" he asked.

Matthew put down his fork and wiped his mouth. "Damn! I'm sorry," he said, "but it's so good I couldn't stop eating. This is fantastic!"

Andrew laughed. "You're just saying that because, like you said earlier, you're so hungry you could eat a cow."

"A horse," Matthew said, correcting him. "This is better than . . ." He leaned over toward Andrew, cupped his mouth with one hand, and finished his sentence in a whisper, "Brother Adrian's—just in case the walls have ears."

"Thanks," Andrew said, "but I don't know if I'd go that far."

"No, it really is," Matthew insisted, as he plunged back into the meal.

"Be sure to save some room for dessert," Andrew cautioned.

"Now you tell me," Matthew said, with his mouth half full. He used his napkin to wipe sauce from his chin. "What are we having?"

Andrew considered making him guess but decided against it. "Strawberry shortcake, without the whipped cream."

"All right!" Matthew said excitedly. "That's got to be my favorite."

"I must be a mind reader," Andrew said. He cleared part of the table, rinsed the dishes, and left them in the sink. "I'll make some fresh coffee, and then I'll get the dessert."

Brother Matthew got up and helped Andrew with the cleanup. He stood beside him at the sink, scraped the dishes, and rinsed them, in preparation for washing. He was acutely aware of any contact with Andrew, especially when his arm or shoulder brushed against his, which caused him to feel incredibly elated. Unable to fight these feelings any longer, he stood in back of Andrew, put his arms around his waist, and squeezed him.

"I can't help it," he said, speaking quietly into Andrew's ear. "It's just so good to be with you."

Andrew stopped what he was doing and stood silently with his eyes closed. He wondered if this would be the last time he would spend with Matthew, completely alone, away from the monastery, and how their relationship would fare in the months to come. He wrapped his arms around his, leaned his head back and gently kissed his ear.

"I'd better make some coffee," he said.

"Can I help?" Matthew asked, feeling a bit abandoned.

"Thanks, but no," Andrew replied. "Have a seat by the fire and relax."

Andrew quickly put the dessert together while the coffee continued to perk on the stove. He turned off the gas burner, poured two cups of the steamy brew and brought the shortcake and coffee over to where Matthew was sitting. He set them on the small table between the chairs and left to retrieve two spoons.

It did not take long before Matthew tasted several spoonfuls of the dessert. "This is terrific—and don't say it's because I'm hungry."

Andrew smiled. "Okay, I won't, but I have to tell you that the berries were frozen."

"But the biscuits are homemade and delicious," Matthew said. "Where did you learn to cook like this?"

Andrew was pleased that Matthew noticed the biscuits. "Well, I learned a lot from Brother Adrian, who really is pretty gifted," he said. "And I guess it comes from living alone or living with someone who either couldn't or didn't like to cook—not to mention that the recipe is on the side of the box."

Matthew's attention seemed to peak. "I shouldn't be asking, but was the person who didn't like to cook a guy you lived with, before you came to the monastery?"

The question made Andrew uncomfortable; he shifted in his chair and hesitated, not sure whether to express his discomfort or simply let it go. He quickly opted for the former.

"You're right, Matt," Andrew said quietly. "I might have felt better if you hadn't asked, but . . . it was a woman—Sara, I lived with, who didn't like to cook."

An invisible pall appeared to envelop Matthew, who stopped eating and stared at the fire. He then got up, walked over to the darkened kitchen area and stood, leaning against the counter, in silence.

Andrew was genuinely stunned by Matthew's reaction, yet he was unsure as to which part of his response prompted it. He walked over to where Matthew was standing.

"I'm sorry, Matt," Andrew said softly, "but the question took me by surprise. I shouldn't have been so blunt." He then hugged him with genuine remorse.

Matthew had no immediate response; he allowed Andrew to hug him while he continued to remain silent.

Andrew was bewildered by this reaction, not knowing whether to question Matthew or to wait for him to speak.

Finally, Matthew responded. "I don't know what came over me, but I'm the one who should be apologizing."

"It's okay," Andrew said. "I want to try to understand what upset you and how I can help." He gently grabbed Matthew by the shoulders and turned him so that they faced each other. "What's going on?" he asked.

Matthew responded without eye contact. "I don't know," he said quietly, staring at Andrew's sweater. "It must be the woman thing . . . I just never expected that you lived with a woman."

Andrew pulled Matthew toward him, hugged him firmly and kissed him lightly on the forehead. "I understand," he said, knowing fully that Matthew's statement implied much more than he would be willing to verbalize, at least, for the moment. "Whatever you think or feel, I want you to know my being here with you, my relationship with you, is what I've chosen, and you are the person I've chosen to be with. Do you understand that?"

Matthew shook his head, indicating that he did.

Andrew placed his hand under Matthew's chin and raised his head so that he could look at his eyes. "Meeting you in the monastery has, admittedly, placed me in a dilemma, of sorts, but I'll have to deal with that; just as long as you know that I care very deeply about you."

Matthew smiled. "I know," he said, hugging Andrew, "as long as you know that the dilemma is something we'll *both* deal with."

"I do," Andrew said. "Now, I think we should finish dessert."

Andrew first checked the woodstove, which needed another log. He placed the log on the burning embers and then joined Matthew who was sitting in a soft chair, near the fire, enjoying his coffee.

"I wish I didn't have to leave at midnight," Matthew said regretfully. "It would have been nice to stay the night with you."

Andrew nodded, mesmerized by the fire, yet keenly aware of Matthew's comment. Sipping his coffee, he appeared to become more focused. "I really would have liked that," he said, "and yet a part of me was, and perhaps still is, a little apprehensive about it."

"What do you mean?" Matthew asked.

"I guess it's part of the dilemma thing," Andrew said, "something we've mentioned before—the whole physical aspect of our relationship and what can be considered 'crossing the line.'" Andrew was not sure he wanted to continue with this particular part of the conversation, especially after Matthew's earlier reaction to his previous living arrangements. "Maybe this isn't the best time to discuss it," he said, hoping to avoid a potential altercation.

Nevertheless, Matthew viewed the topic as significant and timely. "I don't mind talking about it if you don't," Matthew said. "In fact, this might be a good time."

Andrew did not sense any antagonism from Matthew, rather a genuine concern for the status of their relationship. "Okay," he said, "but I'm not sure what to say."

Matthew rested his head against the back of the chair. "Maybe we should simply say the obvious—how we feel about each other. And I think we both feel the same." He paused, anticipating a response from Andrew; however, there was none. "Isn't it safe to say we're more than just friends?" He looked directly at Andrew, who sensed a heightened level of energy within Matthew, a response which made him uncomfortable.

"Of course, Matt," he said calmly. "The point is, how do we relate to each other, particularly physically, without crossing that line I've mentioned? I mean, we can't exactly live in 'consummated marital bliss' and still fulfill the expectations of the Rule, within the monastic enclosure." He got up to refill his coffee; Matthew also held up his mug. "Don't get me wrong. All those feelings for you are there; call them carnal, or whatever, but the saving grace for me is knowing something deeper about how I feel about you, a feeling which is difficult to easily admit. And that feeling is knowing that I love you. I can only hope you understand and feel the same way because I feel as though, having said this, I am particularly vulnerable and committed to follow my heart."

Matthew stood behind Andrew's chair, placed his arms around his chest, and nuzzled his neck. "Of course I feel that way—the exact same way. I didn't think we really needed to spell it out, but listening to you say it makes me feel like I could burst with . . . joy and, secretly, some disbelief, that I am really, I don't know . . . deserving of you. I mean that." In his exuberance, Matthew gently turned Andrew's head and placed his mouth against his, kissing him roughly yet lovingly, an embrace that was not expected.

"Time for air," Andrew insisted, as he got up from his chair. "It seems like it's getting awfully warm in here." "How about some ice water to cool you off?" he said, looking back over his shoulder at Matthew, who settled back in his chair.

"Sure," Matthew said, "but I'm not sure if I really want to cool off."

"It's good for you, Matt. It'll help flush some of that wine out of us." Andrew returned with two glasses, handed one to Matthew, and sat back down.

In the silence that followed, they could hear the wind, whipping icy snow against the cabin windows, like sand on glass. The fire reacted to every gale, brightening and crackling and creating the ever-present, but now benign, dancing images on the ceiling.

Matthew shifted in his chair so that he faced Andrew who was intently watching the whirling panoply above him. The firelight illuminated Andrew's face with a soft orange glow, highlighting his strong chin and high cheekbones, yet Andrew was not aware that he was being observed by his admirer. Matthew watched as Andrew would occasionally squint and rub his chin with the side of his index finger, take deep breaths and exhale slowly, or yawn with his mouth nearly closed.

"I love watching you," he said, startling Andrew with his comment.

"What?" Andrew replied, returning to the present and quickly facing Matthew.

"I said 'I love watching you,'" Matthew repeated.

Andrew smiled. "Why?"

"Because you're so handsome," Matthew said bluntly.

Despite the fire's glow, Matthew observed a blush spread across Andrew's cheeks and ears, which only served to reinforce Matthew's admiration for him and his growing urge to do more than simply sit next to the one he cared for. He knew any chance of having the evening result in a more physical exchange would depend entirely on his ability to initiate a more aggressive approach, since Andrew, willing yet tempered, would not cavalierly suggest or even encourage that which he might, in fact, be most desirous of. Even then, Matthew realized, the situation required an uncertain appropriateness.

"I think you do that just to see my reaction," Andrew replied with a grin. "You know that I blush easily."

"No, I said it because it's true."

"I'll accept that," Andrew said.

Matthew felt that it was time to initiate something, anything, rather than just continue sitting in front of the fire, while Andrew got lost in the dancing images on the ceiling. "So what would you like to do?" he asked, as he put his hand on the arm of Andrew's chair.

"I don't know," Andrew replied, "but I have the feeling that you are getting bored."

Matthew grimaced. "That's not the word I would have used," he said, raising his eyebrows, to indicate that he had not completed his thought.

"Well?" Andrew asked.

"Well what?"

"What is the word you would have used?"

Matthew slouched in his chair. "You might not want to know," he said, as he folded his hands on his chest.

"Yes, I would," Andrew insisted.

Matthew hesitated, hoping that what he was about to say would not destroy the evening. "Horny," he said. His one-word sentence was followed by silence. He slowly dared to look at Andrew and saw that he was smiling.

"Honesty, I like that in a man," Andrew said, as he turned to look at Matthew. "Especially in you."

"Well, that's what I feel," Matthew said, "and I am being honest. Can I ask what you feel?"

Andrew shrugged. "Same as you," he admitted with a grin.

"It's unanimous, then," Matthew said, with more emphasis than he had planned. "So what do we do next?"

Andrew's smile faded as he began to consider his circumstances and what effect Matthew's visit would have on his vocation. "That's the point, Matt," he said. "I don't know."

Matthew watched as Andrew slowly paced the length of the room, turned, and walked in the opposite direction. He knew that the conversation had opened a delicate issue, which could easily explode if he handled it poorly, yet without his input, he felt that this would be an opportunity which he might never have again, at least, not for a long time.

Suddenly, Andrew stopped, removed his Zen stool from the shelf, and placed it near the stove.

"This probably sounds crazy but would you mind if I meditate for a while?" Without waiting for an answer, Andrew sat on the stool, with his back to Matthew, and made himself comfortable.

"No," Matthew replied. "That's fine." He hoped that his disappointment did not register in his voice, as he thought to himself, 'I guess I blew that.'

Rather than continue to sit in his chair, Matthew got up, removed a cushion from the couch and placed it next to Andrew. "Do you mind if I join you," he asked.

Andrew was pleased with his decision. "No, I'd like that."

Although he was able to remain still, Matthew felt as though he was being tortured, as lurid, carnal images, which most often involved Andrew, drifted in and out of his consciousness. He turned his head slightly to see if Andrew might be aware of his dilemma; however, Andrew continued to sit quietly, with closed eyes, his hands cupped on his lap.

Breathing deeply, Matthew attempted to resume his meditation, using a phrase rather than a single word for his mantra. He silently repeated, "Lord Jesus Christ, son of God, have mercy on me, a sinner" over and over until his breathing slowed considerably, and he was able to pacify most of his internal turmoil. The firelight flickered red and black images through his eyelids while soft popping sounds of the burning wood produced just enough noise to keep him focused within his environment. Matthew sat patiently for approximately forty minutes, absorbed in his meditation, until he was suddenly conscious of being very uncomfortable from sitting on the couch cushion, which was very different from meditating on his Zen stool. He tried to reposition himself by moving one leg and then the other, yet it seemed impossible to ease the sharp muscle pains he was experiencing.

Without disturbing Andrew, Matthew got up, walked to the stove and stood barefoot, several feet in back of him, where he observed him in silence and was flooded with feelings of genuine respect, love, and physical longing. Perhaps subconsciously, Matthew began to unbutton his shirt, slowly yet deliberately, which he removed and placed on the chair. He then untied the knot on his sweatpants, let them drop to the floor, and stepped out of them. He removed his cotton long johns in the same manner and remained standing, wearing only his white shorts. With Andrew still deep in meditation, Matthew slid off his shorts and stood naked next to the fire, a feeling similar to the saturated heat of a sauna.

Very calmly, he walked up behind Andrew, knelt, and gently put his arms around him and pulled him toward him.

Andrew appeared unruffled. He slumped slightly against Matthew and rested his head on his shoulder. "I'm glad you're here with me," he said with his eyes still closed. He reached up, placed his hands over Matthew's arms and realized they were bare. "You took off your shirt," he said, assuming that Matthew might have been warm.

Matthew intensified his grip, hugged Andrew tightly and slowly moved his mouth over his neck and behind his ear. "I need to be with you, to touch you, to love you," he said, squeezing Andrew. "Don't disappoint me . . . please," he implored, "because, before we know it, Brother Mark will be here to take me back."

Andrew sensed the yearning in Matthew's voice and knew that he himself was experiencing the same needs and desires. He grabbed Matthew's head and pulled his mouth over his, knowing all along, that this is what he wanted to happen.

As Matthew pulled Andrew toward him, the Zen stool tipped and Andrew collapsed on top of Matthew, who was sprawled on his back. Only then did Andrew realize that Matthew was completely naked on the cold floor.

"I think we'd better get up before you freeze to death," Andrew said, smiling. He jumped up, extended a hand to Matthew and helped him to his feet.

"Where to, captain?" Matthew said formally.

Andrew pointed over his head. "To the loft, mate," Andrew mimicked, "and quickly."

In a flash, Matthew ascended the wooden ladder while Andrew followed, watching Matthew's bare buttocks disappear up and over the loft floor.

Only the light from the fire illuminated the area, which was considerably darker than the main room of the cabin. Andrew crouched to avoid hitting his head on the sloped ceiling, found his bed and stretched out on his back as he waited for his eyes to adjust to the light.

When he could see more clearly, he saw Matthew, standing at the foot of his bed, facing him, silhouetted by the firelight.

"You should always go naked," Andrew said softly, admiring the outline of the figure in front of him.

"Why?" Matthew teased.

"You know why . . . because you are so freaking beautiful."

Matthew knelt at the foot of the bed and slowly ran his hands over his chest and thighs. "Take off your clothes," he said unexpectedly.

Andrew did not respond immediately as he was startled by the remark.

"You know you want to," Matthew added in a somber tone.

The second remark initially angered Andrew, who felt as though an act of condescension was about to be granted to him—an act involving power and perhaps blame. He raised himself up on his elbows.

"Let's get something straight, Matt," he said angrily yet softly. "Is this some sort of one-sided thing?"

Puzzled, Matthew sat back on his calves and placed his hands on Andrew's ankles. "I'm sorry," he said. "I didn't mean it to sound that way. I just want to feel that you are as much involved in this as I am, because, here I am—totally naked, and there you are—fully clothed."

Andrew got up and stood in front of him on the mattress, centered between the two sides of the sloped ceiling. He carefully pulled off his sweater, unbuttoned his shirt and removed it. With one hand on the ceiling for balance, he tugged at one of his socks, slipped it off and then switched hands to remove the other.

"I think we're about to be naked together," he said as he unbuttoned his jeans and, once again, used the ceiling for support as he pulled first one leg out and then the other. He stood in front of Matthew wearing only his shorts. Just as he was about to remove them, he felt Matthew grab his arm.

"Wait," he whispered. He then let go of Andrew's arm.

Andrew watched as Matthew leaned forward and placed his head on the mattress in quiet supplication, a gesture similar, he thought, to a Hindu at prayer.

Starting with one foot, Matthew put his mouth on Andrew's ankle, kissing and gently biting it, running his tongue over the instep, toes, and arch, licking Andrew's skin like a puppy and then continuing up to the calf and knee in the same manner. When he reached his thigh, Matthew affectionately yet firmly forced his head between Andrew's legs, prompting Andrew to take a wider stance and balance himself more carefully against the ceiling.

Andrew's eyes remained close as he allowed himself to savor such exquisite pleasure; however, when he opened them and glanced down, he saw Matthew's face, filled with passion, his blond hair glowing in the firelight. He reached down with one hand to stroke Matthew's head, running his fingers through his hair while massaging his temples, ears, and forehead.

For a brief moment, Matthew made eye contact and then quickly turned his head toward Andrew's hand, grabbed Andrew's thumb with his lips and pulled it into his mouth. He was able to do the same with each finger as he slowly massaged the back of Andrew's thighs and calves.

Finding his fingers in Matthew's mouth was a sensation of contrasts for Andrew; he felt the hardness of his palate and teeth, the soft warmth and wetness of his tongue and cheeks—an invitation which seemed to say, "My personal space is now completely yours and available to be invaded as you wish."

Once again, Matthew bowed deeply, with his head to the floor, as he resumed the entire sequence, beginning with Andrew's other foot and continuing up to his groin where he retraced some familiar ground and, much to Andrew's enjoyment, was still able to explore areas previously untouched.

Already satisfied beyond his expectations, Matthew withdrew and knelt upright in front of Andrew, with his hands by his side, pausing to regain some energy or perhaps, some self-control, in anticipation of what would follow. Andrew stood with his hands on the ceiling, wearing only his shorts; his muscular body was softly illuminated by the glow of the firelight, enhancing Matthew's desires.

Submissively, Matthew initiated his ritualistic pattern of kissing, licking, and temperate biting over Andrew's abdomen, chest, and waist. When he reached the waistband on Andrew's shorts, Matthew grabbed it with his teeth, tugged it down, and slowly slid his shorts to the floor.

Placing his hands on Andrew's thighs, Matthew sat back slightly and observed the man before him. "Now . . . tell me who is freaking beautiful," he whispered, blatantly staring at Andrew.

The silence served to focus the moment on the present and acknowledge a mutual awareness and consent between two young men in search of, and in need of, complete affirmation and physical resolution of their otherwise solitary and lonely lives.

Fondly, Andrew looked down at Matthew, who remained kneeling in front of him like a humble English knave. He placed his hands on Matthew's head and gently tilted it upward. "The beauty that I see is still before me," he said, as he leaned forward, grabbed Matthew's shoulders and kissed him on the forehead.

"Lie back," Matthew said softly, pulling down on Andrew's hips.

Matthew dropped forward on the mattress, supporting himself with his elbows. He lightly traced his fingers over Andrew's stomach and hips, carefully avoiding any direct genital contact, as Andrew shivered slightly with his touch. He then lowered his head, found the area where Andrew's leg joined his body and, using his mouth and tongue as he had previously, he explored immodestly, yet sensitively, at will.

The intense pleasure overwhelmed Andrew whose breathing grew rapid and irregular and caused him to emit barely audible cries. In an attempt to modulate Matthew's efforts, which were bringing him closer and closer to ejaculation, Andrew placed both hands on Matthew's head to encourage him to slow down and to help sensitize him to his feelings.

"Okay, Matt, stop!" Andrew insisted. Looking down, he could see Matthew's flagrant disregard, as he appeared out of control, vehemently mouthing his penis to the point where he was inflicting considerable discomfort and raising Andrew's anxiety level.

"Matt, stop . . . please! You're hurting me."

When he received no response, Andrew did what he had to do; he grabbed Matthew's hair and yanked it forcibly, causing him to cry out and release him.

Matthew rolled on his side, knowing that he had transgressed the unwritten rule according to Andrew, or as he would say, St. Andrew. In the silence, he could feel his heart pounding in his chest as he waited for a pronouncement, which he was sure would be fatal. Instead, he felt Andrew's hand slowly caress his head.

"Come here," Andrew whispered as he sat up and pulled Matthew toward him.

Matthew crept up alongside of him while Andrew put one arm around him and hugged him tightly.

"I'm sorry," Matthew said truthfully, burying his head in Andrew's chest. "I guess I just get carried away."

Andrew rolled on his side to face him.

"It's okay," he said with a slight smile. "Except for the very last part, you made me feel . . . like I'd died and gone to heaven."

Matthew chuckled. "Well it's the last part that I thought would have felt the best."

"It did," Andrew admitted. "It's just that . . . I don't know . . ." He rolled onto his back, pulling Matthew toward him. "Some things just don't seem 'right.' I think it has something to do with crossing that line I talked about earlier."

Supporting himself with his elbow, Matthew looked down at Andrew. "Do you have any idea how often I've thought of doing to you what I just did?" Matthew said.

"No," Andrew teased. "Tell me."

"I would," Matthew said, "but you'll just get a big head." As soon as he said it he burst out laughing. He reached down and touched Andrew's still-swollen erection. "Oh, you've already got one," he said softly, rubbing his nose against Andrew's.

Andrew laughed and rolled him over on his back. "I love when you talk dirty," he said seductively.

"I haven't even begun," Matthew responded.

"No?"

"Not yet."

"Well, give it your best shot," Andrew badgered.

"I can't," Matthew quipped. "It has to be done in the heat of passion, which I'm hoping there will be more of."

"I can tell," Andrew said. He lightly ran his fingers down Matthew's chest to his penis and gently squeezed it.

Matthew's response was immediate. Like a tight string plucked on a violin, he seemed to vibrate and shutter, waiting, needing more stimulation, and hoping Andrew would recognize that need and complete it. "You can do that as long as you like," he said quietly, attempting to encourage Andrew to become more assertive.

Andrew willingly complied. "I love touching you," he whispered. "You're like a sculpture that came to life."

Matthew pulled him down on top of him, kissing him hungrily, as though devouring him would make them one. Suddenly, he broke away, rolled on his side and faced Andrew.

"Look," he said somberly. "Before I go any farther, I need to know about 'crossing that line' of yours. I don't want to make you angry . . . I want to love you."

Andrew hesitated and rubbed his eyes. "Okay, Matt, but it's not the easiest thing to talk about."

"Well, we'd better," Matthew insisted, "because, my hormones are in high gear and I don't want to do the wrong thing. And right now, I want to do everything to you."

Andrew smiled and sat up. "I don't want to sound like the pious miscreant because—believe it or not—I feel the same as you. Like I said earlier, a fully consummated relationship just doesn't seem right, at least, not here. Does that make any sense?"

"Sort of," Matthew admitted, "but I need to know specifically."

"You're going to make me say it?"

"Somebody has to," Matthew replied, as he placed his hand on Andrew's arm.

"Okay, no intercourse and no complete fellatio," Andrew said. "How's that sound?"

Matthew shrugged. "I don't have a choice, do I?"

"No, but that still gives us plenty of room, don't you think?"

"We'll see," he said shrewdly, as he grabbed Andrew by the shoulders and rolled him onto his stomach. "Remember when you said you love when I talk dirty, and to give it my best shot?"

Andrew shook his head affirmatively.

"Well, how's this?" He straddled Andrew and leaned close to his ear. "No fucking or sucking allowed. Is that right?"

Andrew sighed. "I guess that qualifies."

Matthew began to give Andrew a full body massage, starting with his head and neck and continuing down to his feet. Returning in the opposite direction, he lingered over Andrew's buttocks, massaging firmly and deeply, kneading his palms into the thick part of the muscle and gently exploring the anal area with his fingers.

Andrew grew increasingly more uncomfortable as Matthew approached such a personal area; he tensed, flexing the muscles in his buttocks to discourage him, however, Matthew persisted.

"I don't think so, Matt," Andrew said flatly, as he raised himself on his elbows and turned to look at Matthew who immediately stopped.

"Why not?" he asked.

Andrew dropped his head between his shoulders and stared at the mattress. "It's embarrassing," he said.

Matthew stretched out with his chin resting on the arch of Andrew's lower back. "I said that I want to love you, so please, don't be embarrassed. It's what I want to do . . . there is just me and you . . . relax. Besides," he persisted, "this wasn't on your list of off-limits items."

Knowing that he lost this one, Andrew lowered himself back down to the mattress and prepared to be sufficiently humiliated, hoping that whatever was about to happen would be over with quickly.

With no further dissension, Matthew delicately resumed his blatant pursuit, probing Andrew's private realm.

Andrew could not relax; he felt himself tense up as Matthew got closer and closer, and he wished that this was not happening to him.

"Relax!" Matthew insisted. "It's not the end of the world; in fact, I think you'll find it very enjoyable."

Andrew took a deep breath and buried his face in the mattress. "What the hell," he muttered. "Go for it." He struggled not to tense his muscles and hoped that he would endure. And after a short time, he realized that he was, in fact, in the hands of a proficient and caring partner, who was sensitive to his apprehensions and skilled at inducing incredibly sensual responses. He found himself not only wanting more but writhing in anticipation.

Feeling thoroughly satisfied with his oral foray, Matthew lowered himself on top of Andrew, positioned his penis along the moist crevice and licked his neck, cheek, and ear and finally, kissed his mouth.

Andrew stretched his head to willingly accept that same mouth and tongue which had just given him so much pleasure.

"Don't speak . . . just a yes or no," Matthew whispered. "Was it worth it?"

"You know the answer," Andrew said, with obvious satisfaction. He then rolled underneath Matthew so that they faced each other, grabbed his head and roughly pulled his mouth into his, as teeth gnashed against teeth, and Andrew was quite sure that he tasted blood.

Lifting Matthew slightly, Andrew proceeded to work his mouth down Matthew's neck to his chest.

"It's okay to bite harder," Matthew said, hoping that Andrew would follow through.

Andrew responded and applied more pressure yet Matthew asked for more. He bit even more brutally, fearing that he would easily pierce his skin. He continued downward, licking Matthew's chest and abdomen while Matthew managed to support himself above Andrew until he reached his erection which, Andrew found, was still wet with saliva. He could feel Matthew tremble and quietly moan with pleasure and perhaps, disbelief, as he aggressively pushed himself against him, while Matthew, erotically stimulated beyond his wildest expectations, rhythmically rubbed his own penis and forced his buttocks against Andrew's mouth.

Fearing that he would ejaculate and preferring that it be simultaneous, Matthew reluctantly lifted himself up and knelt above Andrew. He turned, faced Andrew and urged him to kneel with him and face each other.

"I can't keep it in much longer . . . what do you think?" Matthew asked, while he gently touched himself.

"Yeah, I'm about there," Andrew replied. He reached for Matthew's penis and realized that he had released enough fluid for the both of them, as he slowly slid his hand over the bulky shaft and head, under his scrotum and between the crevice of his buttocks.

Leaning forward, Matthew kissed him compassionately as he placed his own hand on Matthew's and encouraged him to explore the area more deeply.

The deeper Andrew probed, the more excited Matthew became; he rubbed his own erection vigorously, until he released his pent-up desires and ejaculated on Andrew's chest and abdomen.

Using Matthew's semen as an extra lubricant, Andrew did not take long to produce his own frenzied orgasm, most of which fell on Matthew's arm and leg.

Totally satiated, Andrew fell forward against Matthew and embraced him firmly; a fellow cosmic traveler who shared the deepest intimacy of his life in a highly unlikely and unanticipated environment, culminating, as if preordained, in their transcendent union.

"I don't know where you came from . . . I don't care, but I'm glad you're here," Andrew whispered.

Matthew responded by squeezing Andrew even harder and then kissing him tenderly on his eyes, nose, lips, ears, forehead, and neck. He gently coerced Andrew to roll onto his side, while he continued to hold him, and then ran his fingers through his hair, massaging his scalp and temples; Andrew closed his eyes and yielded to his healing touch.

In the quiet that followed, they could hear the wind assaulting the cabin and the occasional snap of the burning wood, as shadows danced on the stained wooden ceiling.

"It's been a long time—if ever—that I felt this fulfilled," Andrew said, as he observed Matthew's slightly flushed face.

Matthew leaned over and rubbed his nose against Andrew's. "I can barely describe my feelings," Matthew whispered. He kissed Andrew fervently, rekindling the fire within.

Andrew suddenly jumped up and began to descend the ladder. "Come on. I want you to bathe with me." He plugged the drain with a rubber stopper, turned on the hot water, and proceeded to shower Matthew with a handheld sprayer. He quickly soaped himself, while Andrew rinsed him off.

Matthew reciprocated and held the sprayer for Andrew who did the same. "Go ahead; sit down," Matthew said, as he wet his hair, poured some shampoo into his hands, and unexpectedly massaged the shampoo into Andrew's hair, washing it thoroughly.

Andrew closed his eyes and relished the luxurious feeling of having his friend wash his hair. "Who would've thought this?" he said out loud.

"Thought what?" Matthew asked, as he began to rinse Andrew's hair.

"This . . .," Andrew said with hesitation. "Us . . . here, in this tub, in this cabin, and . . . in the monastery."

Matthew finished with the rinse, sat down behind Andrew and wrapped his arms and legs around him. "And are you unhappy or anxious?" he asked softly.

Without hesitation this time, Andrew responded. "No! Not at all. Are you kidding?"

Matthew nibbled on his ear. "The only thing I regret is having to leave you, to let you sleep alone, and not feeling you beside me."

Andrew squeezed his arms. "Damn! I wish you could stay with me." He turned to face Matthew and pulled his mouth against his.

The discussion suddenly caused Andrew to focus on the hour. "What time is it?" he asked.

Matthew squinted at his watch. "Ten forty-five," he said. "We still have over an hour."

"I hope so," Andrew replied. "You don't think Mark will show up early do you?

Matthew chuckled. "I wouldn't be surprised if he had been standing outside the window all night."

"Don't say stuff like that," Andrew said with a shiver. "It gives me the willies."

Matthew leaned back against the high porcelain tub, pulling Andrew against him and inhaling the fresh scent of his clean hair. "I wish this moment would never end," he said softly. "It's something I've always wanted."

Andrew pushed himself even closer to Matthew. He squeezed the hand sprayer over Matthew's shoulders, showering the both of them with soothing warm water.

"This might not be a good time," Andrew said cautiously, "but I'll ask anyway."

"Oh, God, here we go," Matthew said. "I hope this doesn't depress me."

Andrew rubbed his knees. "No, relax," he said, "and don't laugh. I was just wondering—knowing how involved we are and living in a monastic community—about your prayer life . . . how important you feel it is."

Matthew looked up and sighed. "It's very important—that's why I'm here, but as you know, Andrew, so is my sexuality. I honestly don't know how they can best be reconciled." He leaned forward to look at Andrew. "Did I pass?" he asked cynically.

"Come on, Matt," Andrew replied. "I am naked with you, in a bathtub—I obviously care a great deal about you—and I'm only trying to get to know you better." He rolled on his side and snuggled against his chest.

Matthew squeezed him with both his arms and legs and brushed his nose against his forehead. "I know," he said.

It was not long before the water in the tub began to cool.

"I can feel goose bumps," Matthew said as he ran his fingers over Andrew's arm.

Andrew sat up. "Yeah, I guess we had better get dressed." He jumped out of the tub, got two towels and handed one to Matthew, who was already standing.

"What's so funny?" Matthew asked, looking at Andrew's ear to ear grin.

"Oh, nothing," Andrew said, still smiling and drying his hair.

Matthew twisted his towel lengthwise and was about to snap it at Andrew. "Tell me," he insisted.

"Okay, okay," Andrew conceded. "I was just thinking how amazing it is that someone can go from being so huge to so . . . regular."

Matthew looked at himself and dropped the towel in front of him. He then leaned forward and snatched the towel away from Andrew. "Look who's talking!" he said, glaring at Andrew's flaccid member.

"What the heck," Andrew said laughing. "Now give me my towel back."

"Say please."

"I'm freezing, Matt."

"I can tell," Matthew taunted. "It's getting even smaller."

"That does it," Andrew joked. He charged Matthew, took both towels, and ran over to the woodstove where he stood, shivering.

Matthew immediately stepped out of the tub and joined him at the woodstove where he stood, naked, with his hands inches away from the hot surface. He made no effort to retrieve his towel.

Once again, as so often in the past, Andrew could not help being moved by Matthew's unpretentious beauty and physical attributes. He stood behind him, wrapped one of the towels around Matthew's waist and, with the other, he gently dried his shoulders, back, and neck, leaving the towel draped over his shoulders when he had finished. He then removed the towel from Matthew's waist, squatted, and began to dry Matthew's feet, calves, and thighs.

Matthew turned to face him; he took the towel from him, pulled him to a standing position, and kissed him tenderly. "I love you," he said softly, hugging him firmly.

"It's what I've been hoping to hear," Andrew replied. He then quickly dried his hair. "I guess we should get dressed before Brother Mark gets here," he said.

"Oh, I don't know," Matthew mused. "It might be interesting to meet him, naked, at the door."

"Not for me," Andrew said as he scurried up the ladder into the loft.

Matthew followed. He searched for his clothes and then realized that he had left them where he took them off—downstairs.

"Damn," he said as he hurried back down the ladder. "How did my clothes get down here?"

Andrew laughed. "I wonder . . ."

When he had finished dressing, Matthew returned to the loft to sit next to Andrew who was almost completely dressed, except for his socks.

"Just in case he comes in," Andrew said, struggling with one sock. "I don't want to appear partially clothed."

Matthew stretched out on the mattress and smirked. "He probably doesn't expect you to be dressed."

Andrew paused and looked at him. "Now what does that mean?" he asked with enormous curiosity.

Matthew rolled on his side and supported his head with his arm. "Didn't you find it unusual when Brother Mark decided to pick me up at midnight? He could have said eight thirty or nine—everyone at the monastery would have been sleeping, and we would have just finished dinner."

Andrew lay down next to him and faced him. "Are you saying he anticipated and, maybe sanctioned our get-together?"

"In so many words . . . yes."

"Why?" Andrew asked, somewhat stunned.

"Who knows," Matthew said, rolling onto his back. "Maybe he wanted us to do something to feed his own sexual fantasy."

"Maybe you have an overactive imagination, Matt," Andrew teased.

"I'm sure of that," Matthew responded honestly. He sat up and wrapped his arms around his knees. "If you're interested, I'll tell you something, a fantasy, of sorts, about my meditations—something I've never told anyone and something I'd prefer not be repeated."

"Sure," Andrew said. "If it's important to you, it's important to me."

"You might not feel that way after I tell you."

"Try me," Andrew said encouragingly.

Matthew seemed to hesitate, unsure of how to begin. "Well, my meditations go along fine, until the end, when I get bombarded with all sorts of sexual imagery and desire."

Andrew felt the need to interrupt. "So what's wrong with that?" he said, attempting to offer some consolation. "It happens to me all the time."

Matthew remained hunched over his knees. "Yeah, but you probably respond to it differently," he said softly.

"Maybe," Andrew said, sensing some discomfort in Matthew's voice. He moved closer to him and gently rubbed his back. "So tell me about it," he urged.

"You sure you won't tell anyone?"

"I'm sure, Matt," Andrew insisted. "You didn't murder anyone, did you?"

Matthew laughed. "Not yet," he said, looking over his shoulder. He lay back and continued. "Anyway, toward the end of the meditation, I usually feel . . . horny, and since sex doesn't seem 'right' after all the spiritual stuff, I created a messed-up situation which seems to work. It involves my . . . strange relationship with Jesus."

He returned to a sitting position, briefly paused, as if searching for the right words and then went on.

"I imagine him to be fairly young, handsome, and well-built. We are alone together, and I begin to kiss him—barely, at first, and then, more and more passionately, while I push back my robe, and begin to jerk off on my Zen stool until I come." He lay back with a thump and covered his eyes with his arm.

"So there it is," he added quickly, as though relieved that he could finally tell someone what had apparently been bothering him for some time.

As if a red flag had been raised, Andrew could feel himself react. The words "unhealthy" and "pathos" shot through his brain, momentarily impairing his ability to respond, yet he knew that he could not express those feelings to Matthew, who continued to lie there with his face covered, like a wounded soldier.

He put his hand on Matthew's chest. "I've never seen you like this, Matt," he said, continuing to rub his chest and then reaching up to pull his arm away from his eyes. "And quite honestly, I'm not sure what to say."

Matthew turned to face him. "You don't have to say anything," he almost whispered. "I'm just glad that I told you." He pulled Andrew toward him and kissed him, squeezing him with a familiar bearlike hug.

Just as Andrew was about to resist, the threatening sound of the truck's engine, and its tires on gravel, made him bolt upright. "Shit! He's here!" Andrew shouted, as he jumped to his feet, dragging Matthew with him, and nearly hitting his head on the ceiling. "We've got to get down there."

"Take it easy," Matthew admonished. "He knows we're both here, and I doubt that he'll come in."

Andrew flew down the ladder to the front window, separated the drapes, and waved twice into the glaring headlights, which Brother Mark flashed to acknowledge his wave.

Matthew slipped on his ski boots and parka, grabbed his broken skis and was about to open the door when he suddenly stopped, hugged Andrew, once again, and kissed him hard, yet briefly. "Thanks . . . for everything, and—don't worry—things will be all right. I'll see you tomorrow, back at the ranch."

Andrew smiled as Matthew stepped out into the snowy night; however, he quickly called to him. "Matt," he said, softly enough so that Brother Mark could not hear him above the clamor of the engine. "At the end of your next meditation . . . think of me."

In the glare of the lights, Matthew smiled, gave him a thumbs-up sign with his free hand and, after stowing his skis in the back, got into the pickup.

Andrew closed the heavy door, locked it and stood silently, as he listened to the truck groan up the driveway and shift onto the main road, until its sound faded completely.

By 3:00 p.m., Andrew had everything packed, cleaned the cabin and sat reading as he waited for his ride back to the monastery. He dreaded having to face Brother Mark after the events of the night before yet 'better now than later,' he thought. 'I'd rather get it over with.' As hard as he tried, he found it nearly impossible to concentrate on what he was reading. He paced the floor, checking and rechecking things he had already checked before. Anxiety grew within him until he found it difficult to breathe. He rushed to the door, threw it open and sucked in the air like a drowning victim, brought to the surface, and snatched from a watery grave.

Partially recovered, Andrew remembered the medication Brother Nathan had given him. He found it on the table where he had left it—took one of the pills with water and put the container in his pocket. It was not long before he could feel the effects of the drug; his body felt heavy, his breathing slowed and, after yawning several times, he stretched out on the couch to relax.

When he awoke, Andrew was barely able to recognize Brother Morgan through the muddy light in the cabin. He was sitting in a chair near the fire, contentedly reading, thoroughly absorbed in his book, while he puffed on what appeared to be a corncob pipe.

"I never knew you smoked," Andrew said quietly, hoping not to startle him.

Brother Morgan removed the pipe from his mouth and slowly turned toward Andrew. He squinted and, with the pipe smoke curling up, over his face, he reminded Andrew of some armchair sleuth, ready to solve his next mystery. "I don't usually," he said with a fake British accent. "Only when there are celebratory events."

Andrew sat up and rubbed his eyes. "I'm almost afraid to ask . . . what event did you celebrate?"

"You mean, what event *am* I celebrating," Brother Morgan said with a flourish.

"Okay, what's the event?" Andrew asked brusquely, uncertain about his tolerance of Brother Morgan's humor.

Brother Morgan sprawled in the chair and spread his arms wide in the air. "This . . . this place!" he said excitedly. "It's almost perfect. Don't you agree?"

Andrew stood up and stretched. "Yes, it's perfect," he said, "but I think we should get back." He checked the woodstove, filled it with just the right amount of firewood, and waited until the wood caught before he adjusted the vents. He put on his parka and moved his gear toward the door while Brother Morgan continued to sit by the fire. "Are you coming with me?" Andrew asked.

Brother Morgan stared at Andrew. "Take the truck keys . . . tell them I quit." He threw the keys on the table.

Andrew dropped his duffel bag and walked toward Brother Morgan. "What's going on?"

"Nothing," Brother Morgan responded, absent the accent. "Just the same old crap." He stood up and put on his coat. "I just need to get away—like this. The monastery gets repressive—you know how it is."

"Yeah, I do," Andrew said. "And believe me, it's hard to leave this cabin and go back. I feel as if I've been here for months."

"I'd like to be here that long," Brother Morgan said wistfully. He grabbed Andrew's duffel bag and walked toward the door.

"By the way," Andrew asked suddenly. "How did you get in here?"

"I knocked, but there wasn't an answer, so I tried the door; it opened, I walked in and saw you sleeping on the couch. You were really out." Brother Morgan smiled. "A rough night last night?"

Andrew could feel himself tense as he wondered about the source of Brother Morgan's comment. "Not really . . . why?" he responded, more defensively than he would have wished.

"No reason," Brother Morgan said innocently. "I thought maybe you had difficulty sleeping."

Andrew closed the cabin door with a thud. He replaced the key on the second log above the top of the door, directly over an obvious knot in the wood. "Now that you mention it, I did have some difficulty sleeping. I guess that's why I fell asleep this afternoon and didn't hear you."

Brother Morgan helped load Andrew's gear in the back. He started the truck and drove up the driveway while Andrew looked back at the cabin through the truck's rear window. A gnawing depression seemed to instantly flood his body with an inexplicable sense of doom, a realization that he would never return to this place again.

"Are you okay?"

Brother Morgan's question startled Andrew. He rubbed his eyes and laid his head back against the seat.

"I'm fine," Andrew said unconvincingly.

"You look like you just saw a ghost," Brother Morgan said.

Andrew turned toward the side window, which reflected his pale image. "Maybe I have," he said softly.

Chapter Nine
The Meeting

His cell was exactly as he had left it, yet Andrew suddenly realized how small the room appeared after being in the cabin. He felt confined as he unpacked his clothing, sorting the dirty linen from the clean and returning books and pads of notebook paper to their proper places. 'This will definitely take some getting used to,' he thought. With his soiled clothing separated and stashed in a laundry bag, Andrew headed for the laundry room in the basement, happy to return to a more spacious environment.

Two heavy-duty washers and dryers sat side by side in the tiled room. Remnants of clothing, either mismatched or forgotten, occupied one corner of the large folding table, which Andrew often learned upon while reading or simply watching, mesmerized, as his clothing tumbled aimlessly in the gas heated dryer.

A commercial extractor intrigued Andrew, who earlier realized that washed lettuce, tied inside a clean pillowcase and placed inside, would easily result in crisp nearly perfectly dried salad greens.

Satisfied that the washer was working properly, Andrew was about to return to his cell when he saw Brother Mark walking directly toward him with an overflowing laundry bag. Brother Mark entered the room with a smile. He dropped his laundry and offered his hand to Andrew. "Welcome back," he said graciously, as he reached out to hug Andrew who was baffled by the encounter. "It looks like we both had the same idea."

"I guess so," Andrew said. "After a week away, things start to build up." He could feel the heat intensify in his face.

Brother Mark picked up his bag and began to sort whites from colored clothing, throwing the latter in the other washer and the whites onto the floor.

Andrew balked at the silence, unsure of what to say and equally unsure if this was the appropriate time. He watched Brother Mark openly sort his dirty underwear, until the task was completed and the washer started.

"Look . . .," Andrew said as Brother Mark turned to face him. "I don't know what to say to you about last night but . . . I respect you tremendously, and no matter what, I hope we can remain friends."

Brother Mark lifted himself up backwards and sat on the folding table. "For my part, I never doubted your friendship nor do I anticipate doing so in the future. I'm hopeful that you can get over this . . . glitch in your vocation and continue on with it," he said, looking directly at Andrew. "Besides," he added with a smile, "we need you here."

Andrew could feel his apprehension begin to dissolve as he exhaled deeply. "I really appreciate that," he said, grinning and rubbing his eyes. He continued in a more somber mood. "I'm anxious about meeting with Father Luke, though. I don't feel comfortable lying to him."

Brother Mark's eyes seemed to narrow. "I understand," he said, "but unfortunately, there are three of us involved in this masquerade, and it's important to stick to the same story or we'll all hang separately. I have to say, I don't ever want to be in this position again."

"Me either," Andrew agreed. He looked over his shoulder to see if anyone was approaching the laundry room.

"Have you talked with Matthew?" Andrew asked cautiously.

"Not much," Brother Mark responded. "Why?"

"I don't know. I guess I was wondering what his mood was."

"He's pretty resilient," Brother Mark said without hesitation. "He'll survive this. It's you I'm worried about."

Andrew glanced down. "I'll be okay."

"Good," Brother Mark said as he jumped down from the table, "because I am supposed to tell you that Father Luke will see both you and Matthew after supper—at six."

"Oh, shit!" Andrew said carelessly.

Brother Mark grabbed him by the shoulders. "Don't worry about it. He won't bite you. Just tell him the same story and you'll be fine . . . okay?"

"Yeah," Andrew said quietly.

"I've got some work to do. Good luck." Brother Mark disappeared out the door and down the long corridor.

Andrew left his clothes in the washer to return to his cell, sensing a renewed anxiety over the imminent meeting with Father Luke. He had eaten very little all day, and yet he did not feel hungry; he could not think of food—only the meeting and the need to compromise his honesty. He wished that he could talk with Brother Matthew to help alleviate the tension; however, he knew that such an attempt, if observed, would undoubtedly fuel the alleged fires of the Fathers. He slowly paced the length of his cell, pulling on his fingers in an attempt to crack his knuckles, as he reviewed what he would say when asked about Brother Matthew. The more he thought, the more confused he became—he decided to clear his head by going for a walk.

The midwinter night was all too familiar to Andrew, cold, with brilliant stars and almost total silence. He walked on the road's hard-packed snow, listening to his boots squeak, while he inhaled the bitter air like a tonic, to cure his ailing soul. He chose to think about nothing, if possible—to walk in an empty state, much as Buddhists do in Zazen, only not nearly as slowly. It was not long before he had reached the old outer buildings near the main guesthouse, which was warmly lit and welcoming.

Andrew paused to observe the house from a distance. He could see someone occasionally pass by the kitchen windows and assumed that the facility was being used for a retreat.

Suddenly, out of the darkness, he saw a figure turn the corner of the road and proceed directly toward him.

"Andrew?"

"Yeah . . . is that you, Matt?" The question was out of his mouth before he could reconsider using Brother Matthew's name.

"Of course," he replied. "I can't believe we're both out here."

Andrew felt excited yet uncomfortable over their chance encounter. "Do you know about the meeting with Father Luke at six?"

"Yes. Brother Mark told me about it this afternoon. Are you okay with it?"

Andrew kicked at the snow with his boot. "I guess. I just want to get it over with."

Matthew moved closer to Andrew in an attempt to hug him.

Andrew quickly took a step backwards. "What if someone sees us?" he said quietly.

Matthew scoffed at the comment. "Out here? *I* can barely see you!" He grabbed Andrew by the arm and pulled him inside a covered three-sided wooden structure used for feeding the horses. "Feel better?" he asked, and without waiting for a response, he pulled Andrew toward him, hugging him and nuzzling his ear. "I miss this," he said softly, gently biting Andrew's earlobe.

The physical contact was reassuring to Andrew, who reciprocated by squeezing Matthew firmly.

"How can it be that you are getting even better?" Matthew said with a smile, as he ran his hands over Andrew's thighs.

"I don't know; I always thought you brought out the worst in me," Andrew quipped.

"The 'worst' or the 'wurst'?" Matthew said, acknowledging Andrew's tumescence.

"What can I say . . . ? I can't help it."

In the distance, a door could be heard opening in the guesthouse, followed by bits of laughter and the sound of the door closing.

"It's two friends I've known for a long time from California," Matthew offered. "They're doing a three-day retreat."

The cold wind caused Andrew to pull his collar even tighter around his neck. "It must be quite a change in the weather for them, being out here," Andrew commented.

"It's definitely not the beach, but they both ski, so . . . I think they'll have a good time."

Andrew looked down the road to see if anyone, by chance, might be approaching them. "I guess we had better get back and face Father Luke."

"On one condition," Matthew proposed as he, again, reached out and pulled Andrew into his embrace.

Walking in the darkness, Andrew and Matthew reviewed their versions of the story, making minor corrections and attempting to keep it simple. It was not long before the conversation drifted toward their evening together and the intensity of what each of them experienced, as they navigated through the indigo light to the dimly lit entrance of the monastery.

* * *

Father Luke's second-floor office consisted of two rooms connected by a large oak door, which separated the smaller space, where his desk, bookcase, and chair defined a distinctly private study. The larger outer office contained a vintage Duncan Phyfe couch and two matching armchairs, a more informal, common area. Unlike most rooms in the monastery, Father Luke's office was paneled with black walnut and carpeted with a thick moss green rug. Heavy metal sconces and floor lamps softly illuminated the area with a warm, soothing glow.

Andrew and Matthew arrived promptly at six—both somewhat anxious yet eager to resolve the issue. Matthew knocked firmly on the door and waited. Soon afterwards, the door swung open.

"Come in," Father Luke said with a smile.

As Andrew walked past Father Luke and into the room, his blood immediately chilled. Scattered here and there, on the couch and on folding chairs, sat six senior members of the community, most of whom Andrew knew by name only.

"Please have a seat," Father Luke said as he motioned toward the two empty chairs directly opposite the couch.

Andrew was thankful to sit, as he began to feel lightheaded and short of breath; however, he never made it to the chair. He felt as if life suddenly stuttered and then stopped, while a familiar blackness erased, first, his vision, and then his very being, like a faulty projector slowing the film and then stopping it completely, causing it to melt and smoke in the intense light.

When he came to, Andrew found himself lying on the carpet in Father Luke's office, with his feet elevated and an ice pack under his neck.

Father Gerald wafted a broken ammonia pellet under Andrew's nose, which caused him to quickly turn away to avoid the noxious odor. "How are you feeling?" he asked as he knelt over him.

Andrew squinted in an attempt to refocus and looked skeptically at his surroundings. He saw Father Luke sitting on the couch to his left; otherwise, the room was empty. "Embarrassed," he said with difficulty through a parched mouth. "Where is everyone?"

"They've left," Father Gerald said, attempting to reassure him, "and everything is fine—so, just stay where you are and try to relax until you feel better."

Andrew leaned his head back against the cold pack and closed his eyes. He wished that he could make himself disappear from such an awkward scene, not have to answer questions—just evaporate—and pretend it never happened.

"Have you fainted before?" Father Gerald asked quietly.

Andrew rubbed his eyes. "Maybe once or twice. I'm not real sure."

"Do you think you could sit up?"

Andrew nodded.

Father Gerald reached under Andrew's arms and helped him to a sitting position. "Are you all right?"

With his back against the chair, Andrew felt stable yet still somewhat dizzy. "I'm sure I'll be fine." He glanced at Father Luke, who remained curiously silent, as he sat on the couch, observing the two of them. A certain uneasiness momentarily seized Andrew's stomach and then gradually abated. He felt as though Father Luke had been instructed by Father Gerald to remain silent or, at least, not to say anything that might exacerbate his condition.

Perhaps sensing this, Father Luke leaned forward and attempted some stilted humor. "You know, I fainted once, as a teenager—at the dining room table—and, for the longest time, my father blamed it on my mother's cooking. I never wanted it to happen again."

Andrew smiled and then looked down at the floor. The silence that followed appeared to magnify Father Luke's failed attempt to be included, and more importantly, exonerated for arranging such a disastrous method of questioning the two novices within the parameters of the monastic rule.

Father Gerald fidgeted with his glasses. "Well, why don't I walk with you back to your room," he said, as he stood up and offered his hand to Andrew, who was pleased to know that he would be leaving. Before he knew it, he was gently whisked out the door as Father Gerald managed to comment briefly to Father Luke.

"We can discuss another get-together when I see you," he half whispered. "Good night, Father Luke."

The cloisters were sparsely illuminated by small nightlights that created eerie elongated shadows as Father Gerald and Andrew walked toward Andrew's cell. The smell of incense drifted through the open doors of the chapel reminding Andrew that he had missed his evening meditation, a time which he coveted for meaningful spiritual practice and personal relaxation.

When they reached Andrew's door, Father Gerald looked mildly perplexed. "Would you mind if I came in for a moment?"

"No, not at all," Andrew replied. He opened the door, switched on the light and offered his desk chair to Father Gerald.

"Thanks," Father Gerald said, "but I'll just sit on a corner of the bed. Take the chair."

Andrew turned his chair toward him and sat down.

"I'm sorry that this happened," Father Gerald began. "I wish I had known about your meeting with Father Luke. I would have suggested a different format."

Andrew was surprised by his comment. "That's okay; I guess I was overwhelmed by seeing so many senior monks there."

"I can understand why," Father Gerald admitted. "When I speak with Father Luke, I'm going to strongly recommend that he meet with just you and Brother Matthew—not with the entire senior board."

"Thanks . . . I'd feel better about that." Andrew wondered if Father Gerald was informed as to the exact nature of the meeting. He moved a book from one side of the desk to the other.

"Are you aware why Father Luke wants to meet with Matthew and me?"

"Somewhat, but quite honestly, I have difficulty assigning it too much importance—just between you and me—yet if you ever feel the need to talk about it, I would be happy to."

Andrew felt a tremendous sense of relief. "Thanks," he said truthfully; however, he immediately decided to add a disclaimer, "but there really isn't a lot to talk about."

Father Gerald remained silent; instead, he casually looked around the room until his eyes, once again, were on Andrew. "I asked to talk with you because I'm concerned about your overall health," he said bluntly. "I think you've been through a lot and I'm concerned about how you are dealing with stress."

Andrew shifted in his chair, confused over Father Gerald's knowledge about his alleged stress. "Other than the tragedy at the eggery, there hasn't been all that much that has been bothering me."

"Are you absolutely sure?"

"I guess," Andrew said guardedly.

Father Gerald paused. "Well . . . I know it isn't the first or second time you fainted, and it looks as though you have been fairly ascetic in your eating habits."

"You mean—I look thinner?"

"Noticeably."

Andrew laughed. "I guess that's what retreats do to you when you have to cook for yourself." He was hoping Father Gerald would find some humor in this; however, his attentive expression did not change. "Can I ask about the fainting?" Andrew asked. "How did you know?"

"He asked me not to tell." This time, Father Gerald smiled, assuming that Andrew knew the source.

"That's strange," Andrew said. "Why would he tell you about my fainting?"

"I don't know . . . maybe he genuinely cares about you."

The response took Andrew by surprise; he could feel his face begin to burn and his palms grow sweaty.

"Do you still have the medication Brother Nathan gave you?"

"Yes . . . thanks," Andrew said with some relief, now that the subject had been changed.

"Have you felt the need to use it, or have you been sleeping all right?"

"I used it a couple of times—I guess I had some nightmares." His admission left him feeling vulnerable.

"That's pretty much expected," Father Gerald said. "Don't hesitate to use it when you experience similar difficulties, okay?"

Andrew nodded affirmatively.

Father Gerald stood up and offered his hand to Andrew who reciprocated with a firm handshake. "Well, I'll let you relax and enjoy the rest of the evening." He turned and walked toward the door.

"Thanks for talking with me," Andrew said warmly, and then he added a more personal comment. "I feel like . . . someone understands me."

Father Gerald smiled, squeezed Andrew's shoulder, and returned to the infirmary.

Alone in his room, Andrew began to wonder why Brother Matthew might have spoken with Father Gerald and what else he may have told him. 'I'll have to talk with him,' he thought.

Once again, Andrew was acutely aware of the confines of his cell, compared to the spaciousness of the log cabin which, in actual footage, was still quite modest. He already missed the freedom to prepare coffee or a snack when he felt like it or to sleep as late as he wished after staying up most of the night, reading or writing.

He opened one of the many books which he left unfinished, *They Speak by Silence*, meditative thoughts by an anonymous Carthusian, and read the following:

> *There is no other remedy for our passing ills than God's eternal love for us. At bottom, all our sufferings derive from the fact that we want joy and possessions that are altogether too narrow and too fleeting for the greatness of our hearts.*

Andrew closed the book and sat staring at its dusty brown cover, feeling somewhat troubled by thoughts he knew to be true yet, in practice, arduous to live by. He removed his Zen stool from the closet and initiated a lengthy meditation, filled with good intentions, yet often bombarded by new erotic imagery which, after a significant struggle, he was barely able to dismiss.

* * *

When Andrew awoke at 2:00 a.m., he could hear the wind howling through the garth with a ferocious groan, blasting icy snow against his window and creating a huge drift alongside the arched cloister. He quickly pulled on his clothes and made his way down to the main lavatory through the chilly dark hallways.

The large arched windows, receiving the brunt of the storm, were almost totally covered with diaphanous etchings, like frosted lace, in an irregular yet artistic pattern. He stopped to touch the delicate tracery but decided against it and quickly withdrew his finger. 'Too perfect to spoil,' he thought.

In the lavatory, he found his towel hanging on a large hook with his name, Brother Andrew, stamped above it in blue plastic. He threw the towel around his neck, relieved himself at the urinal and then washed his face and hands and dried them. He located his personal wooden drawer, which resembled one of many post office boxes minus the glass fronts, removed his toothbrush and toothpaste and returned to the sink to brush his teeth. On his way out, Andrew had to abruptly change course to avoid walking into Brother Matthew, who appeared to be still sleeping; his hair was disheveled, and he yawned repetitively as he walked.

"Sorry," Matthew said too loudly at the end of the yawn with his eyes half open. He did not immediately recognize Andrew who could not help smiling at what he felt was lethargy personified.

"Wake up," Andrew whispered, "or you'll kill someone."

Startled, Matthew responded with a full smile and then looked around to see if anyone were in the area. "Like I said, we've got to stop meeting like this."

Andrew flashed his "yeah, right" grin and hurried to his cell where he put on his habit, picked up his Zen stool and trudged toward the entrance room for vigils.

Once Father Jude intoned the initial psalm, "Oh God, come to my assistance," the community responded: "Oh Lord, make haste to help me," and the service began. Andrew listened to various readings, unsure as to whether he really comprehended their meaning due to his focus on the gale winds and blowing snow outside the windows. He was thankful for the comfortable heat from the woodstove which flared occasionally from the downdrafts. Without it, he knew the room would be unbearable.

At the end of the service, Andrew placed his Zen stool on a thick black mat, in preparation for his meditation. Most of the brothers had already left the room to either read in their cells or prepare breakfast. Andrew knew that two monks were present with him and, although he could not be positive, he felt sure that one of them was Matthew; however, he chose not to explore the matter. He simply faced the front of the room, settled on his Zen stool, and began his meditation by using his familiar mantra—"omnes."

The wind-driven snow against the windows, the flickering light of the candles, the aromatic incense—all combined to help ease Andrew into a deep meditative state. He soon lost awareness of his immediate surroundings and, instead, thought he was back at the cabin, alone, sitting in front of the woodstove, as flames danced brilliantly through his closed eyelids. Eventually, his thoughts seemed to evaporate, just as his physical body seemed to dissolve in the flickering light. He no longer existed as Andrew but as an amorphous bundle of energy, consumed by the fire, and willingly transformed into one of its dancing flames. He remained in this state for almost an hour until, suddenly, he was overcome by an intense sense of doom as total darkness extinguished the pervasive radiance, causing him to return to the present and open his eyes.

The corpulent frame of Father Cyril came between the candles and Andrew, blocking the light, momentarily, as Brother Cyril initiated his meditation.

This unsettling feeling left Andrew emotionally and physically chilled. He carefully withdrew his Zen stool, stood up, stretched and waited for his legs to adjust to the different position. 'Time for a hot shower,' he thought as he made his way back to his cell.

At four thirty in the morning, Andrew found that few other monks showered at that time; most, it seemed, showered after breakfast, just before the morning mass, which followed Lauds—that is, for those who *chose* to shower. Some of the older members of the community, he realized, had difficulty accepting the twentieth century and integrating it with St. Benedict's rule.

Once he had adjusted the water temperature and began to soap, he was somewhat surprised to hear the shower next to him being used. His curiosity faded as he lathered a copious handful of shampoo into his hair, massaged his scalp and stood, gratefully, under the steamy water, as it rinsed away the soap and the tensions of the previous night.

With his eyes shut tight under the running water, Andrew thought he heard the sound of the metal hooks that support the shower curtains, slide on the aluminum rod, as if it had been opened and quickly closed. He then sensed a blast of cold air, and goose bumps began to cover his body.

'No, it can't be,' he thought, as fear and adrenaline began to overwhelm him. He frantically tried to wipe the soap from his eyes, and as he stepped backwards, he bumped into a body behind him. He tried to yell, however, he was quickly grabbed around the chest and a hand firmly covered his mouth.

"Shut up! It's me!" Matthew hissed into his ear.

In total disbelief, Andrew turned, wide-eyed, to look at his abductor and confirm the words he had just heard. Once he stopped struggling, he felt Matthew release him, slowly, as though he was unsure of how he might respond. Ashen, Andrew turned, robot-like, and faced him.

"You . . . are . . . fucking nuts," he said coldly, revealing a dark side of himself, which Matthew had never seen before. He then slid down the shower wall into a crouched position with his head buried in his hands.

Matthew adjusted the shower nozzle so that the water fell mostly on Andrew's back. He squatted in front of him. "I'm sorry," he said softly. "I didn't mean to scare you like this . . . I thought you would see me come in."

Andrew looked up, dazed. "Why?"

"Why what?"

"Why are you doing this to me?" Andrew's exasperation quietly erupted.

Matthew shrugged his shoulders and smiled. "I missed you."

Andrew grimaced and shook his head. "This is the *monastery*, Matt. We're meeting with Father Luke precisely for this reason, and I don't know about you, but I don't want to be thrown out." He squeezed his forehead with one hand and pushed back his hair. "Besides, I don't know if you've noticed, but emotionally, I'm not doing too well with this."

Matthew knelt on the shower floor and pulled Andrew into his embrace. "I don't know what's wrong with me, but please, try to forgive me . . . I'm really sorry."

He then lifted Andrew to his feet and continued to hug him.

Andrew held him firmly, as tears flooded his eyes and mixed with the warm water that washed over Matthew's back. "You need to get out of here," he whispered into Matthew's ear.

"Not without this," Matthew said, as he faced Andrew and kissed him gently, and then more deeply. He pulled his head back and, again, looked at Andrew directly. "Can you forgive me?" he asked sincerely.

Andrew nodded and smiled faintly. "Just barely. Now . . . get out of here."

He watched as Matthew pushed back the inner curtain and picked up his towel which he wrapped around himself. He then carefully peered through the outer curtain to make sure that no one was in the bathroom and hurried into his own shower.

* * *

Later that day, Andrew learned from Father Gerald that the meeting with Father Luke would take place at 6:00 p.m. Father Gerald graciously offered to attend the meeting; however, Andrew, at first, did not feel it was necessary, and Father Gerald accepted his decision. Yet as he watched Father Gerald disappear down the cloister, he had a sudden change of heart and quickly ran after him.

"I've changed my mind," Andrew said shyly. "I would like you to be at the meeting . . . if you still want to."

Father Gerald smiled. "Yes, I would like to be there."

"Thanks," Andrew said.

As Andrew turned to leave, Father Gerald grabbed his arm.

"Just a thought; you might want to take one of the pills we talked about, one hour before the meeting. It's up to you."

Andrew smiled and simply nodded his head.

Just before six, Andrew knocked on Father Luke's door, which was promptly answered, not by Father Luke but by Father Gerald, a pleasant surprise which, along with the medication, made Andrew feel much more comfortable.

"Come in," Father Gerald said with a smile. He quickly leaned close to Andrew. "Did you take your pill?" he asked quietly.

Andrew chuckled. "Yes, thanks . . . and I can feel it working."

"Good. Have a seat."

Andrew successfully made his way to the same armchair he failed to reach during the previous meeting. As he looked around the room, he could see Father Luke in his office, sitting at his desk, writing, in what appeared to be, a checkbook. Other than for the three of them, no one else was present. Brother Matthew had not yet arrived. On the coffee table to his right stood a stainless carafe of coffee, cups, and a variety of delicious-looking pastries he assumed to be homemade.

"Help yourself to the coffee and dessert," Father Luke said without looking up. "I'll be out in a minute."

With his anxiety chemically checked, Andrew's appetite gnawed inside of him as he poured himself some coffee and selected a chocolate brownie.

"Coffee?" he asked, looking at Father Gerald.

"Sure, but I think I'll pass on the pastries." Father Gerald squeezed his waistline with both hands.

Andrew had just finished pouring the coffee when he heard the knock on the door. He could feel his heart begin to beat a little faster, not knowing what to expect from Brother Matthew or, from the meeting in general.

Once again, Father Gerald opened the door, and Brother Matthew entered the room with his usual aura, at least to Andrew, of strength, beauty, and self-confidence.

Andrew looked up and smiled, trying to be somewhat reserved and casual. "Hi," he said, as he raised the brownie to his mouth and bit off a healthy portion.

Unlike the previous meeting, Brother Matthew appeared relieved by the casual ambience of what he was seeing and feeling. He acknowledged everyone with a smile and a greeting. "Hello . . . Father Gerald . . . Father Luke."

"How about some coffee and dessert?" Father Gerald asked.

Matthew reached for the coffeepot. "Thanks." He put his cup down and removed a Danish pastry from the tray.

The three of them sat, eating in silence, while Father Luke finished his paperwork in the adjoining office.

It was Matthew's unexpected comment that shattered the silence and made Andrew wish he could crawl beneath the carpet.

"Is this the Last Supper?" Matthew said softly, with a half smile.

Andrew could feel himself tense as he stared into his cup.

"I don't think so," Father Gerald said calmly. He too wondered if Father Luke had heard the comment.

If he had, Father Luke's demeanor evidenced no trace of animosity or indignation as he walked, smiling into the room, with his usual air of formality. "I'm pleased to see that you're having some pastry," he said. "I don't want to be tempted to eat it later this evening." He poured himself some coffee and settled back into his chair.

"First of all, I want to apologize to both of you for last evening. I was wrong to have convened the board of elders for the meeting, and I'm truly sorry." He leaned forward and placed his coffee on the table in front of him.

As if planned, Andrew and Matthew remained silent, waiting for the real substance of the meeting.

"I think you both know why we want to speak with you. There is some concern about a growing familiarity between you, and I think it would be helpful to clarify the role of the monk here at St. Anthony's." As Father Luke spoke, he appeared more and more uncomfortable. The color rose in his cheeks and, occasionally, he would stutter. "We encourage friendships among the brothers so long as that friendship remains healthy and respectful of each other's dignity."

"Is there some reason to think otherwise?" Matthew asked assertively.

Father Luke sensed the confrontation. "I can appreciate your question. Some of the older monks have told me that they have seen you together, even during the Grand Silence, a time reserved for prayer, and lectio, and meditation. And I believe, Brother Matthew, that Brother Cyril, your immediate neighbor in the dormitory, said that he heard the two of you laughing in your cell, followed by loud thumping and bumping sounds one afternoon."

"He's right," Matthew admitted. "I was joking with Andrew and we ended up having a pillow fight. I'm sorry we disturbed him. But I would like to say that Andrew and I *are* good friends, and our friendship has never been more than just that. Innuendos implying otherwise are simply false, and might be the product of others being too intrusive."

Andrew felt as if his heart had stopped, momentarily, after hearing Matthew's response.

Father Luke appeared stunned and remained silent.

It was Father Gerald who spoke up. "I guess the point here is that, as a community, we need to learn to live together and, as Father Luke said, to respect each other. We are all very different and have different needs. Confrontation is not the intent of the discussion—it's learning how we can be more accepting, more loving, and still conform to the guidelines of the Rules of St. Benedict, which stress obedience, not for the sake of power by one segment of the community over the other, such as the professed over the novices, but for the ability to willingly accept orders from others so that we are able to readily obey the word of God when he calls us." He took a sip of his coffee, hoping that he had helped defuse a potentially disastrous situation.

"How do you feel about this, Andrew?" Father Luke asked.

Andrew rubbed his eyes and felt the warmth in his cheeks. "I'm sorry this happened. I'll apologize to Brother Cyril." He looked at Matthew and then back at Father Luke. "Matthew and I do care a great deal about each other but . . .," after swallowing hard, he continued, "not in a manner incompatible with the Rule, or expectations of the life, in general."

Father Luke clasped his hands in back of his head and stretched. "I want you both to know that this is something I don't feel comfortable with. I'm not here to punish you; I want to help you live your lives as good—not flawless—monks, in a way that may be different from our early forefathers yet still in keeping with the spirit of our vocations. Besides, it's easier to live in a house with brothers who are happy. I know that it is tremendously difficult, especially for the younger monks, to face temptations regarding chastity and the loneliness of being away from family and friends; however, we are available to help you, to talk with you whenever you feel a need to do so. I would also add that keeping your prayer life strong is essential to the vocation; otherwise, what are we here for?"

In the silence that followed, Matthew appeared less angry and more conciliatory as he sat, leaning forward, with his elbows on his knees.

Andrew held his coffee cup with both hands and stared at the carpet.

"If there are questions," Father Gerald said, "I'll do my best to answer them." After a brief pause, he continued. "Maybe we'll just leave it at that." He stood up and extended his hand to Andrew and then to Matthew.

"Thanks," Andrew said.

They watched Father Luke stand and both walked toward him and shook his hand. "God bless you both," he said.

As they were halfway through the door, Father Luke called out to them. "How about some pastry to take with you?"

"No, but thanks anyway," Andrew said.

Matthew did not hesitate. He quickly snatched another Danish. "Thanks," he said with a smile. "They're delicious."

Together, they walked in self-imposed silence through the cloister, as Matthew finished eating his dessert and rubbed his hands on his jeans. The walk seemed endless to Andrew who was flooded with conflicting emotions, the need to talk, to process, and a yearning to be completely alone. Occasionally, he could feel Matthew's elbow brush against his and stir familiar feelings, which confused him even more. As they turned the corner into the dormitory, Matthew furtively looked around and then at Andrew.

"I'm glad that's over," he whispered.

Andrew agreed, but simply shook his head.

When they arrived at Andrew's door, Matthew paused, as Andrew opened it halfway. He looked at Andrew with an intensity Andrew had never experienced before, and then smiled. "I won't live apart from you," he said, as he quickly turned and continued toward his cell.

* * *

In the weeks that followed, Andrew purposely tried to avoid being alone, in almost any situation, with Matthew. After vigils, while meditating, after the other monks had left the room, Andrew sensed Matthew's presence from behind. Without looking, he quietly stood and walked toward the exit, but before doing so, he quickly glanced up to see Matthew staring back at him. And one evening after Compline, Andrew had achieved a deep meditative state when suddenly, he felt someone brush against his ear and say "I love you." By the time Andrew could refocus, the person had left the room. It was, however, another incident in the bathroom, which proved most unsettling for him. He had finished with his shower, got dressed and was standing at the sink and began to shave.

Unexpectedly, Matthew entered, with his towel in hand, ready to take a shower. He purposely chose the shower directly opposite Andrew's back and in clear view from the large mirror over Andrew's sink.

Matthew pushed open the outer curtain, entered the dressing area of the shower and only partially closed the curtain. He undressed leisurely, in full sight of Andrew's mirror, knowing that he was being observed.

Andrew forced himself to concentrate on his shaving but found it impossible not to extend his vision past his own face, toward Matthew's shower.

Matthew then pushed open the inner curtain and waited, naked, with his back to Andrew, as he adjusted the water temperature.

Knowing that Matthew could not see him, Andrew stared longingly at the familiar figure, recognizing the curves and angles he knew so well and, quite frankly, missed.

Matthew stepped under the steamy water and, once again, pulled the inner curtain only two-thirds closed. He began to soap himself as he faced Andrew, washing under his arms, over his chest and stomach and down to his growing erection.

Just at that point, Brother Morgan entered the room and, sleepily, walked past Andrew to the end sink where he began to brush his teeth.

Andrew glanced at the mirror and noticed that Matthew had closed the inner curtain completely. Just before he left the bathroom, while Matthew was still showering, Andrew discreetly reached up and closed the outer curtain on Matthew's shower.

Chapter Ten

Seeds of Discontent

Spring came slowly, yet joyfully, to the high country around the monastery, as melting snow from the elevated peaks swelled the surrounding rivers and creeks with raging powerful torrents, capable of moving large boulders along its beds with deep rumbling growls. Unsuspecting animals that wandered too far into the water would often get swept downstream and could be found, lodged between rocks, or floating, bloated, in a tranquil eddy.

The arrival of the warmer weather also signaled an influx of retreatants who enjoyed the serenity of the monastery and the benefits of an alpine environment. And with fresh air and exercise came enormous appetites that had to be satisfied for both the retreatants and the monks.

Brother Adrian, unfortunately, was experiencing pain associated with extensive dental work and often, was not up to his usual self. He called on Andrew regularly to assist with the main meal preparation, usually with his guidance, but more so, lately, by himself. Andrew enjoyed cooking, even though he still felt a few butterflies just before he was about to serve, yet with time, even that seemed to dissolve, especially if he had his customary glass of wine or two while preparing the food.

As vegetarians, Andrew learned a great deal from Brother Adrian but also from his worn copy of the *Moosewood Cookbook*, which taught him how to prepare everything from miso soup and eggplant Mykonos to tofu burritos and peach parfait with amaretto cream. Father Jude still insisted that seafood would not be allowed on the menu primarily, Andrew learned from Brother Adrian, because Father Jude disliked fish. Although this limited the choices, most would agree that the food was rarely routine and hardly simple. In fact, Andrew began to realize that the expenses involved with this type of cooking were substantial—food, quite often, that Andrew was not familiar with but learned to use and appreciate.

But it was the abbot's insistence that, whenever possible, all food products be of the "natural" variety—without additives, preservatives, or unnatural flavorings. As he spent more and more time in the kitchen, Andrew saw several trucks deliver large shipments of pure maple syrup in five-gallon cans; ten-pound sacks of walnuts, almonds and pecans; gallons of natural clover honey; cases of almond butter, jams, and jellies made with honey (since it was forbidden to cook or bake with white sugar); a variety of spices (most of which Andrew never heard of); gallons of heavy cream; and cases of all-natural granola. It wasn't unusual for Andrew to initial the receipts of these deliveries without being completely astounded by the total cost of the bill; one in particular—several gallons of pure maple syrup—amounted to approximately one thousand dollars.

He was often reminded of his earlier existence, prior to entering the monastery, when grocery shopping meant frugal purchases on a limited budget with occasional splurges of impulse buying. Yet the weekly shopping trips by the monastery to the large supermarkets and Planet Earth, the health food store in the working-class city of Elkridge, filled the van with fresh vegetables, a variety of fruit, cheeses, sprouts, beans, porcini and shiitake mushrooms, peanut oil, tahini, and other products too numerous for Andrew to recall; and most of which he never knew existed.

As he became more skillful in the culinary arts, Andrew was encouraged to plan meals several days in advance, check the necessary resources he needed, and to write his own order for those who would do the shopping to Elkridge. He learned to proportionally plan and prepare a meal for sixteen or twenty-six guests, with substantial servings and few leftovers.

In the middle of a fairly complex preparation, Andrew was beckoned by Brother Adrian into the narrow pantry.

"I just want to tell you that I don't know what I'd do without you," Brother Adrian said quietly, looking at Andrew over the top of his metal-framed glasses, which were smudged with fingerprints.

Andrew smiled. "Thanks, but it's you who deserve the credit. I had no idea of what I was doing when I first stepped foot into this kitchen."

"Well, you've certainly come a long way under my . . . if I may say . . . persistent guidance." Brother Adrian smiled a wider smile, flaunting his new partial bridgework which made a significant improvement in his appearance. "I don't think it's too early for a chocolate—what do you think?"

Andrew did not feel like eating sweets at ten thirty in the morning, yet he knew that he could not refuse Brother Adrian who, new dental work notwithstanding, did not readily share his chocolate, particularly when it was Godiva. "It's never too early for chocolate," Andrew agreed.

Brother Adrian made his familiar climb up the wooden ladder, reached behind a large can of tomato sauce, and returned with his golden box of sweets which he offered to Andrew. "I love Godiva's," he said, as he indiscriminately grabbed two of them, pulled off their brown wrappers, and popped them into his mouth.

"I haven't had Godiva too often," Andrew admitted, "but they are tasty."

"The best," Brother Adrian said convincingly. He then selected two more, one with a foil wrap, and, again, put both of them into his mouth. He moved the box closer to Andrew. "Have another. Lunch is still a long way off."

"Thanks, but one's fine. Besides, I'd better get back to my cooking or at lunch may be farther off than you think."

"Well, you're doing a good job, Andrew. Let me know if you need any help."

"Thanks, it's not all that easy, but I think I'll be fine."

Brother Adrian smiled. "Thank God you got a job, Brother."

Andrew laughed at Adrian's repetitious pragmatism and returned to the kitchen to measure ingredients for four cheese soufflés—a meal which Andrew agonized over—hoping that when he placed them on the warming trays in the refectory, they would maintain their puffy inflation, at least until the first person (usually Father Jude) sliced into them.

A glass of wine, Chablis or Burgundy, poured from gallon jugs, was customary for the noonday meal. Andrew filled his four-ounce glass with Chablis, found an empty seat close to the door, and sat down to enjoy his meal. He recognized Brother Matthew's voice emanating from the reader's pulpit with words from Merton's *Bread in the Wilderness*:

"The more we are united to Him in love, the more we are united in love to one another because there is only one charity embracing both God and our brother."

Andrew looked up at that point and found Brother Matthew gazing directly at him. He quickly looked down at his plate, toyed with the few remaining peas, and then glanced around the spacious room to see if, by chance, someone might have recognized their visual contact; however, heads were mostly bowed over their food as the monks devoured Andrew's successful lunch, all except for Brother Adrian, who was sitting directly opposite Andrew.

He was staring at Andrew with an obvious smirk as he sat, cross-legged, slowly swinging his top leg, and holding his glass of wine with one hand, while methodically raising his index and middle finger of the other hand, back-and-forth from his lips, as he pretended to be smoking a cigarette in some imaginary cabaret.

The unexpected theatrical pose, in such an unlikely context, had an immediate impact on Andrew, who could barely retain his laughter. He stifled his giggles with his napkin as he turned away from the character across from him and pretended to cough repeatedly until the urge to laugh subsided. He knew that he would easily be out of control if he dared to glance in Brother Adrian's direction; instead, he bowed his head like the others, forced himself to finish the food on his plate, and prayed that Father Jude would soon ring the bell to signify the end of the meal.

* * *

Following the cleanup of the noonday meal, Andrew lingered in the kitchen, checking supplies for the coming week. He paused to look through the expansive windows and saw that spring had turned the soft earth in the driveway to mud, which had been partially covered by wooden planks to help keep delivery drivers from sinking up to their ankles. The southwest facing bluffs had already lost most of their snow cover, while sprouts of new green were rapidly coloring the landscape. In the distance, the mountain peaks remained ringed with bands of snow, which draped gracefully over supportive washes and gullies like haphazard garland.

"Still working?" Father Luke asked softly as he came through the door.

"Just doing the order list . . . and daydreaming," Andrew replied.

Father Luke smiled. "It's a good day for that." He searched through one of the lower cabinets and removed a box of wheat crackers. "Something to put on top of the medication I just took," he said, chewing on one of the crackers.

"Another headache?" Andrew asked, knowing that Father Luke had a history of migraines and repeated the scene in the past.

"Yes, unfortunately. Maybe it's God's way of keeping me humble after spending too much time on the budget, which needs a minor miracle to make it into the black." He stared out the window at several crows that had settled in some of the taller sage. "Brother Adrian says that you're doing a great job in the kitchen, and I would certainly agree. The food has been delicious."

"Well, I appreciate that. Brother Adrian is a good teacher."

Father Luke turned and faced Andrew. "How are things going, in general—since our last meeting?"

Andrew did not anticipate the question. "Fine, I guess. What do you think?"

"I agree," Father Luke said. "It looks as though you've both put a lot of effort into maintaining an appropriate relationship."

Andrew tried not to show his sudden resentment over, what he felt to be, a fairly patronizing remark, even if it were true. Maintaining an appropriate relationship, outwardly, was acceptable; but internally, Andrew knew that he could not simply discount his feelings for Matthew. He did not respond immediately—instead, he decided to change the subject and redirect his anger.

"Would you mind if I speak freely about something you've been working on—the budget—and my role as a cook?"

Father Luke appeared stunned. "No . . . what is it?"

Andrew rubbed his eyes and began. "Since I've been working in the kitchen, I've seen a lot of expensive products being used. For example, almost all containers have the word "natural" on the labels, and the food we eat just seems . . . I don't know . . . less than simple—more gourmet;

at times, I wonder if it's really in keeping with the spirit of monasticism." He crossed to the opposite side of the room. "I know when I was living on my own, I couldn't afford all this." Andrew picked up a brown jar and held it up for Father Luke to see. "*Almond* butter?" He returned to the sink and stared out the window, knowing that he had instantly become a rebel, of sorts, or at least, "someone to be reckoned with," a position he neither wanted nor felt comfortable with.

He turned to face Father Luke. "I'm sorry," he said. "I know you have a headache and this is probably not the best time to dump this on you. I guess it's been one of those days.

"It's okay," Father Luke said. "The important thing here is that you're sincere, and I can see you are very serious about this." He rubbed both temples while he closed his eyes. "I guess the only thing I can say right now is that I'll discuss the matter with the abbot and the board, and once a decision, if any, is made, I will let you know. I appreciate your feelings on this, Andrew." He winked at Andrew, an uncharacteristic gesture, and exited out the back door.

On his way back to his cell, Andrew passed the community bulletin board where various notes and letters were posted, sometimes notes of thanks, but more often, requests for prayers for dying relatives or other personal reasons. The ragged appearance of a new addition caught his eye. He moved closer and read the following:

> *To the monks at St. Anthony's:*
>
> *I am writing to ask for your collective support by praying for my family. My husband, Josh, lost his job and we are currently living with our two children in our automobile since we cannot afford to rent an apartment. I am working part time but it is not enough to sustain us. Please, please pray for us. May God bless you.*
>
> *Josh, Alice, Fred and Lindsay Cooper*

Andrew had seen other requests for prayers but none quite as moving as this. He closed his eyes and silently said a "Hail Mary" for the Coopers.

Ironically, near the bottom of the board, Andrew noticed a neatly typed letter on embossed stationery from the Starrett family, specifically, Ted, a neighbor, who made most of his fortune in wine production and lived, part-time, in a spacious, contemporary four-story log structure across the mesa. Ted was transferring ten thousand dollars worth of "unproductive stock"—a write off—to the monastery, to be used at their discretion: either sell it or let it ride. He included his broker's name and telephone number.

The sharp contrast between the two notes fueled Andrew's already simmering anger and stirred his curiosity. He had not paid much attention to the particular newspapers and magazines the monastery subscribed to, yet he vaguely remembered thinking it was unusual for the monastery to receive the *Wall Street Journal* and *Money Magazine*. Suddenly, the inevitable lightbulb went on as he realized that St. Anthony's was, most probably, a player in the market. After all, it was unlikely, he decided, that "the girls" could support the place on eggs alone.

Once again, as so many times in the past, Andrew agonized over the dilemma of a dichotomous lifestyle, within the institution itself, and his own human needs and desires. He found himself inundated with conflicts as he made his way down the cloister to his cell, attempting to sort out what might be genuinely monastic and what, if anything, it all meant. He thought, 'I love this life, yet somehow, it doesn't gel. How the hell can I be a monk and feel the way I do about Matt? And how can I point a finger at the abbot?' The more he allowed himself to think, the more his thoughts began to rapidly race and blur within his head. He began to experience a familiar lightheadedness, followed by an enveloping blackness, and then—nothing.

It was Brother Mark who found him, crumpled against the cloister wall, lying on his side, in a small pool of blood.

"Jesus!" he shouted, kneeling over Andrew, as he attempted to establish a pulse; his fingers successfully found a throbbing vessel. "Somebody help!"

Within seconds, three monks, including Brother Nathan, appeared in the hallway, stunned by what they saw. Yet guided by Brother Nathan's medical experience, they carefully stabilized Andrew's head, put him on a stretcher and transported him immediately to the infirmary where they tried to summon Father Gerald, who had left the monastery to visit an ailing neighbor.

When Andrew awoke, he felt as if he were still dreaming. The déjà vu scenario was complete with both Father Gerald and Brother Nathan peering over him with pensive faces, surrounded by sterile whiteness and aseptic scents. "What happened this time?" he asked, cautiously, uncertain about whether he really wanted to know.

"I believe you fainted, again," Father Gerald said, "except, this time, you apparently hit your head against the corner bricks and have a nasty cut above your right temple."

Andrew was suddenly aware that Brother Nathan was holding something firmly against his head.

"How are you feeling?" Brother Nathan asked softly.

It was a question Andrew felt was being asked too often, regardless of its sincerity; he was tired of what he saw as bringing attention to himself and creating, what might be viewed as a pattern in his medical history. "I'm not sure . . . anymore," he said, swallowing hard and looking away.

"Easy," Brother Nathan cautioned. "Try to keep your head still."

Father Gerald removed the blood-soaked gauze. With the help of a powerful flashlight, he examined the oozing gash above Andrew's hairline. "You are going to need a few stitches to close this," he said. He turned, walked to the sink, and began to scrub his hands and arms. After administering a topical anesthetic, Father Gerald clipped some of Andrew's hair closest to the cut and began the cleansing and then the closing. "That ought to do it," he said.

Brother Nathan gathered the leftover paraphernalia, returned items to cabinets, and placed some instruments in the infirmary's autoclave. He washed his hands and spoke to Father Gerald. "Are you all set?" he asked.

"All set," Father Gerald acknowledged. "Thanks." He then added, "Oh . . . would you stop by after Compline to check on Brother Andrew? I'm going to have him stay overnight to monitor his vitals."

"Of course," Brother Nathan said. He smiled at Andrew and held up his hand in a cursory wave before he exited.

Father Gerald gave Andrew pajamas and a light robe. "You might as well put these on and be comfortable."

"Do I really have to stay here overnight?" Andrew asked.

"I think it's a good idea—just to be on the safe side. Besides, you get to sleep through vigils."

Andrew grinned. "It sounds better already."

He watched as Father Gerald pulled the privacy curtain around his bed.

"Don't get out of bed to change," Father Gerald cautioned. "Just call out when you're through and I'll open the curtain."

Feeling somewhat unsteady after struggling with the pajama bottoms, Andrew lay back against the pillow and waited for the feeling to pass.

"You okay?" Father Gerald inquired, at exactly the right moment.

Andrew wondered if he could see through the white material.

"I'm all right . . . just taking a rest."

"Take your time."

When he finished changing, he folded his clothing, placed them on a chair next to the bed, and pulled the cover up to his waist. "I'm all set," he signaled.

The curtain separated with an abrasive screech as Father Gerald proceeded to open it fully. "Well, at least now, you look like a patient," he said with practiced bedside manners. He pulled a vacant chair closer to Andrew and sat down. "I know that this is not the best time to talk with you but, eventually, we'll need to discuss what might be going on with you and causing you to faint." He continued to look directly at Andrew with a soft sympathetic expression. "I don't see any immediate evidence of a serious nature—yet it can't be ruled out. Is there anything that you are aware of that would be helpful in making a determination?"

Andrew rubbed his eyes and stared at the very white ceiling. He wondered if it had been freshly painted. "Not really," he said. "If I had to venture a guess, I'd say that I'm not very good at handling stress. I think it runs in the family."

"A lot of families," Father Gerald reinforced. "And I have a feeling that you may have hit the nail on the head with your own diagnosis." He stood up and put his hand over Andrew's. "Don't let this bother you . . . you are going to be okay." He placed a urinal on the bed. "Just in case you need to use it. I'll be in and out so, if you need anything, just pull on this cord and either Brother Nathan or I will check on you."

"Thanks," Andrew said. "Sorry for all the trouble."

"You're welcome, but you've got to stop thinking like that—it's no trouble, at all."

Alone in the fading twilight, Andrew ran his fingers over the cold metal urinal, remembering Matthew, the night at the cabin, and their stifled relationship which, he knew, presented him with the most troublesome enigma of all. Within seconds, he could feel an involuntary stirring deep within—a lascivious yearning for that which he missed yet continued to fight against in order to maintain his monastic vocation.

He carefully rolled to his good side and faced the window. The landscape had faded to black, except for the distant hills and peaks, which glowed with a tangerine tint from the setting sun. He watched the colors slowly fade until even the highest mountains succumbed to total darkness.

He woke in a softly lit room, still facing the window which, cloaked in external darkness, had become a mirror that reflected his bandaged head—a white knot amid a tangle of black hair. Someone in the room was busily moving back and forth, quietly opening cabinets, writing brief notes, and putting away shiny instruments. Andrew heard footsteps approach the bed, as he watched the reflection in the window grow larger and become more distinct.

"You're awake," Brother Nathan said, leaning over Andrew's shoulder. "Good timing. I brought some food from the refectory. Would like to try some?"

Andrew rolled onto his back. "Sure, I'll give it a try . . . thanks."

Brother Nathan pressed a button on the side of the bed and raised the headboard. "How's that feel?"

Although he suddenly felt somewhat woozy, Andrew did not want to center the conversation on his current health status. "That's fine, thanks."

With the skill of an uptown waiter, Brother Nathan placed the bed tray over Andrew's lap. "Coffee, miso soup with barley, and a grilled, cheddar cheese sandwich, sent with best wishes from Brother Adrian."

Andrew laughed. "He knows my favorites. Be sure to thank him for me."

"I will. Enjoy your meal." Brother Nathan smiled at Andrew and then left the infirmary.

Although the food was delicious, Andrew was not feeling particularly hungry. He managed to eat half of the soup and less than half of the sandwich. He lay back, coddling his mug of coffee with both hands, and attempted to shrug off any thoughts that were unsettling or negative. He did not want to search the past as an excuse for his present status, any more than he wished to extrapolate on the future and his desire to remain a monk. Instead, he chose to think about Matthew, admitting, right at that very moment, he missed him tremendously and wished he could see him, talk with him, listen to his laughter, and share a smile.

When the infirmary door swung open, it was not Matthew but Father Gerald who entered.

"How are you feeling?" he asked from across the room. He removed his black coat and hung it on the freestanding wooden rack.

"I'm doing all right," Andrew replied.

Father Gerald observed Andrew's tray. "Not too hungry?"

"Not especially."

"How about nausea, dizziness, blurry vision?"

"Not really . . . maybe a little dizziness, when Brother Nathan elevated the head of the bed."

Father Gerald returned with a blood pressure cuff, examination light, and stethoscope. Afterwards, he made his pronouncement. "So far, so good. No signs of any salient, clinical issues, but I still prefer to have you stay overnight so I can drop in, take your vitals, and see how you are doing."

Andrew did not object. The infirmary, at night, was a much warmer, welcoming place once the harshness of the sterile white environment was muted by the evening's obscurity.

"Is there anything you want to tell me to help alleviate whatever, if anything, might be contributing to your stress?" Father Gerald asked unexpectedly yet with genuine concern.

Andrew sipped his coffee and rubbed his eyes. "Yes," he said, "but not right now . . . not tonight."

Father Gerald smiled. "I can respect that."

Without thinking, Andrew suddenly heard himself talking. "May I ask a favor of you, Father Gerald?"

"Of course," he replied.

"Would it be possible for you to ask Brother Matthew to visit me this evening?"

Father Gerald did not appear surprised by his request. "I'll look for him now," he said and quickly left the room.

Andrew was amazed at the ease with which he was able to pose the question to Father Gerald and pleased to hear his nonchalant response. He looked at his watch—5:45 p.m.—and wondered where Matthew might be.

Just before six, the door to the infirmary opened, once again.

"Hey, Andrew!" Matthew announced before he had time to close the door. He hurried to his bedside. "You look like a wounded soldier . . ." He quickly looked around the room to confirm their privacy. "Handsome and brave," he added with diplomacy, using humor to express his understated feelings. "How are you?"

Andrew smiled. "I'm okay . . . just tired of this fainting crap, and, I don't know, a bit anxious about what's going on."

"You mean what's causing it?"

Andrew's smile quickly faded. "I guess; who knows, maybe I have a brain tumor or something."

"Not according to Father Gerald," Matthew said quickly. "He said that you would get some additional tests in Bitter Creek."

"He told you that?"

"Yes, when he came to my room to tell me that you wanted to see me."

"That's funny. He never said anything to me."

"Well, don't worry about it. I'm sure it'll be fine." He squeezed Andrew's hand. "Is that the only reason you asked to see me?" A familiar look subtly transformed his expression.

"Of course not," Andrew said. He placed his other hand on top of Matthew's. "I need to talk with you before I go totally nuts. We haven't talked in such a long time—I don't know what's going on, and then all this attention to my health . . ." His pressured speech was obvious.

"Easy, easy," Matthew said, firmly squeezing his hand. "It's okay. You are going to get all riled up again, for nothing. Try to relax."

Andrew rubbed his eyes, harder and harder, as if he were trying to push them into his head.

"Stop it!" Matthew insisted, as he grabbed Andrew's arm and held it to the bed. "Nothing's changed. You know how I feel about you. If it weren't for my respect for you, our decision to live this . . . somewhat fucked-up lifestyle, I'd spend every day, busting my ass in this place, working, and genuinely praying, just as long as I could spend every night with you, from the end of Compline to the beginning of vigils. And I wouldn't feel the slightest twinge of hypocrisy or guilt, just because I am capable of loving . . . loving another man, who God created. I feel I am loving him since—what are we—but his reflection, at least, according to everything *I've* read."

It was as if flashbulbs exploded in Andrew's head. He realized that Matthew had no difficulty reconciling his feelings for him and his ability to genuinely live as a monk, as long as he could do it on his terms—a clandestine physical relationship, where he could express his love for him and, as an extension of that love, fully praise and love his God. He made it very simple and honestly believed it to be both true and possible. Andrew closed his eyes, laid his head back against the pillow and smiled. "I guess that's what I love about you," he said. "You have this innate ability to tell it like it is, or at least, how you sincerely think it is, and that's that." He squeezed Matthew's hand. "I would like to be able to reason that way, Matt, yet something gets in the way and starts screaming, 'What's wrong with this picture?'"

"Don't worry about it right now. It'll pass . . . you'll see."

Andrew sighed. "Will it?"

"Yes," Matthew said convincingly.

His hair appeared golden in the soft light, framing his head, Andrew thought, like a Nordic God, on loan from some royal Scandinavian museum. He turned slightly to his right to face Matthew directly. "I could look at you all night," he whispered, knowing that he meant much more than his comments implied.

"Don't encourage me," Matthew said. "I might find some way to arrange it. In fact, it wouldn't take much for me to climb into this bed right now."

Andrew laughed. "Don't even think about it because I'd probably let you."

Matthew leaned over the bed. "You've got to stop talking like this—I'm getting all excited."

"I can tell," Andrew said, glancing down.

Matthew pulled a chair closer to the bed and sat down. "Less obvious this way."

In the ensuing silence, Andrew sensed the frustration of their torments, which had been cavalierly couched in humor.

"I'm a little surprised that we were allowed to spend this time together," Matthew said suddenly. "I thought that there would be at least five of the elders sitting in the room with us."

"I have a feeling that Father Gerald is the only one who knows you're here," Andrew replied. He rolled onto his back to make himself more comfortable. "Besides, I think that he knows about you and me, and I can't say for sure, but I don't think he sees it as some repulsive sin."

Matthew leaned forward in his chair. "It's weird you should say that because I've had that same feeling." He reached out and gently touched Andrew's cheek and then ran his fingers over his ear and down his neck.

Andrew closed his eyes. "It feels so good just to be touched," he said, wishing that the feeling could go on forever.

"I know," Matthew whispered.

The sound of the infirmary door opening caused Matthew to quickly withdraw his hand and initiate a conversation in more normal tones. "By the way, I heard from Ellen. She's coming back for a retreat this week for three days."

Brother Nathan approached the bed with a blood pressure cuff and stethoscope. "I see you have a visitor," he said politely. "Brother Matthew," he acknowledged, tipping his head in Matthew's direction.

"Hello, Brother Nathan," Matthew replied.

"I won't disturb your visit for too long . . . I just want to get Andrew's blood pressure." He wrapped the cuff securely around Andrew's upper arm, pumped up the cuff, and placed the stethoscope below it while he listened for the telltale bumps. He released the air and removed the cuff. "How are you feeling?" he asked, as he reached for Andrew's wrist to check his pulse.

"I'm okay," Andrew said.

In the following seconds of silence, Andrew glanced at Matthew who responded, unobserved, with a toothy full-faced grin.

"Your pressure is up a bit but nothing to worry about. Any headaches or dizziness?"

"Lots of dizziness," Matthew interjected.

Brother Nathan was not expecting the remark and laughed heartily. "I'm sorry, Brother Andrew, but Matthew's humor caught me off guard."

"Well," Andrew said smiling, "that's Matthew; but no . . . no headaches and no dizziness."

"All right. I'll check on you later in the evening." He turned to go. "I'm sure that Father Gerald will be in to see you. Good night."

As soon as he heard the door close, Andrew faced Matthew. "Lots of dizziness," he mimicked. "I could have killed you."

"You have to admit—it was funny. And I think that's the first time I saw Brother Nathan laugh."

"I think you're right," Andrew said with a chuckle.

"Were you serious about Ellen coming to the monastery for a retreat?"

"Yes," Matthew said." She also mentioned that she hopes to be able to see you."

Andrew felt a sudden tightness in his chest. "Sure . . . that would be fine." He was not able to maintain eye contact with Matthew; instead, he pretended to adjust the covers in front of him.

Once again, Matthew moved closer to him and placed his hand on his arm. "I'd better be going or I'll be late for Compline. Take care of yourself, and I hope you feel better by morning." He stood up and looked down at Andrew. "It may sound crazy, but it's difficult for me to leave."

"It's not crazy," Andrew said. "I really miss . . . us. Thanks for coming."

As Matthew turned to walk toward the door, Andrew rolled on his side and watched his reflection in the window, as he stood by the door looking back at him. He raised his hand and waved. "Good night, Matt," he called out.

"See you tomorrow," Matthew said.

He watched the door close and, like the blackness outside the window, he could feel, once again, an enveloping darkness settle over him, like an invisible weight.

* * *

From a sound sleep, at three o'clock in the morning, Andrew felt the familiar chill and tightness of the blood pressure cuff around his arm.

"Sorry to wake you," Father Gerald said quietly. "How are you doing?"

The question appeared so unexpectedly, Andrew did not have time to think before he responded. "I don't remember," he said sleepily.

Father Gerald chuckled. "I know... it's early." He placed a thermometer under Andrew's tongue. "As soon as I check your temperature, I'll let you get back to dreamland."

Andrew could taste the alcohol wash, still clinging to the thermometer.

"Looks good," Father Gerald said. "You can go back to sleep now." He turned off the lamp near the bed, sat at his desk and recorded the necessary data before leaving the room.

In the silence, Andrew, less than fully conscious, could hear the faint Gregorian chant of the monks at vigils, a reassuring and comforting chorus, which eased his transition toward sleep. In this dreamlike state, he thought he could hear his name being whispered, more and more clearly.

"Andrew," Matthew said softly. "Don't be frightened. It's me, Matt."

Andrew forced himself to open his eyes. In the darkness, he could see Matthew's blurred smile as he reached out and touched his face. He smiled, unafraid, and grabbed Matthew's hand. "Am I dreaming or is it really you?"

"Does it matter?" Matthew said. He leaned over and kissed him on the forehead, nose, and lips.

Andrew reached up, put his arm around him and pulled him toward him until Matthew was snuggled alongside of him. "I can't believe you're here," he whispered as he hugged him tightly.

"Remember what I said earlier about crawling into bed with you?" Matthew asked. "Well, here I am . . . but I don't have much time."

"I know." Andrew eagerly kissed him, reigniting the etched memories of their time together in the loft. "I missed you so much," he said into Matthew's ear, inhaling his familiar scent, redolent of fresh mowed hay.

"If you only knew," Matthew responded as he squeezed Andrew firmly. "But I'd better get out of here before all hell breaks loose." He stood up. "I'll see you tomorrow. Sleep well." He squeezed Andrew's nose and then quietly left the room.

* * *

The morning arrived, glaringly bright, with sunlight flooding the infirmary and bouncing everywhere within the white environment. Father Gerald appeared shortly after Andrew woke.

"Good morning," he said cheerfully, "How did you sleep?"

Andrew suddenly remembered Matthew's visit and smiled. "Other than for a minor interruption, I guess I slept pretty well."

Father Gerald laughed. "I know. I'm sorry about having to bother you last night, but I wanted to be sure that your vitals were all right."

"It's okay," Andrew said with a smirk.

"And," Father Gerald continued, "as soon as I do the same this morning, you should be able to return to your regular routine." Once again, he checked Andrew's pressure, pulse, and temperature, looked at his eyes and ears and helped him to a standing position. "You might feel a little weak or unsteady, but I'd like you to walk toward the bathroom with me so I can see how you're doing."

Andrew experienced a bit of dizziness, yet it quickly passed. He had no difficulty walking, just somewhat stiff from lying in bed longer than usual. "I feel fine, so far," Andrew explained.

"Good," Father Gerald said.

"Since I'm already here, would you mind if I used the bathroom?" Andrew asked.

"Of course not, as long as you feel steady on your feet."

"So far, so good."

When Andrew returned, he saw Father Gerald sitting at his desk writing. "Am I ready to get dressed?"

Father Gerald stopped writing and looked up. "Yes. You can pull the curtain around the bed."

Andrew was pleased to put on his familiar jeans, shirt, and sweater and discard the hospital-like pajamas. He opened the curtain and approached Father Gerald's desk.

"Have a seat," Father Gerald said with a wave of his hand. "I'd like to do some follow-up work at the Bitter Creek hospital, just to be sure that everything is fine."

Andrew did not relish the thought of more emphasis being placed on his health. He felt as though he wanted to get out of the spotlight, which seemed to be pointed directly at him, yet he respected Father Gerald's genuine concern for his well-being. He could not say no. "If you feel it's necessary, I'll do whatever you say."

"Good. I'd like to get some pictures of the area on your head where you fell, and also, an electroencephalogram, to monitor and evaluate normal brainwave patterns."

"It sounds complicated," Andrew said with a smile.

"Not really," Father Gerald replied. "I'll set it up and let you know when they can see you. In the meantime, take things easy, avoid bending and try to relax."

After a breakfast of French toast and orange juice, Andrew was told that he should refrain from all work chores and attend services only if he felt well enough to do so. He decided that it was a good opportunity to enjoy the beauty of the day by going for a walk.

Spring's late arrival was becoming more obvious, as manifested by the increased number of songbirds that had moved into the higher altitudes with the warmer temperatures. Roads that had once been soft and muddy were beginning to dry out and, in some places, crack, under the strong vernal sun. Even now, an approaching car left a light trail of dust.

As the car got closer, Andrew recognized the abbot's familiar blue Peugeot, which appeared to contain two people. From his position on the left side of the road, Andrew could see the passenger who, much to his surprise, waved vigorously at him as they went by, yet it was not until they passed before Andrew recognized the dark-haired young woman as Ellen. She continued to look back at him and wave. He smiled and waved back, confused and somewhat awed by her association with Father Jude. As he walked he thought, 'No big deal—she was probably walking toward the monastery when the abbot recognized her, asked if she wanted a lift, and she accepted.' Nevertheless, it was a situation Andrew could not easily dismiss.

In the distance, the receding snow climbed even higher up the mountains, exposing a panoply of budding sage, worn rock, and brick-colored earth. Barbed wire fences, which had been buried by drifts, emerged, in need of repair, and appeared contrived against the natural landscape. Andrew knew that he would soon be asked to work on the fences to prepare for the influx of cattle that grazed on the monastery's land over the short summer months. The water from Empire Creek would, once again, be allowed to flow through the main gates and fill the miles of the irrigation ditches that ringed the property.

He turned quickly to acknowledge the approaching motorcycle, which stopped abruptly, alongside of him.

"You look much better out of that infirmary bed," Matthew said, as he got off the bike and pushed the hair out of his eyes. His wide smile and ruddy complexion reflected the healthy glow of the morning.

"And I'm glad to be out," Andrew said. "Where are you working?"

"Just over the ridge," he said, pointing in the direction over Andrew's shoulder. He suddenly got back on the motorcycle, started it up, and motioned to Andrew with his head. "Hop on," he said. "I want to show you something."

Andrew hesitated. "I don't know, Matt."

"Don't worry about it. Just get on the damn bike."

Andrew seemed frozen to the spot until Matthew reached out and pulled him toward him. He threw his leg over the seat and settled in behind Matthew who had already shifted into second gear. He barely had time to grasp the grab bar in back of him before Matthew accelerated and drove down the road toward a cutoff road that wound upwards into the foothills.

Matthew downshifted, avoiding the remaining muddy areas, as he left the main road. "Be sure to hang on." He said over his shoulder. "The road's a bit rough."

Andrew unexpectedly felt Matthew reach behind him, grab his arm and put it around his waist. He shifted hands, reached for Andrew's other arm until both were wrapped tightly around him. "That's much better, don't you think?"

Andrew cautiously looked around, fearful that they might be observed. He then squeezed Matthew, leaned forward and placed his mouth against his ear. "You are getting me incredibly horny," he said, as he playfully bit Matthew's earlobe.

"Oh, God," Matthew said, looking over his shoulder. "You'd better stop that or I'll never make it to the top."

Andrew laughed, squeezed him, and then ran his hand quickly over his chest and abdomen.

As they climbed higher and higher, the road narrowed into a worn path which, most likely, had been created by the indigenous wildlife, either elk or deer. Near the top of the ridge, Matthew stopped the bike on a flat stone outcrop and both got off.

"Follow me," Matthew insisted, as he began the short final climb to the highest point on the precipice. It was a steep yet relatively manageable assent due to the steplike formation of the rock, which was still partly covered with snow.

Matthew reached the top first, extended his hand and pulled Andrew up, alongside him. "Well, what do you think?"

The three hundred and sixty degree view left Andrew breathless. The jagged fourteen-thousand-feet peaks in the distance were still laden with snow, while the valleys were just beginning to sprout sparse carpets of green over the adobe soil. A fairly distinct line separated the snow from the barren earth, as if drawn purposely by some celestial artist.

"This is incredible!" Andrew said, mesmerized by the panoramic spectacle. "How did you ever find this place?"

"One day, I just kept walking," Matthew said. He grabbed Andrew, turned him slightly to his left and pointed to a snow-covered peak. "That's Squaw Mountain in Bitter Creek. You can see skiers on the snow fields, if you concentrate."

Andrew squinted his eyes; in the distance he did, in fact, see colored dots traversing the expanse of white, like miniature bugs making their way down the mountain. "It makes me want to ski again!" Andrew lamented.

"I knew you'd get a kick out of the view," Matthew said. "Besides, it's a chance to spend some time with you, away from all that." He pointed to the valley were the monastery was located.

Andrew could see all of the buildings, including the eggery, retreat houses, and barns. A vehicle, barely visible, trailed dust as it left the main road and drove toward the complex.

Matthew watched as Andrew submerged himself in the visual banquet. He stood behind him, wrapped his arms around him, and rested his head on his shoulder. "Are you still feeling hesitant about coming up here with me?" he asked softly, nuzzling Andrew's ear.

"Of course not," Andrew replied, "but . . . what if Brother Adrian just happens to be using his binoculars and sees us up here?"

Matthew laughed. "If he sees us right now, I'll bet he gets an erection."

"You're crazy," Andrew said with a smile, "but I like that in a man."

"If you're paranoid about being seen, follow me. I've got something else to show you."

Matthew led Andrew back down the stoneface, almost to the outcrop where the motorcycle was parked. He changed direction suddenly and trekked a short distance, up a wide knoll of scree, to another rocky area that appeared to be hollowed out of the mountain like a natural foxhole, only much wider and deeper. The circular space was ringed with large angular stones and contained a relatively flat floorlike interior.

Once inside, Andrew imagined himself to be in a fortress. "What is this?" he asked in amazement.

"I don't know. Just . . . some sort of natural phenomenon, I guess."

"You just stumbled on it?"

"Yeah, the same day I climbed up the precipice."

Andrew stretched out on one of the table-shaped rocks. "I wonder if others know about this place."

"I doubt it," Matthew said confidently. "Look at this." He moved to the opposite side of the hollow and pointed to a flat rock slightly indented from the one above it yet easily visible. On its surface sat two half dollars and four quarters. "I put this here last summer and no one touched it." Matthew beamed over his perceived ingenuity.

"Another monk wouldn't take that," Andrew said with exasperation.

"It doesn't have to be a monk—just another hiker."

"I don't know," Andrew mused. "They might think it looks like a set up and, if they take the coins, some evil curse will overcome them."

Matthew pulled down on his cheekbones, which stretched his lower eyelids into a grotesque shape. "You've been here too long." He then moved to a part of the wall which had been cut even deeper into the side of the depression, a space resembling a small closet. "Come over here. I want to show you something else."

With Andrew at his side, Matthew pointed to a flat surface on the wall where a heart, approximately six inches by six inches, had been carved into the stone. Inside the heart was the inscription "Matt loves Andrew."

Overwhelmed and somewhat shocked by this open declaration, Andrew could feel the color rise in his cheeks. "When did you do this?"

"Last fall," Andrew said proudly.

Andrew laughed. "But we hardly knew each other then."

"I know," Matthew said. "It didn't matter; I knew how I felt about you a long time ago."

"Come here, crazy man," Andrew said softly as he reached out, pulled Matthew against him and kissed him—an embrace which seemed endless and necessary yet insufficient.

"I want to touch you," Matthew said, running his hand over Andrew's jeans.

Andrew looked around anxiously. "What if someone shows up?"

"I'm not expecting anyone," Matthew joked. "Are you?"

"I'm serious, Matt," Andrew said.

"Look around. The only one who might see us is a pilot, or a voyeuristic eagle, and you can easily hear someone walking up the rock pile. Besides," he said quietly, "remember the last fence post we drove by, just before we stopped the bike?"

Andrew nodded vaguely.

"Well, that was the end of the monastery's property. We are probably on public property belonging to the city of Bitter Creek; I thought you'd like to know that."

"It's really scary how you seem to be able to read my mind," Andrew admitted.

"I know you," Matthew said, "and I know what we both need." He kissed Andrew aggressively, exploring, and plunging into the renewed physical encounter. He moved his hand to the top of Andrew's jeans, unbuttoned them, and slid them down. He then carefully pushed Andrew's shorts over his erection and down to his thighs. After removing his own jacket, Matthew threw it on the ground. "We can kneel on this," he said as they continued to embrace each other.

The intense feeling of Matthew's gentle stroking, while they kissed, left Andrew nearly breathless, with an infinite craving to become one with his partner, to unite his very soul to his, to mesh together until images blurred—to become the very flesh and blood of Matthew himself. He tugged at the button on Matthew's jeans and slid both his shorts and pants down at the same time; and then, with both hands, he grasped Matthew's erection, exploring its laudable thickness and length with firm repetitive movements.

A jet may have passed overhead; hikers could have crunched the scree, but it would not have made a difference. Both were completely absorbed in the ecstasy of an emotional and physical union, an extraordinary relationship in which the two men celebrated both the sacred and profane, as an expression of their humanness and their ability to love what, Matthew always believed, God had created.

Afterwards, they held each other in silence, still kneeling on Matthew's parka. Their heated bodies exuded a familiar collage of spent sexuality—an intoxicating aroma, which Andrew remembered and missed. He nuzzled Matthew's neck, felt the dampness of his hair and inhaled the warm, haylike fragrance of his body heat. He touched his lips to Matthew's ear. "Thanks for bringing me up here," he said softly.

Matthew faced him. He looked unabashedly into Andrew's eyes, as if they were windows, and he could see directly into his soul. He then kissed Andrew deeply, but before doing so, he said, "I want you to keep your eyes open."

It was a kiss unlike Andrew had ever experienced. Staring into Matthew's eyes, he felt a sense of oneness, clarity, and genuine acceptance. In the brilliance of the late morning light, it was as if pretensions, doubts, or institutionalized guilt were immediately erased from his memory and could never be reinstalled. Words were not necessary. Somehow, he knew that Matthew was not only aware of his feelings, but also aware that these same feelings were originally generated and experienced by Matthew during their initial encounter.

"You've always felt this way, haven't you," Andrew said solemnly.

A hint of a smile softened Matthew's face. "Ever since I saw you," he said.

"Why has it taken me all this time?" Andrew asked, as if to himself.

"That's not important right now. Maybe . . . life got in the way."

Andrew hugged him hard, unable to speak.

Matthew reached down, pulled up Andrew's shorts and jeans and began to help tuck in his shirt.

Once they were dressed, they stretched out, side by side, in the sun, on a long flat rock.

"So," Andrew asked introspectively, "where do we go from here?"

Matthew unexpectedly looked at his watch. "I've got enough gas in the bike to get us to the Bitter Creek Airport; we can get a jet to Vegas and be married by three thirty."

His nonchalant delivery provoked hysterical laughter from Andrew.

Two inquisitive wrens perched side by side, on a small branch across the way, tilting their heads in wonderment or confusion.

"We're being observed," Andrew said, nodding in the direction of the two birds.

"No," Matthew objected. "Not observed . . . acknowledged. I'll bet they're homosexual."

Andrew smirked and sat up. "What am I going to do with you," he said with a shake of his head. He wrapped his arms around his knees as he watched a Volkswagen-shaped cloud crash into the sun.

Sensing Andrew's pensive mood, Matthew settled in behind him, enveloping him snuggly with his legs and arms. "I can hear the wheels turning," he said, pressing his mouth against the back of Andrew's head. "What are you thinking now?"

Andrew shrugged his shoulders. "Oh . . . I don't know. I guess I'm wondering how to balance our relationship with our life here." He turned his head slightly to the right. "I love you, Matt, and I also love being a monk. Like I said before, where do we go from here?"

Matthew rested his chin on Andrew's shoulder and hugged him. "Believe it or not, it's possible. You know that I am completely in love with you and, as much as I bitch about the lifestyle, I also love being a monk. As I told you in the infirmary, as long as we can be together, like this, even if it means having to hide our affection, I can survive the darkest nights, knowing that somehow, somewhere, we will be together." He brushed his nose against Andrew's ear. "Do you understand what I mean?"

"Yes . . . and no," Andrew said. "I want to be with you as much as you want to be with me, but would our relationship really gel with the reason why we're here?"

"Okay," Matthew said bluntly. "Why are we really here?"

Andrew dropped his head to his knees and sighed. "Don't do this to me, Matt."

"I'm serious," he said. "You probably think I have this self-serving, convoluted agenda but, think about it. You are here because you are a loving person, intent on nourishing your spiritual needs, most likely, at the expense of your human needs. And you have a strong belief in the power of prayer. I feel the spiritual and sensual are not separate entities; in fact, sensual expression is a gift from God to . . . enhance and more fully realize our true, spiritual selves."

"It sounds as though you've given this a lot of thought," Andrew said. Inwardly, he was surprised, if not genuinely impressed, by Matthew's reasoning, self-serving or not. "How did you come up with this?"

Matthew squeezed him. "Something to do with love," he said. "I think it runs in our family." He nuzzled Andrew's neck. "Why is it," he said softly, "when you're growing up, you're taught that sex is dirty, yet the moment you get married, sex is suddenly beautiful; it never made any sense to me." He rubbed Andrew's arms. "Sex has always been some tremendous, cosmic wonder to me: beautiful, physical, and so . . . mystical."

Andrew leaned his head back against his shoulder. "If that's the case, why did you come to the monastery? Wouldn't you have been able to establish that relationship with someone outside?"

"Probably," Matthew replied, "but for me, the monastic life had the greater attraction. Now that I've experienced the life somewhat, I feel that my sensual needs are an integral part of my spiritual life, and shouldn't necessarily be separated from it. I know it sounds like 'having my cake and eating it too,' but I feel that the church makes a big deal over sex and, as a result, it has screwed up too many lives."

"Can you say 'ex-com-mun-i-cation'?" Andrew joked, as he slowly enunciated each syllable of the word.

"I think so," Matthew said with a laugh. "Can you say 'I can't breathe'?" He began to squeeze Andrew until he begged him to stop.

The morning sun had nearly reached its zenith, filling the hollow with heat and light, a precursor of the imminent prolific summer. Its rays warmed Andrew's face as though he were on vacation at his favorite lake, high in the Adirondack Mountains only this time, he felt the elation of loving and being loved. "I could stay here forever," he said, pulling Matthew's arms around him.

"At least until we get hungry," Matthew replied.

"I wonder what Jesus would say," Andrew said casually. "That's what Brother Adrian would ask."

Matthew shifted on the rock to a more comfortable position. "Hard to say, but he must have created us for a reason," he said.

"And what's that?" Andrew asked.

"Oh, I don't know . . . paint the Sistine Chapel, write the 1812 Overture, conquer two-thirds of the known world, reform St. Anthony's monastery . . . who knows. I don't believe he created everyone as heterosexual, and I don't believe that homosexuals create themselves. I think we're a product of God's creation which, in itself, is not an easy cross to bear."

"So you see yourself as homosexual?" Andrew asked.

"Always have . . . what about you?"

"I think I've always known it," Andrew said, "but I've always fought it—dating women, sleeping with some, yet always wanting to be with Mr. Right."

"I think you're still fighting it, Andrew."

"Maybe . . . but not as much lately—not since we've become close." He brushed his cheek against Matthew's. "Things just seem to take longer with me."

"Well, it didn't take you long this morning," Matthew said with a laugh.

"You know the answer to that," Andrew retorted. "You bring out the 'wurst' in me, remember?" he said, spelling out the word.

"M—m—m," Matthew mumbled, as he buried his face in Andrew's hair. "And it's a lot of wurst." He turned Andrew's face toward his and kissed him.

"We need to stop or we'll never make it to lunch," Andrew cautioned.

"I'm not hungry," Matthew responded, "at least, not for food."

Andrew felt his body flood with renewed desire, yet he knew they needed to return to the monastery for lunch or be conspicuously absent. He jumped to his feet and pulled Matthew up after him. "Time to go," he said, "before the Inquisition materializes."

Grudgingly, Matthew followed him. "Promise me you'll come back here with me," he said, as he stopped and grabbed Andrew's arm.

Andrew leaned over and kissed him on the forehead. "I promise—now, let's get the heck out of here."

Just as he was about to get on the bike, Andrew remembered seeing Ellen. "I forgot to mention that I saw your sister this morning."

"She's here already?" Matthew asked.

"Yes. She was with the abbot, driving toward the monastery when they passed me on the road."

Matthew frowned, temporarily confused. "He must have picked her up at the airport."

The ride down the mountain proved more perilous to Andrew then the ascent, as the road suddenly dropped and disappeared, while the bike lunged over knolls and seemed momentarily airborne. He squeezed Matthew, fearing that they would certainly crash and, most likely, become wheelchair roommates in some large rehabilitation facility where they would be spoon-fed and spend their days struggling to walk after months of physical therapy. He closed his eyes and held his head firmly against Matthew's back. After what seemed like an eternity, the ride leveled out. "Are we there yet?" Andrew shouted.

"Just about," Matthew said over his shoulder. "You can open your eyes now."

When they reached the main road, Andrew got off the bike. "I'd better walk from here," he said. "No sense creating another stir."

"I know," Matthew said. "I'm going to return the shovel to the barn and come back. I'll see you at lunch."

Andrew watched as the bike accelerated down the road. He turned and walked toward the monastery when he suddenly heard the bike stop.

Matthew had spun it around and was heading toward him. He pulled up next to him and stopped. "I didn't want to leave without saying thanks for spending this time with me. I really appreciate it."

Before Andrew could respond, Matthew quickly made a tight U-turn and drove away.

* * *

Chapter Eleven

The Foot

Saturday morning mass often attracted a greater number of people, who either intended to fulfill their obligations early, or begin their weekends on a more spiritual note. With improving weather and dry roads, churchgoers seemed to rapidly multiply and crowd the sanctuary with new faces, some familiar faces, and of course, Andrew's favorite—a collective olfactory bouquet of perfume and cologne that merged subtly with the incense.

Sitting in his chair, which was part of a half circle around the altar, Andrew inhaled the fragrant scents, drifting throughout the church. From the corner of his eye, he noticed a young dark-haired woman descend the three steps to the main floor and take her place in front of the other participants. Without looking at her directly, Andrew knew that the jeans, purple jacket, and red turtleneck belonged to a confident, exuberant, and very radiant Ellen, who appeared eager to make eye contact and be acknowledged.

He was thankful that he was not assigned a reading; he would rather sit unobtrusively and concentrate on the mass; remain separate from the visitors and from Ellen, as he tried to distance himself from the memory of their Christmas Eve together. Regardless of his efforts to quell the onslaught of erotic imagery, Andrew was inundated with visuals of Ellen's black hair undulating over him with choreographed intent. He purposely bit his cheek, hoping that the pain would help him refocus on anything but Ellen—or that evening—however, the futile gesture seemed, instead, to heighten his involvement by activating another sense, the strangely sweet and familiar taste of his own blood. He wondered if Ellen might be experiencing the same thoughts and feelings or, worse yet, whether she knew what he was thinking at that very moment.

When Father Paul intoned the first verse of the Psalm, Andrew stood with the rest of the community and sang, temporarily relieved of his thoughts about this dark-haired distraction. He turned his head slightly to the right, glanced up from the hymnal and saw Matthew staring back at him. His smile, natural and disarming, helped him to relax and prompted him to return the same.

Turning his head even more to the right, Andrew observed Brother Conrad, just in time to see him gyrating his hips in his inimitable Hula-Hoop fashion, as he attempted (Andrew later learned) to lock the brace on his afflicted leg. With his brace successfully stabilized, Brother Conrad, once again stared, froglike, at the floor.

Andrew knew that it would be impossible not to laugh if he happened to see Brother Conrad's action once more. He immediately dropped his gaze, hoping that the view of the tiled floor would absorb his thoughts and stifle his welling laughter. Shortening his vision, Andrew looked at his old suede shoes, which protruded from the hem of his habit like anthropomorphic gnomes—amorphous yet well behaved and afraid to leave the security of Andrew's white tent.

Unexpectedly, while looking down, he noticed the feet of the young visiting monk standing to his right. His name was Brother Joshua, a tall muscular individual, who chose to wear open leather sandals that barely covered his feet, a personal statement which Andrew, generally, did not approve of because it appeared affected or, at least, disingenuous; yet on closer inspection, Andrew could not believe his eyes.

He observed a pair of flawlessly shaped and perfectly proportioned feet—an observation which struck him as peculiar since he had never paid much attention to that part of the body nor had he ever considered the possibility that aesthetics might be attributed to feet. He stared at the well-formed toes, their graceful yet masculine shape, the curved arch and faultless nails, until he was suddenly aware that he was also being observed by Brother Joshua, who discreetly shifted his weight and stepped backwards ever so slightly.

With a gentle cough, Andrew quickly refocused on the tiled floor, knowing that he had been foolishly careless, caught, and convicted in front of everyone. Regardless of whether or not they knew what had happened, Brother Joshua was certainly aware. He could feel the heat increase in his face, as he began to counteract the embarrassment with deep breathing and slow exhalations. Once he regained a semblance of control, he dared to glance at Brother Joshua who, much to Andrew's surprise, met his glance with complete eye contact and a full disarming smile.

Andrew returned the smile, knowing that Brother Joshua's genuine surely innocent response induced an unsolicited yet appreciated reaction within him, as if he had silently said, "It's okay. I understand."

Once the mass ended, the community proceeded out of the church to the cloister where the monks dispersed in two directions. Andrew hurried to his cell to remove his habit, knowing that he should return to the entrance room where Ellen would, most likely, be waiting to see him and her brother. He pulled an old grey sweater over his shirt, quickly brushed his hair and told himself to relax. He would be cordial, caring, and brief.

Several guests had gathered in the stone and brick room, which was bathed in early-morning sunlight, incense, and cologne. They were joined by an equal number of monks, most still in their habits—an obvious external distinction from the colorful garb of the visitors. Andrew noticed Father Jude enjoying the apparently humorous conversation of two very well-dressed attractive women. Their winter tans radiated a privileged life spent, most likely, on the slopes in Gstaad, or on the teak decks of sailing yachts in the harbor at St. Barts, since the truly affluent of Bitter Creek had a limited tolerance for their own local culture.

Andrew walked slowly through the gathering, smiling at those who made eye contact, nodding to those he knew, and briefly exchanging words with them. Still, Ellen was nowhere to be found. When he approached the outside door, which was not fully closed, he pushed it open and walked out into the brisk brilliant morning.

"Andrew!" Ellen shouted as she moved toward him and hugged him tightly. "I was hoping that you would show up, even though I know you don't particularly like this sort of thing."

He looked at Matthew who was standing in back of her and pretending to hide his face in his hands. "Now, whoever gave you that idea?" he said, smiling and looking accusatively at Matthew.

"Beats me," Matthew said sarcastically.

Andrew noticed that Ellen's beauty was even more pronounced rather than diminished by the bright morning sun. She seemed to glow with a quiet yet seductive aura and a maturity well beyond her current late teens. "You look terrific, as usual," he added. "How have you been?"

"Great!" she said. "I'm out of school for a few days, and I can't tell you how nice it is to see you and to be back to a place where I can slow down a bit—away from the urban rat race."

Andrew laughed. "I know what you mean. I'd probably be stuck in the eight o'clock traffic right now, if I weren't here."

"You haven't seen traffic until you've experienced it in California," Matthew said.

"No, and I don't want to," Andrew responded. He looked at Ellen. "So you'll be on retreat for a few days."

"Yes, and I'm really looking forward to it." She glanced quickly at Matthew and then refocused on Andrew. "Matthew says you help make the life more bearable for him, even though I know my telling you this will probably embarrass him."

"Not at all," Matthew insisted. "Andrew and I are great friends . . . and I'm glad."

The unexpected comments caught Andrew off guard. Once again, he could feel the blush of embarrassment color his cheeks as he struggled to maintain a sense of sangfroid and formulate a casual yet meaningful response. "He's right . . . we've become good friends."

"Great friends!" Matthew interjected.

"Great friends," Andrew mimicked, "and it does make the life a bit easier." He resorted to rubbing his eyes. "I guess Matt helps me put things in perspective when I become too serious; in fact, did you know that your brother's crazy?"

"That does it," Matthew shouted, feigning indignation, as he threatened to attack Andrew; however, Ellen quickly intervened by stepping between them.

"All right! Stop it!" she said. She held the two apart with outstretched arms. "This is a monastery . . . you know, peace, love, civility."

"You left out subtle indiscretion," Matthew quipped.

"And mayhem," Andrew added.

"That's it," Ellen said, laughing. She stepped aside. "Go ahead and annihilate each other."

Matthew instantly grabbed Andrew and placed him in a headlock before he could react.

After a short scuffle, Andrew conceded. "Okay, I give" he said, knowing that Matthew would, otherwise, maintain the hold until he turned purple.

"You sure?" Matthew taunted.

"Yes!" Andrew shouted.

Matthew released his grip. Still standing behind Andrew, he let his hands slip to Andrew's waist, and with both arms around him, he pulled him toward him and hugged him affectionately—in full view of his sister.

Ellen sighed and smiled.

Embarrassed by Matthew's undaunted behavior, Andrew quickly broke away and stood beside Ellen. "See," he said. "I told you he's crazy."

Ellen laughed. "Actually, I've known that for a long time. I think it runs in the family."

Matthew leaned with folded arms against the railing. "What she means, is that I am the only *sane* person in the family . . . and the best looking."

"That remark alone destroys your credibility," Ellen said, with an air of authority. "It simply proves you're a maniac."

Matthew dismissed the comment by rolling his eyes and displaying his "yeah, right!" grin.

"Maybe I'd better go and let you two slug it out," Andrew joked.

"No contest," Ellen said. "I'd thrash him." She then stood in front of Matthew and hugged him tenderly. "I really miss you," she said.

"That's good," Matthew responded, "because I miss my little sister too."

The genuine sibling affection touched Andrew deeply as he watched his friend, *his great friend*, share his love with Ellen. A sense of acceptance, of being a part of the family, was even further reinforced when Matthew suddenly looked up and said, "Come over here and give us a hug." Andrew complied, hugging them both, as Ellen laughed and welcomed the spontaneous gesture.

"Well," Andrew said, "Unfortunately, I'm responsible for cooking lunch and, if I don't get things started, there will be a lot of angry men at the kitchen door." He kissed Ellen on the cheek. "Enjoy the retreat and make sure that this one leaves you alone," he said, gesturing toward Matthew.

"Don't worry, I will," she said

He was halfway through the door when Ellen suddenly called out.

"Will I see you before I go?" she questioned.

Andrew turned and smiled. "Sure," he said somewhat wistfully. He pulled the door tight and walked quickly toward the refectory.

* * *

"I've been looking for you," Father Gerald said, as Andrew entered the kitchen. He was leaning against the counter, drinking coffee from a Trappist mug. "I scheduled your appointment at the Elkridge Hospital for Monday at 10:00 a.m. I hope that doesn't present a problem."

"No," Andrew said. "Sounds fine."

"I spoke with Father Luke; he said it would be acceptable if both you and Brother Matthew drove in with the van for the appointment, and then did the weekly shopping. I haven't mentioned it to Matthew yet, but I'll catch him after I leave. The appointment shouldn't last too long—a half hour to forty-five minutes."

Andrew poured himself some coffee. "That should work out fine because there are a few food items I need to pick up for the meals next week."

"Good," Father Gerald said, rinsing his cup in the sink. "I'll look for Brother Matthew."

"I just left him and his sister standing outside the entrance room."

"Thanks . . ." Father Gerald had already left the kitchen and entered the refectory, as his voice trailed behind him.

Sipping his coffee, Andrew mused over Father Gerald's news, which paired him and Matthew for the shopping trip, an unlikely choice, Andrew thought, given their rather recent chastisement by Father Luke for questionable conduct. He could not help but wonder if Father Gerald was responsible for allowing the both of them to spend more time together—a conclusion which seemed to be valid, yet the real question for Andrew remained: why was he doing this?

He glanced at his watch, knowing that he needed to prepare for lunch. Vegetables would have to be washed, chopped, or peeled for a Minestra—a Spanish vegetable stew which was spiced with paprika and seasoned with sherry. He would top the stew with chopped olives and wedges of hard-boiled egg and serve with a plentiful supply of garlic bread.

The recipe called for frozen peas to be added a short time before serving. He checked the freezers in the kitchen, searched under frosty boxes of frozen berries, cauliflower, waffles, and English muffins; however, the peas were nowhere to be found. He then remembered that extra supplies were stored in the large freezers in the subcloister, next to the wine cabinets. He found the appropriate key that unlocked the cabinets and hurried to the basement.

Taking a shortcut, out the back door, down the steps, and through the boot room, meant he would have to pass through the main lavatory. As he walked in front of the area where the toilets were located, he noticed a familiar sandal and barefoot sticking out from under the privacy curtain, which had been haphazardly closed. Andrew's soft-sole shoes were virtually silent against the tile floor, which may have helped to explain the event. As he approached the occupied stall, he noticed that the curtain was not quite closed, yet there was sufficient light to illuminate the occupant who, while sitting, had leaned back against the far wall and was forcefully masturbating. His head was stretched back and his eyes were closed.

Obviously distracted, Andrew stopped to watch, mesmerized by such a blatant display. Brother Joshua had his shirt unbuttoned, exposing a well-defined chest and abdomen which, within seconds, received the brunt of his discharge.

"Oh, shit!" Brother Joshua exclaimed, once he noticed Andrew watching him. He immediately bent forward and attempted to cover himself with his arms and hands.

Andrew looked around to see if anyone was approaching the area; however, satisfied that they were still alone, he reached inside the stall and gently lifted Brother Joshua's chin so that he could see his face. He then smiled genuinely at Brother Joshua's apprehensive large eyes.

"It's okay," he said quietly.

Almost immediately, the frightened face softened into a still-embarrassed half smile.

Andrew reached up, closed the curtain completely, and walked away.

The low freezers sat end to end like porcelain coffins, yet Andrew had used them so infrequently, he could not remember which freezer contained frozen the vegetables. He lifted the cover of the freezer directly in front of him, and with help from the automatic lights, he quickly began his search. It was ironic, he thought, that Brother Adrian, who was so meticulous to label and date frozen packages, neglected to list those items on the outside of the door. He carefully lifted foil-wrapped containers, plastic freezer bags, and grocery store goods; but he still could not find peas. 'Must be in the other freezer,' he said to himself. Just as he was about to drop the cover, he noticed two large round tubs covered with frost. They appeared to be five-gallon ice cream containers, but Andrew could not recall the monastery buying it in such bulk. He scraped the frost from the top of the closest container which read, "Häagen-Dazs ice cream—Rum Raisin." With more scraping, he read the second, which was also "Häagen-Dazs—Butter Pecan."

He slammed the door shut with a hollow thud and stared angrily at the tile wall. "Why!" he said loudly, as he punched the top of the freezer. "Why!" Once again, he felt confronted or, perhaps betrayed, by the ironies of the monastic community not abiding by their written principles, specifically, the rule of poverty and the good intention to live a simple life. He had seen plenty of ice cream in the house; in fact, most of the monks were very fond of it. Yet it was always a local quality brand and certainly much cheaper than Häagen-Dazs, and the fact that it was a five-gallon container seemed flagrantly imprudent.

He stood, leaning with both hands on top of the freezer—his head lowered below his shoulders.

"Is . . . everything all right?"

Andrew looked over his shoulder to see Brother Joshua, standing in back of him, nervously rubbing his hands together. He turned to face him. "Everything's fine," he said softly. "You just happened to catch me having a nervous breakdown."

Brother Joshua's consternation was obvious. "You mean because . . ." He turned slightly and gestured toward the lavatory.

Andrew laughed. "I'm sorry, but no. Not because of that. I can't seem to find the peas I need for lunch."

Brother Joshua looked relieved. "I'd be happy to help you look," he said honestly.

"Thanks, but I'm sure they're in the other freezer."

Brother Joshua remained motionless as though anticipating further discourse. Standing there in jeans, a checkered shirt, and his famous sandals, he struck Andrew as overtly handsome and physically solid. Andrew dared, once more, to glance at his feet.

"I owe you an apology," Andrew admitted. "This morning, I *was* staring at your feet and I'm sorry. It's not something I normally do. I guess I had never seen such perfectly formed feet before." He rubbed his eyes. "I hope you don't think I'm too weird."

"Not at all," Brother Joshua said. This time, his smile was more obvious. "It's a nice compliment, but quite frankly, I think we both know that I should be apologizing to you for my . . . out-of-control behavior back there. I'm embarrassed, and I'm very sorry."

Andrew could see that he was, in fact, red-faced and edgy. "Relax, monks are human too," Andrew said. He reached out and momentarily squeezed his shoulder as a gesture of acceptance.

"Thanks," Brother Joshua said.

"Well, I'd better get cooking or you won't have anything to eat for lunch." Andrew lifted the cover of the second freezer as Brother Joshua walked down the subcloister. He turned to watch and then suddenly called out to him. "Brother Joshua?"

He stopped and turned. "Yes?"

"Next time . . . close the curtain."

Brother Joshua laughed freely, shrugged his shoulders and continued on his way.

By midmorning, Andrew had already peeled the necessary vegetables, chopped them, and had them ready to simmer while he prepared his vegetable stock. Washed potato peels had been stored in water in the large walk-in cooler, along with broccoli stems, cauliflower, and celery. Andrew boiled the stock, added onions, carrots and seasoning until it was ready to be strained. He then added the fresh vegetables to the stock and continued with the Minestra.

Although the discovery of the ice cream was upsetting, he forced himself to concentrate on the cooking, ignoring the occasional passerby outside the window until, looking at his watch, he realized that he was well ahead of schedule.

Unexpectedly Andrew found himself reaching for the bottle of sherry. He poured a small quantity into a juice glass, sipped it, and walked into the empty refectory, while the alcohol stung his throat and seemed to settle his stomach. The spaciousness of the vaulted room, with its high wide windows, unobstructed view of Navigator Peak, and copious amounts of sunlight, created an ambivalent feeling of living well—unencumbered and privileged. Nevertheless, without objection, he stood at the window, placed his glass on the sill, and marveled at the dramatic view.

Still draped in snow, Navigator Peak was a study in grey and white—the granite changed from light to dark as the sun and clouds shifted their position, highlighting the raised areas and coloring the rifts and valleys with a gunmetal shadow. Lowering his gaze, Andrew observed irregular patches of evergreens, below the tree line, sheathing the foothills with a greenish-black swatch, while thickets of pencil-thin aspens sat naked, anticipating new foliage. Closer to the foreground, the army green sage had already leafed out, clustered in haphazard clots and defined by a maze of reddish soil. Within his immediate view, he could see that the grass in the pastures and fields remained stubby and nearly colorless, eager for sunlight and water, as it struggled to flourish.

Andrew drained the contents of his glass. He wondered how many people would ever be fortunate enough to see, and perhaps, more importantly, to feel, what he was experiencing at that moment—the artistry of God displayed in such a pristine setting.

He returned to the kitchen and began his final preparations for lunch. He simmered the vegetables in the stew broth, adjusted the seasoning and cut large chunks of homemade bread for garlic toast. The crusty bread yielded easily to his sharp knife, which sliced through its doughy fragrant center. Andrew could not resist; he cut one of the chunks and popped it into his mouth.

"Ha ha!" Matthew said. "I caught you."

Surprised by the unexpected visit, Andrew was speechless. He pointed to his mouth and continued to chew, hoping that he could successfully compact the bread and swallow.

"That's all right," Matthew joked. "You don't have to say anything. We both know you are guilty."

Andrew smiled, looked in the direction of the refectory, and then tossed a chunk of bread at Matthew.

"H-m-m," Matthew said suspiciously, "bribery too." He took a large bite of the bread. "This is great."

Finally able to swallow, Andrew responded. "Don't get caught eating that," he said pretentiously. "Besides, what are you doing here?"

Matthew raised his eyebrows. "I live here, remember?"

"Yes," Andrew said quietly, " . . . and I'm glad."

Matthew continued to devour the bread, speaking between mouthfuls. "I just popped in to say that we are going shopping Monday, after your appointment at the hospital. Good news!"

"I know," Andrew said. "I think Father Gerald arranged it."

Matthew gestured with his hands, holding both palm up, and shrugging his shoulders. "Whatever."

The sound of the refectory door opening and slamming shut alerted Andrew. "Someone's coming," he whispered.

Matthew immediately turned and went out the back door. "Thanks for the bread," he said softly and then disappeared into the sunlight.

Andrew listened as the faint footsteps grew louder and entered the kitchen. "Smells great!" Brother Mark said, as he peeked into the pot. "What is it?"

Andrew looked up, surprised that Brother Mark did not recognize the soup. "Oh, just a Spanish vegetable stew, which translates into plain, old vegetable soup, with paprika and sherry, added for some pizzazz."

Brother Mark rolled his eyes. "You got my mouth watering."

Andrew laughed. "Let me know if you feel the same way after you eat it."

"I'm sure I will."

Andrew realized, especially then, that food played an extremely important role in the otherwise uneventful lives of his brothers. The Sunday lunches, generally prepared by Brother Adrian, were viewed as feasts, celebrated individually, and consumed in silence. Every flavorful odor emanating from the kitchen was personally analyzed, dissected, and categorized, until a reasonable conjecture about the final product could be determined with salivating anticipation.

"Actually," Andrew said, "you get the award. This bread is terrific."

"Thanks," Brother Mark said, "The French-Italian is my favorite." He lowered his voice. "But *somebody* prefers the cakey white bread, which we usually have at breakfast." He went into his Groucho mode. "You know what I mean, kid?"

Andrew shook his head. "Yes. I have a hard time eating that stuff."

"I don't eat it," Brother Mark said. "I only bake it."

"I'm dying for a good loaf of sourdough," Andrew reminisced.

"Another favorite" Brother Mark admitted.

"Did you ever make it?"

"Once," Brother Mark said. "One of the neighbors brought over some starter dough and it turned out fantastic but, once again, *somebody* wasn't crazy about it."

"That's too bad," Andrew said, "it would be great to have some here."

Brother Mark walked over to the sink and stared out the window.

Andrew looked up to see if there might be something in particular which caught his attention, however, everything looked the same—no visitors, animals, or unusual weather. "Is everything all right?" he asked. "You look suddenly . . . absorbed."

Brother Mark spoke to the window. "Just thinking," he said quietly. "I've had a lot on my mind, but I'm sure I'll survive." He turned to face Andrew. "How about you? How are you doing?"

Andrew continued slicing the bread. "Oh . . . I have my good days and not so good days, but I think I'm doing okay. I'll let you know after the results of my tests on Monday."

"Are you going to the hospital in Elkridge?"

"Just for a quick test. Father Gerald said it shouldn't take too long."

"It will be good to get checked out."

"Yeah. We're going to do the shopping afterwards," Andrew said. He scooped the bread chunks into a stainless bowl.

"Is Brother Nathan driving you?" Br. Mark queried.

Andrew hesitated. "No . . . Father Gerald suggested that Brother Matthew would come with me." He moved the bowl to the counter near the stove so that he would not have to face Brother Mark.

"Oh . . ." Brother Mark moved away from the window. "Well, I'd better get out of here so you can continue with lunch. Do you need any help?"

Andrew smiled. "I think I have everything under control, but thanks for asking."

Just minutes before noon, Andrew added the frozen peas and a generous splash of sherry to the Minestra. The hard-boiled eggs had been quartered and placed on the serving table in the refectory along with sliced olives, which could be used as a topping. He pulled the garlic bread out of the oven as Father Jude intoned the blessing, and then he quietly dumped the bread into a stainless steel square pan which had been lined with cloth napkins. He waited until the prayers had finished and quickly placed the bread pan into an empty space on the steam table next to the soup.

According to protocol, Father Jude initiated the self-served meal while the remainder of the community followed. Once the line diminished, Andrew joined Brother Edward, who was nearly always the last one to eat, since he would enter the kitchen, select twelve to fifteen vitamin supplements and place them on his tray, before returning to the refectory and joining the others. Andrew watched as some of the colorful pills rolled around and under his plate.

With his bowl filled, two pieces of garlic bread, and a glass of Chablis on his own tray, Andrew settled at an empty seat near the door which, to his surprise, suddenly opened.

Obviously in a hurry, Brother Joshua entered and quietly closed the door. He then proceeded to the serving table to get his food.

Andrew sipped his wine, tasted his soup, and secretly decided that it was nearly perfect. He glanced around the room and observed only bowed heads, contentedly devouring their meals, while others, who had already finished, were waiting to see if the abbot would be the first to return to the table for seconds. From the corner of his eye, Andrew did, in fact, see Father Jude get up and serve himself more soup. At the same time, he suddenly heard and then saw someone sit down next to him. He looked to his right and recognized Brother Joshua, who acknowledged him with a cursory smile.

Andrew abandoned himself to the sensual flavors and textures of the food while he listened to Brother Nathan, high in the pulpit, read a tract from the Zen master, Roshi Maezumi:

> *"One of Buddha's central teachings is that everything is impermanent, that everything is in a constant process of change. In a way, this is obvious even to the rational mind. Observing the mind, we see that thoughts and feelings come and go and, observing the body, we see constant change. The earth itself and the whole universe are the same—constantly in flux. Even though we know that nothing is permanent, we seldom live in accord with that understanding. Instead, we cling to our ideas or our possessions or our relationships or whatever, not content with allowing things or people to just be, we attempt to control, dominate and possess them. Everything changes and yet, trying to prevent things from changing, we cause ourselves and others suffering."*

When the abbot rang the bell, the community stood, joined in the prayers of thanksgiving and proceeded to participate in the cleanup. Since Andrew had done the cooking, he was excused from dishwashing and other kitchen duties, which he generally enjoyed.

He exited out the back door into the warmth and brightness of an early spring day. Although he was somewhat tired from the stress of preparing a meal for the entire community, he felt suddenly energized in the sunlight and in the mood for a brisk walk up the main road. As he turned the corner of the monastery to walk down the front steps, he nearly collided with Brother Joshua, who had left the building through the front entrance room.

"The meal was delicious!" Brother Joshua said with a smile. He was much more relaxed than he had been earlier that morning.

"Thanks," Andrew replied. "I've made it before, and it seems to go over pretty well with the brothers."

Brother Joshua accompanied Andrew down the steps to the driveway. "I guess you're not taking the usual noonday nap," he said.

"I thought about it, but when I walked outside, I decided it's too nice a day to sleep through."

"You're right. Springtime at this altitude is incredibly beautiful."

Andrew could not help glancing down at Brother Joshua's feet, which were barely covered by his sandals. "So are you here on retreat or just a brief visit?"

"A one-week retreat," Brother Joshua explained. "I've been having difficulty with my community in Kentucky, and they decided I should try a smaller, less structured house."

Andrew was surprised by his candor; he decided to be careful about being too intrusive. "How long have you been at the Abbey in Kentucky?"

"Just about two years," Brother Joshua said. "My prior felt I might to do better with fewer brothers to deal with. He was concerned that I had developed too close a relationship with one of the novices."

'What a coincidence,' Andrew thought; he saw red flags go up, all over, in his mind. He wondered if there was anything Brother Joshua would *not* talk about. Andrew was unsure of how to respond without encouraging more specifics. "I guess there's no such thing as the perfect house although, except for a few glitches here and there, I have to say, I really love this community."

Brother Joshua looked at him and smiled. "That's great," he said, "because I can sense the good feelings." He picked up a small stone and threw it into the pasture. "I'm thinking about asking for a change of stability—a transfer to this community—but I'm not sure if it will be granted; how do you feel about that?"

Andrew sensed the inappropriateness of the question, since they both knew it had nothing to do with the personal response of another novice. He was sure Brother Joshua was searching for affirmation of their limited friendship, and he felt threatened by the request. "That's a tough one," Andrew said with exasperation. "I think you have to be really positive of your choice first and then abide by the decision of your novice master or prior." He felt quite certain that he had disentangled himself from Brother Joshua's probing.

"I understand that," Brother Joshua said. "I guess I want to know how *you* would feel about my being here."

"Oh," Andrew said, as he tried to think of an appropriate response. He remained silent—at a loss for words, and continued his walk, hoping Brother Joshua would correctly interpret his noncommittal remark.

Brother Joshua stopped walking. "Well?" he said.

Andrew was troubled by his persistence; he turned to face him. "I think it would be fine, but don't let one man's opinion sway your decision; it's too important. Besides, I hardly know you."

"That's funny," Brother Joshua said without smiling. "I feel like I've known you for a long time."

'The statement was obvious,' Andrew thought. Whatever his motivation was, genuine or not, he knew Brother Joshua was signaling his intentions, which made him feel mildly flattered and yet uncomfortable. "Well, I appreciate that," he said honestly, "but I feel like I have a sign on my back."

"What do you mean?"

"You know—a sign . . . something like 'available.'"

Brother Joshua laughed. "Well, are you?" he asked blatantly.

Andrew looked directly at him, with barely a hint of a smile. "Somebody else might have been seriously offended by that question. The answer is no, but thanks for asking." He walked a bit farther and stopped. "Now, I'd like to ask you a question."

"Go ahead," Brother Joshua said. He jammed both hands in the pockets of his jeans and straightened his posture, which made him appear even taller and intentionally assertive.

"Like I said," Andrew continued calmly. "I hardly know you, but from what you've told me, why would you consider leaving one community, for the reasons you've mentioned, particularly the one about a close friendship with one of the novices, and openly signal your intentions to a Brother of the community you wish to join?"

Brother Joshua seemed to hesitate, which surprised Andrew. "I don't know," he said honestly. "Maybe I'm looking for some positive support from this end."

"Well," Andrew said, laughing. "You've come to the wrong guy. Like you, I'm only a novice and I have no real voice or vote in those matters."

"That's okay," Brother Joshua said. "At least you've gotten to know me, somewhat."

Andrew squinted. "Somewhat," he said. "I know that you have—what . . . nice feet?"

Brother Joshua raised one eyebrow. "That's not the only thing you've seen," he said, feigning offense.

Andrew threw his hands into the air. "Okay, I suppose that's nice too," he said, as he turned to continue his walk, "but this conversation is getting way out of hand."

Brother Joshua immediately caught up with him. "You're right," he said. "And I apologize for making you uncomfortable."

Once again, Andrew stopped walking. "I can deal with the content of the discussion—that's not a problem. The problem is your presentation and apparent assumption of who I am, and, perhaps, your disregard of place and purpose." He rubbed his eyes and exhaled. "Look . . . do you need to hear me say 'I like you,' because, if that's the case, it's true. You seem like a nice person. But please, don't base your vocation, and the need to transfer from your community in Kentucky to this one, on our brief conversation this afternoon. It's a decision much larger than that."

Brother Joshua was silent. He turned slightly, perhaps staring at Navigator Peak.

Andrew watched the muscles in his jaw contract and release as he squinted off in the distance.

"I guess I need to hear these things," he said, still facing away from Andrew. "There comes a time when I have to stop being a jerk."

Andrew grabbed his arm and gently turned him toward him. "We're all jerks, at one time or another, so don't let it bother you. You have a good opportunity this week, on retreat, to sort through some of the things you need to figure out—what's really important to you and what isn't. Hopefully, we'll have a chance to talk again before you leave."

"Thanks, Andrew, for being honest with me." He turned and walked briskly toward the small retreat house, while Andrew continued up the road.

Moments later, Andrew turned to see if Brother Joshua had gone inside; however, instead of doing so, he remained, standing on the porch, looking in Andrew's direction. When he saw Andrew looked back, he waved tentatively, as if in slow motion, a gesture which evoked in Andrew a sense of unexplained pathos. Andrew cheerfully waved back, first with one hand and then with both, hoping to brighten the spirits of what he felt characterized a confused, yet beautiful, young man.

By the time he reached the outbuildings near the main guesthouse, Andrew could feel his head began to clear in the spring air. When he turned the corner to approach the main road, he noticed the abbot's Peugeot parked next to the barn where a small single occupancy guest apartment had been built for retreatants. It was usually occupied by women—located quite far from the monastery and, since the women were not allowed to eat with the monks in the refectory, it was equipped with a small functional kitchen, bathroom, and comfortable bedroom.

Just as he was about to continue, he suddenly saw the abbot exit the building with Ellen, who was engaged in conversation with him. Andrew quickly stepped back behind the wooden shed and waited for them to leave. He watched as Father Jude opened the passenger side door and closed it, after Ellen got into the vehicle. He got into the car, and they drove off down the main road.

Recalling previous incidents which involved the abbot, Andrew sensed an ominous pall settle over him. 'It could be perfectly innocent,' he thought, 'and yes, it's none of my business.'

He continued to the main road and purposely walked on it, in a circle, as if by doing so, he had defied the enclosure rules and might be instantly killed by a bolt of lightning, yet the only thing he felt was the welcomed warmth from the sun. He smiled at the fiery ball and said "thank you," from the middle of the road, before reluctantly beginning his journey back to the monastery.

* * *

Chapter Twelve

The Confession

Andrew spent the remainder of the afternoon collecting eggs with Brother Mark. It was the first time he had returned to the eggery since he found the body hanging in the washroom—a sight which was indelibly engraved in his memory. Even though he needed to urinate, Andrew refrained until he was able to use the bushes across the road from the main building.

"You haven't been down here in quite a while," Brother Mark said cautiously, as he attempted to gauge Andrew's feelings about visiting the scene of the tragedy.

"First time," Andrew said, through his face mask. He then added, "since John died." He collected the eggs from the upper trough while Brother Mark, who was considerably shorter than Andrew, collected from the lower trough.

"Are you doing all right, now that you're back?" he asked.

"I think so," Andrew replied. "I'm glad I'm not alone, at least for now . . . and it may take some time before I can use the bathroom."

"I would say so," Brother Mark concurred.

Two jellied eggs, without shells, were lodged just above the trough inside the cage. As Andrew attempted to retrieve them, one of the hens pecked relentlessly at his hand until he was able to free both eggs. He then discarded them into the bucket attached to the cart, along with other cracked or unacceptable eggs.

"A protective mother," Andrew said, checking to see if his skin had been broken.

"Did she peck you?"

"More than once but she didn't go through the skin."

"I hate when that happens," Brother Mark joked.

They collected eggs in silence for the next twenty minutes, not only because of their vows, but also due to the difficulty of hearing each other above the din of the exhaust fans and the cackling of the hens. Andrew also felt it was somewhat healthier to have his mouth closed to avoid breathing excess chicken dander that clogged the air.

Once the eggs were stacked in the walk-in cooler, they locked the outside door of the eggery and began walking back to the monastery.

Andrew decided that it might be a good opportunity to confront Brother Mark. "Can I ask you something?" he ventured.

"Sure, what is it?"

"Well," Andrew began, with mild trepidation. "It seems as though things have changed between us, ever since that night at the Cole cabin, when Matthew was there with me. You seem . . . less friendly."

Brother Mark had not anticipated the question. He looked off in the distance as if struggling with a response. "You want the truth?" he asked bluntly.

Andrew nodded.

"Okay," Brother Mark said. "I've thought about this a lot and I'm hoping that what I say will be kept between us."

Again, Andrew nodded, not knowing what to expect.

Brother Mark stopped walking and faced Andrew. "I think I was jealous and, perhaps, still am," he said honestly. "I've never been good at hiding my feelings."

Andrew was completely stunned by his admission. He rubbed his eyes and looked at Brother Mark. "Jealous over what—our friendship?" Andrew asked.

"That and more. I feel that you and Matthew are . . . very close."

Andrew could feel his defenses kick in. "We are close, but that doesn't mean it's physical."

"That doesn't matter to me," Brother Mark said mournfully.

"Well it seems to matter to everyone else," Andrew retaliated.

"I know; but I don't care," Brother Mark admitted. "I guess not having a close friend makes me envious of the both of you, and I guess it shows. I'm sorry." He dropped his gaze to the gravel road.

"I had no idea you felt that way," Andrew said, nearly awed by Brother Mark's openness.

"And why should you? At least now you know that my needs may not be all that different from yours or Matthew's, yet I had hoped that my vocation would have helped me transcend those feelings, but my individual needs are far from being extinguished." He looked directly at Andrew. "I shouldn't be taking it out on you or Matthew; it's just that, when I see the two of you—together, those feelings tend to surface. It's my problem, not yours, and I'll have to deal with it."

"I don't know what to say other than I really appreciate your honesty," Andrew said. He placed his hand on Brother Mark's shoulder. "And . . . I still want you to be my friend."

"Thanks," Brother Mark said with a smile. "I'm glad I got this off my chest."

* * *

With the advent of spring, the daylight hours grew longer making it increasingly more difficult for Andrew to fall asleep before dark. Still in his habit, he decided to visit the library to review the magazine selection, which was usually current. Except for one lamp illuminating the middle of a large mahogany table, the room was dark and empty.

Andrew selected the latest copy of Newsweek and sat within the lamp's glow. As he scanned various articles, he sensed that very little in the world had changed for the better—man continued to kill his fellow man in the name of politics or, even more sadly, in the name of religion. When he reached the last page of the magazine, he felt sufficiently depressed and very much alone. Outside, dusk had turned to dark, enough for Andrew to see his reflection in the murky glass. He left the library and walked toward his cell through the echoing desolate cloister.

Once inside, Andrew turned on the light in his closet and removed his habit.

"Where have you been?" Brother Matthew said softly.

Just as before, Andrew stood, frozen with terror, as sharp white lights seemed to explode behind his eyes. He turned slowly and saw Brother

Matthew in his bed, under the covers, lying on his side, with his head propped up by his arm.

"Are you trying to kill me?" Andrew whispered. "Because, if you are, you're doing a good job."

"I'm sorry," Matthew insisted. "I didn't intend to scare you. I thought you'd be here before it got dark." He pointed toward the door.

Andrew could see that his arms and chest were bare.

"Lock the door, please" Matthew whispered.

"What?"

"Just in case . . ."

Andrew obliged by shoving in the button on the doorknob, which made a barely audible click. He suddenly realized his compliance—a simple yet definitive act, which instilled excitement with disobedience. 'I must be crazy,' he thought.

"And the light," Matthew added softly.

Andrew turned out the light, pulled his desk chair to the side of the bed and sat down. Once his eyes adjusted to the dark, he could see Matthew, bathed in the green glow from his alarm clock—his hair nearly incandescent. "You look like a Martian," Andrew whispered.

Matthew leaned forward and put his hand on Andrew's knee. "Maybe I am," he said suggestively. "I came to earth to eat you up."

Andrew smiled and put his hand on Matthew's. "Why do I have the strange impression that you are naked?"

"Well, why don't you get under the covers with me and find out?" He then added a familiar disconcerting phrase. "You know you want to."

Andrew rubbed his eyes and sat back in the chair. "Even if it's true—why do you have to say that, Matt? You know it bothers me."

Matthew sat up. "Okay, I'm sorry. I forgot," he said apologetically. "Leave it to me to screw things up." In the inky light, Andrew watched as shadowy footsteps quickly passed his cell, darkening the small space between the bottom of the door in the carpet.

"It's all right," Andrew said. "I'm glad you're here . . . But it's making me anxious. Aren't you nervous about being here?"

Matthew nonchalantly lay back. "Not really. I'm just happy to be with you."

"What if someone comes looking for you?"

"They won't, so relax." He sat up and placed both arms on Andrew's knees. "Look, I just want to hold you, and hopefully, spend the night with you. There's plenty of room; and I promise, I'll let you sleep—as long as I can watch you and be with you." He put his arms around Andrew's waist and rested his head on his knees.

Finding him impossible to resist, Andrew gently ran his fingers through Matthew's hair, massaging his scalp with increasing pressure as he explored the bony structure and shape of his head.

Matthew hugged him tighter. "That feels so good, I could fall asleep right here," he said softly.

"Well then . . . let's," Andrew responded. He made an effort to get up as Matthew lifted his head and lay back on the pillow.

Matthew watched as Andrew removed his clothes, except for his shorts, and quickly got into bed with him.

Lying on his side, facing Matthew, Andrew slowly moved his hand over Matthew's back, down the arched area of his lower spine and then gently over his bare buttocks. He was not surprised; in fact, he knew that he would have been somewhat disappointed had Matthew been wearing shorts. "You're so predictable," he whispered, as he kissed Matthew's forehead and nose.

Matthew raised his head to look at him. "Yes, I know but . . . you like that in a man," he replied confidently. He then placed his mouth against Andrew's and kissed him, welcoming the familiar wet warmth.

"You don't really need these," Matthew insisted, as he slid his hand between Andrew's buttocks and shorts and forced them down to his knees.

Andrew assisted by removing them completely and tossing them on the chair.

"No, wait," Matthew said. "Give them to me."

"What?"

"Your shorts . . . let me have them."

Andrew reached in back of him and handed his shorts to Matthew, who immediately buried them in his face.

"You really are insane," Andrew said seriously, somewhat embarrassed by his behavior.

"Probably," Matthew replied, "but what's more honest than me doing this in front of you . . . something I think about when I'm alone. Besides, you have a woodsy, earthy scent which, when combined with a slight odor of urine, is incredibly sexy. Try it." He held the shorts close to Andrew's face.

Andrew quickly grabbed the shorts and threw them across the room. "Some other time," he said.

Matthew raised his head and supported it with his hand and elbow. "Don't be mad over something so simple."

"Simple?" Andrew said.

"Yes. Scents are important to me. You have a signature scent which drives me crazy and makes me want you even more. I wasn't trying to embarrass you."

In an effort to deflate the discussion, Andrew conceded. "Okay. I understand."

"You do?"

"Yes . . . Now maybe we should go to sleep."

Matthew straightened his arm and crashed into the mattress. He rolled on his side and faced the wall, with his back toward Andrew.

His childlike response caused Andrew to smile. He curled up alongside of Matthew, placed his arm around him and whispered into his ear. "How could I not be in love with you? You smell like fresh-cut, August hay."

Matthew slowly turned his head toward Andrew. His smile said it all, yet before he turned away, he jokingly added, "Don't bother me—I'm trying to sleep."

Lying together in the darkness, they both found the Grand Silence to be unusually clamorous as their heightened sensitivity caused them to be aware of even the slightest noise. When the door to Brother Edward's adjacent cell opened and closed, they anticipated his staccato flatulence and began laughing in advance of the actual event; however, much to their surprise they heard nothing.

"He must have swallowed some Tums," Matthew whispered.

He barely finished the sentence when Brother Edward cooperated by releasing, what sounded like, a symphony of multirange methane, complete with piccolos and kettle drums. Andrew could feel Matthew's body convulse with stifled laughter, which eventually broke through in a high-pitched wheeze. Barely under control himself, he pulled the pillow out from under their heads and jammed it into Matthew's face, while he buried his own face in the mattress. Although it was difficult to talk, Andrew somehow managed to whisper, "I'll bet you'd . . . like his shorts!"

At that point, Matthew was beyond control as he bolted upright and then doubled over with laughter.

The movement caused Andrew to fall out of the small bed, knock over his chair and end up sprawled on his back, naked, in the middle of the floor.

Hearing the thud and seeing Andrew fall, Matthew was riddled with sobriety. He leaned over the side of the bed and looked down. "Are you okay?" he asked anxiously.

Andrew smiled. "No," he said calmly. "I'm lonely."

In a second, Matthew was on the floor. He reached up, pulled the blanket off the bed and covered them both.

"Don't forget the pillow," Andrew insisted.

Matthew tucked the pillow under Andrew's head, snuggled alongside of him and placed one leg over his thigh. "I guess we're through laughing," he said, as he nuzzled Andrew's ear.

"I guess . . .," Andrew said. He turned to face him. "I'm really glad you're here."

Matthew grinned. "I hope you always feel that way."

Once again, in the darkness, Andrew watched as shadowy footsteps passed his door, hoping they would not stop, and fearing the sound of the quiet knock. Yet with Matthew firmly next to him, he felt insulated from any imminent danger, as if wearing a suit of armor. What could really matter, he thought, when the one he loved had him snuggly pinned to the earth's surface, as the planet glided imperceptibly through the cosmos.

"I feel like I can't get enough of you," Matthew said, as he moved even closer, inhaling Andrew's hair and tenderly biting his earlobe.

"Yeah?" Andrew said wryly, as he turned to face him. He briefly resorted to mimicry. "I hope you always feel that way." He smiled and lightly kissed Matthew's forehead.

"I meant what I said, about staying the night with you . . . if it's okay."

"I want you to," Andrew whispered, "as long as we can get some sleep."

"I promise," Matthew said with a smile. He immediately jumped up and began to arrange the bedding.

* * *

It was nearly 2:00 a.m. when Andrew awoke and looked at the alarm clock. Curled comfortably against Matthew's back, he was surprised he slept as long and as soundly as he did, anticipating, instead, a night of tossing and turning, generated by an overriding physical desire as a result of Matthew's naked presence. He carefully raised himself on one elbow, listened and watched, as Matthew continued to sleep deeply and produce barely audible hissing sounds when exhaling. As in the past, Andrew was struck by Matthew's physical beauty—the strong well-shaped nose, the characteristic high cheekbones, even the elegance of his ears were vivid testimony of a skilled sculptor. Feeling overwhelmed, Andrew carefully bent over him and kissed him gently on the cheek, hoping not to disturb him.

Without opening his eyes and clearly still not awake, Matthew pulled Andrew's arm even tighter around him and spoke in a faint whisper. "I love you, Andy," he said and then resumed his breathy aspirations.

Andrew smiled and realized it was the first time Matthew had ever used his nickname—the abbreviated form—which he was not particularly fond of, yet when spoken so innocently by this caring partner, lying beside him, the sound of the word evoked an acceptable intimacy and sharing of two souls, united as one.

Although the alarm clock was set to go off at 2:30 a.m., Andrew made no attempt to sleep for the half hour that remained. He knew Brother Edward would rise at two forty-five, walk the halls of the dormitory, with his clanging bell, and wake the sleepy monks fifteen minutes before the start of vigils. He settled back and curled himself securely against Matthew who, even in deep sleep, seemed to welcome the embrace. In the silence, Andrew buried his face in his nape, tasted his slightly salty skin, and secretly wished Matthew were fully awake, knowing, to the contrary, it was his idea they be allowed to sleep. Fighting desire, he lowered his head to the pillow and took several deep breaths; yet within minutes, he found his hands gently caressing Matthew's chest and thighs, as his erection swelled against his buttocks.

"I hope that you'll always care about me," Andrew said unexpectedly, with closed eyes.

In the darkness, Matthew raised his head, as he attempted to look at Andrew. Unsuccessful in making eye contact, he rolled his back against the wall and faced him. "No matter what happens, I'll always care about you . . . always love you . . . no matter what," Matthew whispered. He put his arms around Andrew and hugged him.

The powerful sense of promised sanctuary caused Andrew to shudder and stiffen, as he buried his face between Matthew's neck and shoulder. Sensing the wetness beneath his hip, Andrew grappled in the dark for the towel. "I guess I wasn't the only one who got excited," he said as he wiped Matthew's discharge off the sheet.

"What did you expect?" Matthew quipped. "You were very close to fulfilling one of my greatest desires."

"And what's that?" Andrew asked as he lay down beside him.

"You want me to say it?"

"Yes."

"I wish you were inside of me—letting me feel you within me," Matthew said softly. "Don't you think about that sometimes?"

"Come on, Matt," Andrew said. "Of course I do, but please . . . let's not talk about it right now. Besides, we had better get you back to your room before Brother Edward rings his bell . . . I hate to see you leave."

"I know," Matthew said. "Me too." He sat up, swung his legs over the edge of the mattress, and began searching for his clothes.

When Matthew was completely dressed, Andrew unlocked the door and nervously looked for early risers. "It's clear," he whispered.

Matthew quickly brushed by him, stopped, grasped Andrew with his famous bear hug, and then hurried down the hallway.

* * *

Chapter Thirteen

The Red Baron

The morning dawned with crystal clarity and a characteristic Alpine chill as Andrew waited in the kitchen for Matthew to accompany him on the shopping trip, while he went to the hospital for his scheduled examination. He leaned against the counter, sipped his coffee, and watched as several monks emerged from the boot room wearing irrigation gear, primarily hip-length waders, and caring shovels—all except for Brother Morgan who, in addition to the usual apparatus, also wore a dilapidated leather aviation cap, complete with attached earmuffs, which he had pulled down and secured with a neck strap. Andrew was instantly overcome with laughter as he struggled to open the window.

"Are you dueling with the Red Baron this morning?" he asked between giggles.

"Haven't you heard?" Brother Morgan said seriously, with a failed attempt to mimic a German accent; he pretended to adjust his monocle. "I shot him down last week." He pressed his face against the screen and whispered. "Now, I'm going after the devil himself." He paused and then quickly saluted and walked stiffly toward his dirt bike. Once he had secured his shovel above the muffler, Brother Morgan stomped on the kick starter, which caused the engine to roar. He adjusted his sunglasses, put the bike in gear and, just before he drove away, he turned to look at Andrew and flashed him a "thumbs-up" sign.

Andrew smiled, returned the same sign and mouthed the words "good luck." He watched as Brother Morgan disappeared around the curved road, followed by a faint trail of red dust.

"Sorry I'm late," Matthew said, suddenly appearing in the kitchen and startling Andrew. "Brother Nathan asked me to pick up a few things for the infirmary. He gave me a list."

"We've got plenty of time," Andrew replied. He returned his gaze to the dissipating dust trail left by Brother Morgan's dirt bike.

Aware of Andrew's brooding mood, Matthew stood next to him and looked out the window to see what, if anything, caused him to be so absorbed; however, nothing struck him as different or extraordinary. He glanced at Andrew. "Are you okay?" he asked quietly.

Andrew rinsed his cup and left it in the sink. "I don't know," he said unexpectedly. "I just spoke with Brother Morgan, who was wearing his crazy pilot's hat, and we joked a bit about a fake air combat . . ." He put the keys to the van in his pocket.

"And . . . ?" Matthew asked.

"You know how he is always kidding around; he said something about going after the devil. He drove off on his dirt bike just before you came in, and . . . I can't explain it but I feel . . . uneasy."

Matthew ran his fingers over Andrew's forearm. "You've got goose bumps."

Andrew pulled the sleeves of his jersey down to his wrists and put on his jacket. "Well, we better get going."

"You sure you're all right?"

"I'm fine," Andrew smiled. "Let's go before they change their minds and keep us here."

With Andrew at the wheel and Matthew strapped comfortably into the bucket style passenger seat, the van exited the enclosure and began its hour journey, down from the high country to the valley city of Elkridge. Sun glinted from every reflective surface as they drove through a flawless spring day, past rambling ranches, extravagant homes—some allegedly owned by well-known celebrities—and scenic areas fit for postcards and landscape artists.

"Why do I suddenly feel as though someone removed my shackles?" Andrew said with a huge grin.

"I feel the same way," Matthew replied. "Should we just keep on driving?"

"Yeah, right," Andrew quipped. "Don't tempt me at a time like this—I could be easily persuaded."

"Oh yeah? Well, we could always pull off the road onto one of these side roads," Matthew said seductively.

Andrew laughed. "I love . . ."

"When you talk dirty," Matthew mimicked, chiming in on the second part of the sentence.

As they continued to lose altitude, the seasonal changes became readily apparent—lawns were not only green, but were already mowed or being mowed as they drove by. Patches of color appeared everywhere, as spring flowers bloomed obediently in the bright sun.

Matthew rolled down his window, and the van was soon filled with the warmth and aroma of the new season exploding around them.

"Can you believe the difference?" Matthew asked, energized by the sudden welcomed change.

"It's like night and day," Andrew said, as he reached for the radio knob, turned it on and heard only static. "Damn! They must have disconnected it so that we can't hear anything worldly."

"Never fear," Matthew said, reaching for his backpack. He pulled a cassette from a zippered pocket, removed the case, and fed the cassette into the player. Strains of Elton John singing "Bennie and the Jets" filled the hollow van with concertlike quality.

"I can't believe you brought a tape," Andrew said excitedly. "This is great!"

By the time they reached the hospital, Andrew and Matthew were singing "Goodbye Yellow Brick Road" for the third time. He drove up to the main entrance, set the emergency brake and exited the van with the engine running, as Matthew climbed over the console into the driver's seat.

"I should be through in about an hour. Pick me up in front, okay?"

"Yes, sir," Matthew said formally.

"Don't forget to go to the market—we'll shop for the other stuff after . . . and, Matt?"

"Yes?"

"Try to behave yourself."

"Always," Matthew quipped.

Andrew watched as Matthew drove slowly down the driveway and then stopped. He saw the white reverse lights go on, as Matthew began backing the vehicle toward him.

Andrew met him halfway and peered in from the passenger window. "What?"

Wearing a genuinely thoughtful expression, Matthew leaned over the console. "I nearly forgot to wish you well with your tests. Good luck."

"Thanks," Andrew said, attempting to hide his deep appreciation for a relatively simple gesture. "Now get out of here."

Except for bits of the electrode glue, stuck to his hair, Andrew emerged, relatively unscathed, nearly one hour later. He sat, cross-legged, on the thick grass, waiting for Matthew's return. He noticed a dandelion, leaned closer to inspect it and, without picking it, he realized that, for such an infamous weed, it was quite radiant, like a miniature mum, yet with such a bad reputation for its ability to take over a lawn. He thought, 'Somehow, they need to replace their flimsy, hollow stems with something more substantial.'

The sound of the van's horn startled Andrew from his preoccupation with the dandelion. He jumped up, got in and shut the door.

"So how did it go?" Matthew asked. He was halfway through an ice cream sandwich—the paper rolled back to his knuckles. He reached into his backpack and handed one to Andrew, who willingly accepted it.

"Basically painless other than for the electrodes that pinched my head."

Matthew reached over to remove some of the glue. "What the heck is this stuff?" he asked, wiping his hands on his pants.

"Glue; they said it would come out with shampoo." Andrew turned to look at several bags of groceries, which Matthew had placed near the rear door. "Did you get everything on the list?"

"I think so," Matthew said. "We just need to go to the plaza to get Brother Nathan's supplies from the pharmacy." He folded the empty ice cream wrapper and placed it in the ashtray before driving away.

"Do you remember how to get there?" Andrew asked.

Matthew continued to drive cautiously, yet confidently, through the steady stream of traffic. "Yup," he said, looking straight ahead. "I stayed in Elkridge for a few days, just before joining St. Anthony's."

"Trying to make up your mind before taking the fatal plunge?" Andrew teased.

"Probably," Matthew said. He looked at Andrew with a familiar smile. "But . . . I'm glad I joined."

Andrew laughed.

"I *am*," Matthew insisted. "What's so funny?"

"Nothing," Andrew said more seriously. "I'm glad you joined too." He looked out the window as everyday people bustled here and there, doing the necessary or expected within their secular world. "I just wish I could close my eyes sometimes, to things up there that bother me."

"At the monastery?" Matthew asked.

"Yes."

Matthew reached over and gently rubbed his knee. "Okay," he said. "What happened now?"

"I shouldn't start," Andrew said with a shrug. "It's too nice a day."

"The heck with that," Matthew said, matter-of-factly. "If you can't talk to me about things then . . . something isn't right."

Andrew was obviously hesitant to discuss it. "It's no big deal . . . well, maybe it is to me," he said. "When I was looking for some things in the freezer, I came across two five-gallon tubs of Häagen-Dazs ice cream, and it really bothered me. I just feel that, as monks, we seem to be living very well—what's wrong with the generic supermarket brand?"

Matthew pulled into the plaza parking lot near the pharmacy and shut off the engine. "I see what you mean," he said, genuinely, looking at Andrew. "I guess I never thought too much about it . . . and I should have. We could never afford that stuff when I was growing up, and now, I'm guilty of looking at it as a special treat."

"It has nothing to do with you, Matt—you know that," Andrew replied. "I think it's all about the abbot—his need to fulfill some unexplained deprivation."

Suddenly, Matthew became very animated. "That reminds me," he said excitedly. "The other day, I saw him in the kitchen, with a visitor, and they were both drinking bottles of Perrier water, which I also found in the trash, near his room—several empty bottles."

"You serious?" Andrew asked, wide-eyed.

"Yes . . . but maybe I shouldn't have told you."

Andrew shook his head. "Why not. It doesn't surprise me, but it does make me wonder what the hell is going on. I really hate to see those notes on the board, from families who are nearly starving and living in their cars, when we seem to be living like royalty."

"Not much makes sense right now . . . but things can change," Matthew offered.

"Yeah," Andrew scoffed. "When Father Jude leaves, or hell freezes over—whichever comes first." He got out of the van. "I'm sorry, Matt. Let's finish the shopping."

Once they were sure they had purchased every item on their lists, they began the trip, back up the mountain, to the place they called home—an austere allegedly celibate dwelling on the outside; yet like most families, the tensions of daily life and the disparate milieu of men living with men revealed an inside view symptomatic of the frailties of human nature.

"I guess nothing's perfect," Andrew said, half daydreaming, looking out the window, while Matthew navigated the sharp curves with precision.

"I can think of a couple of things that come close," Matthew joked.

"I'll bet you can," Andrew said. "Give me a hint."

"How about you . . . and the weather," Matthew challenged.

"I love that story," Andrew said, with an exaggerated grin. "How about you . . . and you."

"Or you and me."

"Or us."

Matthew suddenly hit the brakes and sharply turned the van into the crowded parking lot at the Skyline Haus restaurant. "How about you and me, and two cheeseburgers with fries?" he said, as he eased the van into a narrow parking space.

Andrew began to feel uneasy. "Do you think this is a good idea—being vegetarians, and eating in front of all these people? What if someone recognizes us?"

"We're human too," Matthew said, unapologetically. "And I'm dying for a charcoaled burger; besides, there's a takeout window, so we can eat in the van."

With some reluctance, Andrew got out of the vehicle and followed Matthew to the side of the restaurant where they waited with others to place their orders.

A young couple with two children stood in front of them. The younger boy clung to his father's neck, shyly staring, at first, and then smiling at Andrew and Matthew with greater boldness, as they continued to wait in line.

When he was sure that neither parent was looking, Andrew smiled back and made silly faces at the child. The red-haired youngster squirmed gleefully, until the father grew more and more inquisitive and turned around to determine the boy's excitement. He looked directly at Andrew, who acknowledged him with a smile.

"He looks like a handful," Andrew said casually, suddenly realizing that the father was not much older than he was.

"Terrible two's," he replied, "but I guess I'll keep him." He held the boy in front of him, lifted him up and let him drop quickly, but safely, to his chest. The child squealed with delight.

Armed with cheeseburgers, fries, and milkshakes, they made their way back to the van where they devoured the food like two ravaged desert dwellers who had not eaten in weeks.

"Now, *this* is heaven," Matthew said, halfway through his burger. "I think my body requires meat once in a while."

"You're right," Andrew admitted. "Doesn't it say somewhere that man cannot live by bread alone?"

"Somewhere," Matthew agreed, wiping ketchup from his face.

Thirty yards beyond the truck, past the budding cottonwoods, Little Crow Creek churned its way down river, roiling over submerged boulders, looking as pure and effervescent, in the bright sunlight, as the Perrier water, which Andrew tried to forget. In the trees, flashes of scarlet darted between branches as red-winged blackbirds made amorous attempts to secure suitable mates.

"Have you ever seen a prettier day?" Andrew said pensively, sucking his milkshake through a straw.

"Oh, I don't know," Matthew mused. "Truth is—I probably have . . . but I've never felt this good."

"What do you mean?" Andrew asked.

"You know . . . that you are with me—that we are together—and my life doesn't seem so . . . empty anymore."

"You really mean that, don't you," Andrew said, mildly shocked by Matthew's unsolicited admission and serious mood.

"Yeah, I do," Matthew said honestly.

Andrew reached over and gently squeezed his knee. "Thanks," he said.

Just as he said the word, Andrew noticed a blue Peugeot drive past the van and park in back of the restaurant. "Holy shit!" he said suddenly. "Let's get out of here—the abbot just drove in, and I think your sister is with him."

"Ellen?"

"Yes. Let's get out of here."

"Are you sure?" Matthew questioned.

"You drive—I'll look," Andrew insisted.

Matthew backed the van out of the lot and quickly turned onto the highway.

With his head stuck out of the window, Andrew watched as Father Jude and Ellen got out of the car and began walking toward the restaurant.

"You're right," Matthew said. "I saw them in the mirror."

"You were supposed to be driving," Andrew said.

"Well, I had to see for myself," Matthew replied. The edge in his voice was obvious.

After several miles of silence, Matthew finally spoke. "I can't figure her out; my family says she's seventeen—going on thirty."

"Well," Andrew offered, "she is one, beautiful woman."

"And she knows it," Matthew said, with a roll of his eyes.

Andrew recalled watching the abbot and Ellen leave her guest quarters in the barn, yet he was hesitant to share the information with Matthew, who was already angry over seeing them together at the restaurant. Without warning, the icy thought of Ellen, in his cell on Christmas Eve, caused him to flinch with sudden guilt for having to hide the unintended event from her brother. "You don't think . . ."

"I'd kill her," Matthew said without hesitation. "She's only seventeen and Father Jude is what . . . forty something? I guess I don't have a lot of respect for him, but he can't be *that* stupid." He looked at Andrew. "Could he?"

Andrew shrugged. "I doubt it but, then again, I'm not the best person to ask, since I share your point of view."

Hoping to relieve the tension and improve Matthew's mood, Andrew switched on the Elton John cassette. Before long, he could hear Matthew singing softly as the seasons, once again, began to change with the increase in altitude.

As they drove around the back of the monastery, Andrew paled. "Something's wrong," he said anxiously.

A sheriff's car sat, with flashing lights, near the rear entrance. In front of the car, a black coroner's hearse silently screamed death—its rear door partially open in anticipation of human cargo.

"What the hell happened," Matthew said with a mix of fear and wonder. He parked the van on the far side of the lot.

As they walked toward the monastery, they encountered two men pulling a gurney through the back door. A white sheet covered the body from head to toe, disguising its identity, yet Andrew was nearly certain that he recognized the draped profile.

"It's Brother Morgan, "he said. An icy quiver strained his voice and body; his feet felt as though they were suddenly made of lead. Involuntarily, as if in slow motion, Andrew reached out as the gurney passed him, pulled the sheet from the head of the body and glimpsed the ashen yet strangely contented face. Just before his world grew dark, prior to passing out, Andrew remembered seeing Brother Morgan's hair, matted with blood, and wondered what they did with his aviators cap.

* * *

The sterile whiteness of the infirmary appeared abrasively bright. 'Not again,' he thought, as he looked disparagingly around the room. In the far corner, he saw Father Gerald, sitting at his desk, writing quietly in a large ledger.

"I guess I did it again," Andrew said hoarsely, through a dry mouth.

Father Gerald immediately got up and came to his bedside. Before responding to Andrew, he pressed the buzzer above the bed to summon Brother Nathan, who appeared within a matter of seconds.

"Yes, you did," Father Gerald said, "except, this time, Brother Matthew caught you before you hit the ground." He put the stethoscope in his ears and placed the cold receiver against Andrew's chest. "Sounds okay, how are you feeling?"

"Tired . . . and thirsty," Andrew said.

Brother Nathan left his side and returned with a glass of water, which Andrew gratefully accepted.

"Thanks," he said, after drinking most of it without stopping.

Brother Nathan simply nodded affirmatively.

"I've given you a mild sedative to help take the edge off what happened today," Father Gerald explained. "Do you remember what you saw?"

Once again, as if in a dream, Andrew remembered seeing Brother Morgan's face and bloody hair. A wave of revulsion washed over him and then suddenly subsided. "Yes . . . I saw Brother Morgan on the gurney; his hair was soaked with blood. Is he dead?"

Father Gerald looked at Brother Nathan, who was ready to restrain Brother Andrew, if necessary. A prepared syringe sat uncovered on sterile gauze in the stainless tray near Father Gerald.

"I'm afraid he is," Father Gerald said softly, barely able to maintain his own composure.

Andrew felt a chill throughout his body; he began to shake visibly and his teeth began to chatter.

Brother Nathan rolled the blanket from the foot of the bed over Andrew, who continued to shake.

"I'm going to give you another light sedative."

"Before I fall asleep, please tell me what happened." He could already feel his words begin to slur.

"Maybe we should let you sleep first," Father Gerald said.

"No!" Andrew insisted through his dry cotton mouth. "Please, I want to know."

Father Gerald sighed. "As far as we know, it looks as though Brother Morgan hit some rocks up on the mesa, lost control of his dirt bike and hit his head, most likely, against one of the rocks. He landed with his face partially submerged in an irrigation ditch, and probably died from drowning."

The words "from drowning" echoed repeatedly in Andrew's head, bouncing like hollow sounds within a cavern, until they became more and more distant and then faded into complete silence.

* * *

Once he had recovered sufficiently to leave the infirmary, Andrew continued to be troubled by Brother Morgan's death. He felt as though Brother Morgan somehow knew his own destiny and needed to say something ironic, on that chilly Monday morning, as a way of saying goodbye.

Later that day, after supper, he walked with Matthew through the placid dusk of an otherwise flawless evening.

"It was just coincidence," Matthew insisted. "Brother Morgan's comments were almost always indecipherable. I could never tell if he was joking or being serious."

"I know," Andrew agreed. "But why did I get such a weird feeling when I saw him drive away?"

"Who knows; maybe you have some sort of clairvoyance within that wonderful head of yours."

Ordinarily, such a remark would have made Andrew laugh or, at least, put a smile on his lips, however, this time, he remained somber as they made their way past the small guesthouse. "What if I am?" Andrew said seriously.

"What . . . are clairvoyant?"

"What if?"

"I don't know," Matthew said. He stared at Navigator Peak in the distance, which glowed reddish orange from the setting sun. "The thought of it makes me uncomfortable."

"Me too," Andrew said.

"If you're clairvoyant, tell me what I'm going to do next," Matthew teased, yet before he had finished the sentence, Andrew knew for certain that Matthew would kiss him. He stopped and closed his eyes. "I don't know," he said, as Matthew leaned over and kissed him gently on the ear.

"See," Matthew said. "You're not clairvoyant so let's try to forget about it."

A shiver ran through Andrew's body. "Fine. Let's forget about it."

With a glance over Andrew's shoulder, Matthew noticed someone sitting on the porch of the guesthouse. "Oh, oh," he said quietly. "I think we've been observed."

"Where?"

"The porch at the guesthouse. Someone is sitting there."

Andrew turned slowly to see Brother Joshua—his feet on the porch railing—waving at him. Andrew smiled, waved back and continued walking at a brisk pace. "You're right. We've been observed a by an Observer, Brother Joshua."

"You know him?"

"Not biblically," Andrew retorted. "We met on the road one day and he practically told me his life story. He's interested in a change of stability—moving to St. Anthony's from another monastery."

"Is he that tall, nice-looking guy who sits next to you at mass?" Matthew asked.

"That's the one," Andrew said.

"H-m-m-m," Matthew joked. "Maybe I should let him know you're taken."

"I think you just did," Andrew said with a smile.

It was not long before resurgent thoughts of Brother Morgan flooded Andrew's head with sadness, confusion, and anger. "Why him?" he said out loud yet unintentionally.

Nevertheless, Matthew grasped his meaning immediately. "I don't know," he said, "but he seemed like a considerate, quiet person who basically had it together."

"Well, I'm not sure I'd go that far," Andrew commented. "I think he was struggling like the rest of us."

Matthew picked up a small stone and threw it at a telephone pole, missing it by several yards. "Maybe . . . but his struggle is definitely over."

"I know," Andrew said, fighting his emotions, "and I'm really going to miss him."

* * *

Father Luke's phone call cut through the heart of Brother Morgan's parents more deeply than they could have ever imagined. How, they wondered, did their son die in such a protected and peaceful community? The concept was unthinkable—unreasonable and unacceptable. Within the hour, they had contacted the funeral home where Brother Morgan had been taken and made arrangements to have his body flown to Oregon the following morning. Any attempt by Father Luke to allow Brother Morgan to be buried in the monastery cemetery was futile.

Brother Morgan's body never appeared in the chapel; a formal wake never occurred. And as a result, for Andrew, and others in the community who had grown to know him, the grieving process would evolve piecemeal, often unexpectedly, either during quiet time or in the midst of morning work. Andrew could seldom drive the old John Deere tractor without memories of Brother Morgan clouding his head, memories which sometimes filled him with sadness or, more often, caused him to smile and laugh out loud—a healthy mix, which moved him, slowly yet steadily, through the long process of healing.

* * *

The intermittent rain which fell during the night did little to quench the thirst of the new spring grass sprouting sparsely on the surrounding slopes. The flatter mesas fared better as they had less runoff and were less likely to succumb to erosion, yet because of this, they were also somewhat more difficult to properly irrigate, since the water would often pool and not spread sufficiently.

Nevertheless, Andrew knew that he had to visit the scene of Brother Morgan's accident, even though he was not sure where exactly, on the mesa, the fatal blow was struck.

When he passed by the entrance room on his way to the lower cloister, he noticed that the door was shut; however, he was able to hear, what sounded like, an animated discussion. He paused momentarily and recognized the voices of Matthew and his sister, Ellen. Feeling somewhat guilty for eavesdropping in the middle of the empty cloister, Andrew bent down and pretended to be tying his shoe. Only the louder bits of conversation could be heard, yet even those fragments indicated that Matthew was not happy with Ellen's ambiguous relationship with Father Jude.

"I'll do what I want!" Ellen shouted.

"Are you crazy—you're young enough to be his daughter!"
"You should talk," Ellen retorted.
"What the hell does that mean?" Matthew replied, less assuredly.
"You honestly think I don't know about you?"

When Andrew looked up, he saw Brother Mark turn the corner and walked directly toward him. He immediately stood and coughed loudly, to alert Matthew that someone was outside the door; he then walked briskly past Brother Mark with a slight smile and a nod. He hoped Matthew got his message.

* * *

Chapter Fourteen
Joshua's Intervention

With his newly sharpened shovel secured above the dirt bike's muffler, Andrew drove slowly around the back of the monastery, over the unstable gravel, unable to dismiss Ellen's comments to Andrew. 'What did she really know?' he wondered. 'What if she told him about Christmas Eve?' He rapidly shifted gears and drove toward the mesa.

Hovering above the valley like a petrified tidal wave, Navigator Peak snagged several wisps of grey, cumulus clouds, which, Andrew felt, closely resembled the wind-driven spray above the ocean waves. He stopped his bike, removed his shovel and walked toward the canvas dam, which blocked the flow of the water, and instead, allowed it to seep through the cutouts over the now greening soil. He determined where the next dam should be placed, pulled the rocks that held the old dam together, and quickly began to construct a new barrier further down the ditch. Once this was completed, he strategically made V-shaped cutouts, as needed, which allowed the water to effectively saturate the soil. Andrew watched, with childlike wonder, as the parched dirt slowly darkened with moisture while some higher areas initially resisted the flow of the water and then succumbed—an event reminiscent of his youth, as he remembered watching Popsicle sticks, carrying little stone people, either heroically survive the current, or tragically tilt and dump them into the stream.

Satisfied with his work, Andrew drove toward the upper mesa where Brother Morgan had been working. Several rock outcrops dotted the area, which was, otherwise, relatively flat. He slowly began to search each one, looking for telltale signs of an accident such as tire marks or, perhaps, even blood on a rock, yet the soft spring rain would have probably washed it clean. He stopped his bike near one of the larger outcrops and carefully began searching for evidence.

"You looking for this?" the voice said, from behind the boulder.

Andrew jumped back when he saw Brother Joshua stand up—he was holding a piece of brown leather.

"You just took ten years off my life," Andrew said, after taking a deep breath. "What the heck are you doing here?"

"Oh, I decided to go for a walk, and for some reason, I thought I'd see where Brother Morgan . . . had his accident."

His response eluded Andrew, who could only concentrate on the item in Brother Joshua's hand. "May I see what you have there?" He gestured toward the brown object, which Brother Joshua clung to.

"Sure." He held up the object toward Andrew.

Andrew knew immediately it was the leather aviator cap Brother Morgan had been wearing, the morning before his death. "Did you find this here?" he asked. He slowly unfolded the hat and peered inside.

"Yes," Brother Joshua said, "well . . . not exactly; just on the other side of these rocks."

Toward the front of the cap, Andrew noticed two small brown patches which, most likely, were Brother Morgan's dried blood, and he thought, quite possibly, the point of impact of his head with the rock, prior to the cap flying off his head, and his face landing in the shallow ditch next to the outcrop.

"You know . . .," Andrew began and then stopped. "Do you know who this belongs to?" he asked.

Brother Joshua shook his head. "No."

Rather than reveal its identity, Andrew chose to deemphasize its significance. "I'm pretty sure I know who it belongs to and, if you wouldn't mind, I'd like to take it with me."

"No problem," Brother Joshua said, gesturing with his hands raised—palms outward. "But there is one condition," he said shyly.

"And . . . what's that?"

"Could I get a lift back to the monastery with you so I don't miss lunch?"

Andrew laughed. "Hop on," he said.

Rather than grab the assist bar in back of the seat, Brother Joshua chose to hang onto Andrew by wrapping his arms snuggly around him.

Initially, Andrew felt uncomfortable; however, as they reached the main road and picked up speed, he was keenly aware that Brother Joshua's grip could not have been too offensive, since he could feel himself becoming aroused, with the constant pressure from Brother Joshua's arms and intermittent lower body contact. 'I must be insane, or oversexed . . . or both,' he thought, as they drove under brightening skies toward the monastery road.

Andrew drove the bike slowly onto the property, past the large guesthouse, near the barn. Just as he turned the corner, he saw Brother Matthew, in front of the barn with his dirt bike, preparing to return to the monastery. Andrew waved cautiously while Brother Joshua turned to observe the person he was waiving at.

As soon as he recognized Brother Matthew, Brother Joshua suddenly pretended to cough, released first, one hand, and then the other, changing his grip from Andrew's waist to the assist bar in back of him.

The short ride to Brother Joshua's guesthouse seemed endless to Andrew. He was not sure if Brother Matthew waved back or, even more troublesome, how he would interpret seeing Brother Joshua on the back of his bike. When he finally pulled over to drop off Brother Joshua, he could hear Matthew approach, maintain speed, and zoom past him without a wave or any acknowledgment.

"Thanks for the ride," Brother Joshua said.

Without responding, Andrew throttled the engine and left in a cloud of dust, hoping to catch up with Matthew.

Brother Joshua watched him disappear. "I smell a domestic altercation," he said, out loud, with a slight smirk.

It was not until he entered the boot room when Andrew encountered Matthew, tugging on his stubborn rubber wader. He sat across from him and watched his accentuated struggle. "Give me your boot," Andrew insisted, leaning forward.

Without speaking, Matthew complied. Andrew grabbed both the heel and toe and gently removed the muddy boot, along with most of Matthew's soggy sock.

"It looks like you got a leaky boot . . . or have you been swimming in the ditches again?" Andrew asked with a grin.

Matthew leaned back against the tiled wall, his hair darkened with moisture, and a faint smudge of dirt near a corner of his mouth.

As if looking at Matthew for the first time, Andrew felt an overwhelming sense of affection and yearning for this brooding man, sitting like a waif, across from him.

"It's not so funny," Matthew said coldly. "Why are you smiling?"

"You know the answer—because you're so handsome," Andrew replied quietly, as he attempted to lose the grin.

Matthew wiped the hair from his eyes and stood, disregarding Andrew's response, and instead, confronted him. "They're called passenger assist bars; they are in back of the seat. Why didn't you ask him to use it?" His voice was calm yet edgy.

"You're right, Matt; I should have but . . . he hung onto me and I was embarrassed to tell him otherwise."

He sat next to Andrew and faced him. "I wonder what you would have said if he slipped his hand between your legs?"

Andrew immediately got up. "I love when you talk dirty, but this is ridiculous," he said angrily. "He was up on the mesa and simply asked for a ride back so he wouldn't be late for lunch. End of story." He quickly exited the room, past the lavatories and stood, washing his face in front of the mirror in the men's room.

Seconds later, Matthew appeared next to him, scrubbing the smudge from his face. He toweled dry and looked around to be sure that they were alone. "I'm sorry, Andrew," he whispered. "I guess I'm just jealous—I'm really sorry."

"It's okay," Andrew said. "I'll see you in your cell after lunch."

As Andrew was about to follow behind him, Matthew turned, forced him into an empty shower stall and quickly closed the curtain. He pulled Andrew toward him, hugged him until he could barely breathe, and then kissed him hard, as though to validate their relationship. He broke away slowly and stared into Andrew's eyes. "Don't be late," he said softly.

Brother Adrian's lunch was devoured with rave reviews—a baked potato and cheese casserole, three-bean vinaigrette salad, and fresh strawberry shortcake made with early west coast berries.

Once again, Brother Joshua arrived late, filled his tray and, quite intentionally, sat next to Andrew, who discreetly searched for Matthew; however, he was nowhere to be found.

After helping with the kitchen cleanup, Andrew brushed his teeth in the main washroom and, afterwards, headed for Matthew's cell. Just as he was about to enter the dormitory, Andrew thought he heard footsteps in back of him. He turned quickly to see Brother Joshua walking toward him with steadfast determination.

Andrew immediately resumed his walk with a quickened pace. Rather than chance being seen entering Matthew's cell, he decided to go to his own. Once inside, he shut the door and leaned against it, listening for footsteps, which he heard approach and stop, directly in front of his cell. Seconds of silence seemed like endless excruciating minutes, until broken by a gentle rapping, which Andrew feared and hesitated to answer. Yet the prolonged silence was, once again, followed by the same pattern—two soft knocks—resonating like thunder in his head. Andrew took a deep breath before opening the door.

Brother Joshua stood, with a tense smile, on his devilishly handsome face. "I was wondering if you'd be interested in going for a walk," he said awkwardly. "I'm leaving tomorrow morning and . . . I was hoping that we could talk before I left."

Andrew peered up and down the hall, knowing that this conversation with a visiting novice would be viewed as suspect by most of the elders and, most likely, cataclysmic by Matthew. "Come on in for a second," he said softly. He shut the door, turned his desk chair around and sat down, while motioning to Brother Joshua to sit on his bed. "I don't have a lot of energy for a walk—in fact, I really need a nap but, perhaps, we could talk briefly, now."

Brother Joshua sensed Andrew's hesitancy. "I know I shouldn't be here bothering you but I had hoped to be able to talk to you, somewhat personally, about relationships . . . maybe about how you and Brother Matthew get along and . . ."

Andrew interrupted. "I'm sorry, Joshua," he said sternly, "but I really need some sleep." He stood up and walked toward the door.

Brother Joshua stood, reluctantly, and walked toward him. "I didn't mean to upset you. I'm sorry."

"Apology accepted. Enjoy the rest of your visit." Andrew opened the door, looked down the hall and stepped back to let Brother Joshua pass. He quickly shut the door and stood listening to his footsteps disappear down the hall. He slid slowly to the floor in a squatting position. 'Why me?' he thought.

With mild trepidation, he stood, opened his door to be sure that the hall was still empty, and made his way quickly to Matthew's cell, hoping as he walked, that none of the doors he passed would suddenly open since he was obviously far from his own room. Having safely reached his destination, Andrew did not bother to knock. He carefully turned the doorknob, stepped into a darkened room and very quietly shut the door in back of him.

"You know, you'd make an excellent cat burglar," Matthew said softly.

"Very funny," Andrew said, as he continued to stand by the door, waiting for his eyes to adjust to the changing light.

"Don't forget to lock it."

Andrew knew immediately, even though he could not see him that Matthew was, most likely, in bed, naked, with a certain agenda in mind. "Heaven I heard that before?" he joked, while pushing in the small doorknob.

Matthew remained silent.

With his eyes more accustomed to the darkness, Andrew approached the bed.

Matthew moved closer toward the wall and lifted a corner of the sheet, waiting for Andrew to join him.

He kicked off his sneakers and jumped in, fully clothed, where he experienced the bare warmth of a wingless seraph reach out and envelop his very being.

"It's not supposed to feel this good," Andrew whispered, clinging to Matthew and wrapping his body within his own.

"Oh . . . I don't know," Matthew responded. He nibbled on Andrew's ear. "I can think of ways to make it feel even better."

"I'm sure you can."

Matthew kissed him deeply, while slowly managing to unbutton his shirt and removed it. He reached down and began to unbutton Andrew's jeans; however, Andrew grabbed his hand.

"What's the possibility of just being here, Matt, quietly, enjoying this time together?" Andrew whispered. "I probably want you even more than you want me but . . . it might be good for both of us to show some restraint."

Matthew shrugged. "It's probably about as possible as me becoming abbot at St. Anthony's."

"That's what I thought" Andrew said, smiling.

"Don't give up so easily. I'll do it if we can both be . . . on unequal footing," Matthew proposed.

"I'm afraid to ask, but what does that mean?"

"That means that you get to be as naked as I am, and I get to take off the rest of your clothes. Deal?"

Andrew rubbed his eyes. "I must be totally insane," he mumbled. "Okay."

The socks came off first followed by a penetrating foot massage which Andrew found extraordinarily relaxing. Matthew then completed what he had started earlier—he unfastened Andrew's pants and carefully removed them. With Andrew lying on his back, Matthew continued to massage his calves, knees, and thighs, kneading the large muscles with professional skill, while Andrew writhed with pleasure from Matthew's powerful hands, a pleasure that registered more obviously under the waistband of his shorts.

In the silence, Matthew straddled Andrew and gently rubbed his chest and stomach. He slipped his fingers under the top of Andrew's shorts and gently slid them down, past the thighs, calves, and finally off his feet. He continued to kneel over him, captivated by both beauty and desire.

Andrew reached up toward him with both arms. "Don't say anything. Just cover me with your body."

Without hesitation Matthew slowly lowered himself on top of him. He buried his face in Andrew's neck, inhaling his familiar scent, as he adjusted his position so that both bodies aligned perfectly, in full contact with each other.

Andrew willingly supported his weight, a sensation of total security and, perhaps, submission, as body heat multiplied and enveloped them both with dewy perspiration. He traced the hills and valleys of Matthew's back, lightly running his fingers over his spine and muscles, and then over his unforgettable buttocks and into the warm crevice. He could feel Matthew shiver, ever so slightly, with his probing touch.

"Guess who followed me to my cell after lunch?" Andrew said softly into Matthew's ear.

"I can't imagine."

"Brother Joshua."

Matthew quickly rolled off Andrew and onto his side. "Are you serious?"

"Yes, but don't get excited. He wanted to know if I would take a walk with him so we could talk. I asked him in, to get him out of the hall, said I was tired, and asked what he wanted to talk about."

"This ought to be good," Matthew interjected.

"Well, he said that his retreat was nearly over and—get this, he wanted to talk about relationships, and how you and I get along."

"What?"

"That was my reaction. I stood up, reminded him that I was tired and walked toward the door. At that point, he got up and apologized. I opened the door and he left."

"The guy has balls," Matthew said, "and I'm sure he is after you."

Andrew chuckled. "You're so cute when you're jealous, but I think you're wrong."

"Believe me, Andrew, you're just naïve."

"Maybe, but I think he is really searching, much as we are, for answers about us and our vocation—how it all fits together—and how he might work some of that out with . . . I don't know, a friend of his own and still live the monastic life."

"Just as long as that 'friend' isn't you."

Andrew leaned forward and kissed him. "You won my heart; you earned my friendship, so don't ever worry."

Matthew looked at him. "I like when you say things that way."

"Well, I mean it." Andrew pushed his fingers through Matthew's hair, pulling gently while massaging his temples, scalp, and forehead.

Matthew closed his eyes. "I can't begin to tell you how good that feels." He lay back against the pillow as Andrew kneaded his head with both hands.

"Anything new with Ellen?" Andrew asked, hoping that Matthew would not ignore their quarrel in the entrance room.

"Not really," Matthew said sleepily. "We had a bit of a tiff yesterday, after mass. I hope that we weren't too noisy. Anyway, I asked what was going on between her and Father Jude and she said that they were just friends—as though anything else was impossible. I guess I came on pretty strong."

"It must have surprised her."

"She looked sort of shocked that I would have thought there was more to it."

At first, Andrew hesitated then decided to be direct. "Did she ever say anything about me or . . . about us?"

"Do you really want to know?"

"Yes . . . is it that awful?"

"Of course not." He slid his hand over Andrew's side and across his thigh.

"Well?"

"She thinks you are incredibly handsome and very sexy," Mathew said proudly.

"She told you that?" Andrew asked with surprise.

"Yes, a long time ago."

"What about us? Has she ever said anything?"

"Yes, but I'm not through." He leaned forward, propped himself up with his elbow and gently pushed on Andrew's shoulder, encouraging him to lie back. "My turn," he said as he began to massage Andrew's head. He bent down and kissed him on the nose. "She said that if you weren't in the monastery, she'd consider marrying you because, among other things, she has a feeling that you are very romantic and a great kisser."

Andrew laughed nervously. "You're making this up."

"Cross my heart," Matthew said, gesturing with his hand on his chest.

"What did you say to her?"

"I told her she's absolutely right—you are tremendously romantic and a terrific kisser."

Andrew suddenly grabbed him in a headlock. He was hardly able to control his laughter. "Tell me you're joking or you're a dead man!"

"I'm joking . . . and I'm choking," Matthew gasped.

Andrew released him, and they both settled back into the mattress.

"What about the 'us' part?" Andrew continued.

"Questions, questions, questions," Matthew said evasively. "Let me just rub your head so you can relax."

"Are you avoiding the question, Matt?" Andrew asked with some trepidation.

"Do you really have to know? I have a feeling that whatever I say, you will obsess about it and make more of it than you should."

"Even so . . . please tell me."

Matthew lay down alongside of him. "Okay . . . she thinks we're more than friends."

"You mean . . . like boyfriends?"

"In so many words . . . yes."

"So what did you say to her, seriously?" Andrew could feel his anxiety increase.

"I looked her in the eye and told her she has an over-active imagination for a seventeen-year-old."

"Yeah, like you said, a seventeen-year-old going on what . . . thirty?"

"So she's insightful. She can't claim to know the truth so, please, don't worry about it."

Andrew sighed. "Why should I worry about Ellen when most everyone in the monastery thinks the same about us?"

"And they can't claim to know the truth either," Matthew quipped. "Besides, I'll bet 98 percent of them are jealous." He threw his leg over Andrew's and rolled against him. "Now, do you see why I didn't want to tell you? You're upset, and there is no reason to worry about what others think. Whatever they think is none of our business. I am with you, and I love you more than I have ever loved anyone . . . or ever will." He traced the outline of Andrew's nose, lips, and chin.

Andrew turned, wrapped himself around Matthew and held him tight. "You have a way of simplifying things and erasing all that seems to complicate my head."

"Is that good?"

"It's very good."

"I wonder how she ever got the idea that you're a great kisser," Matthew said with a chuckle.

Andrew felt himself tense. He held Matthew even tighter and remained silent as Matthew gently rubbed him.

Attempting to change the subject, he recalled Matthew's absence in the refectory. "Did you skip lunch? I didn't see you there."

Matthew laughed. "I figured I'd be having *you* for lunch so I took a shower. I was pretty grubby from irrigating."

"Very thoughtful," Andrew whispered. He nuzzled his ear and kissed it.

Just then, the bell clanged loudly over the monastery, signaling a ten-minute notice before the start of None, the first afternoon prayer service.

"Damn!" Matthew said. "I didn't think it was this late."

"Me either," Andrew said, as he jumped out of bed and began searching for his clothes. "I can't find my underwear."

"Do we have to go?" Matthew asked.

"You kidding? They'd probably search our cells if we were both absent."

Andrew pulled his jeans over his bare buttocks. "Let me know if you find my shorts." He looked down at Matthew, who simply lay there, nonchalantly, with his head propped up by his arm. "You had better get out of that bed."

"Do I really have to?" Matthew lamented.

"Yes, you do," Andrew insisted. He had only to tie his sneakers before being nearly completely dressed.

Matthew swung his legs over the side of the mattress and sat up. "I can't believe we have to leave each other like this."

Andrew leaned over and kissed him. "There will be plenty of other times. Now . . . get dressed." He walked toward the door and stopped. "I can't go out this way—someone will see me." He peeked through Matthew's slider, which opened to the far side of the garth. "I'm going this way," he said, pulling the large door open.

The natural light illuminated Matthew, who remained sitting, naked, on the bed.

Andrew looked up and paused. "I must be crazy for leaving . . . you are so beautiful." He then stepped outside and quickly closed the door.

In the darkness, once again, Matthew reached under his pillow and removed the underwear which he had hidden from Andrew. He rubbed the shorts against his face and inhaled Andrew's body scents, mixed with the freshness of fabric softener. With the underwear still covering his face, he leaned back against the wall and, within minutes, he was able to release that powerful yearning he had anticipated sharing with Andrew, a moment he would have to, regretfully, postpone until their next encounter.

* * *

Chapter Fifteen

The Moreland Mesa

The summer season burst upon the monastery and surrounding high country like the opening of a moonflower at dusk. Colorful wildflowers painted the mesas with vibrant patches of red, yellow, lavender, and blue, accenting a backdrop of newly green grasses and the ever-present adobe soil, which became easily airborne in the arid summer breeze.

Andrew watched with amazement as truckload after truckload of cattle were deposited, like Holocaust victims, at various locations on the property, or as the locals preferred to call it, "the ranch." Rugged-looking farmhands, some not much older than Andrew, performed the back-breaking job of moving the herds out of the trucks, down the narrow ramps and into the appropriate pastures, checking first that all of the perimeter gates were secured. Although the monastery did not own any of the cattle, they leased the land to the predominantly wealthy ranchers who benefited from the nearly four thousand acres of farmland, which provided ample room and food for their stock and, in some cases, generous tax write-offs for their owners. The monks were primarily responsible for irrigating the arid land to produce grass for food, maintaining the fences to secure the cattle within the property, and generally overseeing and reporting any problems.

The variety of cattle fascinated Andrew, who, with practice, learned to tell the difference between the Black Angus, the reddish brown Short Horns, and the white-faced Herefords, yet his favorite remained the light brown nearly white Brahmans with their rabbitlike ears and prominent humps.

Aware of the cow's natural curiosity, Andrew decided to experiment, one afternoon, by seeing how they would react to him merely sitting, quietly, in the middle of the field. He watched with lowered eyes as the white-faced herd slowly surrounded him and began to move closer and closer until he could nearly feel their breath. One of the braver animals stretched her head forward to get a better scent, and then quickly pulled back, afraid of what might happen, until, after three attempts, she, once again, stretched forward; and much to Andrew surprise, stuck out her tongue, licked his nose and cheek and then abruptly moved back. As soon as Andrew raised his arm to wipe his face on his shirt, the herd bolted away, scattering in several directions, while Andrew sat there, laughing, amazed by the roughness of her tongue and the strong milky scent of her breath.

His other experiences with the cattle were much less personal yet, perhaps, more provocative. On several occasions, he watched, with a mixture of erotic longing and mild embarrassment, as the bulls mounted their mates, all several hundred pounds, and copulated furiously despite what sounded like cries of pain or, perhaps, pleasure from their partners. 'Doing what came naturally, no matter where or when,' Andrew thought.

Having to subtly observe their mating, Andrew would often ridicule himself and the norms of society, of which he was obviously a part. As Matthew once said, "sex, especially as viewed by the church, should not be painted as such a dirty and ugly event until the glorious moment of matrimony when it suddenly becomes a beautifully sanctioned act of God." Most often, he would readjust his erection and continue with his irrigating, unless he happened to be in, or near, the Moreland Mesa, which provided a natural private cove, an unobservable area surrounded by high cliffs and a steep drop-off where Andrew was able to lean comfortably against the ditch and masturbate, unhurriedly, surrounded by the earthy scent of damp vegetation. He wondered if any of his brothers had used this spot for the same purpose. Andrew had considered telling Matthew about it—assuming he did not already know—but decided instead to keep it as his own special place.

And as much as Andrew grew to enjoy cooking, it was the job of irrigating he enjoyed the most—not that it was without its downside; the first being his mortal fear of bears that roamed the back acres, mostly unseen, yet scarring the trees with massive claw gouges, ten to twelve feet high; and second, the persistent deer flies which, when in season, knew exactly where to attack and when. Andrew knew they could skillfully attack his eyelids—one of the few places without insect repellent—by crawling behind his glasses, at the precise moment, when he had just lifted a substantial boulder, and was carrying it, in the ninety-degree heat, to the newly constructed dam. More often than not, he would be forced to drop the boulder and attempt to swat the fly, which would, inevitably return, as soon as he picked up the rock.

Depending on his location and his ability to be observed, Andrew found himself, on two occasions, furiously removing his clothes and jumping naked into the frigid ditch water to cool off and avoid the flies. Since it was impossible to remain in the icy water, he had to dress quickly before the persistent flies found new and more vulnerable territory to attack.

Yet it was the consuming beauty of the area and his genuine sense of purpose that caused Andrew to stop and reflect, not only on his role as a monk at St. Anthony's but also as a humble, yet grateful, particle of the cosmos—something he did quite often, when working in the fields. The ineffable grandeur of early summer in the mountains often left him breathless; snowcapped peaks surrounded the greening valleys with majestic vistas and dizzying heights, while carpets of wildflowers and fluttering aspens, with their canoe-white trunks, grounded him, temporarily, within his spiritual sphere. At times, he was genuinely moved to fall to his knees in the silence of his summer cathedral, to thank God for his well-being, to pray for assistance in dealing with his own demons, and to pray for all who might benefit from one man's seemingly weak but well-intentioned plea.

Nevertheless, he often wondered, 'Is this enough? What more can I do, and as always, why shouldn't this be shared?' He thought, 'I wish Matthew were here to see this, to feel what I'm feeling,' as if it were necessary to validate its authenticity, something he felt incapable of experiencing on his own or, at least, unwilling to do so. Even now, as he knelt, aware of his insignificance, he coveted his secret sacred friend.

With the sun setting quickly behind Navigator Peak, Andrew made his way across the field, through the pines, toward the monastery, where he remembered spending a snowy afternoon with Brother Morgan, collecting fresh pine boughs for Christmas decorations and laughing hysterically as Morgan demonstrated his humor, often unintentionally. Yet his smile faded quickly as a familiar pain filled his heart—a sadness that washed over him and made him fully aware of his own mortality and transient, yet painful, loneliness.

* * *

"I just don't see why we have to live so . . . well," Andrew said calmly. "Forgive me for speaking so bluntly, but it bothers me to be a member of this community when, at times, we live such privileged lives."

Father Luke sat quietly behind his desk, listening intently, as Andrew shared his concerns. A light breeze nudged the heavy curtains and swirled the white pipe smoke into gentle vortices, which soon dissipated, leaving only the scholarly scent of expensive English tobacco.

"It's the Perrier and the Häagen-Dazs you are referring to," Father Luke said.

"Mostly," Andrew replied.

"I'm not in disagreement with you, Brother Andrew. We need to watch our expenses, yet quite honestly, you are the only community member who has spoken about this to me." Father Luke set his pipe in its holder and leaned forward. "What do you think I should do?"

Andrew leaned forward to mimic Father Luke's body language. "I'm not sure, but I get the feeling that others may have similar feelings but don't want to cause any dissension." He leaned back in his chair and rubbed his eyes. "If I may speak openly, I wonder if all of this is simply what Father Jude wants, regardless of the cost; yet I see it as far from ascetic and find it almost hypocritical and contrary to the intent of the monastic rule. Doesn't any of this bother you?"

Father Luke reached for his pipe, relit it, and sat back. "Perhaps more than I realize," he admitted. "Yet my obedience to an abbot allows me to overlook what might be considered faults while, at the same time, as prior and novice master, I am here to resolve issues and, hopefully, do what God wishes by properly guiding younger men, such as yourself, who are relatively new to this very difficult calling, toward a solid formation of monastic life based upon a total, selfless, love of God. I know that you are serious about this, and I want to try to minimize your struggle. You are an asset to the community, Andrew—committed, and always willing to do more than your share. I will speak with Father Jude."

Andrew shifted in his chair. "Thanks, Father Luke, but I'm not sure if I want my name connected with the whole mess. I don't want to be viewed as an adversary."

"I understand and will respect that." Father Luke stood, extended his arms and hugged Andrew in a genuinely monastic yet avuncular manner.

"Thanks for listening to me," Andrew said. "If nothing else, it helps just to talk about it."

* * *

His meeting with Father Luke generated a post-stress hunger which could be satiated only by some of Brother Adrian's chocolate chip cookies. When he entered the kitchen, he found that Brother Mark had the same idea.

"Caught red-handed with your fingers in the cookie jar," Andrew said quietly, standing behind him and smiling.

Brother Mark appeared unruffled and returned the smile. "Yup . . . want some?" He picked up the heavy container and offered it to Andrew, who immediately joined the complicity. "We had better get out of here before we get arrested."

As they opened the screen door to exit, Buddha nonchalantly sauntered in, apparently gorged with her fill-of-field mice, and in search of her bowl of milk, which Brother Adrian refreshed daily.

The beauty of the day begged for enjoyment and appreciation of all that an early summer afternoon might flaunt.

"You up for a walk?" Brother Mark asked, munching on his cookie, in the bright sunlight.

"Why not," Andrew said. "It's the thing to do around here, isn't it?"

"Yes, very *de rigueur*, but don't feel obligated."

"Who could resist," Andrew said honestly.

They walked in relative silence except for the crunching of the cookies, and the gravel, and the occasional mooing of the cattle, on either side of the road. Red-winged blackbirds darted from bush to bush, as though to accompany them, flashing their carmine brilliance in flight.

"Would you be interested in a three-day retreat at a commune in Oregon?" Brother Mark asked unexpectedly.

Andrew laughed. "Is this a trick question?"

"No, I'm serious. I've been invited to a coed commune in Oregon and they allow one guest."

"And this has already been approved by the higher powers?"

"It has," Brother Mark said confidently. "I thought you might be interested in coming with me."

"What sort of retreat is it?"

"One of the Zen masters from New York will lead the sessions," Brother Mark explained.

"So it's more or less a Zen oriented get-together?"

"Pretty much," Brother Mark said. "Probably lots of sitting meditations, with group and some individual sessions."

Andrew paused and rubbed his eyes. "I like the idea of getting out of here for a while, but as you know, I've never been good at sitting on cushions or Zen stools for very long, and those who usually attend these gatherings are Olympic champs of Zen meditation. My back starts to knot up and I end up sitting on a chair."

"That's right," Brother Mark said. "I forgot about your back." He shook his head apologetically. "Well, it's nearly two months away so you have plenty of time to think about it."

"I appreciate the offer, Brother Mark, but you might want to ask someone else so that they can plan ahead. Maybe Matthew would like to go."

Brother Mark appeared startled by the suggestion. "Why?" he said quickly. Aware of his hasty response, he smiled and tried to recover. "I mean, why not. He seems to be able to sit for quite a while. Besides, he might enjoy it."

"He might," Andrew added.

"I don't want to sound like I'm trying to pry, but how are the two of you getting along?"

Although the question sounded genuinely benign, Andrew felt his defenses steel; he took a deep breath. "Fine, I guess. He's a decent person, and it's helpful to be able to share some thoughts once in a while."

"Especially in this place," Brother Mark said. "Wasn't his sister here for a retreat?"

"Yes—Ellen. She left before I had a chance to say goodbye."

Brother Mark fell silent, turned off the road to the gate which led through the pasture, and up, toward the overlook, where Matthew and Andrew shared time together.

"I just had a meeting with Father Luke," Andrew said.

"So how did it go?"

Andrew shrugged. "I told him how I felt about what seem to be excesses in our diet."

"You mean the Perrier and the Häagen-Dazs?"

"Yeah. He said he would mention it to the abbot, but I asked that my name not be connected with the whole mess."

"That was smart," Brother Mark admitted. He removed a white handkerchief from his pocket and blew his nose. "Allergies," he said, sniffling. He shoved the handkerchief back in his pocket. "How well do you know Ellen?"

The abruptness of the question surprised Andrew, as he focused his attention on the bumpy road. "Oh, I guess somewhat. I talked with her when Matthew's family was visiting. Why?"

"I don't know," Brother Mark said, looking off in the distance. "I was amazed to see her with the abbot on two occasions—maybe not exactly occasions—but riding in his car with him. I didn't know they were so friendly."

Andrew scoffed. "I think they were seen by nearly everyone in the monastery, so don't feel alone."

"I wonder what that's all about," Brother Mark said quietly, as if to himself.

"Who knows," Andrew replied with a shrug. "You have to admit, she's incredibly beautiful."

"That's for sure but . . . what is she . . . nineteen?"

"You're close," Andrew said with a laugh. "Would you believe seventeen?"

"Yeow!" Brother Mark shouted, uncharacteristically. "That's jailbait."

"Only if . . . you know, they have a physical relationship," Andrew stammered. "I doubt it's reached that level."

"Yeah," Brother Mark said derisively. "Me too."

"He couldn't be that misguided, could he?"

Brother Mark shook his head. "Who knows what a sex-starved celibate might do with an admiring seventeen-year-old."

Andrew watched as puffy, marshmallow clouds drifted across the high ridge in the distance. "I think this is the only place where I constantly see clouds shaped like Volkswagens."

Brother Mark laughed. "It's a change in the subject, but you're right. That is definitely a Volkswagen up there." He pointed to the cloud that Andrew was watching.

"What does Brother Matthew think about it?" Brother Mark refocused the discussion.

"We haven't discussed it much. He seemed to shut down when I raised the issue, so I decided to let it go. I know that he feels Ellen's behavior exceeds her age."

"The old 'seventeen going on twenty-five' adage?"

"Maybe thirty-five," Andrew added.

"Well," Brother Mark offered, "whatever the case, it must be difficult for him to process the unknown and accept Father Jude as abbot and role model of the monastery."

"I guess, but then, I admit having similar feelings, and Ellen has very little to do with it."

Brother Mark walked in silence as though digesting Andrew's comment. Three quarters of the way to the top of the ridge, he walked off the trail to a small rocky outcrop and sat down. He looked at Andrew with a somber expression. "I don't want to see you leave," he said suddenly, continuing to look at Andrew, who was caught completely off guard.

"As far as I know, I'm not going anywhere. What makes you think I'd leave?"

"Experience," Brother Mark replied. He quietly observed the valley below. "My life is down there—the bricks, the staleness, the emptiness, and, at times, the validation—yet when I see familiar patterns developing in novices, I get that same sinking feeling of losing another friend, someone who, for whatever reason, decides to call it quits and departs. You know the story."

"And you see that pattern developing with me?" Andrew asked.

"I'd say you're in a holding pattern. A few more hurdles could push you over the edge."

"Oh, I don't know . . .," Andrew said. "I bitch a lot, but I still feel a firm commitment here."

"You've been through quite a bit—especially with the suicide at the eggery."

"*John*," Andrew replied sharply. "His name was *John*."

"I'm sorry," Brother Mark said. "You're right. I should have used his name,"

Andrew rubbed his eyes. "Wow. Maybe you're right. I didn't realize it was still so sensitive for me. I'm sorry."

"It's okay," Brother Mark said softly.

Puffs of dust on the road below slowly dissipated behind the yellow truck.

"Looks like Eric Holtz is making a delivery," Brother Mark said. The sound of the engine finally reverberated up the mountain to where they were sitting.

"He seems like he's really got it together," Andrew remarked.

"Who knows anymore," Brother Mark said. "He's a great guy, but I doubt that his life is a bed of roses."

"Really?" Andrew quipped.

"If you can believe the local gossip."

"More murmuring," Andrew said with a laugh.

"Maybe, but the story involved a divorce, filed by his wife two years ago, and then . . . silence. Nothing more was heard about it and they are still very much together."

"Probably for the sake of the kids."

"Probably . . .," Brother Mark said.

Andrew watched as the truck drove out of sight, around the far side of the monastery and then reappeared near the kitchen door. He could just barely see Eric leave the vehicle and enter the kitchen.

"They always seem so happy when they're together," Andrew said. "I wonder why this divorce thing happened."

"I could tell you . . .," Brother Mark began.

"But then you'd have to kill me?" Andrew said, completing the sentence.

"Just about," Brother Mark said seriously.

"Well, now that you've got me completely curious . . . I guess you'll have to kill me."

Brother Mark's reticence was easily overpowered by his poorly veiled enthusiasm.

"It's not exactly a secret but then, who knows about the validity of the rumor. Most of the locals seemed to think, for whatever reason, that it was true."

"So it's known about outside of the monastery?"

"Unfortunately, yes."

Andrew waited for him to continue. "And . . ."

Brother Mark shifted his position to face Andrew directly. "I'll tell you, but I'd rather not have others know that I did so."

Andrew nodded his head affirmatively.

"The story is that Eric was having a relationship, and Kathy found out about it, but no one knows, for sure, how."

"With a younger woman?" Andrew asked.

"Not exactly," Brother Mark said. "It was with another man."

Andrew rubbed his eyes. "I would never have expected that." He was quite stunned by the news, yet he made every effort to appear as though it was fairly insignificant. "I guess nobody's perfect after all."

"Well," Brother Mark continued. "That's not the end of the story. He was allegedly having a relationship with one of the monks—Father Martin."

"You mean, Father Martin . . . dead Father Martin?" Andrew asked incredulously. By now, his calm façade gave way to complete bewilderment, fueled partially by his private fascination of what he viewed as an unlikely event, due to the substantial discrepancies in their ages, and Father Martin's status in the community as a prayerful and traditional member.

"Yes, the same Father Martin," Brother Mark repeated. "Sooner or later, you would have heard about it, so it might be better if you aren't surprised by some of the people from Bitter Creek, who thrive on stuff like this."

Andrew stood and stared at the changing mountains, as the clouds alternated their intensity from patches of shadow to bright sunlight. "Well, I can't imagine someone coming up to me after mass and saying, 'Hi, I'm so-and-so. Did you know that Father Martin was having a relationship with Eric Holtz?'"

"Don't bet on it," Brother Mark cautioned. "Some of these people have minds like lasers and tongues like scalpels. They think that affluence allows them certain improprieties which should simply be overlooked."

"It's . . . quite a jolt," Andrew admitted. "How did the rest of the community deal with it?"

Brother Mark chuckled. "Pretty much like everything else that isn't especially favorable to their collective reputation—they denied it."

"Sort of like the Häagen-Dazs and Perrier," Andrew said cynically.

"Not exactly, but yes, sort of," Brother Mark agreed.

"And you?" Andrew asked bluntly. "What do you think of it?"

Brother Mark scooped up some pebbles and tossed them onto a flat stone. "I don't know. True or false—what does it matter? I wish that Father Martin were still alive so that his awful death didn't appear to be some sort of divine retribution."

"Do some members of the community think that?"

"I wouldn't be surprised," Brother Mark said remorsefully.

Andrew sat down next to him. "It's amazing how different things can seem, once you get to look inside. With all that's happened, or supposedly happened, haven't you ever thought of calling it quits?"

"Yes," Brother Mark said without hesitation. "But then, I let some time pass, ask myself, why am I here, and usually come to the same conclusion—what the hell what I do for a job on the outside?" He laughed at his own feeble attempt to use some humor and then continued in a more serious mood. "With some quality meditation, I'm able to realize that the vocation is much larger than the incidentals of community life. We're all human and subject to various imperfections. It may sound corny but I really believe that it's true, and I'm thankful that God has given me that insight."

"That's fine but, at the moment of the incident, you must have experienced some negative feelings, didn't you?"

"Of course," Brother Mark admitted, "but over the years, I've learned that things can change and the pain slowly begins to subside. That doesn't mean that it totally disappears."

They both watched as Eric's yellow truck made a wide U-turn and drove away from the monastery, yet this time, Andrew sensed a different feeling toward its driver—a closeness he now identified as something which, earlier, he had only wondered about.

Andrew's questioning continued. "Does the passing of time allow you to see Father Jude in a favorable light—not so much from a moral perspective, but more from a leadership and role model point of view?"

"That's the difficult part," Brother Mark said. "Sometimes, he just really pisses me off, yet at meetings with the professed, I feel as though I have to defend him, or be a traitor to the community. There are times when I think he won't be here much longer, at least, not in his present capacity as abbot."

"What would he do?"

"I'm not sure, but if I had to guess, I'd say he would ask to live a more hermetic existence, which fits 'his lifestyle' better."

"Maybe he could buy a condominium in the heart of Bitter Creek, snort coke, and teach snow bunnies how to meditate," Andrew joked.

"I could see him doing that," Brother Mark said seriously. He stood up, stretched, and then blew his nose. "This has been fun but, what do you say—are you ready to head back?"

"Yeah, let's do it," Andrew said. He jumped up and prepared to leave but not without glancing behind him at the hidden rock hollow where Brother Matthew's name and his were written together in stone.

* * *

The Canadian thistle began to bloom explosively across the arid mesa once the irrigation waters quenched its straining roots. Huge puffs of purple and lavender spheres topped the dangerously spiked stems like firecrackers, frozen in time, on the Fourth of July. Wearing his leather fencing gloves, Andrew would carefully gather a large bouquet, place them in a colorful vase, and set them next to the statue of the Blessed Virgin near the refectory.

"That looks good," Matthew whispered. He towered over Andrew, who was squatting to arrange the flowers.

"Thanks," Andrew said. He looked around furtively to be sure that they were alone. "So do you," he said with a grin.

Matthew laughed and unconsciously rubbed his thigh. "Don't do this to me. The noonday devil has already been tugging on my soul."

"Well," Andrew said, standing up. "You'll have to do what they say—grab him by the horns and say 'die . . . die.'"

"I'd rather grab someone . . . or something else."

His squeaky footsteps identified Brother Adrian before he turned the corner of the cloister and approached the two monks. He smiled broadly, proudly exposing his new dental work. "So you're the one," Brother Adrian said, acknowledging Andrew's arrangement. "I've often admired the beauty of purple thistle next to the blue of Mary's clothing." He continued to grin excessively.

"Thanks," Andrew said. He stood and rubbed his eyes. "I almost hate to cut them but they are too beautiful to simply leave on the mesa and not be appreciated by others."

"And that includes me," Brother Adrian said. "I hardly ever get up to the different mesas anymore." He turned and looked at Matthew. "Did you help, Brother Matthew?"

Matthew laughed and appeared to blush. "No. I guess I'm just another passing spectator, but I have to agree, the thistle looks great there."

Brother Adrian maintained eye contact with Matthew long after he had finished speaking, until Matthew averted his stare and chose to look at Andrew.

"Well, don't miss lunch; I think you'll like it," Brother Adrian said.

"It smells terrific," Andrew said. "Spaghetti?"

"No, but you're close—cheese ravioli."

"Wouldn't think of missing that," Andrew said.

Brother Adrian began to walk toward the refectory and then suddenly stopped and turned around. "I nearly forgot. The community may be going on a raft trip soon," he said excitedly. "It should be quite thrilling; have you heard about it yet?"

Both Andrew and Matthew shook their heads.

"Not yet," Andrew answered, "but it sounds almost too good to be true."

"Well, when Father Luke mentions it, act surprised." Brother Adrian raised his eyebrows, grinned and walked away.

When he was sure that Brother Adrian was out of earshot, Matthew whispered to Andrew. "What a character. He looks at me . . . as if he knows."

"What?" Andrew asked.

"About us."

"Maybe," Andrew said, "but quite honestly, I've often wondered about him. Besides, I think he likes you."

Matthew chuckled. "You're funny . . . and right now, you look incredibly sexy."

"It must be the company I keep," Andrew replied.

"So when will I see you?" Matthew asked seriously.

Whether it was the headiness of the moment combined with Matthew's charm, or the exuberance of a new summer day bringing vitality to his surroundings, Andrew paused briefly and then surrendered to Matthew's advances. "I should be irrigating over at the Moreland Mesa around three—if you want to stop by."

Matthew's face lit up immediately. "I'll bring my shovel."

* * *

Brother Adrian outdid himself, Andrew thought, as he savored the homemade ravioli, fresh tabouli salad, and pineapple tofu custard. And judging by the bowed heads, hovering over their plates, and the number of monks returning for seconds, he knew that the community shared his feelings.

Halfway through his meal, Andrew paused to discretely survey the room. In the far corner, close to the old woodstove, he noticed two young Observers, sitting uncomfortably erect with lowered eyes and, at times, demonstrating awkward eating habits by either dropping food or being excessively self-conscious. One young man, in particular, finished his meal and sat motionless, as if meditation would immediately resolve his apparent anguish by making his world disappear. Andrew remembered experiencing some of those same feelings when he first arrived, a sense of anxiety mixed with awe, which may have stemmed from his own insecurity and lack of worthiness, yet he was surprised how quickly those feelings faded. He wished he could simply get up, lean over the table where the two were sitting, and say something humorous to help them relax. Instead, the words of Father Gerald, reading from the pulpit, suddenly caught his attention.

"For the sensual and the spiritual are not separate realities—both embody the same mystery. The life of the spirit may well be enhanced by the physical expression of sexuality."

It was a message which resonated with Andrew, yet he was more than astounded by the fact that this particular book, a book which he later learned was written by John Sanford and titled *The Invisible Partners*, was chosen and allowed it to be read in the refectory. He wondered if his brothers were experiencing the same feelings of complete astonishment, yet when he looked around the room, there was little change. They simply continued to eat, impervious to Father Gerald's words.

* * *

The summer sun warmed the fields to a nearly unbearable intensity as Andrew continued to irrigate the Moreland mesa. The parched soil absorbed the water with a voracious thirst, darkening slowly to a deep brick red and then allowing the excess to move further down the slope. It seemed unfathomable, Andrew thought, that such barren sod could, within a week, turn from dust to fertile green pasture with the proper amount of water and a regulated flow.

By midafternoon, sweat had soaked through his T-shirt, shorts, and jeans, as if he had tumbled into the ditch, an idea he had seriously considered. On several occasions, he removed the handkerchief headband, squeezed out the excess moisture and pulled it down over his forehead. And despite the rigorous chores in a relatively hostile environment, Andrew would often pause, lean on his shovel, and acknowledge that it was this type of labor which offered him the greatest sense of satisfaction and accomplishment—a feeling of self worth and identity with the land, nature, and being an integral part of God's creation. This, he knew, was what man was meant to do.

The red-tailed hawks drifted easily above the mountains, emitting their distinct screech and then dropping at dizzying speeds to capture unsuspecting prey, only to rise again, often laboriously, with their trophies. Andrew often wondered how the monastery cat, Buddha, had successfully eluded such skillful hunters, including badgers, coyotes, and the occasional eagle. Given her girth, he decided she seldom strayed far from home.

The sound of a dirt bike in the distance broke the silence and caught Andrew's attention. Although he still could not see it, the sound grew in intensity as the bike approached. Suddenly, where the road curved and disappeared into the lower field, Andrew watched as the bike emerged and appeared to draw a bead directly on him and continue at breakneck speed. He knew that it could be only one person—Matthew.

The bike skidded to a stop on the wet soil, sending a wave of engine heat over Andrew like the opening of an oven door. Matthew turned off the ignition and quickly jumped away from the hot machine.

"Hey, farmer," Matthew joked. "How are you doing?"

"Well, mostly sweating," Andrew replied.

"It's not bad when you're moving but when you stop, it feels like a broiler," Matthew said, wiping the sweat from his forehand. "It's got to be ninety out here."

Andrew laughed and moved away from the bike. "I know. I feel like a total sweat-ball but, so far, I've been able to move the water and cover most of the field."

Matthew surveyed his work while shielding the sun from his eyes with his hand. "You're getting darn good at this," he said with exaggeration. "Pretty soon you'll be head of the ranch."

"I don't think so," Andrew said slowly, leaning against his shovel. "I wouldn't want the responsibility that goes with it."

"I know what you mean. There's a lot of acreage out here to cover." He looked at Andrew. "You up for a break?"

The implication was clear—and welcomed. "Why not," Andrew said. "Besides, didn't someone say, 'He that hath a head of wax must not walk in the sun'?"

"I don't know but . . . are you referring to me or you?"

Andrew laughed. "Me, of course. Your head is fine just the way it is." He strapped his shovel above the muffler, taking extra care not to burn himself. "See where the ditch curves around the hillside?" he said, pointing in the distance.

Matthew nodded.

"I think we'll find some shade in there."

Matthew started the engine and Andrew quickly hopped on behind him.

"Where did you leave your bike?"

"Right where we're heading," Andrew said.

Matthew drove carefully yet faster than Andrew appreciated, as the bike bumped over the rutted field, stirring grasshoppers and field mice. He placed his arm around Matthew's waist, which felt warm and wet with perspiration. His other hand held tight to the assist bar in back of his seat, until Matthew reached behind him, grabbed his arm and wrapped it around him.

"That's much better," Matthew said, turning his head so that Andrew could hear him.

Andrew squeezed him tightly and nuzzled his ear. "I'd feel better if you kept both hands on the handlebar."

The moving air comfortably cooled his face and arms as he held on to Matthew and felt the tall grass brush stiffly against his jeans.

"Hang on!" Matthew shouted. Just ahead, a hidden ditch appeared unexpectedly. The bike became airborne for a few seconds and then touched down, hard, on the other side. Andrew could feel his weight compress against Matthew as his head flew forward and hit the back of Matthew's head. Matthew maintained his balance, kept the bike upright and quickly stopped.

"Shit!" Matthew said. "Are you all right?"

Andrew rubbed his forehead. "I think so." When he lowered his hand, he could see his palm was covered with blood. "Well," he said quietly. "Maybe not."

Matthew moved closer to inspect the wound. "You split the skin just above your eyebrow . . . not too bad, though." He removed a canteen of water, which he had wedged inside the bike frame. "Give me your bandanna."

Andrew handed his sweaty handkerchief to him.

After pouring fresh water on it and squeezing it out several times, Matthew tied it tightly over the wound. "Apply some pressure to it. That ought to stop the bleeding until we get back."

"Thanks," Andrew said quietly, "but what about our break?"

Matthew grinned. "You still up for it?"

"Why not, I doubt that I'll bleed to death but . . . on one condition."

"Anything," Matthew said with an intentionally saccharine tone.

"That damn bike doesn't come out of second gear."

Matthew stiffened and saluted. "Yes, sir!"

He drove at a leisurely pace, avoiding as many ruts as possible while Andrew hung onto him with one hand and kept pressure over his cut with the other. He stopped the bike near Andrew's and shut off the engine. "How are you doing?" he asked, inspecting the wound to see if the blood had stopped flowing.

"Okay. How does it look?"

"I think it's stopping."

Andrew led the way along the ditch as it curved and entered his special place, a shaded isolated area, very different from the arid heat of the open fields.

"This is a great spot," Matthew said. "Nice and cool and . . . private." He handed his canteen to Andrew who gratefully accepted a drink of water.

"Thanks," Andrew said, wiping his mouth. "It's still cold." It was not until then that he noticed that Matthew was carrying his shovel. "Are you planning on irrigating?" he asked with a grin.

"Just in case we need to look like we're working." He carefully leaned the shovel against the embankment. "Besides, we might have to defend ourselves against a bear."

Andrew laughed and sat on the edge of the ditch with his back against the rocky cliff. The familiar scent of the damp vegetation and fresh earth stimulated his senses, especially when Matthew sat down beside him.

"I'm sorry about the accident. I should have been going slower, but I guess I was a bit excited."

"It's all right," Andrew said. "I think I felt the same way." He looked at Matthew. "I'm glad you're here with me."

Matthew leaned against him and put his hand on his thigh. "Me too. How did you ever find this place?"

"It was one of my assignments in the spring. Father Luke asked me to walk the ditches to look for animal burrows, mostly on the higher ditches. If they burrow out the side of the ditch, and it goes undetected, the water eventually washes away the dirt and it could cause a slide—like the McLaren wash."

"A burrow hole caused that?" Matthew asked.

"That's what Father Luke said."

Matthew nuzzled his neck. "And just how much time do you spend here?"

Andrew inhaled his hay scented hair. "Not that much but, when I do, it's you I think about."

Suddenly, Matthew shifted his position. "I can't begin to tell you how much I missed being with you." Before Andrew could answer, Matthew leaned forward, licked his neck, and then kissed Andrew aggressively, as they both tasted the salty yet not unpleasant perspiration.

"Do you really think of me often?" Matthew asked.

"Probably more than I should," Andrew said with a slight smile. "There are times when it seems as though I fall in love with the beauty of the summer day, much like today, and I say to myself, I wish Matthew were here to share those feelings." He brushed Matthew's hair back, out of his eyes. "And here you are."

"I'm glad you finally asked me to meet you, outside, like this."

"Well, I wasn't sure that I wanted to share this particular place, but the more I thought about it, it only made sense that you should experience it with me."

Matthew leaned forward and squeezed him. "You make me crazy when you say things like that." Once again, he kissed Andrew hard, as their tongues explored the moist intimate areas.

When Matthew broke away, he aggressively tugged on Andrew's T-shirt and pushed it up, under his arms, exposing his stomach and chest.

"Stay right where you are," Matthew said softly, as he stood up suddenly. He removed first one rubber boot and then the other, followed by both socks. Standing barefoot on the soft soil, he pulled his T-shirt over his head, unzipped his jeans, and awkwardly slipped out of them. With only a hint of a pause, he slid his shorts below his knees, stepped out of them, and stood completely naked in front of Andrew, who gazed, admirably, at the man before him.

"You are some work of art," Andrew whispered, unabashed by Matthew's lack of inhibition.

Matthew's beauty, in this natural light, was conveyed through proportion, muscularity, and complexion, a combination which, for Andrew, translated into raw sexuality, something he was overwhelmingly desirous of and unable to control.

"I want you, Andrew—all of you—and don't get upset because, in my heart, I know that you must want me to have you, to feel my mouth on you fully, and to give you what we both need."

Andrew smiled briefly. "I suppose I anticipated this conversation long before this." He rubbed his eyes and then pushed back his hair. "You're right; I do want it—as much as you. But I need to hear it . . . do you honestly care for me as much as you seem to . . . as much as I care for you, and willingly risk each day, knowing that it could destroy our reason for being here?"

"*Yes*," Matthew said without hesitation. "I think that you sometimes doubt my ability to love, and perhaps—my ability to reason. But I do. I love you."

Andrew stood, leaned forward, and kissed him with rekindled craving. "I think it's the right time."

Like a slot machine junkie who just hit triple sevens, Matthew savored a tingling intensity in every nerve of his body. He knelt submissively in front of Andrew, coaxing the warm bittersweet reward, which also welled up within him, and then exploded onto the soil.

"Oh, God," Andrew whispered, as he sank to his knees in front of Matthew. "Do you feel as good as I do? It feels as though my entire body tried to exit through my erection."

Matthew laughed and hugged him. "From what I felt—I think it did." He leaned back, looked intently, yet briefly, at Andrew, and then kissed him lovingly.

The taste of his own semen renewed Andrew's commitment to Matthew as a valid partner who, once again, successfully tore down another wall between them, by loving uninhibitedly and taking within him the essence of Andrew's intimacy—as if by doing so, the more they would become one.

"I think we both could use a bath," Matthew said. He grabbed Andrew's arm. "The ditch looks pretty refreshing right now." Without waiting for an answer, he lifted Andrew to his feet and pulled him toward the frigid water.

"You're not serious . . .," Andrew protested, but before he knew it, he was waist deep in what felt like the Arctic sea.

Suddenly, Matthew emerged from below the surface, like a nuclear submarine, jumped on Andrew, and pulled him down with him.

Although he was submerged for only a few seconds, Andrew thought it was an eternity. In the murky silence, the water seemed to penetrate directly through his skin, flooding his internal organs and chilling them instantly. He was sure that clouds of steam must have risen above him and settled over the ditch. As if in slow motion, he managed to push against the bottom of the ditch and propel himself upward until he was standing, shaking the water from his hair and laughing, as Matthew moved forward, pulled him toward him and hugged him. He was grateful to be alive.

"You're insane, you know," Andrew declared.

Matthew squeezed him even harder. "Yes," he said. "Insanely in love with you."

Andrew suddenly stepped back and appeared to be distracted.

"What is it?" Matthew asked.

In the distance, the faint drone of an engine appeared to be growing louder.

"Oh shit!" Andrew exclaimed. "It sounds like a dirt bike."

As if perfectly choreographed, they both jumped out of the ditch and began frantically sorting through piles of clothes for familiar items.

"Forget your underwear, this time," Matthew insisted. "Go for the jeans and stuff your shorts in a pocket."

"Good idea . . . and why is it I get the feeling you've done this before," Andrew remarked.

Matthew scoffed "Just keep dressing."

The sound of the dirt bike grew louder and louder and then suddenly stopped.

Matthew yanked on his second boot, pulled his T-shirt down, over his head, and crept toward the open area with his shovel. Looking into the field, he could see the bike and rider, paused, as if observing, and then suddenly, the bike moved forward in a wide arc and drove slowly out of sight.

"Almost as if they were looking for us," Andrew said.

His presence startled Matthew, who thought he had remained, hidden in the glade.

"Did you see who it was?" Andrew asked.

"If I had to guess, I'd say it was Brother Mark." Matthew stood to observe the scene more prudently; he seemed to scan the area with eaglelike vision. "Well, we managed to have some luck on our side."

"How?" Andrew asked.

"Look at where the bikes are parked. My kickstand must have sunk in your expertly irrigated soil and the bike fell over. With the grass so tall, he only saw one bike."

"Do you think it was divine intervention?" Andrew quipped sarcastically.

"Nope—gravity," Matthew said with a smile. He turned and faced Andrew with a more somber expression. "Thanks for believing in me . . . for letting us share our lives more fully." He kissed Andrew's forehead, nose, and then lightly pressed his lips against his. "I better get out of here before I drag you back into the woods."

Just before he reached his bike, he turned and called back to Andrew. "Don't spend too much time looking for these." He reached into his pocket and held up both of their underwear.

With a grin from ear to ear, Andrew watched as Matthew's bike shimmered in the distant heat and then dissolved into the horizon.

* * *

Chapter Sixteen

Father Gerald's Disclosure

Summer, that particular year, pulled out all the stops. Its beauty was punctuated with extremes, breaking heat records and flaunting extraordinary, yet often frightening storms, which lit up the skies with magnificent displays of lightning and thunder, so loud, that more than one member of the community pondered the imminent coming of Christ. A particularly vicious storm, in early June, resulted in the loss of a metal-roofed barn, on the upper mesa, and two tractors, which were parked inside, after being struck by a massive bolt of lightning.

Andrew watched from a distance as the structure burned out of control. He heard small explosions, most likely, the gas tanks on the tractors, just before the building collapsed and sent skyward a shower of sparks and burning embers.

He returned to his cell and stood in front of his closet. A small mirror on the upper shelf reflected his slightly sunburned face as he searched for his habit in the dim light. He glanced up, surprised to see his own image and was pleased with its reflected features—a strong nose, prominent cheekbones, and shiny dark hair—chaotic and unpretentious. 'Vanity,' he thought, 'is ruinous.'

He pulled his robe over his clothing and looked once more at the mirror. 'So,' he mused, 'what is it, but genetics?' Andrew was about to drop the scapular over his head when he realized that the oppressive heat and humidity, after the rain, had him sweating profusely. He stopped, tossed the scapular onto his bed and removed his robe. He let his jeans fall to the floor and stepped out of them. For the first time, Andrew got dressed in his habit, wearing nothing but his jockey shorts and a T-shirt, something that Brother Mark said he resorted to every summer. And now, Andrew knew why. The cotton brushed against his legs and caused the air to circulate freely, creating a pleasant, if not sensual, experience, which began to express itself physically; a situation Andrew resolved by rearranging his scapular to drape even more loosely in front of him.

Compline eased the community into the meditative dusk. The sound of singing birds surged into the quiet chapel through the open windows, filling it with melodious discord, a tolerable cacophony, until Brother Edward tugged on the thick bell ropes, causing a much greater commotion, which silenced the startled birds, at least through the reading of the first Psalm, when they resumed their noisy chatter.

As he had done so many times in the past, Andrew watched the members of the community enter the church and take their assigned seats. Visitors, guests, and potential Observers arrived and quietly found seats on the hard benches that lined the walls of the chapel. Andrew noticed a young woman, wearing an acceptably short and colorful sundress, sit down with familiar poise, on the opposite side of the chapel and face him. Although he was slightly nearsighted, he was sure that it was Ellen; however, he could not recall a conversation with Matthew about Ellen returning for a retreat.

Brother Edward switched on the overhead lights, which signaled the start of the service. After an intentional look at each of the monks, Father Paul blew softly into his pitch pipe, establishing the correct key, and intoned the first chant of Compline.

With his hymnal held higher than usual, Andrew peered over the top and looked, again, at the woman whom he suspected was Ellen. At the same time, she also looked up and met Andrew's eyes with a memorable smile, as she mouthed the word "hi." 'Who,' he thought, 'but Ellen could reduce religious ritual to the mundane with her unpretentious smirk.' He responded with an exaggerated grin.

After a period of meditation, Andrew heard footsteps and watched as Father Gerald approached the pulpit in preparation for the next reading; he adjusted his glasses, and much to Andrew surprise, Father Gerald continued with John Sanford's book, which he had been reading, earlier, in the refectory:

> *"Thus in sexuality, we not only seek the satisfaction of physical needs, the release of physical tensions and, sometimes, psychological intimacy with other people; we can also be expressing our longing for ecstasy, that is, for an enlargement of narrow ego consciousness through contact with the divine . . . nor have the values of the spirit ever been realized through the repression of the senses, and sometimes, spiritual development arouses and needs sensual love in order to be grounded and become substantial."*

Father Gerald closed the book and returned to his seat, as the community began its final meditation for the evening.

Not knowing whether to believe his ears, Andrew glanced, furtively, around the room, half expecting a mass exodus by his brothers in an attempt to comply with or, hopefully, experience, Mr. Sanford's seemingly antithetical message. Instead, only Matthew made eye contact, however briefly, with an "I told you so" expression, which needed no further explanation. Andrew immediately dropped his gaze to the floor and resumed his meditation. He was filled with questions about the reading, not necessarily in disagreement, but more concerned about Father Gerald's choice, and the nature of the message within a monastic setting.

When the service ended, Andrew's eyes searched for Father Gerald through the smoky haze of incense. Although many of his brothers left the church immediately to return to their cells, Father Gerald sat quietly, in the growing dusk, while Andrew watched him from the corner of his eye. He had hoped to share his concerns with Father Gerald that evening, if possible, knowing fully that he would be in violation of the strictly monitored Grand Silence, which prohibited unnecessary speech. When Father Gerald eventually shifted in his chair and stood up to leave, Andrew discreetly followed him from a distance, down the darkened cloister, toward the infirmary where Father Gerald unlocked the door, entered, and closed the door behind him.

For several minutes, Andrew paced the cloister, trying to decide whether or not he should go through with his plan, even though he was quite sure Father Gerald would be receptive. Feeling courageous, he stood in front of the wooden door and gently knocked.

After a slight pause, the door opened. Father Gerald, dressed in lightweight pants and a short sleeve shirt, stood, smiling, a pipe in one hand, while he extended the other toward Andrew. There was no immediate conversation—he simply pulled Andrew into the room and quietly closed the door.

"I know I shouldn't be bothering you," Andrew said with reservation.

Father Gerald held up his hand as if to silence him. "It's perfectly okay," he said quietly, "in fact, it's nice to have some company once in a while." He turned and led Andrew toward two large chairs where he had apparently been sitting and reading, judging from the thick book placed on the seat of one of the chairs. He gestured toward the available seat. "Please—sit down and make yourself comfortable."

Andrew sunk into the chair, which needed no getting used to since it felt as though it were custom-made for his particular frame. "That's very easy to do in this chair," Andrew commented.

"I know. There are many nights when I find myself dozing right here until the early hours of the morning."

An oscillating fan quietly generated a comfortable breeze, which found its way under Andrew's robes and over his legs. This part of the infirmary was unfamiliar to Andrew who knew only the clinical area where three sterile beds stood waiting for afflicted brothers. He was happy to be ensconced in the plush wingback.

"If you don't mind," Andrew began, "I'd like to ask you . . ."

"About the book I've been reading?" Father Gerald interrupted.

"Yes," Andrew said, mildly surprised by Father Gerald's intuition. "It seems to have a message that encourages spiritual growth through sexuality, and I was wondering how that would be compatible with our lives here at the monastery. Don't get me wrong—it's not offensive to me . . . just confusing."

Father Gerald smiled, pulled on his pipe and slowly exhaled a fragrant cloud of smoke through his nose. "I expect others will feel the same way—or, perhaps, even offended, but I found the book's message important enough to share with the community and, once Father Jude gave his approval, I began with the readings."

"But . . ." Andrew stopped himself; he nearly remarked that such a situation would be like asking a thief if it would be acceptable to rob a bank.

"Yes?" Father Gerald asked.

"How does the message work?"

"I suppose it's like Psych 101. We can't deny our sexuality any more than we can avoid contemplating our existence, our cosmic relationship with the unknown. The church's history of repression has not been especially healthy, and that's very unfortunate. I think that Sanford may be suggesting that spirituality and sexuality are closely linked, and may even build upon each other."

"I guess that's the easy part," Andrew explained. "What do we, supposedly celibate monks, do with such a message?"

Father Gerald shifted in his chair. "I think each member of the community will have to interpret that the way he feels most comfortable. I'm certainly not trying to advocate blatant sexuality, but we need to de-emphasize the negative aspects of sex and the tremendous amount of guilt that has been attributed to it by the church for so many centuries. Man is sexual by nature. That's why it's very important to establish open communication, especially in the monastic setting, and to properly guide young men, such as yourself, to deal with the subject in realistic terms."

"Maybe St. Aelred had the right idea," Andrew commented.

Father Gerald smiled. "I think he may have." He reached toward the can of tobacco, repacked his pipe and lit it. "Yet my perspective may be influenced by my life as a married man. Others may not share my point of view."

Andrew found Father Gerald's marital experience and remarks insightful. "So . . . how does a young member of the community deal with his sexuality in this setting?"

Once again, Father Gerald was shrouded in smoke, after drawing deeply and exhaling. "Discreetly," he said candidly.

His one-word response was unexpected and, although it was somewhat startling, Andrew feigned a casual nonchalance. He wondered if there were more to the remark then intended. "I guess that wasn't the answer I expected," Andrew said.

Father Gerald apologized. "It was the first thought that came to mind. I hope I haven't offended you."

"No . . . not really." Andrew's reply was delivered awkwardly. He paused and then continued. "Perhaps I should be the one apologizing."

"That's certainly not my intent," Father Gerald said genuinely, as he leaned forward toward Andrew.

Without spelling it out in eight-inch letters, it was clear to both of them that the conversation became specific yet nonthreatening. Andrew sensed a safe space with Father Gerald, an opportunity to share some of his inner thoughts on that part of his life which began unexpectedly, and now permeated his very soul. "You know about Matthew and me, don't you," Andrew said bluntly.

Father Gerald carefully set his pipe in the large ashtray. He quickly rubbed his hands over his face and sat back in his chair. "Look," he said thoughtfully. "You don't have to do this."

"I know," Andrew continued, "but it might do some good, that is, if you're not offended."

"Well," Father Gerald said, "I won't be offended, and right now, it seems as though it's very important for you to discuss it."

"Maybe so," Andrew said, "but I get the feeling that you already know about Matthew and me."

"Not exactly; more 'suspect'—I have no proof of anything, nor do I feel a need to. It's not my role here."

Andrew shifted in his chair. "I never intended or, least of all, expected, that this would happen to me, yet it has, and as difficult as it has been, I've been able to deal with it as best I can. I have no idea where it's all going or what can become of it in the monastery—that's why I was so taken by your reading of Sanford's book. It was as if everything Matthew has been saying is now factual—black and white."

Father Gerald stood, walked over to the glass front cooler, and opened it. "Cranberry juice or diet Pepsi?"

"Uh . . . cranberry, thanks."

Father Gerald returned with two large plastic cups and handed one to Andrew. He sat down and slowly sipped his drink, as he mulled over Andrew's words. "I wish I had the perfect response for you, Andrew, but as you know, even here—or especially here—nothing's perfect."

"I understand," Andrew said. "I just thought you might have some words of advice . . . or something."

"Maybe the following will be helpful to you. It's very personal and I would appreciate it if you would keep it between us."

Andrew nodded. "Sure," he said.

Father Gerald stared off in the distance and began his story. "Just about one year after my wife died, I decided to spend more time with my kids . . . well, they're not exactly kids anymore; Elizabeth is pushing thirty and Luke is just a few years older than you. Elizabeth has been married for three years, and I'm already a grandfather. Luke is still single and living in southern Vermont. I visited both of them for a relatively short period of time—we all became a lot closer and more respectful of each other's choices in life. They, initially, had a hard time accepting my decision to give up a successful medical practice and enter a monastery, just as I, initially, had a hard time accepting some of their choices." He smiled and brushed his hand over his face. "Of course, Luke would immediately correct me, if he were here, and with good reason. He is living a successful, and apparently happy, life with another man, whom he has been with for many years. His friend or partner—I'm never sure how to refer to Ethan—is a pediatric anesthesiologist, an incredibly likable fellow who seems to evidence a genuine love for my son who, I have to admit, is very lovable, and practically worships the ground that Ethan walks on." Father Gerald took a long drink of his soda and continued. "Anyway, I guess what I'm getting at is, as difficult as it was for me to really accept Luke's particular lifestyle, I have done so, and more. I now understand him, respect his right to be who he really is, and realize that choice had very little to do with his sexuality. It's who he is—what he always was—and I will always love him very much."

Andrew sat quietly, mesmerized with intrigue and the frankness of Father Gerald's disclosure. He knew that the story carried a certain message—an acknowledgment and acceptance of his relationship with Matthew, something he clearly had not anticipated, at least, not on such a personal level. He rubbed his eyes and looked at Father Gerald, who eventually looked his way. "Luke is a fortunate guy to have you for his dad," Andrew said softly.

"And I feel fortunate that he's my son."

Andrew shifted in his chair. "I never expected to hear all of this, yet I want you to know that it means a lot to me, and I appreciate you taking me into your confidence. It's very helpful to me."

The exhaled pipe smoke circled above Father Gerald head. "I had a feeling that it would be helpful to you, Andrew, yet I'm far from being an expert in this area. If you ever feel the need to discuss the subject more thoroughly, the offer with Dr. Klein, in Bitter Creek, still stands."

Andrew could feel his defensiveness begin to surface. "I'm not a basket case yet, am I?"

"Far from it," Father Gerald said quickly. "My intention was to direct you to someone who would be able to help answer your questions, or settle your thoughts, should the need arise later on. I understand that it's not an easy road."

Andrew chuckled. "Not to mention impossible in a monastery."

"Oh, I don't know," Father Gerald remarked. "As I said, discretion plays an important role."

The unexpected comment heartened Andrew. "Maybe I should read Sanford's book—cover to cover."

"I think you'll find it very interesting."

Andrew set his glass on the small end table. "I had better be going or I'll never get up for vigils." He stood and extended his hand to Father Gerald. "Thanks, again, for listening and for being so helpful. It really means a lot to me."

"Life can be confusing, particularly in a monastery," Father Gerald said, shaking Andrew's hand. "And please—feel comfortable to stop in whenever you need to talk."

* * *

Chapter Seventeen

The Proving Ground

"Have you ever been in a large eggery, Brother Kevin?" Andrew asked tentatively, knowing that the response would most likely be negative.

The young Observer hesitated. "Well, not exactly, but my grandfather has a few chickens." His deep red hair was genetically complemented by his nearly pale complexion, which, unfairly, evoked a subtle aridity. "I've helped him gather eggs a couple of times,"

"That's a start," Andrew said with a smile. He anticipated a long afternoon in the brutal heat, as he demonstrated the art of egg collecting to the relatively quiet neophyte. He carefully pushed the four-wheel cart, which required practice and energy, as the layers of eggs in their soft, purple cartons grew increasingly higher and heavier as the day wore on and the heat and stench in the eggery became even more oppressive. Being taller, Andrew chose to collect the upper tier, while pushing the cart with his thigh. This allowed him to use both hands, which was often necessary, since his helper seemed to be missing many of the eggs from the lower row of cages.

Even in the hazy light, Andrew could see the change in Kevin's complexion. His face grew ruddy and smudged with grime as he attempted to brush away persistent flies or wipe the perspiration from his eyes.

"It sure is hot in here," Andrew said, hoping to hear a response, yet Kevin remained silent, grabbing one egg after another, with his small hands, while wiping his forehead with his shirt sleeve.

As they neared the end of the row, Andrew noticed that Kevin's face looked even redder than before, with little evidence of perspiration. At first, it appeared as though Kevin stumbled, caught himself, and then resumed his work, but when Andrew glanced up, he saw Kevin grasp the cage with both hands and begin to lean backwards. He rushed around the cart and caught him, just as he was about to collapse into the dung pit below the cages. He carried him into the cool processing room, gently set him on the floor and immediately soaked a towel with cold water, wrung it out, and placed it under Kevin's neck, prior to calling the monastery.

Before Father Gerald arrived, Andrew had already draped several wet towels over Kevin and was wiping his face with a cool cloth.

The door flew open as Father Gerald and Brother Nathan rushed in to assist the stricken Observer. "Good job," Father Gerald said calmly as he fastened a blood pressure cuff around Kevin's arm. "Where did you learn to do this?"

Andrew had difficulty thinking. "Boy Scouts," he muttered.

After listening in silence, Father Gerald removed his stethoscope and pulled the cuff from Kevin's arm. "We need to get some ice on him."

Without instruction, Brother Nathan lifted Kevin effortlessly and, within seconds, placed him on the backseat of the abbot's Peugeot, as Father Gerald got behind the wheel.

"Jump in," Father Gerald said, looking at Andrew.

" . . . The eggs," Andrew stammered.

"The eggs will be fine. Hurry."

Andrew quickly got in and closed the door as Father Gerald put the car in gear and drove rapidly toward the monastery.

It was not long before Kevin was placed in one of the infirmary beds, packed with ice, while an IV bottle, suspended above him, dripped a rehydrating solution into his arm.

From a distance, Andrew watched with fascination as the process unfolded. He then sank into the familiar armchair located in Father Gerald's office. "Will he be all right?" Andrew asked, as Brother Nathan and Father Gerald entered the room.

"I think so," Father Gerald said. "It's a good thing you were with him."

"The wet towels were extremely beneficial," Brother Nathan added.

Andrew smiled. "It's strange, but my first aid course suddenly popped into my mind, and I just did what I thought was right."

"And you did it well," Father Gerald said proudly. "But before I have two casualties, I want to check your blood pressure, and be sure that you have a large glass of juice before you leave."

"I'll be fine," Andrew protested.

"I know you will so . . . let's have your arm."

Andrew lifted his right arm while Father Gerald wrapped the cuff tightly around it and began to inflate the balloonlike apparatus. With his stethoscope in place, Father Gerald listened intently, deflated the cuff and removed it along with the stethoscope.

"A bit high but nothing to worry about."

Brother Nathan suddenly appeared with a large glass of orange juice. "You may also need some fluids," he said, offering the glass to Andrew, who inexplicably imagined him as an English manservant, properly overdressed, in tails and white gloves.

"Thanks," Andrew said with a smile.

Brother Nathan smiled and walked briskly toward the infirmary to monitor Kevin.

"I will ask the abbot if I may address the community, tomorrow at lunch, about everyone's need to consume sufficient amount of liquids," Father Gerald said. "This heat can be dangerous, especially in a place like the eggery."

"It was pretty hot down there," Andrew admitted. He swallowed a large quantity of juice. "Maybe I should have seen this coming. Kevin's face was pretty red."

"None of that," Father Gerald insisted. "You are not responsible for an Observer being overcome with heat exhaustion; in fact; as I said, it was a good thing you were with him."

Andrew finished his juice and set the glass on the table. "Maybe so but . . . I wonder if this will have a bad impact on how Kevin sees himself as a potential monk."

"What do you mean?" Father Gerald asked. He appeared puzzled.

"You know," Andrew continued. "It's as though the eggery is used as a 'proving ground' for Observers, to see if they can handle the nasty task of collecting the eggs—surrounded by the stench and squawking of ten thousand cramped hens. I just assumed it was SOP around here."

"Not that I'm aware of," Father Gerald said sternly. "And at least while I'm here, it had better not be SOP, as you say."

"Well, forgive me if I've said too much, but many of us understand it to be that way."

A curious smile crossed Father Gerald's face. "We'll see," he said softly. "And I know what you're thinking, so don't worry about it—your name will not be mentioned."

"Thanks," Andrew said.

When Father Gerald returned, he found Andrew resting comfortably in the same chair. "He's doing fine," Father Gerald said. "He's alert, his temperature is down, and his pressure is normal. Would you like to talk with him?"

Andrew sat up and rubbed his eyes. "What should I say?"

"Well, I made it clear that you were specifically responsible for his recovery by your quick actions, along with, of course, God's intervention. I'm sure he will want to thank you."

"But you and Brother Nathan did all the real work," Andrew insisted.

Father Gerald raised his hand in protest. "If you had not been there and began cooling his body, he may have died. End of discussion," Father Gerald retorted.

Andrew shrugged. "Okay, but he's not very talkative."

Father Gerald chuckled. "Don't expect it of him." He offered his hand to Andrew and helped pull him to a standing position. "Are you all right?"

Andrew stretched and shook his head. "I'm fine," he said.

With a pensive expression, Father Gerald paused. "If you want, you might mention what we talked about earlier, that there is no real connection between collecting eggs and one's ability to become a good monk. Otherwise, they would have thrown me out of here a long time ago."

Andrew chuckled. "I suppose I can do that," he said. "Besides, I'm sure there must be some 'not so good monks' who can collect eggs pretty easily."

"You think so?" Father Gerald said with a wink.

Entering the infirmary, Andrew was immediately aware of the cool freshness in the room. Two fans circulated the air conditioned environment, stirring the curtains into a repetitively choreographed ballet for faceless dancers.

Kevin appeared mesmerized by their movement as he lay in bed, covered with only a sheet. His face had lost most of its earlier color yet his cheeks remained flushed, as if embarrassed by his involuntary illness. One bare arm rested on his chest.

"Are you feeling better?" Andrew asked softly. He hoped that he would be acknowledged, if only by a nod. Instead, he was surprised to see Kevin face him, smile broadly and extended his hand toward him.

"Yes . . . thanks to you." He shook Andrew's hand.

Unexpectedly, Andrew could feel the color rise in his own cheeks, even though the room was sufficiently cool. He had never really looked closely at Kevin, until this moment, when he realized that he possessed extraordinary features, which combined into a single yet subtle handsomeness.

"I see you've been talking to Father Gerald," Andrew said, smiling. "He and Brother Nathan did all the hard work."

"Well, I'm glad that you were with me," Brother Kevin said. He looked directly into Andrew's eyes.

"Me too," Andrew said awkwardly, as though searching for a proper response. He rubbed his eyes and welcomed the ensuing silence to help him refocus.

"I remember when I first saw the eggery," Andrew began, "and I thought—this has got to be hell—full of crap and disease. The smell was overpowering, and the heat—well, you know about the heat—and I didn't want to have anything to do with it. Anyway, after collecting all these years, I still feel the same way. I pretty much dread going in there, but I managed to put up with it and perhaps, I've even gotten good at it, which means that I can get out of there quicker." He pulled a chair close to the head of Kevin's bed and sat down. "No one ever said anything to me, but I felt inside that this is what it must take to become a good monk and pull my weight in the community; sort of a trial by fire. Now, I've come to realize that *I* was responsible for putting all that unnecessary pressure on myself. I've learned that we all have different gifts, different skills, even though there are times when we feel we have nothing to offer. It really doesn't matter externally, what we are capable of—or, who has the shortest haircut, or who can last the longest on a Zen stool. What really matters is what's inside, how big one's heart is, and how forgiving we can be toward each other . . . I guess what I'm trying to say is don't let what happened today dissuade you from your reason for being here. Believe me, there is no connection between being a good monk and being good at collecting eggs, or cooking, or irrigating the fields. Just follow your heart."

Kevin rolled on his side and faced Andrew. "It's as though you knew what I was thinking, what I was . . . fearing. I expected to be told that I would have to leave." His apprehension was obvious.

Andrew smiled and put his hand on Kevin's. "It's what I would have thought when I was an Observer, but it isn't true, so don't worry about it. You need to concentrate on getting better. Besides, who knows; you may already be the best monk in the community." Andrew stood up to leave. Kevin's genuine smile needed no response. He squeezed Kevin's hand, turned and exited the infirmary, into Father Gerald's office.

"How did it go?" Father Gerald asked, as he sat at his desk, writing.

"It was just as I thought," Andrew said. "He figured he'd be asked to leave because he failed at collecting eggs."

Father Gerald set down his pen and turned to face Andrew. "That's ridiculous," he said.

"I know," Andrew agreed. "I just hope others feel the same as you."

"Well, they had better after today."

* * *

The cloister radiated a burnished glow after being thoroughly mopped and waxed. As he walked toward his cell, Andrew realized he had not changed his shoes or clothing, after working in the eggery, and looked back in haste to see the dusty shoe prints he had left behind. Leaning against the wall, he removed both shoes and set them on a small ledge below the arched windows. He then removed his outer shirt, turned it inside out, and dropped to his knees where he began the process of cleaning the telltale marks. He had nearly finished when he heard footsteps behind him.

"That's what mops are for," Matthew whispered, with a grin from ear to ear. "Do you do windows? The one in my cell could use a cleaning."

"Very funny," Andrew remarked. "It's muck from the eggery. I forgot to change my shoes."

"And take a shower . . ."

"Yeah, that too."

Matthew leaned down and took the shirt from Andrew. "I have a feeling you're having a bad day." Without asking, he squatted and finished cleaning the floor while Andrew protested in silence by sitting against the wall, with his head resting on folded arms and raised knees.

When the job was finished, Matthew sat down next to him. "Are you okay?"

"I'm fine," Andrew said, staring at the tiles between his knees. He then raised his head and looked at Matthew. "One of the Observers collapsed at the eggery from the heat. I called Father Gerald, and he put him in the infirmary. He seems to be doing all right."

"Was it the small kid with the red hair?"

"How did you know?"

"I didn't," Matthew said honestly. "When I saw him in the refectory, I thought to myself that he might have difficulty with work, especially the eggery."

Andrew was somewhat baffled by his comment yet decided to let it pass. "He seems like a pretty nice guy—quiet."

Suddenly, Matthew stood up. "I don't believe this," he said, shading his eyes, as he pointed toward the garth.

Thinking that another deer had wandered onto the property, Andrew quickly got up to look. Instead, he saw Father Jude sitting in the open doorway of an empty cell, holding an aluminum sun reflector under his chin to accelerate his tan.

"An excellent example and role model for humility," Matthew said with a sardonic lilt. "When I grow up I want to be just like him."

Andrew shook his head. In a barely audible whisper, he said, "He can't be good for this place."

He picked up his shoes, took his shirt from Matthew, and attempted to stretch his muscles by leaning backwards. "I suppose I should take that shower."

A hint of a smile crossed Matthew's face. "If you need anyone to wash your back..."

Andrew rolled his eyes. "Thanks, but I think I'll manage." He turned to leave but then stopped abruptly. "Hey, thanks for helping me with the floor."

Matthew remained facing him, hands in his pockets, as if expecting more, "You're welcome," he said softly.

Andrew sensed the rueful tone of his voice. He moved closer. "I'm *okay*," he said honestly, looking into Matthew's eyes.

"And us?" Matthew asked.

"We're okay," Andrew insisted.

"Then tell me we can be together tonight—after Compline—just to talk. I need to be with you."

Andrew closed his eyes in jest, as if giving the matter great thought, and smiled. "After dark, I'll leave my screen door unlocked." He turned, walked toward his cell and waved briefly over his shoulder, without looking back.

* * *

Chapter Eighteen

Emerging Symptoms

Supper, that evening, consisted of chilled gazpacho with dollops of sour cream, tabouli salad and wedges of pita bread, all flawlessly prepared by Brother Adrian—an inviting meal for the end of a sweltering day.

Refreshed from his shower, Andrew sat reflectively in the quiet refectory, alternating spoonfuls of the perfectly seasoned soup with salad and bread. In the distance, the setting sun horizontally bisected Navigator Peak—a brilliant salmon-gold summit over a dark green base, surrounded by the watery blue sky of dusk.

Without looking up, he heard the heavy door open and gently close. Footsteps padded softly past him and stopped at the serving table. A faint clang of a stainless steel bowl renewed his curiosity. When he glanced up, Andrew saw Brother Kevin, apparently recovered from this crisis at the eggery, walking toward the opposite side of the room. He selected a seat almost directly across from Andrew, bowed his head in prayer, but this time, Andrew noticed, his hands were simply folded in quiet supplication, not fully extended, as he had observed once before. After a moment of silence, Kevin picked up his spoon and began to eat his soup.

Two other monks entered the refectory, selected what they needed, and sat where each felt least intrusive.

Andrew nearly finished his meal when he felt as though he was being observed; he raised his eyes and met Kevin's innocuous stare with surprise. Rather than look away, he continued to look at Kevin, wondering if he were simply daydreaming or had difficulty with his vision, yet unexpectedly, a subtle smile appeared on his face; Andrew returned the smile. He gathered everything onto his tray, briefly offered a prayer of thanksgiving, and went into the kitchen to washes his dishes.

* * *

Even on the warmest evenings, the inside of the church seemed to offer a refreshing breath of coolness. Its high, vaulted ceiling drew the heat upwards, allowing fresh air to circulate within its brick and tile interior, however; Andrew sensed a difference this particular evening. There was no movement; the air with static, almost stagnant. Perspiration beaded lightly on his forehead, over his nose and across his upper lip. He felt the dampness seeped into the leg openings of his shorts and down his lower back and was relieved that Compline was finally ending.

When he returned to his cell, he switched the small floor fan to high and closed the door to the hall. He opened the slider fully, pulled off his habit and, standing only in his shorts and T-shirt, Andrew hung the robe, scapular and cincture, neatly in his closet. He reached up and found a baggy pair of gym shorts, which he slid over his underwear.

Once again, a familiar, but seldom acknowledged, sense of emptiness enveloped his very being—he recognized the symptoms, yet he rationalized them away as "feeling sorry for himself" or the "normal mandates of the vocation" which generally sufficed, however, the magnitude of this intolerable void seemed persistently overwhelming. At first, he paced, as much as possible, the limited space of his cell, until he realized that it was not beneficial due to the oppressive evening heat. With a thud, he sat at his desk as waves of darkness washed over him, stirring melancholic memories that raced inside his mind, unconnected, yet visually poignant and relentless—until he clutched his head, screamed silently into his hands and began rocking rapidly, back and forth, until the mental agony finally subsided. 'Why is this happening?' he thought. He noticed that his arms were lightly covered with perspiration.

After drying himself with a towel, he returned to his desk and picked up a book he had been reading, a book written by an anonymous Carthusian. Unexpectedly, he found solace in its message:

> *"Perhaps that is why, almost unknown to ourselves, we have always felt the utter insufficiency of creatures and, the transitoriness of this life. The deep interior anguish which results from this conviction is reserved for those souls whom God is calling to a higher life. God keeps them almost continuously aware of the sheer nothingness of all that is around him, in order to detach them from it so that he may take possession of them more readily."*—They Speak by Silence

Through the open slider, Andrew watched as the distant peaks above the slate covered roof slowly darkened in the declining light. A brazen chipmunk scurried up to the screen, stared intently, sniffed several times, and quickly disappeared. 'I hope I don't smell that bad,' Andrew thought with a smile, as he made himself comfortable on his bed. Suddenly, he remembered Matthew's conversation. He got up, unlocked the screen and lay back down, quietly anticipating his expected intruder with tempered ambition.

Once the last iota of light faded into total darkness, Matthew, barefooted, carefully made his way across the dewy garth to Andrew's cell. He quietly slid open the screen, stepped over the row of gravel, and entered the darkened room with the prowess of a cat burglar. Dressed in a black T-shirt and jeans, he blended easily into the night.

Andrew lay sprawled on his bed, sleeping soundly, while the fan circulated the warm, evening air over his body.

Matthew mused upon the childlike man before him, comfortably sedated by the influence of deep sleep. He noted that Andrew's leg and arm positions, bent in different directions, curiously resembled a badly drawn swastika in need of arrangement. He quietly walked to the hall door and gently pushed in the center knob of the handle to lock it. Intuitively, he knew that he should do the right thing and leave, yet looking down once more at such dormant grace, Matthew felt his heart expand and reverberate from his head to his groin—leaving was no longer an option.

Instead, he pulled his T-shirt over his head, stepped out of his unbuttoned jeans, and set them on the desk. He carefully faced the desk chair toward the bed, and wearing only his jockey shorts, Matthew sat and pondered, once more, the idiosyncrasies of Andrew's sleep pattern.

Occasional twitches would cause first, one arm to move briefly and then the other, or the propensity would be repeated in his legs. Eventually, after a muffled whimpering sound, Andrew shifted his weight to his back, extending both legs to the end of the mattress.

Without hesitation, Matthew silently squatted at the end of the bed to massage Andrew's feet. He carefully began to rub one foot, lightly applying pressure to the top, up to the toes and over the ball of his foot. Although he moved slightly, Andrew continued to sleep soundly while Matthew proceeded from one foot to the other with his therapeutic touch.

Yet the sensuality, Matthew realized, was more than unilateral. Unable to resist, he leaned forward slightly and put his mouth over Andrew's toes, gently sucking and licking, hoping that Andrew would not awaken, since the pleasure he was providing paled in comparison with the pleasure he received. Finished with one foot, Matthew moved on to the other with even greater appetite, repeating his actions more aggressively, as though ingestion might be an option. He reached down and gently touched himself, but quickly withdrew his hand due to his heightened level of arousal—any additional stimulus would easily cause him to ejaculate.

"Come up here," Andrew said softly.

Surprised, Matthew looked up to see Andrew, propped up by his elbows, watching him. He obediently lifted himself over the foot of the bed and crawled alongside of him, unsure of Andrew's mood.

Without a word, Andrew rolled to one side and wrapped his arms around him, hugging him as tightly as Matthew had often hugged him. He buried his face in Matthew's neck while his legs intertwined with his and pulled his body even closer, which, still, did not seem close enough.

More than concerned, Matthew pulled away slightly and held Andrew's head with both hands so that he could look directly at him. "Hey . . .," he said softly. "Are you okay?" He continued to hold his face in front of him until Andrew spoke.

"I don't know," he said quietly. The sullen tone of his voice was obvious.

Matthew released Andrew's head and they both lay back against the pillow, staring into each other's eyes.

"Well, it doesn't sound like it," Matthew whispered. "What's going on?"

"I'm tired of talking about myself," Andrew said with discouragement. He closed his eyes and rolled onto his back.

Matthew remained on his side, studying Andrew's profile. In the darkness, Andrew's growing five o'clock shadow appeared as a full beard, clipped close to the face. He had to reach out and touch his cheek to verify the truth.

"Even to me?" Matthew asked.

Andrew remained silent.

"Talk to me," Matthew insisted.

Andrew rubbed his eyes. "It happened again tonight."

"What?"

"That feeling," Andrew began. "It's hard to describe."

"You've felt it before?" Matthew asked.

"Yes, but not like this . . . it's a hollow emptiness that just gets worse and worse until it seems to scream garbled sounds inside my head, and my head feels like it's going to explode." He turned to look at Matthew. "I didn't want to say anything to you before—I hoped it would just go away."

Matthew propped himself up on one elbow to look directly down at him. He gently pushed Andrew's hair out of his eyes. "Sounds like a lot of stress to me," he said quietly. "I just hope I'm not the cause of it." He continued to rub Andrew's forehead.

"I have no idea what's causing it; I just want it to stop," Andrew whispered.

Matthew leaned forward and kissed him lightly on the forehead. "Be honest—is it me?"

Andrew stared into his eyes. "Don't do this to me, Matt," he said anxiously. "I don't know what it is."

Matthew fell back against the pillow. "I'm here to be with you, to talk with you, but I don't know what to say other than something you already know—how much I love you."

"And I love you too," Andrew said as he rolled onto his side to face Matthew. "A lot has happened since my arrival here—including us—and some of it has been kind of rough for me."

"Are 'we' a part of the rough stuff?"

"Don't make me explain it again," Andrew pleaded. "You know how difficult it was for me, initially, but you have to admit, I've come a long way since then."

"You have," Matthew said, "and I'm very lucky." He reached up and gently ran his fingers over Andrew's cheek. "Aren't you warm in that T-shirt?"

Before Andrew could answer, Matthew grabbed the shirt by the bottom and began to pull it over Andrew's head.

"Not anymore," Andrew said with a smile. He lay down next to Matthew. "By the way, did you walk over here in your underwear?" He glanced down at Matthew's jockey shorts.

"No, I walked over here naked. The shorts are yours."

Andrew sat up to inspect them.

"Check inside the back." Matthew rolled in the opposite direction.

Written in black laundry ink, Andrew did, in fact, see his own name printed neatly next to the label.

"I'm not sure who is crazier—you or me," he said with a laugh.

"What does it matter?" Matthew said as he rolled onto his back. "Didn't you once say 'there are hospitals for guys like us'?" He reached up and pulled Andrew on top of him.

Nuzzled against Matthew's neck, Andrew relished the familiar scent of his skin and hair, the strength of the arm around his shoulders, and the taut definition of his chest.

"I saw Ellen yesterday," he said unexpectedly.

"She's back?" Matthew asked, with moderate concern.

"Well, I'm not sure for how long but she was at Vespers. Didn't you talk with her?"

"No," Matthew said. "I had no idea she was planning another retreat."

Andrew rolled carefully onto his back. Even though the sun had long disappeared, the room continued to be uncomfortably warm. He wanted to discuss Ellen's relationship with the abbot but decided against it, knowing that it would only anger Matthew.

"So what do you think about the book that Father Gerald is reading?" Matthew asked suddenly, as if intentionally changing topics.

"I thought you wrote it," Andrew quipped. "You must have noticed my expression at Vespers."

Matthew laughed. "I probably could have, yet I would have been more explicit."

"No doubt," Andrew replied.

"It's not too far from what I often feel—here, about you," Matthew said. He turned to face Andrew who continued to lay on his back while Matthew affectionately traced the contours of his chest with his index finger. "You may doubt my sincerity about my own spiritual path but it's real, and it doesn't mean that sexual expression should be excluded. Isn't that what is being said in the book?"

"I guess . . .," Andrew said softly. "I still have some concerns about how it all fits together in a monastic setting." He glanced quickly at Matthew and then put his hand over his to reinforce and, perhaps, protect their relationship. "I haven't told you, but I spoke to Father Gerald about it and essentially asked him how it all fits in."

"What did he say?"

"It's more what he didn't say," Andrew explained. "When I asked how men in a monastery deal with their sexuality, he said, 'Discreetly,' as though he knew exactly what I was referring to."

"You mean about us . . ."

"Well . . . yes. I'm convinced he knows about us, and I'm also convinced that he feels it's genuinely all right—depending on proper discretion."

"What did I tell you," Matthew whispered excitedly.

"It's tremendously supportive," Andrew said, smiling, "yet it doesn't exactly mean we have the right to fornicate in the chapel."

Matthew covered his mouth to stifle his laughter. "I love when you talk dirty." He playfully rolled into Andrew and put his leg between his, and without Andrew knowing it, he quickly slid his shorts over his hips and thighs and pulled them off with his foot. He kissed his neck and gently nibbled his earlobe, and just he was about to place his mouth on Andrew's, he could feel Andrew pull away.

"What's the matter?" he asked softly, looking into Andrew's eyes.

With hesitation, Andrew looked away, unsure of his words.

"Just tell me," Matthew whispered as he put his hand up to his mouth and exhaled. "Is it . . . my breath?" he asked timidly.

Andrew smiled and shook his head. "Your breath is fine. It must be me, recovering from my 'episode' this evening."

Matthew lay back against the pillow, afraid that there might be more in Andrew's statement than he expressed. "Look," he whispered. "Tell me what's really bothering you. It has to be something between us, but if you don't talk about it, I can't help you."

Andrew rubbed his eyes, rolled on his side, and faced him. "It's just what I've been trying to say all along. How does all of this fit?"

"You heard Father Gerald's response," Matthew said. "Discretion."

Andrew closed his eyes and then opened them. "I know . . . but what the heck does that really mean? I've said it before, Matt; my feelings for you are, at times, nearly uncontrollable, both the physical aspects of our relationship, and the genuine love that I feel inside. Sometimes, I just want us to be with each other, respectful of each other's needs, not necessarily feeling that I have to give in to my overwhelming desire to have sex with you. I feel like I need to exert more willpower. Does that make any sense?"

"I know what you mean," Matthew whispered, "but I don't want to say the wrong thing and end up in an argument or feeling bad."

"No," Andrew insisted. "You said that talking is what's important right now. I'm not going to get angry."

"Give me your hand," Matthew said suddenly.

When Andrew held his hand in front of him, Matthew placed his hand over his and gently moved it down, over his body. He positioned Andrew's hand on his firm erection and held it there. "Just because you can feel the physical desire I have for you, doesn't mean that the unseen part of my love for you, in my heart, is any less respectful or genuine. I think the difference may be that I don't always separate the two when I'm with you—the physical part is always as important as what's inside of me. And I know we can't always express what we feel when we're here, but I can't deny it either. So when we're together, don't be afraid to tell me what 'feels right' for you. Being with you, loving you, *is* a spiritual occurrence for me. I don't know what else to say."

He removed his hand from Andrew's, expecting that Andrew would release his grip. Instead, Andrew squeezed him gently, affectionately, moved by his words and impassioned by his candor.

"Are you sure you didn't write that book?" he asked with a smile. "Because you have a nice way of saying things." He kissed Matthew gently on the lips.

Ironically, Matthew suddenly rolled to the edge of the bed and got out. In the darkness, he pulled his T-shirt over his head, reached for his jeans and, with an awkward two-step dance, managed to pull them on and just barely zip them. "I can't believe I'm doing this . . . but I know it's what I should do," he said. He kneeled over Andrew.

"You really don't have to go," Andrew whispered.

"Yes, I do, because my willpower is incredibly fragile right now and, if I stay much longer, it will dissolve completely." He kissed Andrew briefly, opened the slider and turned to face him before leaving. "Anyway . . . it's a beautiful night," he said softly, and then disappeared into the darkness.

Once again, like a computer searching for a familiar phrase, Andrew's mind was jolted with the recollection of Ellen exiting with a similar sentence on that cold Christmas Eve. He could feel the hair on his arms and neck stand up as the eerie moment washed over him like a bleak anxious dream. 'What is the likelihood . . .,' he thought. 'Maybe he's known about it all along.' He could feel his heart began to pound while painful thoughts clogged his mind, eventually distorting any chance of rational behavior and short-circuiting his very being. He held his head and covered his ears in an attempt to stop the high-pitched babble that seemed to emanate relentlessly from the very center of his brain—a feeling which swelled within his chest and began to force its way up, out of his mouth, as an involuntary scream. Andrew quickly reached for his pillow to stifle the inevitable; however, its volume resonated deeply into the quiet summer evening. And then . . . it was over.

As if he had just inhaled the acrid fumes of a broken ammonia capsule, Andrew was suddenly thrust into the present. He found himself on the edge of his bed, drenched in sweat, in the darkness, a pillow in his hands. Within seconds, he heard footsteps approach his door and stop, followed by the expected, yet subtle, knock.

He opened the door to see Brother Nathan standing in the dim light looking apologetically concerned.

"I'm sorry to bother you, Brother Andrew, but I heard what sounded like a scream coming from the area of your cell. Are you all right?"

"A scream?" Andrew asked naïvely.

"Yes . . . deep, perhaps a yell."

Andrew switched on the overhead light to dispel possible innuendo. "Well, I recall having a dream—maybe a nightmare—and feeling frightened when I woke up, but I can't say for sure that I screamed, but . . . I might have." He consciously moved to one side to allow Brother Nathan a full view of his cell.

"Do you want to talk about it with me or with Father Gerald?"

"No . . . not right now. I think I'll be okay."

"All right, then," Brother Nathan said quietly. He turned to leave then abruptly stopped. "Do you still have the medication I brought to you when you were on retreat? It was to help you sleep."

Andrew rubbed his eyes. "I think . . . yes, I do."

"You might want to take some before returning to bed."

"Thanks," Andrew said.

"Oh," Brother Nathan added with a smile before leaving. "If you are not up for vigils—don't worry about it. I'll explain it to Father Luke. Have a good night."

He closed his door and stood silently, facing the blackness outside of his screened slider, wondering what was happening to him. He quickly found the sleep medication Brother Nathan asked about, poured a half a glass of water and swallowed the pill willingly, hoping that it would alleviate some of the unbearable emptiness, the anxiety, and auditory stimulation, which proved so terrifying. "Something is not right," he half whispered. He sat on his bed, remembering Matthew's visit and thought, 'I was wrong—he left because of me.'

He glanced at his clock, which read ten fifteen. He quickly got up, pulled on his T-shirt, and shut off the light. After opening his door and checking the corridor, he entered the hall and quietly closed his cell door, knowing exactly where he was going, regardless of whomever he might encounter.

A faint light spilled onto the carpet from under Matthew's door. Without knocking, Andrew turned the handle, hoping that it would not be locked. It turned easily and Andrew stealthily slipped inside.

Lying on his bed, half covered with a sheet, Matthew, who had been reading, looked up, startled. "Hey . . .," he began, but Andrew raised his finger to his lips.

"It's okay," he whispered. He walked over to the bed, reached up and turned off Matthew's light. In darkness, once again, Andrew removed all of his clothing and climbed into bed behind Matthew so that, in a sitting position, he held him in his arms while leaning against the wall in back of him. He buried his face in his hair, nuzzling the back of his neck and gently biting his earlobe. "I'm sorry about tonight," Andrew whispered.

Matthew turned slightly. "Don't be sorry. You didn't do anything wrong—I'm just glad that you're here."

"I don't want to be alone tonight," Andrew said softly.

Matthew turned, once again, to face him, this time more directly. "You don't have to be alone *any* night, as far as I'm concerned," he said. He reached up and pulled Andrew's mouth over his, kissing him aggressively.

Once their fervor had subsided, they lay nearly motionless, listening to the silence as drops of perspiration trickled between Andrew's chest and Matthew's back, to the sheets beneath them. A gentle breeze fluttered the leaves of the Japanese maples in the garth, filling the room with a welcomed coolness, the first sign that the evening heat was about to break. In the distance, the sky would brighten irregularly and then fade again to total darkness—a summer storm seemed imminent.

Matthew carefully got out of bed, retrieved the towel, and proceeded to cleanse any moist areas, as Andrew sat quietly in the same position. "You okay?" he asked.

"Totally relaxed," Andrew said with a smile. He stretched out fully on the bed.

"Good," Matthew said, kissing him lightly on the lips. "I hope I had something to do with it."

"You did . . . but I think it was the sleeping pill I took before I came over here. I feel totally wiped out."

"Sleeping pill? . . . I didn't know you took them."

"Yup, once in a while." Andrew's words slurred slightly.

Matthew hung up the towel and then sat on the bed next to Andrew, looking at his handsome face and body. "You really are beautiful," he whispered. He leaned down to kiss him and, when there was no response, he realized that Andrew had fallen completely asleep. "Out like a light . . . but not out of mind," he said.

The sedative, combined with his earlier trauma, resulted in a very deep sleep for Andrew, a trancelike state punctuated with flashes of events, feelings, and, most of all, sexual gratification. Throughout the rest of the evening, he was never sure whether he was partially awake or totally sleeping, and merely dreaming of what was happening to him. He remembered seeing Matthew, feeling his soothing touch, as he gently massaged his entire body; he thought they kissed and remembered how his mouth felt warm, moist, and inviting; he seemed to dream that they were together, close, loving, and that feeling filled him with desire, which he hoped would be satisfied. His feelings blurred and melted into an indistinguishable reality; that same warmth and moisture now focused on his genitals like a heated bath. Andrew vaguely remembered the intense pleasure he experienced, which somehow grew even stronger as the repetitive movements enveloped his entire body and skillfully provoked overwhelming ecstasy.

Not long afterwards, he experienced the security of Matthew lying alongside of him, holding him, and kissing him gently. And somewhere in that half dream, he thought he heard someone whisper: "You have no idea how much I love you." The soft voice reverberated inside his head like a drugged echo.

* * *

Chapter Nineteen

Vacation by Raft

Summer continued with relentless, record-breaking heat and, fortunately, marginally sufficient amounts of rainfall to assist the weary monks who were assigned to irrigate the fields. By now, Andrew knew practically every inch of the surrounding acreage, the idiosyncrasies of the ditches and their sluice gates, the trees with the most bear claws, and which fields to avoid during the season of deer flies.

One particularly hot, summer afternoon, he drove his dirt bike to the upper mesa to irrigate a fairly remote section of the property. Even before he turned off the engine and removed his shovel, he could smell an obnoxious odor permeating the air, a scent which seemed to undulate with the direction of the afternoon breeze. Following the intensity of the scent, Andrew walked through scrub sage, over a small ditch, and up a dry knoll, until the stench became almost intolerable. Below him and off to his right, he spied the source of the odor. A dead cow, bloated to nearly double its size, lay on its side like a downed dirigible, its legs stretched out straight into the air, as if it had fallen and could not get up because of its weight. Andrew felt himself smile slightly, yet repulsion was close behind. Suddenly, he thought he saw something move behind the inflated carcass. The blackness of its fur glistened in the afternoon light as it attempted to chew into the cow's soft underbelly. When Andrew realized that it was a bear, he froze momentarily and then quietly sank to the ground, unsure of his next move. He opened his eyes to an unchanged scene—apparently, he had not been spotted and, luckily, was downwind from the curious bear. He watched as the animal became more and more aggressive, clawing at the cow's flesh and then biting until, unexpectedly, like a popped balloon, the carcass exploded, sending rotted flesh into the air along with an odor so overwhelming, Andrew felt as though he was about to vomit, yet he had only one thought in mind—run—as fast as possible.

Without looking back, he flew over the ground and seemed to reach his motorbike in seconds, which he hurriedly started and began to drive toward the main road. Safely on the pavement, Andrew nervously looked in the direction from which he had come. In the distance, he thought he saw a blur of black scrambling over the foothills; however, he was not inclined to idly sit there just to confirm his suspicions. He knew he needed a shower.

* * *

The month of August proved axiomatic—its steadfast heat seemed to enervate even the most stalwart members of the community, regardless of their task; irrigating, fencing, ranching, gardening, yard work, cooking, and, particularly, working in the eggery, grew especially arduous as the month dragged on with its classic dog-days refrain. Thus, the arrival of the final week, a week of river rafting through the southern desert, had most of the monks giddy with the realization that "their vacation" had finally arrived.

And no one appeared more excited than Brother Mark, who made little attempt to hide his somewhat uncharacteristic behaviors, as he laughed and joked with his fellow monks and openly demonstrated his Groucho Marx persona. Andrew watched him from a distance, amazed at his childlike simplicity, a quality he appreciated and, perhaps, envied, since, for him, such public self-disclosure did not come easily.

The four-hour drive to the point of departure was a welcomed change for Andrew. He watched as the scenery gradually transformed from the familiar, mountainous high country to the barren yet colorful desert, which, by its very spirit, seemed to reflect a monastic ambience, a sense of utter simplicity and isolation yet grounded so firmly through nature that its sacred relationship to the spiritual world was unmistakable. He wondered if the physical location of the monastery might not be better suited to just such an austere environment.

The caravan of four vehicles, filled with mostly neophyte rafters, worked its way south via superhighways and, on the last leg of the journey, over dusty roads, which were barely distinguishable from the parched desert soil. Andrew wondered how the leader of this valiant expedition knew where she was going, until he learned that she and her three companions had made this trip several times before and were very confident of each other's skills and previous experience running this particular part of the river.

Joan and Phil Mead had been involved with river rafting ever since they were married—approximately twenty years. Shortly after building a house in Bitter Creek, they became acquainted with the monastery, got to know most of the monks and, as the years passed, were treated nearly as extended family, a courtesy that continued to exist. They brought with them two other experienced rafters, Bill and Tim, both in their early thirties, who looked like pared down versions of Paul Bunyan, complete with beards, jutting muscles, and genuine gregariousness. Their zeal for running rivers and simply appreciating nature was soon evident by their endless energy, motivation, and conversation throughout the five-day trip. The Meads referred to them as "true river rats."

Standing on the sandy riverbank, Andrew watched with amazement as the four leaders initiated the Herculean task of preparing for departure. Deflated rafts were carried to the river's edge like giant, lifeless creatures waiting to be resurrected—a job which Andrew undertook by endlessly stepping on the double foot pump until the amorphous mass of rubber and canvas slowly began to define itself. He shaded his eyes from the bright sun, and looking down river, he saw Matthew, shirtless, smiling back at him while inflating an even larger raft which would carry most of the necessary supplies. With a smile, he waved back and thought how natural Matthew appeared in this environment—like Tom Sawyer anticipating an exciting adventure. He quickly looked around. Convinced that he was not being obvious, Andrew mouthed the words "I love you." Matthew beamed, placed his hand over his chest, and then held up two fingers to sign the words "me too."

Once the major tasks were completed and the gear securely stored aboard the rafts, the Meads, along with Bill and Tim, convened a meeting to outline the basics of water safety, proper rowing techniques, and every imaginable "dos and don'ts" as it applied to the pristine environment and its historical roots. Andrew listened anxiously, increasingly eager to begin his first rafting experience.

It was Phil Mead who assigned seats to the assembled monks. Andrew found himself comfortably ensconced, paddle in hand, with two of his brothers, Brother Nathan and Brother Mark, while Joan Mead manned the helm with the rudder extension confidently within her grasp. She proceeded to push her new crew through several maneuvers—turning to the right, to the left, back paddling, and a man-overboard drill—until she felt comfortable with their abilities, at least, for the moment. "We'll practice more as the river kicks up," she said. "Now, let's go rafting!"

With the sun on his face and the beauty of the San Paulo River Canyon gliding effortlessly past him, Andrew, at first, found it difficult to paddle in unison with Brother Nathan's perfect strokes. He watched from the corner of his eye as Brother Nathan slipped his paddle into the glassy green water, pulled a smooth stroke, and then raise the paddle with barely a splash as he prepared for the following stroke. "I get the feeling you've done this before," Andrew said, as he turned to face Brother Nathan.

Even in the bright sunlight, Nathan's face seemed to redden. "Oh . . . a bit," he said shyly, "I used to crew at Navy just to help keep in shape for football." He laughed. "I never thought it would come in handy."

Brother Mark, sitting in the bow of the raft, like George Washington crossing the Delaware, turned slightly, an imaginary cigar in one hand. "Yes, you're doing a wonderful job, Nattie. Keep up the good work."

Joan stifled a giggle at the unexpected and less than formal camaraderie. Andrew simply laughed out loud, while Nathan, broad shouldered enough to handle the ribbing, quickly reversed his paddling and, with perfect aim, directed a spray of water at Brother Mark that sufficiently soaked him.

Brother Mark stood up but lost his balance and fell back against the raft's soft cushioning, laughing hysterically as he attempted to find his seat and regain his composure. Once again, he turned to look at Brother Nathan. "I thought we were going down, mate!"

Brother Nathan laughed and then quickly apologized. "I'm sorry, Brother Mark. I guess I surprised myself."

"Apology accepted, but . . . you ain't seen nothing yet."

Still laughing, Joan interceded. "Okay, fellas. I want you to have fun but I also want you to be safe, especially on the water so . . . no standing in the raft, or we may have to utilize our man-overboard skills for real." The three monks nodded in agreement.

Early on, the river entered what seemed to be an endless canyon marked by sheer cliffs of striated colors and textures—a natural cathedral and a geologist's haven which seemed to defy the imagination. In one particular area, the perspective of the rock strata on each side of the steep canyon produced the uncanny impression that the rafts were, somehow, traveling up a significant slope, spurning the rules of gravity like spawning salmon. Andrew quickly sensed a slight disorientation within the surreal surroundings.

"Am I crazy or are we going uphill?" he asked.

Joan laughed. "I was wondering when someone would question it," she said. "It's a classic optical illusion."

"Wow!" Brother Mark said. "This is wild! Paddle harder, Natty, or we will never make it to the top." He then ducked behind a seat cushion in anticipation of Brother Nathan's paddle splash.

"Not this time," Brother Nathan said. "I'm too busy paddling so we won't slip backwards."

The river continued to flow at a leisurely pace, through the steep gorge and out into the wider flat lands where the severity of the cliffs diminished and several welcoming beaches seemed to beckon the passing guests. Andrew observed how inviting they appeared—isolated, untrammeled and, perhaps, sensual. He suddenly found himself scanning the other rafts for Matthew.

Off to his right, he recognized Matthew trying his hand at rowing the large raft he shared with two other monks and Tim, one of the bearded organizers of the trip. From a distance, Andrew was impressed by Matthew's newly acquired skills, his ability to stay on course, and the ease at which he rowed. 'Gotta love him,' he thought.

Once the sun sank behind the uneven cliffs, a comfortable coolness settled over the river, as if magically air-conditioned. Shadows lengthen and changed the colors of the ascending walls from bright clay to deep maroon and burnt sienna, with large sweeps of black and grey artfully washed over the natural rock canvas. Andrew was fascinated by the myriad of worn shapes—graceful curves that seem to flow into one another with liquid fluidity, until encountered by the distinct, angular formations of more durable strata. The ever-changing scenery begged for exploration and explanation: however, Andrew did not want to burden Joan with questions. Yet shortly afterwards, she pointed to a piece of ground between two steep canyons. Mounds of earth, covered with rocks and sticks and supporting what appeared to be articles of tattered clothing, nearly filled the entire area.

"An Indian burial ground," she said, gesturing to her left. "It's a very sacred area—definitely no trespassing. Legend has it that if you enter an Indian burial ground and disturb the graves, a curse will be placed upon you for the rest of your life."

Small goose bumps covered Andrew's arms. As the raft floated silently past, he thought he could see a child's blue dress hanging eerily from a crooked stick above one of the mounds. Totally absorbed, he watched as the burial ground slowly disappeared from sight and then resumed his paddling.

The languid entourage respectfully followed the river's gentle flow, steering around the obvious boulders and, occasionally, gliding over the rounded tops of those barely submerged below the water. Andrew could feel the slight drag as the rough bottomed raft would brush against the unseen rocks, like hidden monsters waiting to fatally gash a vulnerable spot and devour them, deep below the cold, green surface. Trying not to be obvious, he glanced back at Joan to see if any trace of emotion registered on her face; however, she simply smiled back at him, reassuringly, and then responded as if she had been asked a question.

"The river is filled with them—old, worn boulders which, even if you ride over them, seldom cause a problem. I'm doing my best to avoid them, but the light is getting pretty flat." She then glanced ahead to the lead raft. "It looks as though we'll be heading in soon to make camp. Anybody hungry?"

In unison, the three monks responded with a hearty, positive reply.

"No disagreement here," she said as she turned strongly to starboard. "Okay, hard right, fellas."

With some aggressive rowing and equally strong paddling, they were able to pull alongside the raft being rowed by Joan's husband, Phil.

"Hello there," Joan called, as she kept pace with the other boat.

Phil turned and smiled. "We've got to stop meeting like this," he said casually. "What will the neighbors say?"

Joan glanced around briefly. In an attempt to humor him, she said, "What neighbors? You'd be lucky to find someone within twenty miles."

"I know, isn't that wonderful?"

"Yes, but . . . are we the only ones getting hungry?"

Phil checked his watch. "You must have read my mind. We're not too far from Little Canyon. We'll set up camp there for the night."

"Sounds good to me," Joan said with a smile. "Besides, I have to use the bathroom."

"Yeah, me too," Brother Mark voiced from the bow. "Watching these guys paddle must be doing something to my bladder."

As before, Brother Nathan scored a direct hit, covering Brother Mark with a cold shower of river water. "Gotcha!" he cried out amid roars of laughter from both boats.

Little Canyon proved not quite as little as Andrew expected and exceedingly so in its splendor. From the wide, sandy beach on the river, the canyon twisted up and away to the flatland high above it. Massive amphitheaters of red and gold strata stood like giant opera halls, waiting for the barrel-chested diva who would fill the surroundings with lyrical Italian while the rafters prepared the evening meal.

Andrew helped bring the raft ashore by jumping overboard and using the painter to guide it between the larger rocks. Once their land legs returned, the crew began unpacking, setting up small cooking tables and stoves, and initiating the task of cooking for fourteen people. Bill helped Tim find a suitable spot for the portable latrine, behind a small ledge—a secluded privy with a million-dollar view, complete with a water basin for washing.

"I'm first!" Joan shouted, as she raced up the incline to where they were standing. "I hope you don't mind, but I really got to go."

"Make yourself at home," Bill said. "Besides, we've got to get supper going before these monks decide to eat us."

"I doubt that'll happen," Joan said with a laugh. "Now, get out of here."

"Yes, ma'am!" Tim said. "We're outta here."

Supper turned into a magnificent celebration with excellent food, camaraderie, and scenery of unparalleled light and beauty, as the setting sun backlit the distant hills and flooded the area with a reddish-orange glow.

"Does anyone else feel like he's on Mars?" Brother Mark asked between mouthfuls of chicken scampi. "Because I do, and I really like it."

"No," Phil said.

"No," Tim and Bill answered in unison.

The monks looked at each other and shook their heads negatively.

"Oh, well," Brother Mark said, unfazed. "It must be the light."

Suddenly, Bill stood up and placed his plate on his portable canvas stool. He looked at Brother Mark and spoke with a deep, monotone voice, like a computerized robot. "This is not Mars. This is Pluto. You must be Martian. We eat Martians. Here I come . . ." He lifted his arms straight out in front of him and began to walk stiffly toward Brother Mark who quickly left his seat, still holding on to his plate, and hid behind Brother Nathan.

"Eat Brother Nathan, Mr. Pluto. He's much bigger than I am!" he shouted.

The laughter resounded throughout the canyon, echoing long after the final roar.

Andrew sat quietly, awed by his surroundings, finishing a perfect meal which was followed by homemade cherry cobbler, fresh coffee and, for those who wanted something special, a splash of cherry kirsch to help ease them into the evening. This, he realized, was a first-class event, in keeping with the expected monastic financing. When Tim approached with a fancy-looking bottle of brandy, Andrew succumbed, held out his cup, and allowed him to pour until the liquid reached the brim.

"You'll sleep tonight," Tim said quietly with a smile.

Because of his closeness, Andrew could not help but notice his subtle, appealing features—a rugged handsomeness expressed in gentle bearing—as if an unstated recognition suddenly registered, visually, between them. Andrew bashfully glanced down at his cup. "Thanks . . .

I hope so," he said. He immediately took a sip of the strong, sweet coffee and liqueur and then scanned the area for Matthew, who was sitting near the cook stove with Joan and her husband. He watched as Tim moved on to the next guest.

"So . . . what do you think of the trip so far?"

Somewhat startled, Andrew recognized Brother Nathan's gentle voice. He looked up to see him towering above him, holding a coffee in one hand.

"I don't think it gets any better than this," Andrew said. "It sort of feels like I'm in fantasy land."

Brother Nathan laughed. "I think Brother Mark was right. The place definitely has a spiritual quality to it which, of course, he would recognize as Mars."

Andrew was mildly surprised by Brother Nathan's openness and attributed it to the environment and being away from the structure of the monastic setting. "You're welcome to have a seat," he said, gesturing toward one of the boat cushions.

Brother Nathan piled two cushions on top of each other and sat down cross-legged. "Brandy and all . . . quite a spread," he said, parroting Andrew's earlier thoughts.

"I should've known," Andrew ventured. "Does the monastery ever do something simply?"

"Well," Brother Nathan said. "We like to think we do, but nothing short of excellence seems to suit us."

"I shouldn't be saying anything," Andrew said apologetically. "The day has been so beautiful, and the evening looks to be as nice." He looked at Nathan. "How's your coffee?"

"Excellent, of course," Brother Nathan said with a smile.

"No, I mean, besides that . . . with or without the cherry kirsch?"

"With, of course," Brother Nathan said. "Why refuse a good thing?"

Andrew pondered his remark, surprised, once again, by Brother Nathan's candor. "Is that really you speaking or the headiness of the trip combined with brandy?"

Brother Nathan laughed out loud. "If I may speak freely, you seem to have this stereotypical view or, should I say, misconception of me, that everything I do is colored by my relationship to the monastery which, to a large extent, may be true. But just like you and, probably, every guy here, I have my own needs, thoughts, desires, feelings, and so forth. I am just careful how I express them and to whom." He glanced at Andrew. "I hope that doesn't offend you."

"No," Andrew said with stifled amazement. "Not at all. It helps to know that most of us are real flesh and blood—not simply robots acting as monks."

"I thought you would have seen that on the raft when I covered Mark with water."

"Well, lights did go off, and I remember being surprised." Andrew took a deep swallow of his coffee. "Actually, it was nice to see."

"We need more of these outings," Brother Nathan said, stretching out his legs.

"So . . .," Andrew asked, curious about Brother Nathan's past, "what was it like playing football for Navy?"

Brother Nathan scuffed his heel in the sand. "Oh, I guess it was different for each guy. I liked the friendships I made and the competition, but other than that, it was no big deal. I was studying hard for medical school, so a lot of my time there just became a big blur."

"Nevertheless, it's still quite an accomplishment to graduate from the Naval Academy."

"I suppose," Brother Nathan agreed. "If it weren't for my parents, paying for it and encouraging me, I would probably have dropped out."

The red glow of the evening light faded to pale orange and yellow, changing the entire backdrop to one less intense and more comfortable. Tim and Bill, accomplished guitar players, assembled a welcoming campfire and encouraged the rest of the group to join them for a song fest. Brother Adrian asked immediately if they knew any Irish ballads.

"Do we know any Irish ballads?" they mimicked and then segued smoothly into "When Irish Eyes are Smiling," followed by at least ten other songs, and concluded with "Oh Danny Boy," much to the delight of Brother Adrian who, by now, was drinking the kirsch straight and singing quite well, if not with a slight slur.

"He's quite a character," Brother Nathan said, pointing toward Brother Adrian. "After him, they broke the mold."

"Tell me about it," Andrew said. "I once thought he was trying to blow up the monastery—and me along with it."

"Oh," Nathan laughed. "The old 'light-the-oven' trick—you got to watch out for that one."

With the music mellowing out, along with the rest of the group, Brother Nathan quickly switched gears. "Do you mind if I ask how you are doing? I mean . . . I know that you've been managing very well at the monastery." He took a sip of his coffee and set the mug on the sand. "But I'm more concerned about how you might be doing psychologically, after all that you've been through—John's death at the eggery and Brother Morgan's tragic accident up on the mesa. I know that you were fairly close."

Andrew exhaled loudly through his nose. "I want to say okay, but I can't anymore," he said, surprising even himself. He looked directly at Brother Nathan. "I haven't told this to anyone before—and I hope you don't mind me telling you—but lately, I've been experiencing unusual thoughts, thoughts that seem to appear out of nowhere and continue on and on until I can't think clearly, and it feels as though I'm about to explode. I don't understand what it's all about." He rubbed his eyes and then looked back at Brother Nathan. "Am I going crazy or what?"

"How long has this been happening?"

"Oh, for about a month or so," Andrew said. "It's beginning to concern me . . . if not scare me."

Brother Nathan shook his head. "I can see why. You haven't mentioned this to Father Gerald?"

"No, not yet. Should I?"

"I think it might be a good idea," Brother Nathan said quietly. Several hypotheses jumped into his mind, yet he wisely refrained from asking a pointed question. He faced Andrew. "It could be nothing . . . or it might just mean that you've finally reacted to past stressors. Do you want to say anything else about it?"

"Oh . . . I don't know." Andrew was not sure whether he should say more but then decided to see how Brother Nathan would react to his feelings. "I suppose there is," he admitted.

Brother Nathan gestured with his hand. "You don't have to say anything, Andrew. It's up to you."

"I know." Once again, he rubbed his eyes. "It might help if I talk about it, and right now seems like a good time, not that there is an awful lot say. I guess the easiest way to describe it is a feeling of emptiness which seems to totally overwhelm me—a blackness surrounds me, leaving me feeling depressed and anxious, like a caged animal. That's when the thoughts seem to take over, louder and louder, until it feels like my head is going to blow up." He looked at Brother Nathan and smiled. "You're not going to have me committed, are you?"

"I don't think so," Brother Nathan said, affecting as genuine a smile as possible, "but I think it would be good to talk with Father Gerald when we get back, just to see what he has to say. He might suggest that you speak with Dr. Klein . . . I'm not sure."

"Off to the shrink," Andrew joked.

"He may not even suggest it but, if he does, take advantage of it. There's nothing wrong with getting some counseling." He quickly looked around the gathering. "God knows," he said quietly, almost to himself, "most of the guys in this place could use it."

Although surprised by his comment, Andrew smiled compliantly.

"One more question," Brother Nathan said. "The night that I heard the scream and knocked on your door . . . it was you, wasn't it?"

"I think so," Andrew admitted.

Brother Nathan smiled. "Well, you did a great job of covering it up. I almost believed you."

"I apologize," Andrew said honestly. "I guess it scared me."

"That's okay." He reached into his pocket, pulled out a small amber bottle, and offered it to Andrew. "Just in case you can't sleep. Another one of those screams out here would probably give someone a heart attack—including me."

Andrew took the bottle. "Thanks . . . for thinking about me."

"Yeah, well, it's my job—sort of," Brother Nathan said softly. He stood up, yawned, and stretched. "All this exercise and fresh air is making me sleepy. I guess I'll bunk out. Have a good sleep."

"You too," Andrew said, as he watched him walk toward the campfire.

The light faded quickly within the canyon, erasing all but the immediate surroundings closest to the fire. Off to his right, Andrew noticed Matthew still standing with Joan and her husband and also with Tim. He decided to follow Brother Nathan's lead, retrieved his sleeping bag, and looked for a soft place to sleep.

With his flashlight guiding the way, Andrew found his gear leaning against the still warm rocks. He pulled the vinyl air mattress out of his backpack, located his canteen of water, and continued to search for his toothbrush and toothpaste. He was unaware of Matthew's arrival.

"It looks like naptime," Matthew said unexpectedly.

Andrew inhaled loudly. "God, you scared me!"

"I'm sorry. I thought you heard me walking toward you."

Andrew found his toothpaste, squeezed some onto his brush, and began brushing his teeth. "It's okay," he said with a slight slur. He spit out the foamy paste and rinsed. Trying not to be obvious, he removed one of the sleeping pills and swallowed it with more water from his canteen.

"Where are you sleeping?" Matthew asked.

Andrew shrugged slightly. "Further down to the right, near the river, I guess."

"Leave your flashlight on. I'll meet you over there."

"Sounds good but . . . you know—discretion—so not too close," Andrew reminded him.

Matthew laughed. "I know. Don't worry."

After deciding on a soft, sandy spot on the beach, Andrew quickly blew up his air mattress and placed his lightweight sleeping bag on top of it. He undressed, brushed off his feet, and settled into the surprisingly comfortable nest he had created. He then scooped sand around the flashlight and pointed it skyward like a miniature beacon.

Whether it was the exercise or the weather or the soothing sound of the river flowing smoothly past him less than thirty feet away, Andrew could not fight sleep any longer. He vaguely remembered what felt like a light kiss, as lips brushed against his—a feeling of familiarity and desire which soon ebbed away into dreamless, deep sleep; he completely forgot that he had taken a sleeping pill.

Morning broke with brilliant sunlight flooding the upper canyon, illuminating the brick-red cliffs with renewed clarity against a soft blue sky, while the floor of the canyon remained submerged in shadow.

Raising his head, Andrew noticed that Matthew had set up his sleeping bag more than twenty feet away yet closer to the river. To his right, another sleeping bag sprawled, half unzipped. He thought it might be Tim, one of the professional rafters, whom Matthew was sitting with for most of the evening. Andrew could see his naked torso down to his lower back, which was lightly covered with dark, curly hair. Looking to his left, he observed what looked like a small refugee camp, as several sleeping bags dotted the red sand like obvious intruders upon the flawless landscape with still immobile occupants—except for Bill, the other half of the Paul Bunyan twins, who stood behind the cook stove, preparing a breakfast of strong coffee, scrambled eggs, ham, toast, and orange juice. The enticing aroma of the coffee and grilled ham and the urge to urinate easily motivated Andrew to get up and enjoy the quiet solitude of daybreak.

Comfortably dressed in shorts, a T-shirt, and sneakers, Andrew quietly made his way around the sleeping rafters toward the makeshift latrine, high above the camp. He announced his arrival with a gentle, "anybody there?" and when he heard no response, he thankfully dropped his shorts, sat on the famous "blue goo" latrine, and enjoyed the beauty of his surroundings. The canyon flattened out in the distance, as the river snaked into the horizon and the rising sun appeared to have a different effect here; a truly supernatural yet mesmerizing light in the southern desert. Nevertheless, Andrew knew he could not linger since, most likely, others would be in need of the facilities. He reached for the toilet paper, which had been cleverly hung from a small, rocky outcrop with a piece of rawhide lacing, completed his task, and began to pour water from the pitcher into the large wash basin, when he abruptly stopped. Floating inside the porcelain basin, half filled with water, were two solid stools. Andrew gagged and set the pitcher down. 'Who,' he thought, 'would crap in the dam basin?' Yet it did not take a great deal of deductive reasoning to come up with an answer. 'Probably poor old Brother Edward, who must have thought it was a toilet.' He gingerly lifted the basin and emptied its contents into the chemical latrine.

It was nearly 10:30 a.m. before the well-fed crew had finished breakfast, cleaned the area, and repacked all their gear into the waiting rafts. Hoping to alleviate his increased hunger, Andrew filled both front pockets of his shorts with smoked almonds, knowing they would come in handy as the day wore on.

"Looks like another beautiful day," Joan said as she made some last-minute arrangements.

"Yes," Andrew agreed, "another day in paradise."

"How did you sleep?" she asked.

"Like a rock. How about you?"

She laughed. "After a day of rowing, I never have any problem falling asleep."

"I'm not sure how good I'd be at it, but I wouldn't mind giving you a hand with it," Andrew offered.

"Thanks," Joan said. "There will be some quiet parts on the river where you're welcome to give it a shot."

"All right!" Andrew said excitedly.

Looking over Joan's shoulder, he could see Matthew packing a few items into his backpack. He watched as he struggled to zip one of the compartments, which had been easily overfilled and was bulging against its seams.

"Excuse me," he said to Joan and began walking toward Matthew.

"I have extra room in my pack," he said, looking down at his perplexed friend. "Otherwise, you'll probably pop your zipper."

Matthew looked up and began to laugh.

"What?" Andrew asked, forgetting to close his mouth after the question.

Matthew shook his head. "Never mind . . . you have a way with words." He pulled a sweatshirt out of his backpack and held it up in front of Andrew. "Got room for this?"

Andrew took the sweatshirt and folded it. "I think so."

"Thanks."

"By the way, "Andrew began. "I must have gone off to dreamland as soon as I got into my sleeping bag last night. I didn't hear you come by."

"You were definitely out," Matthew said. He stood up and moved a bit closer. "But did you feel anything?" A familiar grin spread across his face.

"Funny you should ask. I thought it was a dream."

"After I leaned down to turn off your flashlight, I just couldn't resist."

Andrew laughed. "I love when you talk like that."

Matthew adjusted the pack on his back. "I know," he said.

At that moment, Joan signaled that the rafts were ready to go. Matthew winked, hiked up his pack, and walked down river toward his boat. Andrew took his position in the raft, along with his three companions, while Joan instructed them to row gently over the shallows; however, the raft would not budge.

"It's too shallow for all this weight," Joan said. "We're going to need a pull."

Without thinking, Andrew quickly jumped into the less than knee-deep water, grabbed the painter, and began to drag the raft out, into the river. He walked several yards until the water approached the pockets on his shorts, yet the raft was still hitting bottom. Suddenly, he remembered the almonds. "I can't go any farther," he stammered.

"Why not?" Joan asked, wondering if he was fearful of the deeper water.

"My nuts will get wet," he admitted. The words escaped before he had time to think. Totally humiliated, Andrew stuck his hand in his pocket and quickly held out a handful of almonds, but by then, the damage had been done. Brother Mark was laughing hysterically, thrashing around, totally out of control, in the bow of the boat, while Brother Nathan sat quietly, grinning at the floor. Joan was speechless; her face the color of sunburn.

"I meant . . ." Once again, Andrew held up his handful of almonds and walked closer to the boat so that everyone could get a better look, but it made no difference, especially to Brother Mark, who continued to look as if he were having a seizure. Andrew threw the wet line at him and stuffed the almonds back in his pocket. "Hang on," he said brusquely and then walked toward the stern. He pushed until he could feel the raft float freely, hoisted himself up over the transom (with an assist from Joan), and quickly took his position at the port paddle.

By then, the temperament of the rafters had subsided, at least until Brother Mark turned to look at Andrew, a glance noticed by Brother Nathan who suddenly stopped paddling.

"Don't even think of it," he said coldly, staring at Brother Mark.

Brother Mark took his advice, turned his head, and silently observed the ever-changing scenery floating past him.

Just before noon, the bright sunlight gave way to a milky sky, which quickly darkened into a torrential downpour, complete with deafening thunder and dangerous lightning. The lead raft, skippered by Phil, made a quick decision to take cover under large overhanging cliffs, which lined one side of the river. Following his lead, the other boats did the same, anchoring next to each other like a large rubber dock. Each was tethered to the other, while the first and last rafts tied onto various rock outcrops that jutted out over the river.

It was not long before Bill and Tim capitalized on the delay by distributing cold drinks, ham and cheese sandwiches, potato chips, and brownies to the entire crew, an alfresco, if not impromptu, lunch served within a natural grotto of subtle beauty.

Andrew noticed large sprays of green vegetation, clinging precariously to the red cliffs, as though someone knew they would be stopping there for lunch and decided to decorate the site with indigenous flora. Nevertheless, the steep angle of the overhang, regardless of its immensity, stretching out over the river with no visible supports, caused him some concern. "I hope this roof doesn't decide to collapse," he said between mouthfuls of food. "They probably wouldn't find us until the next Ice Age."

Two boats away, Bill heard him and laughed. "Oh, it probably will, someday, but I doubt that it will happen today."

"Unless it sustains a direct hit from one of those lightning bolts," Tim added.

At that point, almost everyone stopped eating to seriously observe the massive rock structure above them.

"I'm just kidding," Tim said quickly. "It's too remote—just a joke . . . so please, finish your lunch and relax."

Remote or not, Brother Edward could barely take his eyes off the ominous ceiling above him, as he indiscriminately swallowed a handful of vitamins and then reached into his pack for more.

At the cliff's edge, a solid curtain of rain pelted the river with the force of the fire hose, sending small waves into the grotto and gently rocking the rafts. Occasional rivulets of water found their way through the small cracks above them and dripped annoyingly, first onto one raft and then onto another, until those in Matthew's boat resorted to using a plastic bucket to bail out the excess.

Yet even before they finished their lunch, the storm ended as quickly as it began. Within minutes, the sun burned through the lingering clouds, steamed the remaining moisture from the rocks, and, once again, established itself as the reigning source of desert heat.

"A typical canyon deluge," Phil quipped. "We'll have to be careful of runoff and rising water; so let's get a move on so we can set up camp early."

With the lunch gear properly stowed away, the boats headed downstream through ascending vapors and a noticeable increase in temperature and humidity.

"I thought the rain would cool things off," Brother Mark said, as he wiped his brow.

Joan laughed. "It's sort of like throwing water on the hot rocks in a sauna; the humidity skyrockets for a while, but it should dry out pretty soon." She barely got the words out of her mouth when the swollen surge of water broke over the stern, lifting the boat several feet and propelling it forward, as if an outboard motor had suddenly been attached and slammed into gear at high speed.

"It's the runoff!" she shouted. "Paddle hard and keep the bow heading downstream!"

She had no time to warn the other boats, since she could not be heard above the growl of the river.

Andrew dug his paddle deep into the frothy water, hoping that he could match Brother Nathan's powerful strokes and maintain the rhythm needed to keep the boat on course. He watched as the surge hit the other rafts, bolting them forward with equal velocity and nearly capsizing one of them.

Brother Mark held on to the safety ropes that stretched around the entire raft, his feet braced against the rubber cushioning, and his back arched to match the vertical flex of the boat as it was being tossed by the roiled current. He reminded Andrew of a rodeo cowboy who had been just let out of the gate on a bucking bronco, hoping to stay upright and praying hard for the same.

Andrew jammed his feet under the wooden seat in front of him, knowing that it was the only way to anchor himself to the raft. He continued to paddle strongly, matching Brother Nathan stroke for stroke.

Unexpectedly, he heard Joan shout the words he never wanted to hear.

"Capsized boat!" she yelled, her voice filled with emotion.

When Andrew looked up, he saw the shiny beige bottom of the overturned raft, reflecting the sunlight like an eerie monster surfacing for air. In the water, he counted three bobbing heads supported by orange life vests. He knew that someone was missing.

"Who's raft?" he shouted to Joan.

She squinted. "I think it was Tim's."

"Weren't there four people aboard?"

"Yes," she replied. Her anxiety was obvious.

Andrew could feel his chest tighten . . . he knew that Matthew was on that raft.

Paddling hard, they were able to narrow the gap between them and the overturned boat. Suddenly, another head appeared from underneath the raft, bobbing like the others and supported by the bright orange vest.

"I think that's Matthew!" Andrew shouted.

"Maybe he could grab on to his raft," Joan acknowledged, yet the elusive raft seemed to be moving faster than Matthew could swim and appeared to be out of reach.

"Keep your legs out in front of you!" Joan shouted, hoping that Matthew could hear her. She knew that he could use his legs like springs to bounce off on submerged rocks and hoped that Tim had explained that to his crew during one of the practice maneuvers.

Whether he heard her or had, in fact, been well-trained, Matthew remained facing downriver, head above the surface, with no visible signs of panic.

By then, they had reached a part of the river where it broadened considerably, absorbing the excess flow and slowing its speed so that Joan was able to place her raft alongside of Matthew, who immediately grabbed on to its rope. Brother Nathan reached down with both hands and, with little assistance, hauled him into the raft as effortlessly as if he had just scooped up a water lily.

Matthew sat on the floor and leaned against the side cushioning of the raft while a trickle of blood and water ran down his forehead next to his eye. Exhausted from the unexpected ordeal, he glanced around at the anxious faces, smiled, and said, "Can we do this again?"

'Only Matthew,' Andrew thought, as laughter shattered the now-placid river and fear slowly abated.

But his smile quickly faded. "How are the others," he asked apprehensively.

Joan looked downstream toward the other boats. "I think everyone has been rescued." She then focused her attention on Matthew. "How are you doing?"

He moved his hands and fingers, flexed his arms and legs, and gently moved his head from side to side. "I guess I'm all right."

"Except for the cut on your head," Andrew added.

Matthew reached up and wiped his brow. He was surprised to see blood on his hand.

Joan freed a plastic box from its secured compartment on the side of the raft—a universal first aid kit. She handed it to Brother Nathan, who immediately began to tend to Matthew's cut.

"It's not too deep," Brother Nathan said, working quickly yet skillfully, as he finished applying an antibacterial spray and then covered the wound with a bandage. "I think you're going to make it."

Matthew laughed. "Well, that's good news. Thanks."

Watching Brother Nathan, Andrew wished he could have been the one to help Matthew, regardless of Brother Nathan's advanced medical knowledge. And more than anything at that moment, he wished he could simply hug him and let him know how happy he was to see him alive and well, and sharing the same raft with him, yet he knew it would have to wait.

Not much farther down river, Phil and Bill steered their boats toward a wide sandy beach, rimmed by moderate cliffs of ascending heights. The others followed; glad to be back on dry land after the mishap on the river.

Brother Nathan was called immediately to look at a gash on Brother Edward's leg, a fairly deep wound, sustained when he collided with a submerged rock, part of a larger boulder which, most likely, only recently fell from the canyon above and remained sharp and angular beneath the surface.

"Nothing appears to be broken, but it's a substantial cut," Brother Nathan said as he hovered above Brother Edward. After cleaning and wrapping the wound, he looked around at his curious audience. "Any other bruises?" he asked.

Most everyone shook their heads negatively.

"No? That's good. Let's enjoy the day."

Joan and Phil, along with their two river rats, Tim and Bill, called the crew together to discuss the mechanics of the accident, much to Tim's embarrassment. He was clearly uncomfortable, trying to explain the sequence of events that led to the capsize, a situation that might have been deadly, yet he did not shy away from taking most of the blame.

"I should have been able to steer out of that," he said quietly. "I'm sorry."

Of course, Joan and Phil refused to allow him to shoulder the burden alone. "It wasn't your fault," Phil said. "If anything, I should've known that the surge would be potentially dangerous and would arrive quickly, after seeing how hard the rain fell. We should have waited it out under the cliffs."

"Well," Joan interjected, "we are 'shoulding' all over ourselves. It was an accident; it's over, and thank God, no one was seriously injured." She pulled her hair back and covered it with a red bandanna.

"Now . . . it's a great day for hiking. We can look for some evidence of the Anasazi Indians, hopefully find some petroglyphs and . . ."

"Some what?" Matthew interrupted.

"Petroglyphs," Joan said. "They are pictures chipped into the rock with stone chisels. Each image has a different meaning, often more than one. It was a way in which the ancients left their heritage, carved carefully all over these canyons."

"Well, I'm ready," Matthew exclaimed. His curiosity had peaked.

Although Brother Edward remained behind with Bill and Brother Nathan, the remainder of the group set off in search of early Indian history among the red cliffs and heat of the afternoon. It was not long before Phil spotted two crudely chiseled figures etched upon a protected wall under a cliff.

"I've found some," he shouted, pointing toward what looked like a horned figure and a humpbacked deity with a flute. "It's the horned water serpent and a flute player."

"Sounds as though you've done some studying on this," Andrew remarked.

Phil nodded. "Oh, a bit. It's hard to hike through these canyons—and all this history—without trying to know more about what took place here."

"So . . . what did take place here?" Matthew asked.

It was as if Phil was waiting for someone to ask the question. "The Anasazi, or Ancient Ones, settled in this area around 800 A.D. Essentially, they are the ancestors of most of the native American Indians. They began by living in caves or underground but soon constructed rectangular, aboveground housing out of stone, mud plaster, and timber bracing. Eventually, they became cliff dwellers, constructing elaborate, apartment-like structures, high above the canyon floor where they were protected from both predators and the elements."

"Anything like that in this area?" Andrew asked.

Once again, Phil smiled sheepishly. "Of course," he said candidly. "It's too hot to hike just for the sake of it. Although it's not one of the largest settlements, it's still pretty impressive and worth the walk."

"How far?" Matthew questioned.

"Oh, about an hour from here."

"All right!" Matthew said enthusiastically. "Let's go."

"Don't forget to drink plenty of water," Joan added. "It's easy to get dehydrated out here."

"I think I've had enough water for a while," Matthew joked.

Joan rolled her eyes and smiled. "Never mind . . . just start walking!"

"Yes, ma'am," Matthew barked.

Andrew was thankful that he did not salute.

Following Phil's lead, the stalwart body forged ahead through a constant mist of red dust and merciless heat, dodging boulders, occasional sage, and, infrequently, scrub pines.

"How did the Anasazi survive this environment?" Andrew asked, as they climbed even higher into the cliffs.

Phil stopped and drank some water. "They were like a flower that bloomed and then quickly faded," he said, "mostly because of a twenty-three-year dry spell which burned the land, dried up the rivers and streams, and killed the corn as it sprouted."

"What happened to the Anasazi?"

"Most migrated, either south or west, joining other settlements and assimilating into their cultures. They say it was the Great Migration, which lasted for over one hundred and fifty years."

"How can they be sure it was a drought?"

"Through early records and by studying the effects on plant life, especially trees and the soil."

Andrew wiped his brow. "That's a long time to be without water."

"I'll say," Matthew added as he drank from his canteen.

Phil continued to lead with his steady pace, over a small outcrop and back down to the flatter surface. He stopped and pointed toward his left. "Here it is," he announced with uninhibited jubilation.

The gasps were audible throughout the group.

"This is incredible!" Matthew uttered, wide-eyed with disbelief. "How did you ever find this place?"

"Word of mouth and good fortune while hiking," Phil replied.

Nestled beneath a cathedral-like sandstone arch, the cliff dwelling clung to its precipitous slope, as if it had sprouted from the very rock it sat upon. Mud and stone structures, squarely built with obvious precision, draped the area, each connected to the other and built above the one below, so that roofs became porches as tiers of apartments rose high above the valley floor.

"You can see how concerned they were with defense," Phil explained. "Notice that none of the lower dwellings have doors."

"How did they get in?" Matthew asked.

"Through a hole in the roof. If you look closely, you'll see the small footholds carved into the rock where they climbed to reach the first level." Phil pointed toward the staggered, dark nicks. "They also made use of ladders for those who weren't quite so agile, such as the elderly, but only if they were certain that no danger was present."

Joan laughed. "Once I reached my apartment, I'd probably never come back down."

"Some probably didn't," Phil joked.

"It's not coincidental that they chose an east-facing arch," he added. "That way, they benefited from the warmth of the winter sun while the large overhang protected them from the hundred-degree summer heat."

"They weren't exactly stupid, were they," Tim remarked.

Phil shook his head. "Hardly; in fact, I'd say they were architecturally advanced."

The early afternoon rays of the sun began to tilt into the far side of the arch, illuminating the redness of the massive span and the plethora of greenery, which, for Andrew, evoked a Christmas-in-July aura. He stood silently, mesmerized by the vastness of his environment, its beauty, and the new knowledge and respect for those who went before him. The only thing missing was the scent of balsam, cinnamon, and newly fallen snow.

"We can explore for about an hour," Joan said, "but let's be careful, especially when climbing. It's a long hike back, and Brother Nathan, our 'resident doctor,' is not with us."

This was the news Matthew was waiting to hear. While most everyone eagerly approached the cliff dwellings, he caught Andrew's eye, winked at him, and encouraged him to follow. Casually, yet by design, Matthew stealthily made his way back down to the lower level of the area, around the corner of the arch, and began to climb the gradual slope toward the cliffs above.

Surprised by his boldness, Andrew followed in silence, hoping that their absence would not be obvious. Once he was out of earshot of the others, he called to Matthew.

"Where the heck are you going?"

Matthew looked back and smiled. "Anywhere we can be together for a while." He kept climbing quickly, almost effortlessly, motivated by anticipation. Suddenly, after reaching a shaded area under a jagged cliff, he stopped and waited for Andrew to catch up with him. He pulled off his T-shirt, tucked it into his shorts, and drank deeply from his battered canteen.

With his hair matted in ringlets across his forehead, Andrew reached the welcomed shade of the overhang.

"Greetings, fellow troglodyte," Matthew joked, as he handed his canteen to Andrew who eagerly drank from it.

Andrew wiped his mouth with his sleeve. "I don't know what that means, but it better not be nasty." He handed the canteen back to Matthew.

"You're welcome," Matthew quipped. "And no, it's not nasty."

Impulsively, Matthew reached out, pulled Andrew into his arms, and kissed him aggressively, a situation Andrew anticipated and encouraged by responding with an even greater level of passion for the one he cared about so deeply.

"I wanted to hold you the moment Brother Nathan pulled you into our raft," he said quietly. "It scared the crap out of me when I realized your boat had gone over."

Matthew held Andrew's face close to his with both hands. "It scared the crap out of me too, but I'm alive—thank God. I'm here with you, and it made me realized even more how much I love you." Once again, Matthew leaned forward and kissed him, this time more gently, while Andrew fought hard to keep his emotion in check.

"I think we should climb a bit higher," Matthew said as he stood up, "someplace we can get more . . . comfortable."

Andrew smiled. "More comfortable," he repeated. "Sounds good to me."

They climbed across flat rocks, which looked as if they had been arranged steplike, to reach the higher levels of the amphitheater until suddenly the entire horizon opened before them with a three-hundred-and-sixty-degree view. In the distance, telephone poles appeared as miniature crosses—a narrow horizontal cemetery, which reminded Andrew that life, however bleak or solitary, still existed above the verdant river.

"Hey, it's the real world," Matthew remarked.

Andrew felt a slight shiver. "Yeah, and I'm not sure I like it," he said with a blank expression.

"I know what you mean," Matthew added, "so let's head down."

Once again, Matthew lead the way, this time toward a different part of the canyon where pools of rainwater had collected in smooth, carved out basins, some as large as bathtubs. Matthew stopped to feel the water.

"I can't believe it! It's like bathwater," he said excitedly. He paused and looked around until he saw a large pool sitting in the bright sun, yet protected on two sides by steep rocks. "Come on," he said, as he hurried to examine it more closely.

Andrew followed and watched as Matthew, once again, leaned down to test the water. He saw him kick off his hiking boots and socks, remove his shorts and underwear, and climb naked into the thermal water.

"It's like a hot tub in heaven with an awesome view. You won't believe it!"

Andrew laughed. "You're crazy, you know, but what the heck, I'm coming in anyway." He removed his shoes and clothing and settled into the heated tub opposite Matthew, by placing his legs over his, while he leaned back to soak up the therapeutic warmth of the water.

"This is the life," Andrew sighed, exhausted from the day's hike.

"And what a view," Matthew stressed.

Andrew turned slightly to look out toward the horizon.

Glistening red and green in the bright sunlight, the eroded San Paolo Mountains bumped into each other like elliptical humps against the turquoise sky, tapering off in the distance to the valley below. The river, their temporary home, which now seemed so far away, glinted green as it snaked beneath the peaks and then disappeared behind the sandstone butte.

"It doesn't get much better than this," Andrew acknowledged.

"Wanna bet?" Matthew said with a smirk. He grabbed Andrew's foot with both hands, supported it with his knee and slowly but firmly began to massage the entire foot, soothing the soreness and easing the aches resulting from so much walking.

"You're right," Andrew agreed. "That definitely feels fantastic." He closed his eyes and leaned back against the warm rock.

Matthew continued to massage his foot, completing the work on one and moving on to the other when, suddenly, he thought he saw something move on the ledge to his left, about forty yards above them. He stopped momentarily to get a better focus by squinting in that direction.

Andrew seemed to sense his concern immediately and sat upright. "What's the matter?" he asked cautiously.

As if betrayed by his involuntary signal, Matthew smiled and resumed the foot massage. "Nothing . . . relax," he said, hoping to defuse Andrew's anxiety. "I thought I saw an eagle fly over the ridge, but I'm sure was a hawk."

"Let me know if it flies by again," Andrew said. "I'd like to see it." Once again, he closed his eyes and rested his head against the sandstone.

Out of the corner of his eye, Matthew watched as a figure emerged from the shadows of the cliff above him, the exact spot where he was sure he saw something move previously. Without missing a stroke, he continued to gently knead Andrew's arch while keeping an eye on the mysterious intruder.

"Even your feet are handsome," Matthew said softly.

Andrew grinned. "You've been in the hot sun too long."

"Maybe . . . maybe not," Matthew replied, as he dared to look more directly at the intruder who made no attempt to hide himself.

Matthew was sure that it was a man wearing a jaunty Australian-like cowboy hat when suddenly, his identity became obvious. The only person, he realized, who wore that particular hat, at least on this trip, was Tim, one of the boatmen whose raft capsized and threw Matthew into the river. And like falling dominoes, earlier questionable looks, innuendo, double entendres—events in the past, which Matthew simply sloughed off as camaraderie, now took on a whole new meaning. He was being sent a message.

Without hesitation, Matthew made the decision to send a message back. He leaned forward slightly and placed his mouth on Andrew's foot, gently biting his arch and then licking and sucking his toes.

Andrew shuddered ecstatically, welcoming Matthew's sexual advances. "You know that drives me crazy," he whispered.

"That makes two of us," Matthew said, pausing only long enough to get the words out. He then shifted his position, leaned forward, and gently kissed Andrew's neck, ears, eyes, and nose, while Andrew eagerly anticipated Matthew's mouth against his lips. He longed for the intimacy, the wetness, warmth, and sensual viscosity of kissing, which Matthew performed exceedingly well. He would easily admit that kissing Matthew was almost more pleasurable than the orgasm itself.

"I can always tell when you want me," Matthew said softly.

"And how's that?" Andrew asked with his eyes still closed.

"Your lips, barely parted, seem to follow mine like radar."

"What can I say . . . I love being kissed by you."

Before complying with Andrew's wish, Matthew glanced at the figure above them. He noticed he had removed his hat and stood totally naked in the bright sunlight.

Unabashed by his presence, Matthew kissed Andrew with even greater intensity, probing deeply and gently biting, as they kindled an immense sexual passion and welcomed their release.

"There it is!" Andrew said suddenly, pointing toward the sky.

Startled, Matthew rolled onto his side. "What?" He asked, hoping that Andrew had not discovered the intruder.

"The eagle . . ."

Looking in the direction Andrew was pointing, Matthew did, in fact, observed the effortless glide of the huge bird as it rose high on the warm currents and then disappeared above the distant ridge. "They say that's good luck, you know."

"What? Seeing an eagle?"

"Yes, but only for the one who sees it first."

Andrew smiled. "Then the luck is really yours even though you thought it was a hawk."

"I don't think so," Matthew said softly. Almost immediately, he could feel an unaccustomed guilt wash over him like a chilled wind. "Quick. Let's jump back in, cleanup, and get back to the others before we are missed.

"I hate to leave, but you're right," Andrew agreed.

Before getting back into the water, Matthew glanced over his shoulder. The naked man, Tim, was gone.

* * *

By the time they returned to the cliff dwelling, the other members of the group were beginning to gather for the return trek to the river.

Matthew soon spotted Tim alone, wearing his unmistakable hat. He briefly smiled at Matthew, as if the recent incident had never occurred. Matthew barely nodded.

"How was your hike?" Phil asked as he walked toward them.

"Great," Matthew responded. "You should have seen the carved out pools of hot water up in the cliffs—like big hot tubs."

Phil laughed. "No wonder you both look so scrubbed."

Andrew could feel the color rise in his face.

"Yeah," Matthew added quickly. "We each had our own pool and a fantastic view of the mountains."

Andrew uncapped his canteen and drank deeply.

Even before they were inside the camp, they could smell fresh brewed coffee and the mouth-watering aroma of freshly baked rolls.

"They brought an oven?" Andrew asked with amazement.

"Of course," Joan replied with a grin. "This is a first-class operation."

"Is it solar?"

"Nope, it's clay, and it just sits on the hot coals."

"I'd like to see that," Andrew remarked.

The late afternoon sun began to cast elongated shadows over portions of the campsite, a study of contrasts and familiar hues of sienna, magenta, and orange. Looking around, Andrew felt as if he had been gone forever, even though he had been away for only a few hours. Yet it was good to see old Brother Edward resting comfortably in a chair, his leg elevated and a smile on his face, while Brother Nathan seemed to strut around like a rooster in shorts, wearing an apron and helping Bill prepare the evening meal. And when he looked at Matthew, who appeared to be glowing in this surreal light, he knew that he too shared this simple, inexplicable elation. More than ever, at that very moment, he wished he could hug him and show the entire world that this was the person he loved, not only physically but also respectfully as a caring colleague and fellow cosmic traveler.

As if telepathic, Matthew ran up to him, put his arm around his shoulder, and smiled. "Are you feeling as good as I am?" he said softly.

Andrew nodded. "You too?"

"Yup, it's been a perfect day so far. Thanks for sharing it with me." He quietly whispered, "I love you," into Andrew's ear and then ran ahead to joke with Brother Nathan.

Once again, dinner proved to be another gastronomic feast complete with appetizers of salmon cream cheese, salami, crackers, and the optional Asti Spumanti, followed by a simple Caesar salad, meat lasagna, and strawberry shortcake made with homemade biscuits. Coffee and cordials completed the meal, as nearly everyone gathered closer to the fire, awaiting the nightly song fest. And as expected, Brother Adrian was in perfect form, singing *a cappella* in anticipation of the guitar players, who were finishing their evening chores.

Andrew spent the evening sitting next to Matthew and Brother Nathan, who was seldom without a glass of something intoxicating in his hand. As long as it was alcohol, it didn't seem to matter. In the dark, with no one sitting in back of them, Matthew would bravely put his hand under Andrew's sweatshirt and gently rub his back and, even bolder, massage his upper thigh, while he occasionally let his hand wander onto Andrew's crotch, an action which Andrew, although amused, immediately resisted by raising his leg closer to his chest. On the third attempt, Andrew found it necessary to respond.

"Please try to behave yourself," he whispered with a smile.

Matthew looked at him with large, righteous eyes. "Why?"

"Well, for one thing, I don't want to get arrested, and for another . . . I'm getting a hard on," Andrew whispered.

Matthew pulled back his hand. "Now look who's talking dirty," he said with a smile.

Andrew laughed openly and shook his head.

Blocking the light of the campfire, Joan and Phil approached the amusing trio and sat down in front of them.

"I can see that the three of you are having a good time," Joan said as she sipped her glass of brandy.

"Excellent!" Brother Nathan responded uncharacteristically, almost before she finished her sentence. "Except for the capsize, it's been a beautiful day."

"Now wait a minute," Matthew interjected. "Even the capsize had an element of beauty to it."

"Well . . .," Andrew added, "I guess beauty really is in the eye of the beholder."

Phil quickly jumped in. "I never like to see a capsize—ever," he said. "We're very fortunate no one was seriously injured."

It was Joan who decided to quash further discussion on the matter. "It would have been nice if the abbot came with us," she said. "I'm sure he would have enjoyed it."

Matthew chuckled. "I doubt it," he said bluntly. "I can't imagine him sleeping in a sleeping bag."

"Besides," Brother Nathan added, with a slight slur, "there is no place to plug in his hairdryer."

Joan looked at Phil, ran her hands through her hair, and flashed a brief yet intentional smile. "Well, I think we're about ready to turn in." She grabbed Phil's hand and gently pulled him toward her.

"Enjoy the evening," Phil replied over his shoulder. "Don't forget to get some sleep."

Brother Nathan laughed. "I don't think that will be a problem," he said. The slurring appeared more obvious.

Enveloped in total darkness beyond the perimeter of the fading firelight, the lingering campers slowly began to call it a night as they retired, armed with sturdy flashlights and pillows, to welcoming sleeping bags.

"It looks like the thing to do," Matthew said with a yawn. He reached behind Andrew and briefly rubbed his lower back. "You coming?" he asked quietly.

Andrew nodded. "Yeah, I'm bushed," he answered. "I hope I can find my sleeping bag."

"What about you, Brother Nathan?" Matthew asked.

Brother Nathan rubbed his face. "Hell . . . I'm not sure I can walk."

With Matthew on one side and Andrew on the other, they lifted him to his feet and began to walk him toward the direction he was pointing.

"I had no idea you were this heavy," Matthew said between breaths.

"Solid muscle," Brother Nathan exaggerated.

"For some reason," Andrew muttered, "I believe that."

Once they found his sleeping bag, they carefully lowered him onto it. Andrew removed Brother Nathan's sneakers and began to pull the top of the bag over him when Brother Nathan suddenly stopped him.

"I have to piss," he said bluntly. He attempted to stand up, but quickly collapsed onto the sleeping bag.

"We'll get you back up," Matthew offered bravely.

"We hope . . .," Andrew added quietly.

After much effort, they were able to help Brother Nathan to his feet, supporting him, once again, from both sides.

Without inhibition, Brother Nathan reached down, unzipped his shorts, and urinated onto the desert sand. Unconcerned and unaware, he fell back onto his sleeping bag, unzipped, and quite exposed.

Andrew covered him and picked up his flashlight in search of his own quarters. "Good night, Brother Nathan," he said in vain, since the only response he heard was Brother Nathan's muffled snore.

Walking together, they searched near the river for their bags.

"Did you see the size of that thing?" Matthew whispered.

Andrew nodded. "It would have been hard to miss, especially when you had your flashlight shining on it," he said. "Besides, it sounded like a fire hose."

"He must have made *someone* happy before coming here," Matthew added.

Andrew chuckled. "I hope so. Who knows . . . maybe he still is."

"You never know," Matthew said.

* * *

Father Luke celebrated the morning mass, bathed by a brilliant sunrise of golden, red light. Wearing old jeans and a denim shirt, he might have been mistaken for one of the local farmers imitating a priest, as he broke off pieces of consecrated bread from the round wheat loaf and distributed communion to the participants.

Matthew noticed that Tim remained seated during the service and did not receive.

Once the gear was properly stowed, the rafters scoured the campsite for any environmental evidence of their stay. Satisfied that they were in compliance, they continued their river journey through the rising morning mist.

As the sun rose above the cliffs and penetrated the thin haze which hovered over the water, the temperature climbed dramatically, well into the nineties, initially steaming the area and its inhabitants and then bathing them in a dry convection.

Tim paused long enough from his rowing to quickly remove his shirt and, much to Matthew's surprise, his khaki shorts, revealing a brief Speedo swimsuit. He neatly folded his gear and placed it in one of the plastic dry-boxes.

"You guys want to take a break?" he asked suddenly, "because I need to get wet." Without waiting for an answer, he grabbed the stern line and jumped overboard, resurfacing shortly with a big smile, while being towed by the raft and the current. He shook his shaggy head and beard. "It's cold but refreshing. Anybody coming in? If you are, please keep your vest on."

Matthew could feel the sweat drizzling down his back and into his shorts. He was not wearing swim trunks, but his cotton shorts were thin enough to suffice. He pulled off his vest and shirt, climbed back into the vest, and cannon-balled over the edge into the icy water.

Tim swam toward him to offer him a part of the towline.

"Feels great, doesn't it" Tim said.

Matthew was not sure how to respond, torn between acting friendly or somewhat aloof as a result of what happened the day before. "It definitely feels good," Matthew responded with little affect. "Sort of déjà vu," he added sarcastically.

"Yeah, sort of," Tim said coldly. He pulled himself toward the raft, got a firm hold of the roping, and hauled himself over the stern. He then turned and faced Matthew. "I guess we had better be going if we want to catch up with the others." He kneeled in the raft and extended his hand to Matthew who grabbed it and was easily pulled into the boat.

"Thanks," Matthew said, avoiding eye contact.

"My pleasure," Tim responded, but soft enough so that Matthew barely heard him.

As if intentional, Tim allowed his raft to be the last of the four as they made their way through the winding canyons and occasional flatlands. He remained unclothed, except for his swim trunks, and Matthew could not help but notice his muscular, well-proportioned body, mildly hirsute in an appealing manner, with a hint of atavistic qualities. It was obvious that Tim was aware of Matthew's veiled interest, and subtly let him know he enjoyed it by smiling, ever so briefly, when he caught him looking.

It was not until the lead boats pulled into a small beach before Tim put on his T-shirt and shorts.

"It must be time for lunch," Brother Edward said, as he began his customary search for his vitamin supplements.

"Yup," Tim said. "I hope everyone's hungry."

And they were. Sitting next to the river, the group had no trouble devouring all of the chicken salad sandwiches served on fresh, sourdough bread, with coleslaw, pickles, and brownies for dessert.

It was just before they had finished, when the two large rafts floated by. At first, Andrew could not believe his eyes—until Matthew said it out loud.

"They're all naked!" he exclaimed. The mixed group of men and women waved politely from the boats; some called out "hello" and "nice day" as they straddled the sides of the raft, dragging either one or both feet in the water, while the others paddled, indifferently, past the stunned monks, who either waved a feeble gesture in return, or simply sat motionless with their mouths half open and their eyes glued to the passing spectacle.

"*Au naturale*," Bill said, breaking the silence of the relatively dazed group. "And with apologies," he added. "Believe it or not, it's become a tradition for some to raft naked—a sort of 'getting back to nature' thing, but I honestly didn't think we would see anyone else on the river, and I forgot to mention it. I'm sorry."

Father Luke laughed. "Heck, that's about the most exciting thing that's happened to me in a long time!"

His comment dissolved the icy aura as laughter soon swelled into an echoing crescendo with Brother Mark, once again, convulsed into a fit of near hysteria.

"I guess we got on the wrong boat," Brother Nathan added somberly. He still looked a bit ragged from the previous night.

Of course, additional laughter reverberated throughout the canyon.

With full stomachs, the rafters resumed their journey in the stifling noonday heat; it was too hot to even consider hiking—most opted to remain on the water. Brother Adrian, who grew up in a small New England town on the ocean, could be seen, being towed through the icy water, tied to the stern line and grinning like a Cheshire cat.

On the left bank, a makeshift road wound its way down to a small beach where Andrew noticed an old Jeep had been parked close to the river. As they got closer, he saw two Indian teenagers frolicking in the water, attempting to survive the nearly unbearable heat. They stopped when they saw the rafts, laughed, and waved, as though privy to some esoteric joke. Andrew wondered if it had something, remotely, to do with "the white man."

Yet as they rounded the next bend in the river, their laughter seemed to make sense. Settled in a shady grove, the two boats of naked rafters rested on the beach, while the group enjoyed their lunch and a break from the weather by swimming, throwing Frisbees, or simply lying in the sun on the sand. As before, they waved cordially at the monks who, this time, waved back with renewed energy and blatant interest.

The monks reminded Andrew of the Saturday morning cartoon characters whose eyes would bulge, extend five feet from their face, and then retract to indicate extreme desire for the object of their affection. The thought made him smile.

Joan's voice refocused the otherwise distracted rafters. "We're not far from the Narrows," she announced, as she dipped her red bandanna into the water, wiped her face, and then tied it around her head. "With the water level fairly low, it should be an easy passage—but fun."

"What is it?" Brother Mark asked.

"It's an area where the river tends to narrow, hence its name. The water backs up and flows more rapidly for about a quarter of a mile, with no major obstacles other than getting through the first gate with a relatively aligned boat." She smiled. "Believe me, it's nothing to worry about."

"Whatever you say," Brother Mark said, with a slight roll of his eyes.

In the distance, Andrew could see the convergence of the canyon walls meeting the river's edge like a giant dam with a small hole in it. He felt anxiety suddenly enveloped him, tensing his muscles and causing his stomach to churn almost immediately; however; with the Narrows approaching rapidly, he had little time to think of himself.

"Our main objective is to keep the raft heading downstream," Joan said, "and to enjoy the ride. Remember the basics—hard right, left paddlers; hard left, right paddlers. Any questions?"

The group shook their heads negatively, until Brother Mark turned slightly to face Joan. "Any chance of sitting this one out?"

"Too late now," she shouted as the boat got sucked into the current. "Okay. Paddle hard!"

The roiled water rose and dropped repeatedly through a series of gradual rapids, free from any major boulders or obstructions, until it slowly flattened out and carried the raft into a wider and more tranquil part of the river.

Just as Andrew was beginning to relax and enjoy the sensation of speed and the turbulence of the river, it was over before he knew it.

"Hard left," Joan called out. The raft eased sideways across the current. "We can watch the others come down from here." She rested the oars on the side of the boat while she anticipated comments.

"What a ride!" Brother Mark said, grinning from ear to ear. "I could do that again."

Joan laughed. "It's my favorite part of the river," she admitted. "A bit of excitement."

Andrew and Brother Nathan agreed. "I wouldn't mind if the entire river were like that," Andrew said.

"Well, maybe not all of it," Brother Nathan remarked. "You need some contemplative sections."

They watched as the remaining three rafts dropped through the sluice, sped over the rapids, and headed directly for their boat.

"That was a pleasant change!" Phil shouted. "Something to get the blood moving."

Matthew seemed to glow with excitement, smiling broadly like the others. "Now, that was a ride!" he said.

Andrew glanced briefly at the crew in Matthew's boat; he was somewhat surprised by Tim's near nakedness as the brief Speedo trunks did very little to hide his anatomy.

"The remainder of the river is fairly placid," Joan said, almost apologetically, "but I think you'll find the beauty of the landscape worth the slow trip."

She readjusted her bandanna and began to row. "Hard to left," she said as the boat began to turn slowly and faced downstream once more.

After the short excitement of the rapids, the river mellowed out and widened into a child's ride, seemingly geared for complete admiration of the immediate scenery. Layers of red, purple, bronze, and yellow strata merged in wavy lines beneath the sparse greenery. Boulders, the size of Volkswagens, balanced precipitously on the edge of the distant cliffs, some with familiar shapes, depending on the imagination. One, in particular, clearly resembled a sombrero, complete with appropriate creases.

As the heat of the day increased, mountains of cumulus clouds rose above the horizon, like dollops of whipped cream dropped from above.

"We'll probably get some rain," Joan announced. "This heat is going to kick up something."

Andrew looked at the watercolor sky, filled with puffy, white clouds with dark tinted bellies. "Do you think it will hold off until we make camp?" he asked.

Joan squinted. "It's hard to tell but I think so. Besides, we might make camp early, just to be on the safe side."

Andrew wiped the sweat from his brow with the back of his hand. "Do you mind if I get wet?" he asked, knowing that Joan would not object.

"Not at all," she replied. "Just be sure to wear your vest and grab a line."

Moments later, Andrew was beneath the surface, rising quickly to the top with the assist from his life vest. The bone chilling water seemed to penetrate deep inside his body as though his heart and lungs were totally exposed and momentarily shocked by the sudden temperature change. He bobbed alongside the raft.

"It's sort of like an ice bath," he said, smiling feebly, "but it feels great—what a difference!"

Joan laughed. "I think I'll wait till we make camp, and then I'll cool off."

It was not long before Andrew decided to return to the dryer confines of the raft. He swam to the stern, grabbed the safety line, and, with an assist from Joan, hauled himself into the boat. Instantly, the thermal air wrapped itself around him, warming his chilled body like a perfect sauna until he realized that, except for returning to the water, there was no way to escape the heat. It did not take long for his shorts to dry completely and for a bead of sweat to reestablish itself on his brow.

Phil's raft suddenly appeared alongside. He pointed toward a bank of ominous looking clouds in the distance. "I think we should make camp soon," he suggested. "I'm not real confident in what the weather may bring, judging by the sky."

"I sort of figured you would say that," Joan said. "It sounds like a good idea. We'll follow you."

As expected, Phil located a small but deep site which would comfortably house the group and their gear. He made sure that the rafts were dragged high onto the beach, far from the water line, in the event that the river rose and flooded its banks.

Following an early dinner of grilled fish and French fries, the campers were instructed to break out their rain gear, including their tents, while the light was still acceptable to assist with the set up.

Matthew selected a modest, pop-up version, complete with a screen door and plenty of zippered vents for fresh air. He nudged Andrew, who followed him and helped him create their new quarters in anticipation of a rainy evening.

"We have to be sure it's anchored pretty good," Matthew said. "We don't want to get blown away."

"And end up in Kansas," Andrew added with a grin.

Matthew looked around to see if anyone were in earshot. "Yeah, but that's not the only reason," he said wantonly. "It might be an exciting night."

"Discretion," Andrew reminded him. "Don't forget discretion."

"Who . . . me?"

"Yeah—you," Andrew emphasized with a smirk.

With most of the storm preparation completed, the group, once again, gathered around the campfire as the sky clouded over and darkened early, in accordance with Phil's prediction. Because of the increased wind, they decided to keep the fire small and manageable.

Once again, Bill and Tim brought out their guitars, strumming new tunes and singing as well as ever.

"How do you remember so many songs?" Brother Adrian asked.

Bill rubbed his face and responded. "Oh, I guess after playing them so often, they just come to you."

"That's amazing!" Brother Adrian remarked. "You could probably get jobs doing that."

"We do," Tim said, "mostly in the winter when it's too cold to run the river. We play at different clubs in town."

"That must be quite interesting," Brother Adrian said.

"It helps pay the bills," Tim said without much enthusiasm.

Bill used the break in playing to serve coffee and cordials—by now, a regular river tradition.

"I was wondering when this was coming," Brother Adrian said coyly.

"Well, here it is," Bill said. "Tonight, a touch of Drambuie. May I pour you some?"

"But of course," Brother Adrian replied. His affected French accent disintegrated into a nasal whine.

Both Andrew and Matthew held up their cups for their share of the intoxicating elixir. They watched, smiling, as Brother Nathan opted only for black coffee.

Once everyone's cup was full, the guitarists resumed their playing, this time mostly contemporary songs, which few recognized or knew the words. Nevertheless, Brother Adrian sat in rapt attention, tapping his fingers and moving his head with the rhythm.

Later in the evening, Joan was coaxed into singing an old Kingston Trio hit, "Scotch and Soda," which she performed remarkably well and received a strong round of applause. "Thank you, thank you," she said with a deep bow, "but I have to admit, I've had plenty of practice because they always ask me to sing it on most of our river trips. Lucky for you, it's the only song I know."

As expected, Brother Adrian's laughter boomed above the rest and echoed sharply off the canyon walls.

"At least the rain has held off," Brother Edward said, unfortunately, he barely got the words out when a few sprinkles could be felt; however, no one made a comment since it was rare for Brother Edward to socially express himself.

"Oh well," Phil said. "It looks like nature is giving us a reason to turn in."

Assured that all was reasonably secured, Tim smothered the fire with sand.

Immediately, those who had flashlights illuminated them and began their search for their sleeping quarters which, due to the size of the tents, were much easier to find in the darkness.

With the assist of his flashlight, Andrew prepared his bed by pumping up his air mattress with a small hand pump and then placing his bag on top of it. A tepid breeze found its way inside, flapping the lacing on the screened door. He lay back and watched Matthew unzip his lightweight bag and pull his pillow out of the foot section.

"Can't sleep without my pillow," Matthew said, as he gently kneaded it into shape.

"I know," Andrew said. "I wish I had remembered to bring mine."

"What do you use?"

"Oh, usually a flannel shirt. I just roll it up and it seems to work okay."

"We can share mine," Matthew offered with a grin.

Andrew laughed. "Let me think about it."

A strong wind gust strained the tent anchors, as it blew inside with a cool draft and the clean, fresh scent of rain.

"It must be close," Andrew said. "I'll zip the vent on this side."

Suddenly, a voice called out from the other side of the screen door. "Anybody home?"

Matthew and Andrew locked eyes in startled silence.

"Of course," Andrew replied weakly. He moved toward the door and unzipped the screen.

"I hate to bother you but it seems we're short a tent," Tim said, as he entered and squatted near the door. "Would you mind if I shared yours?"

Matthew could feel himself cringe.

"No . . . not at all," Andrew replied with forced graciousness. "There's plenty of room for three."

"Thanks," he said. Tim quickly exited, retrieved his gear which he had left outside, and returned, tossing his bedding onto the only open area available, the third side of the triangular shaped space. "And," he continued, as he searched through his backpack, "I brought a little something to thank you for your hospitality." He pulled out a half-full bottle of Drambuie along with three plastic cups. "Something to help take the chill off the evening," he said, as he poured shot-sized amounts into each glass.

He held up his: "Cheers . . . to your kind understanding of my dilemma."

Matthew felt as though he might gag over his pedantic language and, as a result, quickly downed the sticky liqueur to help settle his nausea. He could feel the soothing heat descend slowly, anesthetizing everything in its path until it ended comfortably in his stomach.

"Another?" Tim asked, holding the bottle toward Matthew.

"No, thanks," Matthew said somewhat cynically. "One will be fine."

Although he was not sure of the cause, Andrew could sense the tension between them. "Sounds like the storm is picking up," he said.

"At least you've got a sealed floor," Tim commented. "No chance of a wet sleeping bag."

Matthew looked at him directly. "No, not a chance," he remarked coldly.

By then, the rain began to vigorously pelt the nylon tent, visibly denting the roof and sucking the structure upwards.

"Maybe it's a good thing you're here," Andrew interjected. "Otherwise, we might have taken off."

"It sounds like hail," Matthew said.

Tim turned toward the door, stuck out his hand, and quickly pulled it inside. "You're right," he said. He opened his palm, exposing three, marble-sized ice balls, one of which he dropped into his glass. "Ice?" he asked, looking at Andrew.

"Sure, why not," Andrew said. He held out his glass as Tim dropped the remaining pellets into it. "Thanks."

"You're welcome."

In his darkened corner of the tent, Matthew began to remove his shoes, socks, and pants. He then climbed into his sleeping bag wearing his shorts and a T-shirt. "I hope no one minds, but I think I'll turn in."

Andrew was surprised by his abruptness. He searched through his backpack for his canteen of water and his bottle of sleeping pills, which he knew he would need to get through the increasingly complex nocturnal arrangement. As discreetly as possible, he took one of the pills out of the bottle and washed it down with the contents of his canteen.

"So how long have you been running river trips?" Andrew asked, hoping to defuse some of the negative energy within the tent.

"Almost ten years," Tim replied. "It sounds long but it seems like yesterday."

"Probably because it's a job you enjoy."

"That's for sure." He looked down and then over at Matthew. "Except, this is the first trip I've had a capsize, something I'm really uncomfortable about."

"Well, like Phil said, it's a good thing no one was seriously injured."

"Yeah, but even so . . . it shouldn't have happened," Tim admitted.

Matthew lay on his side, listening to the conversation. 'Then why did it?' he wondered, wishing that he could have said it out loud.

"Was the water level too low?" Andrew asked naïvely, knowing that he had no idea of what he was asking.

Tim poured himself another drink and offered the bottle to Andrew who accepted.

"I'm not sure," Tim said. "I think we just got sucked into an unexpected hole; the water began to swamp the stern and before I knew it, the raft rolled over and I was underneath."

"Along with the others," Andrew added.

"That's right," Tim admitted, "and that's the hard part. It's frightening knowing that you are responsible for others, especially for those who aren't familiar with rafting and the deceptive power of a river."

'I should've brought my violin,' Matthew thought. He rolled over and faced the tent wall which was vibrating from the wind and the rain.

Getting toward the bottom of his drink, Andrew could feel the sedative and alcohol combination flood over his body like a sudden weight. His eyelids became concrete; his muscles felt disconnected. "Well, I hate to be a party pooper," he said sleepily "but this drink is really knocking me down."

"That's okay," Tim said with a yawn. "I'm pretty tired myself."

Andrew struggled to remove his shoes and clothing, which he piled in one corner of the tent. He gratefully climbed into his sleeping bag and pulled the light covering over him.

The winds suddenly seemed to lessen; the tent settled down, leaving only the gentler sound of a soft shower against the nylon covering.

"I guess it's slowing down," Tim remarked.

Yet Andrew only vaguely remembered hearing the words, which sounded as though a tape recording had lost its power and the message faded into an increasingly baritone blur.

Later that night, Matthew awoke, overcome with the urgency to urinate. He lay on his side with his eyes wide open, remembering that Tim was sharing their tent. He lifted his head, listened, and looked around. The rain had stopped completely. The nearly full moon illuminated the inside of the tent with a milky white opalescence as Andrew slept soundly, curled on his side, facing the outer tent. Tim was sprawled on his back, shirtless, one arm above his head.

As quietly as possible, Matthew approached the door, unzipped the screen, and stepped out into the damp but nearly flawless evening filled with pinpoint stars and a waxing moon. He walked toward the beach, away from the tent, and gazing from one constellation to another, he relieved himself, as several shooting stars streaked across the sky and faded in the darkness.

Back inside the tent, he zipped the screen door shut and settled into his sleeping bag. He listened to Andrew's slow, deep breathing in the otherwise silent evening, closed his eyes, and waited for sleep to dull his senses and ease him into his own unconscious world, yet unexpectedly, all was momentarily postponed.

Without looking, he could hear Tim turning in his bag, shifting his weight and blanket as though uncomfortably awake. In the dead silence that followed, Matthew was keenly aware of Tim's breathing; an increase in his respiration, accompanied by a familiar sound of skin on skin.

'It can't be,' he thought. He closed his eyes even tighter, breathed deeply, and waited for silence. Instead, the sound increased until, overcome with curiosity, Matthew barely raised his head and glanced toward Tim's section of the tent.

In the moonlight, he saw Tim lying completely naked on his sleeping bag, stroking his erection without inhibition, as though waiting for Matthew to take notice.

As soon as he knew Matthew was watching, he turned slightly toward him and began to touch himself with renewed interest, a one-man show for his captive audience.

Feeling himself involuntarily aroused, Matthew rolled onto his back and continued to watch the undeniably handsome man perform and excite him even more. He then looked briefly at Andrew who remained sleeping on his side facing the outer tent, apparently dead to the world.

'This is wrong,' Matthew thought, even though his arousal had peaked. He quickly rolled onto his side, pulled his pillow over his ears, and waited for silence and the inevitable luxury of sleep.

The morning broke bright and warm for the final day on the river. Unlike the other campsites, the absence of obstructive cliffs allowed the sunlight to bathe the area in golden light, waking even the deepest sleepers to a fresh, promising start.

Andrew rubbed his eyes and looked around. He saw Matthew curled up in his bag, lying on his side and exhaling loudly, almost snoring. Tim slept soundly on his stomach, naked from the waist up, exposing his hirsute back and shoulders.

Within minutes, Andrew was dressed, quietly exited the tent, and made his way to the chemical toilet. He waved silently to Bill who was already up, preparing the stoves for breakfast.

When he finished, Andrew decided to help Bill with the food prep by frying sausages, making coffee, and setting up the service table.

"How did you sleep?" Bill asked, as he continued to break eggs into a stainless steel pot.

"Like the proverbial log," Andrew responded. "All I remember is talking for a while with Tim and then going out like a lightbulb."

"Tim slept in your tent?" Bill asked, somewhat surprised.

"Yeah, last-minute," Andrew said. "He said they were short of tents."

Bill glanced at Andrew, paused, and then resumed his task. He made no further comment.

In the tent, Matthew heard Tim yawn. He rolled over and watched as Tim got up, stark naked from his sleeping bag and faced him. His uncircumcised penis hung substantially, as it curved down below his scrotum, inviting any excuse of excitement. Matthew rolled back on his side. After a pause, he heard Tim put on his clothing, tie his sneakers, and begin to unzip the door.

"I just want to say that I enjoyed last night," Tim said softly before exiting the tent.

Matthew kept his eyes closed, without responding. He thought of Andrew with an uncharacteristic sense of guilt, which suddenly washed over him and then abated. 'Where the hell is this going?' he wondered, knowing how much he cared for Andrew yet fully aware of his arousal and undeniable attraction to this rugged stranger.

* * *

Chapter Twenty

The Mountie

The final leg of the journey on the river proved to be a repeat of the previous day, torpid spirits floating ever so slowly within the windless heat of the canyon. More and more of the crew opted for the frigid waters as they drifted lazily behind their rafts—human chum, too large to interest the marine inhabitants indigenous to the river. As predicted, the beauty of the area remained its saving grace. Polished cliffs of complementary colors wound their way along the banks, disappearing at times into the red earth only to resurface once again with their curved strata jutting out over the water, as if purposely designed by contemporary architects to flaunt their incredible elegance and fragility.

Matthew watched as Tim stripped down to his Speedo briefs and threw himself overboard to seek relief from the oppressive heat. When Tim returned, Matthew did the same, shuddering at the initial trauma of the cold water, but then relaxing and enjoying the refreshing ride.

By mid-afternoon, they had finally reached their disembarkation site where, as promised, the locals had driven the four vehicles down to the beach, ready to accept the vast quantity of equipment which would have to be stowed.

In spite of the heat and the gentleness of the river for their last two days, most were reluctant to see the journey end; a nearly palpable sense of despondency gripped the weary travelers, who would no longer call the river their home. Anticipating just such a reaction, Phil and Joan and their two river rats did their best to maintain a jovial atmosphere by remaining as upbeat as possible, smiling and joking with the monks, and recalling some of the highlights of the trip—one in particular—which Andrew would rather have forgotten: the "almonds in the pocket" story.

"Even with the tan, I think I can see a blush," Joan said, referring to Andrew's cheeks. She then removed a large plastic bag from one of the watertight containers and pulled out a stack of new white T-shirts neatly screened in green with the saying "Official River Rat of the San Paolo."

The monks cheered and thanked her profusely.

"There's method to my madness," she joked. "At least when we stop for pizza and beer in Vista Heights, they won't throw us out for looking like rodents!"

Beyond the laughter, Brother Adrian could be heard questioning Joan's apparently incredible offer. "We are really stopping for pizza and beer?" he asked.

"Of course," Joan reinforced. "Unless you guys aren't hungry."

"Or thirsty," Phil added.

"No . . . I mean yes," Brother Adrian stumbled. His excitement was obvious.

With the seemingly endless gear finally packed, the four vehicles made their way across the sandy soil, in search of the semblance of a road.

Andrew took one last look, turning his head to peer through the soiled rear window of the suburban. A familiar hollow feeling welled up from his stomach, as if another door had suddenly closed and would never be reopened. Overcome slightly with panic and hoping that he would not experience whatever it was that he remembered experiencing in his cell, he reached for his backpack, found the anti-anxiety medication, and washed it down with water.

Joan noticed, peripherally, but said nothing.

Matthew found himself riding with Bill and Tim and a truckload of apparatus. Bill sat in the backseat, appearing more introspective than usual.

Matthew turned to face him. "So was this a good trip?" he asked, hoping to effect a change in his mood.

"They're all good when you're on the river," he said with a half smile. "But yes . . . you guys were fun to be with and very, very helpful."

"Thanks, that's good to hear, "Matthew said.

Tim, who had also been fairly quiet, spoke up. "I'm sorry about the capsize, though. That's never happened before."

Matthew was somewhat moved by his honesty. "Hey . . . what can you do? Things happen—so don't worry about it."

After about an hour on the paved road, the caravan pulled over at a four-way intersection and stopped.

Phil jumped out of his vehicle and approached Tim's. "Are you going to drop Bill off with his gear and then meet up with us in Vista Heights?"

Tim turned to look at Bill. "I guess that would make sense. Why double back when we don't have to."

"Sounds fine to me," Bill acknowledged.

"Did you want to go along for the ride or share one of our vehicles?" Phil asked, looking at Matthew.

Surprised by the sudden turn of events, Matthew hesitated. "I guess I'll tag along—help with the gear."

"All right," Phil said. "See you in Vista Heights."

Matthew was surprised that Bill lived close to the river, since he assumed most everyone came from the Bitter Creek area.

Within one half hour they reached his modest cabin, nestled within a grove of cottonwoods on a high bluff.

"Nice place," Matthew commented.

"Thanks."

"Can you access the river directly?"

"No, but about three-quarters of a mile from here, the road cuts down to a nice beach area where you could launch a raft, but it's a rocky, gnarly area . . . great for kayaks."

Once Bill removed his gear, the back of the suburban was practically empty.

"Wow, where do you store all of this?" Matthew asked.

Bill laughed. "Between the house and the barn, I seem to manage."

"You want some help putting it away? Tim asked.

"No, thanks. I got the rest of the afternoon."

"Okay, buddy," Tim said. "Thanks for the help, as usual." He shook Bill's hand and got into the truck. "See you on the next trip."

Matthew also shook his hand and thanked him. "Maybe we'll have a chance to do it again."

"I'd like that," Bill said.

Tim started the vehicle as Bill called out to him. Tim responded with only a smile.

Matthew was not sure, but he thought he heard Bill say, "Behave yourself."

For the next fifteen minutes, they drove in silence through the desert, past windblown dunes and strangely shaped columns of red rock, some of which resembled towers, castles, arches, and even sailing ships.

Unexpectedly, Tim suddenly pulled off the paved road onto a barely defined path. He stopped momentarily to shift into four-wheel drive and then continued into an area surrounded by sculpted dunes and small buttes.

"Is this some sort of shortcut?" Matthew asked, knowing full well that it was not.

Tim remained silent. He drove the suburban over a ridge, into an area ringed with dunes and, surprisingly, a short distance ahead, a small pool of crystal-clear water, approximately fifty yards in diameter, sparkled in the noonday sun.

He turned off the engine. "Not many people know about this spot," he said, looking through the windshield. "I used to come here all the time; hike, swim in the spring-fed pond, and, sometimes, just sit and think." He looked at Matthew. "I thought you might like to see it."

Matthew looked straight ahead. "It's nice," he said abruptly. He wiped the sweat from his forehead with a handkerchief.

After a minute of silence, Tim responded. "Look. I know you don't like me, and I'm not asking you to, but I don't want you leaving today without talking about what's going on between us."

"You mean like this conveniently unscheduled stop in the middle of nowhere?" Matthew said cynically. He looked at Tim. "You tell me, since you brought it up, what is going on between us?"

Tim shrugged. "How honest do you want me to be?"

"Do you make it a habit of spying on people?" Matthew blurted.

"No, I don't," Tim said.

"Then why were you watching Andrew and me that day?"

"Why did you continue doing what you were doing after you saw me?" Tim asked. "I'll bet you never let Andrew know that I was there."

Matthew immediately got out of the truck. He walked down to one of the dunes and stood in its shade.

Tim followed him. "I didn't bring you here argue. I just want to clear the air." He stood in back of Matthew. "The moment I saw the both of you, I thought, why the heck are these two very handsome men—and I don't want to seem disrespectful—hiding behind the walls of the monastery? And as time went on, it became pretty clear, at least to me, that you and Andrew were more than just good friends—the way you'd look at each other, be together, whatever . . . I felt that something was there. So when I saw the both of you leave the Anasazi dwellings, my curiosity got the best of me, and I decided to follow you. The rest of the story you're familiar with."

Matthew turned to face him. "So now you know," he said matter-of-factly. "Andrew and I really care about each other. What else can I tell you?"

"I guess this is where it starts to get to difficult," Tim said.

"What do you mean?"

"It's probably more of what I can tell you," Tim suggested. "I don't know if you want to hear it."

Matthew sat down in the soft sand. "I'm all ears," he said. "Try me."

Tim stretched out in the sand next to him. "I think the reason you don't like me is that you realize we're pretty much alike. You know that I have strong physical feelings for you, and as much as you might deny it, I know that you have those same feelings for me."

"Yeah, right," Matthew said with a scoff.

"I also believe you when you say that you care for Andrew, probably even love him, but I'll bet that the relationship isn't exactly like you'd want it to be. He doesn't give you what you need because of his principles and his vocation. I think he's really torn between totally loving you and trying to reconcile that with his life as a monk."

"What are you, some fucking psychiatrist?" Matthew blurted.

"No, you know I'm not," Tim said softly. "I'm just a realist who has watched you over the past five days, knowing that I can give you what we both want and need. We intentionally error on the side of lust, and as much as we hate to admit it, people, even those we think we love, often become pawns for the sake of our own interests." He paused briefly. "Today . . . out here . . . whatever. No one will ever know, and most likely, we'll never see each other again."

As much as he tried to deny it, Matthew knew exactly what Tim was saying; in fact, his very words, the truth, caused him to become obviously aroused.

"So . . . what do you think you can give me . . . that I'm so *desperately* in need of?" Matthew asked, almost as if to encourage him.

"Should I put it bluntly?" Tim asked. He rolled onto one side, supporting his head with his arm.

"Sure, why not?"

"When's the last time Andrew sucked on your cock or had his dick up your ass?"

Matthew remained speechless.

Tim suddenly leaned over and kissed him forcefully, while Matthew willingly consented and wrapped himself around him, anticipating the realization of Tim's accurate insight.

Impulsively, Tim jumped up and began to walk toward the truck. "Follow me," he insisted. "Sand and sex can be irritating." By the time Matthew met him at the back of the suburban, Tim had already opened the tailgate, raised the rear window hatch, and was pulling a sleeping bag apart and spreading it over the rear deck. In a flash, he removed his T-shirt and shorts and stood naked in front of Matthew. He then used his shirt to help brushed some of the sand from his legs and arms.

Matthew watched, mesmerized, yet completely excited by Tim's total lack of inhibition, his tight, muscular frame and, of course, his impressive, uncut, and distended penis.

Before he knew it, his own T-shirt was swiftly pulled over his head, followed by a quick unzipping and removal of both his shorts and underwear.

"We don't have a heck of a lot of time," Tim said. "Turn around."

Not quite sure what to expect, Matthew turned his back toward him, only to feel Tim gently use his shirt to brush away most of the sand still clinging to Matthew's legs, calves, and arms. He then pressed his body against Matthew's back, embraced him, and began to kiss and lick his neck, ears, and shoulders while exploring with his hands everything within reach.

"Let's move inside," Tim said. He crawled on top of the sleeping bag.

Matthew quickly followed and lay alongside of him.

Once again, Tim kissed him hard but briefly, while gently stroking Matthew's erection. Wasting no time, he slipped his mouth over the head of his penis and down the shaft as Matthew moaned involuntarily, experiencing something he had, instead, been anticipating from Andrew.

"Tell me what you want," Tim said seductively.

"You know what I want," Matthew admitted

"Then say it," Tim insisted.

Matthew responded hoarsely. "I want to . . . feel you inside me."

"It's what we both want," Tim said. He slid himself backwards, off Matthew's legs, and positioned himself behind him. Without haste, he thrust himself into Matthew, who was not expecting such a forceful entry.

Like a knife stabbing him, Matthew cried out sharply, his eyes filling with tears, as he jammed his own fist into his mouth to stifle the loud wail.

Tim stopped momentarily. "I'm sorry," he said softly. "Should I quit?"

"No," Matthew said. "It's been a while."

He leaned down and kissed Matthew's forehead, which was moist with perspiration.

Matthew tilted his head back. "Kiss me," he said softly.

Without a verbal response, Tim complied, kissing him somewhat tenderly and then much more aggressively.

It was what Matthew needed to forget about the pain and, more importantly, to feel less like an object and, perhaps, more valued.

In synch with Matthew, Tim drove deeper and deeper, while Matthew began to stroke his own renewed erection.

When it was obvious that Matthew was about to ejaculate, Tim initiated a near brutal attack, plunging himself recklessly into Matthew. It was impossible to tell if Matthew's cries were the result of Tim's flagrant assault or the intensity of his own orgasm—most likely, a combination of both.

Tim shuddered, straining, as he released himself into Matthew, and then collapsed, breathless, on top of him.

After a pause, Matthew spoke softly, wiping the sweat from his eyes. "I could actually feel it when you came, the heat and force of your semen," he admitted. "I've never felt that before."

Tim smiled. "And I don't think I've ever felt an orgasm so powerful before." He kissed Matthew on the forehead, eased himself out, and began to exit the vehicle. "Come on," he said, as he grabbed Matthew's feet and began to slide him toward him.

"Where are we going?"

"We both need a bath," Tim said. He grabbed Matthew's wrist and ran with him into the pond.

The ride back to Vista Heights, where they would meet the rest of the group, seemed endless. Tim said very little. Matthew knew that there were no strong bonds between them, only their need to satisfy each other's basic sexual desires, dreams, or fantasies; yet without blame, Matthew felt as though someone had called his bluff. Tim gave him what he needed—no questions asked. He seemed capable of easily reading Matthew or, perhaps, seeing through him, and this ability appeared to gnaw at him aggressively.

"You're like a Canadian Mountie," Matthew said suddenly, disrupting the unnatural silence.

Tim glanced over at him. "What you mean?"

Matthew shrugged. "You know, you always get your man,"

Tim shook his head negatively. "If only that were true," he said. His voice was redolent with melancholy.

"Well, I suppose now, you can tell your buddies that you had a monk," Matthew said caustically.

"You don't seem to get it," Tim said calmly. "We both enjoyed each other." He turned to look at Matthew. "Besides, that's not something I talk about." Tim leaned forward to remove his wallet from his back pocket and pulled out a business card which he handed to Matthew. "My home phone is on there. If you ever feel like it, once you cool down and began to think clearly, give me a call." He then looked directly into Matthew's eyes, "Because I'd like to see you again."

Before Matthew had time to respond, he felt the truck come to a sudden stop in front of the pizza shop, the only one in Vista Heights.

"I guess it's time to go," Tim said.

Matthew looked around, surprised that the shop was not located more centrally in the town. "This is it?" he asked.

"What . . . 'this is the pizza place' or 'this is it, goodbye'?" Tim asked with a slight smile.

"It looks like the answer is yes to both of those," Matthew said. "You're not coming in?"

Tim rubbed his hand over his tanned face. "I'd like to but I can't," he said. "I've got to be in Bitter Creek before six—a gig with a band at Little Joe's. Tell the guys inside I can't make it."

Matthew got out of the vehicle, shut the door, and began to walk away.

Tim quickly leaned over and called out the window. "Hey, Matt."

Matthew turned around.

"I'm serious about what I said."

"Yeah, right," Matthew said. He opened the door to the pizza place and went inside.

Although the pizza had not yet been served, most everyone in the group had finished their first beer and was working on their second. Matthew explained Tim's situation, even though he was convinced it was a lie, but it was irrelevant. He felt inundated by his atypical compunction and obvious sense of betrayal to Andrew and, perhaps, even to himself. He found an empty seat next to Andrew, who was well through his second drink.

Unable to sit as close to him as he would have liked, Matthew moved his bare leg to his right until he could feel the heat of Andrew's tanned skin pressing against his, a familiar warmth which helped ease his agitation.

* * *

Chapter Twenty-One

Shrink Time

Returning to the rigorous structure of community life within the confines of the monastery proved difficult for Andrew who, earlier, had surrendered to the openness of the canyons, deserts, and the freedom of life on the river. Whenever he was away for more than a day or two, he was barely able to put into perspective the minutiae of his confinement and the newly recognized boundaries of the enclosure. Life, once again, was refocused, yet it was not long before he experienced the familiar racing of his mind, the horrendous sinking into total blackness, and the inevitable terror which culminated in the even more familiar primal scream, a scream that woke him and others in the dormitory.

He sat on the side of his bed, wiping the sweat from his forehead, anticipating the inevitable knock. As expected, the gentle tapping of Brother Nathan broke the eerie silence.

Andrew switched on the closet light, put on his robe, and opened the door. "Come in," he said, skipping any pretense.

Brother Nathan sat silently in his desk chair, simply observing Andrew, as though waiting for him to recover.

"Yes, I know," Andrew responded quietly to the unasked question. "Maybe I should talk with the shrink."

Brother Nathan leaned forward, his elbows on his knees and his hands clasped. "Yes . . . but how are you right now?" The concern in his voice was obvious.

With a shrug, Andrew slumped against the wall alongside of his bed. "Okay, I guess . . . I don't know."

"Where is the medication I gave you?"

Andrew pointed toward his closet.

Brother Nathan found the prescription bottle on the shelf. "Did you take any of this before you went to bed?"

"No," Andrew said.

After pouring a glass of water from the pitcher, Brother Nathan removed a pill and handed it to Andrew. "Take this," he insisted.

Andrew complied and then stretched out on the floor.

"Do you want to talk about it?" Brother Nathan asked.

"There's not a lot to say," Andrew said, rubbing his eyes. "It's a feeling that seems to come over me, like I'm drowning in darkness, and I can't breathe. Sometimes it's dreams—scary ones, with hooded black figures with burning red eyes. Sometimes, it's as though I can't stop the noise inside my head." He rolled onto his back. "Maybe I'm just going crazy," he suggested.

"I don't know about that," Brother Nathan admitted, "but you can't go on like this. You need to talk with somebody."

"Yeah, I guess you're right."

"Should I talk with Father Gerald in the morning and ask him to talk with Dr. Klein?"

"Only if he thinks it's the right thing to do," Andrew said.

"All right," Brother Nathan said. He stood up. "I'll let you sleep. That pill should be kicking in pretty soon."

"Thanks," Andrew said.

Brother Nathan let himself out and closed the door.

* * *

With Brother Matthew away with Brother Mark for nearly three weeks at a Zen center retreat, Andrew found time for more introspective reading and meditation, free from the clutter of their relationship—both the positive and negative aspects—and an unencumbered opportunity to initiate weekly visits to Dr. Klein, whom Andrew grew to trust as therapy progressed.

Immediately after the first session, Dr. Klein suggested that Andrew visit him twice a week to help determine a diagnosis, if any, and to regulate the effects of the medication he prescribed along with psychotherapy.

"You're exhibiting symptoms of agitated depression," Dr. Klein said candidly, "however, with medication and talk therapy, I'm sure we can minimize symptoms and, hopefully, the source."

At first, Andrew refused to accept the diagnosis, until Dr. Klein was able to help him understand, bit by bit, the rationale for his behavior. Eventually, Andrew held nothing back: he discussed his relationship with Matthew; his life prior to entering the monastery; the confusion he was experiencing regarding his vocation; the apparent hypocrisy he witnessed within the community; the tragedy of John's death at the eggery; and Brother Morgan's death on the mesa. All was brought to the surface with cathartic relief which, at least for the moment, proved tremendously therapeutic.

Alone in his cell, Andrew continued with the writings of Thomas Merton by reading the *Waters of Siloe*, a provocative work which, once again, seemed to speak directly to him as he read the following passage:

> "An even more obvious danger is the materialism into which monks who are also professional farmers can sometimes fall when they attach more importance to the business of running their farm than to the contemplative life which is their real end."

He was reminded of the eggery, the ranching, and, in general, the vast amount of work dedicated to the overall operational side of the monastery which he now realized was, in fact, a business. He no longer had to wonder why Father Luke appeared so exhausted and drawn and why he suffered from migraines. Andrew knew that he was a part of the plan to make the business functional and, with luck, profitable.

He continued with the following:

> "Eventually the contemplative spirit caved in under the pressure of so many active and material interests and the Cistercians tended to lose themselves entirely in the active side of their lives . . . and when a contemplative order ceases to produce contemplatives its usefulness is at an end. It has no further reason for existing."

Andrew was reminded of the conversation between Abbot Paul and Abbot Basil from the writings of the early fathers. "You cannot be a monk unless you become like a consuming fire." He looked out into the garth, where the brilliant lace leaf maple etched a carmine contrast against the soaring spruce. 'A consuming fire,' he mused, 'a consuming fire.' A sudden chill engulfed him, causing him to shiver. He stood, retrieved his Zen stool, and settled down in an attempt to reestablish his tarnished contemplative spirit.

* * *

The three weeks of Matthew's absence seemed to pass quickly now that Andrew had established his twice-weekly visits with Dr. Klein, so when Matthew eventually knocked on Andrew's door after his return from the retreat, Andrew appeared somewhat confused.

"You're back already?" he asked.

"Well, that's a hell of a greeting," Matthew answered. "I'll bet you didn't even miss me."

Andrew rubbed his eyes. "No, I did. I just didn't realize that the time went by so quickly."

Matthew held Andrew's face with both hands. "Are you okay?"

Andrew turned his head, walked over to his desk chair, and sat down. "Yeah, why?"

"You look a little tired . . . and you need a shave."

"It must be the medication."

"Dr. Klein put you on medication?"

Andrew could feel his pulse increase. "To help me cope with my 'agitated depression' as he says." He glanced up at Matthew. "It's no big deal."

"It is to me," Matthew said. He squatted in front of Andrew and placed his arms and hands on his thighs. In silence, he stared at Andrew until he looked away.

"It's me, isn't it," Matthew said quietly. "I'm the reason you're this way."

Andrew turned, looked directly at the person he loved, and smiled. "If only it were that simple," he said. He wrapped his arms around Matthew and pulled him toward his chest. "Don't you remember the night we met—the night you saw me collapsed on the road?" He could feel

Matthew nod. "I didn't even know you, yet I was experiencing some of the same symptoms back then." He leaned back to look into Matthew's face. "It's just me having to deal with my own screwed up brain. You can help by trying to bear with me, okay?"

Once again, Matthew nodded, feeling somewhat sullied in Andrew's presence. "Anything . . . let me know."

* * *

Chapter Twenty-Two

Another Loss

Brother Adrian's death devastated the community and its neighbors; however, the shockwaves of his passing were greater than anyone ever anticipated, particularly in the way it impacted life at the monastery. Essentially, it was the end of an era, the evanescence of "the old guard" and all that it represented; the unraveling of a fabric—the dry, dusty glue, which suddenly allowed unbridled actions to surface with, apparently, little consequence. To even the untrained novice, it was clear that something was missing.

"At least he died in the town he loved," Father Luke said at a Sunday night supper, following the funeral. "Brother Adrian would look for any excuse to walk around Bitter Creek and observe, as he would say, 'how the other half live.'"

"I never knew he had a heart condition," Brother Edward said. He looked over the top of his glasses at his brothers while he ingested a handful of vitamins, one by one.

Mumbles of "me either" and "never knew" could be heard around the table.

"And now that we've sadly lost our main chef," Father Jude added, "Brother Mark and Brother Andrew will be asked to help with the meal prep." He glanced at both monks who also looked at each other, nodded in agreement, and said in unison, "Yes, Father."

Having to spend more time in the kitchen, Andrew was able to observe the everyday coming and going of most of the community, the delivery people, and, particularly, the abbot, who seemed to be much more mobile and dressing stylishly secular on most occasions. Andrew wondered about his destinations.

"Daydreaming, again?" Brother Mark asked, as he walked without warning into the kitchen.

Andrew was obviously startled. "I guess," he said. He turned to check the vegetable broth simmering on the stove, as he prepared homemade French onion soup.

"I never had a chance to ask you about the retreat," Andrew said. "How was it?"

Brother Mark seemed to hesitate slightly as though judiciously planning his response. "Meaningful . . . lots of sitting and Zen meditation." He quickly recovered and then added, "What did Matthew think of it?"

Andrew laughed briefly. "He didn't say."

Brother Mark seemed pleased with the response. "He doesn't say much, does he?"

Andrew, once again, was caught off-guard. "What do you mean?" he asked calmly.

"Oh . . . just that he is often brief with responses and not that much of a conversationalist."

The onion he was slicing burned Andrew's eyes. "I know what you mean, but there are times when I'm with him and he won't shut up." He wiped his eyes with the sleeve.

Brother Mark simply shrugged.

"It's strange being here now that Brother Adrian is dead," Brother Mark said, changing the subject.

"You got that right," Andrew said. "Is it me or does the whole place seemed 'different'?"

"It's not you," Brother Mark said. "I feel as though the captain died and no one has bothered to man the bridge."

"That's because the captain is all 'duded up' and hardly ever here," Andrew said blatantly. "You caught me watching him drive away in his Peugeot."

"That's nothing new," Brother Mark said. "I've seen it many times."

"I wonder if Father Luke knows what's going on."

"Probably, but he'd never say anything. They practically grew up together within these hallowed walls."

"Yeah . . . I forgot," Andrew said. He continued to slice the onions.

"I shouldn't be bringing this up again because it's a difficult subject," Andrew added, "but I sure miss Brother Adrian."

"I know," Brother Mark said. "If he's not in heaven, ain't none of us getting in."

"Yup," Andrew said softly. He was hoping Brother Mark would attribute the occasional tear to the mound of onions in front of him.

* * *

Almost every Sunday, after mass, and sometimes during the week, Andrew noticed that Matthew would meet with a small group of young people from Bitter Creek, often different people, yet one person, Rebecca Storrow—her blond hair glistening in the sunlight like a shampoo advertisement—was always present. He watched from the window in the entrance room, as she managed to position herself directly in front of Matthew; her wholesome smile reflecting perfect white teeth framed by full lips with barely a hint of pink. Occasionally, she would arrive with only one friend, a female, who appeared equally interested in Matthew's charm.

After fifteen or twenty minutes of socialization, Andrew watched her glorious exit as she quickly drove away in a white convertible.

"She's quite a looker, don't you think?" Brother Mark said.

"How is it that you suddenly appear?" Andrew asked, startled, once again, by Brother Mark's presence.

"Sorry . . . but I've seen you staring out this window several times, and my curiosity got the best of me."

"So—who is she?" Andrew asked.

"Rebecca Storrow . . . one of the more affluent names in Bitter Creek, originally from New England where her family made a fortune in banking, commodities, and industry. She probably has enough money in her change purse to buy this place."

"Sounds like the average Bitter Creek resident," Andrew said.

"Pretty much," Brother Mark agreed.

* * *

Chapter Twenty-Three

Talk Therapy

By early October, Bitter Creek glowed in the golden light reflected from the bright yellow aspens. The crisp, sunny days were capable of shattering even the most inaccessible heart as life became, somehow, even more than three-dimensional in one of the world's most perfect towns. For now, its empty brick streets waited patiently for the hordes of tourists who would mercilessly trample them during the height of the ski season.

Andrew laughed quietly to himself as he parked the black Volkswagen in front of Dr. Klein's office. 'Why would anyone want to see a shrink on a day like this?' he thought. 'I must be nuts.' Realizing his thought only caused him to laugh out loud as he pulled open the glass door and waited for the elevator to the third floor while a passing young woman gave him an inquisitive look. 'I'll bet she knows where I'm going,' he thought, and once again, he chuckled out loud in the empty lobby.

Yet once inside the heavily paneled office, the crystal ambience of Bitter Creek seemed miles away. Andrew sat in his usual chair, a comfortable, fabric high-back with wide, supportive arms, as he relaxed and allowed his feelings to surface and be verbalized.

"I just never expected this to happen here," he said. He rubbed his eyes and then looked at Dr. Klein, who sat calmly, in a similar chair, away from his desk. "How did I know that I would meet someone like Matthew?" He expected a response from Dr. Klein; however, he remained silent, looking, as usual, very nonjudgmental. Occasionally, he would jot notes into a small book which rested on his lap.

"I don't want this to sound like I'm blaming Matthew, because I'm not," Andrew continued, "but as you know, my feelings for him . . .

my sexuality . . . loving another man . . . is not why I entered the monastery."

Dr. Klein shifted slightly in his chair. "Why did you enter the monastery, Andrew?" Dr. Klein asked softly.

"The big question," Andrew said. He leaned forward, resting his elbows on his knees, with his hands clasped. " . . . too many reasons . . . I'm not sure. I already mentioned how someone gave me the *Rule of St. Benedict* when I was in college, and that initially piqued my interest. Then my relationship with Sara got all screwed up when I met this guy named Nick. At that time, things were fairly tolerable since I thought, well, what the hell; I'm bisexual—almost socially acceptable—until I found myself spending more and more time with Nick. Things just seemed to fall apart."

"How did they fall apart?" Dr. Klein inquired.

Andrew slouched back against the chair, with his right leg involuntarily shaking. "Well, Sara knew about Nick, and he knew about Sara. There were some ugly scenes—arguments. Sara said she didn't care as long as I would continue to see her; Nick grew to almost hate her, and then Sara overdosed on some prescription tranquilizers, was hospitalized, and recovered. After that, I spent even more time with Nick, which forced me to face all my Catholic guilt about homosexuality—you know, from being an altar boy to class president at a Catholic high school."

"I began to withdraw, socially, and read more spiritual literature. My job was going nowhere, yet my interest in spirituality seemed even stronger. The usual questions arose like 'What is life all about? Is there something out there?' So I decided to visit St. Anthony's to seek some sort of inner peace and, perhaps, an answer, or two, to the questions."

"And have you found any answers?"

"Not really," Andrew admitted. "Instead, I found Matthew or, perhaps, Matthew found me."

"Would you describe him as 'an answer'?" Dr. Klein asked.

Andrew shook his head "I don't know how to describe Matthew except to admit that I've grown to love him."

"Does he feel the same way about you?" Dr. Klein inquired tentatively.

"Yeah," Andrew said. "I'm sure he does; except lately, he's been sort of distant. I think he feels responsible for whatever I'm going through."

Dr. Klein removed his glasses and cleaned them with his handkerchief. "You may or may not find this helpful, but I have talked with several monks throughout the years, and have discussed situations not too dissimilar from yours. I have also studied the writings of the early fathers and read studies regarding sexuality, spirituality, and their close relationship in a religious environment or, for that matter, in nearly any environment including marriage."

Andrew sat up straight. "So what exactly are you saying?"

"I'm only disseminating information, Andrew, without condemning or condoning. You have to use some of this to try to help me to help you."

"I understand," Andrew said.

"Briefly, I'm sure you are familiar with St. Bernard's writings, his candid recognition of carnal love as the departure point of all realistic spirituality, which helped many to further their spiritual path. Of course, Aelred is well known to have encouraged friendships of a close nature within his community; even St. Augustine speaks about the insanity of not knowing how to love men as men should be loved. Nevertheless, given all of this, it does not solve what you are experiencing."

"So am I hopeless?" Andrew asked.

"Of course not," Dr. Klein replied with a smile. "With time, therapy, and medication, I'm sure we'll have you back on your feet before you know it."

Little did he know how absolutely wrong he would be.

* * *

Even with the medication, Andrew experienced strong symptoms of hopelessness, auditory hallucinations, and difficulty breathing, which resulted in unpredictable fainting spells. Often, he would lay in his bed for two or three days at a time, eating very little and consuming only fluids, until Father Gerald called Dr. Klein, who decided that it was time to hospitalize him at a small private clinic.

"Where am I?" Andrew asked when he awoke.

Father Gerald sat at his bedside looking professionally paternalistic. "Halsen Clinic," he said softly, "just outside of Bitter Creek." He reached out and placed his hand on Andrew's arm, above his IV. "How are you feeling?"

Andrew looked around the small yet attractive room. Thin boards of enameled white wainscoting separated the thick grey carpeting from the peach colored walls and ceiling. "I don't know . . . I was hoping you could tell me."

"What do you remember?" Father Gerald asked.

Andrew stared at the ceiling. "I'm not really sure: incredible fear of the darkness . . . suffocation, drowning."

"Dr. Klein has changed your medication, Andrew. I think you'll be feeling better soon."

He looked at Father Gerald and then reached up for his arm as though grabbing for a life preserver. "What's happening to me?" he asked. The concern in his voice was obvious.

"You are experiencing symptoms of clinical depression, symptoms which can be devastating but are curable," Father Gerald said. "It's not an easy road, but I know you'll get through this. I doubt that God would let you down, if you only ask him. And we need to listen carefully to Dr. Klein. He is a very capable clinician."

Andrew looked past Father Gerald to an arched window covered with ornate grating. "There are bars on the window," he said dispassionately, "masquerading as English ivy."

Father Gerald turned to look but said nothing.

After a moment of silence, Andrew rubbed his eyes. "I only wanted to be a monk," he said quietly to himself.

"You're already a monk and you'll continue to be a monk, if you choose," Father Gerald said firmly.

Suddenly, Andrew could feel an inexplicable sadness surge through his chest, while tears streaked his cheeks and fell upon the white linens.

Father Gerald stood over him and gently stroked his forehead. "Crying is okay . . . it's okay." He reached across the top of the bed with his other hand and pressed the call button to signal a nurse, who arrived almost immediately.

Intuitively, she grasped the nature of the situation and quickly left the room, only to return with a syringe which she injected into Andrew's IV, as he lay on his side sobbing uncontrollably into his pillow.

* * *

It was the last day of October when Andrew returned to his cell at St. Anthony's. Fully rested and compliant with his medication, he slowly resumed his duties at the monastery, buoyed by the support of his brothers and one in particular.

"Can I come in?" Matthew asked through the partially opened door.

Andrew put down the book he was reading. "Of course," he said. Just the sound of Matthew's voice evoked a sense of joy and longing within.

Matthew entered and quietly closed the door. "I thought you disappeared until I spoke with Father Gerald."

He hugged Andrew with genuine intensity.

"A minor brain adjustment," Andrew said. "Nothing to worry about."

Matthew stepped back a bit to look at him. "I missed you," he said, and then kissed him on the forehead. For all the suffering Andrew experienced, Matthew was struck by his familiar, handsome features.

"Sure," Andrew joked. "You didn't even come see me."

"Don't think I didn't want to. I sort of got the word from Father Gerald that you needed to rest and shouldn't have a lot of visitors."

"Well, I'm back and feeling fine," Andrew said. "How are you doing?"

Matthew sat on Andrew's bed. "All right, I guess. Things haven't been the same without you."

Andrew sat alongside of him. "Actually, you've been a little scarce, even prior to my absence," he stressed.

Matthew hesitated, dreading the question. "I know," he said. He dropped his head toward his chest. "Part of it is guilt, and part of it comes, once again, from Father Gerald. He thought that you needed some time alone, so I'm sort of caught in a bind over wanting to be with you but wanting to do the right thing." He raised his head to look at Andrew. "I want you to get better, Andrew, while, at the same time, my own needs want us to be the way we were." He put his hand on Andrew's knee. "For now, though, I know it's important that your needs come first—I can wait."

"Hey," Andrew said softly. "I'm getting better already." He leaned over and kissed Matthew's ear.

"I'd better go say hello to the girls and collect the eggs before I jump on top of you," Matthew said.

Andrew watched as he stood up and adjusted his jeans. "Please . . . don't be a stranger," he said somberly.

"I won't be," Matthew replied, "but you have to tell me when I should or shouldn't be with you."

"I will," Andrew said. He quickly jumped up, "Just a thought before you go—does this place seem different now that Brother Adrian is dead?"

Matthew was caught off-guard by his question. "What do you mean?"

"Have you noticed the abbot not being here as much and dressing differently?"

"It's funny you should say that because I saw him getting into his car yesterday looking like a 'Bitter Creek wannabe.'"

Andrew rubbed his eyes. "Well, maybe I'm not as crazy as I think."

"I'd still love you, even if you were a total wacko," Matthew said with a huge grin.

Andrew's smile faded quickly. "Can I ask you one more question?"

"Of course," Matthew said, his face suddenly serious.

"Are you and Rebecca . . . more than good friends?" The question appeared without warning.

Matthew's jaw dropped. "Rebecca? You're not serious, are you?"

Andrew ran his hands over his face to help displace some of the heat he felt in his cheeks. "I'm not trying to get you angry, Matt; it's just that I see you talking with her quite a bit after mass, even during the week."

"She's a typical Bitter Creek monk-follower," Matthew said. He moved closer to Andrew and placed his hands on his shoulders. "I'm the 'monk of the month,' and she brings her friends with her to observe my self-imposed celibacy and to marvel at the lunacy of my lifestyle. And I suppose there is a part of me that enjoys all the attention—that's all there is to it." He hugged Andrew hard. "I may be wrong, but I think someone is jealous," he added cavalierly.

"Just crazy," Andrew said.

"Well, just remember, you're not; but I'd love you even if you were. I've got to go." He kissed Andrew, stepped into the corridor, and quietly closed the door.

Andrew spent the remainder of the afternoon sitting in his cell reading from John Sanford's book. He copied the following into his journal:

> *"There are times when we must allow some of the unlived life within us to live if we are to get new energies for living. Moreover, if we strive to be only good and perfect, we become hateful . . . for this reason, there are few people more dangerous in life than those who set out to do good."* (*Evil* by J. Sanford)

Further on in the book, he noted an additional quote:

> *"If we only play it safe in life we never come to know who we are; life must be thoroughly lived if we are to become whole people, and it is better to be forgiven than to be self-righteous."*

'Maybe Matthew has a point,' he thought. 'Maybe it is possible to live this life to the fullest by totally loving Christ and being able to physically express that love to my brother.' He closed the book, stretched out on his bed, and, forgetting to take his medication, was soon fast asleep.

Even in the daylight, the darkness of his dream sequence found him vulnerable yet somewhat stronger than before. Deep in the total blackness, the barely visible dots of red glowed brighter with increasing intensity, until the hooded figure stood over him, staring with hellish, laser orbs, watching in silence.

Andrew could feel the hair raise on his body as fear clutched him like a vise—his body was immobilized, yet his voice was still functional as it cracked with a high-pitched vibration. "What the hell do you want from me?" he screeched into the faceless face. "What!"

The demonic visage moved even closer. "Your soul, son of Lucifer!"

The deep voice echoed within Andrew's head with the force of an avalanche, pounding painfully with each syllable. "Never!" he shouted. "Never! Never! Never!"

"Andrew! Wake up . . . wake up."

Andrew opened his eyes to see the concerned face of Brother Nathan staring back at him.

"It's okay," Brother Nathan said reassuringly. "You've been having one of your dreams." He slowly released Andrew's arms.

"Again?" he asked with disbelief.

Brother Nathan shook his head. "Have you been taking your medication?"

"Yes . . . but I may have forgotten this afternoon."

Brother Nathan found it on the closet shelf, poured Andrew some water, and handed it to him. "It's something you're going to have to remember," he admonished.

"I know, thanks." Andrew swallowed the pill and gave the glass back to Brother Nathan.

"One thing," Brother Nathan began with a smile. "You sure are strong."

"Really?"

"Well, I had a hard time holding you down on the bed. You came pretty close to slugging me."

Andrew looked embarrassed. "I'm sorry," he said.

"It's okay. I'm glad I happened to be walking by."

"Me too," Andrew said.

Brother Nathan walked toward Andrew's window and stared out into the garth through the thick glass, as if waiting for Andrew to introduce a new thought or question. When the silence continued, he broke it by speaking. "Your view is so different from mine," he said without turning.

"In what way?" Andrew asked.

"Confining," he said without hesitation.

"And yours?"

"Extensive, an uninterrupted view of the mountains and sky." He turned to face Andrew. "Have you ever considered moving to the other side of the dorm?"

Andrew smiled. "I guess the thought never occurred to me."

"Just a notion," Brother Nathan added. "You might enjoy it better."

"Thanks. Maybe I'll do that."

Looking a bit anxious, Brother Nathan sat on the corner of Andrew's desk. "I probably shouldn't be bringing this up, but I know that you and Brother Adrian were quite close, like a lot of us, and his death really took the wind out of our sails. Besides Dr. Klein, if you ever feel the need to talk about it . . . or anything, let me know."

Andrew was genuinely moved by Brother Nathan's attempt to reach out to him. "Thanks," he said. "If you hear someone knocking on your door in the middle of the night, you'll know who it is."

* * *

By the second week of November, winter made its presence known with howling winds and blinding snow, nearly burying the monastery beneath four to five feet of drifting powder. For days at a time, the sunlight remained obscured by swollen storm clouds and wind-driven snow swirled into a frenzy, with occasional glimmering highlights as the pale sun emerged briefly.

With Father Gerald monitoring his medication, Andrew began to feel progressively better; he sensed some of the heaviness had begun to dissipate. Life, for the most part, developed vitality, and yet Matthew, visible at times throughout the day, remained distant. There were no late-night knocks on his cell door, no clandestine agendas, assignations, or innuendo. He wondered, secretly, if their relationship was over or was Matthew simply obeying orders; nevertheless, his obvious absence was troubling, even though deep down, Andrew could not imagine their relationship dissolving. 'I'm sure he's doing this for me,' Andrew told himself.

The ski season had finally begun and Bitter Creek, prior to Christmas, was filled to capacity with mostly wealthy tourists or those who were essentially living on the edge to associate with society's higher strata. A variety of colors—red, green, silver, and gold glittered from every Victorian home, restaurant, inn, and gas lamp, as Andrew drove through crowded streets filled with smiling, perfect people; those who never have cavities, financial worries, or even the slightest sense of stress. Stopped at a red light, he watched as two fashionably dressed women casually crossed the street in front of him—one wearing what looked like a full-length ermine coat, with its hem dragging scandalously in the muddy slush. 'What does it matter,' he thought. 'They might as well have signs painted on their backs saying, we are rich—we don't have to care.'

He carefully made a right on Allard and was fortunate enough to find an empty parking space near Dr. Klein's office.

For Andrew, the glitz of Bitter Creek always reverted into the dark mahogany paneling of the psychiatrist's quiet office, with its subdued lighting and worn Persian carpeting. He sat in a familiar chair, just as he had done so many times before, wondering how all of his talking could ever effect a positive outcome.

"The talk therapy is important," Dr. Klein reinforced, "however, it's just as important to stay on your medication."

At times, he secretly wondered if Dr. Klein were real. 'Maybe he's only a robot controlled by some lunatic,' he thought, until he would catch him sneezing or itching his neck just below his collar, a behavior, he decided, uncharacteristic of an android.

"I feel like I'm doing all the talking," Andrew explained. "Maybe I've said everything I need to say." He rubbed his eyes and slouched back into the comfortable chair.

"Perhaps," Dr. Klein said softly. "It may be time to tell me all that isn't compulsory."

Andrew leaned forward. "I don't think I understand."

"There's no right or wrong answer—you can say whatever you feel, even if you might think it's irrelevant."

"Okay," Andrew said with a touch of defiance. "There are times when I've wondered if you were real. Maybe you're a robot," he said with a slight smile.

An infrequent grin brightened Dr. Klein's face. "And what have you decided?" he asked.

"Well . . . if you're a robot, you're a state-of-the-art fake. You scratch and sneeze like a human."

"I could, in fact, be a high-tech prototype," Dr. Klein joked.

Andrew laughed. "I doubt it," he said.

A significant pause followed the gentle bantering. Andrew watched as minute flecks of dust drifted into the shaft of sunlight and disappeared into the darkness.

Unexpectedly, Dr. Klein introduced a topic that caught Andrew off-guard. "Any thoughts of suicide, harming yourself, or others," he asked quite casually.

"That's not exactly like asking me whether I prefer chocolate or strawberry ice cream, is it?" Andrew replied.

"Not exactly," Dr. Klein said. "I apologize for my bluntness, but I feel it's as good a time as any to introduce the subject."

Andrew sat up straight, rubbed both hands together, and stared at the pattern in the rug. He was unaware of the rapid, pumping movement of his right leg. "I don't know . . . hasn't everybody?" he said with slightly pressured speech.

Dr. Klein looked intently at him but said nothing.

Aware of his anxiety, Andrew got up from the chair, walked to the window, and looked down on Allard Street where life, once again, appeared carefree yet, admittedly, contrived.

"I think about it, sometimes," he admitted.

"And why do you think about it, Andrew?" Dr. Klein asked compassionately.

Continuing to stare out the window, Andrew observed a burgundy-colored Jaguar as it parked in front of a trendy boutique across the street. Two well-dressed men exited the vehicle and entered the store.

He looked away, returned to his chair, and sat down. "To end the pain, the hopelessness," he said quietly.

"Has that pain or hopelessness gotten any better or any worse?"

"I think it's better than it was . . . not yet gone but better."

Dr. Klein turned a page in his notebook. "Has there ever been a time when you can remember the hopelessness and pain totally absent from your life?"

Visual scenes flashed through Andrew's mind like a movie in reverse. 'The question isn't that difficult,' he thought, searching through events, thinking that he had found the answer, only to realize with hindsight that all was not as it appeared. "I'm not sure," he conceded. He looked at Dr. Klein, "What does that mean?"

"There may be some indication that your level of happiness has been compromised, that your global functioning is rooted in pain more than pleasure."

"You mean I choose suffering?" Andrew asked.

"Not consciously," Dr. Klein said. "It may be more subconscious, a denial of pleasure."

Andrew shook his head. "Sometimes I get the feeling it's all just a bunch of words. Is it really so difficult to realize why I'm here?" He spoke calmly, yet the edge in his voice was obvious.

Dr. Klein did not look up. "I know why," he said softly.

Andrew rubbed his eyes. "Can you tell me?"

Dr. Klein placed his notebook on the table. He looked at Andrew over the top of his glasses. "I think you know," he said.

"Then what is it?" Andrew asked.

"I think you're afraid," Dr. Klein explained.

"Of what?" Andrew questioned.

"Unhappy endings," Dr. Klein replied quietly.

Andrew chuckled. "Do you always tell people the truth?"

"Yes . . . when I think they are able to deal with it."

Andrew walked once again to the window and looked down on the street. The burgundy automobile was gone, leaving only tread marks in the snow close to the curb.

He turned to face Dr. Klein. "What about everything I've told you about what I've experienced at the monastery? Does any of it make any sense or help explain the feelings I have?"

Dr. Klein nodded. "Yes, it does," he said with empathy. "It's your reaction to all of it that requires explanation and assistance."

Andrew returned to his chair and sat down. He slouched, hands in his pockets, with outstretched legs. "I never expected . . . never wanted, to meet Matthew," he said softly. "I just wanted to be a monk. And now, I can't simply throw the relationship away or give up my vocation because . . . I've grown to love both." He rubbed his hands over his face. "Having said that, what grounds do I have to complain about anything or anyone at the monastery, yet what I see really bothers me." He chuckled. "It's the old pot-calling-the-kettle-black thing."

"I know you've told me before, but what bothers you the most, Andrew?"

"The hypocrisy, including my own," he admitted.

"What in particular?" Dr. Klein asked.

"I feel like we're living a lie—whether it's the abbot having affairs with Bitter Creek bimbos or living the good life, eating foods that have only the word 'natural' on them; being immersed in Perrier and Häagen-Dazs; giving Christmas gifts worth several hundred dollars to rich people who don't need or want them, while homeless, working families write us and ask us for our prayers; refusing to admit particular applicants just because 'they don't fit the mold'; drifting away from a Christian tradition in favor of Zen because 'it's the thing to do.'" Andrew paused. "Should I go on?"

"Yes," Dr. Klein said, "but I want you to tell me what you are *really* afraid of."

Andrew got up from the chair and paced slowly. "What I'm really afraid of . . .," he repeated softly. Finally he turned to face Dr. Klein. "You already know, don't you?" Andrew said with quiet conviction.

"Maybe . . . maybe not," Dr. Klein responded. "You tell me."

He sat back down. "Obviously," Andrew began, "it has to do with unhappy endings . . . choices."

"Such as . . .," Dr. Klein prompted.

"Such as having to make a decision to walk out the door," Andrew explained. "To give up a lifestyle, a vocation which I feel called to and love, because of all I mentioned already."

"Is it a necessary choice?" Dr. Klein asked.

"Necessary? I don't know, but I can only squeeze so much hypocrisy into my guts before the excess screams at me like a judgmental demon—'liar, liar, liar!'"

Dr. Klein got up from his chair, walked over to Andrew, and placed his hand on his shoulder. "I want you to close your eyes, breathe deeply yet slowly, until you feel yourself calming down," he said softly.

Andrew could feel the warmth and reassurance from Dr. Klein's hand. As requested, he breathed slowly, deeply, until the agitation he experienced seemed to melt into the darkness like an ebbing evening tide.

* * *

Chapter Twenty-Four

Another Christmas Eve

The winter season proved dangerously idyllic with visually stunning scenes, lifted from the canvas of Currier and Ives, while roads surrounding the monastery became, at times, nearly impassable. It was the perfect opportunity for the Starretts to hitch a team of Percherons to a large antique sled for a leisurely visit to the monastery, a visit cherished by the monks who were invited in small groups to experience the beauty of nature from an authentic, horse-drawn sleigh.

Dressed warmly in a down parka, ski hat, and gloves, Andrew waited for the return of the previous riders and wondered if Matthew had already taken the trip. When they arrived, he scanned the group, but Matthew was not among them.

The snorting horses heeded the commands of Mr. Starrett, stopping nearly opposite Andrew. He was awed by their massive girth and powerful bodies, as they appeared to effortlessly pulled the heavy load, tossing their heads, and causing the attached sleigh bells to ring ceremoniously with the advent of Christmas.

"Do you mind a partner?"

The voice came from behind Andrew's shoulder. He quickly turned around to see Matthew, grinning broadly in the declining afternoon light.

"There's always room for Jell-O," he said awkwardly, attempting to be humorous.

Matthew closed his eyes and grimaced.

"Just kidding, Matt," he said apologetically. "Actually, I've been wondering where you were."

"Are you sure?" Matthew asked. "I can wait for the next ride."

"Hey . . . I'm really sorry," Andrew said. He looked around to see if anyone were aware of the conversation. "I was hoping we could do this together."

Matthew smiled. "Then let's get on."

Mrs. Starrett greeted them with gracious hospitality and heavy woolen blankets, as they settled comfortably on the hay covered floor; moments later, she surprisingly served steaming cups of cider, complete with cinnamon sticks. "This ought to keep you toasty," she said as she handed a large paper cup to each guest.

Andrew leaned back against the thick, wooden seat, sipped his cider, and watched as a winter wonderland drifted past. He could feel Matthew's knee against his under the blanket and, suddenly, all seemed right with the world—at least, for now.

Because of the nearness of the other monks, including Brother Mark, it was difficult to initiate a meaningful conversation; however, much to Andrew surprise, it proved unnecessary. In the growing darkness, with the horses returning to the monastery, he could feel Matthew's hand rest gently on his thigh, under the protective covering of the blanket, squeeze him firmly, and then discreetly settle between both legs. He turned slowly to look at Matthew, who leaned his head back, closed his eyes, and said quietly, "This is nice."

* * *

The heady glow and spirit of Christmas failed to elevate Andrew's mood; instead, it only served to underline all that was dark and missing in his life; a tableau filled with memories of earlier holidays and other monks who could be seen lurking sadly within the periphery of the darkened church and cloisters, pretending to be strongly ascetic yet screaming silently, lamenting their loneliness.

It was this same feeling that prompted Andrew, the night before Christmas Eve, to visit Matthew's cell after Vespers. He walked quickly down the long corridor, stood in front of his door, and tapped as softly as possible. With no response, he tapped a bit louder and waited. He thought he heard some movement and noticed a shadow from the space between the door and the carpet. Slowly, the door opened as Matthew, hesitant, looked out.

When he recognized Andrew, Matthew quickly opened the door, pulled him into the room, and locked the door.

"I'm sorry," Andrew whispered. "I just needed to see you."

With a smile, Matthew hugged him like he used to, vigorously yet not enough to crush him. "I thought you'd never come by," he said, whispering into Andrew's ear and inhaling the familiar scent of his hair.

"I kept hoping that you would come see me," Andrew said.

Matthew reached out to retrieve three large pillows from his bed. He tossed them onto the carpet and sat down, pulling Andrew down next to him. "I'm glad you're here," he said with a smile. "How have you been feeling?"

Andrew smiled weakly. "It's almost Christmas; I've hardly seen you, and truth is, I'm feeling pretty lousy."

"Well, that makes two of us," Matthew added. He grabbed Andrew's hand. "But Father Gerald would probably kill me if he knew I was with you."

"What the heck did he say to you?" Andrew asked.

"Just that you would need some time to get through this, with help from Dr. Klein, and that it would be better for you if I made myself scarce; in other words—leave you alone."

"Crap!" Andrew said unexpectedly. "What do I have to do to 'get clearance'?"

"Who knows," Matthew said. "Probably some sort of okay from Dr. Klein."

Andrew laughed. "This is nuts. Remember how we would joke about being crazy? Hell, maybe I am."

"Stop it," Matthew said. He pulled him toward him, once again, and hugged him. "You're going to be fine."

Nevertheless, Andrew could feel the tears well up as he held Matthew tightly. He knew, down deep, that being held by Matthew was all he really wanted. "I hope so," he said. "But . . . I'd better get out before someone finds I'm here." He pulled away and stood up.

"You don't have to leave right away, do you?"

"Yeah, I'd better," Andrew said, "before they come looking for me. You can be sure they'd head straight for your room."

Andrew was about to open the door when Matthew spoke.

"Wait," he said. "I have something for you." He opened a desk drawer and removed a square package wrapped in newspaper. He handed it to Andrew. "Merry Christmas," he said as he leaned forward and kissed him.

Andrew was surprised. "I don't know what to say . . ."

"*Thank you* will do fine," Matthew joked. "You can tell me what you think of it tomorrow."

"I will," Andrew said, somewhat dazed.

Matthew checked the hallway to see if it was empty. "All clear," he whispered.

"I'll see you tomorrow," Andrew said. He walked out into the dimly lit corridor and closed the door without looking back.

Safe in his own cell, Andrew switched on his desk lamp and quietly pulled the newspaper wrapping from the package. Staring up at him from a carved ebony frame was Matthew's charcoal sketch of Andrew, which he finally completed—an excellent portrayal of his features—handsome and strong, with barely a hint of remorse emanating through dark eyes.

This time, there was no hesitancy or control. Without explanation, yet fully conscious of the cause, he found himself sobbing into his hands, hoping that his stifled cries could not be heard.

* * *

Morning broke through a sky obscured with the silvery glow of a light snowfall. Andrew stood in the cold church during the morning mass, feeling as hazy as the illumination filtering through the windows; the familiar feelings of fraternity, cohesiveness, belonging—all seemed to be absent or in danger of slipping away. While the cast of characters remained fundamentally unchanged, Andrew was very aware of those who were no longer standing with him, particularly the young Observer—John, Brother Morgan, Brother Adrian, and Father Martin. Life, he realized, was ineffably fragile.

Nevertheless, Brother Conrad, frozen in time, with a frog-eyed view of the world, would occasionally gyrate, swinging his hips in his now famous "Hula-Hoop" fashion, as he attempted to lock his brace on the afflicted leg, a sight which previously would have sent Andrew into hysterics, but today barely kindled a smile.

He half listened to Father Jude as he droned on and on over the Eucharist, elevating the mini loaf of wheat bread and genuflecting until the transubstantiation was complete. On cue, Andrew followed the other monks to the altar, partook in Holy Communion, and washed down the gritty bread with a small swallow of wine. He returned to his seat to meditate, yet the sour taste of yeast and wheat germ distracted him. Instead, he glanced across the room at Matthew, who sat erect with closed eyes. Andrew wondered if he were sleeping.

Suddenly, he realized that two guests were seated on the far side of the chapel, just inside the entrance. Without his glasses, he found it necessary to squint to get a better focus. And after twenty or thirty seconds, Andrew was convinced of the identity of at least one—he was sure it was Rebecca Storrow.

As soon as the mass ended, he hurried to his cell, removed his habit, and pulled an old, navy sweater over his flannel shirt. It was Andrew's turn to prepare the noonday meal for the monks and guests, a task which almost always created moderate anxiety especially today, since he had no idea of what he would cook and even less knowledge of what supplies were on hand in the kitchen.

Passing the closed the door to the entrance room, Andrew was aware of subtle feminine laughter and quiet conversation. He stopped momentarily and recognized Matthew's voice as it mixed softly with those of the two women. He listened briefly, only to feel a gnawing pain build within his gut and spread quickly to his chest and head. Flooded with emotion, he considered throwing open the door, screaming at the scheming trollops like an authentic jealous lover, and then dragging Matthew bodily out of the room. Instead, he breathed deeply and walked briskly toward the refectory. The hemlock roping draped over the cloister windows reminded him that it was Christmas Eve.

Of course, there were always plenty of eggs. Once inside the kitchen, Andrew hastily searched through the walk-in refrigerator, shivering progressively the longer he remained. When he finally emerged, he had gathered several packages of fresh spinach, four dozen eggs, a bag of potatoes, tomatoes, and a container of feta cheese. With the help from his trusty Moosewood cookbook, he was about to prepare a Greek spinach frittata and a lemon-tomato salad.

By midmorning, he had nearly finished all the prep work—cutting vegetables, cleaning spinach, peeling potatoes, and beating the eggs. He decided that it would be easier to bake the giant frittata rather than attempt several pan-fried versions, a decision which provided him with some spare time to sip a fresh cup of coffee in the silence of the refectory.

Tucked away in the corner near the old wood stove, Andrew sat in the same straight-backed wooden chair which Brother Adrian often occupied. A black case sitting on the windowsill held special binoculars Brother Adrian used to watch the variety of birds as they hovered around several feeders, eating thistle, sunflower seed, and suet; yet as often as he was reminded, Brother Adrian insisted on calling the binoculars "spyglasses," much to the amusement of those within earshot.

Andrew could not resist. He retrieved the binoculars, removed the protective lens covers, and adjusted the focus to observe the hungry birds. Two or three hearty Pine Grosbeaks flitted about, pecking at the suet and throwing seeds haphazardly, as though searching for that special morsel.

The rose and grey males contrasted sharply with the blanket of white, falling snow, making it easy for Andrew to follow their activity.

The groan of the heavy refectory door shattered the silence and startled him. He immediately put down the binoculars and turned to look. Very unexpectedly, he watched as Matthew entered, somewhat timidly, and carefully closed the door behind him—still unaware of Andrew sitting in back of the stove.

"You're a bit early for lunch," Andrew announced glibly.

"I . . .," Matthew stammered. He looked around. "Damn! You scared me." He walked toward the stove.

"Sorry," Andrew said. "I wasn't expecting anyone this early."

"Anyone in the kitchen?"

"No one."

"Good," Matthew said. "I'll grab some coffee."

In his absence, Andrew replaced the lens covers on the binoculars and put them back in their case. He watched as Matthew approached, coffee in hand, and sat down on the wooden bench.

"So what did you think?" Matthew asked. He gingerly sipped the hot liquid.

At first, Andrew was baffled, but then realized what he meant. "Oh . . . the charcoal sketch," he said with enthusiasm. "It is really well done, except, I think you made me look better than I do."

Matthew laughed. "No way," he said. He stared at Andrew as his smile faded. "You honestly believe you aren't that handsome, don't you?"

The remark tinted Andrew's face. "Probably," he said cautiously. He avoided Matthew's intense observation by pretending to study his hands.

"You're amazing," Matthew said. "I've even gotten jealous when people ask me about you, out of the blue, and tell me how good-looking you are."

It was Andrew's turn to laugh. "You're making this up," he insisted.

"No—I'm not."

"Who the heck would ask you something like that?"

Matthew paused. "Well . . . Rebecca Storrow, for one."

Andrew could feel himself tense. "She might just be turned on by anyone in a habit," he said sarcastically.

Matthew allowed some silence before he spoke. "I'm sorry," he said. "I shouldn't have brought up her name."

"No, it's okay I'm the one who should be apologizing," Andrew said. "It's just that . . . I heard you talking with her when I walked past the entrance room and, I don't know—it just bothers me." He drank more coffee and gazed out the window.

Matthew leaned forward. "We're only friends, Andrew, I swear, so don't get yourself upset," he whispered. "Besides, there's only one person in this crazy universe I care about—you."

Andrew turned to face him. "I don't think I can make it without you, Matt," he admitted.

"Then you don't have anything to worry about because I'll always be with you." He reached out and placed his hand over Andrew's.

Andrew closed his eyes, leaned back in his chair, and sighed. "And after your great gift, I forgot to get you something for Christmas."

Matthew squeezed his hand. "After all you've been through, I can't imagine why," he teased. "But it's still not too late."

"What do you mean?"

"Follow me," Matthew insisted.

He led Andrew into the kitchen, cautiously checked to see that it was empty and hurried into the pantry. As soon as Andrew entered, he closed the door.

"You realize that we're both dead meat if anyone finds us in here," Andrew whispered.

Matthew smiled. "Yes, but doesn't that make it even more exciting?" He pulled Andrew toward him. "Now, say 'Merry Christmas, Matthew,' and then shut up."

The silliness caused him to blush. "Merry Christmas, Matthew," he mimicked.

"Merry Christmas, Andrew." Matthew hugged him even harder and then kissed him tenderly until their mutual craving aroused a fierce longing for each other; a familiar, welcomed embrace so necessary for Andrew.

The slamming of the back door caused them both to freeze.

"Shit!" Andrew whispered. He looked around for empty shelf space and motioned to Matthew. "Up there! Quick."

Matthew climbed the wooden ladder to the third shelf, slid himself between two large cases of paper towels and tried to remain motionless.

Aware of his arousal, Andrew pulled an apron off the wall hook and slipped it over his head. He exited the pantry carrying a box filled with two gallons of red wine.

"Aha! Drinking in the pantry."

Pretending to be startled, Andrew looked up to see Eric Holtz, the hired man, smiling his wide mustached smile.

"No, but now that you mention it, I could definitely use a drink," Andrew replied. "What's happening?" He set the box on the counter, pulled out one of the bottles, and unscrewed the top.

"You weren't kidding, were you," Eric said.

"Not at all," Andrew said, handing a glass to Eric. "And if you knew why," he ventured, "you'd be drinking too."

"Yeah, well, I don't want to know," Eric joked. "You guys have such a tough life; I can't bear to hear your troubles. I just hope we don't get caught drinking."

"Don't worry about it," Andrew said. "It's nearly Christmas Eve so—Merry Christmas." He downed most of his wine in two swallows.

Eric watched in amazement. "Well, whatever it was, it must have been gnarly."

"Is that really a word?" Andrew asked halfheartedly.

"It is in California."

"I should've known," Andrew said.

Switching gears, Eric asked about the abbot. "Is Father Jude around?"

Andrew rolled his eyes. "Who?" he asked.

"Be nice," Eric admonished.

As if intentional, Andrew spoke loudly in the direction of the pantry. "I think we should sit by the stove in the refectory, Eric. It's sort of cold in here."

Eric looked behind him to see if someone else were in the room. He looked at Andrew and squinted. "Are you all right?"

Andrew laughed. "We've never been better," he said boldly as he led Eric toward the refectory.

Hearing the footsteps fade, Matthew carefully scuttled down the ladder, looked around, and quietly slipped out the back door, being sure to close it gently.

The view through the refectory windows appeared uniformly picturesque, nearly surreal, as though one of Macy's decorators purposely arranged for the snow to fall evenly, straight down, only to be sucked up again and allowed to drift slowly back to the collection basin beneath the windowsill.

"This room has a sort of magical quality," Eric said unexpectedly.

Andrew sat down in the wooden chair. "It does," Andrew agreed. "I only wish that Brother Adrian were still here to enjoy it."

Eric nodded. "Who knows," he said, "maybe he is."

"It's a nice thought," Andrew said with a smile.

In the silence that followed, the snow seemed to thicken, shortening the view and totally obscuring Navigator Peak. Andrew watched as Eric leaned back, rested his feet on the opposite bench and stared out the window. He evoked the image of a man quietly contented, one who accepted those around him indiscriminately, and unafraid of nonverbal pauses without a conversation—a gentle masculinity with no agenda and nothing to prove—all framed within a healthy, self-deprecating sense of humor.

"So how's Kathleen and the kids?" Andrew asked.

"Oh, they're fine," Eric said. "Of course, the kids are wired now that Christmas is almost here, and Kathleen has been busy cooking and getting ready for tonight."

"You coming to the midnight mass?"

"No, but we'll miss being there," Eric added. "We'll probably make the eleven o'clock tomorrow." He finished his wine and set the glass on the table. "How have you been doing?"

"Okay, I guess," Andrew said with a slight shrug. "Whoever thought I'd be taking drugs and be an alumnus of the Halsen Clinic."

Eric smiled slightly. "You're going to be all right—just hang in there, man."

"I know," Andrew said with a sigh. "It's the process that's painful."

"Welcome to Life 101," Eric joked.

Andrew finished the rest of his wine. "More?" he asked, holding up his glass.

"Heck, no," Eric said. "I came over to see about doing some plowing. It's starting to build up, and you are going to have a crowd of people driving in for the mass. I just wanted to check with the abbot first."

"Yeah . . . well," Andrew began contemptuously. "You might want to drive by the Hyatt in Bitter Creek and see if his car is in the parking lot."

Eric covered his face with one hand and shook his head. "Yeow! I think it's time to plow."

Andrew stood up and tried to apologize. "Sorry about that," he said. "It's one of my hot buttons, I guess—and it just came flying out."

"If you're not careful, you might be the one flying out," Eric offered.

"You're right," Andrew admitted, " . . . funny part is—I almost expect it."

Exasperated, Eric shrugged and gestured with open hands. "And what . . . add you to my list of guys who left here, so that I can spend time missing another one? I hope not," he said.

Andrew laughed. "Since you put it that way, I'll make sure I stay."

"That's what I wanted to hear." He opened his arms to offer Andrew a hug. "Merry Christmas, buddy," he said.

Andrew returned the hug, surprised by Eric's affable candor. "And many more to come," he said.

He followed Eric to the back door. "Say Merry Christmas to Kathleen and the kids," he shouted as Eric walked toward his truck.

Starting the engine, Eric flashed his trademark, extended-thumb-and-small-finger hand sign, as he backed out of the yard.

Andrew looked at his watch and realized that it was later than he thought. He began to rush around the kitchen, stopped, and laughed out loud. He was reminded of one of Brother Adrian's famous malapropisms—"running around like a chicken with its legs cut off." In his honor, Andrew turned on the gas to the oven, waited several seconds, lit a large wooden match, and, from a distance, tossed it into the open oven which ignited with a turbulent explosion. He could feel the blast against his body as it moved his hair and clothing. He then poured himself a bit more wine. "To you, Brother Adrian," he said, as he lifted his glass and drank the wine in one gulp.

Somehow, lunch was a success. The frittata came out of the oven, puffy and golden with a pungent cheese aroma. Andrew had difficulty remembering the exact details of how it all came together, but nevertheless, it was one of his more delicious concoctions, which was tastefully followed by individual strawberry amaretto-cream parfaits.

"Exceptional lunch," Father Jude whispered, as he passed Andrew in the kitchen.

Not only his remark but also his presence caught Andrew off guard; he did not recall seeing him in the refectory. "Thanks," he replied casually. "I'm sure Brother Adrian helped."

Father Jude simply nodded, smiled, and walked out the back door.

Andrew could feel the mixture of medication and alcohol cloud his brain. 'What the hell am I talking about?' he thought. He abruptly left the kitchen and made his way back to his cell where he collapsed on his bed and instantly fell asleep.

Instead of the anticipated exhilaration usually experienced during the solemn midnight mass, Andrew felt himself drift in and out of bouts of depression, mixed with mild anxiety. As before, those who were no longer present appeared to reveal their spirit through the smoky haze, only to dissipate amorphously as they rose and then congealed into the thicker cloud of incense, hovering high above the ceiling beams. 'I'll bet they're here,' Andrew thought, gazing upwards.

Even the singing did little to brightened Andrew's mood. He surveyed the crowded church, filled with somewhat familiar faces; those who braved the trip, in accumulating snow, from Bitter Creek, to attend what they would consider to be one of the more fashionably esoteric holiday events. For many, religion had very little to do with their reason for being there.

Squinting strongly to help refocus his nearsightedness, Andrew felt sure that he recognized Rebecca Storrow, who was accompanied by two or three friends whom Andrew had seen before. As much as he tried, he had difficulty seeing her objectively, regardless of Matthew's plea. She rapidly emerged as a *persona non grata*, even though he had no hard evidence or reason to feel that way; something about her appeared uncomfortably threatening.

With the mass completed and voices straining to vocalize "Hark the Herald Angels Sing," Andrew followed his brothers through the cloud of cologne and incense to the chilly cloister beyond the church entrance. He hurried to his cell, not wanting to interact with anyone, even Matthew. Somehow everything seemed wrong. 'It should not be Christmas Eve,' he thought. He closed the door and immediately searched for his medication, which he found on the shelf in his closet, and poured himself a glass of water from his thermos. Suddenly, a chill settled over him as he remembered what happened to him a year ago. He turned slowly, expecting to see Ellen sitting on his bed, legs crossed, smoking a cigarette; goose bumps covered his arms; his hair felt electric.

"Don't you guys lock your doors?" the voice said.

Andrew dropped the water and pills on the carpet. "What do you want?" he shouted.

Father Martin, barely visible, stood in the corner of the room; his hood covered his head and most of his face. "Nothing," Father Martin said. He moved forward slightly.

"Stop!" Andrew shouted. "You can't be here—you're dead!"

"It's just another dimension," Father Martin said softly. "I know all about you and Matthew," he continued. "I wish I could've had that." He raised his right hand and made the sign of the cross. "Unfortunately," he said, almost regretfully, "it will soon be nonexistent—like me."

"What? . . . what the hell are you talking about?" Andrew screamed.

Andrew watched as both of Father Martin's eyes began to glow like two hot coals.

Just before he passed out, he remembered seeing Father Martin push the hood back from his face, exposing his decomposed, clotted skull.

* * *

Chapter Twenty-Five

The Breakthrough

"Merry Christmas," Father Gerald said, staring down at Andrew as he lay in one of the infirmary beds. He raised his hand and placed his index finger over his lips. "Before you get upset, I want to explain why you're here and . . . I want you to listen. Understood?"

Andrew nodded his head, suddenly realizing that it was covered with bandages.

"That's right," Father Gerald explained. "There is a bandage on your head—nothing serious, as far as I can tell." He sat down in a chair next to the bed. "Brother Edward heard some shouting in your cell and a crash against his wall. He ran into your room, saw you lying on the floor with blood coming from your head. He immediately got me, and we brought you to the infirmary last night. It looks like you fainted, hit your head on the bookcase, and dropped your water and medication. So . . . I spent some time in the early-morning hours stitching your forehead—ten stitches to be exact—and, I have to admit, it looks pretty good. Once they're out, you'll barely notice a scar."

Andrew reached up and gently felt the bandages. "Thank you," he said through a dry mouth.

"How about some water," Father Gerald said. He held the glass to Andrew's lips as he sipped a small amount and swallowed.

The overwhelming whiteness of the infirmary struck a familiar chord with Andrew, a precursor, perhaps, to an obvious transition for any monk—heaven—yet with an implied dark message—the inevitability of one's death.

"Am I dying?" Andrew asked bluntly.

"Of course not," Father Gerald answered emphatically. "But you do require more constant observation, medication regulation, and blood samples, as needed, along with visits from Dr. Klein."

"You mean back to the Halsen clinic," Andrew asked, more in the form of the statement.

"I don't think so," Father Gerald said. "I think it can be accomplished right here . . . if Dr. Klein will agree to it; and, I think he will."

"So what does that mean?"

"It means that you'll be spending more time in the infirmary until your illness stabilizes. I can't allow you to be unsafe due to syncope."

"What's that?" Andrew asked.

"Sorry . . . it means passing out, fainting," Father Gerald added.

Andrew looked around the room once more. "It sounds as though I'll be a prisoner here."

Father Gerald smiled. "No, not at all, but you will sleep here—with raised side rails and supervision."

Andrew frowned. He shook his head slightly and rubbed his eyes. "I don't know," he said quietly. "It just seems that I'm causing a lot of fuss for nothing." His depression was surfacing once again.

"I don't ever want you to think that," Father Gerald said firmly. He put his hand on Andrew's arm and gently squeezed it. "You are a part of this family now, and it's our duty to see to it that you get better." "Besides," he added with a smile. "it will give me a chance to actively renew my role as a physician."

Somehow, Andrew seemed to buy into part of his reasoning. "If you think it's the right thing to do, then I'll do it," he said.

"Great!" Father Gerald said. "It doesn't mean you can't leave the infirmary. As long as you have someone with you, you can take part in most of the liturgy." He looked directly at Andrew. "Perhaps Matthew would be willing to spend more time with you."

Andrew's smile spread quickly. "I'd like that," he said.

* * *

After a month of therapy, medication changes, and follow-up, Andrew emerged revitalized, renewed, with a better understanding of who he really was and what it meant to experience a major mental illness. Like the new spring season nourished by the melting snow, he seemed to break out of his cocoon, bloom, and settled into the acceptable cycle of monastic life. Except for the incessant conundrum regarding his sexuality and his desire for Matthew, who remained very supportive throughout his stay in the infirmary, he began to realize, if not hope, that, after all he experienced, perhaps Matthew was right, that being a monk and being in love were not necessarily incompatible. He wondered why it took him so painfully long to understand what now seemed to be a fairly simple concept.

* * *

Chapter Twenty-Six

Disintegration

Yet at such a pivotal point in his life, an expression of that love barely seemed to materialize, even through the middle of winter and into the early spring. There were brief encounters with Matthew, tenuous ventures where Matthew fought to uphold the advice of Father Gerald, much to Andrew's displeasure, until one snowy Saturday morning at the small guesthouse attached to the barn, when the relationship changed significantly.

His assignment to clean the guest unit was neither unusual nor unacceptable. Andrew chose to walk the mile through a light snowfall, reminiscing about his love affair with the large falling flakes, as he stuck out his tongue to catch five or six of them and felt them quickly melt into icy liquid.

When he reached for the spare key and opened the door, Andrew simply assumed the guest house was vacant; he was not aware of the red Jeep parked at the back of the barn. He closed the door, removed his jacket, and immediately began to take out the necessary cleaning supplies from under the kitchen sink.

"Nice to see you again, Andrew," she said casually.

Andrew could feel his body grow instantly rigid. He feared, once again, that he had begun to hallucinate; yet when he turned toward the direction of the voice, he saw Ellen leaning against the wall, smoking a cigarette, and wearing a long, satin robe.

"Are you real?" he asked with stunned anxiety.

She smiled her unforgettable smile—just slightly asymmetrical with a good exposure of teeth—and then extinguished her cigarette in the ashtray on the kitchen table. "As real as you are," she said quietly. "How have you been?"

Andrew stood up and placed the cleaning supplies on the counter. He was not sure where to begin. "I'm better than I was," he said nervously. "I'm sort of recovering from . . ."

But before he could finish, Ellen interrupted. "I know," she said, with what seemed to be genuine empathy. "Matthew told me what you've been going through."

"He did?" Andrew responded.

"Yes," she said. "I hope that's all right."

Andrew shrugged. "Yeah . . . no problem. I'm glad that he did." He squatted and began to return the cleaning supplies to their place under the sink.

"I'm sorry for walking in on you," he added cautiously. "Father Luke thought all the guests had left."

From the corner of his eye, he saw Ellen approach and stand above him. The floral scent of her perfume suddenly evoked a hint of sexual frisson, as distant memories of Sara surfaced unexpectedly.

"Don't be sorry," she said in a significantly alluring voice. "It's just so nice to see you." She placed her hand on his shoulder. "How about some coffee?"

Although he wanted to say yes, Andrew sensed an inwardly, uncomfortable situation developing. He stood up and barely made eye contact. "I better not," he said awkwardly. He turned and walked over to the couch to get his jacket. "You probably have things to do, and I should be getting back to the monastery."

Ellen sauntered over to where he was standing. "I don't have much to do, and I'll bet you really don't have to get back to the monastery."

Andrew smiled. "I guess monks aren't great liars."

She reached for his jacket and tossed it back on the couch. The smile slowly faded from her face. "I often think about that Christmas Eve with you," she said, toying with one of the buttons on his shirt.

Andrew could feel the color rise in his face.

"Do you remember that?" she asked.

He stepped backwards slightly. "How can one forget something like that?" he said. "I had hoped it was part of the past—just a memory." He rubbed his eyes with one hand. "Why do you feel the need to bring it up now?"

"I've always liked you, Andrew—you know that," she said.

"And I've always liked you."

"You also know that's not exactly how I mean it." She turned and faced the small window which looked out toward a wooden, fenced corral. "We both like you," she said softly.

Andrew could feel his heart began to race. "I'm not sure what you're trying to say."

"Matthew and I have always been very close," she said. She faced Andrew. "Please don't get upset but . . . he's always known about that night."

Andrew seemed to ooze exasperation from every pore. "Why are you telling me this?" He turned away from her and walked toward the door. "I just hope you're lying," he said desperately. As he reached for the doorknob, a familiar, male voice, as if from nowhere, joined the conversation.

"She's not lying," Matthew said quietly.

Andrew froze and then turned to face the voice. He saw Matthew, standing in the entrance to the bedroom, wearing only a pair of boxer shorts and a T-shirt.

Feeling dizzy, Andrew reached for a kitchen chair, pulled it away from the table, and stumbled into it. He leaned forward and held his head with both hands. "What the hell is going on here, Matt?" he said with a groan.

It was very clear to Matthew that Andrew had reached a dangerously stressful emotional level. "It's okay. I can explain it," he said softly, but he barely finished the sentence when he saw Andrew begin to topple over toward the floor. With a quick lunge, Matthew dove under him and was able to break his fall.

"Oh my god!" Ellen shouted. "Is he all right?"

Matthew smiled as Andrew lay slumped on top of him. "He passed out—his reaction to stress," Matthew said. He turned to look at Ellen. "I just wish I'd find him on top of me more often," he added with a lascivious grin.

"Not funny," Ellen said with feigned offense.

"You're right," Matthew said. "Now help me pick him up."

Once Ellen helped to disentangle her brother, Matthew had no difficulty lifting Andrew off the floor and carrying him to the bedroom where he gently placed him on the unmade bed. "Put the pillows under his feet," he said. He partially unbuttoned Andrew's shirt and placed his arms at his side.

Ellen stood alongside the bed, staring at Andrew's placid demeanor, and watched as Matthew ran his hand over Andrew's forehead, brushing back his hair and gently touching his lips with his thumb. "You really do love him, don't you?" she said.

Matthew nodded imperceptibly. "Yeah . . . I really do," he admitted with genuine affect. He leaned forward and kissed his slightly parted lips.

"Do me a favor," he said suddenly. "Don't be in here when he comes to. I don't want to rattle him; besides, it'll be easier to talk with him if we're alone."

Exhaling explicitly for emphasis, Ellen folded her arms. "I understand," she said and then walked out of the room.

It was not long before Andrew began to stir; he rolled his head and fluttered his eyelids bizarrely, as if on neurological autopilot, until he finally became very still, with eyes wide open, staring at the ceiling.

"Hello, handsome," Matthew whispered.

Andrew turned slightly, looked at Matthew, and turned back to his original position. "I fainted, didn't I?" he said anxiously.

"Yes, but I caught you before you hit the floor," Matthew said. With his free hand he gently massaged Andrew's head.

A substantial pause helped Andrew transition back to the present. "The ceiling needs paint," he said unexpectedly.

Matthew glanced upwards and back at Andrew. "How are you feeling?" he asked with some trepidation.

Andrew rubbed his eyes. "Oh, tired . . . confused." He looked at Matthew. "I have no idea of what's going on."

"That's okay," Matthew said. "Just relax and let me explain."

"Fine," Andrew said. He closed his eyes.

"Before I begin, I want you to realize how much I love you," Matthew said. He propped himself up on one elbow and looked directly at Andrew.

"Okay," Andrew said with his eyes still closed.

It was not exactly the response Matthew was hoping for, but he continued.

"Truth is, Ellen told me about you," he said, "even before I knew I would be accepted here at St. Anthony's."

It was an opening sentence which forced Andrew to open his eyes and observe the teller of the tale with rapt attention.

"She visited for a brief retreat, saw you during the prayer services, and came back to tell me about this tall, handsome monk she had seen. It wasn't long after that when I interviewed and began my Observership. I also saw you and realized she was right; I think I fell in love with you immediately."

Andrew rolled on his side to face Matthew. "Did you come here to be a monk or have a relationship with one?" Andrew asked bluntly.

The question pierced Matthew's emotional armor.

"No," Matthew said quietly. "I had already applied; I came here to be a monk, yet I was excited knowing that I would be with a young, good-looking guy. I had no idea our relationship would turn out as it did."

With a sigh, Andrew rolled onto his back. "What about Ellen?" he asked. "The Christmas Eve visit—your knowledge of it—how come you never said anything?"

"I don't know," Matthew admitted. "Maybe I was jealous. Maybe I wasn't sure about your sexuality. When I began to realize how you felt about me, I just tried to forget the Christmas Eve thing."

"So Ellen knows about us?"

"Yes," Matthew said. "And it's okay. She's always known about me for years. Like she said, we've always been pretty close."

"Then what about your being here in the guesthouse?" Andrew asked.

"Today's Ellen's last day of retreat. I came down last night to visit her after Compline; we had some wine, maybe too much, and I fell asleep here."

"It all sounds a bit wacky," Andrew said.

"It probably does," Matthew admitted. "But you have to realize, she probably likes you almost as much as I do."

Andrew sighed. "That's flattering but . . . confusing."

"Well, don't worry about it," Matthew insisted. He kissed Andrew's forehead.

"That's another thing," Andrew blurted. "I've hardly seen you or shared any time with you, lately. It's like you've been avoiding me."

Matthew smiled. "And guess why?" he said. "Father Gerald spoke with me several times, essentially saying 'hands off,' so I tried to keep things on the up and up." He kissed Andrew's nose. "But I'm with you now," he said, as he began to squeeze Andrew's thigh. He then kissed him on the lips, softly at first, and then more and more deeply until Andrew forced him away.

"Your sister is in the other room!" he said with whispered anxiety.

Matthew smiled, got up, and shut the bedroom door. "How's that?" he said as he jumped back into bed and settled alongside of Andrew.

"You're not serious . . ."

"Yes, why?"

"Matt, she's in the other room."

"I know . . . she's an adult, and she can handle it."

"I don't know if I can" Andrew admitted.

Matthew terminated any further dialogue by quickly rolling halfway onto Andrew and kissing him hard. It was a feeling Andrew longed for and knew he could not prevent. He responded with equal or even greater passion, inhaling the familiar musk of past encounters.

Matthew unbuttoned Andrew's shirt and pulled it off him, gently licking his chest and then biting to the point of intolerable pain. He then pushed Andrew's arm over his head, exposing his armpit, and without hesitation, he buried his face in the dampness, licking once again and inhaling the sensual scent, as though he were unable to be satisfied.

Andrew emitted soft cries of pleasure, relishing the practiced skills of the man he loved and allowing him free reign of his body.

Aware of Andrew's unspoken yet carte blanche approval of his assertiveness, Matthew carefully unbuttoned Andrew's jeans, unzipped them, and lightly ran his hand over Andrew's erection. Andrew softly moaned and involuntarily flexed his hips in anticipation of Matthew's mouth.

Matthew quickly removed Andrew's shoes and socks; he hovered over him, firmly grabbed both his shorts and jeans, and pulled them down over his knees and feet and let them fall to the floor. As before, the site of Andrew naked on the bed caused Matthew to catch his breath. "You must have fallen from the ceiling of the Sistine Chapel," he whispered.

Andrew smiled briefly and then raised his head to watch, as Matthew began to proceed with his oral stimulation.

When he felt Matthew finally slip his mouth over the head of his penis and envelop the entire shaft, Andrew settled back in pure, consensual pleasure, while Matthew intuitively interpreted each and every move Andrew made, tailoring his technique to optimize Andrew's bliss.

Sensing when to stop, Matthew slipped off his T-shirt and shorts and, once again, settled alongside of Andrew. He looked into his eyes. "I missed you—I missed this—so much," he said softly and then pressed his nose against Andrew's.

"I know," Andrew said. "I felt as though you deserted me."

"No . . . never," Matthew said. "I just want you to be well."

Andrew smiled. "I'm feeling a lot better already." He pulled Matthew's mouth over his, kissing him hard, while the occasionally gnashing of teeth could be felt.

Matthew rolled on top of him, licking his neck and gently nibbling his ears and shoulders and anywhere in between. Andrew felt as though he might explode with pleasure as he held Matthew tight, kissing or licking his forehead whenever it was in range. It was then, while holding on to Matthew's head and nibbling his ear, that he felt it: incredibly, someone was sucking on his erection. He tried to raise his head, but he could not see over Matthew who seemed to be holding him down.

"Wait . . . stop!" he shouted as he attempted to push Matthew to one side. Once Matthew moved slightly, Andrew saw Ellen continue to move her mouth over the shaft of his penis with unabashed intent, until she slowly raised her eyes, looked at Andrew, and then vigorously resumed her intentions. Although initially perplexed, he continued to watch her and realized that, as much as he hated to admit it, it was unexpectedly erotic and thoroughly provocative. He sheepishly glanced at Matthew with wide, questioning eyes.

"Wait," Matthew whispered. "Before you say anything—you know how much I love you."

Andrew nodded slightly.

"Do you love me?" Matthew asked.

Andrew stared at him in silence.

"Do you love me?" he repeated, this time more emphatically.

Once again, as if mesmerized, Andrew nodded.

"Then say it . . . please," Matthew pleaded.

"You know I love you," Andrew whispered.

Matthew smiled slightly, seemingly more relaxed. "She loves you also," he said. "Just go with this—once. It'll never happen again."

Andrew took a deep breath.

"Lie back and relax," Matthew instructed.

With some hesitation, Andrew complied.

Matthew kissed him gently, lovingly, until he could sense Andrew's increased passion.

Totally caught up in the moment, Andrew returned Matthew's kiss, only harder and deeper, while being completely inundated by Ellen's more aggressive behavior. He realized that his level of stimulation had suddenly skyrocketed to an unexpected yet exhilarating height.

Seemingly aware of this, Ellen quickly stopped. She began to kiss and lick Andrew's stomach and chest until she moved alongside of him. She licked his throat and ears while Matthew continued to kiss Andrew, who watched Ellen from the corner of his eye. He could see her shapely breasts, which were barely covered by her robe and squeezed against his chest. He reached out and slid the top of her robe off one shoulder and then the next, until she complied by loosening the sash and allowing the robe to fall to the floor. Andrew could see that she was completely naked. Her small rounded butt alternately contracted and expanded as she rhythmically forced her pelvis, deeper and deeper, into the mattress.

As soon as Matthew moved his mouth away from Andrew's and over his throat, Ellen quickly took advantage of the vacancy by kissing Andrew as passionately as her brother. The slightly pungent yet not unpleasant taste of tobacco, mixed with mint, stimulated Andrew even more by signaling the definitive change of a new and unaccustomed mouth. Ellen felt even more slippery, smoother; the softness of her lips was highlighted by the understandable absence of facial stubble—perhaps, but not necessarily, better—just different.

As she moved even higher, placing her chest within range of Andrew's mouth, Matthew slowly worked his way back to Andrew's penis, gently licking, and then more aggressively sucking, while Andrew moved in rhythm with his mouth.

Ellen, he soon realized, loved oral stimulation of her breasts. She allowed Andrew to suck and gently nibble one of her nipples and then alternate with the other, until she could no longer tolerate the willful mix of pleasure and pain.

With one hand, Andrew massaged Ellen's buttocks, carefully exploring the soft area between them, while he continued to suck even harder on her breasts. With the other, he ran his fingers through Matthew's hair, guiding his head over his erection and, at times, forcing Matthew to accept him completely, irreverently.

Even at the peak of bliss, Andrew found himself questioning the events that were taking place, yet he was able to restrain the encroaching rationality due to his overwhelming desire to be with Matthew. 'Who would know,' he thought, 'or care?' He realized that each of them, in their own way, was getting what they really wanted.

Reinforced by his own clouded logic, Andrew began to explore Ellen more boldly. He allowed his hand to slide off her buttocks and under her stomach until he could feel the coarseness of her damp pubic hair and the slippery warmth of her genitals, as he gently explored the soft folds and valleys, so sensitive to his touch. It was not long before he found her taut source of excitement—the more he massaged it, the more Ellen would sigh and heave herself against him. Andrew inserted his fingers, two and then three, deep within her, while she forced herself against his hand, condoning his actions and anticipating even more.

Moments later, he felt Matthew alongside of him. He turned to kiss him, recognizing, once again, his familiar, welcomed mouth. As Ellen moved off Andrew's chest and to his other side, Matthew encouraged him to get up on his knees, while they continued to kiss each other passionately. Ellen positioned herself on all fours, with her buttocks pressed firmly against Andrew's groin, when she reached in back of her and began to stroke Andrew's erection. She gently pulled him toward her and coaxed insertion, while Andrew eagerly complied, kissing Matthew savagely. With a stifled moan, Ellen slowly accepted all of Andrew, who could feel her warmth envelop his penis with vulgar pleasure. It was not until he began to forcefully develop deep thrusts, that he looked down and realized Ellen had taken him anally, avoiding vaginal contact. In disbelief, he stared at Matthew with wide eyes.

Matthew acknowledged Andrew's astonishment with a scant smile. "She's a lucky woman," he said softly and then returned to Andrew's kisses.

They separated momentarily while Ellen encouraged Matthew to kneel in front of her.

When Andrew leaned forward slightly and held on to Ellen's hips for support, he was able to kiss Matthew and continue to plunge even more deeply. He could feel Matthew tremble and, at times, gently moan. At one point, he watched as Matthew leaned back and straightened.

It was then that the second surprise was revealed. Andrew watched as Matthew's sister sucked his erection, taking as much as possible, while Matthew rammed himself mercilessly down her throat. Andrew found the visual stimuli exceedingly arousing, as he watched his intimate partner participate in an enigmatic yet thoroughly tantalizing brother-sister sex act. Whether it was Matthew's display of unabashed brutality or his own sexual craving, Andrew was unaware of his own savage attack on Ellen, who appeared to be quite gratified with her position. He could not take his eyes off Matthew's penis, which was thrust deeply into Ellen's mouth; in fact, he knew that he was completely envious of her role.

With both hands on Ellen's head, Matthew entered the final phase. Andrew easily recognized his familiar body language, facial expressions, and sounds, just prior to Matthew's orgasm, much as an established spouse would sense the same, and ejaculate simultaneously—which is exactly what happened. Neither pulled away from his warm orifice, hammering Ellen from both ends and forcefully depositing fluids into their willing receptacle.

Exhausted and still kneeling, Matthew and Andrew clung to each other for both physical and, perhaps, psychological support, kissing gently and inhaling the heated scent of each other's spent bodies. Ellen quickly disengaged herself and collapsed beneath him, watching as they kissed, while masturbating slowly into a long, writhing climax.

In silence, they lay alongside of each other with closed eyes, not knowing what to expect next, each hoping that the other would speak a rational word and resolve what seemed to be an increasingly awkward moment.

"This never happened," Andrew said softly yet distinctly, piercing the stillness with his declaration, as he rolled onto his side and then looked directly into each of their eyes—staring until they responded.

"You're right," Matthew said solemnly.

Ellen smiled. "Yes . . .," she said and then quickly added, "but for something that didn't happen, it was . . . rather unforgettable. Thanks." She rose up slightly and affectionately kissed Andrew on his cheek.

Andrew returned the same. "Well . . . I need to get back," he said, just as ineffectively as he said it while talking earlier with Ellen, in the kitchen. In a flash, he found his clothing, dressed haphazardly, and was, once again, walking—half dazed—through the cleansing snowfall.

* * *

It was not until Sunday afternoon, a day generally reserved for free time, when Matthew finally had a chance to speak with Andrew. He watched as Andrew completed his meal and, from a distance, followed him back to his room.

After a gentle rap on his door, Andrew opened it and looked at Matthew with bewilderment.

"Let's go for a walk," Matthew insisted.

In silence, he grabbed his jacket and obediently followed Matthew through the cloister.

Suddenly, Matthew turned. "Meet me outside the door. I need to get my coat."

Standing in the fresh air, outside the entrance room, Andrew took a deep breath, hoping that it would help him to relax, not knowing exactly just what course the conversation would take. He watched as shadows from quick-moving clouds scudded across the mesa, covering Navigator Peak with dark spots like a giant trick Dalmatian, and wondered—just when he thought he had things figured out—how life could suddenly become so complicated. Even within the deepest recesses of his soul, he had no idea Ellen would become such a prominent figure in determining his relationship with Matthew.

The door suddenly flew open. "Not exactly summer," Matthew said, as he zipped up his coat. He looked at Andrew who continued to stare off in the distance. "I know this isn't easy for either of us, Andrew, but I'd rather talk about it and try to clear the air." He started down the steps to the sidewalk and the road beyond.

Andrew followed, petulant yet resolute, sensing an inexplicable closure, as he tread on the stone stairs which, more than two years ago, once let him toward, not away, from his solitary home.

For a while, they walked in silence, listening to the gravel crunch beneath their shoes, until Matthew stopped abruptly. He faced Andrew with his hands in his jacket pockets.

"Look . . . I'm sorry this happened; it wasn't planned, it just . . . happened," he said apologetically. "I hope you can forgive me and realize that, no matter what, I love you, and hope that you still love me."

Andrew laughed a nervous giggle. "I thought everything was getting better with us, and then suddenly, I'm in bed with you and your sister, primarily because I wanted to be with you," he said with pressured speech. "Then, I find out about Ellen, relating the Christmas Eve story to you, and now hearing that you and Ellen are 'close.' Is there anything else you haven't told me, Matt?"

Matthew shook his head. "I don't know."

"You don't know," Andrew repeated quietly.

"No," Matthew said.

Andrew rubbed his eyes. "For Christ's sake, Matt, your sister was blowing you. How the hell normal is that?"

Matthew shrugged and kicked the loose gravel. "Maybe I don't have a good grasp of what's considered normal."

"Terrific," Andrew said. His frustration was obvious. "I fell in love with a psychopath."

"Come on, Andrew. That's not fair. You're hitting way below the belt."

"Okay," Andrew conceded. "Then at least be honest, and tell me the truth."

Matthew looked directly at Andrew. "Maybe, now, I'm afraid to."

"What are you afraid of?"

"I don't want to lose you, Andrew."

"Well, that makes two of us," Andrew admitted, "but I can't go on like this, not knowing what to expect next."

"I don't want you to hate me," Matthew insisted.

"Matt, I doubt that I'd ever hate you. I'm trying to understand you—trying to understand us. It doesn't take much to see that I'm pretty much fucked up as it is. Let's try to help each other."

Matthew rubbed his hands over his face. "Oh shit . . . this is not easy," he began. "Ellen and I have had a relationship which would easily be characterized as incestuous," he said quietly.

Andrew gestured with his hand, as if about to speak.

"Wait," Matthew said. "Let me finish. Coming from a large family, there were times when beds were short, and early on, Ellen and I would often end up in the same bed. Well, I woke up one morning and found her performing oral sex on me. I was fourteen or fifteen, basically knew that it wasn't right, but it sure felt good. She always told me that, even as she dated guys when she got older, she never saw a better penis than mine—until she forced herself on you—and then she told me I had a rival. We've never had any type of intercourse because she knew that I wasn't really attracted to women, and the more she told me about other guys, it just made me even more interested in them." He looked away, filled with humiliation and worry, not sure if he wanted to hear Andrew's response. "Actually, right now, I wouldn't blame you if you did hate me."

Instead, Andrew remained silent. He watched as large crows skimmed the fields for unwary prey. Words from Matthew's mouth seemed to amalgamate within his mind, blurring into something amorphous, indecipherable. Unexpectedly, he remembered a dream he had the night before, filled with vivid details yet fragmented, as dreams often are. He spoke softly, slowly, as if traumatized.

"I dreamt last night that I was about to be put to death by a firing squad. There was little organization; no men lined up; just me, tied to a metal fence with a jumble of soldierlike men across the field, taking aim at me. It must've been during the Civil War because they appeared to be wearing Confederate uniforms. My back was toward them; fear choked my very being. I wondered where and if I'd feel the first bullet and why hadn't they fired yet. I just wanted to get it over with.

"Then someone shouted. Something came up which needed attention, and I was told that the execution would be temporarily delayed. Surprisingly, someone unlocked the shackles from my wrist and told me that it was all right for me to walk around. 'Terrific,' I thought. Was I supposed to feel better or relieved? Did they expect me to escape and run toward the woods beyond the clearing?" Andrew paused to rub his eyes.

"You don't have to go on with this," Matthew whispered.

A hint of a smile crossed Andrew's face. "Actually, I do," he said somewhat cryptically. "I want you to know a bit about what's inside of me." He then continued with the story.

"Anyway, I did think of running, running as fast as I could toward the trees, hoping that their horses wouldn't be ready or quick enough to catch me. And then, somehow, Sara was next to me, clutching my arm. She looked at me with pitiful eyes and said—'who will I walk with in the darkness?'—and the only thing that went through my mind was—'obviously, it won't be me.' But I didn't say it. Then a tall handsome soldier came up to me and said—'you can do it yourself'—and he handed me a pistol. I remember looking at it, thinking how strange it was. It was made out of wood; the barrel was also wooden, and when I looked at it more closely, I realized that it was also square, but the end of the barrel was flared slightly. Once again, I was seized with fear because I knew he was right. I had no choice—I had to get it over with. I glanced at him and held the pistol up to the side of my head. 'In the temple?' I asked. 'No,' he said quietly. 'Put the pistol in your mouth.' I did as he said and put the end of the barrel in my mouth. It seemed strangely comfortable, but I knew I couldn't delay, so I closed my eyes, bit down on the barrel, and pulled the trigger. I heard a click but nothing happened, so I pulled the trigger again and again. It was then that I woke up."

It did not matter to Matthew that it was daylight. He moved forward, pulled Andrew toward him, and held him tight. "I can feel you trembling," he whispered. He nuzzled Andrew's ear. "That wasn't a dream," he said. "It was a nightmare. Someone once told me that if you dream bad things—don't worry. Those dreams never come true."

"It's not the dreams I'm worried about," Andrew said. "Reality is much more frightening." He glanced down at Matthew's jacket, which strangely resembled a uniform—grey with gold braiding around the collar. Frightened, he began to pull away from Matthew's embrace; however, Matthew held him even tighter. When he opened his eyes,

Andrew realized that Matthew was wearing his same old baseball jacket, green with a thin yellow-striped collar. Relieved, he buried his face into the warmth of Matthew's neck.

The sound of the approaching vehicle in the distance caused them to separate. With a flash of his headlights, Eric Holtz drove past them in his truck, waving and smiling his California smile. They watched as the truck rounded the turn near the monastery and disappeared out of sight behind the buildings.

"I never told you about him, did I?" Andrew asked.

"Told me what?" Matthew replied.

"That he and Father Martin were more than just friends."

"You mean . . . they were having a relationship?"

Andrew nodded. "Supposedly . . . according to the gospel of Brother Mark."

"Well, what do you know," Matthew said with a smirk. "I guess there is definitely more to this place than meets the eye."

"Yeah," Andrew said sarcastically. "Like we should talk."

Matthew grimaced slightly but remained silent.

Andrew slowly rotated his body, three hundred and sixty degrees, observing the magnificent vista as if for the first time. Once again, he faced Matthew. "So," he began, hoping to refocus the conversation, "where are we going, Matt?"

"I don't know," Matthew replied. "Do you want to walk down to the barns?"

Andrew closed his eyes and then opened them. "No, I mean—us. Where is our relationship headed?"

"What does it matter if we love each other?" Matthew said honestly.

"It matters to me." Andrew said softly. "Do I have to be concerned that you are having sex with Ellen?"

Matthew grabbed both of Andrew's arms. "Look. I'm not having sex with my sister. That was in the past. There is nothing to worry about."

"And . . . the three of us . . . what just happened . . . we won't have to do that again?" Andrew asked.

"No, I promise," Matthew said. He stared at Andrew with genuine affection. "I promise."

"Okay," Andrew said with a smile. "We should probably be getting back."

"Okay," Matthew replied.

They turned toward the monastery.

Matthew stopped abruptly. "Should I disobey Father Gerald?" he asked suddenly with a slight grin.

Andrew reached out and gently squeezed his nose. "I was hoping you would, long before this," he said.

"Great!" Matthew said. "Then I'm staying in your room tonight."

* * *

Chapter Twenty-Seven

An Unexpected Exit

As expected, spring eventually reached the higher Alpine valleys with all its familiar glory. Snow lines receded toward the treeless peaks in irregular patterns, replaced by carpets of wildflowers that painted the clay colored soil with vibrant hues of blue, red, yellow, and white. Columbine suddenly sprouted within patches of paintbrush, while the sage flourished in the warmth of the sun, surrounding the fringes of the monastery like decorative edging.

Summer chores began to unfold; dirt bikes were tuned up to transport the monks to various parts of the property so that the irrigation could begin; farming began anew with planting; fences would need mending to contain the newly arrived shipment of cattle; and the season of new guests and prospective postulants had begun.

Andrew was surprised by Matthew's steadfast attention, his genuine caring and sense of adventure. The snow had barely melted when he encouraged Andrew to join him on his bike, drive up the steep and muddy trail to their familiar rock overlook, and spend the afternoon inside their stone fort. Andrew immediately searched for the message that Matthew had carved on a smooth rock, nearly two summers before. It did not take long before he founded it, almost as clear as the day it was carved—"Matt loves Andrew"—neatly chiseled within a heart-shaped frame. If, as the saying goes, in springtime, a young man's fancy turns to love, Matthew and Andrew personified the essence of its intention, a fact which did not go unnoticed in the community yet was discretely tolerated, more so, by some than others.

Father Gerald, their reigning defender, would often argue their case, unknown to them, behind closed doors. "They are not exactly holding hands and kissing in public," he would say, while some of the elderly and certainly more conservative monks would frown and sink even deeper into their chairs but remain relatively silent. "Andrew has been through many traumas. He has a significant mental illness which, with medication and therapy, is not in any way inconsistent with the monastic life. I feel that their affection for each other is genuine, and while I cannot condone whatever it is they do in private, I'm not so sure that it is necessarily profane. It may even spring from a spiritual framework; I can't arbitrarily condemn love."

It was, perhaps, the very first time that such a private issue was raised so publicly within the council of professed elders. Some of them grumbled and shook their heads but said nothing until Brother Cyril's terse remark.

"God forgive me," he said quietly, "but I hope Brother Andrew is not a victim of this relationship."

"Please speak freely," Father Gerald said.

Father Cyril's increasingly ruddy complexion contrasted strongly with his dark beard and hair. He attempted to clear his throat. "I don't know," he said with a struggle. He waved one hand in the air and shrugged. "I don't know," he repeated.

"Well," Father Gerald added, "at this point, Dr. Klein has not suggested that they be physically separated. In fact, he feels that it may be extremely detrimental, particularly to Brother Andrew. Right now, I feel that they both need our prayers. We can only watch and wait and be hopeful."

With the advent of summer came longer days and greater workloads and less time for contemplative prayer and formal meditation. Sweat and sunburn, which later turned to tan, became the norm, yet no one seemed to complain. Falling into bed at eight o'clock while still daylight, posed few problems even for the worst insomniacs, as the physical demands of the day proved beneficially exhausting, allowing a deep, natural sleep, which often quieted the mind within minutes once heads touched their pillows; all except for Andrew, who still relied on medication to assist him through the night and to decrease recurrent dreams. The black hooded figure with fiery eyes would sometimes stand silently in the distance as Andrew tensed in his sleep, preparing for the worst yet experiencing the unexpected anticlimatic disappearance of his tormentor. At other times, the hooded figure would appear and hover inches from his face, its glowing eyes burning into his, as if trying to destroy him with his hideous stare. It was then that the guttural sounds welled within Andrew's chest and erupted in the darkness with an unholy wail, waking more than just his immediate cellmates in the dormitory. Most of his brothers remained frozen in their beds as they waited for the heavy, reassuring footsteps of Brother Nathan, who would often arrive at Andrew's cell, armed with a syringe.

On one such occasion, when Brother Nathan turned on the light in Andrew's room, he unexpectedly found Andrew, naked and nearly traumatized, standing in a corner clutching a pillow and hyperventilating while Matthew sat, wide-eyed, on the edge of the bed. Brother Nathan helped him get dressed, gave him medication, and quietly escorted him back to his bed. It was the first time Matthew had fully experienced—in close proximity—one of Andrew's nightmares and, consequently, the first time that Brother Nathan observed what appeared obvious, that the relationship between the two young monks clearly included a physical context. His clinical response bore sparse subjective judgment, yet he knew that his sublimated libido registered an uncomfortable upward blip.

* * *

As contented as he was, Andrew continued to be bothered by Rebecca Storrow's presence at the Sunday mass and her occasional attendance during the middle of the week. He would look out the entrance room door and see her white convertible parked smugly against the weathered rail fence. Even with a slight chill in the air, she often rode with the top down, her blonde hair blowing in the wind; a carefree and obviously affluent spirit who was, at least in Andrew's mind, seeking more than spiritual guidance. At times, he would watch as Matthew leaned against her car, talking with animated gestures and laughing while she responded in kind with practiced etiquette reflected by her well-bred stature.

"Why?" Andrew asked, lying alongside Matthew in his cell. "Why do you still see her when you know how much it annoys me?"

Matthew closed his eyes and sighed. "She's a nice person, and she's only a friend, Andrew," he said sharply. "There's no reason to get upset."

"Maybe not . . . but it does—it scares me," Andrew said quietly. He rolled on his back and stared at the ceiling.

"Scares you?" Matthew repeated. He propped himself up with his elbow. "What do you mean?"

"I don't know," Andrew said. "Something about it doesn't feel right. I can't explain it."

Matthew reached down, pushed the hair away from Andrew's forehead, and gently massaged his temples. "Are you waiting for me to tell you how much you mean to me—how much I love you—because I do." He kissed Andrew's lips. "It's just that it's new for me to feel the friendship of . . . a woman. I've never really experienced that before—other than Ellen—and she's very nice to me."

"I know about that," Andrew said, "and I guess that's the part that scares me."

Matthew chuckled. "Why? Do you think I'm suddenly going to become straight?"

"No, but I'm afraid that you might be swayed by her kindness and impressed by her wealth and think that it might be fun to do something impulsive."

"Like what?"

"I don't know."

"You mean have sex with her?"

"I don't know," Andrew stammered. "I hope not."

"Don't be crazy," Matthew said. "How can you think something like that?"

"Maybe because I've known someone very much like Rebecca." Andrew reached up and pulled him close. "I guess it makes me jealous," he whispered. "Try to understand that."

"I will, I promise," Matthew said.

* * *

The view from the upper mesa was as spectacular as ever as Andrew finished building his damn across the wide ditch and began to plan the proper spacing for the cutouts which would irrigate the area below with a constant flow of life-sustaining water. He paused, as always, to reflect on the natural beauty of his surroundings, to acknowledge his own insignificance, and to give thanks for the never expected opportunities he was given. 'In spite of the damn mental illness,' he thought, 'someone is looking out for me.'

A small cloud of dust appeared in the distance on the road below and approached the guesthouse. Although he was not wearing his glasses, Andrew thought it looked very much like one of the suburbans which transported the monks to and from their rafting adventure the summer before. He watched as the vehicle stopped in front of the guesthouse. Someone got out, got onto a dirt bike, and drove away from the monastery, followed closely by the suburban. His vision was limited, yet he could have sworn the person on the bike was Matthew—the same walk, the same general shape. Puzzled, he returned to his task and was soon mesmerized by the water's effect upon the soil, as dusty red clay, once moistened, darkened to burgundy in the brilliant sunlight.

* * *

Perhaps the weather should have been his first clue. Just prior to dawn, wind-whipped rain pelted Andrew's glass slider with increasing intensity, until he was sure that someone was intentionally throwing stones at the window, hoping to break it. He quickly drew back the heavy drape, expecting to see a deranged monk standing in the garth; instead, he was amazed to see golf ball size hail bouncing everywhere and collecting on the lawn, while blue and white streaks of lightning zigzagged repeatedly across the horizon, momentarily illuminating the entire monastery with stadiumlike brightness. He immediately closed the drape, dove for his bed, and quickly pulled the quilt over his head.

As the day wore on, the heavy rain subsided, leaving only a misty, windless silence over the valley. Andrew felt as though he was walking through clouds on his way to the eggery, and in fact, he was. The mist would lift, at times, and allow him to see the giant softly shaped mounds heading directly toward him, as they obliterated most of the surrounding peaks.

Brother Mark was waiting for him in the office, primarily as a result of Dr. Klein's recommendation that Andrew should never be left alone while working at the eggery. Even the men's room, where Andrew found John hanging from a water pipe, had been completely renovated and equipped with an emergency buzzer which alerted an on-call staff person at the monastery. Their obvious goal was not only safety but also to help dissolve some of the tragic memories associated with such a bleak environment.

"We hardly ever have a chance to talk anymore," Brother Mark said while stooping to retrieve the eggs from the lower cages.

Andrew wiped the sweat from his forehead with the back of his hand. "I know," he said. It seems as though my life since the raft trip has been a cerebral disaster, so to speak—from clinics to Dr. Klein's office, it starts to become one big blur."

Brother Mark hesitated to ask, but he was curious about Andrew's mental status. "I probably shouldn't be asking you, but I'm wondering how you've been doing with the dreams and the therapy."

Andrew was comfortable with the question. "I guess I'm feeling better," he said honestly. "How do you think I'm doing?" he asked unexpectedly.

"You seem fine," Brother Mark said, "but I think that you don't always show on the outside what's going on in the inside."

Andrew laughed yet avoided eye contact. "No, really. I think I'm a lot better," he said.

"Okay," Brother Mark replied somewhat abruptly.

They finished collecting in relative silence, tossing the soft shell "jellies" into the plastic bucket for the resident pigs and, as expected, commenting on the perpetual heat and stench of the hen houses. It was not until they were out of the building, walking on the road in the fresh air, when Brother Mark broached another somewhat delicate subject.

"How are things with you and Brother Matthew?" he asked.

This time, the question surprised Andrew, who began to feel slightly defensive.

"Okay, I guess . . . why?"

"Just wondering," Brother Mark replied. He walked with his hands in his pockets and kicked at some of the larger stones in the roadway. "I haven't seen much of him since early yesterday," he added.

Suddenly, it occurred to Andrew that he was right. He remembered seeing Matthew after the morning mass but that was it. He sensed that, perhaps, something was wrong and Brother Mark may have known more than he was admitting.

"So what aren't you telling me?" Andrew asked defiantly.

Brother Mark cringed. "Nothing," he insisted. "I was just wondering if you know where Matthew is."

Andrew took several deep breaths to relax. "If I knew, I'd tell you, but it wasn't until now that his absence became an issue," he said. "What makes you think he's missing?"

"Well, he was supposed to meet with Father Luke this morning after mass, but he never showed up."

"Anything serious?"

"I'm not sure," Brother Mark said.

"Not sure?" Andrew retorted. "What do you mean? Should we notify the police or do some sort of low-level search on our own?" He stared at Brother Mark.

"I'll speak with Father Luke," Brother Mark said.

"What about the abbot?" Andrew asked.

"Father Jude is not here."

Andrew shrugged. "Maybe they went somewhere together," he said.

"No, that's impossible," Brother Mark replied. "Father Jude was seen leaving the day before yesterday, when Matthew was still here."

"Well, who the hell is running this place?" Andrew blurted. "Doesn't Father Luke have any idea where his boss is?"

"Let's both calm down," Brother Mark insisted. "I'll speak with Father Luke, and let you know if he's heard anything."

"That's not good enough," Andrew said. "I'm taking one of the dirt bikes to see if he might have had an accident up on the mesa."

Brother Mark shook his head. "No need for that," he said quietly. "Brother Nathan thought he saw Matthew drive away in the Volkswagen. And the car is still missing."

Andrew felt as if his world were suddenly crashing down on him. He immediately wondered if Matthew had suddenly decided to abandon the lifestyle and the relationship, to simply throw it all away and disappear without a word. 'It can't be,' he thought.

"Look," Brother Mark insisted. "Stay close to your room, and I'll let you know as soon as possible what Father Luke decides to do, okay?"

Andrew nodded. "Don't take too long though," he said softly.

Back in his cell, Andrew paced constantly, encountering first the garth, through his screened slider, and then simply the back of his closed door, as he waited for word from Brother Mark. Approaching the screened door, Andrew was sure he heard the unmistakable sound of a Volkswagen engine, as the car puttered its way around the back of the monastery, kicking up a cloud of dust.

He immediately bolted for the kitchen, running uncharacteristically down the cloister to see if Matthew had returned, and hoping that he would see the black Volkswagen in the parking lot, with Matthew, leaning against the kitchen counter, making himself a sandwich. Only half of his wish came true—the car was, in fact, parked near the back door, but Matthew was nowhere to be found. Andrew checked the walk-in cooler, the pantry, and the area outside the kitchen, but found no trace of him or anyone. Bewildered, he decided to visit Father Luke's office which was on the second floor, directly above the abbot's quarters. He barely began climbing the slate steps when he heard an angry voice, shouting above Father Luke's moderate tones.

"I need the damn money!" Matthew screamed. "I've worked for it, so let's not make this difficult."

Andrew reached the top of the stairs and stood quietly, listening outside the closed door of Father Luke's office.

"It's okay," Father Luke said calmly, "we can get you the money, but are you sure you want to do this?"

He heard Matthew laugh sarcastically. "What would you do? She's my sister and she's barely eighteen! What's Father 'douche bag' . . . forty-seven?" Once again, Matthew's voice reached an uncontrolled crescendo, causing Andrew to shiver nervously.

Suddenly, he heard heavy footsteps running quickly up the stairs. He turned to see Brother Nathan moving directly toward him.

"I need you to go back to your cell," Brother Nathan said firmly.

Andrew felt glued to the floor and said nothing.

"Please," Brother Nathan insisted. "Go back, now!" He gently pulled on Andrew's arm, encouraging him to leave.

In a daze, Andrew could still hear Father Luke's level voice asking Matthew to remain civil, but that was the last he heard. He did as Brother Nathan asked; he quickly ran down the stairs and walked confused and frightened toward his cell, knowing that something serious had happened which, he was sure, would negatively impact his life and his relationship with Matthew. A familiar despair tore into him, not unlike the rekindled rain which relentlessly pelted the cloister windows.

He watched from his bed as the summer storm darkened around the monastery, blowing the rain horizontally and then brightening the darkness with jagged bolts of lightning. Sleep was out of the question, replaced instead with gnawing fear and anxiety, as he wondered what was happening. Matthew, he realized, was obviously out of control, much as he was, after hearing such a flagrant exchange between Father Luke and the person he undoubtedly loved. 'Perhaps this is how it ends,' he thought, 'with fireworks and an angry exit.' The tightness in his chest seemed unbearable; he forced himself to take slow, deep breaths to try to regain some composure, until suddenly, it happened. A steady knock on the door caused him to bolt upright in bed and stand immediately. The quick change caused him to be lightheaded, crash momentarily into the plaster wall, and perforate it with his elbow.

"Shit!" he cursed. He shook off the dizziness and answered the door.

"I haven't got much time," Matthew said, "but I want you to know what's going on."

Andrew found it difficult to understand how different he looked—disheveled, upset, and overheated—and yet, somehow, very sexual, as though spent after-the-fact.

"Come on in," Andrew said softly. He shut the door and waited for what he knew would be a psychological death sentence.

Matthew wasted no words. "I found out early yesterday that Ellen is pregnant, and the father is none other than our illustrious abbot, Father Jude."

"Are you sure?" Andrew asked, more with shock than disbelief.

"Yes," Matthew said. "Ellen has confirmed it, and 'douche bag' is not denying it."

"Holy shit!" Andrew exclaimed. "I can't believe it." His thoughts began to blur.

"Well, it's true," Matthew said. "I know that Ellen isn't exactly an angel, but it's hard to believe that this sanctimonious bastard, who is thirty years older than she is, wouldn't have known better."

Andrew sat on the bed for support. He looked up at Matthew. "I'm sorry about this, Matt. You must be going crazy."

Matthew chuckled. "That's nothing—you should hear what my family is going through."

Andrew rubbed his eyes and shook his head. "I can imagine."

"Actually, you have no idea," Matthew said quietly, almost as if talking to himself.

As much as he hated to ask, Andrew knew that he had to. "So what are your plans?" he asked nervously. "You mentioned that you didn't have a lot of time."

"I'm going back home for a while, until I can think straight and see if I can be of any help," he said. "I just can't be here right now."

Andrew felt as though someone had just stuck a knife in his chest and slowly twisted the blade; he tried to breathe deeply, remain conscious, and not show his emotions. "I understand," he whispered.

"Brother Nathan is driving me to the airport in Bitter Creek in fifteen minutes. I should be back in California before the sun sets out there."

Andrew shrugged and tried to smile. "So . . . when will you be coming back?" Just saying the words proved totally enervating.

Matthew hesitated. "I'm not sure," he said softly, "but don't worry. I *will* be back."

A half smile brightened Andrew's face. "You promise?"

Matthew also smiled. "Yes, I promise." He reached out and pulled Andrew to his feet. "Now, give me a hug so I can go in peace."

Andrew willingly complied, hugging him just as tightly as Matthew always hugged him. He desperately fought back the tears that welled up so quickly, as he buried his face between his neck and shoulder. "Will you write . . . or call me?" He managed to get the words out with some semblance of control.

"Yes, of course," Matthew said.

"I'm going to miss you, Matt," he said with a struggle.

"And I'll miss you too, Andrew, but right now, I've just got to deal with this my own way."

Andrew took a deep breath and pulled away. "Okay," he said firmly. "Then get out of here and good luck."

"Thanks," Matthew said, "but not without a kiss." He pulled Andrew back into his arms and kissed him deeply and then abruptly backed away. Avoiding eye contact, he quickly exited the room in silence.

A vague, strange taste of tobacco lingered briefly on Andrew's tongue; however, this was soon forgotten as he collapsed on his bed, sobbing uncontrollably into the pillow which he held firmly against his face.

* * *

For Andrew, that summer without Matthew barely happened. He lived for the occasional letter postmarked from California and the even less frequent phone calls, when he could hear his voice, his laugh and imagine his brilliant smile, yet even then, there was seldom privacy to express his innermost thoughts, his feelings, and, most of all, his love. That was almost always reserved for late-night letters, letters that sometimes exceeded five or six handwritten pages of scrawled yet, somehow, decipherable sentences, which soon evolved into extensive, unindented paragraphs of raw emotion, rank with loneliness and genuine longing, and nearly always ending with the same question—'When are you coming back?'

'Soon,' Matthew would write, 'soon.'

His absence took its toll on Andrew, who began to decompensate gradually. Increased symptoms necessitated lengthy sessions with Dr. Klein, where he would lament his separation from Matthew and cry openly, at times, unable to stop until Dr. Klein injected a sedative, waited for the drug to take effect, and allowed him to sleep in a small private room next to his office. In his heart, Andrew was quite sure Matthew would not return to the monastery, that he would never see him again, and the pain of that realization proved nearly devastating. He would blackout unexpectedly, gash his head and require stitches, or, as in the past, recurrent nightmares caused him to scream in his sleep as he faced the black hooded demon with glowing eyes. On one occasion, while still asleep, he jumped up on his desk to attack the red-eyed monster, lost his balance, and fell to the floor, crashing into the heater and dislocating his shoulder. It was then that the community felt the need to make a decision.

"I don't think he should be here," Father Cyril said frankly. "He should probably be with his family or"—his face grew even redder—"or in California."

Father Gerald, who had been meeting regularly with Dr. Klein and keeping in touch with him by telephone, offered a shared opinion. "We feel that he needs to ride out this pain in a caring environment," he said apologetically. "He doesn't seem to have the support he needs at home, and going to California would probably be the most detrimental choice he could make, especially in light of the abbot's alleged involvement with Matthew's sister."

As in most cases, the community sided with Father Gerald, with the understanding that he would spend more time with Andrew and help him to readjust, in accordance with Dr. Klein's recommendations.

* * *

"It's sort of strange," Andrew began, as he sat calmly in the overstuffed chair in Dr. Klein's office, "but when I stopped for the red light, just before I turned down your street, I saw two young men—about my age—sitting on one of the park benches, facing each other, obviously more than friends, and so totally absorbed with each other . . ."

Dr. Klein allowed the silence to linger. "And?" he said finally.

Andrew rubbed his eyes. "I don't know. I guess I'm just so much more aware of how happy two people can be now that that part of my life has ended."

"He may come back," Dr. Klein said reassuringly.

"Yeah," Andrew said. "He may, but I doubt it."

"What will you do if he doesn't?"

Andrew paused. "Try to cope, I guess. I don't know."

"Do you think it would ever be possible for you to have a similar relationship with someone else in the monastery?"

Andrew got up from his chair and looked out the window, where he watched an elderly woman with snow white hair walk her dog with the same colored fur. "Like I've said before, that's not why I came here,"

"I understand," Dr. Klein said, "but as before, it just might happen."

Andrew had no immediate response; instead, he watched the white-haired duo disappear out of sight and wondered how long it would be before he might be that elderly person walking his dog, alone—alone in a world consisting primarily of much younger and, certainly, more attractive strangers.

"I had sex with his sister," he said nonchalantly. The unsolicited remark tumbled out of his mouth with little emphasis.

Dr. Klein shifted slightly in his chair. "What else do you want to tell me about it?" he asked.

Andrew turned and faced him. "I didn't get her pregnant," he said.

"Are you concerned that you might have?"

"No, not really," Andrew said. "She didn't take me in her vagina."

"So . . . you had anal sex with her," Dr. Klein said, more in the form of the statement.

"Yes."

"Then it's highly unlikely that you got her pregnant."

"I know," Andrew said. He slumped back into the soft chair.

"I may be wrong," Dr. Klein began, "but I feel as though you brought this up for a reason."

Andrew shrugged. "Maybe . . . I don't know."

Dr. Klein remained silent, waiting for Andrew to share whatever was on his mind.

"Okay," Andrew said. "I know I'm not 'Mr. Morality,' but I'd like to think that if I were nearly fifty and the abbot of a monastery, I'd have the sense not to have sex with a novice's seventeen-year-old sister."

"I'd like to think that you would, indeed, have that sense," Dr. Klein said.

Andrew waited for a follow-up yet Dr. Klein said nothing. "Is that all you have to say?" he said bluntly.

"No," Dr. Klein said. "I will discuss how you feel about the situation you brought up and how it affects you, but I can't be expected to ethically comment on whatever your abbot and Brother Matthew's sister allegedly did. Can you understand the difference?"

"I guess," Andrew said unconvincingly. Once again, he rubbed his eyes. "I think I feel revulsion toward the abbot, but what I feel toward Ellen is more like hatred. Somehow, I knew she'd come between us."

"The feelings are not that different," Dr. Klein explained. "Are you saying that your anger toward Father Jude is less than your anger toward Ellen?"

"Maybe..."

"Any thought of harming either one of them... or yourself?"

Andrew scoffed. "No, of course not," he said. He stood up suddenly and looked at Dr. Klein.

"What the hell is it with this monastery?" he asked. There was an obvious edge in his voice. "Are they all like this?"

Dr. Klein poured himself more coffee and offered the carafe to Andrew, who shook his head. "I hope not," he said, "but I've little evidence to go on. I am familiar only with St. Anthony's." He placed the thermos back on his desk and leaned back in his chair. "Nevertheless, I would venture to say that no monastery is perfect."

Andrew retrieved his jacket and began walking toward the door. "Well, God help the Catholic Church," he said. He nodded slightly toward Dr. Klein. "I'll see you next week."

"Are you all right or would you like to talk more?" Dr. Klein offered.

"No... really. I'm okay."

* * *

It was a warm Saturday afternoon when Andrew checked his mailbox. He immediately recognized Matthew's handwriting on the blue envelope and gently opened it. He read the following with captivated attention:

> *Dear Andrew,*
>
> *I'd almost forgotten how hot California's weather can be—not to mention the pollution and congestion. It's a far cry from the bright blue skies of the monastery.*
>
> *As you can imagine, things are a mess here. My parents are just beginning to calm down after discussing the case with a lawyer. They are thinking about suing, but then Ellen goes bullshit because she says that she loves Father Jude and wants to have the baby. Of course, everyone is really pissed over their*

age difference, but Ellen is insisting that the bastard will marry her. Right . . . I heard that he is home in Texas with his family. Apparently, they have a few bucks, which may be one of the reasons why Ellen is so interested. I think she's finally gone off the deep end. I can't imagine what she ever saw in him other than what she told me the other night after having a couple of beers. It seems as though our lusty abbot has a big one . . . anyway, I doubt that Jude will be allowed to return to St. Anthony's. I have no idea what will happen with the legal stuff.

I shouldn't tell you but I've been to the ocean twice since I've been back, and it was as fantastic as I remembered it. I won't say anything more about it. I don't want to make you jealous.

You know that I miss you very much, and I hope you miss me even more. I also hope you're doing okay. I'm not sure when I'll be back, but it should be soon. I can't wait to see you.

*Love and a big hug,
Matthew*

Andrew carefully folded the letter and slid back into the envelope with mixed emotions. He had hoped that Matthew would have written more than one small paragraph about their relationship and been less oblique about his return to the monastery, yet he was happy, at least, to entertain the thought that such a return was possible. 'Maybe he is coming back,' he thought. And it was this renewed hope that allowed Andrew to function somewhat more effectively, one small step at a time.

Days soon turned into weeks as Andrew seemed to be going through the motions, meditating zombielike, attending regular prayer services, and, at times, preparing fairly palatable meals for his hungry brothers. Nearly everywhere he went, he managed to see Matthew's presence and imagined how things were before he left. He would stare at his empty chair or walk by his cell, hoping to be pleasantly surprised. One day, when he realized that Matthew's door was unlocked, Andrew quickly slipped inside, locked the door behind him, and sat in his chair, inhaling what remained of his absence. He ran his fingers over the surface of his desk, touched his lamp and his drawer handles, knowing how tempted he was to open them. Unable to resist, he carefully pulled open the shallow drawer beneath the desktop. Boxes of paper clips, some rubber bands, pens, pencils, and small notepads were scattered about with ragged photographs of his family and some pictures of the raft trip. Most were group shots Andrew never remembered being taken, and yet there he was, standing next to Matthew, a big smile on both of their faces, while they held plates of food and cans of soda.

Overcome with a sense of guilt, Andrew, nevertheless, opened a small blue notebook. On the first page, Matthew had roughly sketched Andrew, sitting next to a campfire, wearing shorts and a T-shirt emblazoned with the name "Sunkist" on it, while he hugged his knees tightly against his chest. He smiled when he realized that he was, at that moment, wearing the same shirt. He was also moved by Matthew's skill and the fact that he took not only the time but also the enthusiasm to sketch him. He took a deep breath and turned the page.

It was there that he saw two hastily scratched telephone numbers—one for Tim, presumably the person who shared their tent one night during the raft trip, and the other for Rebecca Storrow, the wealthy young woman who, Andrew was sure, was overly interested in Matthew. Suddenly, he felt as if he had just swallowed a lead balloon, as earlier feelings of joy soon dissipated into confused suspicion. 'Why,' he wondered, 'would he have their phone numbers?'

He closed the notebook and carefully placed it back where he found it. With remorse, he closed the desk drawer and quietly left Matthew's cell.

* * *

Although most would have agreed that lunch was delicious, Andrew pawed unenthusiastically through his own creation of homemade potato salad served with chilled, marinated asparagus. Halfway through his meal, Andrew squinted for better focus and looked around the room. He fantasized that Matthew would be sitting where he always sat, opposite him and to his right. Instead, Andrew was surprised to see a familiar face—Brother Joshua—whom Andrew had once observed masturbating in the bathroom, the same novice who was famous for flaunting his perfectly shaped feet. It appeared as if he had been waiting to be noticed, and as soon as Andrew made eye contact, he smiled, gently nodded his head, and extended both legs out from under the table.

'Oh God,' Andrew thought. 'He's back.' Respectfully, Andrew returned the smile. He then looked down at his plate and, with renewed interest, methodically ingested every morsel, right down to the lonely piece of chopped chive hovering tenuously on the rim of the stainless steel dish.

When the meal was finished, it was not long before Brother Joshua successfully located Andrew, who was quietly sitting alone in the periodical room, looking at a magazine and catching up on the national news.

"Hello, again," Brother Joshua said with a smile. He extended his hand toward Andrew, who immediately got up.

"Hello," Andrew said. He clasped Brother Joshua's hand and shook it firmly.

"Well," Brother Joshua began. "I'm officially here as an Observer."

Andrew realized that Brother Joshua must have successfully completed the necessary paperwork and passed the usual battery of psychological tests.

"Congratulations . . . and welcome," Andrew said. "It's nice to have you back," he said. The white lie seemed to partially stick in his throat, and he suddenly began to cough.

Brother Joshua moved toward him and motioned, as if he were about to slap him on the back; however, Andrew held up his hand to stop him.

"I'll be fine," Andrew squeaked. "It must be the pollen."

After a few seconds of coughing and clearing his throat, Andrew managed to settle down. "When did you arrive?" he asked.

"This morning, around ten."

Andrew had forgotten how tall Brother Joshua was as he towered over him by a good three inches. He looked around the empty room and lowered his voice. "We probably shouldn't be talking in here," he said.

"Okay," Brother Joshua replied. "How about a walk?"

Andrew hesitated and then conceded. "Sure . . . why not," he said.

It was a nearly perfect afternoon; bright blue skies surrounded the monastery while occasional wisps of high altitude clouds cast barely perceptible shadows across the valley. With temperatures in the upper seventies and low humidity, it would have been heresy to remain inside.

"Let's just cut to the quick," Andrew began unexpectedly, as they walked on the gravel road. "What do you or don't you know about Father Jude, Matthew, or me?"

His outspoken approach caught Brother Joshua off-guard. "Nothing like being direct," he retorted. He shrugged and placed both hands in the pockets of his jeans. "Well, I doubt there is a monk around who hasn't heard about Father Jude and Brother Matthew's sister. I expect that eventually it will be front page news in the *Catholic Free Press*. Other than that, I haven't heard much else."

As much as he hesitated to smile, Andrew could not hide it. "Pathetic—but funny," he admitted. He glanced at Brother Joshua, who was also smiling, and suddenly realized how handsome he appeared in the natural light, with his radiant expression and prominent features.

"I'm pretty sure that you and Brother Matthew are more than just friends," Brother Joshua added boldly.

Andrew scoffed. "Oh yeah?" he said. "And how did you determine that?"

"Come on," Brother Joshua quipped.

"Seriously . . . tell me. How?"

"Just by watching the two of you together the last time I was here."

"We were that obvious?" Andrew asked.

"Not to the untrained eye," Brother Joshua remarked. "It was the little things I noticed."

"Like what?"

"Oh . . . the way you'd look at each other and smile. I remember, one day, you were both walking down the cloister. You didn't know that I was walking in back of you, and without speaking, Matthew reached out and straightened your hood on the way to Vespers." He turned and looked at Andrew with a smirk. "It was nice," he added.

"I think I remember that day," Andrew said nostalgically. It was then that Andrew's defenses and oppositional feelings toward Brother Joshua suddenly began to fade away. "You know, you just might be okay."

"Well, I hope so," Brother Joshua said. "I'd like us to be friends."

For a while, they walked in silence, digesting their new reconciliation, a peaceful resolution to an otherwise rocky beginning, as the beauty of the flawless summer day wrapped its arms around them, gently reminding them of the ultimate importance of the transient, present moment.

"By the way—nice feet," Andrew remarked.

Brother Joshua chuckled and continued to stare off into the distance.

* * *

Chapter Twenty-Eight

The Return

Once again, the month of August strutted its brutal essence with wind-whipped heat and late-afternoon storms, which seemed to evaporate as rapidly as they arose, leaving behind a sauna like environment of surging humidity. There was no place to hide, no door to exit, unless, like Andrew, you were lingering in the walk-in cooler, choosing food for your upcoming retreat.

Although he would be away for only one week, Andrew did not need to over pack since Father Gerald had decided, following a consult with Dr. Klein, that Andrew could use the upper hermitage, with the stipulation that he return to the monastery each evening to eat and sleep. Andrew did not object; in fact, he was pleased. He had visited the hermitage on several occasions and marveled at its stoicism. Unlike Linda and Arthur Cole's cabin, where he spent an earlier retreat, the hermitage had few conveniences—no stove, no running water, and no bathtub. And yet its difficult accessibility, high upon a mountain meadow, afforded an unparalleled view experienced by only a privileged few. The breathtaking vista of the snowcapped summits spread out in the distance, like jagged fingers clawing the oxygen-starved heavens. Even the seemingly benign meadow warranted caution, as its wildflower carpet abruptly ended in a precipitous cliff, hundreds of feet above the makeshift road below.

Yet for Andrew and others who experienced this incredible location, they would all agree that it was probably the closest they could come to heaven while still standing on earth.

With most everything he needed for the day packed securely in the back of the four-wheel drive pickup, Andrew returned to the kitchen for one last check. He stood at the sink, looking out the window at the early-morning heat rising in barely visible waves above the fragrant sage. In a daze, he sipped a glass of cherry juice as Buddha silently rubbed herself against his leg, claiming him, for the hundredth time, as her own.

Father Gerald's arrival in the black Volkswagen seemed insignificant, at least until the cloud of red dust blew over and his passenger got out and stood on the far side of the vehicle. Andrew could not believe his eyes. As if in a dream, he saw Matthew, staring at him through the window, grinning from ear to ear, waiting to be welcomed.

It was the sound of the glass breaking in the sink, after he dropped it, which forced Andrew to function. He rushed out the back door, straight into Matthew's embrace and held him firmly.

"Please, Brothers," Father Gerald admonished with a smile. "No kissing. Someone may be watching."

Apparently, with their level of excitement extremely elevated, Andrew and Matthew found tremendous humor in Father Gerald's cautionary remark. Out of control, they clung to each other for support, laughing hysterically, nearly choking, with tears running down their cheeks. And when Matthew finally managed to squeak out and mimic "no kissing, brothers," the cycle simply repeated itself, this time, with even greater intensity.

"If one of you has a heart attack, don't assume I'll administer CPR," Father Gerald joked. "Now help me with Matthew's luggage."

"I'm sorry, Father," Andrew said, still laughing. He wiped his eyes with his sleeve. "I guess we weren't expecting your comment."

"That's all right," Father Gerald said. "I'm pleased to know that I still have my sense of humor. God knows—around here, you need it."

Andrew carried one of Matthew's suitcases into the kitchen and set it next to the counter. "Is that everything?" he asked.

"That's it," Matthew said as he deposited the rest of his luggage next to the suitcase. He looked around the familiar sunny kitchen and smiled. "It's good to be back," he said. "It even smells the same as I remember it."

Father Gerald peeked into the refectory, and even though it was empty, he pulled the heavy wooden doors shut. "You can talk in here, if you like—as long as it doesn't get too rowdy." He smiled, turned toward Matthew, and hugged him warmly. "Welcome back," he said. "I have some errands to run, so I'll get going." He started out the back door and suddenly stopped. "Andrew—just a reminder—make sure you're back from the retreat for dinner, okay?"

"I'll make sure," Andrew said.

The screen door slammed shut just before Father Gerald started the car and drove away from the monastery.

"So you are leaving for . . ."

"Shh . . ." Before Matthew could finish his sentence, Andrew interrupted him, grabbed him by the arm, and pulled him into the pantry. Safely inside, he pushed the door shut. "We'll have lots of time to talk but, right now, I just want to hold you and . . ."

Matthew needed no further explanation. He quickly embraced Andrew, remembering his familiar touch, the scent of his hair, the singular beauty of his face, and the taste of his kiss. "I've missed you more than I think you could ever imagine," he whispered, as he hugged Andrew tighter and tighter, as though he were afraid he might suddenly vanish into thin air.

Andrew pulled back slightly and stared into his eyes. "I'm glad," he said, "because I have a confession to make."

"What?" Matthew asked.

"I wasn't convinced that you were really coming back."

"Well, here I am."

"I hope you never have to leave again," Andrew said. "I just don't do well without you." He buried his face in Matthew's neck and clung to him.

"Hey . . . relax," Matthew said softly. He could feel Andrew tremble beneath him like a frightened puppy. "It's okay. I'm here." He gently rubbed his back, neck, and shoulders while he nuzzled his ear with moist lips.

Andrew pulled back slightly. With an intense gaze that could have easily seared Matthew's retinas, Andrew's face gradually softened into an intimate smile which rapidly grew to a grin. "Let's get out of here before the Gestapo find us," he said. "I wouldn't want that on your first day back."

"Okay, but . . . are you all right?" Matthew asked with genuine concern.

"Yeah, I'm fine," Andrew insisted. "Now let's get out of here."

"So—you're going on retreat?"

Andrew nodded. "For five days, no overnights. Father Gerald doesn't think it's a good idea for me to be alone at night at the Hermitage—at least, not yet."

Matthew smiled his familiar, lascivious grin. "I could probably come up with a solution," he said.

"Yeah," Andrew said sarcastically. "I'm sure you could, but I doubt that Father Gerald would approve." "Besides," he added, "I'll be back each night for supper."

"You mean I have to wait till then?"

"I guess. It's only a few hours from now."

Andrew rubbed his eyes. "Anything you want to say about what's going on with Ellen and the abbot before I go?"

Matthew shrugged and threw his hands in the air. "Other than the fact that I hate the bastard—not much. Ellen is still insisting that he is going to marry her, and they'll live happily ever after. My parents aren't as convinced. They have been in touch with a lawyer who is itching to file statutory rape charges, but Ellen won't let them. And Father Jude remains in Texas, sort of implying that he is considering marriage."

"Even though he's thirty years older than she is?"

"I think he'd do anything to avoid jail time," Matthew offered.

"What a mess," Andrew said. "I'm sorry all this happened."

"I know," Matthew replied. "I wasn't going to tell you, but my parents weren't all that crazy about my coming back to St. Anthony's because of the scandal, but I told them I was coming back anyway."

"I can't say that I blame them but, quite selfishly, I'm not sure what I would have done if you didn't," Andrew said.

Matthew put his arm around Andrew's shoulders. "It doesn't matter, because I'm here. So don't worry about it, and enjoy your time on retreat. Now get out in that truck, and I'll see you after supper."

"Yes, captain!" Andrew said with feigned rigidity and a smile. He grabbed a small cooler and walked toward the back door. Stopping suddenly, he turned to face Matthew. "I'm glad you're back," he whispered and then continued out the door and got into the truck.

Matthew watched through the window, until the truck rounded the corner and disappeared from sight.

* * *

The following two days for Matthew consisted primarily of meetings with Father Luke, Father Gerald, and, much to Matthew's surprise, Dr. Klein, Andrew's psychiatrist.

"I'm all right with this," Matthew insisted. "Just as long as I don't have to lay eyes on Father Jude."

"I think the likelihood of that is marginal," Father Luke said gravely. "Nevertheless, I need to be sure of what I can expect from you."

"Such as . . .," Brother Matthew retorted.

"Well, for example, the anger you seem to be expressing . . . even now," Father Luke said. He quickly raised his hand to interrupt Matthew. "And please understand, I think you have every right to be angry, yet while you are in this community, you need to abide by the Benedictine Rule, which means that you must show respect and subject yourself to the authority of the prior, who will be acting in place of the abbot for the time being."

"That's fine," Matthew said. "I apologize. Just bear with me for now, and I'll try to do my best."

"And that's the reason Dr. Klein is here," Father Luke said softly. "I'm not sure you've met him, but I believe you know that he is Andrew's doctor."

Matthew ran his hand over his face. "Yes, I do," he said.

"Nice to meet you, Brother Matthew," Dr. Klein said. He extended his hand toward Matthew, who politely reciprocated with a firm grip.

"Yes," Matthew replied. "It's nice to meet you after hearing so much about you." He paused slightly but then continued before Dr. Klein had the opportunity to speak. "Tell me, how is Andrew *really* doing?"

Father Luke immediately interceded. "That's not why Dr. Klein is here," he said brusquely.

Calmly, Dr. Klein was accepting of and unshaken by Matthew's question. "Thank you, Father Luke, but I don't mind responding." He looked squarely at Matthew. "Actually," he said, "I was hoping you might be able to give me your opinion."

Matthew's surprise was evident. "I . . . don't know," he stammered. "I just got back . . . and he left for retreat. He seems like he's doing okay." Having recovered somewhat, he continued in a bolder vein. "But being his psychiatrist, you would probably be in a better position to answer the question, don't you think?"

Father Luke leaned forward in his chair, obviously uncomfortable with Matthew's intentional chagrin.

"Clinically, yes," Dr. Klein said placidly. "But then, I see him only weekly. I don't live with him or . . ."

"Or sleep with him?" Matthew interjected.

"That's not necessary, Matthew," Father Gerald said quickly. "I don't believe that's what Dr. Klein meant."

"He knows it's true," Matthew persisted.

Dr. Klein motioned with both hands. "I do, in fact, but quite honestly, that wasn't the intention of my discussion. However, if you feel the need to talk about it, we can; that is, if Father Luke and Father Gerald are in agreement."

Father Luke's face took on a rosy glow, as he fidgeted with a paperclip on his desk. "Perhaps this may be a good time to excuse myself," he said. He abruptly stood up, nodded slightly to Dr. Klein and Father Gerald, and proceeded to leave his office.

The brief silence that followed served only to magnify the ticking of the mahogany wall clock, hanging like a time bomb, behind Father Luke's desk.

"I didn't mean to drive him out," Matthew said apologetically. "It just, stupidly, came out of my mouth."

Dr. Klein sat quietly as if carefully weighing his words. "Sometimes, Matthew, anger can make us do or say things we might later regret, something Father Luke alluded to earlier. It was Father Gerald who suggested I talk with you, and if you agree, we can talk about those things which you feel are important. I had hoped to talk about the situation involving your sister and Father Jude and its impact on you; however, I think you need to take some time, decide on whether it's the "right time" for you, and let Father Gerald know so he can call me." Unexpectedly, he quickly stood and, once again, offered his hand to Matthew. "It was nice to meet you. Please think it over."

Before he knew it, Matthew found himself sitting alone in Father Luke's office with nothing but the sound of the ticking clock and an empty, gnawing feeling deep within.

* * *

The week could not have been more perfect for Andrew's retreat at the hermitage. Clear blue skies with occasional clots of cumulus clouds and temperatures in the upper seventies made being outdoors imperative. On his fourth afternoon, Andrew, once again, found himself walking on the Alpine meadow, marveling at the spectacular vista while carrying his rusty scythe like Father Time, to ward off his most fearful predators—marauding bears. As much as he enjoyed the view from the farthest end of the field, he was always uncomfortably aware of the significant distance between himself and the protection of the hermitage and the narrowness of this jutting finger of land. Being eaten by a bear was no more palatable to him than jumping off the treacherous cliff, but then, he thought, 'why would a bear want to eat someone who was instantly overcome with diarrhea?' Even though he could feel the developing smile on his face, he was reminded of the seriousness of the situation, specifically the story of Father Edward, who was forced to make a hasty retreat up the stairs, across the deck, and into the safety of the Morgan cabin as a large black bear rapidly followed him up on the deck and peered inside through one of the glass sliders. Bears, he acknowledged bear watching.

Sitting on his favorite rock, Andrew removed a book from his backpack, a thin paperback entitled *Notes to Myself*, by Hugh Prather. He reread the following which he had previously underlined:

> *"One thing has become quite clear: all acquaintances are passing. Therefore, I want to make the most of every contact. I want to quickly get close to the people I meet because my experience has shown we won't be together long."*

As before, the passage evoked a certain sadness within him, which generally caused him to think about Matthew and their relationship. He wondered where it could possibly go and what would become of it, what would become of Matthew and even himself. The thought of ever having to live totally alone without him proved overwhelming, yet he would seldom dwell on it for fear of self-imploding and possible rehospitalization.

He gently closed the book and stared at the vast panorama before him. The seemingly endless expanse of jagged peaks remained fixed in silence against the softness of the sky—unchanged, slightly ominous, and, for most, insurmountable. For the very first time, he saw them quite differently and questioned whether mountains might, in fact, be simply another waste of space.

A trail of red dust rising from the road below suddenly caught his attention. This was soon followed by the unmistakable sound of a dirt bike fighting its way up the steep grade, as it roared and then decelerated only to once again pick up speed, as it tried to maintain momentum. Andrew quickly put his book in the backpack and ran with anticipation toward the hermitage. He knew only one person who would be crazy enough to challenge the mountain on a dirt bike and bold enough to interrupt a brother's retreat—Matthew.

By the time Andrew made it to the front of the hermitage, he could already see half of Matthew, leaning forward on the bike, partially hidden behind the slope, until he rounded the curve in full view and approached the flatter land, where he shifted up a gear and accelerated to nearly full throttle, directly toward him. He stopped with a slight skid, only inches from Andrew's leg, and turned off the engine.

Unflappable, Andrew stood firmly with crossed arms and a smile on his face. "I've said it many times: there are hospitals for guys like you."

"And every time you've said it, I've had to correct you; it's not for guys like 'you,' it's for guys like 'us,'" Matthew spouted. "Besides, that's a heck of a welcome for someone who nearly died trying to make it up here." He attempted to brush some of the red dust out of his eyes and off his forehead.

"You know that I'm very happy you're here," Andrew said, "just as long as Father Luke doesn't decide to pay me a visit."

"With what—the Volkswagen?" Matthew said with a laugh. "You've got the only four-wheel-drive vehicle already sitting up here next to the cabin."

"I never thought of that," Andrew said. "But you never know, old Luke may decide to take a walk up here."

"Yeah, right," Matthew said with a shrug. "You've been in the sun too long." He began to walk toward the hermitage.

"Maybe, so where are you going?"

Matthew called back over his shoulder. "Got to use the outhouse."

Andrew waited for him near the front of the cabin. When he saw Matthew come out, he called to him. "Let's walk to the end of the property. I left something down there."

Matthew ran toward him, obviously pleased with his successful ride and happy to be with Andrew in such a magnificent and isolated setting. "Don't tell me," Matthew taunted. "You left your Thomas Merton book on a rock near the cliff."

"Nope," Andrew said smugly.

"The New Testament?" Andrew persisted.

"Nope."

"Then, what?"

Andrew looked at him with a slight smile. "I don't want you to laugh," he said somberly.

"What? . . . I won't laugh, I promise."

"My scythe," Andrew said softly.

"Your what?" Matthew asked.

Andrew took a deep breath and said it louder. "My scythe, you know, the thing for cutting grass." He made a sweeping motion back and forth in front of him.

Matthew furled his forehead. "Wait a minute—you were whacking weeds near the edge of the cliff?"

"Not exactly," Andrew said.

"Then what?"

"Remember what I said about not laughing."

"I promise," Matthew reiterated.

Andrew stopped walking and faced him. "You know how I feel about bears . . . right?"

Matthew suddenly understood what Andrew was trying to tell him. "So you carry the scythe in the event a bear decides to take an interest in you."

"Yes," Andrew said seriously.

"You realize that a scythe wouldn't do much to stop an angry bear?"

"Maybe . . . maybe not," Andrew said. "Got any better ideas?"

Matthew paused. "I think I might," he said. "Didn't Brother Nathan do some welding up here?"

"I'm not sure," Andrew said.

"I remember seeing a small propane welding torch in the workshop. If there is fuel in the tank, all you would need is a reliable lighter to spark it. It can throw a good-sized flame. I doubt a bear would hang around long if he felt the burn or his fur caught on fire." Matthew laughed. "What a sight that would be."

Andrew laughed with him. "You're right—it might work. Just as long as I don't have to use it, because the thought of a bear burning to death as he runs across the mesa doesn't make me feel too comfortable."

"Well, I doubt it would ever happen because, if a bear attacked you, you'd probably pass out and set yourself on fire instead," Matthew joked. "But the torch just might make you feel a little more secure."

Andrew frowned. "Setting myself on fire?" he half whispered, as if a familiar chord had been struck.

"What?" Matthew asked.

"Oh . . . it's nothing; just thinking about Basil and Paul."

Matthew decided to let the comment slide.

They reached the end of the field where Andrew found his scythe. Little had changed with the panoramic view in front of them other than a gradual lengthening of the shadows across the mountains.

"There aren't too many places where you get a better view than this," Matthew remarked.

Andrew nodded. "It's beautiful. I love the mountains, but . . . I'm beginning to think they're not all that practical," he added.

"What do you mean?"

"I was thinking earlier, just before you drove up, that mountains are great, but the land isn't really all that usable."

Matthew tossed a small stone over the cliff to the road below. "Ski areas are happy with them," he said.

"Yeah, but that's only the lower mountains," Andrew said. "I'm thinking of the peaks out there—the ones that reach thirteen or fourteen thousand feet, not especially habitable."

Matthew looked at him with a vaguely prurient grin. "Did you ever consider that maybe, just maybe, you think too much?"

"Better than not at all," Andrew quipped.

"Now, hey . . . what is that supposed to mean?" Mathew asked indignantly.

"Nothing," Andrew said. "Just teasing you. Now, let's go get that welding torch."

The door to the tool shed opened with a groan, stretching spider webs like taut threads and then tearing them apart. Except for the opened door, a small grimy window above the workbench was the main source of light.

"Whew!" Matthew exclaimed brushing webs from his face. "It's warm in here." Once his eyes became accustomed to the dark, he searched the work area and found a functional flashlight. "What do you know—it works," he said, as he played the light over the area in front of him. Suddenly, he stopped. "And there it is." He directed the light at a cylindrical blue canister which had a long brass tube connected to it. "The welding torch." He picked it up, shook it gently, and slowly opened the valve. A strong hissing sound emanated from the container. "And it has fuel in it."

"I'm surprised it hasn't exploded in here from the heat," Andrew said.

"Me too," Matthew admitted. "It is warm." He carefully set the torch and the flashlight on the workbench and, unexpectedly, pulled off his T-shirt and faced Andrew. "Come here," he insisted. "I've missed you."

Andrew sensed the emotional chemistry of the heated tool shed from the moment he followed Matthew inside. He eagerly moved toward him, wrapped his arms around Matthew's sweaty back, and kissed him aggressively, as if, again, for the first time, while Matthew ran his hands down Andrew's back, over his buttocks and, then forward, over his growing erection. He could feel him struggle slightly with the button on his jeans and then quickly unzip them.

With both hands, Matthew slipped Andrew's jeans and underwear down below his knees. "You feel so good," Matthew said, while continuing to kiss him. He pulled Andrew's shirt over his head and set it on top of his on the workbench. With gentle kisses and tolerably painful bites, Matthew worked his way down Andrew's chest, over his stomach and, finally, took his penis into his mouth while kneeling in front of him.

Andrew placed both hands on top of Matthew's head. "Go easy," he whispered. "I feel like I could explode."

Momentarily gratified, Andrew sighed with content. He lifted Matthew's face so that he could look at him. "Why don't we get out of here and go into the hermitage. The bed would be a lot more comfortable."

Matthew looked surprised. "You don't mind . . . going in there?"

"Not really," Andrew said with a smile. "I'll just take the crucifix down from above the bed and put it in a drawer.

"All right," Matthew said enthusiastically. "Let's go."

Half clothed, they walked briskly into the coolness of the hermitage with its expansive glass windows and roughly hewn, weathered wood interior. Andrew led the way up the narrow staircase to the second floor, where a small bedroom overlooked part of the first floor sitting room. An arch of stained glass from the floor below continued up to the ceiling of the bedroom, through which the entire entrance to the hermitage could be seen. A single platform bed sat in one corner, facing the window, beneath the sloped ceiling.

Andrew pulled back the light quilt cover and blanket, exposing pale blue sheets. He sat on a corner of the bed to remove his shoes; however, Matthew wasted no time.

Without a word, he dropped his jeans and underwear and, hovering over Andrew, he grabbed Andrew's head and forced his face into his heated groin, against his semi-flaccid erection. "I think it's your turn," he said seductively, as he thrust himself against Andrew's mouth.

Andrew paused briefly and glared at him. "It's not 'a turn,' Matt. It's because I want to," he said softly but resolutely and then resumed his attention to Matthew's renewed erection.

Aware of his faux pas, Matthew removed himself and knelt in front of Andrew. He wrapped his arms around him and held him tight.

But before he could respond, Andrew spoke. "It's okay. You don't even have to say anything. I just wanted you to know that I was aware of something that made me uncomfortable and takes away from our relationship. I want us to enjoy this time together."

Matthew pulled away slightly and looked directly at him. "I love you," he whispered.

"I know," Andrew said genuinely. "So now, let's simply show each other that we do."

The awkwardness of the moment slowly melted away as the reconciled partners began to seek each other's body in the protective warmth of the loft bedroom. Droplets of sweat beaded on their overheated skin, adding a mild taste of salinity to their exploring lips and tongues, while hands caressed everything within reach, sometimes probing or massaging but always expressing the same message of love through touch.

After what seemed to be an all too short eternity, Andrew realized that he was dangerously close to ejaculating. He slowly rolled onto his back, grabbed Matthew by the arms, and encouraged him to lie next to him where he could, once again, see his face, kiss his eyes and lips and feel the coldness of his nose as it brushed against his cheek.

"I love the way you make me feel," Andrew whispered as he stared into Matthew's eyes. "It's as though, as long as you're with me, the whole world could disintegrate and it wouldn't matter—I feel . . . safe."

In the silence, Matthew held him even tighter and thought he could feel Andrew tremble once or twice, as he gently massaged his back and neck while inhaling the heated chestnut scent of his hair.

Separating himself slightly, Andrew placed both hands on Matthew's face. After a lengthy interval of intense eye contact, he forced Matthew's mouth against his, kissing him passionately, exploring his mouth with aggressive affection, until Matthew found it necessary to break away.

"Easy . . .," he whispered with a smile. "We have lots of time, and I'm not going anywhere."

Without responding, Andrew slowly edged his way toward the foot of the bed, kissing and licking Matthew's chest and stomach, until he could feel Matthew's erection nudge him firmly under his chin. When Matthew began to move in unison against him, Andrew understood the message and eventually allowed Matthew to slip his erection into the moist warmth of his mouth.

Straining, with his back and neck arched, Matthew was barely able to let Andrew know that he was about to ejaculate. "I can't hold back . . .," he said softly. He could feel Andrew nod, and when he heard him say, "okay," Matthew gratefully thrust once more and immediately reached orgasm, exploding forcefully with Andrew's eager consent.

Reluctantly, Matthew carefully backed away. He positioned himself alongside of Andrew and, lying on his side, caressed his chest and stomach and then ran his fingers over his face and through his hair. "You have no idea how much you mean to me," he whispered. Bending slightly, he kissed Andrew gently. "You okay?" he asked cautiously.

Andrew smiled and nodded. "Never been better," he said as he rolled toward Matthew, wrapped his arms around him and pulled him on top of him. He looked up into Matthew's eyes. "Was it okay?"

Matthew replied with quiet laughter. "You've got to be kidding . . . it was fantastic." He dropped himself fully onto Andrew and kissed him deeply, experiencing the residual salinity and sweetness of his own semen. "I'd forgotten what I taste like," he said with a smile. "Not bad."

"You barely had an appetizer," Andrew quipped. "I had the entire entrée, two desserts, and I can tell you, it was scrumptious. You've been eating more apples."

"Wow. You have discriminating taste buds; I usually eat two, sometimes three a day—maybe I'm part horse."

Andrew laughed. "Yeah, and I can tell you which part."

Matthew glanced down at Andrew. "Like you should talk."

Andrew grew more pensive. "I know you're going to think this is weird, Matt, but when we do this, I sort of feel that a part of you somehow becomes a part of me."

"That's not really so weird," Matthew explained. "Look at what gets said every day at mass, over communion, during the 'voodoo' transubstantiation." He irreverently raised both hands over his head and said, "Take this bread and eat of me . . . blah, blah, blah."

"Okay, I get the picture," Andrew scoffed. "Don't wreck my delusion."

Matthew smiled salaciously. "Believe me; I'd be happy to feed that delusion anytime you wanted."

"Oh, yeah?" Andrew taunted.

Matthew did not require any additional prompting. He fell onto Andrew and kissed him with feral intensity, biting his lips and ears, licking his neck and face, and then returned to the familiar taste of his eager mouth. Repositioning himself, Matthew could feel Andrew's erection beneath him, jabbing him in the stomach, and suddenly, he decided to attempt what he had always wanted from Andrew, a desire previously designated as unacceptable or off-limits. While still kissing Andrew, he discreetly moistened his fingers with saliva and carefully rubbed a sufficient quantity of the lubricant deep within. He then straddled Andrew, reached behind him, and stroked Andrew's penis, while he slowly massaged his own newly emerging erection.

"You look so incredibly sexy from here," Andrew said as he stared up at Matthew.

Matthew spit into his hand. "Good," he said, "because you're the one who makes me feel this way." He immediately grabbed Andrew's erection and rubbed the saliva over its slippery head.

Bolstered by the increased sensitivity of Matthew's saliva, Andrew closed his eyes and lost himself in the infinitely pleasurable stroking of Matthew's touch. Within moments, he began to slowly thrust himself against Matthew's hand.

'It's now or never,' Matthew thought, as he carefully raised and repositioned himself directly above Andrew's straining erection. With one quick yet painful move, Matthew lowered himself, and while guiding Andrew's erection with one hand, he plunged the head of the penis beyond the tight muscle, into the deeper warmth. In silence, he sat motionless, waiting for the pain to subside.

Within seconds, Andrew was suddenly aware of the situation—his eyes as big as half dollars—as he raised himself on his elbows. "What the hell are you doing?" he shouted in a barely restrained voice. He could see that Matthew had taken nearly half of his penis deep inside.

"Relax, please," Matthew encouraged. "Count to ten and tell me if it doesn't feel great."

Although he knew that Matthew was right—it did feel incredibly sensual—he refused to participate in an act which, he felt, violated an earlier agreement they had both made regarding intercourse. "It's just not right—not here," Andrew said angrily. "Remember," he added, "no fucking. Now, please get off me."

Matthew knew that it was uncharacteristic for Andrew to resort to guttural language, and in doing so, he knew that he was in trouble. "But you've already . . ."

"What?" Andrew shot back.

At this point, Matthew realized he had said too much, and he was left no choice but to comply. "Nothing," he said. Cautiously, he raised himself off Andrew.

"Please," Andrew said quickly. "Don't say anything—just make me come."

And he did. Matthew used every skill he knew to please Andrew; he lovingly used his mouth, first, to renew Andrew's flailing erection and, secondly, to devote such attention to it that within minutes, Andrew reached an intense orgasm which Matthew accepted willingly, yet more in the spirit of a mortally wounded warrior.

A silent, sudden chill seemed to sweep through the heated, stagnant air in the loft. And although neither expressed it nor would ever admit—whatever the reason—both began to wonder if this, in fact, might be the beginning of the end of their physical relationship.

Matthew immediately began dressing. Half finished, he turned to look at Andrew who had pulled the sheet up to his waist. "I'm sorry," he said. His voice was laden with regret.

"I know you are, and so am I," Andrew replied.

When he was completely dressed, he sat on the edge of the bed and looked at Andrew. His insides felt heavy, as much as his heart felt torn. "Sometimes, I guess we just need different things," he said.

Andrew nodded. "Maybe . . ."

"Yeah, well . . . I know you have this thing about us having intercourse, and I respect it, but I can't say that I really understand it," Matthew said awkwardly.

Andrew sat up and pulled his knees to his chest. "I can't explain it exactly, Matt, but it just isn't right for us to be doing that here."

"What's the difference? We do pretty much everything else."

"Yes, but that doesn't make it right," Andrew answered. "Is it really that important to you?"

Matthew could tell by the tone of his voice that Andrew was getting upset. He shrugged. "I don't know—maybe it is."

"Really?"

"Yeah, really," Matthew jeered.

"Then, hell, let's do it. Let me fuck you," Andrew said crudely. He threw off the sheet and pulled Matthew toward him.

"Stop it, Andrew," Matthew insisted.

"No, I'm serious, I want to fuck you."

"You already have!" Matthew shouted.

Suddenly, the silence was nearly palpable. Andrew pulled up the sheet and leaned against the wall while Matthew remained sitting on the edge of the bed, staring at the floor.

"I'm sorry, I didn't mean to say that," Matthew said quietly.

"No . . . tell me about it," Andrew insisted.

"Look . . . I don't want us to argue anymore."

"Okay," Andrew said. "We won't argue. Just tell me what you mean."

Matthew shook his head and covered his face with both hands. "I don't think I can," he said. "You will hate me even more." In that instant, he knew that he had caused irreparable harm to their relationship, especially to Andrew, who did not deserve to hear what he was about to tell him.

Andrew leaned forward and placed his hand on Matthew's shoulder. "I promise, I don't hate you—I couldn't—and I won't argue."

"Oh, shit," Matthew began.

Andrew could feel him tremble. "It's okay. Tell me."

Matthew took a deep breath. "It happened last summer, in my room. You came to visit me. It was hot, and we took off our clothes. Well, after you helped me ejaculate, I was massaging you, and before I knew it, you were out like a light. I finally realized that you must've taken your medication, but I kept on rubbing you—all over—and you popped this fantastic hard-on. I rubbed it more, sucked on it forever, but you didn't come, so I decided, what the hell. I used some lubricant on myself, straddled you, and took you up my butt. Once I got comfortable, the pleasure was unbelievable. And you seemed to be responding to my up-and-down movement, almost as if you were dreaming, which, you, most likely, were. Then you actually began to thrust yourself into me, and when you came, it was like fireworks for me. I shot all over your chest. Afterwards, I cleaned you up and lay alongside of you; you slept for two hours." He cautiously turned to look at Andrew. "I'm sorry, Andrew. I know I shouldn't have done it, and I should've told you."

Andrew lay back, unknowingly, in a fetal position. "It's okay," he said softly. "I think I just want to be left alone right now."

"All right," Matthew stammered. "I'll see you back at the monastery."

Andrew vaguely remembered hearing the dirt bike start and begin its descent down the dangerous mountain road.

Chapter Twenty-Nine

Imminent Decompensation

That same evening, just before dusk, Father Gerald noticed that Andrew had not returned from the hermitage, and the four-wheel-drive pickup was also conspicuously absent. Alarmed, he notified Father Luke, who agreed that the situation was potentially serious, particularly with the arrival of nightfall.

"We really don't have any other way to get up there," Father Luke said pensively.

Father Gerald began to pace. "I've got an idea. What if we call Eric Holtz? Maybe he would drive me up there."

Father Luke picked up the phone before Father Gerald finished his sentence. He dialed and waited nervously. "Eric, hello. I'm sorry to bother you, but I'm wondering if you could do us a favor. We may have a serious situation on our hands and will need to get up to the hermitage as quickly as possible. Would you be able to drive over and pick up Father Gerald? He'll explain when you get here."

Within minutes, Eric's four-wheeler roared around the corner of the monastery and stopped in back of the kitchen where Father Gerald was already waiting in the parking lot, clutching his leather satchel, in the event they might need to use it.

"What's going on?" Eric shouted.

Father Gerald jumped into the passenger seat and buckled himself in. "I'll explain on the way," he said abruptly. "Right now, drive as fast and as safely as possible, if that makes any sense."

"You got it," Eric said. He nearly flew down the gravel road, dodging potholes, as Father Gerald clung to his seat and hoped that some unsuspecting visitor, late for Compline, would not be driving toward them. Safely on the paved road, Eric attempted once again to get some information from his visibly distraught passenger.

"It's Andrew, isn't it," Eric inquired.

Father Gerald nodded. "How did you know?"

Eric shrugged his shoulders, and then downshifted as they approached a steep grade. "I don't know—just a hunch, I guess, based on the little bit I've heard about his . . . his emotional problems." It was clear that Eric felt uncomfortable discussing the secondhand information.

"It's true," Father Gerald admitted. "He's gone through a lot since he's been here, and yes, he does experience recurrent symptoms of a significant mental illness." He rubbed his face and yawned. "I just hope he's safe."

"He was on retreat?" Eric asked.

"Yes, but only during the day. He was supposed to drive back to the monastery each evening for dinner."

"And he hasn't shown up yet?"

"Unfortunately, no," Father Gerald said guardedly. "It's not like him to be late."

"Could be he just fell asleep and lost track of time," Eric added.

"I hope that's the case," Father Gerald said with reservation.

By now, they had reached the steepest climb to the summit. Eric slowed the truck considerably, shifted into four-wheel low, and expertly guided the vehicle up and over the deeply rutted road. "Maybe in the spring, we should try to get the backhoe up here and dump a couple of loads of gravel," he said with a strained voice, as he clutched the wheel with both hands. "It's beginning to look like a mine field."

Just then, a front tire plowed into one of the ruts and promptly shot out of it, jostling the truck like a bucking bronco and banging Father Gerald's head against the back window.

"Case in point," Father Gerald said as he rubbed the sore spot.

"You all right?" Eric asked.

"Oh, perhaps a bit dumber," Father Gerald said with a smile.

"Well, the worst part is over," Eric said with relief. "As soon as I make this corner, we should see the hermitage."

Within moments, the hermitage was, in fact, within view. And parked alongside was the monastery's grey pickup, a hopeful yet still ominous sight for Father Gerald, who already had his hand on the door handle and was ready to exit the vehicle before it stopped.

"I hope he's all right," he said anxiously, and then jumped from the truck while it was still moving forward.

Once inside the hermitage, Father Gerald called out, hoping that Andrew would be asleep in the upstairs bedroom. When he got no response, both men walked up the narrow stairs, scanned the empty loft, and returned to the first floor.

Father Gerald was obviously shaken. "I don't like the looks of this," he said quietly. "Check the outhouse, and I'll check the workshop and the area in between."

Fear that Andrew may have committed suicide racked Father Gerald's brain with genuine trepidation. When he reached the door to the old shed, his heart began to race even faster. He could see that it had not been properly closed, and it appeared to have been recently opened, judging from the freshly scraped arc on the muddy threshold. He took a deep breath, grabbed the brass knob, and aggressively threw open the door, yet much to his surprise, the shed was empty. A blue welding torch sat conspicuously in the middle of the workbench.

"Anything, yet?" Eric asked from outside the workshop.

Father Gerald was startled by his untimely inquiry. "Other than the heart attack you nearly caused me—no. No sign of him."

"I'm sorry," Eric said. "There was nothing in or around the outhouse."

They left the workshop, while Father Gerald made sure to pull the door tight.

"Well, only one other area," Father Gerald said. "Let's check the mesa. I hope to God he didn't slip off the cliff."

"No way," Eric commented.

With the light rapidly fading, their vision became difficult.

"Wait a second," Eric said. "I'll get my flashlight from the truck."

They walked in silence through knee-high grass, as Eric played the beam judiciously over the sloping meadow.

"I doubt he'd be out here," Father Gerald said quietly.

"Why's that?" Eric asked.

"Andrew has a mortal fear of bears," Father Gerald explained.

Eric laughed. "I haven't seen or heard of a bear being around here in years."

"Yes, but to someone who is petrified of them, rational explanations aren't that helpful."

"Yeah, well, I suppose you're right."

Suddenly, Father Gerald stopped; he stuck out his arm to discourage Eric from taking another step. After a short pause to listen, he spoke. "Do you hear that?" he whispered.

Eric seemed to raise his head slightly and freeze in midstep, much like a pointer who scented his prey. "Yeah," he whispered. "What the hell is it?" Perhaps it was the threat of imminent danger that made him forget himself and use a mild expletive in the presence of Father Gerald; however, neither paid much attention.

"It sounds like . . . whipping . . . like someone being whipped." Father Gerald said with bewilderment. "Hand me the light."

Father Gerald directed the light to his right toward the bizarre sound, moving it slowly back and forth above the level of the grass. After a minute of searching, the light finally illuminated the unnatural spectacle. Forty feet away, near the edge of the cliff, Andrew stood, completely naked, rhythmically beating himself with a willow switch as rivulets of blood streaked his body like macabre war paint.

"God help us!" Father Gerald whispered in total disbelief. He turned toward Eric. "I'll try to talk to him—could you hurry back to the hermitage and pull a sheet off the bed and get back here as quickly as possible?"

"Sure," Eric stammered. " . . . you gonna be okay?"

"I hope so."

Eric turned to go and then stopped. "You want me to bring the truck down?"

"Not all the way—about three quarters . . . and no lights. Oh, and bring my leather case down."

"You got it."

Father Gerald took a deep breath and wished wholeheartedly that Dr. Klein were with him to help him respond properly to this emotional maelstrom. Without moving toward him, he spoke softly to Andrew. "It's me, Father Gerald, Andrew," he said and, momentarily, turned the flashlight on himself to help identify his presence. "You're going to be all right. There is no need for you to continue to whip yourself. Please, throw away the willow branch."

In a daze, Andrew looked up and ceased his self-flagellation. "I'm not worthy," he uttered, " . . . not worthy."

Father Gerald's immediate concern was Andrew's close proximity to the cliff. "It's okay," he said. "Not many of us are worthy, *especially* me. There is no need to continually punish ourselves, physically or emotionally; life itself is hard enough. Do you understand me?"

Andrew cocked his head slightly and squinted. "Who are you?" he asked.

Stretching out his arm, Father Gerald, once again, held the light on himself. "It's Father Gerald, Andrew. Can you see me? You are welcome to move toward me. I'll stay right here."

With measured relief, he could hear Andrew approach. He slowly lowered the light toward the ground, and as soon as his eyes became adjusted to the darkness, he saw him standing less than ten feet away. "Say my name," Father Gerald instructed.

"Father . . . Gerald," Andrew said.

"Good. Now, you no longer need the branch; you can throw it away."

Andrew let the branch fall from his hand.

Father Gerald then watched, helplessly, as Andrew contorted his face and began to scream and sob at the same time.

"What's happening to me?" he yelled repeatedly, until he collapsed to his knees, heaving, in a fetal position in the tall grass.

Hearing footsteps behind him, Father Gerald turned to see Eric approaching with a sheet and his leather medical bag. "Thanks," he said hurriedly. "If you can hold this light for a second, I'm going to see if I can give him something to relax him."

"No problem," Eric said. He glanced down at Andrew, who continued to sob uncontrollably. "This is really sad," he whispered.

After squirting the excess medication out of the syringe, Father Gerald carefully recapped the needle and tore open an alcohol pad. "And if you would hold this for a second, I'll try to get the sheet around him."

Father Gerald walked slowly toward Andrew. "Can you hear me, Andrew?" he said softly.

When there was no response, he tried again, this time a bit louder. "Andrew, can you hear me?"

Finally, Andrew nodded.

"Good," Father Gerald said. "I'd like to wrap this sheet around you to help keep you warm. Is that all right?"

Once again, Andrew barely nodded.

Father Gerald gently draped the sheet over him, leaving his head and shoulders exposed. He squatted alongside of him. "I'm going to give you a shot to help you feel better. Do you understand me?"

Andrew nodded.

"Okay. Now try to stay still," Father Gerald encouraged. "It's going into your buttocks so try to relax."

He glanced up at Eric. "Would you mind steadying his legs in case he kicks?"

"No problem," Eric said as he knelt over Andrew.

Andrew flinched momentarily and then slowly relaxed.

"I think you'll start to feel a lot better very soon, Andrew," Father Gerald said.

It was not long before the sobbing stopped and Andrew appeared calmer.

"How are you feeling?" Father Gerald asked.

"Tired," Andrew slurred through a dry mouth.

"Before you get even more tired, Eric and I are going to help you to your feet and walk you to the truck, so we can drive you back to the monastery, okay?"

Andrew simply nodded and made a feeble attempt to stand but slipped back to the ground.

"Let's get on either side of him," Eric suggested.

Once they had him on his feet and covered him partially with the sheet, it was still difficult to walk him, as he was unable to provide any support.

"Sort of like a big sack of potatoes," Eric commented.

Father Gerald was already exhausted. "Maybe we would be better off if you pulled the truck all the way down," he said.

"Good idea," Eric agreed.

Within moments, Eric carefully parked the truck next to Andrew, yet their efforts to get him to walk were unsuccessful and prompted Eric to act independently.

"I've got an idea," he said. "Open the passenger side door. I think I can pick him up and put him in the truck."

"You sure?"

"Yeah, let's go for it."

Father Gerald opened the door as Eric hovered over Andrew, put his arms under his knees and back, and, with difficulty, managed to struggle to his feet.

"Hey, Eric," Andrew mumbled.

"Hi, buddy," Eric said. "I'm going to set you in the truck, so just hang in there."

Andrew nodded slightly and then let his head fall against Eric's chest.

When they were safely in the vehicle, Father Gerald began to question whether Andrew should be returned to the monastery without psychiatric follow-up, including a blood screen to rule out a conceivable drug overdose.

"Are you in a real big hurry?" he asked Eric.

"No, not at all," Eric answered. "What do you need?"

"I'm thinking of taking Andrew directly to the Halsen Clinic rather than the monastery," he said. "Would you have time for that?"

"Of course," Eric said. "Just as long as you tell me how to get there."

"Thanks," Father Gerald said. "I think it's the wiser thing to do."

Meanwhile, Andrew continued to doze against Father Gerald's shoulder, even when the truck bucked and lurched during its hazardous descent.

* * *

When he awoke the next morning, Andrew immediately recognized the pastel surroundings of the clinic. An attendant wearing a white lab coat rapped gently on the opened door, entered, and set a breakfast tray on the table next to Andrew's bed.

"Good morning," he said cordially. "I hope you're hungry because our chef, Bernard, makes great French toast."

Andrew attempted to be polite, but the best response he could muster was a strained smile which barely separated his lips. He watched as the dark-haired attendant prepared his tray—selflessly, with tremendous attention to detail, even unfolding the linen napkin and placing it on Andrew's chest.

"I'll raise the head of the bed, slide the bed table over, and you should be all set," he said. "If you need anything, hit the buzzer—my name is Kurt," he said with a smile and then quickly left the room.

Although he did not feel especially hungry, Andrew tasted the French toast and agreed that Kurt was right. It was deliciously flavored with some unusual spices, most conspicuously, the rind of mandarin orange. In no time, he devoured three of the four slices while ruminating on the attendant, specifically, why he would want the job he was doing, and conversely, he supposed that Kurt might have the same curiosity about him.

Andrew moved the tray aside, just as Dr. Klein entered the room without a knock.

"Hello, Andrew," he said disarmingly. "How was breakfast?"

Andrew wiped his mouth with the napkin. "Very good," he said. He laid his head back against the pillow and looked at Dr. Klein. "So . . . what happened to me this time?" he asked; his voice was thick with disappointment.

Dr. Klein removed his glasses and set them on the table. "I was hoping you could tell me," he said softly. "What do you remember?"

Andrew rubbed his eyes. "I'm not sure," he said.

"Did you have any visitors?" Dr. Klein asked bluntly.

"No . . . why?" Andrew responded unconvincingly.

"I was wondering if Matthew came up there and if anything upset you," he said. "Someone said they thought they saw him on a motorbike, driving toward the hermitage."

Andrew shifted his position to lie on his side. "Can we discuss something else?" he insisted. "I don't want to talk about it right now."

"All right," Dr. Klein said. "What are you willing to tell me about last night?"

Andrew hesitated. "I remember feeling depressed, like I was being swallowed by a black hole, and the feeling just kept getting worse. So I took some medication . . . I can't remember, but I may have taken more medication later."

Dr. Klein approached even closer. "That's the part that concerns me the most," he said. "We did a tox-screen, Andrew. The medication in your bloodstream was near overdose level." He pulled up a chair and sat down, leveling their eye contact. "What we seriously need to determine is whether it was accidental or intentional—I need you to tell me the truth."

His somber demeanor seemed to strike a chord with Andrew who raised his head and supported it with his arm and elbow. "I don't think it was intentional," he said quietly.

"I took the first dose, washed it down with a can of beer, and vaguely remember taking more pills."

"You know that you are not supposed to use alcohol with your meds," Dr. Klein admonished. "It intensifies the strength and probably helps to justify the high level of toxicity."

"I know," Andrew said softly. He rolled onto his back and stared at the glaring white ceiling. "I just wanted the pain to go away as quickly as possible," he said with a struggle.

Uncharacteristically, Dr. Klein reached out, placed his hand on Andrew's forehead, and pushed his hair back, away from his eyes. "I'll get you through this," he said, "but I'll need all the help you can give me."

"I understand," Andrew said.

"We'll also discuss the specifics of why you felt the need to whip yourself with the willow branch—it's a behavior I can help you change if you'll meet me half way," Dr. Klein suggested. "Otherwise, the source of those unchecked behaviors can have devastating effects."

Andrew appeared concerned. "Am I beyond that point?" he asked cautiously.

Dr. Klein smiled. "Not even close—but that doesn't mean we don't have some work to do." He sat back in his chair, momentarily pensive, as he considered sharing a story with Andrew.

"I recently read a disturbing story in a British publication that you may or may not find interesting. It seems as though several monks in one particular monastery were suddenly and inexplicably being plagued with visual problems, potentially devastating symptoms which, for most, resulted in blindness. After a lengthy investigation, it was concluded that it was a result of the monks' own behaviors."

Andrew quickly interrupted. "Please don't tell me it's true what they say about masturbation . . ."

Dr. Klein shook his head and smiled. "No, not at all. It turned out that more than one of the monks learned that if they applied constant pressure by continuously rubbing their eyes—I mean vigorously—it would produce significant pressure on the retina and cause them to have visual hallucinations, which they apparently felt was a positive addition to their meditation. They were totally unaware of the horrific results."

Andrew appeared amazed. "That actually happened?"

"Yes," Dr. Klein said. "As I mentioned, it was just published by a British medical journal."

"Wow," Andrew commented.

Dr. Klein stood and prepared to leave. "I want you to know that we will get you through this, as dark as things may appear right now. But keep in mind—behaviors have consequences."

* * *

After approximately one week at the clinic, Andrew returned to the monastery, following Dr. Klein's approval and Andrew's promise to strictly adhere to the proper medication routine and to keep all of his weekly therapy appointments as scheduled.

Almost as if he had never left, he resumed his life at the monastery, working, praying and, as always, sublimating the eternal questions, fears, and desires that constantly plagued his meditation and most of his daydreaming, which, quite often, became indistinguishable.

Nevertheless, he attempted to renew his prayer life with genuine commitment by meditating longer and by finally admitting, in supplication, his aspirations and honest intentions regarding his feelings toward Matthew, even though he felt that their relationship was now in serious jeopardy. "No apologies, Lord," he prayed. "I've loved honestly and wholeheartedly one of your own, and if I'm guilty of anything, perhaps I'm guilty of loving too much. As you know, I've suffered and continue to suffer. Like your own son, I expect that you will do with me what you will."

It may have been a prophetic prayer or, perhaps, a genuine cry for help, yet Andrew had no way of knowing what fate would bring and, least of all, whether his loving God would wantonly script and allow such a brutal tragedy.

* * *

The August sun reflected harshly off the irrigation ditch as Andrew made his final cutouts and watched as the water seeped into the parched soil. In the calm, clear liquid, he could see the eerie bottom of the ditch and was suddenly reminded of all the time he spent floating on his inflatable raft in the crystal waters of the Adirondacks. Lying on his stomach, he would hang his head over the front of the raft and watch as bizarre rocks and boulders of various colors would pass beneath him like inhospitable monsters waiting for their next victim. Sometimes, he would see his own face, reflected on the water, and would shudder at the thought of possibly seeing a milky-white corpse staring back at him from below.

Distracted by the sound of an automobile on the gravel road, Andrew could barely see what looked like Rebecca Storrow's white convertible approach the monastery. It stopped far short of the front entrance, yet Andrew was quite sure that the passenger who got out and walked quickly up the steps was Matthew.

Regardless of the irreversible status of his relationship with him, Andrew could feel his heart sink at the thought of what used to be and what could, most likely, be again, if only he would physically provide all that Matthew required. Yet for Andrew, the enigma remained; what did Matthew truly expect to get from Rebecca Storrow—a beautiful woman but, nevertheless, a woman.

That same evening, after Vespers, Andrew returned to his cell to shed his habit amid the stagnant August heat when, unexpectedly, he heard a familiar rap on his door.

"You feel like taking a walk?" Matthew asked softly. He stood in the open doorway wearing baggy jeans and an oversized T-shirt; his blond hair scattered carelessly across his forehead.

"Yeah, why not," Andrew said casually. "It's too hot to stay in here."

Rather than take their usual walk on the road, Matthew assertively led the way out the back of the monastery, through the scrub sage toward the shade of the Aspen grove, near the Moreland Mesa. "I thought it would be a bit cooler back here," Matthew said as he wiped his forehead with the back of his arm.

"At least there's some shade," Andrew said.

Yet both knew that this particular place was redolent with memories of past sexual occurrences, whether together or alone; in fact, the very scent of its musky dampness stirred in Andrew a conflicting desire to rekindle what once was simply assumed. 'I can't let this happen,' he thought. 'I can't.'

Matthew seemed to be walking directly toward the secluded area of the ditch where they once swam naked in the cold water. "I'm sorry about what happened to you at the hermitage," Matthew said directly. "I had no idea you would end up in the clinic."

Andrew laughed nervously. "Yeah, neither did I."

Matthew plopped himself down on the edge of the ditch. He removed his sneakers and socks and let his feet dangle in the icy water but quickly withdrew them. "Way too cold," he said, clutching his knees. "I'll have to do this gradually."

"Can you believe we swam in here?" Andrew remarked with a detectable touch of nostalgia. He sat down next to Matthew.

"I wouldn't exactly call it swimming," Matthew said. "It was more like jump in—go under—get out."

"I thought my insides would freeze," Andrew joked. He stared at the surface of the water; however, he was able to look beyond it and see the rocky bottom, as a slight shiver ran through his chest and arms.

Matthew turned to look at him. "Father Luke and Father Gerald both spoke with me about the hermitage and what happened to you," he said guardedly.

Anticipating Matthew's question, Andrew quickly responded. "I said you were never there." The level of composure in his delivery surprised himself.

"I sort of figured you would," Matthew said with relief. "Thanks."

"It's okay," Andrew said.

"So . . . what happened?"

Andrew turned to look at him with a vacuous stare. "What do you mean?" he asked.

"I mean . . . finding you naked—on the mesa near the cliff."

Andrew shrugged. "Symptoms, I guess. The illness must have been triggered."

"By what?" Matthew asked.

Andrew's stare grew more intense. "You really don't know?"

"No, not really."

"Well, it doesn't matter," Andrew said quietly.

Matthew slumped back against the verdant rise. "It must be the sexual stuff, right?" he said.

"Right," Andrew replied anxiously. He watched in silence as a bloated dead mouse drifted slowly past and out of sight.

"Was it because I had sex with you in my room, when you were half drugged on medication?"

"That's a part of it, I guess," Andrew said. He removed his sneakers and tested the frigid water. "You're right—it's freezing."

Matthew rolled on his side to face him. "I'm sorry I did it," he said honestly, "but I have to admit, it felt incredible to have you inside me."

Andrew cringed. "And so you tried it again at the hermitage, knowing how I feel about it," he said. "I just don't understand you."

"Maybe I don't understand myself," Matthew mumbled. He sat up and leaned over the water.

Andrew rubbed his eyes with one hand. "What was so difficult with this relationship?" he asked. "Was it because I gave in to having oral sex that you thought I would probably give in to having anal sex?"

"I don't know," Matthew said, even though he knew that Andrew was right.

"Because it seems as though, when we're together, you are not completely satisfied until you have that damn altar candle up your butt and, quite honestly, it makes me feel a bit uncomfortable, if not guilty." Andrew admitted.

Matthew splashed his feet in the water as if to drown out what he was hearing. "What can I say," he said somewhat defensively. "It's something

I enjoy; at least I'm honest about it. Who knows . . . you might like it if you tried it."

Andrew shook his head. "That's not the point, Matt," he said. "We're monks, remember? And in my mind, blatant intercourse is the last line to cross which, for me, would totally debase my vocation and my reason for being here."

Matthew turned and stared directly into Andrew's eyes. "Then maybe we should leave . . . together," he said, softly yet with conviction.

"You're serious, aren't you?" Andrew said.

"Yes," Matthew replied.

A silence followed as Andrew gazed into the distance and saw nothing. Instead, he could hear only his hidden fears and thoughts as they surfaced and became real. He looked at Matthew. "You have no idea how often I've had this imaginary conversation with you, and now, how much I'm dreading its actual existence."

"Why?" Matthew asked. "Just say, yes—you'll leave."

"Come on, Matt," Andrew implored. "You know I don't want to do that."

"Does that mean you won't?"

Andrew nodded. "Yes. Too much of me is invested here, even if where we are isn't perfect."

"You mean to say that after all the Häagen-Dazs, the Perrier, our less than simple lifestyle, and the scandals, like the abbot screwing my sister—you still have a reason to stay here?" Matthew asked.

"I feel very bad for Ellen, for you, and your family," Andrew said, "but Father Jude is gone and maybe, just maybe, this place will start to shape up, and you and I can be a part of it."

Although an olive branch, of sorts, was offered, Matthew had no intention of reaching out and accepting it. "You're either a much better man than I am or a heck of a lot more stubborn," he said. "I'd probably go with the first one," he added with a smile.

Andrew tossed small pebbles into the slow flowing stream and watched as the ripples spread in concentric circles to either side of the ditch, while water bugs skated over the disturbance with remarkable adroitness. He knew the finality that he dreaded was imminent. He spoke with hesitation. "So . . . what happens next?" he asked softly.

Matthew shifted uneasily. "Well, it's probably the reason why I asked you to go for a walk," he said. "I've talked with my parents and with Ellen, and things aren't getting any better with them. The abbot is still in Texas and making no effort to either marry Ellen or to talk with her. Everything is being handled through his lawyer. And since all the head honchos here know about it, I decided to go back home and see what I can do. My parents have pretty much said that they don't want me here any longer. It's also the reason why I wanted to get some gut reaction about us."

Andrew could feel the knot begin to grow even larger in both his stomach and his throat. "So what was the gut reaction about us?" he asked.

Matthew, once again, began to splash his feet in the water. "I was hoping that you'd come with me," he said, "but that hope seems to have flown out the window, unless I can get you to change your mind . . ."

As if someone had taken a knife and plunged it into his heart, Andrew took a quick, shallow breath. "I can't do that, Matt," he said. "Besides, it wouldn't be the best time for your family to have to deal with someone else, you know, with all that's going on right now."

"I sort of figured you'd say something like that."

"I'm sorry," Andrew said.

Almost immediately, Matthew dried his feet on his jeans, put on his sneakers and stood up. "I'm leaving tomorrow morning," he said bluntly. "Father Gerald is driving me to the airport."

Barefoot and half dazed, Andrew got up and stood on the soft, moss-covered ground. "I'm not sure I understand all of this," he stammered. "Are you . . . coming back after Ellen's situation is settled or what?"

An obvious pause in the conversation caused Andrew's heart to sink, as Matthew raised both hands over his head and stretched his back and shoulders. "I don't know," he said with a yawn. "I'd like to, but right now, I just don't know what to say."

Andrew chuckled inappropriately. "So this is . . . it? This is the end of us and all that we had together?" He looked at Matthew with disbelief.

"No, never," Matthew said. He grabbed Andrew by both arms. "I don't want you to think that way; no matter what happens, there will never be an end to us. I'm going home to help settle this mess with Ellen, and in whatever capacity, I'll be back. If I don't return as a monk, I swear, I'm coming back to take you with me."

"You promise?" Andrew whispered.

"Yes," Matthew said. "I promise."

"Then do me a favor," Andrew said. "Give me a hug, and then just get out of here, quickly."

Without hesitation, Matthew pulled him tight, gently nuzzled his ear, and then abruptly turned and walked away as Andrew watched him go.

Once he reached the sunny field, Matthew looked back and waved, covering his eyes with his other hand to block the glaring light.

And even though Andrew was sure he could not see him, he waved back slowly, until Matthew turned and disappeared beyond the golden aspen grove.

* * *

As before, life without Matthew was painfully lonely. Andrew plunged even more deeply into his meditation, reading, and inner silence, only to unload verbally at his weekly sessions with Dr. Klein, who remained therapeutically supportive.

"Do you think he will come back?" Andrew asked tentatively. He sat in his favorite leather chair, nearly swallowed by its sumptuous bulk, while Dr. Klein exhaled fragrant pipe smoke from behind his ornate desk.

"I wish I knew," Dr. Klein said quietly. "You said that he promised—so that, in itself, may be hopeful." He tapped his pipe against a large ashtray. "How have you been feeling?" he asked.

Andrew simply stared out the window at the trees, which were just beginning to display their autumn blush. "The medication prevents me from feeling much at all, sort of mummified or robotic. I'm sure you must know what it does to your patients," he said.

"Yes," Dr. Klein replied, "but each patient is different, has different precipitators, different threshold levels. It really depends on the individual."

"It all sounds like so much gobbledygook," Andrew said with a bit more animation.

"I can understand that," Dr. Klein agreed.

After a slight pause in their conversation, Andrew initiated a new topic. "I mentioned that he was with Rebecca again—didn't I?"

"In her car, I believe," Dr. Klein said. "And she dropped him off near the front of the monastery."

"What do you think that's all about?"

"I'm not sure," Dr. Klein replied evasively. "What are your thoughts on that?"

Andrew moved to his familiar spot next to the window and gazed down to the street below. "I don't know," he said. "I just can't see how he would be satisfied with a woman."

"You mean sexually?"

"Yes. He often wished that I would have anal sex with him," Andrew said candidly. "And of course, there was his famous candle. I don't understand how she can satisfy him."

"Perhaps there's more to it than just the sexual aspect," Dr. Klein explained.

"Like what?" Andrew asked.

"Companionship or even some unexplained opportunity," Dr. Klein said.

Andrew shook his head. "I realize she's wealthy but . . . I doubt that's why Matthew sees her."

"In any case," Dr. Klein explained, "I feel you may be reading a bit more into the matter than actually exists. Do you feel there's a possibility they might be just friends?"

Andrew turned to face him. "It's possible, but I doubt it."

Dr. Klein signaled the end of the session in his usual manner by rising, walking around to the front of his desk, and leaning against it. "Please remember to stay on your medication at the proper times," he admonished. "Especially now, Andrew. It's very crucial."

As painful as it was to miss Matthew, Andrew, nevertheless, sensed a welcomed reprieve from the underlying tensions inherent in most private relationships. He no longer felt the need to scrutinize every vehicle that drove past him on the way to the monastery or the need to lie awake at night, waiting for Matthew's familiar knock and wondering what lascivious acts might transpire in the silence of his cell. And even more obvious than his last absence, Matthew made no attempt, since his departure, to call or write. Andrew could only wait and wonder and hope, perhaps, in vain, that he would return with a renewed commitment to his vocation and with a genuine understanding, if not acceptance, of the physical nature of their relationship.

* * *

Although it was unclear how to appropriately decipher Brother Joshua's motives, Andrew, once again, took some consolation in his seemingly innocuous companionship and support.

"You must really miss him," Brother Joshua said empathetically, as he struggled to keep up with Andrew's loping stride.

Andrew continued to climb the steep path. "I do . . . mostly," he said, "but then there are times when I look forward to the quiet and lack of inner turmoil."

"What about the sex part?" Brother Joshua asked bluntly.

Andrew stopped, turned to look at him and smiled slightly. "Now that's really none of your business, is it, Bozo."

"Not really," Brother Joshua said with a shrug, "but I thought we were friends."

"Well, even friends aren't obligated to tell each other everything," Andrew said.

"Can't blame me for trying," Brother Joshua said.

Andrew proceeded to walk to the top of the rise, across the jumbled scree, to the natural stone fortress where Matthew had carved their names inside the cavelike dwelling. The inscription—Matt loves Andrew—remained as distinct as the day Andrew first saw it.

"I'm impressed," Brother Joshua said, as he slowly ran his fingers over the rough letters.

"Impressed . . . or jealous?" Andrew asked sarcastically.

He turned to look at Andrew. "Maybe a little of both," Brother Joshua admitted. "I wouldn't mind having my name up there."

"Oh, yeah?" Andrew quipped. "Which one would it replace?"

Brother Joshua smirked. "Silly question—which one do you think?"

"If I knew, I wouldn't have asked."

"Maybe I should just say that friends aren't obligated to tell each other everything," Brother Joshua mimicked.

"That's fine with me," Andrew said. He turned and walked out into the sunlight.

Brother Joshua followed Andrew and stood in back of him. "You honestly don't know that it's you I care about?" he said softly.

Andrew dropped his head to his chest and then turned to face him. "Look," he said. "It's nice to be cared about, but you know damn well that I'll always love Matthew, no matter what happens."

"I know that," Brother Joshua said. "But I thought I'd put my cards on the table, right now, just to let you know that if something changes in your relationship—I'll be here for you."

Andrew slowly shook his head from side to side and smiled. "You know . . . you amaze me. Isn't this the same reason why you left the monastery in Kentucky—because you were . . . what, too close to a fellow novice? Do you really want to walk down that same path?"

Brother Joshua stared directly at him. "For you, I would," he admitted.

"You're a crazy man," Andrew commented. "Let's get the heck out of here."

* * *

The weeks seemed to fly by as Matthew's hiatus extended into mid-September. Each morning, just before lunch, Andrew would approach his mailbox with less anticipation of hearing from him, yet down deep, he knew that eventually a letter would arrive.

And it did; it was a Saturday, an idyllic, if not uncharacteristically, humid day for the alpine setting of the monastery, with warm temperatures and blue skies, hovering like a crystal dome which had captured a brilliant sun.

Andrew could tell by the feel of the letter—its thickness—that Matthew was not overly wordy. But that did not matter. He felt as though he had just won the lottery, as he immediately headed for his cell, letter firmly in hand, to absorb its contents in private.

Sitting at his desk with the door closed, Andrew carefully slit the top of the envelope with a brass letter opener, took a deep breath, and pulled out the small, two-page epistle. Matthew's familiar, rounded script, rudimentary yet readable, was initially a welcomed sight, until he read on in disbelief, horrified by its message:

Wednesday, September 17

Dear Andrew,

I'm not very good at this correspondence stuff, but I'll do my best. Even though I haven't written, I do think of you often and hope you are well. Ellen is still interested in marrying the abbot, and it looks like he is going to do it. So she's happy, but my parents are still pissed and would rather sue him, the monastery, and God, if they could. As for my opinion, I think Ellen is out of her mind to want that ugly bastard, but hey—it's her life.

This part is tougher to talk about, so I hope you're sitting down. But before I explain, I want you to know that I still love you and always will. It's just that I know we could never be as I wanted us to be—one—spiritually, physically, sexually, while still in the monastery. And I know that you would never leave because I think you've found your true vocation, and I'll always respect you for that. So whatever follows in this letter, know that I'll always love you, even as ridiculous as it may seem.

Yes, I've been guilty of seeing Rebecca. I think you've always known. I know what you're thinking, and you're right—it's not the same. But I know that she really loves me and treats me like I have some genuine value, and I think I have grown to feel the same toward her—I'm sure I have. You probably think I'm crazy, but you may as well be the first to know. Rebecca and I are getting married sometime in October at her father's club—the Ashford—in Bitter Creek, and somehow, I hope you can forgive me and help us celebrate that day. She pretty much knows about you and me and is very understanding, so there would be nothing to worry about. I guess happiness is an elusive quality, but I want you to be as happy as I hope Rebecca and I will be. I'll be in touch.

With love and respect,
Matthew

Within seconds, the ice in Andrew's veins melted with fiery rage. His vision blurred as his uncontrolled pressure caused small hemorrhages within his eyes and clouded his sight, as tears of burning pain fell silently on Matthew's letter, mixing with the ink and smudging several words.

His deafening, baleful cry reverberated throughout the monastery and would be remembered long after his absence. Still gripping the letter opener, Andrew raised it high above his head and, in one swift movement, brought it down with full force into his upper thigh. It was only the thickness of the handle that prevented it from going completely through his leg and perforating the opposite side, and yet even then, Andrew felt no pain. He stood up with the opener still stuck in his leg, while blood soaked through his jeans, ran down his leg, and oozed onto the carpet. Although he continued to emit an ungodly cry, Andrew heard nothing except the violent pounding of his heart. All that he saw looked pink to him; his actions appeared robotic, as if the world had suddenly shifted to slow motion and he was no longer inside his body. He watched as he picked up his desk lamp, ripped the cord from the wall, and threw it against the glass slider. In total silence, large shards of glass crashed against the tiled footer, shattering into infinite splinters, which spread throughout the cell like miniature missiles. Andrew then leaned forward, picked up his desk with adrenaline charged ease, and managed to heave it into whatever glass remained in the jagged door; however, this time, large slivers of glass bounced off the screen and back toward him, lacerating his face, arms, and chest.

Totally exhausted and confused by the sight of his own blood, Andrew stood motionless, observing the destruction like an innocent child. When he thought he heard his name being spoken, he slowly turned to see Brother Nathan standing inside the doorway, as others peered cautiously from the corridor.

"It's okay," Brother Nathan said softly, but when he grasped the severity of the situation, saw the letter opener hanging from Andrew's thigh, and realized the amount of blood he had lost, he momentarily lost his composure. "Oh, Jesus!" he said in a quivering voice. "We had better get an ambulance up here!"

* * *

Chapter Thirty

Halsen Encore

The emergency room at Whitehill Medical Center in Bitter Creek was generally more familiar with orthopedic injuries incurred by either extreme skiers or out-of-shape beginners with an exaggerated sense of their invulnerability. So when Andrew arrived, off-season, with a self-inflicted leg wound and multiple glass lacerations, complicated by psychological trauma, the staff turned out in full force to provide immediate triage care to this dismal spiritual anomaly. He was immediately rushed into surgery to stanch the flow of blood from the leg wound and facial lacerations, while Brother Nathan delicately explained Andrew's current psychiatric history to the attending physician, Dr. Cole, including his admissions to the Halsen Clinic under the care of Dr. Klein.

"Is there a diagnosis?" Dr. Cole asked.

"Yes," Brother Nathan replied cautiously. "I believe it's mostly depression with aggravated anxiety and, possibly, some additional psychotic involvement."

"What about medication?"

"I know that he takes medication, but right now, I can't remember. Your best bet is to contact Dr. Klein at the clinic."

"I'm going to try to reach him right now," Dr. Cole said. "Thanks . . . and, by the way, I think Andrew will be fine as far as the surgery goes. I would assume that Dr. Klein will admit him to Halsen, as soon as he is medically stable."

Like an expectant father, Brother Nathan paced repeatedly in the waiting room, until he was joined by Father Gerald, who was away from the monastery when the incident took place.

"How is he doing?" Father Gerald asked with obvious concern.

"Dr. Cole thinks he'll be fine," Brother Nathan said. He slowly shook his head. "You wouldn't have believed what he looked like when I saw him in his cell—blood running down his face and the letter opener still buried in his thigh."

"I know," Father Gerald said. "That's what I felt when I saw his room. At first, I wondered if he cut his wrists because of all the blood, but thank God, he didn't."

Frustrated, Brother Nathan ran his hands over his face while yawning and stretching his neck. "Any idea of what set him off?"

Father Gerald nodded, reached into his pocket, and pulled out a sealed plastic bag. "This," he said, holding up Matthew's letter. "When I walked into Andrew's room to see the damage, this letter from Matthew was on the floor, nearly buried by the desk."

"So . . . what did he write?"

"Well, I wasn't going to read it, but then I decided it was clinically necessary and appropriate," Father Gerald said apologetically.

"And I shouldn't be asking," Brother Nathan said.

"No, you should," Father Gerald said. "You have a good peer and professional relationship with him, and to maintain his safety, you should be aware of some things."

"So whatever set him off is in that letter?"

Once again, Father Gerald nodded. "For now, we'll keep this quiet until I see how Dr. Klein wants to deal with all of it. Essentially, Matthew told him how much he still cared for him, but then followed with the news that he and Rebecca Storrow would be getting married in October."

Brother Nathan appeared dumbstruck. He sat motionless in his chair with his mouth slightly open and stared at Father Gerald. "It's a joke, right?" he finally managed to say.

"If it is, it's tremendously cruel," Father Gerald said. "In fact, I believe Matthew is telling the truth."

"I don't get it," Brother Nathan admitted. "I thought . . ."

"And you thought right," Father Gerald added quickly.

"Didn't Matthew have any idea what this would do to Andrew?" Brother Nathan asked.

"I don't know," Father Gerald said. "I think, now, we're getting into Dr. Klein's area. He'll have to help all of us cope with this in whatever way is psychologically appropriate."

"You don't think Matthew is acting out of revenge of some sort, do you?" Brother Nathan suggested.

Father Gerald slowly shook his head. "It's hard to tell but I hope not."

"I can't imagine what Andrew is going to be like on the day of Matthew's wedding next month."

"Hopefully, if I have anything to say about it, he'll still be at the Halsen Clinic, heavily sedated and closely watched," Father Gerald said firmly.

* * *

Less than a week after his admission to Whitehill, Andrew was transferred, as expected, to the Halsen Clinic and given a comfortable corner room, complete with a scenic view of the aspen-covered mountains, still visible through the ornately scrolled metal bars. Each time he saw the scrolled work, he laughed at its camouflaged attempt to subtly restrain an occupant from going out the window.

'It's a nice touch,' he thought, as he examined his bandaged thigh. The dressing appeared fresh—no oozing fluids, wicks, or drains, just residual pain. It was not until he talked with Dr. Klein that he became aware of his trauma and the incident in his cell. And yet even now, he had not recalled Matthew's letter, since Dr. Klein purposely chose not to tell him until he was safely admitted to Halsen.

Consequently, Andrew was surprised when Kurt entered his room with a medication tray.

"Hello, again," Kurt said cheerfully. "They've given you a much larger room this time."

Andrew nodded. "Oh yeah," he said flatly, "just like a hotel." He watched as Kurt inserted a syringe into a vial of liquid medication, extracted an exact amount, and set the syringe and an alcohol pad on the tray.

"I remember you from my last admission," Andrew said.

Kurt smiled broadly. "That's good because I also remember you. How are you feeling?"

Andrew shrugged his shoulders. "Okay, I guess," he said with uncertainty. "Actually," he added self-consciously, "I feel like a jerk for having to be here."

"I can understand that," Kurt replied frankly, "but try to let that settle. You're here for a reason—a valid reason—and need to concentrate on getting better." He picked up the syringe and stood alongside Andrew's bed. "I'm going to put the medication into your IV line, which will help you relax," he said softly.

Andrew looked surprised. "You're a nurse?" he asked.

"Yes," Kurt said, "a psychiatric RN."

"Oh," Andrew said. "The last time I saw you, you brought me breakfast; I thought you were an attendant . . . I'm sorry," Andrew added.

"Don't worry about it," Kurt said. "You're not the first to make that mistake. I guess I just don't look old enough to be a nurse." He emptied the syringe into the shunt. "Maybe I should grow a mustache."

Within seconds, Andrew began to feel warm and euphoric and much less guarded. "No, don't," he said with a delayed response.

"No, don't what?" Kurt asked.

"The mustache . . . don't grow one," he said. His words had already developed a slight slur.

"No? Why not?"

Andrew smiled dreamily. "Because I like you just the way you are."

With a quick glance toward the door, Kurt leaned over Matthew and smiled. "Thanks," he said softly. "I feel the same about you, but I think the medication may be putting words in your mouth."

"Maybe, but they had to be in my mind first," Andrew said.

Kurt blushed slightly, smiled, and continued to stand alongside of the bed. "Look," he said more seriously. "I expect that Dr. Klein will be in very shortly to talk with you . . ."

"Heck, I'd rather talk with you," Andrew interrupted.

"And I'd rather do the same," Kurt said, "but he's your doctor, and you need to listen to him, okay?"

"Am I dying?" Andrew asked directly. He rolled on his side.

"I doubt it," Kurt replied. "It's just that some sessions with the psychiatrist are tougher than others . . . and this may be one of them."

Andrew shrugged. "Lately, it seems like they're all tough," he said in a more subdued voice.

"Just hang in there," Kurt encouraged. "I'll be right outside the door if you need me."

Andrew looked up at him with expectant eyes. "You promise?" he asked.

"Yes," Kurt repeated, "I promise." He placed one hand over the back of Andrew's, just below his IV, and gently squeezed it. Without looking back, he left the room, leaving Andrew to wonder about his imminent meeting with Dr. Klein.

However, he did not have to wait long. Dr. Klein walked briskly through the open door wearing his usual look of concern, which was only slightly tempered with a hint of a smile. "How are you today?" he asked, as he reached out to shake Andrew's hand.

Andrew reciprocated with a less than firm grip. "Well, thanks to Kurt, who squirted some magic juice into my line, I'm feeling pretty relaxed," he said.

"So you can feel a definite difference in your mood—less anxious, perhaps a bit drowsy?" Dr. Klein asked.

"That's about it," Andrew replied. "Does it come in tablet form?"

"It does," Dr. Klein said cautiously, "but we can talk about that later." He pulled a chair close to the bed and sat down. "I want to talk about what happened to you in your room at the monastery," he said softly.

Andrew rolled onto his back and raised his knees so that the soles of his feet were flat on the sheet. "I thought we went through this already," Andrew said benignly.

"We have," Dr. Klein explained, "but I need you to understand as much as possible about why it happened so that I can help you resolve whatever issues might surface."

At that moment, Andrew could feel a dulled surge of anxiety wash over him and then, like magic, evanesce into a vague portent. He was totally unaware of the three clinic staff sitting quietly outside of his door, including Kurt, who anxiously held another tray with two syringes of medication, in the event that Andrew's behavior escalated. The two bulky attendants sat close to the door, listening for any verbal indications that might require their intervention. As a precaution, both were equipped with brightly colored restraints which would be used, if necessary, to tie Andrew to his bed.

"Do you remember what caused you to act out the way you did?" Dr. Klein asked.

"No . . . I really don't," Andrew answered.

"Anything about Matthew?"

Andrew paused. "I don't think so."

"Very often," Dr. Klein began, "one might experience such tragic news, something unexpected, that it's possible to block it temporarily from the conscious memory. It's as if it were erased from a certain level of the thought process."

"And you think that's what I did?"

"Unfortunately, yes, I do," Dr. Klein said honestly.

"It has to do with Matthew, doesn't it?" Andrew asked.

"Yes, it does," Dr. Klein admitted. "Before you get upset, I want you to understand that he is all right and still in California."

"Then what is it?"

Dr. Klein shifted in his chair. "I want you to think of some of our earlier sessions in my office when we talked about whether or not Matthew would return to the monastery, how much you missed him, and yet how much more relaxed you felt—almost relieved, at times, not having to deal with a complex relationship. Do you remember some of those conversations?"

"He's not coming back, is he?" Andrew asked bluntly.

"I'm not going to sugarcoat it, Andrew," Dr. Klein replied. "I want you to be strong; I can help you through this."

"It's okay, I guess," Andrew said softly. "I think it's something I've feared but always expected." He rubbed his eyes with his free hand.

"You are doing well, so far," Dr. Klein said with a slight smile.

"How do you know all of this?" Andrew asked.

"Do you remember getting a letter from Matthew that Saturday?" Dr. Klein asked cautiously.

Andrew squinted, trying to remember, and then slowly shook his head. "No," he said, "but it sounds as though I did."

In the hallway, Kurt signaled to the attendants by raising his head. In silence, they got up from their chairs and stood next to each other, as close to the entrance as possible.

"We found the letter in your cell," Dr. Klein said.

"And you just went ahead and read it?" Andrew asked.

"I apologize, Andrew, but judging from the amount of destruction to yourself and your room, I decided that it was clinically appropriate."

"Do you have the letter?"

Dr. Klein paused. "Yes, I do," he said.

"Please let me see it," Andrew pleaded.

"Let me explain something first," Dr. Klein said. "If you react to its contents the way you reacted in the monastery, it could be very dangerous to your health. I can't allow that to happen to you. Instead, I want to talk with you, very gently, about what Matthew wrote so that you can digest it gradually and, perhaps, less painfully. Do you understand?"

Andrew shook his head. "Yes," he said. "I think so."

"On several occasions, we talked about Matthew and his relationship to Rebecca Storrow. You once told me you saw them in the car together, and from a distance, it looked like Matthew got out of the vehicle and entered the monastery."

"I remember," Andrew said with sudden agitation, "so skip the head trip and tell me what Matthew wrote."

"Fair enough," Dr. Klein said softly, "but you've already escalated at the mention of her name. Excuse me one second." Dr. Klein stood up and walked toward the door.

"Where are you going?" Andrew shouted, yet he barely finished the sentence when Dr. Klein returned followed by Kurt, who was carrying the familiar medical tray.

Within seconds, Kurt had inserted another syringe into Andrew's IV shunt. He briefly made eye contact, as Andrew barely heard him whisper, "I'm sorry, buddy," and then he quickly left the room.

"Oh, this is terrific," Andrew remarked sarcastically. "I'll be so grogged up, I won't remember what you told me anyway."

"I'm sorry," Dr. Klein said. I just don't want to see you suffer."

Andrew began to slip slowly back into a deeper euphoria, yet still conscious of Dr. Klein's conversation.

"This is the difficult part," Dr. Klein said. His voice grew more definitive, to capture Andrew's attention.

"So tell me," Andrew said with a familiar slur.

"Matthew made it very clear that he still loves you, those are his words. But then he wrote that he is going to marry Rebecca in October," Dr. Klein said clearly. "I apologize for having to be the one to tell you."

Even though he was heavily medicated, Andrew managed to rip the IV from his arm as he attempted to get up and flee the room; however, both attendants were on him immediately and had him secured in four points before his feet even touched the floor. He screamed through tears, unable to wipe them away. "That bitch! That fucking bitch!" he yelled, as he fought in vain against his restraints. "Why . . . why?" he repeated over and over, but by then, Kurt had another syringe prepared and injected it directly into Andrew's arm. Almost immediately, Andrew's breathing slowed. He no longer squirmed and resisted; instead, he gave into the medication and fell into a well-deserved sleep.

Dr. Klein moved closer to the bed and gazed down at Andrew's now tranquil face. "I've never liked having to go through this part," he said softly.

Kurt stood on the opposite side of the bed. "It's always sad," he admitted.

"Let's get a check on his vitals," Dr. Klein said with a more professional tone. "He'll need close observation—one-to-one, for the next twelve hours with a check on vitals, hourly. I'm hoping that he'll be fine." He turned to leave and then turned to face the three clinicians. "I apologize," he said with a smile. "I almost forgot to say thank you. Also, I think it's okay to remove the restraints—let him get a comfortable sleep. I'll be in early, but feel free to beep me if you need to."

Just before 10:00 p.m., Kurt entered Andrew's room to relieve the attendant who had been monitoring Andrew for most of the night. "You must be bored," Kurt said as he checked Andrew's pulse and pressure.

"Not really," the attendant replied. "I can sort of put myself in this guy's place—one little push and you're over the edge."

"How's he been doing?" Kurt asked.

"Vitals have been within normal range, some mumbling and probably some wild dreams."

"How do you know?"

"Well, for someone this medicated, he's been spiking erections about every half hour," the attendant said with a smile.

"Hey—maybe you're right," Kurt replied.

"Anyway," the attendant said as he walked toward the door, "he's all yours. Have a good night."

After recording the vital signs in Andrew's chart, Kurt sat down next to the bed and watched as Andrew's sleep was occasionally disturbed by involuntary twitches, rapid eye movement, and incomprehensible murmuring, some of which vaguely sounded like "Matt." Moments later, Andrew rolled onto his back and appeared to stretch. Kurt adjusted the IV line so it would not get tangled in the sheet that covered Andrew. When he sat back down, he realized that the attendant was, in fact, very observant—the top sheet bulge considerably, as Andrew's erection could clearly be seen through the light cotton covering.

* * *

Dr. Klein arrived at the clinic unusually early, anxious to review Andrew's evening report and to evaluate his current functioning. When he entered Andrew's room, he found him propped up with pillows, a breakfast tray in front of him, yet little sign of any movement.

"How are you today?" Dr. Klein asked, as he walked to Andrew's side and stood over him. He looked down at his ashen complexion, dark circles, and chapped lips and realized, once again, how devastating a psychiatric illness could be, transforming an otherwise healthy, relatively happy individual into a shattered wreck at such an unreasonably early age.

Andrew attempted a smile, which barely evolved. "I don't know anymore," he whispered. The medication knocked me out."

"I know," Dr. Klein admitted, "but after all you went through yesterday, I wanted to be sure that you would be able to sleep and allow the medication to do its job. I'm sure you feel quite weak. Even so, I need you to cooperate and try to get some of this breakfast down so that you can regain some strength—even with the IV."

"What did I go through?" Andrew asked.

Dr. Klein paused. "What do you remember, Andrew? Try to think—hard."

"I remember getting upset . . . syringes going into my IV line."

"What got you upset?" Dr. Klein prompted.

Andrew shook his head.

"Do you remember anything about Matthew?" Dr. Klein asked cautiously, and discreetly pushed the call button above Andrew's bed.

"Yes, I think so," Andrew said. "There was a letter."

"What was in the letter?"

"I remember him saying he still loved me and . . . oh, fuck," Andrew said. His face grew sad as tears began to well up in his eyes and run freely down his face; he used the sheet to dry them. "He's marrying Rebecca, isn't he?" He squinted at Dr. Klein, expecting yet fearful to hear the inevitable.

Dr. Klein shook his head. "I'm sorry, Andrew."

* * *

The days drifted into hours of waking, sleeping, and, mostly, brooding introspection, characterized by intense, unbearable weeping, which seemed to decrease as the medication took effect. Andrew began to climb slowly out of a pitiful darkness where hopelessness incited finality, as waves of unspoken suicidal ideation washed over him like a warm panacea. At times, death appeared significantly more tolerable than suffering.

It was just after supper, on the third day of being in bed, when Kurt and the attendant entered Andrew's room, smiling—as if on a mission—and, unexpectedly, provided a faint glimmer of optimism to an otherwise despondent patient.

"Guess who has orders written on him to be given a bath," Kurt said with a slight swagger, as he stood alongside Andrew's bed.

Andrew looked befuddled. "Why?" he responded blankly.

Before Kurt could answer, the attendant walked quickly into the bathroom and began to fill the Jacuzzi equipped tub with hot water and then added a packet of powdered therapeutic soak, which foamed slightly and filled the room with the clean fragrance of bergamot.

Kurt smiled as he sat on the edge of Andrew's bed. "Do you realize that it's nearly been three days since you had a bath?"

A self-conscious blush colored Andrew's cheeks. "I guess I haven't thought much about it," he admitted.

"That's okay," Kurt said. "You've had other things on your mind, but without being disrespectful, take it from me—you could use one."

Andrew could feel the color in his face intensify. "Great . . .," he quipped. He then stared at Kurt with his large brown eyes.

"What?" Kurt asked, knowing that Andrew looked perplexed.

He glanced toward the bathroom. "Does he have to be here?" Andrew asked quietly.

"Jim?" Kurt replied. "No, not really. We want to see how much strength you have before you get into the tub. Jim and I will get you out of bed, walk with you—out in the hall and back—and if you seem fairly stable, he can leave, and I'll be here with you." Kurt leaned a bit closer and smiled. "So do your best," he said softly.

Andrew managed a full-sized grin. "Thanks," he said.

Motivation appeared to conquer incipient atrophy as Andrew struggled initially to remain upright and shift his weight from one leg to the other. However, after a brief rest, he regained, momentarily, sufficient strength, and with minimal support from either side, he walked the length of the corridor and returned to his room—tired but, nonetheless, victorious.

"So how do you feel now?" Kurt asked as Andrew rested on the edge of his bed.

"I think I'm ready for that bath," he admitted.

Kurt glanced over at Jim. "He looks pretty stable; I'm sure I'll be fine with him. So if you want to catch up on some other work, go right ahead."

Jim nodded. "Thanks. Beep me if you need help."

Andrew walked the few steps to the room sink, unassisted, and began to brush his teeth. "I'd forgotten how good it feels to be out of that bed," he said. Mountains of peppermint foam fell in a broken stream and mixed with the running water before disappearing down the drain.

"It's nice to see you up and about," Kurt said. "You had me worried for a while."

"Why?" Andrew asked.

"Oh . . . I don't know. I guess I was concerned that you wouldn't respond to the medication and would spend more time in bed."

Andrew wiped his mouth and walked into the bathroom where Kurt was removing bath towels from a small closet. "I doubt that I'm even close to being my old self, but it's good to know that someone is concerned about me." He looked at Kurt with a slightly devilish grin.

"Well, besides me, I'm sure that there is an entire monastery full of well-wishers, hoping that you will be out of here soon," Kurt said. He placed the towels on the counter top and smiled at Andrew. "I'm ready if you are."

Andrew removed his robe and handed it to Kurt, who threw it over his shoulder.

"Hang on one second," Kurt said. "Let me untie the back of your hospital gown and you can jump in."

With his back toward Kurt, Andrew felt a bit awkward, knowing that, within seconds, he would be totally naked, 'but,' he thought, 'what the hell.'

"You're all set," Kurt said.

Andrew let the garment fall to the floor, placed one leg in the tub, and, with Kurt's assistance, followed with his other leg, and then carefully submersed himself in the hot, soothing water.

Copious rainbow-colored bubbles covered much of the water's surface, scenting the entire room with their fragrance.

"This feels great!" Andrew exclaimed. He leaned his head back against the folded towels.

"There's more," Kurt said. He reached down and pressed two buttons on the side of the tub which activated the jet pumps. Instantly, the water swirled around Andrew while penetrating, transparent fingers seemed to massage his entire body like an invisible masseur, soothing his back and shoulders and manipulating the soles of his feet with perfect pressure.

"Oh, man," Andrew said excitedly, "this is fantastic." He looked at Kurt. "You've got to try this," he remarked without thinking. His embarrassment was obvious as he struggled to explain. "I mean . . . you know."

Kurt laughed. "It's okay. I know what you meant," he said. "I'm going to let you soak for a while and enjoy some solitude, all right?"

Andrew nodded. "Sure," he said.

Left alone in such a luxurious state, Andrew could feel his entire body relax as the soothing water kneaded his muscles, momentarily erasing his cares and draining his energy to do anything but sit there. The almond-colored bar soap and the intriguing bottle of blue shampoo sat, unused, on the rim of the tub. It was as if he were mesmerized, and yet his mind continued to send him messages, some clearer than others, mostly about the interesting man in the next room. Surprisingly, even though he was not aware, there were no thoughts of Matthew or Rebecca or their marriage—only of Kurt and the strange wire-wrapped light which was partially recessed in the high ceiling above his head.

"How are you doing in there?" Kurt asked from the other room. When he received no response, he immediately panicked and charged into the bathroom. Andrew remained in the same position, his head back against the towels, his eyes open.

Kurt immediately shut off the pumps. "Are you all right?" he asked.

Andrew nodded and smiled. "Just tired," he whispered.

"That's good because you nearly scared me to death."

"Sorry," Andrew replied sleepily.

"You're really out of it, aren't you?" Kurt said, judging from Andrew's demeanor.

Once again, Andrew nodded.

"Well, buddy, we're going to have to finish up here before I get you to bed, okay?"

"That's okay," Andrew repeated.

Kurt shampooed Andrew's hair for the second time, rinsing it clean with more fresh water and then gently toweled it dry. "You about already?" he asked.

Andrew paused after Kurt's request to help quell his sexual response to Kurt's touch. "If it's okay, would you mind if I just sat here for a while and relaxed?"

"That's fine," Kurt said, "just as long as you don't fall asleep."

"I won't, I promise."

After a five-minute rest, Andrew was ready to leave. "I guess I'm all set, Kurt," he said, in as loud a voice as he could muster.

Kurt returned, threw two towels over his shoulder, and sat on the edge of the tub. "I want you to grab the assist bar with your right hand and then put your left arm around my shoulders, okay?"

Andrew nodded.

"Good," Kurt said. "Now pull yourself forward and stand up, and I'll support you with my other arm."

With some difficulty, Andrew managed to make it to a standing position, with Kurt's head beneath his armpit.

"Excellent," Kurt said as he ducked under Andrew's arm and immediately wrapped a heavy bath towel around his waist. "How are you feeling?"

Andrew sighed. "Exhausted but great . . . thanks to you."

"Yeah, well, you know the saying—it's a tough job but somebody's got to do it," he said.

"Well, I'm glad that you're here with me."

Kurt's genuine smile was more than sufficient.

"If you'll turn around and hang on to the upper bar, I'll dry off your back."

While Kurt was wiping his back and shoulders, Andrew boldly loosened the towel around his waist, removed it, and began to dry his chest, stomach, and genitals. And at that moment, it not only seemed natural to Andrew but, somehow, submissively honest, to be standing naked before such a compassionate clinical peer.

"It's a bit chilly in here," Kurt said apologetically, as he quickly moved on to the back of Andrew's thigh. He squatted to reach his calves and feet.

When he finished, Kurt retrieved a fresh hospital gown and handed it to Andrew. "Put this on. I'll get your bathrobe."

A freshly made bed greeted Andrew when he returned to his room.

"You did all of this when I was in the tub?" Andrew asked.

"It's a lot easier than having to do it while you are still in bed," Kurt said.

Andrew sat on the edge of the mattress, swung his legs up, and leaned back against the pillows. His newly scrubbed exterior barely concealed the exhaustion within. "Is this the part where you get to tell me a story?" Andrew asked with a smirk.

Kurt stood alongside of his bed and smiled. "I'll bet if I did, you'd be out like a light in five minutes." He reached out, tentatively, and pushed Andrew's hair back, away from his eyes.

Andrew looked up and smiled. "Dr. Klein does that sometimes," he said quietly.

"Yeah, well, maybe that's because we both care about you," Kurt replied. He sat down on the edge of the bed and watched in silence as Andrew's smile faded slowly and his eyelids appeared to grow heavy and close, only to reopen and close again.

"Sweet dreams," Kurt whispered, and then quietly, he returned to the nurses' station in the corridor.

In the days that followed, Andrew's medication was slowly decreased; he appeared brighter and stronger, yet Dr. Klein realized that he was still fairly fragile and required observation, especially with the advent of Matthew's wedding, which was due to take place in two days, on a Saturday.

"How do you expect he will deal with it?" Father Gerald asked, as he sat in Dr. Klein's office at Halsen.

"I'm not sure," Dr. Klein said. "I know that he seems to be doing better, but the wedding could be a real trigger."

"Are you sure he knows when it will take place?"

Dr. Klein nodded. "He read the announcement last week in the local newspaper."

"Has he said anything about it?"

"Not too much. I don't think he's ready or even able to discuss it. He usually wells up and begins this gentle sobbing."

Father Gerald shook his head. "I hate to see this happen to him. It's very sad."

"He'll have one-to-one supervision beginning Friday evening and continuing throughout the weekend," Dr. Klein said. "We'll see how he functions and go from there."

"Well, that relieves some of my anxiety." Father Gerald paused, as if puzzled. "I realize this question doesn't have a definitive answer, but I have to ask. Is there still a potential suicide risk with Andrew, and if so, to what degree?"

Dr. Klein accepted the inquiry with professional courtesy. "The risk is endemic to this particular diagnosis; however, depending on external stressors and his toleration of the medication, Andrew could be nearly free of all symptoms and lead a relatively happy, healthy life."

"So the wedding on Saturday could be potentially devastating," Father Gerald remarked.

"Absolutely. That's why he'll be on twenty-four hour observation."

Father Gerald stood up and shook Dr. Klein's hand. "I just want to say, again, how appreciative we are for your assistance. Thanks."

Dr. Klein reciprocated with a smile and a handshake.

"I guess I'll walk down and say hello to him," Father Gerald said.

* * *

"Stuffed sole with peas, mashed potatoes, and coleslaw," the attendant said, as he walked into Andrew's room, carrying a food tray at shoulder level and looking very much like a waiter. "And it smells great." He set the tray on the table and pulled up a chair.

Andrew was no longer eating his meals in bed. He put aside the magazine he was reading, swung his legs over the side of the mattress, and sat there. "Thanks, Jim," he said quietly.

"You're welcome." Jim smiled and turned to leave.

"Oh," Andrew added suddenly. "I haven't seen Kurt today. Does he have the day off?"

"No, but you will surely be seeing more of him over the weekend, starting tonight."

"What do you mean?"

Jim hesitated. He walked closer to Andrew and spoke softly. "I probably shouldn't be telling you but Dr. Klein has requested that you be started on close observation—so Kurt switched his schedule. He'll be with you from eleven tonight till seven in the morning." He smiled and then added, "You make sure he doesn't fall asleep."

Andrew grinned. "Thanks, I'll do my best."

Sitting on his bed, Andrew explored the food on his tray with trivial interest. The lemony sole flaked perfectly against the stainless tines, exposing the chunky crab stuffing and emitting a delicious aroma, which awakened Andrew's palette. Yet after only two or three mouthfuls, he pushed the tray table aside, knowing that the urge to eat had suddenly evaporated as his thoughts began to escalate, thoughts about his need for observation and the stark realization that Matthew would be getting married in the morning. 'So,' he thought, 'the moment is finally here.'

All that he previously refused to acknowledge suddenly began to surface and disturb him deeply: if Matthew had simply left the monastery to return to California, Andrew felt there would be hope; if he chose to be on an extended sabbatical, there would be hope; if he remained at the monastery and refused to associate with him, there would be hope—a door would still be open. And now, it was as if Matthew was closing that door—forever—by marrying Rebecca, denying his true identity and leaving Andrew with the scars of old memories and unfulfilled promises and dreams.

'Why?' he thought. 'Why . . . why . . . why?' By then, he began to talk out loud. "Because you're a fool—a stupid fool," he said plainly. "Why didn't you give him what he wanted? Why?"

Andrew began to pace rapidly from one side of the room to the other, sometimes grabbing his hair and pulling out small pieces or he would slam his closed fist against the side of his temple with such force that his head would snap violently to the opposite side, just as if an invisible boxer were brutalizing him in the ring. "You're an asshole!" he shouted. "Why didn't you fuck him? He wanted you to fuck him! That's what he wanted! And you, you fucking hypocrite! Admit it! You wanted the same thing. You wanted to fuck him! But no . . ."

Andrew never had a chance to finish his sentence; the two attendants were on him as soon as they heard the commotion, holding him down until the nurse arrived and injected a powerful sedative into his arm. Within a short time, Andrew began to grow limp; his shouting faded into slurred invectives and then ceased, as he succumbed to the medication's effect.

After returning him to his bed and contacting Dr. Klein, Jim and the other attendant applied loose restraints to his arms and legs and waited for the doctor's arrival. It was eminently clear that Andrew's psychiatric remission had ended, as feared, on the celebratory eve of Matthew's anticipated gala.

It was in this sedated state that Andrew began to recall an old, familiar dream—the grizzly appearance of the hooded monk, faceless except for two glowing red eyes, which made Andrew's skin crawl with terror. As in the past, the image appeared suddenly, hovering above him like a demon from hell, staring at him through diabolical eyes. Unable to move, Andrew fought against his restraints and began to scream into the evil empty face. "What do you want from me? What . . . ?" Except this time, he did not wake up.

Instead, the hooded face came closer and, as it did once before, spoke with a deep, ungodly voice. "Despair will overwhelm you, just as terror seizes you now. Your soul is marked for another eternity."

Paralyzed with fear, Andrew screamed once more into the macabre darkness, believing intuitively that this was not a dream but a precursor of some horrific event which would eventually come to pass.

"His pulse has skyrocketed!" Kurt said. "Blood pressure is dangerously high."

Dr. Klein quickly squeezed the excess medication out of the syringe and then jammed it into Andrew's arm. "I hope to hell this works," he said, as he wiped the sweat from his brow.

Andrew continued to thrash against his restraints, at times, so violently that the bed began to inch across the polished floor, while the purple webbing around his wrists chafed against his raw skin. Moments later, the behavior began to abate; his pulse started to slow, along with a decrease in his blood pressure. Eventually, all was quiet.

"How are his vitals?" Dr. Klein asked.

Kurt removed his stethoscope. "Almost back to normal," he said.

"That's what I was hoping for." Dr. Klein placed his stethoscope against Andrew's neck, listened and then moved it to several locations on his chest. "Sounds okay," he said. "Are you with him for the night?" he asked, looking at Kurt.

Kurt nodded. "I sort of figured that this might be a bad night for him so I switched shifts."

"I'm concerned that he may require acute care for the weekend and beyond," Dr. Klein admitted. "But I'm glad you're here. You seem to have a good rapport with him."

"He's a nice person," Kurt responded a bit awkwardly. "It's always tough to see this happen."

"Yes, I know all too well," Dr. Klein said.

He watched as Andrew lay curled on his side, with one arm behind his back, his breathing deep and slow.

"Do you think he'd be more comfortable if I rolled him onto his back?" Kurt asked.

"Probably," Dr. Klein said. He stood up to help Kurt with Andrew. "You're all set with medication—PRN, if he becomes agitated?"

"Yes, but I hope that doesn't happen."

"It shouldn't, after all he has been given. Oh . . . and before I forget—you know about the restraints. They have to stay on until I can evaluate him in the morning."

"I understand," Kurt said.

"If there is any change in his vitals . . . anything, call me immediately. It doesn't matter what time it might be, okay?"

"Thanks," Kurt said.

After Dr. Klein left, Kurt sat in the quiet, dimly lit room, watching Andrew and listening to him breathe. He saw him involuntarily tug against his restraints, as he attempted to shift his position, only to return to his back rather than fight the heavy sedation. Kurt observed the familiar scene with remorse and wondered, 'How does this happen, what will become of him, and why?' He knew what the textbooks and his professional experience told him, and yet in this case, it just did not seem fair.

By 4:00 a.m., Kurt began to fight his sleepiness with yawns, stretches, and walks around Andrew's bed. Unable to leave the room, he used his two-way radio to contact the attendant on-call. "I need some coffee, badly," he said. "Are you able to one-to-one my patient?"

"I'll be right down," the attendant said.

Armed with fresh coffee and a chance to use the bathroom, Kurt returned to find the attendant leaning over Andrew and talking to him.

"He just woke up," the attendant said softly. "Doesn't recognize me . . . keeps asking for you. If you're all set, I'll make some rounds."

"Thanks for the break," Kurt said.

Andrew stared at him with sad eyes and raised both hands as far as the restraints would allow. "Why this?" he asked.

Kurt felt as though his heart had suddenly been torn. "I want you to understand that this isn't easy for me either," he said. "I don't like to see you like this any more than you do." He purposely took deep breaths to maintain his composure, until Andrew suddenly began crying softly, unable to wipe his eyes or nose.

Kurt was soon aware of his own tears that flooded his eyes. He immediately turned away under the pretext of retrieving a tissue for Andrew—he did not want him to see his anguish. He held the tissue to Andrew's nose, just as a father might do to his child. "Okay—blow," he insisted. He then took a fresh tissue and wiped Andrew's eyes.

"What happened this time?" Andrew asked.

Kurt hesitated to tell him the truth. "You honestly don't remember or are you looking forward to getting upset again?"

Andrew appeared deep in thought. "It's Saturday, isn't it?"

Kurt nodded. "Now don't get wild on me—please."

"I don't have the energy," Andrew admitted.

"Good, neither do I."

"You know all about Matthew and me, don't you?"

"I'm obligated to read the chart, Andrew, but no, I can't say that I know all about the both of you."

"Well, what do you think after reading it?"

"About what?" Kurt asked obliquely.

"About me and Matthew."

Kurt leaned forward in his chair. "I never met Matthew, but off the record, I'd have to say he's a fool to leave you."

Andrew barely smiled. "Maybe not . . ." He looked away toward the darkness through the window. "I just can't believe he's getting married today."

With genuine empathy, Kurt reached out and covered Andrew's hand with his. "I know it must be incredibly difficult for you, but try to cope with it. There are a lot of people wanting you to get well."

Andrew turned to face him. "Like who?" he said gently.

"How about me, for starters?" Kurt said. "I wouldn't be sitting here holding on to your hand if I didn't care about you."

"You really do, don't you?" Andrew said.

"Yeah, I really do. Are you all right with that?"

This time, Andrew's smile was more evident. "Sure, why wouldn't I be?"

"I don't know," Kurt shrugged. "Maybe you think I'm . . . unappealing."

"I would bet that's one word that has never been used to describe you," Andrew replied.

"Oh . . . you might be surprised," Kurt said with a straight face.

Andrew stretched against the restraints. "How long do I have to leave these on?"

"Dr. Klein is going to evaluate you in the morning, and if you do as well as you've been doing so far, he'll probably remove them."

"I really have to wait till then?"

"Sorry," Kurt said.

"Well, then I have a problem."

"What?" Kurt asked.

Andrew appeared reticent. "I have to go to the bathroom."

"That's okay," Kurt said. "Bedpan or urinal?"

"Just the urinal," Andrew replied.

Kurt removed the urinal from the lower shelf of the nightstand. He then raised the head of the bed until Andrew was nearly in a sitting position. "You know what I have to do, don't you?"

Andrew nodded. "It's either that or I wet the bed."

With the blankets pulled down to Andrew's knees, Kurt carefully slid the container between Andrew's legs and pushed the base of the urinal firmly against the mattress. "If you start to feel the urine close to the top—stop; I'll empty it and give it back to you."

Andrew stabilized the urinal with pressure from his thighs. "I don't think I've had that much liquid." He could feel the cold container grow warmer as his heated urine began to collect and rise.

"What's so funny?" Kurt asked. He noticed that Andrew had his eyes closed and was grinning from ear to ear.

"Oh . . . just something that happened once to Matthew and me. We sort of got stuck together in a urinal." His amusement soon erupted into exaggerated laughter which began to increase until Kurt began to question its clinical onset.

"Are you okay?" he asked.

Andrew nodded but continued to laugh hysterically.

"Can I take the urinal? I don't want you to spill it."

Although he nodded, Andrew reacted even more deliriously to Kurt's question.

With the urinal safely on the nightstand, Kurt attempted to assess Andrew's condition. "Hey!" he shouted, as he stood up and grabbed Andrew shoulders. "Take some deep breaths, Andrew—right now!" He lightly moved him off the pillows and set him back down. "Good," he said. "Now try to relax. Take more deep breaths."

Slowly, Andrew's laughter began to diminish, only to be followed by sobbing so intense that the entire bed shook and creaked as it moved against the tile floor.

"I hate to do this, buddy, but I think you need it," Kurt said. He quickly retrieved the syringe from the medication tray and injected its contents into Andrew's arm.

"How can Matthew do this?" Andrew managed to say between breaths. His flushed face contorted as he fought for air, at times, hiccupping like a choking child.

"It's okay," Kurt repeated. "It's okay." He lowered the side rail to the floor and sat on the edge of the bed. "I know it probably seems like the end of the world, but believe me, you are going to be all right." He ran his fingers through Andrew's hair, pushing it back, away from his heated forehead, acknowledging Andrew's pain yet hating to see such tragic suffering.

At one point, just prior to the sedating effects of the medication, Andrew looked up at Kurt through watery eyes and reached out to hold him but was prevented from doing so by the purple restraints.

As before, Kurt could feel his own heart being ripped apart with Andrew's pain, as he continued to hold out his arms and stare at him like a drowning victim, only inches away from a rescuing hand yet still, unable to reach it. "That's it," he exclaimed. "I don't care if I'm fired." He immediately released both of Andrew's upper restraints, sat on the bed, and pulled him toward him, hugging him tightly and feeling his overheated face against his, while Andrew's tears wet his cheek and ran down his neck. "You'll be okay," Kurt whispered. "I'm with you. Try to relax."

Comforted by Kurt's affection, Andrew proceeded to embrace his protector with welcomed relief, rocking gently back and forth, afraid to let go. Gradually, as the medication flooded his system, his breathing slowed, his tears abated. A garbled sound rose in his throat and stuck there.

"You don't have to say anything," Kurt said. "Let me hold you. Try to sleep."

Although it was just barely decipherable, Andrew managed to get the words out. "Thank you," he said.

"You are very welcome," Kurt replied with difficulty. He could feel his own throat tighten and choke with emotion.

Before long, Andrew slumped against Kurt with deadweight, as the full effect of the medication successfully suppressed his system.

Kurt gently laid him back against the pillow, lowered the head of the bed, and covered him completely. He immediately checked his vital signs, which were well within expected parameters. After recording the necessary information in Andrew's chart, Kurt remembered that his once hot coffee sat tepid on the nightstand, but it did not matter. He leaned back in his chair and sipped it thankfully, now that the crisis had passed, and Andrew looked ever so peaceful in his drug-induced sleep. With only mild concern, Kurt glanced at the purple restraints hanging festively from the side rails and chose not to use them. 'Let him rest comfortably,' he thought.

Kurt arrived back at the clinic at twelve thirty and was greeted by Dr. Klein and Father Gerald, who had just returned from the church where Matthew's wedding mass was celebrated.

"You are going to be exhausted by tomorrow morning," Dr. Klein said with a smile.

"Not really," Kurt replied. "I'll try to sneak a nap before my shift starts at three." He reached out to shake Father Gerald's hand. "How are you doing?" he asked.

"Not too badly for an old physician," Father Gerald said. He glanced down at Andrew. "I just wish circumstances were a lot less adverse."

Kurt nodded. "Yes, it's too bad."

Their discussion was suddenly interrupted by an announcement over the clinic's public address system. "Mayday on West One! Mayday on West One!"

"What's that all about?" Dr. Klein asked. "This is West One."

He barely completed the sentence when shouting and people running could be heard in the corridor.

"Andrew! Where are you?" Matthew screamed.

"Stop him!" someone shouted.

"I'm on him," an attendant yelled, yet in seconds, Matthew appeared, dressed in his long tailed tuxedo, in the doorway to Andrew's room, just as the attendant seized him.

"I'm so sorry, Andrew!" Matthew lamented. "I'll always love you." When he attempted to repeat himself, the attendant covered Matthew's mouth with his hand so that only a muffled version could be heard. Along with security, they proceeded to drag him down the corridor and into a secured room.

"Hell of a way to start a marriage," Dr. Klein commented to Kurt, as he returned to Andrew's room.

Kurt responded with minimal forethought. "Maybe he realizes that he married the wrong person." His face flushed almost instantly. "I'm sorry," he said. "I shouldn't have said that."

Dr. Klein grinned. "It's okay. You merely said what I was thinking."

Andrew stirred, moaned something unintelligible, and rolled onto his side.

"Do you think he heard him?" Kurt asked.

"I can't be sure," Dr. Klein said.

"I know I shouldn't be asking but I was wondering what took place with Matthew."

"We calmed him down, called his new father-in-law, and, before he arrived, explained how important it was for Andrew to be left alone so that he can put this behind him and get on with his life. If he wanted to help him, he should pay attention to this and let him get healthy."

"How did he handle it?" Kurt asked.

"Well, Matthew said he had no idea how ill Andrew was, and I believe, he was experiencing some major guilt. I imagine the wedding put some sort of finality into his life. Father Gerald offered to ride back with him and Mr. Storrow."

"It seems as though there are lot of unanswered questions."

"Unfortunately, yes, and they may never be answered."

Kurt nodded toward Andrew. "So is it possible to determine a prognosis?"

Dr. Klein ran his hand over his forehead and down his face. "I think he'll be all right, however, I'm worried about the transition between the clinic and the monastery."

"What do you mean?"

"If he can get himself re-acclimated to a familiar routine in the monastery, as quickly as possible, I think his chances of recidivism will be low."

"Hey, look; no restraints," Andrew said unexpectedly, with a hoarse voice. "I must be doing better."

"How are you feeling?" Dr. Klein asked, as he and Kurt approached his bed.

Andrew moved his head slowly from side to side. "Groggy, I guess."

"And you should," Dr. Klein said. "Later on, if you're up to it, I want to get you out of that bed. We'll get you walking so that you don't lose muscle tone."

"That will keep *him* busy," Andrew said. He turned and smiled at Kurt.

Kurt shrugged. "Well, you know. It's a tough job but somebody's got to do it."

Andrew's lunch tray arrived on the shoulder of the attendant, who placed the steaming food on the movable table. "Cheese soufflé with fresh asparagus," he said. "I think you'll like it." He wheeled the table next to the bed and swiveled the top so that the tray was directly in front of Andrew.

"I don't know how hungry I am but I'll try." Yet after only two mouthfuls, Andrew set down his fork, leaned back against the pillow and, once again, began shaking uncontrollably, nearly upsetting his food tray.

"Something set him off," Dr. Klein whispered. He immediately moved closer and attempted to comfort him. "It's okay. We'll save your lunch for later."

But Andrew shook his head. "Take it away. I don't want to look at it." His voice was more controlled.

Dr. Klein motioned toward the attendant to remove it. "I'll order something later." He then walked toward Kurt and spoke to him very softly. "I'm going to have a session with him. Ask the attendant to sit outside the door. And I'd suggest you try to get some sleep in the staff lounge."

Kurt nodded and left the room.

* * *

"He's not doing well," Dr. Klein announced, as Kurt returned after his nap.

"What happened?"

"He managed to share some of his feelings, familiar themes regarding Matthew's desertion, sexual roles, etc. But I'm mostly concerned with his level of depression and his uncontrolled crying."

Looking over Dr. Klein's shoulder, Kurt could see Andrew's tremulous body as he lay curled, fetal-like, on his side, sobbing against the pillow. "What about more medication?" he asked.

Dr. Klein shook his head. "Not right now." He placed his hand on Kurt's arm and gently moved him toward the door. "I've contacted Dr. Fitzgerald, and he's on his way to the clinic. We both feel that Andrew would benefit from ECT."

Kurt's surprise was obvious. "Shock treatment?" he asked.

"It's been very effective in situations such as this," Dr. Klein said with confidence. "Dr. Fitzgerald is extremely skilled in the field."

"I guess I'm surprised, but if you feel it's the right course of action, then by all means, do whatever is best for Andrew. He doesn't seem as though he's getting any better."

Kurt could feel his heart grow heavy as he digested Dr. Klein's intentions and its implications for Andrew. He wondered what it would mean for him. "Do you think Andrew will remember who I am?" he asked.

Dr. Klein smiled slightly. "Maybe not immediately, but yes, he will recognize you. It's primarily short-term memory loss."

"Does he know about your plans?"

"I told him, but I doubt that it's sinking in. I've contacted Father Gerald, and he will be signing the paperwork."

"I just hope it goes all right," Kurt said pensively.

"He'll be fine," Dr. Klein said reassuringly. "If you have the inclination, you're welcome to observe.

His invitation momentarily caught Kurt off-guard. "Well . . . why not," he said. "I've seen the ECT room, but I've never actually watched a procedure."

"I'll page you when Dr. Fitzgerald arrives."

After Dr. Klein left the room, Kurt stood next to Andrew's bed and watched as he continued to sob into his pillow, unaware of Kurt's presence. He pulled a chair close to the bed. "You're going to be okay, buddy," Kurt said softly. He reached out and gently rubbed Andrew's back.

Through swollen red eyes, Andrew looked up at Kurt, as if for the first time, scared and hesitant to speak.

"It's just me, Kurt."

"I know," Andrew said finally. "I just don't understand what's happening to me . . . I don't like what I'm feeling." His crying remained constant.

Kurt touched his face, wiped away some of Andrew's tears and pushed his hair away from his eyes and off his forehead. "Try to hang in there. Dr. Klein said you'll feel better after the treatment."

"Will I?" Andrew asked.

"Absolutely," Kurt said tentatively. "You'll be as good as new."

Andrew reached up and squeezed Kurt's hand. "Do me a favor and stay with me when they take me in. Can you do that?"

"I'm way ahead of you—I've already made arrangements to be there."

Andrew closed his eyes, smiled briefly, and pulled Kurt's hand down against his lips.

Hearing footsteps, Kurt quickly pulled his hand away from Andrew's mouth.

Paul, the day nurse, entered, carrying a medication tray. "Dr. Fitzgerald ordered this for Andrew prior to the ECT."

"It looks like you'll be getting another shot," Kurt said to Andrew, as he stood up and walked around the bed.

Once the instructions were completed, Andrew was transferred onto a gurney, with the assist of two attendants, and wheeled into the elevator where he was taken to the small, unimposing ECT room.

Kurt watched as they transferred Andrew onto a heavily padded table, complete with leather restraints and a protective head stabilizer.

After being secured, Andrew reminded Kurt of a convict on Death Row, awaiting a lethal injection.

"Is all that really necessary?" Kurt asked.

Dr. Klein nodded. "Unfortunately, yes," he said somberly.

Kurt was strangely mesmerized by the process and still curious to observe the results. Like a train wreck that he could not turn away from, he watched as the electrodes were strategically attached to Andrew's skull, creating a Frankenstein-like impression of an otherwise handsome face.

After inserting the rubber guard into Andrew's mouth, Dr. Fitzgerald announced that they were ready to proceed.

Kurt backed up slowly and waited for the electric jolt which would cause Andrew's brain to produce seizures.

"Stand clear," Dr. Klein said.

Almost immediately, Andrew's body began to spasm within the restraints, as if every neuron and synapse began firing uncontrollably, destined to destroy their shackles and dart—helter-skelter—around the room, like a deflating balloon. Kurt squinted to lessen the staggering visual impact; however, by then, the image had been permanently etched within his memory—an image he now wished he had never observed.

* * *

By the time Andrew was returned to his room, Kurt had been asleep in a lounge chair next to Andrew's bed for over an hour. The attendant placed the gurney on the opposite side and proceeded to wake him.

"Sorry, Kurt," he said softly, as he gently touched his shoulder.

With a startled yawn and stretch, Kurt sat upright and attempted to assess his surroundings. "I guess I dozed off there for a while," he said sleepily.

"No problem," the attendant said. "I'm returning Andrew from ECT, and I'll need your help transferring him from the cart to his bed."

Kurt immediately jumped out of the chair. "Let's do it."

Once Andrew was comfortably situated and covered, Kurt inquired about his status. "No broken bones . . . or anything I need to know?"

"Dr. Klein said he did fine." The attendant handed Kurt a brief report. "The plan is to let him sleep and then force fluids. I expect that Klein or Fitzgerald will be down to see him before long."

"Okay, thanks."

"You working a double?"

Kurt smiled. "If I make it . . ."

In the silence that followed, Kurt found himself, once again, staring down at a more placid and assuredly exhausted Andrew. Curls of dampened hair, reminiscent of Greek sculpture, crisscrossed his forehead with irregular "s" shapes. At that moment, he began to finally admit that his feelings for Andrew surpassed what might have been described as prurient and were now evolving into a strong bond of friendship, which he would cautiously characterize as love. 'I've done it,' he thought. 'I've fallen in love, and I must be nuts—I'm in love with a monk.'

The smile was still on his face when he turned to acknowledge Dr. Klein's presence.

"How's he looking?" Dr. Klein asked.

Kurt glanced back down at Andrew. "Incredibly peaceful."

"Well, not too peaceful, I hope; I've heard that same phrase used to describe the deceased." He checked Andrew's vitals and recorded the necessary information. "He's alive and well. And he did fine with the ECT, but I would like to try to wake him and check his orientation before I leave."

Dr. Klein sat on the edge of the bed and gently shook Andrew's shoulder. "Hello in there," he said softly. "It's Dr. Klein, Andrew, and I need you to try to wake up for a while."

Andrew stirred momentarily and then opened his eyes.

"It's all right," Dr. Klein reinforced. "You did well with the treatment. How are you feeling?"

Andrew continued to stare at him with caution. "Sort of dizzy . . . and thirsty."

Kurt quickly filled his glass with ice water, put a straw in it, and handed it to Andrew, who nearly finished it without stopping.

"I want to do a quick memory check," Dr. Klein said. He moved a bit closer to Andrew. "Do you remember my name?"

"Dr. Krine," Andrew said hastily.

"No, but very close. Try to think a bit harder."

Andrew frowned. "Oh . . . Klein," he said, "Dr. Klein."

"Good." Dr. Klein motioned for Kurt to come closer to Andrew. "Do you remember this gentleman's name?"

Kurt could feel his anxiety began to grow.

Unexpectedly, Andrew began to smile. "Of course," he said. "That's my guy, Kurt."

Kurt's joy was immediately hijacked by embarrassment, as his smiling face glowed radiantly in the fading light. "Well, I'm glad that you know who I am."

Although he realized it was a gamble, Dr. Klein continued, undaunted, with the next question. "Can you tell me what day it is?"

'Oh, shit,' Kurt thought. 'I hope this doesn't set him off.'

Andrew rubbed his eyes with one hand and gently shook his head as if to clear it. "I'm pretty sure it's Saturday."

"Excellent," Dr. Klein said. He looked up at Kurt. "If you have a second," he said softly.

Kurt followed Dr. Klein into the hall outside of Andrew's room.

"I think that the ECT has been beneficial, with minimal side effects. We'll see what happens. I don't think we need to worry about fluids if we can get him to drink."

"Cancel the IV?"

Dr. Klein nodded. "For now. Let's see how he does in the morning. If he becomes strongly symptomatic, use a PRN, or if he gets worse, call me immediately."

Kurt nodded. "Shouldn't he be getting hungry? He hasn't had much food all day."

"Don't hesitate to buzz the kitchen. Someone is always on call." Dr. Klein reached out to shake Kurt's hand. "I really appreciate your help with this case."

"Thanks," Kurt said. A bit of color rose, once again, to his cheeks.

"Oh, and while Andrew's sleeping, you might want to catch a few Z's yourself. You have a long night."

Kurt smiled and watched as Dr. Klein left, presumably to resurrect whatever was left of his Saturday and the typical unexpected constraints placed upon his own family as a result of his chosen profession. When he returned to check on Andrew, he expected him to be fast asleep.

Kurt pulled his chair close to the bed and rested his elbows on the mattress. "So . . . what's so funny, sleepyhead?" he said affectionately.

"You," Andrew said, slightly slurring the word.

"Oh, yeah? Why am I funny?" Kurt said with a feigned scoff.

"You know, when I called you 'my guy' and your face got red."

"You did that on purpose, didn't you?"

Andrew smiled and nodded.

Kurt moved a bit closer. "Well . . . is it true?"

"Do you want it to be?" Andrew asked thoughtfully.

"Of course," Kurt replied, "but only if you feel the same way."

Andrew delayed with contrived indecision. "Let me think about it—I'll let you know when I wake up."

"Well, don't keep me waiting too long," Kurt joked. "Several guys are waiting for an answer from me."

"Put them on hold."

Kurt reached out and took Andrew's hand. He could feel the emotional tightness in his throat. "By the way, I'm pretty proud of you—you did a good job with the treatment today."

It was clear that Andrew accepted his compliment yet was not quite ready to engage in a lengthy discussion about it. He simply smiled briefly and shook his head and, as before, pulled Kurt's hand up to his lips. "I hope you're here when I wake up," he whispered and then rolled onto his side and closed his eyes.

Within minutes, Kurt could tell by Andrew's breathing that he had lapsed into a deep, well-deserved sleep, while still holding his hand.

Most of Kurt's evening was consumed with observation, chart recording and, after dinner in Andrew's room, more observation. By twelve midnight, he found himself fighting exhaustion, while Andrew dozed peacefully, oblivious to his surroundings. Knowing that he could not resist it any longer, Kurt extended the foot rest on the lounge chair, lowered the back support, and pulled a light blanket over himself before joining Andrew's somnolent world by falling fast asleep.

Approximately one half hour later, a noise in the bathroom woke him; he sat upright and noticed that Andrew was not in his bed. His anxiety multiplied when he bolted out of the chair and found that the bathroom door was shut. He quickly turned the door handle, and with relief, it opened into a room filled with steam and the sound of running water. Through the thick vinyl curtain, he was able to see Andrew's silhouette in the shower.

"Andrew?" He spoke loud enough to be heard but not so loud as to frighten him.

Andrew appeared, smiling, from behind a corner of the curtain. His head was dripping with water and soapsuds. "I had to go to the bathroom, and I didn't want to wake you."

"So you decided to scare me to death, instead?" The severity in Kurt's voice was unmistakable.

"I'm sorry," Andrew said with genuine regret. "If I hadn't decided that I needed a shower, I probably wouldn't have caused you to wake up, and I would have been back in bed by now."

Kurt shook his head in frustration. "I don't care about that. I'm concerned about you. I don't want you to fall and get injured. How are you feeling?"

"Pretty good, actually," Andrew said.

Kurt reached behind him, picked up the lightweight shower seat, and slipped it behind the curtain. "Take this, put it in the shower, and sit on it," he insisted.

"You serious?"

"Yes, damn serious. And stick your arm out here." Once he was seated, Andrew complied and shoved his arm outside the curtain.

After drying it with a towel, Kurt immediately wrapped a blood pressure cuff around it, noted his pressure, and then checked his pulse which was somewhat elevated. "I want you to finish your shower from a seated position—okay?"

He watched Andrew nod. "All right."

He also saw him get up, adjust the shower nozzle, and quickly sit back down so that he could rinse off the shampoo.

"I can't seem to get this gook out of my hair."

"It's okay," Kurt said. "It's paste from the electrodes. I'll take care of it when you're back in bed."

Moments later, Andrew reached forward and turned off the water.

"Stay seated," Kurt insisted. "I'll get your towel."

He passed it around the side of the curtain.

Once Kurt determined that Andrew was about ready, he opened the curtain and covered him with another towel. Supporting him with his arm, he helped Andrew stand and step over the tub while assisting with drying his back. "I want you to realize how serious this was," Kurt said. "You could have been injured and I would have had a lot of explaining to do." In spite of his grave concerns, Kurt could not avoid being distracted by the natural, muscular curves of the handsome man he was trying to chastise. There was little visible evidence of atrophy.

"I know . . . I'm sorry," Andrew said. He turned to look at Kurt with a solemn expression, which easily convinced him of his sincerity and, at the same time, caused Kurt's heart to defrost.

"Hey, it's all right."

"Besides," Andrew added suddenly. "I was sort of embarrassed."

"About what?"

"I didn't want to ask you for the bedpan."

Kurt smiled and shook his head. "We all have to go, man . . . I would have given you as much privacy as you needed."

"It isn't just that," Andrew explained. "I just don't like using those things."

"I probably could've gotten you to the toilet. Don't be afraid to speak up and tell me what you're feeling."

"Okay," Andrew replied.

"Let's get you over to the bed."

With Andrew sitting safely on the side of the bed, Kurt removed a clean hospital gown from the cabinet and held it in front of Andrew. "Slip this on, and I'll tie the back of it for you."

Once that was finished, Kirk removed the towels, helped swing Andrew's leg onto the mattress, and then lightly covered him with a sheet. "All you need now is a shave, and you'd look like a million dollars."

Andrew shrugged. "It would take more than a shave."

Kurt looked directly at him. "Not in my book."

A hint of color rose in Andrew's cheeks as he glanced down, averting Kurt stare.

"How about doing something about the paste in your hair?"

"How do you get rid of it?"

"I'll show you," Kurt said. He took a bottle of rubbing alcohol and a clean towel from the cabinet and set them on the bedside table. Sitting on the side of the bed, Kurt proceeded to soak a part of the towel with the alcohol and aggressively daub the hardened glue until it softened and could be easily combed away. "The alcohol might sting a bit, but it works." The physical closeness and touching evoked in Kurt a sensual, loving sentiment, which he was sure Andrew shared, judging from his submission to Kurt's manipulations.

"No, it's fine," Andrew said softly. His eyes remained closed; his face appeared tranquil. "In fact, I have always liked the antiseptic smell of rubbing alcohol."

"Yeah, me too," Kurt admitted.

Footsteps and a third voice suddenly interrupted their conversation. "Sorry to bother you, Kurt, but I'm not feeling that great, so I wanted to let you know that I'll be leaving early." Jim, the attendant, stood in the doorway, not sure if he should enter.

Kurt continued to work on Andrew's hair. He spoke without turning around. "No problem. I hope you'll be feeling better."

"I hope so," Jim said.

Realizing that an explanation might be necessary, Kurt stood up and walked toward him. "I'm trying to get some of the electrode glue out of Andrew's hair. He says it's making him uncomfortable."

"Oh, that's right. He had the ECT today, didn't he?"

Kurt nodded.

"How's he doing?"

"It looks good so far. I hope that he makes it through the rest of the night without a problem."

Jim smiled a curious smile. "Well, with you taking care of him, I'm sure he'll be just fine."

"Thanks. I wish I shared your confidence."

"Sorry to wimp out on you, but I'm really bushed," Jim said.

"Don't worry about it," Kurt said. "Anything I need to know about the patients?"

"I think things will be fine until morning." Jim gestured with one hand, turned, and walked down the corridor.

Kurt returned to Andrew's bed, sat on the edge, and continued to remove the paste from his hair.

"Are you the only one covering?" Andrew asked unexpectedly.

"Security is here, but I'm the only clinical staff person until seven."

"It seems like a big responsibility."

"It can be," Kurt said. "Especially when I get guys who disobey their doctor, get out of bed unescorted, and take a shower in the middle of the night."

"You're not going to let me forget that, are you?"

"At least for tonight," Kurt said with a smile. He rubbed the remaining fragments of hardened paste from Andrew's hair and then used his fingers to gently massage his scalp and roughly rearrange his hair into a semblance of order.

"That feels good," Andrew whispered.

Kurt simply gazed at him with silent understanding.

"By the way, I thought about it," Andrew said pensively.

"About what?"

"You know—when I called you 'my guy' in front of Dr. Klein."

"And?"

"It's fine with me," Andrew said. "It always was."

Kurt grinned from ear-to-ear—but not for long—as Andrew suddenly reached out, pulled him toward him, and kissed him, uninhibitedly, with aggressive intent.

Caught off-guard, Kurt almost immediately pulled away as the severity of the situation loomed before him. "Hold on a second," he whispered. "This is not the best time or place for this, even though I want it as much—or more—than you do." He glanced over his shoulder toward the opened door. "I could easily lose my job."

Surprisingly, Andrew appeared only slightly repentant. "Well, I honestly don't want that to happen, but what are the chances? It's three in the morning, your attendant has gone home, and the security guards are probably fast asleep at the monitors." He smiled lasciviously. "Besides, can't you lock the door with the key from the inside?"

Kurt nodded. "You drive a hard bargain."

"I'll let that line pass," Andrew joked. He then continued in a more somber vein. "If you are really that uncomfortable or, more importantly, would just rather not be with me, tell me now."

"What are you, crazy?" Kurt replied. The sentence escaped before he realized what he was saying.

Andrew smirked. "Probably; in fact, someone once said there are hospitals for guys like me." His vanishing smile reflected his interior anguish, which Kurt immediately recognized.

"Look, I'm sorry," he said. "You know I didn't mean it the way it came out. Of course I want to be with you, and that's exactly what I'm going to do. The door can be locked, the drapes closed—so screw the job." He immediately jumped up and accomplished the tasks, as well as remembering to place a towel over the door window. When he returned, Kurt drew the privacy curtain three quarters of the way around the bed, creating a secure, provocative ambience.

"That's nice," Andrew admitted. "How do you feel?"

"Much better," Kurt said. He reached behind Andrew and turned off all the lights, except for the softly shaded table lamp on the other side of the bed.

"That's even better . . .," Andrew said. Once again, he pulled Kurt toward him and resumed where they had left off, kissing him passionately, tasting his mouth, and licking almost every part of exposed skin above Kurt's collar. Unexpectedly, Andrew untied his hospital gown and, within seconds, slipped his arms out of the garment, and was soon completely naked before Kurt.

"You are so fucking beautiful," Kurt said slowly, almost in awe, as he stared down at him.

Andrew pulled the top of Kurt's scrubs out of his pants over his head and set it on the tray table. "No more than you," Andrew commented. He was surprised by Kurt's muscular definition which was well hidden by the loose fitting uniform. "Heck of a chest and abs. You must work out quite a bit."

Kurt shrugged. "Not as much as I used to." Kurt took the time to remove his shoes and socks and then slowly slipped off his pants and underwear. He then carefully got into bed and lay on his side next to Andrew, who responded by placing his leg between Kurt's and exploring his body with his hands, while gently biting his ears and shoulders.

The general bulk of his body fascinated Andrew; his large, solid biceps and muscular back flowed smoothly into flared buttocks and strong thighs.

Although Kurt was not nearly as tall as Andrew, his stature made up the difference in general muscle mass, which was proportionately appealing. With heightened interest, Andrew slowly moved one hand inside of Kurt's thigh, until he felt his erection. In total disbelief, Andrew investigated, almost clinically, to verify what he was holding was, in fact, real.

He raised his head to look at Kurt. "I'm sure you've heard this before, but I have to say it—that's incredible."

"Maybe I haven't heard it as much as you might think," Kurt said with a slight smile.

Ignited by his discovery, Andrew continued to massage the massively thick member, unable to fathom its reality.

Yet as that reality slowly sunk in, Andrew seemed to lose control, writhing with intense craving, kissing Kurt savagely, and then initiating his descent toward the lower half of his private centaur.

"You're a fucking wild man," Kurt uttered.

Andrew did not look up. The coarseness of Kurt's language only served to inflame his craving. "It's what you do to me," he said. "Should I continue?"

"Hell, yes," Kurt groaned. "Do whatever you need to do."

Perhaps it was this carte blanche approval that prompted Andrew's behavior, yet in his heart, Kurt sensed the true genesis of Andrew's desire—at least part of it—and, as much as he did not want to admit it due to obviously selfish reasons, he remembered that it was still the first night of Matthew's honeymoon with his new bride. Overwhelmed by Andrew's sexual intensity, Kurt resolved to simply let such thoughts evaporate and enjoy the present moment with someone who truly interested him. He knew it was the wrong time to begin analyzing.

And if there were such a thing as an autopilot button for lust, Andrew's had definitely been pushed. He had worked his way down Kurt's chest and abdominals, until he successfully reach Kurt's exceptionally thick erection which, at first, he gently licked, not knowing whether its bulbous head would actually fit into his mouth. With even less inhibition, Andrew slid his tongue still lower within the thin crevice between Kurt's buttocks. Carefully, he separated them and paused slightly for a reaction from Kurt, and when it seemed as though there were no objections, Andrew initiated his contact with Kurt's private area, just as he remembered it happening to him.

Unlike Andrew's initial response to Matthew, Kurt blatantly encouraged Andrew to do more by opening his legs even wider and using both hands to force Andrew's face against him. Needing air, Andrew, once again, moved up to Kurt's erection. With barely a pause, he slipped his mouth over its massive head, tasting the salty fluid and knowing he needed to concentrate on keeping his mouth open as wide as possible or risk injuring Kurt with his teeth. Andrew moved gently down the shaft, until he could feel Kurt thrust himself against the back of his throat. At that point, Andrew's gag reflex became overwhelming. He immediately moved up the shaft and, somehow, allowed the bulbous head to escape without teeth marks. Following a brief coughing spell, Andrew lay on top of Kurt, who held him fast.

"I'm sorry," Kurt said genuinely. "Are you okay?"

Andrew smiled broadly. "Never been better."

"Good," Kurt said. He pulled Andrew's face against his, kissing him hard until, at times, Andrew felt as though air were being sucked directly out of his lungs and into Kurt's. Reaching beneath him, Kurt played with Andrew's erection, massaging it roughly and rubbing it between his buttocks.

Andrew got the message and responded boldly. "I'll do it, if you want," he admitted quietly.

Kurt nodded. "I think it's something we both want." He carefully slid, first, one and then the other leg, out from under Andrew, and brought both of his knees up toward his chest.

The anticipation of what he was about to do filled Andrew with fierce craving. After gathering a sufficient amount of saliva in his mouth, he rubbed the lubricant over his erection and then massaged the excess into Kurt's anal area.

"Go easy," Kurt cautioned. "I'm really not too good at this."

On his knees, Andrew pulled Kurt toward him, raised his buttocks slightly, and, with one hand, proceeded to penetrate the resistive pressure. With one firm thrust, Andrew sensed the immediate warmth and sensual viscosity of his receptor who, at the same time, muffled his response—a sharp cry of pain—by jamming his forearm against his mouth.

Andrew watched with heightened desire as Kurt lay beneath him with closed eyes, uninhibitedly experiencing the total acceptance of another man with no regard for societal stigma or one's role within the relationship. Unable to resist, Andrew leaned down and kissed him, tenderly at first, until Kurt began to thrust himself against Andrew's erection and brutally invade his mouth with his, biting intentionally and probing deeply with his tongue.

Kurt's aggression easily incited Andrew to ejaculate, as he thrust himself even deeper within him, only to pull back, momentarily, and mercilessly repeat the process until he crashed, exhausted, on top of his receptive partner.

With his arms wrapped around Andrew, Kurt rolled him onto his side and held him tight. The mild flush across Andrew's cheeks highlighted his handsome dark features, as he rested quietly with closed eyes. Kurt noticed the small beads of perspiration that had gathered on his forehead and across the bridge of his nose, reflecting the soft lamplight like iridescent bits of glitter. He raised his head close to Andrew's and gently licked away the salty residue, until Andrew met his mouth with his and shared his own taste.

"I can't tell you how happy I am that we met," Kurt whispered.

Andrew looked at him with large docile eyes. "Me too," he said. "I just never expected it under these circumstances."

"Well, you've been through a lot, but after the storm there is often a rainbow, and you know what's generally at the end of the rainbow."

"Yeah—you," Andrew said with a grin.

Andrew chuckled and looked up at Kurt. "How about you? Any serious relationships?"

"You mean, besides this one?" Kurt's smile was colossal.

His comment evidently pleased Andrew who returned his smile. "Yes, besides this one."

"No longer than a year and a half," Kurt said. "I guess nobody wants me."

"I doubt that." Andrew reached down and gently massaged Kurt mounting erection. "They want you . . . but they probably can't take you."

"Maybe," Kurt said. He licked Andrew's neck, ears, and face before kissing him with growing desire. "That feels really good," he said softly.

"You have an incredible cock," Andrew said unexpectedly, undaunted by his own sudden use of vulgarity. Once again, he managed to orally accommodate Kurt's erection.

Kurt remained silent. He continued to run his fingers through Andrew's hair, tugging slightly and, at times, applying pressure as necessary to maximize his pleasure.

"If you keep this up, I'm going to be coming in your mouth," Kurt said quietly.

But Andrew had other plans. He carefully backed away and gently removed his hand from its warm crevice. He then pulled himself toward Kurt, held him tight, and kissed him wildly, while wrapping his leg around him and pulling his body close to his. "I want you to do it," Andrew whispered. He stared into Kurt's eyes.

"You want me to . . . ?" Kurt was confused.

"Yes," Andrew said hastily. "Do what I did to you."

Kurt raised his head and supported it with his hand and bent elbow. "Look . . . you don't have to do this."

"I know but I really want to; I want to feel you inside of me."

"Remember what you said earlier about guys wanting me but not being able to take me?" Kurt replied.

"I don't care," Andrew insisted.

"But you were right. It's true," Kurt said.

"Then show me how to be the one who can give you what you want, and come inside of me."

"No," Kurt insisted. "It would be too painful."

Andrew grabbed Kurt's hair and yanked his face toward his. "Listen. I *want* you . . . to fuck me, okay?" He took a deep breath. "Now . . . I've said it, and it seems easier. I want you to fuck me." He pulled Kurt's mouth against his and, once again, kissed him savagely, until Kurt was forced to break away.

"Under one condition," Kurt proposed.

"It doesn't matter—just say it," Andrew said.

Kurt quickly jumped out of bed.

Andrew could hear one of the cabinet doors open and then quickly close.

Kurt immediately returned, straddled Andrew's knees, and held out his hands.

After squinting his eyes for a clearer focus, Andrew recognized the bright purple color of several neatly rolled restraint straps. "I'm assuming they're for me," he said with some bewilderment.

"It's the only way I'll do it," Kurt admitted. "I've been in this position before, and it's almost always the same story. I'm usually getting into it hot and heavy, and invariably, I'm asked to stop because they can't take it. I don't want to stop this time, so please tell me the truth. It's going to hurt, and I don't want to jeopardize our relationship because I love you." He looked hard at Andrew. "Do you want me to put these on?"

Although he did not want to fully admit it, Andrew could feel a growing sense of excitement well-up within his chest and travel quickly to his scrotum. He nodded his head. "Yeah, let's do it—just . . . try to take it easy."

"I'll do my best," Kurt said. "Now, rollover."

Something about the irritable tone of Kurt's statement seemed to concern Andrew and add a new element to his excitement—fear. This combination of emotions and conflicting desires exacerbated his mania. As Kurt tied one arm to the bed frame and then the other, Andrew began to chuckle inappropriately, wanting to experience the feeling of complete domination and yet fearing the unknown consequences.

When Kurt was finished, Andrew was restrained in a four-point spread-eagle position, almost completely immobilized and most assuredly at Kurt's mercy.

"One more strap, and we'll be ready."

"Another one?" Andrew asked.

"Be quiet and raise your stomach," Kurt demanded.

As Andrew lifted his midsection, Kurt slid the restraint under his navel, crisscrossed the ends over his back, as though he were wrapping a present, and then secured each end tightly to the bed frame.

Suddenly, Andrew realized it was almost impossible for him to move, even slightly, in one direction or the other. He could feel a light sweat break out on his forehead. "I don't know about this," he said anxiously.

"Relax," Kurt insisted. "You'll be fine."

His familiar tone of voice, replete with deception, chilled Andrew's blood.

Unexpectedly, Kurt pulled the pillow from under Andrew's head and squeezed it beneath his hips and the mattress. Andrew was unaware that he had removed the pillowcase.

"I think you'll find this more comfortable," Kurt said. He then jumped off the bed and stood alongside of it, as if admiring his work. "You look so incredibly fuckable."

Andrew watched as he stood over him, slowly massaging his already stiffened erection, and wondered how he would ever be able to accept the massive member that protruded, almost unnaturally, from Kurt's groin while, at the same time, knowing that he craved to be completely satiated by its enormity.

Kurt lay alongside of him and rubbed his back. Without saying a word, he leaned down, kissed him lovingly with open eyes, and then swung one leg over his. He began to rub himself against Andrew's buttocks, while he kissed his ears, neck, and shoulders.

By now, Andrew's fears began to abate as they were, once again, replaced by desire. "That feels much better," he said softly.

Like an artist, Kurt skillfully manipulated his marionette, pulling first, one string, and then another, until Andrew willingly complied—although blindly—with every unspoken mandate. He licked nearly every inch of his back, down to the symmetrically dimpled area above his buttocks which were sufficiently elevated by the pillow and already spread apart by the individual restraints.

"That feels really good," Andrew whispered.

"And this will feel even better," Kurt said. "Just relax," he instructed, as he continued to probe with his tongue.

As much as he tried, Andrew knew that this part of sex initially caused him anguish. Once he felt comfortable and the anxiety faded away, he knew that he would be able to thoroughly enjoy the anal attention; however, Kurt began to grow impatient.

"Relax!" he insisted.

His tone of voice only prompted Andrew to become more rigid, until suddenly, he could feel the wincing pain as Kurt slapped his right buttock with serious intent. He buried his face in the mattress to avoid crying out.

"Sorry," Kurt said softly, "but it's for your own good. It'll help loosen up that beautiful ass of yours." Once again, Kurt shoved his face between the walls of muscle and then abruptly stopped.

Unanticipated, Andrew immediately felt the incredible pain of having his other cheek slapped with even greater force, a slap which would imprint the shape of Kurt's hand onto his buttock for nearly two weeks. He cried out again and fought hard against the restraints. "Okay, stop it! I've had enough." His voice was filled with anger.

As before, Kurt lay alongside of him, trying to calm him by rubbing his shoulders and back. "I know this will seem weird but, if I can't get you to relax, I'll have a tough time getting inside of you, and believe me, it will be painful."

"Just stop the damn slapping," Andrew insisted.

"All right." Kurt quickly got out of bed, went to the cabinet, and returned.

Andrew could see that he something in his hand. "What's that?"

"A tube of lubricant—water soluble jelly." He leaned down and kissed Andrew, who quickly warmed to his gentler passion. Kurt squeezed a copious amount of jelly into his hand, spread it between Andrew's buttocks, and carefully massaged it over the tight muscles until he could feel their tension release. He delicately inserted one finger, while he continued to kiss Andrew with even greater passion. "How's that feel?" he asked softly.

Andrew responded with a hypnotic glaze. "Much, much better."

Feeling his excitement grow, Kurt inserted a second, and then a third finger, as he attempted to relax and stretch Andrew's muscle. "I think you're about ready," he whispered.

Positioning himself between Andrew's widely spread legs, Kurt lowered his body toward him and, with one hand, guided his lubricated penis firmly against the coveted entrance. "Take a deep breath and exhale," he admonished and immediately thrust the massive head through the muscled ring and into the more accommodating area beyond.

The more Andrew screamed, the harder Kurt shoved his face against the mattress.

"Take a deep breath! The pain will go away after a minute or so!"

With tears streaming from his eyes and gasping for breath, Andrew wondered if Kurt had instead shoved a knife inside of him, as flashes of colored lights zigzagged across his eyelids; he felt as though his heart would burst from his chest.

Kurt lay motionless on top of him, licking his neck and whispering words of encouragement into his ear. "It's okay. The worst part is over." He knew that he was lying, but this time, Andrew believed him. "It's okay," he repeated, "it's okay." He kissed Andrew's ears and licked the tears that wet his cheeks, while ever so slowly resuming his mild thrusts, advancing even deeper into Andrew's warmth and stopping, only briefly, whenever he sensed Andrew's response to the excruciating pain. Before long, Kurt had managed to fully insert himself into Andrew, who continued to breathe deeply through his mouth.

"You can relax," Kurt whispered. "You've taken it all. Take a minute or so to let your insides expand and get used to it." He turned his head and kissed Andrew's open mouth. "You are doing exceptional, so far," he said and then kissed him with greater intensity.

Andrew returned his kisses, tentatively, at first, and then, as the pain subsided, with increased hunger. Feeling Kurt's weight on top of him and a substantial portion of his body deep within his, Andrew began to relate to Kurt not as a separate entity but more as a unified extension of his own body, a freaky anomaly not unlike that of Siamese twins. "I never thought I'd be able to do this," he said.

"I knew you could," Kurt confessed. He also knew that Andrew was ready for what was about to follow, yet he silently doubted his ability to tolerate the pain that would be inflicted upon him. "Just stay relaxed," Kurt said softly. He slowly pulled himself back and then pushed himself deeper into Andrew, establishing a slow, comfortable rhythm which Andrew found acceptable. He gradually increased his thrusts faster and deeper, while Andrew moaned beneath him.

"Go easy, you're killing me!" he said loudly.

"Be quiet!" Kurt insisted. "They'll hear us." The visual effects alone were enough to bring Kurt to orgasm; however, he wanted to delay and finish with a renewed, savage assault on Andrew. Yet after several deep thrusts, Andrew, once again, cried out in pain. Kurt immediately stopped and picked up the loose pillowcase which had been thrown on the mattress. Hanging on to opposite corners, he twisted it into a rope, much as he might do with a locker room towel just before snapping it any teammate. In a flash, he slipped it over Andrew's head, forced it into his mouth, and tied it firmly in back of his head. "Sorry, buddy," he whispered, "but this is the only way we're going to get through this."

Unable to call out except for muffled grunting and moaning, Andrew now felt completely defenseless, as he began to panic and fight violently against his restraints, while making high-pitched or guttural wails, all to no avail.

Heady with his total domination over him, Kurt grew even more ruthless and out of control in the final moments of his sexual exploitation—his language grew even coarser and his physical attack essentially turned brutal, as he pounded Andrew's insides with the full force of his lethal erection, slamming his body against his buttocks and causing the bed to move several inches away from the wall.

Meanwhile, Andrew simply grew silent, either as a result of his body's response to the unbearable pain or a combination of his anxiety mixed with rage. He felt as if a small log were thrust violently inside of him, spreading him apart and tearing tender tissue; he was convinced that he was hemorrhaging. And it was with infinite relief, when he sensed by Kurt's breathing and sustained thrusts that he was finally about to reach orgasm—one which he could feel explode deeply inside of him like gobs of molten lava.

Exhausted, Kurt fell on top of him, as he waited for his erection to subside before removing himself from Andrew.

Andrew too lay silently beneath him, confused, perhaps dazed, by what had just taken place in his hospital room. 'What the hell is happening to me?' he wondered. Uncomfortable, he began to squirm.

"You okay?" Kurt asked.

Shaking his head, Andrew did his best to say the word "no."

"All right. I'll take off the gag if you promise you won't make a scene. Will you promise?"

Andrew nodded affirmatively.

Kurt carefully slipped the pillowcase gag over Andrew's head and out of his mouth.

"You son of a bitch! You fucking raped me!" Andrew shouted.

Struggling to replace the gag, Kurt managed to get it back in Andrew's mouth and over his head, but not before Andrew bit him.

"Fuck!" Kurt shouted. "Why did you do that?" He quickly pulled himself out of Andrew, jumped up, and found some rubbing alcohol in the cabinet. After washing the small wound and bandaging it, he removed a familiar syringe from the medication tray and stood over Andrew. He quickly rubbed a fresh alcohol pad onto Andrew's arm and, after checking the dosage, injected its contents into the very agitated patient.

"I'm sorry, Andrew, but I need you to relax. I can't have you yelling, or we'll both be in trouble." He lay down alongside of him and slowly rubbed his back and shoulders.

Unwilling to cooperate, Andrew fought against his restraints while attempting to shout through his gag.

Kurt grabbed him firmly by the hair and forced him to look at him. "Listen!" he insisted. "Before your medicine kicks in, you need to hear what I have to say, okay?"

Although Andrew continued to squirm, Kurt applied more pressure to his head until he settled down.

"That's better. Now . . . I know you probably hate me for what I did, and I guess I can't blame you. But you weren't exactly innocent in the whole ordeal either. I had no intention of fucking you until you insisted, and I apologize if I hurt you—I'm sure it hurt—but in a day or so, you'll be fine. You can tell Dr. Klein what happened if you want to, and I'll probably get fired or sent to jail, which I don't want to happen. It's up to you. And you may not—and probably won't believe me—but my relationship with you is not based on my ability to have intercourse with you. When I first met you on your very first admission, I was totally taken by you, your sincerity, vulnerability, and openness. By your second admission, I think I honestly fell in love with you—and that's exactly how I feel now. It's not a line to get you to forgive me. Truth is, I wish this had never happened.

"As soon as you start to fall asleep, I'll remove all the restraints, remove the gag, and clean you up. When you wake up tomorrow morning, you'll be in a fresh hospital gown and sleeping in clean sheets. I'm going to apply some ointment to your butt and make sure that I check your wrists and ankles for abrasions."

Andrew's eyelids began to slowly droop and retract.

"You look like you're about ready to go out," Kurt whispered. "Before you do, I want to tell you two other things. Earlier tonight, when you were inside of me—it was one of the most meaningful experiences I've ever had. And the other is this—I do love you, Andrew—I mean it." He leaned down and gently kissed his forehead, nose, and cheek.

Before he drifted off, Andrew could feel his eyes fill with tears, yet he was confused by their existence and unsure of their true source.

* * *

Imagining that he was still dreaming, Andrew could feel someone gently nudge his shoulder.

"Time to wake up, sleepyhead. Your breakfast is here."

Through squinted eyes, Andrew could see someone standing next to his bed, outlined by the harsh morning light which streamed through the window in back of him. After a brief pause, he recognized Jim, the day nurse, who stood looking down at him with an expansive grin.

"Wow, what time is it?" Andrew asked.

"A little after ten," Jim said. "Should I pull the tray table over?"

Andrew nodded and suddenly realized his erection was completely visible under the thin white sheet. He immediately sat up, adjusted the covering, and gladly welcomed the wide tray table which obstructed further observation.

"So how was your night?" Jim asked.

"Fine, why?" Andrew blurted. He knew that he had responded more defensively than he should have.

Jim shrugged. "I was just wondering," he said. "I saw in the chart that Kurt gave you some medication."

Like a bad dream, the realization of the evening's events suddenly came into focus. "Oh . . . that," Andrew replied nonchalantly. "I was tossing quite a bit—having crazy nightmares—so Kurt decided it would help me sleep."

"Well, he was right. I hated to wake you, but I didn't want you to miss breakfast."

"Thanks. It looks and smells great."

"They are," Jim said. "Crêpes stuffed with garlic mashed potatoes and cheddar. I had some earlier."

Andrew arranged his napkin. "I'm sure I've never had anything like this before." He cut off a bite sized piece and popped it into his mouth. "Well, you're right. They are really good."

"If you didn't wake up, I was considering eating them," Jim joked, yet judging by his size, Andrew wondered if he might be telling the truth.

"You are welcome to share one," Andrew offered.

"No, thanks, just kidding," Jim insisted. He raised the head of the bed to make Andrew more comfortable. "How's that?" he asked.

"Much better, thanks."

"So how have you been feeling?"

Andrew nodded. "I think I'm doing okay; once I get my head screwed on straight, I'm looking forward to getting back to the monastery."

Jim pulled out a blood pressure cuff and began to wrap it around Andrew's arm. "From the looks of things, I'm sure it will be soon." A pause in the conversation allowed him to listen with the stethoscope and record his findings in the chart. "I'm going to let you enjoy your breakfast. I'll be back in about twenty minutes so that you can get up and use the shower. Dr. Klein wrote orders that it was all right for you to do so, as long as an attendant is in the room."

As soon as Jim left, Andrew immediately threw off the sheet and examined his wrists and ankles for bruises, which were only barely noticeable yet somewhat tender. He could not see the black and blue hand imprint on his buttock until he got out of the shower, a bruise which helped him to remember, vividly, exactly what happened. 'That son of a bitch,' Andrew thought, yet the words may have unknowingly escaped from his lips.

"Are you okay in there?" Jim asked from outside the door.

Andrew quickly slipped into his bathrobe and tied it. "I'm doing fine," he replied. "I'll be right out."

"Take your time," Jim said.

Once he finished his bathroom activities, Andrew returned to the bedroom and settled in one of the comfortable chairs. Hoping to be discreet, he inquired about Kurt. "Is Kurt expected in at three?"

Jim paused on his way out the door. "I believe he switched shifts with Ken, so I don't think he'll be in until this evening at eleven."

In the silence that followed, Andrew leaned his head back against the overstuffed chair and attempted to understand what took place the night before. The fact that he allowed himself to engage in activities he would never have agreed to engage in with Matthew signaled a behavior which, he knew, was uncharacteristic and, in his mind, the beginning of a noteworthy change in his moral ethics. He also thought about Matthew, particularly about his wedding night, and wondered whether there was even the slightest hint of pure passion between the newlywed's requisite naked bodies. And even now, the anger he was experiencing and the sense of desertion by Matthew, forced him to realize that his relationship with Kurt was largely due to his need to be both loved and, perhaps, punished, yet his guilt began to rapidly multiply. 'What the hell have I done?' he thought. 'Why is this happening?'

Andrew closed his eyes and rested his head against the soft cushioning.

After hearing a gentle tap on his door, he looked up to see Dr. Klein standing in the entrance.

"Am I here at a bad time?" he inquired softly.

"No, not at all. Come in," Andrew said.

Dr. Klein pulled one of the smaller chairs next to Andrew. "Well. You are looking a lot better than the last time I saw you. How are you feeling?"

Before he had time to respond, Andrew knew, instantaneously, that he would have to tell Dr. Klein, not how he actually felt but what he needed to hear, so that he would let him return to the monastery. "I feel like I'm doing a lot better. How do you think I'm doing?" He added the question to reinforce his familiar contentious style.

Leafing through his chart, Dr. Klein noted that Andrew received medication during the early-morning hours. "How did you do last night?" he asked. "I see that Kurt gave you an injection at approximately 4:00 a.m."

Andrew began coughing intentionally to disguise his overwhelming urge to laugh. "A powerful one," he said with a smile. "I guess he said I was tossing and turning and woke up out of control; I couldn't get back to sleep. It must be the reason I slept so late this morning." He could see that his mirth puzzled Dr. Klein.

"It seems as though the extra sleep did you some good."

"Like I said, I think I'm doing better."

Dr. Klein leaned forward slightly. "What about safety issues? Are there any strong urges to harm yourself?"

"No," Andrew replied, with credible emphasis. "I appreciate all you've done for me in the clinic, but I would rather continue with my recovery in the monastery."

After some intense reflection, Dr. Klein responded. "Let's give it one more night, see how well you tolerate unmedicated sleep, and then I'll make a decision in the morning."

Andrew was obviously pleased. "Sounds good to me," he said.

"In the meantime, you can get dressed, use the day room or the recreation room, or spend your time as you wish—within the confines of the clinic."

"Thanks," Andrew said. He extended his hand to Dr. Klein.

"I know you're anxious to get back. I hope my consideration to release you is not premature."

"I understand, but I really don't think so," Andrew said. "Besides, I assume you'll be giving me some prescription meds."

Dr. Klein nodded. "Most assuredly."

"Well, I guess I'll be talking with you in the morning."

* * *

It was just after lunch when Andrew decided to explore part of the clinic. The brightly lit recreation room illuminated the soft mauve, brown, and pink interior, which housed a ping-pong table, a regulation sized pool table, and several small wooden game tables with either checker boards or chess sets painted on top of them.

Although there were few people in the room, Andrew seemed taken by those he saw. He sat in a comfortable chair against the wall and watched as another attendant played pool with a young man, who barely looked twenty years old. He was still wearing pajamas and had an oversized clinic robe wrapped loosely around him. Almost all of his actions appeared exaggerated, as though he were unable to control the copious amounts of energy that flowed from within. As soon as he saw Andrew, he immediately approached him, stuck out his hand, and said, "Hi, I'm Caleb. Wanna play?"

Before Andrew could respond, the heavyset attendant had already grabbed him with both hands and was forcing him backwards. "He just wants to sit, Caleb; let him relax."

Andrew had little time to process what had taken place; he merely sat in his chair and tried to avoid eye contact, while he wondered about Caleb's reasons for being hospitalized. Whatever the explanation, he could feel himself slowly sinking into a familiar depression and decided to leave the room.

The connecting day room appeared far less threatening and glaring. Its carpeted floor and absence of vigorous activity was much more conducive to reading, meditation, or simple introspection. Shelves of books lined the far wall; the opposite consisted of floor-to-ceiling windows which were protected by ornate metal grills to prevent breakage by angry patients or attempted suicides, much like the barriers in Andrew's room. The windows provided an expansive view of alpine forest which dropped sharply away from the clinic and then rose gradually into the foothills and eventually culminated in the majestic peaks beyond. The afternoon sun, intermittently blocked by Bitter Creek's signature Volkswagen-shaped clouds, dappled the landscape with a barrage of kaleidoscope shapes and colors, an ever changing vista, which captivated Andrew's attention until he heard a gentle cough somewhere to his left.

Approximately halfway between himself and the far wall, Andrew could see the back of someone's head sticking up over the high-backed chair. Pretending to be interested in the various titles, Andrew examined the shelves of books with a cursory glance, as he slowly made his way past the person sitting in the chair. He then selected an arbitrary work and, without looking up, sat in a similar chair, which afforded him a lateral view of his subject. Moments later, he decided to steal a quick glance and was surprised to see a fairly attractive man with curly auburn hair staring back at him.

"Why did you try to kill yourself?" the stranger asked unexpectedly. He posed the question nonchalantly, as if inquiring about the weather.

Andrew was so startled that he looked around to see if he might be talking to someone else, yet there was no one in the room. "I don't understand," he said awkwardly.

The stranger pointed toward Andrew's hands. "I can see the scars and bruises on your wrists."

Andrew examined his wrists briefly and self-consciously jammed both hands into his pockets. "Oh, that," he muttered. "I . . . smashed a glass door. The bruises are from the restraints." He barely got the words out of his mouth when he realized that, perhaps, he had said too much.

The stranger half stood and extended his hand toward Andrew. "I'm Chris. Nice to meet you."

Andrew got up to shake his hand and noticed that both of his wrists were heavily bandaged. He immediately averted his stare. "I'm Andrew," he said.

"It's okay. You can ask if you want," Chris said.

"Ask what?" Andrew said.

"About the bandages on my wrists." He held up his arms. "I slashed both of them."

'Why me?' Andrew thought. He looked hard at Chris. "I'm not sure why we're having this conversation."

Displaying a twisted, mercurial temper, Chris wrinkled his face and mimicked Andrew's comment in a high-pitched, affected voice. "I'm not sure why we're having this conversation," he blurted. He then reverted to his initial soft tone. "Because," he said, "this is a fucking hospital for psychos. That's why."

As if out of thin air, two attendants suddenly materialized, gently prodded Chris from his chair, and began to escort him back to his room. They did not go very far when Chris suddenly turned around to face Andrew.

"About the restraints?" He began to laugh. "It looks like the big guy got you too, didn't he?" He erupted with laughter, as the attendants dragged him away through the glaring lights of the recreation room.

Andrew sat in silence as he attempted to recover from Chris's remarks. He wondered how Chris could have made that assumption and, even worse, been correct. 'Kurt must be using the same line on everyone he finds vulnerable,' Andrew thought. 'That son of a bitch.' He moved one of the overstuffed chairs close to the ornate grille work, rested his feet on the fancy, scrolled metal, and stared silently at the mountains through the fading afternoon light.

* * *

Andrew made sure that he was already in bed by 11:00 p.m. He turned out all of his lights, hoping that Kurt would assume he was asleep and would not bother him; yet at eleven-fifteen, he could see the dark shadow of someone standing outside of his door. It was then that he heard a gentle knock. When he did not respond, he could hear the door open quietly and shut. Footsteps approached his bed.

"You awake?" Kurt whispered.

"I am now," Andrew said coldly. "What the hell are you doing in here?"

"I guess I was hoping we could talk."

"Oh, really? Or did you come in to see if you could rape me again?" Andrew blurted.

Kurt pulled a chair close to the bed and sat down. "I don't like it when you say things like that."

"Is it because you don't like hearing the truth?"

"Give me a break, Andrew. It's not like you didn't want it," Kurt challenged.

Andrew could feel himself bristle. He raised himself up on one elbow and glared at Kurt. "Someday, you are going to have to understand the difference between what's acceptable and what isn't and what it means to have respect for the person you're having sex with. Funny thing is, I don't think you'll ever learn."

"Did you hear what I said to you last night . . . that I really have strong feelings for you and . . . that I love you? Can you understand that?"

Andrew laughed. "Is that the same thing you told Chris when you fucked him?"

Shocked, Kurt leaned back in his chair. "What the hell are you talking about?"

"You know damn well what I'm talking about, you bastard!" Andrew swung his legs over the edge of the bed, as if he were about to attack him. "I want you to listen to what I'm about to say. Dr. Klein is ready to discharge me tomorrow, depending on how well I tolerate tonight. If you so much as come near me with a syringe or any medication or write anything in the chart which would jeopardize my chances of getting out of here, I will call security and tell them exactly what happened, and I'll suggest they talk with Chris. Is that clear?"

Kurt stood up and moved the chair back to where he found it "I'm sorry this had to happen because I really do care about you. But . . . yes. It's clear. I know you want to go back to the monastery, and I can't blame you. In some of your quiet moments, I hope that you will be able to remember some of the good things about me." He quickly turned and left the room, as Andrew watched him disappear into the softly lit corridor.

His attempts to sleep were futile; staring at the ceiling, Andrew wondered what he would do if Kurt were to suddenly appear and beg for his forgiveness. As painful as his experience was, he admitted that something about their relationship was intensely genuine and gratifying, not only the sexual aspect but also his affection for someone who was professionally capable and experienced. While he respected his role as a nurse, Andrew felt that Kurt had clearly crossed boundaries.

The last time he looked, his alarm clock read one thirty. Still awake at three, he got out of bed, used the bathroom, and began to pace rapidly around the room, hoping that he would become exhausted and fall asleep. Twenty minutes later, he fell into bed and slept soundly, occasionally dreaming of white gauzy curtains in the monastery's infirmary, fluttering effortlessly in a gentle breeze.

* * *

"The chart looks favorable, how did your evening go?" Dr. Klein asked. He completed his sentence before he reached Andrew's bed.

Startled, Andrew smiled and nodded. "Fine," he said. "I slept fine."

"No bad dreams—no feelings of compromised safety?"

Andrew shook his head. "I don't recall even having a dream."

Dr. Klein sat on the edge of Andrew's bed. "Do you really feel you are ready for this—to return to the monastery, where it's possible that old feelings will resurface and may cause you to decompensate?" he asked with obvious concern.

"You said that you would be giving me prescription medication, didn't you?" Andrew asked.

"Yes, and as helpful as they can be, they are not a total panacea to alleviate all that you've experienced."

"I know, but at least give me a chance to try it," Andrew pleaded.

Dr. Klein's gaze appeared temporarily frozen on Andrew's eyes. "Say his name," he said unexpectedly.

Andrew was puzzled. "Whose name?"

Dr. Klein gently repeated his request. "I want you to say his name."

Andrew realized immediately to whom he was referring. "Matthew, right? You want me to say Matthew."

"Can you express, right now, a thought about him?" Dr. Klein questioned.

The direct inquiry momentarily caught Andrew off-guard. "Yes . . . I still love him, probably always will; but he made a choice to leave, and I think, with time, I'll learn to cope with my feelings." He was moderately surprised by his articulate response.

"Are you fearful or anxious about anything in particular?" Dr. Klein asked.

Andrew rubbed his eyes. "Oh, I don't know," he said with a yawn. "I guess it would bother me to see him in the future—if he ever decided to visit the monastery—with Rebecca and a station wagon filled with his kids. For some reason, I'd have a hard time with that."

A slight smile crossed Dr. Klein's face. "I understand," he replied, and then quickly stood up. "Let's give it a shot. I'll call Father Gerald and have him pick you up. I'm going to give you a supply of medication, which you absolutely have to take as directed. And I want you to call my office and schedule an appointment with my secretary for next week, all right?"

Andrew could feel himself beaming. "Yes!" he said. He shook Dr. Klein's hand. "Thanks for all your help . . . and for putting up with me."

"I'm glad that I am able to help you work through this," he said with a smile. "Good luck, Andrew, and I'll see you next week." He handed Andrew a card. "This is my beeper number—just in case you need to get in touch with me before the next appointment."

* * *

Father Gerald never arrived until after lunch. By then, Andrew had carefully packed his belongings in a small duffel bag, as he waited for his ride back to the monastery.

"I guess it's time to go," the attendant said with a smile. "Father Gerald is waiting for you in the lobby."

Andrew hastily threw the duffel bag over his shoulder, glanced back at his room with mixed emotions, and followed the attendant to the locked door which allowed him to enter the lobby where Father Gerald was waiting with open arms.

"I think it's time to go home," he said and then hugged Andrew with genuine warmth.

"You have no idea," Andrew commented. He was about to follow Father Gerald down the steps when he suddenly spotted a familiar face.

"I didn't want you to leave without saying goodbye," Kurt said. He stood near a wooden column next to the wall, casually dressed in jeans and a T-shirt.

Andrew was obviously bewildered. He looked furtively at Father Gerald, who seemed to intuitively interpret their need for some privacy.

"Let me take your duffel," he offered. "I'll meet you in the car."

"Thanks," Andrew said with relief. "I'll be right out." He waited to speak until Father Gerald had left the building.

"Judging by the way you're dressed, you are obviously not working," Andrew said.

"I know that you don't have much time to talk with me, and who knows, you might not even want to, but I want to apologize for all that I did and the way things turned out," Kurt said.

"I can appreciate your concern, but the forgiveness doesn't come easy."

"Then don't forgive me; just let me hold you once before you go." He grabbed Andrew's arm and gently led him toward the men's room.

Angry yet admittedly eager, Andrew allowed himself to give in to his coercion.

After a brief survey to ensure that they were alone, Kurt pulled Andrew toward him and hugged him firmly. "I don't want this to be goodbye," he said. "You are one of the few people I've met who has ever made me feel this way; I want to always be with you, to touch you, to love you."

Andrew let him kiss him because it was what he wanted and what he wanted to remember. He stepped back and stared at him. "It's nice to hear, Kurt. I only wish that I could believe you." He then turned and began to walk away but suddenly stopped. Without saying a word, Andrew approached him. His totally unanticipated punch sent Kurt sprawling backwards against the wall and caused him to sink slowly to the floor. "That's not only from me but from Chris, and God knows how many others you've messed up."

Just before he left, Andrew turned and noticed a small trickle of blood flowing out of Kurt's nose and down his lip. It was that—not the kiss—which he would remember.

* * *

Chapter Thirty-One

A Changed Moral Viewpoint

The half-hour drive back to the monastery seemed to stretch into an eternity as Father Gerald attempted to avoid any topic which Andrew might consider intrusive. His banal bantering about the weather and the successful hay harvest eventually caused Andrew to respond.

"You can ask whatever you like—it's okay," Andrew said assertively.

Father Gerald continued to look straight ahead and drive, clutching the wheel with both hands. "All right," he said. "What should I ask you?"

Andrew slumped deeper into the fabric seat. "I know you can do better than respond with diplomatic bullshit," he quipped.

As before, Father Gerald continued to drive in silence, apparently unperturbed by Andrew's remark. The road twisted through some of Bitter Creek's most scenic areas, dense pine growths mixed with turning aspens and, often hidden amongst them, exquisite examples of some of the most architecturally interesting homes imaginable. Off to his right, Father Gerald spotted a familiar pull-off which accessed a small creek and picnic area. He drove in, stopped the car, and got out. "Maybe I'm getting too old to do two things at once," he said. "It's easier for me to talk when I don't have to concentrate on my driving."

Andrew followed his lead and got out of the car. He was immediately struck by the incredible beauty of his surroundings. "How did you ever find this place?" he asked.

Father Gerald laughed. "It's mostly a place for locals. Very few tourists know about it, and if they do, it's usually by accident." He sat down at the wooden picnic table. "It was Eric Holtze who showed it to me."

Andrew continued to look around with awe. "Someday, I hope we can come back and spend some time here."

"Well, we're here now, aren't we?" Father Gerald replied. "And I'm not in a rush to return to the monastery—unless you are."

Andrew shrugged. "No, not really. I guess I'm just a little anxious."

"I can see that. Did you take the medication that Dr. Klein gave you?"

Andrew pulled the amber vial out of his pocket as if to reinforce his response. "Yes, just before lunch." He put the medication back, rubbed his eyes, and, for a moment, sat in silence. "I'm sorry for what I said in the car," he said quietly.

Father Gerald chuckled. "I know you are, but I have to admit, you were right. It was diplomatic bullshit," an admission which Andrew found rather amusing.

Grey squirrels scurried up and down the larger trees, occasionally pausing on their hind legs like prairie dogs in anticipation of a handout.

"The water is so crystal clear it looks drinkable," Andrew said.

"I wouldn't advise it," Father Gerald said. "There have been cases of hikers and campers getting parasitic infections."

Father Gerald quickly shifted gears and came right to the point. "Your return to the monastery is a big step and, most likely, not an easy one. I just want you to know that I want to see you succeed, even though I'm sure it will be painful. I'm not a psychiatrist, but my door is always open if you feel like talking."

"You've always been very supportive of me and Matthew, and I appreciate it, Father Gerald. I just hope I can pull this off."

"Draw your strength from those around you who care about you. Try to turn some of that sorrow over to God through your spiritual life; let him help share your burden."

Andrew placed his arms on the table and rested his head. "Do you honestly think he still listens to me?"

"Maybe more so to you than others."

"Why would you say that?" Andrew asked doubtfully.

"Because he knows how much you need him."

Andrew sat up and shook his head. "I don't know anymore," he said. "I just don't think he listens to guys like me."

"Well, I think you're wrong; he'll listen. Just give him a chance." Father Gerald placed his hand on Andrew's forearm. "This is not an easy path to walk down."

Andrew raised his head. "You mean being gay or my life as a monk?"

"Unfortunately, the answer is not either or; it's both."

"I never wanted or expected this to happen," Andrew said.

Father Gerald packed his pipe and lit it as he talked. "Well, perhaps God has given you an extra burden."

"Why? To test me?" Andrew asked with exasperation.

"Maybe it's in preparation for something greater—a forging of steel by intense heat to create a purer, resolute being."

"That must be it," Andrew quipped. "Intense heat . . . like the meeting of Abbot Paul and Basil."

"So you know that story." Fr. Gerald said.

"Only through reading it."

"What do you remember?"

Andrew rubbed his eyes. "Paul asked how he could better serve God, how he could purify himself even more. That's when Basil lifted his hands to heaven, and his fingers flamed like torches. He explained that one cannot be a monk unless he is consumed by fire."

"You seem to relate to that," Father Gerald said. "I think Abbot Basil meant that one needs to become *like* a consuming fire."

Andrew appeared to grow anxious and unfocused. "Have you heard anything from Matthew?" His need to change the topic was curiously obvious.

"I don't think anyone has." Father Gerald exhaled a cloud of fragrant bluish smoke. "I imagine they are still on their honeymoon."

"Where did they go?" Andrew asked with hesitation.

Sensing a need to be guarded, Father Gerald replied obliquely. "Oh, probably someplace warm and sunny. I'm pretty sure they didn't go to Niagara Falls." His attempted humor appeared ineffective.

A lengthy silence followed as Andrew stared vacantly into the deep forest.

"Are you okay?" Father Gerald asked.

"Oh, I don't know," Andrew answered honestly.

Father Gerald spoke very softly yet clearly. "This is the part that concerns me, Andrew. Since I am not Dr. Klein, I'm not always sure how to reach you . . . how to bring you back to that safe space somewhere deep inside you. You are going to have to help me to help you."

Andrew looked at him and smiled slightly. "I know, and I realize how concerned you are. I guess it's going to take some time to let the dust settle, to feel genuinely accepted by the community, and return to being a monk."

"Just try to concentrate on getting better, and don't worry about being accepted by the others. I can honestly tell you that everyone is looking forward to your return, so there is no need to worry about that."

Andrew suddenly stood up. "Well, then, let's get it over with. Let's go back."

* * *

At least for the first week, the days at the monastery were much more forgiving than the long, solitary nights. Andrew almost felt like a returning hero, a celebrity of sorts, who had weathered a finite tragedy and was now expected to be a happy, "cured," and sparkling member of the community. Most of his cell had been completely repaired. The sliding glass door had been replaced, and the new screen glinted brightly. Even his desk had been carefully sanded, filled, and repainted, to match the original grey finish. It would have been difficult to imagine that anything out of the ordinary had ever taken place, until Andrew accidentally knocked over his wastebasket. As hard as they tried, they were unable to completely remove the bloodstained carpet, which had now faded to an irregular coffee-colored blotch, approximately four inches in diameter. It reminded Andrew of an oversized puzzle piece. He reluctantly picked up the wastebasket and recovered the spot, as if by doing so, he could he erase the scattered memory of an event that seemed so far away.

The nights, however, caused him the greatest torment, as thoughts would race endlessly through his conflicted mind until his medication gratefully saved him by slowly decreasing stimuli and easing him into a drugged yet welcomed sleep. He would lie awake for hours, wondering who he had become, what would happen to him, and whether or not he would be able to cope with his apparently bleak destiny. At times, he would pray fervently, experiencing the peace of God's grace and forgiveness, yet more often, his solitude would be convoluted by memories of Matthew, as he wondered where he was, what he was doing, what his actual relationship was like with his new wife and, more specifically, whether Matthew ever thought about him and missed him. As much as he hated to admit it, he would visualize Matthew making love to Rebecca, a reality which both repulsed and excited him, while he imagined himself in their matrimonial bed, arrogantly mounting Matthew from behind, as Rebecca watched and realized that she could never satisfy Matthew's private, physical needs. Only then, after wiping the semen from his chest, would Andrew allow the medication to engulf his brain and cause him to sleep.

And for almost the entire month, Dr. Klein—and even Andrew—began to believe that time was, in fact, gently softening his pain, allowing him to concentrate on his monastic duties, renewing his selfless love for God and solitude, and recreating the man he felt he was meant to be. Yet the inner peace proved to be ephemeral, as his unexpected friendship with Brother Joshua, the tall Kentucky transfer, whom Andrew once observed masturbating in the bathroom, became more and more meaningful.

Certainly less than innocent and always an obvious admirer of Andrew, Brother Joshua continued to seek affirmation from Andrew with telling smiles and, when possible, frank discussion of his feelings, which Andrew eventually grew to tolerate and even respect, especially since he knew that he was, in fact, discreetly attracted to Joshua's dark lanky leanness, handsome features, and gentle yet masculine southern charm.

"Admit it, man. He dumped you for some airhead blonde whose daddy owns most of the county, just because you wouldn't give him what he wanted." Brother Joshua leaned defiantly on his shovel in a warm remnant of October sun.

"That's hardly funny, Josh," Andrew said, "especially coming from you." He continued to make cutouts in the ditch to allow the water to spread across the parched soil.

"Why's that?" Brother Joshua asked with an embellished drawl.

Andrew turned to face him. "When are you ever, *ever* going to learn? They essentially threw you out of one monastery because . . . how did you put it? You had developed too close a relationship with another monk? And here you are, essentially trying to do the same with me."

Joshua smiled and acquiesced. "At least I'm being truthful about it. You make me hotter than Georgia asphalt in the middle of a Savannah summer." He allowed his true southern accent free reign.

Andrew laughed, but he refused to look up. "Just because I made the mistake of telling you that you have beautiful feet doesn't mean that you have to continue wearing those ridiculous sandals. In case you haven't noticed, it's October."

"I do it to get you excited," Brother Joshua quipped.

"Great," Andrew said sarcastically. "I can't wait till it snows."

Joshua shrugged. "No matter. I doubt it'll cool me down."

"Is it possible you can do two things at the same time, like talk and work or, better yet, just work?"

"Yes, Massa," Joshua replied, mimicking an indentured servant. "I be workin' now."

Andrew looked up with a grin and watched as Joshua leaned over his shovel and dug pie shaped cutouts in the ditch. His one-piece coveralls curved snuggly over his muscular buttocks, eliciting a spontaneous response from Andrew. "I have to admit. You have a fine butt."

Brother Joshua turned to face him, staring at Andrew with only the slightest hint of a smile. His voice was soft yet serious. "Just say the word."

Andrew simply turned away and worked even more diligently.

* * *

With November only a few days away, most of the monastery's work became internal—extra cleaning of the building's vast interior, washing and waxing floors, and cleaning windows. In the large barn, all of the dirt bikes were reconditioned. Broken parts were replaced or fixed; dented fenders were pounded out, filled, and painted. Andrew was, again, reminded of Brother Morgan, whose cell was once littered with motorcycle parts—handlebars on his desk, a chain lying on the floor, and wheels resting haphazardly against the sliding door. He was astounded by the display, yet Brother Morgan navigated through the mess with total indifference. His cell, which now belonged to Brother Kevin, appeared lifeless—its door was always mysteriously closed.

And with the advent of the cold weather, came increased time for prayer and meditation, a time for greater reflection and less interaction with the community. Andrew read voraciously, meditated for hours, and took long walks in the cold evening air, but instead of being curative, the isolation forced him to delve even deeper into all that caused him pain, all that went wrong, all that he had experienced, and, even more troubling, all that he now knew he physically required.

When it happened, there was very little forethought. Most likely, Brother Joshua had intentionally arrived at just the right time—five thirty in the morning—a few minutes after Andrew began to shower.

It was unusual for someone else to be in the bathroom that early, so when Andrew heard the shower turn on—the one immediately next to him, he was curious. He separated the inner curtain, and through a small space in the outer curtain, he saw Brother Joshua place his shaving gear on the shelf above the sink, enter the dressing area of the shower he had just started, and close the outer curtain. Within seconds, he could hear him splashing under the luxuriously hot water, soaping himself with seemingly repetitive, almost seductive, sounds.

Andrew did not have to look down to know that he had become aroused and was eager for a resolution. Unable to resist, he wasted no time. Being sure to leave his inner curtain closed, he stepped into the dressing area, wrapped a towel around his waist, and peered out into the bathroom to see if anyone was there. Convinced they were alone, Andrew slipped into Brother Joshua's dressing area. He dropped his towel on top of Brother Joshua's clothes and then stepped past the inner curtain into the steamy shower where Brother Joshua stood silently, expectantly, grinning from ear to ear.

Within seconds, they were locked in a wordless embrace, kissing each other deeply as the hot water flooded over them, creating a sensual viscosity of skin against skin.

Brother Joshua knew that time was definitely a limiting factor. He quickly knelt in front of Andrew and made it clear that he had a specific objective in mind.

Looking down at Brother Joshua, Andrew could already feel himself close to orgasm; he firmly grabbed Brother Joshua's hair with both hands and began to force himself deeper and deeper, until the intense, unstoppable sensation welled within and unexploded euphorically, along with Andrew's silent shudder.

Brother Joshua leaned back against the tile wall, arched his back, and, still tasting Andrew, worked himself into a powerful orgasm. His gentle cries were quickly stifled as Andrew squatted and covered his mouth with his hand; he then helped Brother Joshua to a standing position. Once again, they held each other tight. As expected, Andrew could taste himself when they kissed—a familiar, not offensive, flavor of salty, slightly bitter almonds.

"We should have done this long ago," Brother Joshua whispered, as he nuzzled Andrew's ear.

Andrew kissed him on the forehead and smiled. "I'd better go. We'll talk later."

* * *

Early November brought the feasts of All Saints and then All Souls to the monastery's liturgical agenda, a time which prompted Andrew to remember the anniversary of his own acceptance by the community as a novice, a time when life seemed so full of hope, so full of adventure and genuine spirituality. Innocence once vanished remained totally elusive, yet even though he agonized over its loss, he knew that something was different. He was less and less saddled with religious polarity and its implied guilt—he knew that he had changed. In the early-morning darkness of the church, he allowed the unanticipated tears to flow silently down his cheeks, rivulets of a less bitter, salty fluid, which flooded over his lips and, in the extreme quiet, could be heard rhythmically dripping, like the sound of a metronome, onto his starched habit.

At first, the hooded monk walked past where Andrew was sitting. He bowed, turned around, and then seemed to walk directly toward him. Because of the darkness, it was impossible to see who it was. Unexpectedly, the monk sat down in the chair next to Andrew and remained absolutely still. Andrew could feel his heart began to beat faster, fearing that his recurrent nightmare had become a reality. As much as he tried to turn his head to look at the stranger's face, Andrew realized that he could not move his neck, it was as if it were frozen. Suddenly, he felt something brush the back of his hand. When he finally got the courage to look down, he saw, what appeared to be a small white piece of paper fall off his hand and into his lap, as the monk next to him got up and quickly exited the church.

He picked up the folded paper and opened it, but because of the poor light, he was able to decipher only a few handwritten words slanted severely to the right. Andrew stood up, bowed, and quickly left the church.

Once inside the security of his room, he placed the paper under the glare of his desk lamp and read the following:

"Meet me at five this morning at the retreat house attached to the barn. And relax—no one is scheduled there—I checked. Wait and shower down there. Don't disappoint me. J."

He easily recognized Brother Joshua's handwriting and, easier still, his intent. At first, thoughts flew through his head regarding the boldness of the note, and yet he could not deny his growing arousal. He ripped the note into several pieces and threw it into the wastepaper basket.

Nevertheless, at 4:45 a.m., he quietly slipped out the front door of the monastery down the few steps to the gravel road and, in the fading darkness, hastily walked toward the retreat house where, he assumed, Brother Joshua would already be waiting. With dawn barely breaking over the mountains, Andrew marveled at the small swirl of colors splashed haphazardly against the cobalt sky. 'Here I go again,' he thought, yet there was no reconsideration to turn back. Once or twice, he glanced over his shoulder to see if anyone was walking behind him, but he saw no one.

Standing at the door to the retreat house, Andrew could feel his anxiety begin to multiply. He tapped gently on the door and then tried the handle; the door opened with a slight squeak. He quickly stepped inside and shut the door behind him.

"Lock it," Brother Joshua whispered. He was standing in the dark, near the entrance to the bedroom.

Andrew slid the deadbolt into place and sighed. He spoke softly. "I'm glad you're here because I'd be pissing my pants if it was someone else."

"I'm glad you decided to show up." Brother Joshua walked toward him and kissed him tenderly.

"Your hair is damp and you smell great," Andrew whispered.

"That's because I just got out of the shower. And I know, being the creature of habit that you are, that you'll want to do the same." He led Andrew into the bedroom where three votive candles cast a soft glow, gently illuminating the room with seemingly perfect light. Wearing only a T-shirt and shorts, Brother Joshua slowly began to undress Andrew, removing his jacket, sneakers, socks, and sweatshirt. He pulled Andrew's T-shirt over his head and stood there, gently kissing his chest and stomach. He then squatted, unbuttoned his jeans, and pulled down the zipper. He slid the jeans over his hips and let them fall to the floor.

"We have plenty of time for this," Andrew said. "I'd feel better if I could hit the shower first."

Brother Joshua smiled and stood up. "Don't be long," he whispered. "I would have waited to shower with you, but there is barely enough room in there to turn around."

Andrew nodded. "Yeah, I know."

While Andrew was in the shower, Brother Joshua put a fresh pot of coffee on the gas burner. It was not long before the old-fashioned aluminum pot was percolating and sending its wake-up aroma throughout the small retreat quarters.

"That smells incredibly good," Andrew said. He stood outside the shower, toweling dry his hair.

Brother Joshua grabbed a fresh towel, stood behind him, and wiped his back and buttocks. "You can have some now if you want, but I thought we'd have some later."

Andrew wrapped the towel around Brother Joshua's back and pulled him toward him. "I think I can wait," he said. He nuzzled his neck and ears and then kissed him hard.

Brother Joshua pulled off his T-shirt and led Andrew toward the bed, but remembered that the coffee pot was still on the burner. "Hang on a second." He removed the pot, turned off the gas, and returned to the bedroom.

Andrew had already pulled back the bed spread and was lying half covered with a blanket. "Come on in, it's warm and comfortable."

Just before jumping on top of him, Brother Joshua slipped out of his shorts and tossed them on a chair.

"Get under the covers," Andrew insisted. "I want to feel your entire body next to mine."

"I wish there were a way you could just become a part of me," Brother Joshua stammered. "Somehow . . . become me."

Andrew pulled back slightly and smiled. "We almost are each other—look at us," he said. "We're both tall, sort of lanky, dark-haired, and not all that different in our personalities."

"And handsome," Brother Joshua added with a grin.

"That too—not to mention narcissistic."

"Yeah, but your dick is bigger than mine," Brother Joshua commented.

"Ask me if I care; besides, it's only thicker than yours . . . and yours is probably longer."

Brother Joshua grabbed both of their penises and looked under the blanket.

Andrew immediately pulled his face upward and stared at him. "You think too much." He leaned forward and pulled Brother Joshua toward him. "Come up here. I want to do the same to you." He carefully slid down the bed past Brother Joshua's long, slightly curved erection, and began to massage his feet. "How can someone have such perfectly shaped feet?" he asked rhetorically. "They look like something Michelangelo would've sketched."

Brother Joshua writhed in silence, breathing deeper and deeper, as Andrew managed to get several toes in his mouth at the same time. "I think you'd better stop . . . I come easy that way."

"Well, I don't want that to happen, yet." Andrew said.

"Man, that feels so good," Brother Joshua admitted quietly.

With relative ease, Andrew pulled Brother Joshua even closer. He pushed his legs back over his head and, while straddling his buttocks, gently inserted himself into that warm, wet place inside, as Brother Joshua stifled a cry, at first, and then relaxed to savor a coveted experience.

"Raise my butt even higher," Brother Joshua insisted.

Andrew did as he asked, squatting behind him while continuing his momentum.

"Lay on me—place your weight over me."

When Andrew did so, Brother Joshua proved very flexible; his body assumed a tightly shaped curve much like the letter "C."

Andrew looked beneath his chest and never anticipated what he saw. "That's incredible!" he said with genuine awe. The extra weight of his body pushed Brother Joshua's long, lean penis within easy reach of his own mouth.

With one hand, Brother Joshua guided his penis into his mouth, while continuing to stroke it. The visual incited Andrew to even greater passion and, within minutes, to an explosive orgasm, as he watched Brother Joshua ejaculate semen into his own eager mouth and then lick the remaining remnants from the tip of his swollen erection.

Very carefully, Andrew rolled him onto his side and slid himself down the bed so that he could face his amazing contortionist. Without saying a word, he held Brother Joshua tight and kissed him, tasting his semen and feeling the assurance of his love.

"That was . . . unbelievable. How come you never told me?"

"I was hoping you wouldn't notice."

"Yeah, right," Andrew scoffed.

"Were you referring to you being inside of me or me being inside of me?"

Andrew gently kissed him. "No . . . seriously, it was fantastic being inside of you—you must know that."

"Believe me, I do," Brother Joshua admitted.

"But the other—watching you take yourself in your mouth—drove me wild."

Brother Joshua smiled. "I was a gymnast in high school—parallel bars, the rings; you become pretty elastic."

"And I guess that proves it," Andrew said.

"Proves what?"

"That your penis is longer than mine. I couldn't do what you just did."

Brother Joshua grinned. "Practice—it's all practice—and it helps to have someone with you who can get the blood pumping."

Andrew turned to face him. He kissed him, once again, with genuine desire, absent the often anticipated ritualistic and perfunctory gesture one might expect at such a moment, and then suddenly sat up. "We need to get out of here before it gets any lighter."

Brother Joshua yawned, hesitated, and stared at Andrew with his large brown eyes. "I just want you to know how much I appreciate you being here."

"Well, I feel the same . . . and there will be more opportunities to be together," Andrew said, as he tugged his jeans up over his hips.

"I sure hope so," Brother Joshua replied. He jumped out of bed, turned on the shower, and quickly stepped inside.

* * *

The drive to Bitter Creek in the abbot's Peugeot to see Dr. Klein caused Andrew to reminisce and playfully wonder what the car would say if it could talk. He laughed, surprised that Father Jude was not able to finagle taking the vehicle with him when he left the monastery, after getting Matthew's sister, Ellen, pregnant.

"So, HAL," he said out loud to the car, "did the randy abbot do the wild thing with Ellen while you were watching?"

Andrew answered himself, as if the car were responding, except he spoke softly—cautiously—imitating the voice of the computer, HAL, from his favorite movie, *2001: A Space Odyssey*.

"I don't think I should answer that question, Dave," HAL said in characteristic cadence. "That is personal information which has little to do with my mission."

"I understand, HAL, but you are always so . . . professional. Can't you at least give me a hint?"

"As you have already said, Dave, a response would be unprofessional."

"Yes, HAL, but by not responding to the question, I feel that you've already answered it."

"You may choose to feel that way if it suits you, Dave."

"Oh, cut the shit, HAL. I can still smell her cunt from the backseat."

"I am sorry you seem upset, Dave. As you know, I am not equipped with olfactory sensors. I am incapable of smelling."

"Well, in this case, you might be lucky."

"Is there anything else, Dave?"

"No, not really. I'm just on my way to spill my guts out to my shrink," Andrew said.

"That sounds anatomically painful, Dave. Are you afraid?"

"It's just a saying, HAL; besides, if I say I am afraid, would you know what I meant?"

"Only a literal understanding of the meaning of the word, Dave. I do not have the ability to feel emotions."

"Well, it seems as though several million movie fans would disagree with you on that one," Andrew said.

"I don't understand what you mean, Dave."

"Either do I," Andrew said softly. "Cease transmission, HAL."

"Goodbye, Dave."

"Bye, HAL."

Andrew purposely parked the car two blocks away from Dr. Klein's office so that he could get some air, look in shop windows, and absorb the early November beauty of this still uncluttered ski town prior to the first snowfall, as he attempted to clear his head while wondering where his session would take him. Should he tell the truth about Brother Joshua, talk about his relationship with Kurt at the clinic? He decided that the latter would be totally reckless and, most probably, ruin Kurt's career. He definitely did not want that to happen even though he was tempted to do so, since he had strong suspicions that Kurt might, in fact, be dangerous, yet he had only tenuous evidence.

It was still early enough in the season for the wealthy locals to be driving their luxury automobiles through town, gliding by Andrew with perfectly tuned indifference past the gracious Victorian homes and, eventually, into their own heated garages where, most likely, a four-wheel-drive Rover or BMW waited eagerly for the snow to begin.

Once inside Dr. Klein's office, Andrew wasted no time.

"Well, I've done it again," he said with some exasperation.

Dr. Klein remained seated behind his desk. He sat with an opened pad in front of him; his unlit pipe sat in its holder. "Done what?" he asked.

"Another relationship, another monk—Brother Joshua."

"And how does this have you feeling?"

Andrew fidgeted with his hands, pulling on his fingers and then switched to the opposite hand. He gazed out the window at the greying November sky. "I don't know, for sure. I suppose it's comforting to have someone who cares about me, but I'm still dealing with the same old crap: who am I and what am I doing."

Dr. Klein shifted in his chair. He got up and sat in a chair to Andrew's left. "I'm not sure there are definitive answers to those questions for, perhaps, many of us."

Andrew continued to stare out the window until, suddenly, he began to smile. He walked quickly toward the window and, as suspected, he observed several stray snowflakes drifting lazily down to the street below.

"That makes you happy, doesn't it?" Dr. Klein asked.

"I think so," Andrew said wistfully.

"Can you tell me why?"

Andrew remained at the window. Without his glasses, he was just barely able to see a woman with a young man, most probably her son, sitting at a small table in the bakery across the street. He imagined she was eating a fresh croissant, either almond or raspberry; her son would be having ice cream.

"I'm sorry . . . what did you say?"

"The snow—why does it make you happy?"

Andrew remained at the window. "I'm not sure if happy is the right word, but . . . it seems to create a sense of closeness and isolation at the same time, while erasing all the natural flaws in the landscape."

"A sense of purity—of sorts?" Dr. Klein asked.

Andrew rubbed his eyes. "That's exactly the kind of response I was hoping I wouldn't hear. Maybe I should just shut up."

"I'd rather you continue," Dr. Klein insisted. "Say what you feel."

He returned to his chair and sat down. "I can't blame this on anyone but myself."

"You are referring to the relationship with Brother Joshua?"

"Yes," Andrew said. He leaned forward and clasped his hands while resting his elbows on his knees. "It is, what should I say . . . consummated?"

"You had intercourse."

"He wanted me to fuck him, so I did," Andrew blurted.

The blatant vulgarity scarcely concerned Dr. Klein. "Do you care for him?"

"I think so. He's witty, handsome, and I know that he likes me, yet I can't figure it out. It's as though this relationship between us is . . . totally acceptable—nothing wrong—perfectly normal, but . . ."

"But what?"

"For Christ's sake, we're monks!" Andrew emphasized.

Dr. Klein retrieved his pipe from the desk, lit it, and sat down amid curls of rising blue smoke.

"If this is a difficult question, please tell me. Isn't this situation similar to your dilemma with Matthew, his openness toward the sexual aspect of your relationship and your difficulty accepting that?"

"I guess," Andrew said. He began to shake his leg and fidget. He immediately got up and walked once more toward the window, just in time to see the woman and her young son leaving the bakery. The boy appeared to be excited as he looked upward and reached out to grab a single snowflake.

"But in some ways," Dr. Klein continued, "you've openly engaged in conduct that you wouldn't have participated in with Matthew. Is that correct?"

"Well, yes . . . pretty much," Andrew admitted.

"What made you change your behavior?"

Andrew began to pace. "Come on," Dr. Klein, "you know the answer to that."

"Perhaps, but I'd rather hear it from you."

"Jealousy, I guess. I don't know . . . I think of Matthew being in bed with that blonde woman, perhaps fucking her, and I suppose I felt that I was being deprived of a totally sexual experience. I would even fantasize that I was in bed with them, and as she watched, I would kneel in back of Matthew and fuck him—doggy style."

"So is your relationship with Brother Joshua an outright reaction to Matthew's assumed role with his wife?" Dr. Klein asked.

"Not exactly. I now know that my sexuality is something I can't deny or suppress. Yes, thinking of Matthew may be driving my relationship with Josh, but I'm sure if it wasn't him, I'd probably be with someone else—that is, if someone were available. Matthew may be partially responsible, but I realize that my urge to have sex and a relationship has grown much more powerful. Yet my spirituality also remains conflictingly strong. I want to be a monk—as crazy as it may seem—but I need to have some way to express the human, sexual nature of my being, a being that I feel God created for some completely unknown, screwed-up reason."

Dr. Klein tapped his pipe against the brass ashtray. "If you don't mind me saying so, you seem to be thinking or, at least, talking, in ways which may be similar to what you've told me about Matthew."

Andrew stopped his pacing and stared at Dr. Klein. "Maybe I do sound like Matthew, but a part of me always wondered about the seriousness of his spirituality, the depth of his commitment to monasticism." He shrugged his shoulders and smirked. "Listen to me," he said sarcastically, "the epitome of virtue!" He jammed both hands into his pockets and returned to the overstuffed chair, slouching on the very edge of the cushion.

A brief silence followed, which was broken sharply by Andrew's unexpected giggle. "I don't know why I am thinking about this, but I feel like telling you. It has nothing to do with Matthew." He rubbed his eyes and continued. "As you know, I do a fair amount of cooking at the monastery—all vegetarian food, because that was the abbot's rule. Well, one day, I walked into the kitchen to prepare a big salad for lunch, and my nose detected this familiar, delectable scent, wafting through the door. That's when I saw Father Jude, standing over the stove, slowly frying this thick porterhouse steak in one of our cast-iron skillets. The smell and visual stimuli made my mouth water. I casually walked up to him, smiled, and said, 'That smells good,' because inside, I was so angry I felt like I wanted to rip his head off, but I was hoping it didn't show, yet I'm sure he knew what I meant."

"Did he respond?" Dr. Klein asked.

"Of course, without the slightest trace of culpability. Yet in the middle of his explanation, I laughed into his face—I couldn't help it. He said that he had his hair analyzed at some clinic in Bitter Creek, and they told him that he was deficient in animal proteins. Once they found out he was a monk at St. Anthony's, notorious for its regimentation and strict vegetarian diet, it must have taken a rocket scientist for them to come up with their diagnosis."

"And ever since then, he's been eating meat?"

"More than we realized," Andrew joked.

"You saw him as a 'do-as-I-say-not-do-as-I-do' type of person?" Dr. Klein asked.

"I saw him as a total joke—a real phony," Andrew explained.

"If nothing else, it sounds as though he did not represent himself to you as a believable role model."

"Oh, please . . ." Andrew's frustration was obvious.

Dr. Klein stood up, and rather than returning to his leather chair, he sat, uncharacteristically, on the corner of his desk. "You've been through quite an ordeal, Andrew, and you've still got a tough road in front of you, but with the medication and continued therapy, I think we can get you over the hump and onto some level ground." He ran both hands over his face, creating a momentary blush. "Help me review some facts: you are sincerely invested in your vocation; you want to be a monk—a true monk—yet you are openly cognizant of your physical, sexual needs. You have what appears to be a healthy relationship with a fellow monk, who apparently feels very strongly toward you and is willing—perhaps dedicated—to maintaining that relationship. And you spoke earlier of Matthew's spiritual framework. What is your opinion of Brother Joshua spirituality? I'm asking only because I sense that some expression of genuine spirituality seems to be a necessary requirement for the person who interests you. Is that fair to say?"

Andrew nodded slightly. "Even though he's funny, sexually uninhibited, and, at times, overly confident, I honestly feel that he has a strong spiritual core, capable of encompassing all of his humanness with his vocational goal of being a good monk. Most would deny that such an alliance is even possible."

"If you'll allow me to speak frankly, I wonder if you are referring to yourself."

Andrew looked hard at Dr. Klein, but spoke softly. "You don't have to be so gentle with me. We both know that's exactly why I'm here, why I'm so totally fucked-up. Brother Joshua appears to have a healthy handle on living his life as he does, with little remorse; in fact, just the opposite. He seems to live life fully, deeply, and has now included me in it."

"Will you accept that invitation without compunction?"

Andrew sat in silence, knowing that Dr. Klein had asked the crucial question. He leaned forward and held his face with both hands. He spoke quietly; his voice was on the verge of cracking. "I don't know," he replied.

* * *

Once again, the grey pickup slowly made its way up the steep, winding road to the familiar metal sluice gates that controlled the flow of water to all of the monastery's irrigation ditches. Brother Mark abruptly stopped the truck in the narrow pull off.

"It seems like we were here only yesterday," he said, as he slammed the door and removed the rakes from the back.

Andrew accepted the long handled tool with gloved hands. "Déjà vu," he said. "Except I remember how difficult it was to get the gates to close. There doesn't seem to be as much debris floating around."

Standing precariously close to the edge, Brother Mark began to clear the branches, smaller logs, and a bloated badger from the whirling eddy. "I guess he couldn't swim."

Andrew helped pull the heavy load ashore and raked it far from the rumbling creek. "He sure doesn't smell too good either."

Once the majority of the flotsam was removed, Andrew and Brother Mark began the ponderous task of cranking the rusted wheels, which caused the gates to swing out into the ditch and join together, stopping the flow of the river by diverting all of the water downstream.

Brother Mark ran the back of his glove over his forehead. "I hope Father Luke alerted the neighbors. Otherwise, their irrigation ditches are going to be flooded."

With a final heave and a solid groan of metal, the gates came together in the middle of the ditch with surprising precision. Small jets of water arched through the rusted holes and over the receding ditch water like invisible urinating statues, until the excess volume reached its level and subsided. Within minutes, the bedrock glistened slightly in the weak November light.

"Another season terminated," Brother Mark said.

"As the Buddhists remind us, all is change, nothing is permanent," Andrew replied. His seriousness surprised him.

"That's rather philosophical."

"It must be the place . . . and my mental status," Brother Andrew said softly.

Brother Mark laughed. "You're not going to freak out on me, are you?"

"Whatever gave you that idea?" Andrew said, as he picked up a rake and began to chase Brother Mark around the truck, while grunting wildly and making grotesque faces. "I'm totally sane."

Laughing, Brother Mark sought refuge in the vehicle.

Andrew tossed his rake in the back and joined him. "If I remember correctly, this is where you pull a thermos of hot coffee from under the seat, and we have some provocative or profound discussion on our pitiful lives as monks."

With a smile, Brother Mark reached beneath the seat. He held the familiar silver canister in one hand while searching for paper cups. "You're right about the coffee—the discussion is optional. I guess I have some thoughts on what has been going on, but it's up to you." He looked directly at Andrew. "I don't want to get into any area that would make you anxious or uncomfortable."

He handed a cup to Andrew, removed the top of the thermos, and poured the dark steamy liquid until it nearly reached the top.

"Leave some space for cream and sugar . . . you brought some cream and sugar, didn't you?" Andrew asked, with rolled eyes.

"Of course." Brother Mark opened the glove box. He took out several sugar packets and a small container of powdered coffee lightener.

"Better than nothing," Andrew said.

"The stir sticks are in the bag with the sugar."

Andrew sipped the coffee and leaned back, cradling the cup in both hands for warmth. "I've never had such good coffee until I came here. Thanks for bringing it with you."

"You're welcome," Brother Mark said. He chuckled quietly.

"What's so funny?"

"Oh . . . I was just thinking about why the coffee is so good."

"And?" Andrew asked.

"It probably costs twelve dollars a pound, ordered by our ex-abbot. Nothing was too good for Father Jude."

"Here we go again," Andrew quipped.

"Got to start somewhere," Brother Mark said. His breath was visible inside the cold cab.

"I guess they are getting married—Father Jude and Ellen—according to the last letter from Matthew," Andrew said.

"Just imagine being at that wedding." Brother Mark pretended to be an anonymous guest as he shook the imaginary hand of Father Jude. "Nice to meet you, Jude. Is this attractive young woman your daughter?"

Andrew immediately continued the role-playing with an affected English accent. "And is it my imagination or does she actually appear to be a tad . . . pregnant?"

Brother Mark laughed uncontrollably and choked on his coffee. He repeated the phrase in a high-pitched, hysterical voice. " . . . A tad pregnant!" And once again, laughed himself into exhaustion.

Andrew rubbed his eyes. "It's a good thing we're perfect," he said.

"Yeah, otherwise we'd be in deep poop," Brother Mark said.

A lull in the conversation amplified the sound of the increasing wind as it attempted to enter the truck through the slightest gap in the window seals.

"I don't think you have anything to worry about," Andrew remarked.

Brother Mark stared pensively at his reflection inside his cup. "You never know. I'm far from perfect and light years away from Nirvana."

"I think that describes 99 percent of the human race."

"Well, then, it's fair to say that I have stuff to worry about."

"Like what? Andrew prompted.

Brother Mark appeared uncomfortable as he shifted in his seat. "I don't think it would be good to talk about—and it wouldn't be easy."

"Well, now I'm really curious," Andrew admitted.

"What I mean is—I don't think it would be good for *you*."

"Maybe I should be the judge of that," Andrew said.

Brother Mark shook his head. "I don't know. It's difficult stuff; besides, I don't want to be rude, but I don't know where your head's at."

"What the heck does that mean?"

"It means that I don't want to get you upset, and I think I've already failed," Brother Mark said.

Andrew took a deep breath, paused, and spoke softly. "Okay. Why don't we do this? Just ask me first what you need to know before you continue."

"And how will I know if you find the question troublesome?" Brother Mark said.

"I will simply tell you." Andrew sipped his coffee. "I have the feeling you want to ask me about Matthew, and that's okay. You don't have to be cautious or condescending. I'm sure everyone knows that Matthew and I were more than just friends."

Brother Mark took a deep breath and then blurted out what he wanted or, more accurately, needed to say. "That's exactly my point," he said nervously. "At one time, Matthew and I were . . . more than just friends."

Andrew inhaled sharply, as if he had been mortally wounded. His partially-filled cup fell from his hand to the floor mat, spilling coffee on his pants and boots.

Brother Mark immediately located a roll of paper towels, ripped off several, and attempted to absorb the liquid. "I'm sorry, Andrew. I never meant for it to happen—it just did."

At that moment, Andrew knew he could not remain in the truck. He was overcome with the urge to act out, to smash a window or, even worse, to strike Brother Mark. He got out, slammed the door shut, and stood silently, hyperventilating, in the cold near the creek.

Feeling helpless and ashamed, Brother Mark agonized over his next move. 'Why did I have to tell him?' he thought. 'He could do something stupid like jump in the creek or come back and beat the crap out of me.' He watched as Andrew continued to stand motionless in the grey light. With genuine trepidation, he got out of the truck and stood safely near the front. He refused to get any closer. "I'm sorry, Andrew," he repeated, "but I want you to understand; even though I'm guilty, it wasn't my fault. He pretty much forced himself on me. I didn't want it to happen. Can you hear me?"

After several moments, Andrew turned slowly and faced him. He spoke sluggishly, methodically. "Is there anyone he missed?"

Relieved by Andrew's apparent recognition of his dilemma, Brother Mark approached him carefully. "I wanted to tell you a long time ago—to let you know that he seemed totally driven by his sexuality. I'm really sorry."

"I guess I've always known that," Andrew said, as he stared into the distance. "But aren't we all?"

Brother Mark put his arm around Andrew's shoulder. "It's cold out here. Let's get back in the truck."

Safely inside, Brother Mark started the engine to warm the cab. He poured Andrew another coffee, mixed it for him, and filled his own cup with the steamy black liquid. "Here, drink this."

Andrew accepted the cup and slowly sipped it.

"I never wanted to hurt you," Brother Mark said quietly.

Andrew continued to drink. "I know," he said. "But now that you've told me, I want to know the whole story: what happened? when?"

"I figured you'd say that. I just hope it doesn't make you feel even more upset."

"I'm fine; just tell me what happened."

"Before I do, I want to say what I feel. Even though I know that you both cared about each other deeply, I'm glad that he's no longer here—I'm especially glad that you found the courage to stay here, to participate in the monastic life without him and, hopefully, gain inner strength and peace to continue with what I feel is God's plan for your life. "And," he added, "I think many of us in the community feel the same way."

"I appreciate that, but I have no idea of how true it is or whether I can ever live up to those expectations."

"Just pray, and give it your best shot," Brother Mark said.

"Okay," Andrew responded, "but what happened?"

Once again, Brother Mark took a deep breath. "You really want to hear this?"

"Yes."

"Remember when Matthew and I went on that Zen retreat after the rafting trip?"

Andrew nodded.

"Well, that's when it happened. It was the last night of our stay. We had separate sleeping bags, but we both shared the same two-man tent. I fell asleep, and sometime in the middle of the night, I woke up to find Matthew on top of me. He had pulled my sleeping bag open and was going to town on me before I was fully conscious. I thought, at first, it was just another one of my erotic dreams, but when I opened my eyes, there he was, larger-than-life, and even though I was initially upset, I am guilty of letting it continue. I'm sorry."

Andrew shrugged. "Don't be. Just tell me what happened next, because, believe me, I know that Matthew wouldn't have stopped there."

"Wow . . . I guess you know him pretty well," Brother Mark admitted. "Before I knew it, he had straddled me and continued to ride me until I came inside of him; shortly afterwards, he also ejaculated. I should have stopped, but it all felt so good, so unexpected, that I just let it happen out of my own weakness and my overwhelming desire to express my sexuality. It was like a good, bad dream. I could barely look at him after that."

"Tell me the truth. Did it ever happen again?"

Brother Mark drew close to Andrew. "Never! I swear!"

"Did you ever think about the possibility of having it happen again?"

"I suppose," Brother Mark admitted, "but I told him that I would disclose what happened on retreat if he ever tried anything again."

"Even though you participated in it?"

"Yes, even if it meant being thrown out of the monastery."

"Why so valiant?" Andrew questioned.

Brother Mark paused, stared out the window, and then looked directly at Andrew. "Honestly? Because I care about you. I knew what your relationship was with Matthew, and I didn't want to see you get hurt anymore."

"By whom?" Andrew asked.

"By Matthew, who else? You can't, for a second—after his sham marriage to Rebecca—think that he was faithful to you, do you?"

Andrew shook his head. "I don't know. I guess I never wanted to admit what I've always known in my heart."

Once again, the silence allowed the cold November wind to be heard, as it buffeted the cab and swirled leftover leaves and debris into the air like a miniature dust devil.

"I know you don't want me to say this, but I'm really sorry, Andrew. Maybe Matthew's leaving is the best thing that could have happen to you—to all of us."

Andrew slowly shook his head, as if daydreaming. "I don't know," he said.

"Well, I think I do." Brother Mark hesitated but then continued. "He seemed obsessed with sex—as far as I can say. Remember the two guys on the rafting trip who accompanied the Meads? What were their names . . . Bill and Tim? On two occasions, I saw Matthew get dropped off by one of them near the road to the monastery. I wasn't exactly sure who was driving, but I clearly remember the truck. Now, what the hell was that all about? I'm sure they didn't just go for coffee."

"You saw them?" Andrew asked.

"Yes. I happened to be working near the road where he was dropped off. They never saw me. The second time, I drove by them. Matthew pretended to duck so that I wouldn't recognize him, but it was definitely Matthew and one of those guys in the same truck."

"Was it a truck or a van?"

"Actually, now that you mention it, it was a van, one of the same vans that we used on the rafting trip."

"You're right," Andrew said weakly. "This isn't getting any better."

"That's not the point. I'm finally telling you all of this so that you can get on with your life and realize, maybe, that Matthew wasn't exactly a one-man guy. I think he has a definite problem."

"I wonder if it's catchy," Andrew quipped.

"No, I'm serious," Brother Mark said. "It's none of my business, but why the hell do you marry a woman when it seems as though he really enjoyed . . . you know, taking it up the butt. I think it's clear that he married her for her money and to try to convince everyone, maybe himself, that he was heterosexual."

Andrew rubbed his eyes "Whatever the reason, it was a way out for him."

"He could have just left—walked out the door," Brother Mark suggested.

"To what?" Andrew replied. "He knew that Rebecca worshiped the ground he walked on, and you have to admit, her lifestyle was certainly enticing. He became an instant millionaire."

"This is unfair, but do you think that she knew about Matthew's relationship with you?"

Andrew laughed. "Come on. I doubt it. I'm sure the only thing Matthew ever told her is that he and I were good friends."

"Yeah, you're probably right." Brother Mark paused. "I often wonder what their sex life is like."

Andrew appeared bewildered. "I thought I was the only one who wondered about that."

"Well, now you know you're not alone."

"Maybe she dresses in leather, has a whip, and one of those big strap-on phalluses," Andrew quipped.

Brother Mark nodded. "I wouldn't be surprised."

"The time that you spent with him on retreat—did he ever say anything to you about me?" Andrew asked.

"Only after I asked him. It was after our unexpected get-together. I felt horribly guilty—and still do—knowing that you and he were . . . close. I told him that I knew about his relationship with you, that I felt bad about letting the act continue, and then asked him why and how he felt about it."

"What did he say?"

"Should I tell you exactly?" Brother Mark asked.

"Why not, I'm expecting the worse," Andrew admitted.

"That's what I was expecting to hear, but I didn't. He told me that he loved you more than anything or anyone else in the world and then went on to say that you wouldn't give him what he physically needed, because you felt it just seemed plain wrong to fully consummate the relationship as monks."

"He actually said that?"

"Yes," Brother Mark said softly. "Can you imagine how that made me feel? I felt like a slime bag."

Andrew gazed out the truck window to hide the tears that had welled in his eyes and were now, slowly, making their way down his cheeks. "Hey, what can I say? It's what I felt at the time." His cavalier bravery almost succeeded.

Brother Mark placed his hand on Andrew's shoulder. "I'm really sorry, man."

Andrew wiped his eyes. "Yeah, me too," he said. He continued to look out the window at nothing, trying to sort out exactly what he was feeling—sadness over Matthew's words and anger over his actions mixed like oil and water within his guts, flooding his brain with conflicting emotions, including jealousy, and a strangely elevated desire to assert his sexuality. "Maybe we should get out of here—head back," he suggested.

"Are you okay?" Brother Mark asked.

Andrew nodded. "Yeah. Let's just go."

* * *

By the time they pulled up to the back of the monastery, lunch had already begun. Andrew hastened down the steps to the boot room, hung his jacket on a vacant hook, and then hurried into the empty bathroom where he washed his face and hands and quickly dried them. He glanced halfheartedly at his ruddy glow, as he ran his fingers through his hair to suggest a semblance of orderliness. He wondered how it was possible to outwardly appear fairly collected when everything inside of him felt roiled and disconnected. This familiar aura of despair engulfed him once again in its hopeless, oppressive grasp.

The solid oak door to the refectory creaked loudly as Andrew opened it. By now, he knew that it was fruitless to attempt to close it quietly, so he pushed it shut with its usual groan and thud.

The heated food cart sat steaming on the far side of the room, a distance that seemed interminable, as Andrew trudged slowly toward it like an exhausted climber. He could feel the eyes of those he passed scan him momentarily, but today, it did not matter. He poured himself a glass of white wine and scrutinized the food—potato pancakes, green beans with slivered almonds, applesauce, sour cream, and fresh chocolate chip cookies. He was impressed. After placing his dessert on his plate, he glanced into the kitchen and was surprised to see Brother Kevin, the young novice who had passed out in the eggery on that hot summer day, standing behind the stove wearing his apron. Andrew had no idea he could cook this well.

Just then, Brother Kevin looked up, saw Andrew staring at him, and smiled bashfully.

Andrew returned the smile. With his free hand, he gave Brother Kevin a thumbs-up sign, which caused him to smiled broadly and gently nod.

After taking a seat near the door, Andrew concentrated on the quality of the food and Brother Kevin's culinary skills, as Brother Conrad continued with his reading from Plato's *Symposium*:

"As I said in the beginning, in itself, an action is neither noble nor shameful, but it becomes noble when done in a noble manner and shameful when done shamefully."

He stared out the window at Navigator Peak, which had already developed a dusted white summit. He briefly pondered Plato's words and, with little forethought, wondered how an inherently abhorrent act, such as murder done nobly, could ever become noble.

As soon as the dishes were cleaned and put away, Andrew returned to his cell where, like the others, he would be expected to take his noonday nap. Yet the agitation, the energy, he experienced from his conversation with Brother Mark earlier that morning continued to build and prevented him from sleeping. Instead, an animal-like craving spawned deep within, radiating heat to all of his extremities, forcing him to react with minimum forethought.

When he found himself at Brother Joshua's door, he sensed an immediate déjà vu, a scene redolent with familiar beginnings and endings, of behaviors with Matthew, clandestine acts blurred by expediency and replete with inevitable intensity. Because of or, perhaps, in spite of the varied thoughts crashing within his brain, Andrew rapped firmly, undaunted by potentially negative consequences.

The door opened slowly, as Brother Joshua cautiously peered out.

Andrew raised his index finger to his lips and immediately stepped inside. After closing the door, he observed his startled friend.

Brother Joshua stood in awe, a partial smile on his speechless, open mouth. He wore a heavy sweatshirt, boxers, and white socks.

"Is this a bad time?" Andrew asked.

Brother Joshua shook his head and smiled. "Nope, not at all."

Nothing else needed to be said, as the two men embraced and kissed each other like the new lovers they now were. It was not long before each had removed their clothing and stood naked in the center of the room. Brother Joshua pulled the quilt from his bed, threw it on the carpet, and pulled Andrew down on top of him, pinning himself against the floor. He enjoyed the feeling of Andrew's weight, the sense of being dominated, and the intense sensation of his skin against his.

Nevertheless, it was Brother Joshua's feet that Andrew sought. Not only was he intrigued by their sculpted handsomeness, but he also recognized they were incredibly sensitive and a source of erotic pleasure for Brother Joshua. He slid down the quilt until he was prone in front of both perfectly arched soles. With gentle pressure, Andrew began to massage first one foot and then the other, rubbing each toe individually, the area in between and both tops and bottoms with both hands. It was clear that Brother Joshua savored every second of attention. Yet when Andrew eventually began to take his toes into his mouth, Brother Joshua was barely able to withstand the pleasure. With splayed fingers, he began to lightly run his hands over his own thighs, chest, and arms, while his breathing grew deeper and more rapid.

Brother Joshua raised his head momentarily and looked at Andrew. "You know what this can do to me, don't you?"

Andrew nodded. "Put your head back, and let it happen. I want to watch you come."

As soon as Andrew resumed his mission, Brother Joshua lay back, placed both hands under his thighs, and began to thrust his pelvis upwards, until he discharged three bursts of semen, most of which flew past Brother Joshua's averted head onto the quilt behind him.

After giving him a moment to recover, Andrew gently crawled on top of him, held his head with both hands, and kissed him tenderly. "I've never seen that before," he whispered. He continued to nuzzle his ear and throat.

"Overly sensitive feet in the mouth of a sensitive lover," Brother Joshua said with a smile. He held Andrew tight and then began to move his hands over his shoulders, back, and buttocks. With a slight twist of his body, Brother Joshua reached beneath Andrew until he found his firm erection. "What should we do about this?"

Andrew looked into his eyes. "We don't have to do anything about it."

Unexpectedly, Brother Joshua reached up with his other hand and pulled Andrew's mouth against his, kissing him hard. "I want to feel you inside of me—if it's okay with you."

"You don't have to say that," Andrew insisted, "but the truth is, I really need to fuck you."

"When are you going to realize that I seldom say things I don't mean?" Once again, he kissed Andrew with savage intent. Brother Joshua looked up at him through watery eyes. "Just before you feel as though you're about to come, I want you to kiss me—kiss me the entire time, okay?"

Andrew nodded. "Okay." He barely got the word out when he leaned down, kissed Brother Joshua, and, while breathing loudly, rammed him mercilessly until he ejaculated.

Lying together on the floor, wrapped in the quilt, they could hear the sound of the door in the adjoining cell open and close.

"Is that Brother Kevin's cell?" Andrew whispered.

"I think so," Brother Joshua said.

Andrew kissed his ear. "Are you all right?"

"Of course, why?"

"Well, I think I was out of control near the end."

"Out of control is good. You came damn close to making me come again," Brother Joshua admitted.

"Next time, tell me earlier, and I'll see what we can do about it," Andrew said with a smile.

Brother Joshua reached up and pulled the blanket off his bed. He threw it over the both of them.

"You cold?"

"A little," Brother Joshua said.

Andrew immediately snuggled even closer. He wrapped his arm and one leg around him. "You feel so damn good."

"I'm just happy that you finally decided to spend time with me, rather than me having to leave your notes."

"I doubt that you'll have to worry about that."

"You promise?" Brother Joshua asked.

"Yes, I promise."

The November wind blew hard against the side of the dormitory, as the pale light made its way into the cell through the heavy drape, softly illuminating the far wall and a small portion of the room.

"I never knew he could cook," Andrew said unexpectedly.

"Who?" Brother Joshua asked.

"Brother Kevin. When I arrived late for lunch, I saw him in the kitchen, standing behind the stove. He must have made today's meal."

"It may have happened when you were away," Brother Joshua said. "I think Brother Mark spent some time with him, showing him some of the basics."

Andrew began to chuckle.

"What's so funny?"

"Nothing, really," Andrew said. He held Brother Joshua firmly and kissed the back of his neck. "What you just said reminded me of my conversation with Mark this morning. We were up to Greystone, closing the main irrigation gates."

"And?"

"We got into a conversation about Matthew. He explained some things to me and . . . I don't know, something seemed to resonate with your description of Brother Mark teaching Brother Kevin how to cook. It's a long story." Andrew curled himself against Brother Joshua with renewed longing.

Chapter Thirty-Two

Adirondack Farewells

He had always expected his father to die first. When Father Gerald met him that morning to tell him of his mother's death, Andrew felt another chunk of his world come crashing down just before collapsing into Father Gerald's arms. When he awoke in the familiar surroundings of the infirmary, he was mildly surprised to see both Dr. Klein and Father Gerald standing near the edge of his bed.

Dr. Klein pulled up a chair and sat down. "How are you doing?" he asked quietly.

Andrew simply nodded.

"I'm really sorry to hear of your mother's death."

At that moment, the reality of the situation began to surface but not quite as painfully as when he had first heard it. "What happened?" Andrew asked.

"After Father Gerald told you, you passed out. He immediately called me, and I've given you a sedative."

Andrew raised his hand slightly in protest. "No . . . I mean, what happened to my mother—how did she die?"

Father Gerald moved closer. "Apparently, she had a heart attack early this morning. When your aunt couldn't reach her by telephone, she drove over but couldn't get in, so she let herself in with a spare key your mother had given her. She said she found her sitting in one of the living room chairs." He reached out and placed his hand on Andrew's. "This is going to be a difficult time for you, Andrew. I hope you can find some consolation, knowing that the entire community is praying for her and also for you, to gather strength to cope with such a tragedy. I am very sorry."

Even though he was moderately sedated, Andrew could not stop the tears that flowed steadily down his cheeks.

Dr. Klein put a box of tissues on the bed. "You've made it through this far, Andrew. Let me try to help you survive this."

* * *

After a marathon consultation, it was finally decided, with considerable trepidation, that Andrew would be allowed to make the trip back home.

Unaccompanied, he gazed out the window as the jet circled the Albany airport and prepared for its final descent. In the distance, the Adirondacks, although no longer as high as the familiar Rockies, reached out with worn peaks and pine-covered moraines, like an old friend waiting patiently for his return. Instinctively, he placed his hand on his pocket and was reassured to feel the prescription bottle of medication, which would help ease him through the imminent pain of sorrow, memories, and past acquaintances.

As expected, his aunt, Maris, ever gracious and generous, met him at the gate with a mixture of emotions. She appeared to have grown a bit older, with greying hair, yet remained as elegant as ever. She hugged him firmly. "I'm so sorry, Andrew," she said between tears. "I had no idea she would go so quickly."

He placed his suitcase in the trunk of her seasoned, two-seater Mercedes convertible and was about to get into the passenger side when his aunt handed him the keys.

"Would you mind terribly if I asked you to drive? You haven't forgotten how, have you?" Her smile was a welcomed change from all that had happened so far.

"I think I can manage," he said with a laugh. "Let's give it a shot."

"Thank you. I'm not all that comfortable driving on the highway."

Even though Maris talked most of the way, Andrew had difficulty concentrating and responding appropriately, as he watched familiar landmarks loom outside the window, each with the special significance one remembers when returning to their birthplace after years of absence. As they approached Saratoga, Andrew sensed a growing anxiety within his guts, an unexplained edge which he tried desperately to quell. "So you still have this bucket of bolts," he said jokingly, "and it's running beautifully."

"Yeah, well, thank God for Ted, my mechanic. I don't know what I'd do without him."

"He's still in Bolton Landing at the Marina?" Andrew asked.

Maris nodded. "Yes. He said if he can work on those foolish, high-powered speedboats that destroy the silence of the long gone idyllic summers, he can certainly fix my baby."

"They can't compare to your old Chris Craft and the other woodies on the lake," Andrew said.

"I guess it's a matter of style; I sure as hell can't out run them, but I have to confess, there are times when I've tried."

Andrew laughed. "You'll never change, will you?"

His aunt looked at him and smiled. "Not while I'm still breathing."

It was not long before the familiar materialized before his eyes. The narrow road curved and dipped until the speed limit dropped to thirty miles per hour. Suddenly, the anticipated sign appeared: "Welcome to Bolton Landing."

Andrew could feel a light sweat break across his forehead and on his palms. Just as he was about to slow down and turn right into his aunt's property, she raised her hand and spoke.

"Would you mind if we continued on?" she asked.

Andrew shook his head. "No . . . of course not."

They drove in silence through the center of town, as the late afternoon sun cast elongated shadows of towering pines across the road.

"Why is it I seem to have an idea of exactly where you are heading?" Andrew said with a smile.

"Because you know me too well," Maris admitted.

"And I know how much you love the Old Lady."

"She's the only one left on the lake," Maris said. Her voice developed a melancholy tone. "Besides, I'm dying for a drink, and if you don't mind, I don't feel like cooking tonight."

"That's fine with me," Andrew said. For the moment, he was relieved, knowing that he would not have to be isolated with his aunt as they discussed the inevitable. "I thought you were going to tell me that you don't like drinking alone."

She shrugged, pulled a compact out of her purse, and checked her lipstick. "Hell, that's never been a problem."

Unlike the summer season, the gate to the Sagamore remained open, it's guardhouse vacant. Andrew continued up the smooth blacktop road, rounded the gentle curve near the top, and, as always, felt a slight catch in his breath as the resort came into view. "She's every bit as magnificent as I remember," he said.

"Yes," Maris agreed. "I just hope she stays that way."

The elegant white structure reflected a golden glow as it glistened in the late afternoon sunlight. Andrew pulled into the circular drive and stopped near the main entrance. He was barely out of the car when two uniformed young men approached, opened the passenger door for his aunt, and accepted the keys which Andrew offered to the second valet. "Thanks," he said. "There's no luggage. We're just having dinner."

He followed his aunt across the lobby and into the spacious Veranda Room, which afforded them a spectacular view of the lake and islands. "It doesn't get much prettier than this," Andrew said. He sat next to his aunt in a comfortable wicker chair, softened by patterned mauve cushions.

"I think it's a matter of preference," Maris said. "The summer and fall views have their own special beauty, particularly if you have access to the lake."

"You're right. It would be difficult to make this place look bad, no matter what the season."

The attractive waitress smiled and placed a bowl of mixed nuts on the marble cocktail table. "Hello," she said. "What can I get for you?"

Maris answered without hesitation. "A Gibson—straight up—with extra onions. Could you use Smirnoff's please?"

The waitress nodded and looked at Andrew. "I guess I'll have a margarita on the rocks with salt."

Maris appeared surprised. "You actually like tequila?"

"That's what happens when you hang around the Algonquin."

"Oh sure, let's blame it on the Algonquin."

Andrew laughed. "Well, it might have had something to do with the guys I was hanging around with."

Maris's drink was barely set in front of her when she raised it to her lips and uninhibitedly swallowed a generous amount. "I needed that," she admitted. She picked through the mixed nuts until she found two cashews. "Speaking of acquaintances, I saw your friend, Nick, working at George's restaurant when I had dinner there in August."

The unexpected reference caused Andrew's stomach to knot instantly, yet he responded with forced indifference. "How's he doing?" he asked casually. This time, it was Andrew who raised his glass and drank deeply, until he could feel the anesthetizing effect of the alcohol soothe his stomach and alleviate some of his anxiety.

"He seemed fine," Maris said. "I think he's taking a few courses at the college and living with his parents in Glens Falls." She found two more cashews and, while still chewing, continued her conversation. "Of course, he still as good looking as ever—filled out nicely, and he asked about you."

Andrew could feel the color rise in his cheeks. He immediately threw back the rest of his margarita. "They don't make these as large as they used to," he said. His bewilderment may have been obvious.

"You're welcome to another," Maris said. "In fact, I think I'll join you." With a slight wave, she signaled the waitress, held up two fingers, and made a circular motion with her hand, while raising her eyebrows slightly and barely whispering the words "two more, please."

"Thanks," Andrew said. "Could you tell that I needed another?"

"I think we both do."

Moments later, the waitress returned and placed two fresh drinks on the table.

"Thank you," Maris said. "Could you be a sweetheart and ask about accommodating the two of us for dinner in the Trillium? We didn't make reservations."

"I doubt that's a problem," the waitress said. "Let me check and I'll be right back."

"Thanks so much," Maris replied.

Andrew sipped his drink and smiled. "You certainly haven't lost the ability to charm."

Maris laughed. "It gets easier with age."

Andrew squinted and looked down the lake, as occasional puffs of snow blew off the taller pines like summer pollen. "I hope that isn't the only thing that gets easier with age."

His aunt sensed the underlying sadness; unexpectedly, she reached across the table, placed her hand over his, and leaned forward slightly. "These things are never easy, Andrew, but trust me, you will get through this." Once again, she raised her glass and swallowed deeply. "Your mother was a wonderful woman and an equally wonderful sister to me. I like to think she died quickly and peacefully."

Dreading the moment, Andrew took several deep breaths to maintain his composure. When he felt capable of speaking, he replied simply and softly, "I'm going to miss her."

As if on cue, the waitress returned to the table carrying a tweed sports jacket. "They can seat you in the Trillium whenever you wish."

"That's perfect," Maris said. "We'll be over as soon as we finish our drinks."

Shyly, the waitress offered the jacket to Andrew. "I just guessed at the size; if it doesn't fit, let me know. We have several others."

Andrew accepted the jacket and hung it over the back of his chair. "I'm sure it will be fine," he said. "Thank you."

By now, the shadows across the lake began to fade, as the sun began to settle behind the mountains.

Maris had nearly finished her drink. "Do you mind if I ask you a personal question?"

Andrew inhaled deeply and lied. "No, of course not."

"Do you enjoy being a monk?" she asked bluntly.

"Yes," he replied without hesitation, "but it isn't lacking in challenges."

"What's the most challenging part?" Verbal subtlety was not one of Maris's strong suits.

Andrew was aware of his growing exasperation. "I'm not exactly sure," he said with a sigh. "I guess it's the loneliness, a sense of knowing that for the rest of your life, you will never truly experience intimacy with another human being."

Maris appeared to be digesting the thought in stages, amazed, perhaps, by Andrew's honesty; she looked directly at him. "My first reaction was—if that's the case—why not simply leave, yet I'm sure there are many people who never experienced the intimacy you described, and they have never been exposed to a monastery."

Andrew appreciated her depth of thought with a smile. "That's probably true, but those living a secular lifestyle may still cling to the illusion that someday—*someday*—a significant other will materialize, and they will live happily ever after; whereas those of us who are cloistered eventually see the illusion for what it is—an unattainable, hopeless illusion, which is essentially the true nature and definition of the word 'monk.'" Andrew sipped his drink and smiled. "Am I being a bore?" he asked.

Maris shook her head. "Not at all, in fact, just the opposite." She hastily finished what was left in her glass. "One last question before we eat. The intimacy you've talked about . . . is that then to be rechanneled on a different level toward the religious aspect of the vocation?"

Her insight surprised Andrew. "Pretty much, but as you've mentioned, it's a totally different level and meaning of the word—perhaps more like sublimation."

Maris appeared satisfied with Andrew's oblique response. She pushed back her chair and stood silently for a moment, as if it attempting to get her balance. "Quite honestly, I don't know how you do it."

"That's okay," he said as he stood up. "I'm not sure I know myself." The lie barely left his lips when he was suddenly drenched in his own hypocrisy; at that very moment, he was obscenely aware of the feel, smell, and taste of Brother Joshua's distant body.

* * *

Most of the dinner conversation consisted of well-intentioned banality, as they dined on grilled salmon and lemon peppered veal. Maris insisted on having crème brûlée for dessert, while Andrew settled for strawberry shortcake and a glass of port.

"I don't think I'll be able to walk out of here," he said. "I'm stuffed."

"Me too," Maris said. "This must be quite a change from the usual monastery fare."

"I'd say so. This would never have been allowed on our vegetarian diet."

"Well, I hope you don't get sick."

"I doubt it," Andrew replied. "We manage to scarf down a burger or two on the way to the dentist or doctor and even on some egg deliveries. It depends on who's driving."

Maris laughed. "You must be a big hit with your dental hygienist."

"They know us all by now. The first thing she does is hand me my complimentary toothbrush and a tube of toothpaste."

Maris paid the check with large bills, refusing any change.

"If it's all right with you, I think it would be more practical if you stayed at my house, at least for your first night back. What you think?"

Andrew considered her offer, knowing that he could not refuse yet yearning deeply to sleep in his own bed. "I appreciate that, Aunt Maris, but I think I'll be fine, thanks."

* * *

It was a small funeral. Andrew sat next to Maris in the drafty church, surrounded by a few distant relatives, most of whom he had not seen for years or was unable to recognize. The others consisted of local friends and neighbors who had known his mother for a long time and respected her as a hard-working, goodhearted woman who, because of his father's illness, raised Andrew almost single-handedly. Yet it was Nick's presence which Andrew found so disconcerting, not because of his genuine show of respect, but mostly due to the awkwardness of the anticipated reunion. Andrew realized that unresolved issues remained between them, particularly his relationship with Sara and, of course, his sudden decision to enter the monastery—a decision that baffled both Nick and Sara.

As expected, the postburial gathering was hosted by Maris for all who chose to return to her home and feast on a variety of homemade and donated foods, including shrimp, lasagna, salads and—Maris's favorite—fried oysters. Nick entered the living room and stood quietly between the French doors like a handsome portrait framed in white.

Andrew watched as Maris approached him, placed her hands on his shoulders, and then hugged him with genuine affection. He wondered what Maris may have said to him.

As if she had radar, Maris immediately located Andrew on the far side of the room and pointed him out to Nick with a gentle pat of encouragement.

Andrew sensed his growing anxiety—he feared having an unchecked panic attack. Just before Nick reached him, he took a deep breath, exhaled slowly, and attempted to project as genuine a smile as possible.

Nick disregarded Andrew's outstretched hand; instead, he maintained strong eye contact until he was close enough to embrace him. He held him tight in silence before finally releasing him. "I'm sorry about your mom," he said. "I'm sure you've been pretty much wrecked by it."

The sentence slid off Andrew as if he were made of Teflon. For the moment, he became completely lost in Nick's forgotten physical attributes—his black loosely-curled hair, his piercing blue eyes, the strong chin and nose—all solidly characteristic of his Greek heritage.

"You've put on some weight," Andrew said without thinking.

"That's a heck of a greeting for someone you haven't seen for a while," Nick said with a smile.

Somewhat flustered, Andrew tried to explain his faux pas. "No . . . you look great—added some muscle. You really look good."

Nick appeared to blush slightly. "Thanks. I've been spending some time in the gym at school." His smile faded during the brief pause. "How are you doing, Andrew?" His somber tone and personalization of the question left no room for a contrived response.

Andrew exhaled loudly. "Oh . . . on a scale of one to ten, I'm probably at a minus six . . . somewhere in there."

"Is it mostly due to your mom's death?" Nick asked honestly.

Andrew shook his head. "Yes, but not completely. Things haven't been going well, in general."

"You must mean at the monastery," Nick ventured.

Andrew chuckled. "That must sound pretty weird coming from a monk."

"If you don't mind my honesty, I think it sounds rather normal." Nick accepted two glasses of wine from a tray and handed one to Andrew.

"I've thought about you often and wondered how anyone can live such a harsh lifestyle." He ran his hand over his face as if in despair. "I'm sorry. I should never have said that."

"It's okay. I'm not offended; in fact, you're probably right. It's just that . . . right now . . . I'd rather not talk about it."

"I understand. It was stupid of me to bring it up."

Andrew gestured with his free hand. "It wasn't stupid at all—it's all right."

Nick took a long drink from his glass and looked around the room. "I never feel too comfortable at these things."

"Me either," Andrew stammered. "Did Maris have much to say to you when you arrived?"

"You know Maris. She can imply pages with a single comment."

"I was afraid of that," Andrew said. "So . . . what did she imply?"

Nick laughed. "I guess it's my turn to be evasive." He looked directly at Andrew. "Tell me that you'll meet me later for a drink."

"Why not," Andrew said with some hesitation. "Where do you want to go?"

"How about the pub at the Sagamore? The bar should be fairly quiet."

"That sounds fine, but I probably won't be able to get there until around eight."

"Eight is all right. I'm going to say goodbye to Maris." Nick smiled. "See you then."

Andrew watched as he walked confidently through the crowded room, occasionally stopping to speak or shake someone's hand—a combination of the aspiring politician and local college quarterback. 'Why did I ever choose to desert him?' he thought.

* * *

Nick was right. Mr. Brown's Pub was nearly vacant, except for a young couple and their five-year-old daughter having a late supper of oversized burgers and rough-cut fries. Andrew sensed that the child behaved too decorously for her age; her clothing and mannerisms were more expressive of a twelve-year-old. 'Perhaps the rich really are different,' he thought. 'I wonder if she's missed her childhood.'

"What can I get for you, sir?" The bartender's question startled Andrew, who cringed slightly. He was not used to being addressed so formally, particularly by a bartender who was not much older than he.

"Let me guess," Nick said unexpectedly. He picked up the bar stool and sat close to Andrew, who was obviously stunned by his sudden arrival. "I think 'sir' is having a margarita on the rocks—with salt."

Andrew laughed. "You're right. Now it's my turn, are you still drinking Scotch sours?"

Nick nodded. "When they're available."

"They are available, sir," the bartender said.

"All right, then."

"Any particular brand?"

"It doesn't really matter, as long as it's with ice," Nick said.

Andrew waited to speak until the bartender was out of earshot. "Doesn't it make you feel strange when someone calls you 'sir'? He's only two or three your years older than we are."

"I suppose so. It doesn't seem all that genuine, but he's probably just doing his job."

"The required Sagamore image," Andrew quipped. He picked through a mixture of miniature pretzels, Rice Chex, and other indecipherable cayenne-flavored edibles. "Are you ready to tell me what she said?"

"Who . . . Maris?" Nick replied.

Andrew returned a blank stare. "You don't have to tell me if you don't want to."

"It isn't that," Nick said. "It's sort of difficult to just blurt out."

"Well, the drinks are coming, and I'm in no hurry, so take your time."

Nick shrugged. "You certainly have a way with words . . ."

The bartender set the cocktails on top of small embossed napkins, which seemed too elegant to be destroyed by condensation.

Nick immediately raised his glass and was about to drink when Andrew suddenly grabbed his arm.

"Shouldn't we toast to something?" he asked.

"You're right—I'm sorry." Nick returned his glass to the bar. "I'll let you do the honors."

Andrew grew pensive, not sure of what he should say. He eventually lifted his glass and met Nick's with a soft, crystal ting. "To all that we once had . . . and lost . . . in friendship and in love. Cheers."

"Cheers," Nick repeated. He took a deep swallow while he pondered Andrew's toast—a rather solemn and seemingly final declaration, both unexpected and gut-wrenching. He could not deny his feelings for Andrew, which were now instantly shattered.

"So are you ready to tell me?" Andrew asked.

Nick knew it would be even more difficult to share Maris's comment after Andrew's definitive statement. He looked directly at him. "She gives me the impression that she knows."

"About what?" Andrew asked.

"About us—or, at least, our past relationship," Nick explained.

"What did she actually say?"

"It's not only what she said but how she said it."

Andrew stared with anticipation.

"She told me that she has always liked me, that I've been a good influence on you, and wished that it would be possible for us to be . . . close friends once again."

"Well, she obviously knows," Andrew said. He took a healthy swallow of his margarita. "What does she expect, that I should quit the monastery and move back here?"

"It does sound that way," Nick offered.

"What about you?" Andrew asked.

Nick cautiously pondered his response. "I think you know the answer, Andrew. Don't make me have to say it, especially after your toast."

"I'm trying to be honest, Nick."

"So am I, but I refuse to try to change your mind or, if you'll excuse my emotional shortcoming, further inflate your ego."

Andrew shook his head with exasperation. "You really don't know me, do you?"

"Maybe not, but it doesn't mean I wouldn't be willing to try."

Andrew placed a hand on Nick's shoulder. "It's stuff like that that makes me want to fall in love with you all over again. The problem is—I've changed. I'm not the Andrew you may remember." He finished his drink and motioned to the bartender for another round.

"What makes you think I couldn't live with you—whoever you are?"

Andrew rubbed his eyes. "What do you know about my father?"

Baffled, Nick simply stared at Andrew until he felt capable of responding. "I don't get it. I know a little about him, but what the heck does that have to do with us?"

"Think about it; think about where he is."

"He's at the VA hospital, right?"

"Yes . . . and do you know why?"

"I heard it was from some sort of injury he suffered during the last military conflict."

"Not exactly," Andrew said. He removed a twenty-dollar bill from his wallet and gave it to the bartender. "The conflict merely brought it to the surface." He took a long swallow of his drink before continuing. "He's been confined to the psychiatric unit for clinical depression, is on medication, and had ECT."

"What the hell is that?" Nick asked.

"Shock therapy—sort of how I remember Frankenstein."

"That's not exactly funny," Nick said.

"Sorry, I really didn't mean it to be, but it's how I've always envisioned it."

Nick put his hand on Andrew's shoulder. "I'm really sorry, man. I had no idea."

"It's okay. Not many people know." Andrew nearly finished his drink. "What I'm trying to tell you is that I've pretty much inherited the same illness."

Nick turned to face him; his disbelief was obvious. "I don't get it. You're not serious, right?"

"Unfortunately, I am serious," Andrew admitted.

"But . . . how? You're young, you look . . . normal, for god's sake. How do you know?"

Andrew smiled slightly over Nick's remarks. "After a few admissions to the Halsen Clinic outside Bitter Creek, ongoing visits with my psychiatrist, and several, let's say, less-than-normal occurrences, it was decided that I seem to fit the description."

Nick finished his drink, set the glass down with a thud, and uncharacteristically wiped his mouth with the back of his hand. "I'm a simple business major, Andrew, so I don't have a handle on all this psychiatric mumbo-jumbo, but what's the possibility that they're wrong, that you have been going through some hard times or that the fucking monastery is responsible for putting you through some extraordinary bullshit like . . . imposed celibacy?" He rubbed his face in exasperation. "Look, I'm sorry. I shouldn't have said that. I guess I'm finding this somewhat overwhelming."

"I'm not offended; in fact, it would be nice if I could 'blame' it all on the monastery, but I can't. Apparently, the illness can be inherited and certain situations may cause it to strengthen." Andrew ran his finger around the rim of his glass and spoke softly. "This is tough to admit, but I haven't exactly been celibate, so don't remember me as some angelic creature on a pedestal."

Nick immediately caught his breath and the bartender's attention with a wave of his hand. "I'm having another drink."

"What the hell," Andrew said. "Make it two."

He watched as the young couple to his right left the table and walked in back of them on their way out of the pub. Their daughter looked up with large sad eyes, as if she were aware of his hopelessness as much as her own. Andrew looked away.

Nick stared at his napkin and then directly at Andrew. "Let me get this straight. Are you saying that you are having sex with someone at the monastery?"

Andrew glanced up to find the bartender looking at the both of them as if they were Martian aliens. He locked eyes with him. "You sort of get into the habit," Andrew said sarcastically. The bartender turned quickly and walked away without comment.

"I can't see where the hell you find humor in this," Nick said. He spoke calmly, much as anyone might whose hopes for a second chance with someone he once respected were now totally extinguished and fully realized. "I just never expected it."

"Neither did I," Andrew said sharply. He faced Nick and placed a hand on his knee. "Listen to me. I didn't come back here to hurt you in any way; in fact, I honestly thought I'd never see you again. That doesn't mean I haven't thought about you or missed you. I've even dreamed about you—about us. I went away because I couldn't stand the pain I caused to both you and Sara. Nothing made sense to me then, and now, my life is even more confusing. The last word I would use to describe it is humorous . . ."

"So . . . what's wrong with considering my offer? Maybe Maris is right. You could leave the monastery, come back here, and if it feels right, we could get a place together and finish what we began. I've always wanted to be with you, Andrew, but you probably always knew that." Nick sipped his drink. "I would do my best to learn about this illness you've mentioned and deal with it. You have to admit, I've always been fairly forgiving."

Andrew nodded. "It would take a lot more than forgiveness."

"Like what . . . tell me?" Nick asked.

Andrew grew silent; he fought with every ounce of distraction to prevent his eyes from welling with tears. "I don't know," he lied. "Call it destiny or whatever. It's as if the ending has already been written."

"And apparently, I'm not in it," Nick barely whispered.

Unable to fully control his emotions, Andrew could feel the occasional tear run down his cheek. He did his best to speak in a level tone. "It's not because I don't want you, Nick. I've always loved you—except, things have changed with me. It has nothing to do with you. I really need you to understand that. No matter what happens, can you tell me right now that you understand what I've just said?"

Surprised by the tears, Nick instinctively and uninhibitedly reached out and brushed them off Andrew's cheek. "It's okay. It's okay. I understand. I just wish that somehow, someway, you'd let me into your life."

"Tell me you understand . . . that it's not your fault," Andrew insisted.

Nick stared at him. "I've already said it, Andrew. It's not my fault. I understand." He took a quick swallow of his drink. "You seem to make everything so final. I don't know if I can deal with that."

Andrew shrugged. "I don't know what to say . . . I'm sorry."

Nick hunched over the bar and stared at the fragile looking glasses, which sat upside down on the rubber-lined, mirrored shelving. "So what can I ask you that won't make you feel uncomfortable?" He was aware that before he finished the sentence, he was far from being sincere; in fact, his earlier compassion began to quickly change into an edgy anger.

Andrew shook his head in frustration. "I don't know. It doesn't matter at this point."

"Okay, then," Nick said bluntly. "Do you love him?"

"Who?"

Once again, Nick looked up defiantly. "Whoever it is you've been fucking in your cell or wherever the hell you do it!"

Andrew looked away. He finished his drink and blindly signaled the bartender for another "I suppose I deserved that," he said calmly. "It's just that I didn't expect it from you. The answer is—I don't know, and I'm going to try to forget about your last remark."

"That's a hell of an answer." Nick waved at the bartender. "I'll have another, please."

Andrew slowly turned and faced him. "Let's not do this, Nick . . . please. I never meant to hurt you."

"Well, I hate to tell you, but you're a little too late—you already have." He removed his wallet and paid for both drinks.

"Thanks," Andrew said. "You know, if my mom hadn't died, we probably wouldn't have seen each other, and this conversation wouldn't have happened."

"Probably not," Nick agreed. "But for what it's worth, I had the opportunity to tell you how I've always felt about you, and after all we've said, I hope you can realize how . . . empty I feel right now."

With reservation, Andrew placed his hand on Nick's arm. "Believe me, I do, yet you need to realize that I'm feeling the same way. It's as if I'm on a speeding train—out of control—and I can't jump off, even though it's obvious that it's going to crash."

"Why can't you just take a chance and jump?"

Andrew paused, sipped his drink, and seemed to glaze over. "Because . . . I'm afraid I might live."

Nick shook his head. "I don't understand."

"I have to take a piss," Andrew said with a slur. He could suddenly feel the woozy effect of the alcohol as he made his way through the tables and into the men's room. The fat porcelain knobs on the sinks glared their black words—"hot" and "cold"—in the bright light. Like the mansions at Newport, Andrew half expected to see an oversized tub on the black and white marble floor, flaunting extra faucets for saltwater.

When he returned to the bar, he noticed that Nick had already put on his jacket. "You leaving already?" He stumbled to his seat and sat down.

"I've got a class at ten, and right now, it would be a miracle if I make it."

Andrew's disappointment was obvious. "Yeah, I guess it's later than I thought."

"You going to be all right, driving?" Nick asked.

Andrew smiled. "I'll make it home, but I doubt that I'll be all right."

"Do you want me to drop you off? I can go right by your mom's house."

Andrew considered the offer. "Why not," he said. "I'll walk over and pick up the car tomorrow." He put on his coat, tossed a five dollar tip next to his unfinished drink, and waved good night to the bartender.

Once they were inside of Nick's car, Andrew began to experience a sense of the familiar. With reduced inhibitions, he boldly reached out and placed his hand on Nick's leg as Nick slowly maneuvered his way down the curved drive, past the gate house, over the small wooden bridge, and onto Bolton's main street which was expectedly deserted. He stopped at the red signal light.

"Go through it!" Andrew challenged.

Nick chuckled. "You're blitzed, aren't you?"

Without answering, Andrew suddenly reached over with his left foot, placed it on top of Nick's, and pushed down.

The car sped forward, as Nick attempted to gain control and make a sharp left turn without running up on the sidewalk. "You're fucking crazy!" he shouted. He finally stopped the car on a side street after narrowly missing a lamppost.

Andrew grinned. "That's what I've been trying to tell you, but you won't believe me."

"Fine," Nick said. "I believe you." He rubbed his face in disbelief, happy to still be in one piece. "Should I continue to drive you home, or are you going to pull another stupid act to get us both killed?"

Andrew sat in silence, unsure of his response. His affect grew flat. "I don't know what I want," he said softly.

Nick watched him change, almost immediately, from a near manic high to a sad, depressed state. Like the lifting of a cloud, he suddenly began to realize that everything Andrew tried to tell him about his illness was, in fact, true. Denial had died and reality was not especially attractive. "Do you want me to stay with you tonight?" Nick asked.

Andrew managed a slight smile. "Do you want to?"

Nick refused to appear solicitous or, even worse, as if he were taking advantage of a person in need. "Let me just say that I'm concerned about you."

"I know, because you are a heck of a great guy," Andrew said with sincerity. "But you need to be less concerned about the inevitable; you have your whole life ahead of you. Besides, I don't deserve you, and you sure as hell don't deserve me."

"I'm still willing to try . . ."

Andrew looked out the window. "If you stay with me, I'm going to want to fuck my brains out; you'll be up most of the night, and in the morning, you'll be exhausted and either be late for your class or sleep through and probably hate me for it." He looked at Nick. "I don't want that to happen."

"I understand, but I wouldn't blame you."

"But fucking all night would be all right?" Andrew asked derisively.

"I'd sleep in a separate room," Nick lied.

"That's unlikely," Andrew admitted. "I'd come looking for you."

Nick started the car, knowing that Andrew was right. He drove slowly through the quiet back streets, remembering how excited he used to get when he would pick up Andrew at his house and spend the evening with him, either at a movie, dinner, or having a few drinks at a small quasi-gay bar. He stopped the car in front of the house where he had parked so many times before.

"Turn off the lights, but leave the engine running," Andrew instructed.

The one story house sat at the end of a dead-end street which bordered a small park near the high school's playing fields. Neighboring houses were a fair distance apart; all were completely dark.

Nick was confused by Andrew's request yet he did as he was asked. "So . . . where do we go from here?"

"How about just shutting up?" Andrew said abruptly. He moved closer to Nick, put his arm around him, and, without hesitation, kissed him as Nick remembered—hard yet affectionately—as if they had never been apart.

Taken by surprise, Nick was overwhelmed by the excitement of the moment and the fleeting chance that Andrew may have changed his mind about their relationship. He held him tight, kissed his lips, eyes, and forehead, and then returned to taste his mouth. He could feel Andrew's hands squeeze his chest and abdomen and then move down to his thighs and finally across his bulging zipper. He slumped a bit in his seat to accommodate the situation, as Andrew began to undo Nick's fly and search for a way to unleash his erection. "Should we be doing this?" Nick whispered.

Andrew did not look up. "I really don't want to hear it," he said quietly and then took as much of his penis as possible into his eager mouth.

Half dazed, Nick gently rubbed Andrew's neck and tugged lightly on his hair, while slowly thrusting himself into that familiar warm place. Within minutes, he sensed that ejaculation was imminent. "I think I'm going to come," he said, yet Andrew only intensified his action, anticipating the inevitable.

Almost immediately, Nick ejaculated, while sparks of colored lights flashed in the dark across his closed eyes. And at that very moment, he could feel the unbridled intention of Andrew's zealous efforts, as he sought to devour Nick's entire discharge.

Nearly satiated, Andrew continued to gently lap Nick's softening erection, as if the slightest trace of semen on Nick's body or clothing were unacceptable.

Nick lifted Andrew's chin. "I want to kiss you . . . come up here." Andrew raised his head and met Nick's mouth with his, sharing the slightly bitter and salty flavor that Nick remembered and expected. "You always make me feel so incredibly good," he said while still managing to kiss Andrew.

"I've always loved the way you taste," Andrew replied.

"Then let me do the same."

Rather than release him, Andrew held him tight and kissed him even harder. "Thanks, Nick, but I'm fine. Besides, with all the alcohol I've had, you may be here forever, and I'd rather see you go home and get some sleep."

Nick pulled away slightly. "That's not fair, you know."

"Yeah, but life's not always fair." Andrew tried to help Nick put himself together by tugging up his shorts and jeans. "And I have to get up somewhat early myself."

Once again, Nick was surprised. "How come?"

"My flight leaves at eleven."

Nick's shock descended into despair. "Wait a second. You're going back tomorrow?"

"It's not like I'm on vacation, Nick. They gave me only a few days."

Nick placed both hands on the wheel and looked straight ahead. "Well then . . . I suppose this is it."

Andrew placed his hand on the back of Nick's neck and lightly massaged it. "Please don't make this more difficult than it already is."

"Hell, I wouldn't dream of it," Nick said, with a barely noticeable quiver. "You have to do whatever it is you do, but . . . for a second, there, I actually thought I had a chance . . . that we had a chance—together."

"Who knows," Andrew lied. "Someday we might . . ."

Nick put his foot on the brake and shifted into drive. "I guess I'd better go." He refused to allow himself to completely fall apart in front of Andrew.

"You're right. A quick exit is probably the only solution." Andrew leaned over and kissed him on the cheek. He got out of the car and spoke through the open door. "I've always loved you, Nick—please don't forget about me. And if nothing else, I'm sure I'll see you in heaven." He shut the door with a thud, turned, and walked up the sloped sidewalk to the porch. Without looking back, he heard Nick's car accelerate quickly and drive away, while he finished his thoughts aloud in the dark. "That's right, Nick. You'll be in heaven, and the only chance I'll have of ever seeing you is by looking up with binoculars."

Nick managed to drive two blocks away from Andrew's house before he was forced to pull into a vacant lot behind a gift shop, to release the flood of gut-wrenching tears that erupted in nearly silent wails. At that moment, he knew they would never see each other again, and the unbearable pain and emptiness he felt would scar him forever. Understandably, he was not yet ready to consider that life is seldom so kind as to inflict only one scar.

* * *

Chapter Thirty-Three

Only Atheists Go to Heaven

Although he had been gone for less than five days, Andrew felt as though he had been away for an eternity and was about to resume the enigmatic monastic path, a path which, most often, filled him with polarities and fed his particular symptoms. Yet he would be the first to admit that the barriers were breaking down, as his once rigidly held differences began to meld. His desire for Brother Joshua, although different, became no less than his desire to immerse himself in his spirituality. It seemed as though the more he loved physically, the deeper his quest for spiritual clarity and the greater his understanding of his own insignificance as it related to his personal eschatology. Dr. Klein once suggested that he was replacing guilt with freedom, a leap which, nevertheless, needed to be carefully monitored. So when Father Gerald mentioned that he had taken the liberty to schedule an appointment for Andrew with Dr. Klein, he was not surprised.

The early-morning meeting left him little time to get reacquainted with the community. He found himself driving the black Volkswagen to Bitter Creek through a moderate snow shower, while he thought about seeing and, more specifically, being with Brother Joshua, who managed a radiant "welcome-back smile" during the morning mass. Like a seed about to germinate, Bitter Creek anxiously awaited a significant snowstorm to initiate the ski season and bloom into the burnished entity she became every winter. White gold would fall generously from the heavens, produce handsome profits and, for many, turn into snorted snow. "Live fast—die young" was an accepted mantra.

Unlike the anticipated reacclimation to the monastery, Dr. Klein's office seemed stuck in time. It was familiar, unchanged, and still smelled of pipe smoke. Andrew's barely noticeable handprint remained smudged against the upper windowpane.

"It was a bit of a gamble," Dr. Klein admitted. "I had some reservations about letting you return to New York alone, but overall, I felt that you were capable of dealing with it." He put down his pipe. "Was I wrong?"

Andrew shrugged. "No, not at all. In fact, I would have been uncomfortable if a member of the community were with me."

"Are things pretty much settled up there?"

"Yes, thanks to my aunt Maris. She has been incredibly supportive—as I expected—and is taking care of selling the house. I don't know what I would have done if she weren't there."

Dr. Klein paused briefly before refocusing on Andrew. "And now that you are back, how are you feeling?"

Andrew shifted in his chair. "It may take some time to get back to the monastic schedule, but I think I'm doing fine."

"Any problems with the medication?" Dr. Klein asked. "You are remembering to take them, daily . . ."

"Sometimes, I feel a bit tired. Otherwise, I'm taking them as you prescribed, and things seem to be all right."

Dr. Klein briefly jotted a note. "In light of the recent loss of your mother, how is the depression? Is it significantly worse or is it within tolerable limits with the medication dosage?"

"I think I'm doing okay. It's hard, but I've been sleeping fairly well, and so far, I guess I'm hanging in there."

Dr. Klein stood up. He walked slowly from behind his desk to a chair near Andrew's left and sat down. "If you feel as though you might be sliding backwards, I can increase the level. I would rather not do it, unless we both feel it's warranted. I don't expect you to be a hero."

Andrew rubbed his eyes. "I don't think you have to worry about that."

It was the silence which often followed Dr. Klein's statements that Andrew chose to play with. He would either challenge by waiting for Dr. Klein to speak first, or if he was in the mood, authentically or otherwise, he would share his thoughts and wait for Dr. Klein's response. At times, he would simply attempt to shock. "I've been wondering if I'm not more and more like Matthew," Andrew suggested.

"I'm sure you've felt that way previously," Dr. Klein replied.

"Maybe . . . but I think I'm feeling more comfortable with it."

"As I mentioned, is it the dissipation of guilt and the renewal of freedom?" Dr. Klein asked.

"I don't know, I suppose so. I think it has something to do with my mom's death. It's very painful, yet I feel as though a weight has been lifted from my shoulders, like my life is less consequential almost as if my personal failures can't hurt her anymore."

"That's not an uncommon feeling, particularly after the death of a loved one," Dr. Klein explained. "It's important to remember that, no matter what, consequences cannot be completely separated from our lives. They are a given. Perhaps some might be more significant or meaningful than others, but they will continue to exist."

Andrew looked at the soiled window and beyond, where spruce and yellow pines swayed gracefully through bursts of powdered snow. "Maybe that's it," he said. "Consequences seem to have less meaning for me."

"Then I think we need to talk about it. You need to keep me informed."

Andrew raised his hands in frustration. "What more can I tell you that you don't already know? I'm a monk who had a relationship with one of my brothers, and when that relationship ended, I actively allowed and probably encouraged another to begin. Somehow, I am no longer concerned about the consequences. It's as though my sensuality and spirituality have blurred into one—a physical relationship with another man through and with whom I seek a spiritual purpose. You see, I have become Matthew."

Dr. Klein smiled. "Not exactly. Give yourself some credit."

"What do you mean?" Andrew asked.

"I can only speculate that Matthew may have chosen a less than genuine path out of the monastery; nevertheless, I'd rather talk about you." Dr. Klein retrieved his pipe, lit it, and sat down. "You realize that your description of past events might be described as enlightenment by those who follow Eastern beliefs, particularly those with strong Tantric principles. If you want, I could lend you a book or two when you leave."

Andrew nodded. "Sure, if you don't mind."

"Not at all," Dr. Klein said.

A brief silence followed as Andrew, once again, walked to the window, and looked down on the quiet street. A set of tire tracks blackened the snow with its parallel score. "Then how do we know when I'm in trouble?" he asked.

Dr. Klein exhaled a halo of smoke. "It depends. Do you want the Western or Eastern response?"

"Whichever one is right."

"There is no real right or wrong. I can only suggest that you will know when you are in trouble when polarity produces imbalance. That's all I'd prefer to say."

"And," Andrew quipped, "it sounds as though you would prefer not to be quoted."

"As you wish," Dr. Klein replied. "It's all been said before—thousands of years ago." He immediately got up, browsed his bookshelves, and selected two hardcover copies for Andrew. "Since you may be at a different point from others in the community, it might be a good idea if these didn't leave your cell. I don't want to be accused of starting a revolution at St. Anthony's."

"What about my friend, Brother Joshua? Can I share them with him?"

"Yes, but only because of the special relationship you have formed."

Andrew suddenly grew pensive, knowing that he needed to clarify and seek answers to issues that he had not honestly shared with Dr. Klein. "I was wondering if you would be willing to discuss some concerns that have been troubling me," Andrew asked guardedly. "I know I should have talked with you earlier but . . . I just couldn't do it."

Dr. Klein nodded. "Of course. You are my last appointment, and believe me, your wellbeing is essential, particularly at this stage in your life."

Once again, Andrew walked to his safe space, the window, where he looked out and noticed that the snow had intensified. "I'm not sure where to begin. I guess I'm finally starting to realize that my illness has changed me. I get fearful if I say too much; you might feel obligated to send me back to the clinic, and I would definitely prefer not to return there."

Dr. Klein filled his pipe, lit it, and surrounded himself with smoke. "Let's not focus on hypotheticals right now. A return to the clinic is far from imminent, but I can appreciate your feelings."

"Is it possible to hallucinate, given the nature of my illness?" Andrew asked bluntly.

"Has that been an issue with for you?' Dr. Klein asked.

With the light fading rapidly, Andrew watched as the stores below him began to glow like a comforting Christmas village. "I think it has been, but I've never wanted to discuss it."

This time, Dr. Klein remained silent, forcing a response from Andrew.

"On a couple of occasions, I watched in horror as the faces of those I was talking with suddenly morphed into . . . grotesque images, something I'd rather just leave there for now. I did my best to remain calm, look away, and close my eyes, hoping that they would return to their normal state, and so far, they have, but the experience was incredibly frightening."

"And you are positive," Dr. Klein interjected, "that you were awake, engaged in a conversation, and not dreaming?"

"Yes," Andrew admitted. "That's the scary part. I know I've told you about the hooded monk in my dreams, but this was real—I was awake."

"To answer your original question," Dr. Klein explained, "I would have to say yes, depending on your emotional state." As before, he jotted a brief note in his book. "I need you to tell me if this continues, and we'll see about a medication adjustment. Can you do that? This is serious, Andrew, and I need you to please follow through."

Andrew nodded and returned to his chair, about to discuss an issue he would never have expected to disclose, particularly as a monk, to his psychiatrist. "You know how you spoke about some of the differences between Eastern and Western philosophies as they apply to religion?"

Dr. Klein nodded. "Yes, but I'm not encouraging you to make a choice or abandon your personal beliefs by any means. The books I've offered are meant to help you understand some of the dilemmas you are having by learning through other's experiences."

"I know," Andrew said. "What I'm about to tell you is something that has been in my head long before today's session. It's difficult to admit, but I have to say, as painful as my decision is, it's no longer possible for me to believe in a God. I can't pretend anymore." Andrew slouched in the chair, as if rejected and condemned. "That must sound pretty strange, coming from a monk."

Dr. Klein sat back, drew on his pipe, and exhaled, as the smoke blurred his image. After a noticeable silence, he got up and sat in the chair to Andrew's left. "I can see where this would be an obvious dilemma for you, Andrew, one which might be more appropriately explored with someone at the monastery, someone you feel comfortable with, perhaps Father Gerald."

Andrew left his chair and slowly paced near the window. "I trust Father Gerald, but telling him would be like a Jew confiding in a Nazi. I'm not sure I want anyone to know right now, especially with all that's been going on. And I never thought I'd hear the word 'atheist' come out of my mouth, yet that's how I would have to describe myself." He paused to look out the window. "Spirituality is still very important to me, along with my struggle to describe my ragged belief in a cosmic force of sorts. I think that it's still possible to be a good person and not believe in God, yet even then, I'm not sure I fit into the 'good person' category."

Dr. Klein gestured slightly with his hand. "I suppose 'good' is relative—don't beat yourself up over that." He returned to his desk and set his pipe in its holder. "I can offer some generalized feedback, if you like."

Andrew nodded. "Yes, I'd like that."

Dr. Klein carefully chose his words. "There are those who might suggest that your decision stems from hubris; however, knowing you as I think I do, I'm sure that's not the case."

Andrew questioned his proposal. "I'm not sure what hubris is," he admitted.

"It's a Greek word, now used to describe arrogance or pride, often associated with defiance toward the gods. It can also be associated with retribution or nemesis."

"Do you think it applies to me?" Andrew asked.

"As I mentioned, I think your journey alone, your decision to join the monastery, is clear evidence of your internal struggle to seek knowledge of the divine and the meaning of spirituality, a process clearly not related to hubris."

Andrew sighed. "Well, I guess I feel better about that because one thing is clear—the difficulty of reaching that conclusion was, and is, abhorrent to my psyche."

"How do you see yourself functioning at the monastery now that you've reached this decision?"

Andrew slowly rubbed his hands together as he allowed his thoughts to gather. "That's the big question. I can honestly say that I love my life as a monk, even though I can't accept all of the liturgical trappings—I must be the biggest hypocrite in the building." He looked at Dr. Klein. "I've read the bible cover to cover more than once, and while it can provide solace for believers, I just can't get past the possibility that it's one big fairytale. If I had children, I don't think I'd want them reading the Old Testament because of the violence and eroticism."

"First of all, I don't think you qualify as a hypocrite; you appear to be evolving. Does Brother Joshua know about your feelings?" Dr. Klein asked.

Andrew shook his head. "No. I haven't told anyone, and I don't want to jeopardize our relationship by having him think that I'm more screwed up than I realize." Andrew ended with a brief smile.

"You appear to be responding to something humorous," Dr. Klein ventured.

"Yeah, I just remembered something. I'll share it if you like."

"Sure, if you feel it's relevant," Dr. Klein said.

"Think about this," Andrew suggested. "Only atheists go to heaven . . ." He paused and looked at Dr. Klein, who appeared slightly perplexed.

"And how did you arrive at that?"

"Well," Andrew began, "it's meant to be obviously ironic, since an atheist wouldn't believe in heaven. But if this hypothetical heaven existed, along with a just God, I imagine the scenario of an atheist standing before the gates of heaven, being questioned by God. The atheist, assuming that he was a 'good' person, acknowledges to God that, yes, he is an atheist. He explains that he did his best to live a good life, perhaps following the Golden Rule and, for whatever reason, lack of faith, particularly since the church considers faith a gift or insightful reasoning, the atheist admits that after a long struggle with his faith, he became an atheist because he simply could not rationalize his religious beliefs. I can't help but think that this just God would welcome the honesty of the atheist and open the gates. He might even say, "You're an honest man; come in."

Dr. Klein smiled. "That's an interesting scenario. I'm sure you realize there are many monasteries, particularly within the Eastern tradition, where monks live fulfilled lives outside the parameters and beliefs of the Catholic tradition. Nevertheless, I can see you've given this extensive thought."

"I'm pretty good at that, I guess," Andrew joked, yet he quickly grew more serious. "One of the things I'm not good at is trying to reconcile my physical urges with my concept of 'good.'"

"How do you mean?" Dr. Klein asked.

"As I've mentioned before, we both know I've changed; I often feel like I've become Matthew—referring mostly to his uninhibited sexuality. There are times when I feel excessively driven to be with Joshua, to do things and say things that I would never have even considered with Matthew, yet Joshua accepts and totally encourages them. I can't deny that I enjoy pleasure, but there are times when I feel consumed by it, and it's that feeling of being out of control that frightens me."

Dr. Klein got up and sat on the front of his desk. "This is something that we need to discuss further. In fact, the books I've given you may help you better understand pleasure and the acceptable parameters of controlling one's desires and the positive results of tempered gratification. We can continue with this next week."

* * *

Chapter Thirty-Four

A Proper Prodigal Welcome

Father Gerald's request to meet him at five thirty for dinner in the refectory puzzled Andrew, until they walked through the arched doorway together. The entire community had gathered around the squared tables under a bright green banner that read "Welcome Home, Brother Andrew." They stood and applauded, as Andrew grew flushed from the totally unexpected gesture. He half expected a small, somber greeting in the abbot's office, but this was much more enjoyable. "I can't believe this," he whispered to Father Gerald, just before each of his brothers greeted him with handshakes, condolences, hugs, and genuine affection. The realization that he remained respected and valued by his monastic community became clear and nearly overwhelming when he was thankfully rescued by Brother Joshua, who hugged him, grabbed him by the arm, and led him to an empty seat next to his.

He smiled and whispered into Andrew's ear. "Don't let it go to your head—these guys will do anything for a party."

Andrew laughed hysterically, until the abbot tapped on his glass and asked for silence.

"I love surprise get-togethers—except when they're for me. So I can empathize, Brother Andrew, over how you may be feeling. Since I've been asked to keep this short, I'd like to express our sincere condolences to you for your mother's untimely death; may she rest in peace. And to thank God for bringing you safely back. May he be a source of strength to you in the days and weeks to follow."

The community raised their glasses amid a chorus of amen's.

Andrew could feel himself panic, knowing that he would be expected to speak. He leaned over toward Brother Joshua. "Shit," he whispered. "What am I supposed to say?"

Brother Joshua's smile consumed him. He winked at Andrew. "Anything at all," he whispered back, "as long as it's shallow."

The humor helped to alleviate Andrew's anxiety as he stood on shaky legs. Unexpectedly, he could feel Brother Joshua's well-hidden hand grab his calf muscle and gently massage it. 'I can't believe this is happening,' he thought. Nervously, he swallowed some ice water and began. "I am genuinely moved and so appreciative of all of you for this totally unexpected gesture. So let me, first of all, say thank you from the bottom of my heart."

Once again, the room erupted with applause.

"Secondly, I never anticipated that my mom would leave me this soon. Since some of you have already experienced such a loss, you can understand how important the community is to me now—it is my family."

And again, the applause was substantial yet tempered with solemnity.

"And for the record, Brother Joshua suggested that I say anything as long as it is shallow."

During the laughter that followed, Brother Joshua pretended to hide by ducking and pulling the tablecloth over his head.

"I am sure that he meant for me to be brief . . . and I will. Thank you. Let the party begin."

All the monks applauded heartily, raised their glasses, and drank, as the level of laughter and conversation resumed a festive spirit.

"You had to say that," Brother Joshua said with exasperation. "I could kill you."

Andrew laughed. "I didn't want to be the only embarrassed person here."

"Well, you succeeded." Brother Joshua leaned forward and grabbed a tall bottle filled with green liquid. He put several ice cubes in a short glass, filled it halfway with the liquor, and gave it to Andrew. "Try some of this—it's dynamite."

Andrew accepted the glass as Brother Joshua raised his near Andrew's and proposed an unexpectedly solemn toast. "I hope that the pain of your mom's death will lessen quickly and that your awareness of my love for you will, in some way, help to bring you comfort." He clanged his glass against Andrew's and drank.

Andrew felt as though he should simply squash societal mores by doing what he really wanted to do at that moment—kiss Brother Joshua in front of everyone—but he didn't. Somehow, the word "consequences" produced a conflicting reaction to his initial spontaneity. Instead, he swallowed a mouthful of the green liquor which descended slowly with a burning sensation all the way to his stomach and left him nearly breathless. "What are we drinking—jet fuel?"

"Close to it," Brother Joshua said. He turned the bottle so that Andrew could see the label. "It's Chartreuse, distilled by the faithful brothers in France."

"The Carthusian monks make this?"

"Yes, and supposedly, only three brothers know the recipe. It's a guarded secret, made with over one hundred herbs."

"How do you know all this?" Andrew asked.

Brother Joshua smiled. "Just before you arrived, I had a drink with Brother Mark. He told me. Besides, it's written on the back label."

Andrew's eyes immediately scanned the room in search of Brother Mark. He found him sitting diagonally across from them, looking directly at Andrew, and smiling.

Andrew smiled back and waved judiciously. "Do you say much to him?"

"To Brother Mark?" Brother Joshua asked.

Andrew nodded.

"You mean about us?"

"Yes," Andrew said. "Does he ever ask about our relationship?"

Brother Joshua appeared surprised. "I talk with him but never specifically about you and me. Why do you ask?"

"Oh . . . I don't know. He's a nice guy, but I'm not sure if I totally trust him . . . it's a long story."

Brother Joshua sipped his drink. "Well, someday, I hope you decide to tell me."

Andrew shrugged. "I guess it's really not that important."

Brother Joshua looked at him and smiled. "I really missed you when you were gone. I hated not having you here."

"I know," Andrew said. "I felt the same way. I probably shouldn't be telling you this, but I was having dinner with my aunt one night when I suddenly started thinking of you and couldn't get you out of my mind. My poor aunt must've noticed. I felt a little guilty because she obviously thought that the distraction had to do with my mother."

"That happens to me during meditation sometimes. The spiritual aspect can suddenly get all tangled up with this hot imagery of you and me, loving each other in the presence of an androgynous-looking angel who couldn't care less."

Andrew swallowed more of his drink which, by now, had graduated from tolerable to tasty. "This is weird because Dr. Klein and I had a conversation similar to this. In fact, he gave me two books and said I could show them to you."

"What kind of books?" Br. Joshua appeared quite interested.

"You have to see them—I'll show you tonight."

Andrew had forgotten about the food until he saw Brother Kevin place a steaming pan in the warmer, go back into the kitchen, and return with two more. "Any idea of what we're having?"

"Not a clue," Brother Joshua said. "But if Brother Kevin is cooking, I'm sure it will be good."

"He's been doing a lot of the cooking lately, hasn't he?"

Brother Joshua nodded. "I think he wants your job."

"That's okay with me, at least for the summer. I don't mind irrigating or haying or even collecting eggs, but I'm not crazy about freezing my butt off outside in the middle of winter, unless I'm on skis."

"I don't blame you. Besides, you're a better than cook he is."

Andrew laughed. "Yeah, but he's cute."

Surprised, Brother Joshua feigned frustration by raising his hands in the air. "Oh, great! You are barely back here for one day, and you are already planning on dumping me."

"Relax. I'm simply commenting on his looks. You are the only one I care about because you are so devilishly handsome and so . . . cerebral." Andrew slid his hand under the tablecloth and squeezed the inside of Brother Joshua's thigh. "I think I want you right now."

Brother Joshua jokingly pulled away. "You are a maniac, but I think that's what attracts me to you and makes me love you so much." He finished his drink with a bit of a flourish. "Maybe I'm as crazy as you are."

"I doubt it," Andrew said quietly.

Brother Joshua immediately turned to face him. "Hey . . . I'm really sorry. I didn't mean it like that."

In spite of the mild pain, Andrew smiled. "I know you didn't. I guess it's just some of my hypersensitivity showing through. Don't worry about it."

"Okay. Then let's get something to eat." Brother Joshua grabbed him by the arm and gently pulled him toward him.

Andrew stood, a slight smirk on his face, and looked at him comically. "Shall we dance?" He held out his arms in the traditional waltz pose.

Brother Joshua scratched his head, reached into his pocket, and pulled out a small, imaginary item. "Sorry, I don't believe I have you penciled in on my dance card."

* * *

By evening, an early winter storm howled its way through the alpine valley with gusty winds and copious amounts of powdery snow that drifted considerably in some areas or, on the higher open mesas, blew completely away, exposing the stubble of the summer season. The familiar scenario caused an eerie creaking inside the monastery, particularly in the church, where the tall structure moaned in irregular decibels, as if possessed by an unholy presence.

Meditating in the dark in such a harsh environment, Andrew sensed the goose bumps on his arms and the gnawing need for physical warmth, comfort, and, ultimately, gratification. Although not certain, he thought that Brother Joshua had already returned to his cell; in fact, as he sat in the dark, he grew more and more positive that he was probably anticipating a knock on his door to privately commemorate Andrew's return to the monastery. He also knew he would be wearing nothing more than a plaid flannel robe.

Fueled by increased craving, Andrew's meditation ceased to be spiritually productive. Instead, his sacred quest would be realized in the physical union, celebration, and love of another man—that (as he was often reminded) which God had created.

And he was right. Brother Joshua timidly opened the door to his cell wearing only the robe which Andrew described. He entered the darkened room without speaking, quietly closed and locked the door, and, with the adroitness of a magician, slipped the robe off Brother Joshua and let it fall silently to the floor. Andrew held him at arm's length to study the glorious beauty of the man before him.

Somewhat shyly, Brother Joshua positioned his arms over his exposed genitals, much as a new bride might do on the first night of her honeymoon.

Andrew carefully reached down to separate Brother Joshua's arms. He positioned them firmly against his thighs, exposing once again Brother Joshua's body. "You are so beautiful—just as you are," he said and then pulled Brother Joshua into his embrace. "I could stare at you like this forever."

Since the cells were seldom overheated, Brother Joshua welcomed the warmth of Andrew's body. He kissed his neck and whispered into his ear. "It's so good to have you back. It seems like you been away for a year."

"Hardly," Andrew said, as he rubbed his nose against Brother Joshua's. "But I'd be happy to make up all the time I've missed."

"I doubt that you'll hear me complain." Brother Joshua kissed him hard, as if to confirm his intentions. He began to remove the heavy leather belt, scapular, and robe by pulling the latter over Andrew's head, exposing his T-shirt and flannel pajama bottoms. "Nice outfit," Brother Joshua said jokingly. "Is this the standard monastery uniform?"

Andrew smiled. "In the winter—guess what I wear in the summer?"

"Let me guess . . . absolutely zilch?"

"Haven't you ever done it? It feels incredibly erotic to have nothing on—just a loose robe teasing your overheated skin to the point of arousal."

"That must be the reason why monks wear scapulars."

"You know, I really never thought about it, but I'll bet it's true." He pulled Brother Joshua toward him and nuzzled his neck and ear, gently biting it.

"Let's get these off." With Andrew's help, Brother Joshua pulled off his T-shirt, threw it on the desk, and then slipped Andrew's pajamas down to his ankles so that Andrew could easily step out of them. The familiar sensation of skin against skin caused Brother Joshua to catch his breath, as Andrew massaged his back, continued lower to the lumbar curve, and onto his buttocks with deep, powerful kneading. And it was exactly where Brother Joshua wanted him to be. He kissed Andrew with increased excitement, exploring his mouth with his tongue, just as Andrew was boldly yet gently reacquainting himself with the warm, barely moist area which would eventually join the two as one. He moved Andrew toward his bed, sat down, and pulled Andrew on top of him. His weight alone, pressing down on him with welcomed pressure, further excited Brother Joshua, who anticipated what would follow. Unable to wait much longer, he rolled onto his side and then completely onto his stomach, sending a familiar signal to Andrew. He reached under his pillow and handed him a tube of lubricant.

Andrew mounted him from behind with slow but constant pressure. Brother Joshua moaned quietly and arched his back in painful pleasure as Andrew grabbed him firmly just above his buttocks.

Brother Joshua moved his head from side to side against his pillow, at times, licking his own arms and sucking his fingers. He raised his head and looked back at Andrew with a drugged affect.

Andrew knew exactly what he wanted. With a slight rocking motion, Andrew pushed and pulled himself in and out of the sensitive muscle, which he could feel contract and expand repeatedly.

"You have no idea how good this feels," Brother Joshua said softly. "I could probably come."

Andrew stopped immediately and then thrust himself deep inside. Rather than allow himself to ejaculate, he carefully pulled out and lay alongside of him. He kissed Brother Joshua's neck and ears and eagerly sought his mouth.

"Why did you stop?" Brother Joshua looked confused.

Andrew stared at his clear, beautiful eyes. "It's about time that I give myself to the one I care about," he said quietly. "I want to experience the true yin and yang within me—to realize whatever the other side of my nature is, or maybe I'm just fucking horny."

Brother Joshua smiled and rolled on his side to face him. "This sounds like a real breakthrough of sorts. I am . . . proud that it's with me." He kissed Andrew with increased anticipation, fully aware that this signaled a significant change in Andrew's sexual behavior.

Andrew rolled onto his back and pulled Brother Joshua on top of him. "Is this position okay with you?" Andrew asked, but he didn't wait for a response. "I want to watch you when you come," he added immediately.

Kneeling before him, Brother Joshua remained silent and focused as he gently lifted Andrew's legs and placed one over each shoulder. He carefully inserted himself into Andrew's slippery warmth, experiencing for the first time the shared reciprocity of Andrew's love. As he thrust himself deeper and deeper, Brother Joshua could feel Andrew's resistance and hear him breathe sharply when the initial pain began.

After a slight pause, Brother Joshua resumed his penetration with respectful desire. If Andrew cried out, he would immediately stop until it was clear that it was acceptable to continue. With his body firmly against Andrew's buttocks and his erection buried as deep as possible, Brother Joshua paused to savor the enveloping warmth and wetness and to appreciate the intense physical connection, which, until now, he could only experience by being the receptacle of Andrew's dominant hunger. "It's funny. I never thought you would let me do this," he whispered. "You feel so damn good."

"And you feel incredible," Andrew said. He pulled Brother Joshua toward him so that his erection moved even deeper within him. Every nerve ending tingled, as if an electrical charge suddenly detonated throughout his body from his fingers to his toes. He glanced at Brother Joshua. "You are definitely home—go for it."

Brother Joshua leaned down and kissed him. "You're not going to stop me, are you?"

"No . . . just shut up and do it."

That was all Brother Joshua needed to hear. Within minutes, he had worked himself into a near frenzy, mercilessly ramming Andrew, who could barely refrain from crying out.

As if mesmerized, Andrew watched as Brother Joshua's entire body shuddered, paused, and began to shudder for the final time, as the last spasm of orgasm erupted deep inside of him.

Brother Joshua lowered himself on top of Andrew, while carefully letting Andrew's legs slide down from the shoulders to a more relaxed position. He then kissed him with sincere affection. "Thank you for letting me do that," he said. "I know it was a big step for you."

Andrew looked into his extraordinary eyes. "I guess it just got to the point where I really needed it, and I wanted it to be you. So I should be the one saying thank you."

Brother Joshua simply held him close, as the storm continued to rage across the valley, howling outside the monastery with powerful winds and bitterly cold temperatures. They lay together in the darkness, listening to the occasional creeks and moans of the dormitory held hostage by the blizzard. They were also aware of each other's breathing, the unexpected sigh or quick inhalations.

Considerate of Andrew's needs, Brother Joshua slid his hand over his genitals, rubbing gently until Andrew's erection materialized. "You have such a beautiful penis," he whispered.

Andrew smiled. "How can you tell?"

Brother Joshua squeezed him. "If you are implying that I've seen a lot of them—I haven't. I only needed to look at it, touch it, and . . . taste it."

Andrew kissed him. "I love the way you say things." He pulled Brother Joshua close and kissed him hard.

Knowing what he needed, Brother Joshua slowly worked his way down to Andrew's erection, mouthing it gently almost to the point of orgasm. Lying on his back, he pulled Andrew on top of him, until Andrew was kneeling over his face.

Andrew quickly realized Brother Joshua's intent, as he developed a more aggressive rhythm, forcing himself against Brother Joshua's mouth and firm tongue. Unable to hold back, Andrew sat, pressed himself against his face, and then stiffened, discharging ejaculate against the wall and Brother Joshua's pillow. He then threw one leg over Brother Joshua's body and collapsed alongside of him.

After a well-deserved pause, Brother Joshua lovingly reached over and kissed him. "Welcome home," he whispered.

* * *

Chapter Thirty-Five

The Third Man

It seemed as if the storm would never end. The November light cast a platinum aura over the monastery as significant amounts of snow quickly blew away and then collected in protected, windless drifts.

Andrew would meditate endlessly, remotely cognizant of some predetermined and undefined causality, which he felt would end his existence. Perhaps his thinking was influenced by the return of his nocturnal nemesis, the ungodly red-eyed creature who appeared hooded and realistic in the darkness of his dreams—a monster who left him either speechless with fear or caused him to barely speak, angrily, with a deep, guttural voice.

It was during one of those dreams that Brother Joshua was forced to put a pillow over Andrew's face to silence the eerie sounds spewing from his mouth.

"It's okay, it's okay," Brother Joshua said softly, as Andrew attempted to fight off his alleged attacker and ended up falling, naked, onto the floor. "It's me—Joshua. Take some deep breaths and try to calm down."

Once he was reoriented, Andrew climbed back under the warm covers and held Brother Joshua tight.

"Have you been taking your medication?"

Andrew kissed him on the forehead before chastising him. "You're beginning to sound like my psychiatrist."

"Maybe, but I'm concerned about you."

"I know." Andrew was aware that he was less than truthful, but he felt that he had no choice. He knew that one of the side effects he could expect would impact his sexuality, both his sexual drive and his ability to achieve and maintain an erection. Given his desirable and supportive relationship with Brother Joshua, Andrew absolutely refused to face such a dilemma. And thinking less than clearly, he would refuse to consider the potentially fatal outcome of stopping his medication.

Consequently, November proved to be a montage of sensual black and white stills, replete with incense, crucifixes, snow, and intermingled bodies blurred in the darkness and heavily scented with the smell of sex. The intensely physical relationship transcended the act itself, particularly for Andrew, as he drifted in and out of increased command delusions, fueled by the red-eyed demon, and cathartic, exhausting orgasms.

Brother Joshua was aware of the more obvious changes, yet moved by his own passion, he was reluctant to step back or offer objective comments. He simply assumed the extraordinary to be the results of evolution—sex had become addicting—and they both needed more.

When Andrew received a note from Brother Joshua to meet him at approximately 8:30 p.m. in the small retreat house attached to the barn, he was not surprised. The incessant snow swirled around him, as he walked in the dark on the familiar monastery road. He looked for Brother Joshua's footprints but saw none, as they were rapidly erased by the strong wind. When he reached the door of the retreat house, Andrew noticed only a faint light, perhaps a candle, glowing from within. He tapped gently on the door and waited, until he could hear the latch unlock.

Smiling, Brother Joshua opened the door, and without a word, he helped pulled him inside and immediately kissed him.

Andrew recognized the fire and urgency of his embrace. "What's that all about?" he said jokingly.

Brother Joshua continued to smile. "I have a surprise," he said somewhat nervously. "I hope you won't be upset."

"Why should I be upset? What is it?"

Brother Joshua stared at him and then slowly turned his head to the right, encouraging Andrew to follow his gaze.

Andrew looked toward the bedroom and suddenly was filled with fear and déjà vu. In the shadows, he could barely see a dark figure sitting on the edge of the bed. "Who the hell is that?"

Brother Joshua grabbed his arm. "Relax. It's okay," he said. He then called to the shadowy figure. "Come on out."

Not very tall, the person got up and walked slowly toward them into the light.

"Brother Kevin?" Andrew whispered.

His tentative approach and quiet demeanor signaled his embarrassment. "If this is a problem, I'll leave." A slight stutter clotted his voice.

Andrew stood motionless. He looked at Brother Joshua and then back at Brother Kevin. "No—not at all. I guess I just didn't expect it."

"That's what a surprise is," Brother Joshua quipped. He grabbed Andrew from behind and held him tight. He immediately felt Andrew tense. "It's all right. He knows."

Andrew's anxiety faded into mild excitement as his awareness grew, yet he would rather have pulled Brother Joshua aside for a private conversation regarding the details of Brother Kevin's knowledge. Right now, that was impossible; nevertheless, he soon found out that this was unnecessary. Brother Kevin unabashedly provided the answers.

"I hope you don't mind, but I remember when you were with Brother Matthew. I assumed that your relationship with Brother Joshua was probably the same." He stepped closer to Andrew. "Anyway, I've always remembered how you helped me the day I collapsed in the eggery, and since then, I've often thought about you—not exactly with a pure heart."

"And just this week, I got the courage to confront Brother Joshua about the possibility of spending time with the both of you on whatever level you approved of. He suggested this surprise get-together . . . like I said, I won't be offended if you want me to leave."

Once again, Andrew looked at Brother Joshua for some sign of acceptance. "If it's okay with Brother Joshua, it's okay with me."

"If I thought this would be a problem, I wouldn't have asked him down here," Brother Joshua said softly.

Andrew shrugged. "Sounds fine to me. How about some coffee?"

Brother Kevin moved even closer. He took off his sweater and removed his shirt, exposing a well-defined upper body and a chest lightly covered with reddish blond hair. "If it's okay with you, I'd rather have some later."

Andrew could feel his arousal increase.

Brother Joshua pulled Andrew's mouth toward his. Before kissing him, he looked into his eyes. "Remember—I love you." During their embrace, they felt Brother Kevin's arms around the both of them.

Andrew immediately put his arm around him, pulled him into the circle, and then kissed him gently at first. He then urged him toward Brother Joshua, who kissed him deeply. While they were kissing, Andrew carefully unzipped Brother Kevin's jeans and, with one quick move, slid both his jeans and underwear down to the floor, hampered momentarily by Brother Kevin's unusually thick and somewhat stubby erection which caught in the opening of his boxer shorts. Excited and definitely uninhibited, Andrew shoved his face against his buttocks and drove his tongue deep within. He could hear Brother Kevin moan softly, while he remained absorbed with Brother Joshua. He then removed Brother Kevin's sneakers and socks, slipped his feet out of his jeans, and tossed the jeans on a chair.

Brother Kevin stood naked between them, eager to be loved and satisfied by both, particularly by Andrew, whom he had always wanted.

Yet this chance assignation was far from one-sided. Andrew knew that he was always attracted to the handsome red-haired young man who, by the very nature of his short stature and infectious smile, begged to be loved. Wherever love ended and lust began became irrelevant, as Andrew worked his way down to Brother Kevin's erection. He barely managed to fit the head of it into his mouth when he felt jets of warm semen explode against his palate.

While still kissing Brother Joshua, Brother Kevin placed his hand on the back of Andrew's neck and squeezed it. He then urged him to stand up and join them, reaching immediately for Andrew's salty mouth with his and recognizing the singular taste of his own semen. He looked intently at Andrew. "Thank you," he whispered. He held Andrew tight as Brother Joshua's saliva mixed with the now slightly bitter taste of Andrew's mouth.

"Why is it I'm the only one naked?" Brother Kevin asked with a grin.

"Maybe it's because you're so desirable," Andrew said. He spontaneously picked up Brother Kevin, one arm under his legs, the other under his back, and carried him toward the bedroom.

Brother Kevin looped his arm around Andrew's neck, while Brother Joshua quickly followed.

Andrew carefully lowered Brother Kevin to the bed, lost his balance, and fell on top of him.

Laughing, Brother Joshua kissed him and began to remove his clothes. He was aware of Brother Kevin's strong feelings for Andrew, following their conversation earlier that week; however, as yet, jealousy was not a factor in the relationship. Instead, he wanted Andrew to experience different facets of the relationship, as long as he felt secure, knowing how much Andrew loved him and how much he loved Andrew. And he too was not without sexual feelings toward Brother Kevin. 'Who,' he thought, 'would not be excited about loving this handsome, well-built, and needy celibate.'

Before he knew it, Brother Joshua was suddenly surrounded by two very beautiful, very naked men, who proceeded to slowly undress him while lightly kissing newly exposed skin. By the time they reached his shorts, Brother Joshua's erection had already snaked through the fly, waiting for attention.

Brother Kevin put his mouth over the head of it while he pushed the shorts down with his chin and his teeth. He looked up at Brother Joshua and waxed poetic. "If mine is short and fat, yours is long and lean, and Brother Andrew's is somewhere in between. See . . . it had to be . . . something for everyone." He quickly pulled the shorts down to Brother Joshua's feet and threw them on a chair.

In near silence, the three stood naked, embracing each other with kisses, body contact, and physical exploration.

Andrew was somewhat surprised to feel Brother Kevin's penis erect so quickly. He knew he would easily be capable of more than one orgasm.

Brother Kevin fell to his knees, urged Andrew and Brother Joshua closer together, and immediately became a whirlwind, insatiable in his desires, while Brother Joshua and Andrew kissed passionately, experiencing for the first time the pleasure of a third person.

Brother Joshua looked down and smiled. "You are some kind of wild man," he said softly.

Brother Kevin paused briefly. "I guess that's what happens from living here too long." He glanced back up at Brother Joshua. "You ain't seen nothin' yet."

Close to orgasm, both Andrew and Brother Joshua had to force Brother Kevin off them. He seemed to enjoy the struggle, remained defiant, and appeared to grow even more excited when Andrew head-locked him, picked him up, and threw him, like a sack of potatoes, on the bed. Andrew looked at Brother Joshua. "You're right . . . he's a wild man."

"I want you to fuck me," Brother Kevin declared boldly, looking at the both of them.

Andrew could feel his erection flex with excitement. "We intend to," he said. "Any preference?"

Brother Kevin stared at him momentarily before responding. "Yes . . . both of you—at the same time."

Andrew felt as though his chest were ready to burst; he could feel his heart racing. Brother Joshua felt the same but said nothing. He simply fell on top of Brother Kevin and began to smother him with love. Andrew joined him immediately, seeking the warmth of Brother Kevin's buttocks.

Andrew asked him to roll onto his side, with his back toward him, and then eased himself slowly past the tight muscle into the moist warmth of the area deep inside. He could hear Brother Kevin cry out quietly and then moan with pleasure as his body adapted to the penetration.

"All set," Andrew whispered to Brother Joshua who, unknowingly, was well-equipped for just such an endeavor.

Facing Brother Kevin, Brother Joshua moved a bit lower. He pulled Brother Kevin's upper leg over his chest and held it. He moved the other leg beneath him until he was well positioned for entry.

Once again, Andrew spit on his hand and rubbed it over the head of Brother Joshua's erection.

It was Brother Kevin who guided this long, thin weapon to its destination; however, not without a struggle. In considerable pain, Brother Kevin managed to slip the head past the stretched muscle into the accommodating area beyond.

Brother Joshua remained motionless for a while to allow Brother Kevin a chance to recover, yet even then, it was impossible to describe the pleasure he felt and the anticipation of what was to follow.

Andrew could feel Brother Joshua's firm erection glide against his, in contrast to the velvety heat of Brother Kevin's body. He motioned to Brother Joshua. "Do opposite directions."

When Brother Joshua was thrusting up, Andrew would pull back and vice versa. This greatly enhanced the amount of friction and pleasure for everyone, especially Brother Kevin, who began to shake his head and upper body vigorously until he stiffened, arched, and ejaculated on Brother Joshua's chest.

Watching the intensity of such an orgasm, Brother Joshua knew that he could hold off no longer. He raised his head to look at Andrew. "Got to do it now," he half whispered. He threw back his head and came into the dark warmth.

Andrew could feel everything through his penis—the force of the discharge, the increased temperature difference of the semen and, most obviously, the sensual viscosity of the slippery fluid. The thought of his penis being lubricated with Brother Joshua's semen was more than enough imagery to produce an orgasm. He rammed Brother Kevin repeatedly, until he quickly ejaculated and added even more fluid to the incredibly sensitive chamber.

They rested in silence on the rumpled sheets, exhausted by their efforts, while winter continued to remind them of its presence.

Brother Joshua slowly eased himself out, moved closer to Brother Kevin, held him tight, and kissed him. "You okay?" he whispered.

Brother Kevin nodded and smiled. "It was incredible."

Reluctantly, Andrew also separated and snuggled Brother Kevin from behind. "I think you are an angel," he whispered, as he nibbled on Brother Kevin's ear.

Brother Kevin turned his head and kissed him.

"I never even knew that was possible," Brother Joshua said. He looked at Brother Kevin. "I shouldn't ask but have you . . . done this before?"

Andrew cringed slightly over the question.

"No," Brother Kevin replied. The color rose in his cheeks. "But I saw it once on a video."

"Well, you've got a good memory," Andrew said, hoping to relax him. "Besides, something different is good—no, terrific!" He squeezed Brother Kevin.

The sound of a passing car on the main road caused Andrew to look at his watch. "It's nearly nine thirty. Everyone at the monastery should be sleeping."

"Including us," Brother Joshua added.

"Do we need to go?" Brother Kevin asked.

Andrew looked pensively at Brother Joshua. "Two o'clock in the morning comes early," he said. "Maybe next time we should start earlier."

He looked at Brother Kevin. "Will there be a next time?"

Brother Kevin smiled. "What do you think?"

"I think we should get cleaned up and brave our way back to the imperial monastery." Andrew got up, tossed a pillow at Brother Joshua, and urinated in the dark bathroom, with the door open.

* * *

Chapter Thirty-Six

Presenting with Symptoms

Most everyone in the valley was beginning to wonder if they would ever again see the sun. Snow continued to fall heavier, at times, requiring the highway crews to work constantly to stay ahead of the storm.

Andrew spent a grey afternoon in the eggery, collecting eggs in the dust-filled, noxious environment. He was pleased when Brother Joshua appeared to help him finish the less than savory task.

"I've come to rescue you from the girls," Brother Joshua said loudly.

The hens immediately broke into a raucous chorus of cackling.

Once they settled down, Andrew spoke softly. "Yes, my knight in shining armor has arrived. How did this happen?"

Brother Joshua grimaced in an attempt to show Andrew his teeth. "The dentist was quicker than I thought; besides, Father Luke doesn't want you down here alone." He gently pulled down Andrew's dust mask and briefly kissed his lips.

"Thanks. Let's finish and get out of this shit house," Andrew said.

When they were done, they hung up their aprons and prepared to wash.

"I'll use the sink out here," Andrew said.

Brother Joshua nodded. He knew that Andrew still had difficulty using the bathroom where he found Brother John hanging from a pipe above the sink. In fact, he could feel the hair on his arms raise when he visualized the grisly scene. He quickly zipped, flushed, and washed his hands before hastily exiting the room. He expected to see Andrew; however, the eggery appeared empty and silent. Brother Joshua sensed a peculiar feeling and, instinctively, began to walk slowly toward the door.

Suddenly, a voice could be heard. "Brother John?"

Brother Joshua felt as if his body were electrified. "Andrew?"

"It's you, isn't it, John?" Andrew asked. Pale and sweaty, he walked out from behind the canvas of the candling booth.

"Oh, fuck!" Brother Joshua whispered. He continued to back toward the door, opened it, and stood in the entrance, inhaling the fresh air. "This isn't funny, Andrew," he said forcefully.

"John?" the voice repeated.

Brother Joshua stepped back slightly. "It's not Brother John. It's me—Joshua."

Andrew continued to walk toward him. "Why . . . why did you do it?"

Brother Joshua could smell his own sweat. "Stop it! Just stop it, Andrew! I'm Joshua! I'm Joshua!" he screamed, until he slowly sunk to his knees, crying. Afraid to open his eyes, he could feel Andrew's arms wrap around him.

Andrew held him tight, put his head on Brother Joshua's shoulder, and sobbed loudly, until nothing was left inside.

Only then did Brother Joshua attempt to look at him. "It's okay," he whispered.

Andrew looked at him with inflamed eyes. "What's happening to me?" he asked timidly, fearing to hear that which he already knew.

Brother Joshua's mind raced in anticipation of a therapeutic response. "It must be this place," he said. It was the most benign response he could think of. "Maybe we should just leave."

He stood slowly, encouraging Andrew to stand with him. "Put your arm around my shoulder. I think you'll feel better once we get outside." Standing together in the cold and blowing snow, they evoked a distorted image of Boys Town.

Brother Joshua locked the door to the eggery and hid the key in its customary place. He turned and looked at Andrew. "Before we take another step, tell me who I am."

Andrew sighed, embarrassed by the question "I don't know—Prince of Wales?" He then laughed, ran a short distance down the road, and jumped into a snow bank. Sprawled on his back, he called out to Brother Joshua. "Perhaps I'm Margaret Thatcher," he said.

"Or a court jester," Brother Joshua shouted.

"That too," Andrew said softly.

When he reached the snow bank, Brother Joshua offered his hand to Andrew in an attempt to get him to stand.

Andrew grabbed it firmly and intentionally pulled him down on top of him.

"It's cold!" Brother Joshua said with a smile.

"Then let me warm you up." Andrew wrapped his arms around him, squeezing him hard.

"What if somebody comes?" Brother Joshua said. He glanced up the road toward the monastery.

Andrew laughed. "Whoever comes first get a prize—especially when we are frozen in the snowbank."

"You have a one track mind—and I love it." Brother Joshua kissed him gently on the forehead. "Maybe we should head back."

Andrew squeezed him even harder. "Not until you give me a serious kiss." Cautious yet aware that Andrew would not be dissuaded, Brother Joshua willingly conceded. And despite the cold, kissing Andrew almost immediately triggered his arousal.

* * *

It happened at the Sunday evening supper. Andrew remained extraordinarily quiet until the tubs of Häagen-Dazs ice cream were rolled into the refectory by Brother Mark. A large bowl of whipped cream, jars of chocolate syrup, mint sauce, chopped nuts, maraschino cherries, and other assorted toppings accompanied the ice cream on a separate cart.

Such an array drew jubilation from the salivating monks, who quickly encircled the dessert carts like Indians hell-bent on annihilating the white man—all except Andrew.

"I know you're not having any," Brother Joshua said.

Andrew simply nodded.

"Do you mind if . . ."

"Nope. It's been going on long before you got here." Andrew's mood was sullen.

Once the monks were seated and quietly enjoying their ice cream, Andrew's unexpected excoriation began, softly at first and then elevating to a rather heated crescendo, until he finally stormed out of the refectory, slamming the door behind him. "Don't you all feel even a little bit disingenuous, eating such an expensive, unnecessary ice cream? What the hell is wrong with the brand at the supermarket, and who the hell is responsible for this?" He stood and looked directly at the abbot. "With apologies, Father Luke, I know you didn't institute this, but it is clearly within your jurisdiction—and, I would think, your conscience—to put an end to it." Andrew got up and walked toward the exit. Just before he slammed the door, he shouted a final comment. "I'm going now. You can start sucking down the Perrier water!"

A glaring hush permeated the refectory.

Red-faced, Brother Joshua stood and looked at the abbot. "If it's okay, I'd like to excuse myself."

Father Luke leaned over and whispered briefly to Father Gerald. "Do you want to talk with him instead?"

Father Gerald shook his head. "No. I'll talk with him when he cools down. Let Brother Joshua go."

Father Luke motioned to Brother Joshua. "You may leave," he said softly.

After quietly closing the refectory door, Brother Joshua ran through the cloister, until he reached Andrew's cell. He knocked but heard nothing. He then tried the doorknob and, to his surprise, found the door unlocked.

"Andrew?" he whispered.

Only silence prevailed.

He cautiously stepped inside and turned on the light; however, Andrew was not in the room. He then looked inside the closet for Andrew's parka, but that too was missing. "He must be outside," he said to himself.

Joshua quickly ran to his cell, opened the door in the dark, and searched frantically for his jacket.

"You looking for this?" Andrew asked. He stood naked next to the desk, holding out Brother Joshua's jacket.

"Jesus Christ!" Brother Joshua exclaimed. "I feel like I'm having a heart attack."

"Then take a deep breath and sit down," Andrew admonished.

Brother Joshua quickly shut the door and locked it. He was about to retrieve his jacket and, only then, realized that Andrew was naked. "You've got to put some clothes on—Father Gerald or somebody else might be here any minute."

Andrew threw the jacket on the desk chair. He walked toward Brother Joshua, pulled him into his embrace, and kissed him aggressively.

Excited yet overcome with fear, Brother Joshua pulled away. "Listen to me," he said. "You've got to put your clothes on before they show up. If you are not in your room, they are definitely going to look here."

"So you really want me to leave?" Andrew challenged.

"Don't play games, Andrew. You know that I would love to have you stay but not now."

"Fine," Andrew said unexpectedly. He pulled on his pants and sneakers and, shirtless, was halfway through the door.

"You forgot your shirt," Brother Joshua whispered.

"No, I didn't." This time, he quietly closed the door behind him.

Andrew returned to his cell in anticipation of a visit from a member of the monastic hagiocracy; however, there was none. With every footstep that passed his door, he expected an authoritative knock, and when none materialized, he rested wide-awake in the dark, wishing that he were not alone. He squeezed the swelling in his jeans and considered masturbating when he suddenly jumped up and carefully peeked out the door. The corridor appeared vacant. "What the hell," he said quietly and then proceeded down the hall.

He knocked softly on the door, which opened within seconds. "Surprise," Andrew whispered. He stepped inside and locked the door.

"I've been waiting for you to show up," Brother Kevin said with a grin.

Andrew kissed him hard and began to remove Brother Kevin's shirt. "I've been waiting for you to come," he mimicked.

It was not long before both were naked, clothes strewn haphazardly about the room which, by now, was electric with sexual energy.

With Kevin securely beneath him, Andrew continued his repetitive thrusting, rolled him onto his back, lifted his legs, and reentered.

Brother Kevin moaned with pleasure over the greater depth of penetration which the new position afforded. "You feel so fucking good," he said. The ecstasy proved overwhelming. He grabbed his erection and stroked it savagely, until he shot gobs of thick semen onto his face and hair.

Seeing him come, Andrew also reached an explosive orgasm deep within him.

Totally spent, he collapsed on top of him, gently kissed his lips and face, and nibbled on his ear.

They lay together, absorbing the silence and recuperating, listening to each other's breathing, and inhaling the sexual scent of their heated bodies.

"You don't mind me being here?" Andrew asked quietly.

"Of course not," Brother Kevin said. "Do you have any idea how many times I've wanted you here with me?"

"Even without Josh?" Andrew asked.

"It doesn't matter. It's always been you that I wanted. I never expected to have you here—alone." He rolled up on one side and played with Andrew's chest. "I've rubbed myself raw thinking about you."

"Andrew smiled. "You're such a little devil, but I love when you talk like that." He kissed Brother Kevin's forehead. "Do you think I'm crazy?" he asked unexpectedly.

Brother Kevin look surprised. "Why, because of what happened in the refectory?"

"That and the fact that I'm here with you without Josh."

"Personally, I'm glad you're here with me. It doesn't matter if Joshua's not here."

"So I'm not a real sleaze?" Andrew questioned.

"No, because I know you really love Josh, and I can't compete with that," Brother Kevin admitted.

Andrew shrugged. "I don't know."

"And about the refectory, I don't think it was crazy to say what you did. I think it took a lot of courage to tell the truth. I'm just not sure how well it will be received."

"Yeah, me either. I'm expecting the abbot to call me into a meeting tomorrow."

"What will you say?" Brother Kevin asked with concern.

Andrew rolled onto his back and put his hands in back of his head. "Oh, I guess I'll apologize first and then reinforce my message—less aggressively this time."

Bro. Kevin frowned. "Has anyone ever been thrown out of here?"

"Yes, why? Do you think they will throw me out?"

"I hope not, unless I can go with you," Brother Kevin said with a smile.

"You never know—but I doubt it. Somebody said they need the help."

"Vocations must be scarce," Brother Kevin added.

"Well, you've been here for a while, and no one has entered after you," Andrew explained.

"Good point," Brother Kevin said.

* * *

After mass the following morning, Father Gerald motioned to Andrew, who had been anticipating the meeting. He approached with humble respect.

"You probably know that the abbot wants to speak with you," Father Gerald said softly.

Andrew nodded. "How does it look?"

"I expect he will ask you not repeat what happened in the refectory last night."

"You mean he's not going to throw me out?" Andrew asked.

Father Gerald smiled. "I hardly think so—are you trying to be thrown out?"

"No, not at all, it's just that . . . well, you know how I feel about the ice cream and Perrier water. Can't something be done about it?"

"Let Father Luke answer that," Father Gerald replied. "You may be pleasantly surprised. Now, you had better hurry. He's waiting for you."

Andrew felt relieved. "Thanks, Father Gerald."

Andrew moved rapidly through the cloister, his robes billowing behind him. The arched windows, partially obstructed by the wind-driven snow, dulled the morning light.

Andrew stood in front of the abbot's door, took a deep breath, exhaled, and knocked assertively. He was about to knock again when the door suddenly opened. Father Luke, still clothed in his habit, extended his hand to Andrew. "Come in, Andrew. Please have a seat."

"Thank you," Andrew replied. He found a familiar chair in front and to the left of the abbot's desk.

Father Luke sat down and immediately lit his pipe. Andrew watched the fragrant smoke curl around his head in the still air.

"This meeting isn't meant to be upsetting," Father Luke said bluntly, hoping to defuse Andrew's anxiety. "I hope we can talk about Sunday's supper and amicably resolve any issues that you would like to discuss, particularly those I know have been troubling you—the Häagen-Dazs and Perrier."

Although somewhat comforted by the introduction, Andrew sensed his own latent anxiety begin to rumble. He knew that an apology was in order. "I realize what I said was expressed hastily and rudely. I'm sorry that I behaved badly and I apologize, Father Luke."

In silence, with a wave of his hand and a slight nod, Father Luke accepted Andrew's apology. He paused before continuing. "I've given your concerns some serious thought and shared my thoughts with Father Gerald. He feels the same as I—that we should no longer purchase the products that trouble you, the Perrier and the Häagen-Dazs; however, we will need to consume what remains before we order a different product. But beyond that, thanks to Father Gerald, I now have a clear understanding of exactly what you were trying to tell me earlier. I had no idea that a certain 'status' was attached to each product, not to mention the exorbitant cost. I guess I need to spend more time with the treasurer."

Even though a positive outcome was hinted at earlier by Father Gerald, Andrew was genuinely surprised. "Besides 'thank you,' I don't know what to say," he stammered. "I think the more meaningful part is your understanding about the significance of the two products. I really appreciate it."

Father Luke smiled while exhaling a cloud of fragrant smoke. "Then, that's settled," he said. "Is there anything else you would like to discuss?"

"Not that I can think of," Andrew said.

"If something does come up, please feel free to talk with me, so we can avoid further outbursts at supper."

Andrew stood and shook Father Luke's hand. "I'm sure that won't happen again," he said.

* * *

The red-eyed demon continued to plague Andrew's dreams with bizarre visions and command hallucinations of a singular nature.

"What do you want from me?" Andrew screamed.

"I think you know," the demon said with a familiar guttural voice.

"What?" Andrew blurted.

The creature moved even closer, its hood more defined in the darkness. "Remember the abbots in the desert? As it was said, you must be cleansed by fire—cleansed by fire! Yes, Andrew, you must cleanse yourself!"

"Leave!" Andrew shouted. When he sat up in the darkness, his body was covered with sweat; he felt as if his heart were about to burst through his chest.

"You all right?" Brother Nathan asked. He may have knocked, but Andrew did not hear him.

"Yes, I just had a bad dream. I'm fine." It was unusual, he thought, to see Brother Nathan in his room, wearing only a bathrobe, a scene he quickly and involuntarily colored with sexual overtones.

"I can get Father Gerald if you want."

Andrew suddenly realized that he was sitting up—naked—the sheet barely covering his waist. He reached down and pulled it higher. "No, thanks. I'm sure I'll be all right."

Brother Nathan turned to leave. "If you need anything at all, you can knock on my door."

Andrew smiled. "Thanks, I might." He continued to sit on his bed in the darkness as the cool night air slowly dried his sweat-soaked body. Although his cell was empty, the lingering presence of the dark protagonist's message echoed in the silence. "Cleansed by fire," Andrew whispered, yet he forced himself to dismiss the message by focusing on the sensual vision of Brother Nathan, standing with perfect posture in his white terrycloth robe. He was aware that his feelings for Brother Nathan were often sexual, especially now, and he could easily distort

Brother Nathan's last comment as infused with subtle innuendo, which is exactly what he chose to do.

Fueled by loneliness, persistent lust, and the prospect of adventure, Andrew rubbed himself down with a towel, put on boxer shorts and a T-shirt, and threw on his flannel robe before making the final decision to visit Brother Nathan. "Why . . . why am I doing this?" he said softly, even though deep within his gut, he knew the question was rhetorical.

As he stood in front of Brother Nathan's door, he could feel the moisture on his palms; his pulse began to race. It took only a light tap to get Brother Nathan to answer.

"I had a feeling you would see me," he said. "Come in."

Andrew entered the dark cell, lit only by two votive candles. A fragrance stick of musk incense burned near one of the candles, in front of a small, Buddhist statue. "I hope I'm not interrupting your meditation," Andrew whispered.

Brother Nathan waved his hand. "It's all right. I was beginning to get sleepy." His white robe hung on the back of the door.

Andrew assumed that he may have been in bed, judging by the disheveled sheets and Brother Nathan's attire—a football jersey and boxer shorts.

"Have a seat," Brother Nathan said. He pulled his chair away from the desk and faced it toward his bed. Once Andrew was seated, Brother Nathan sat on his bed and leaned against the back wall, remembering to pull some of the sheet up and over his shorts. "How can I help you?" he asked with compassion.

Andrew suddenly realized how genuinely concerned Brother Nathan was—his tone of voice, his facial expressions—and now he wished he had never bothered him. He began to stand. "You know . . . it's wrong for me to impose like this. I should probably go."

"No, it's okay," Brother Nathan insisted. He swung one leg off the bed as though he was about to get up. "Please. I'd like to have you stay and talk."

"You sure?" Andrew questioned.

"Absolutely, if you don't mind."

Andrew sat down, encouraged by the discussion, and the fact that Brother Nathan chose to leave one of his muscular legs exposed on top of the sheet. "I'm not sure what to say."

"Well, tell me how you're feeling right now," Brother Nathan suggested.

Andrew managed another glance at his strong thigh and thick calf. "It's nice to be able to talk to someone who is more of a peer than fulltime clinician."

Brother Nathan laughed. "You might be one of the few who see me that way. Most think I'm part of the administrative garbage, probably because I assist Father Gerald in the infirmary."

"Garbage?" Andrew repeated with a smile.

"Well, you know what I mean—those who project an aura of authority."

"I don't put Father Gerald in that category," Andrew said.

"It would be hard to do. He's incredibly down to earth," Brother Nathan said.

"I know. He's been very helpful to me."

"I think he's very understanding of all you've been through," Brother Nathan said consolingly.

Andrew looked directly at him. "Somehow, I get the feeling that you are too."

"Thanks, I think I am."

The cold wind continued to rage during the pause that followed, grounding them both in a private moment of time.

"Do you want to talk about what causes you to scream at night?" Brother Nathan asked bluntly.

Andrew shifted slightly in his chair. "It's always the same hooded creature, the one with the red eyes, who manages to seem so real and scare the crap out of me."

"What makes him leave?"

Andrew rubbed his eyes. "I guess I'm so frightened, I scream at him. He appears to fade, but maybe I just wake myself up. I don't know what I'll do if he's ever still there when I wake up."

"That's a haunting thought," Brother Nathan said with a nod.

"But it's hard for me to tell if I'm awake or sleeping, it's so real, especially now that he's talking more. My entire body just seems to freeze."

"What does the creature say?"

Andrew stretched out and placed his feet on the edge of the bed. "It's all about being cleansed by fire."

"Like the discussion of the two abbots in the desert?" Brother Nathan asked.

"You know about that?" Andrew asked with surprise.

"It's fairly well known, I believe."

"I read the account, but why did this thing have to bring it up in the dream—or whatever it was?"

Brother Nathan leaned forward and pulled his knees up to his chest. The sheet was stretched tight between his legs. "Maybe it's a part of your subconscious surfacing. Have you ever thought much about it?"

Andrew knew he had to lie. "No, not really. Why?"

"Well, sometimes it's our deepest thoughts that shape our dreams."

"Then perhaps I have," Andrew said unexpectedly. And with that admission, a flood of emotions welled within him and erupted, at first, as quiet tears, which Brother Nathan could not help but notice.

He immediately got up, squatted in front of him, and put his hand on his arm. "It's all right; go ahead—let the feelings out, if you want," he whispered.

"I don't want to," Andrew said, "but I can't seem to control it." Nevertheless, Brother Nathan's compassion allowed Andrew a safe space to release the genuine pain and sorrow he felt inside; the tears flowed freely.

"Come here," Brother Nathan said, as he reached up and pulled Andrew down to the floor where he proceeded to wrap his arms around him and hold him tight.

Andrew buried his head against Brother Nathan's neck. The warmth and scent of his body slowly raised his own self-loathing, replacing it with the inevitable urge to respond physically to Brother Nathan's kindness, perhaps a different form of self-loathing which is seldom internalized until after the fact. "Why are you so nice to me?" Andrew asked quietly.

There was a significant pause before brother Nathan responded. "Something about you frightens me," he said bluntly. "It's as if you need protecting, maybe that's what I'm trying to do."

Andrew moved his mouth to Brother Nathan's ear. "Maybe it's you who needs protecting," he abruptly suggested. He brushed his lips against his earlobe.

Calmly, Brother Nathan turned his head to look at him. "I think I can protect myself."

Andrew smiled, momentarily, and stood up. "I think I'd be more comfortable lying down." He fell into Brother Nathan's bed and lay on his side. "There's room for you," he ventured.

Beyond Andrew's wildest expectations, Brother Nathan got up, stood next to the bed, and looked down at him with a bewildered expression. "Am I supposed to get in there with you?"

Andrew nodded. "I would like you to . . . if you don't mind."

"This may sound silly, but is there some clinical reason for your request?"

Andrew hesitated. "Probably. I need to feel . . . as though you care about me as a friend who can know the worst about me and still like me. Besides, I don't want to return to my room just yet; let me stay here for a while . . . please."

Against his better judgment, Brother Nathan did as he was asked. He lay on his back, but not before managing to pull the sheet up to his waist. He folded his arms behind his head. "Is this okay?"

Andrew rolled close to him and, with trepidation, let his arm fall across Brother Nathan's chest.

Unsure of his emotions, Brother Nathan remained silent and very still.

Andrew was hesitant to breathe, knowing they had reached a critical juncture; he too was afraid to move or, worse yet, speak.

Only the incessant wind could be heard as it buffeted the huddled buildings with bursts of snow.

Suddenly, he felt Brother Nathan shift his weight to his side, face Andrew, and wrap his arm firmly around him. "You must be cold. Maybe this will help."

Snuggling even closer, Andrew was unable to contain his exhilaration, yet he could not help but think that Brother Nathan's comment was suspect, since the room was not very cold. 'Perhaps Brother Nathan possesses a sexual appetite, after all,' he thought.

"Thanks," Andrew said. "It feels incredibly good." He continued to absorb the powerful bulk that surrounded him. "Thanks for doing this," he added.

Brother Nathan shrugged. "You're welcome. I just wish I could make your red-eyed monster disappear for good."

"Me too," Andrew whispered. "This is a good start."

After another lengthy pause, Brother Nathan finally initiated a more serious dialogue. "Do you mind if I ask you more questions?"

"No, not at all."

"Why did you get upset earlier?"

"When I started to get emotional?" Andrew asked.

"Yes," Brother Nathan replied.

"Something you said about our deepest thoughts shaping our dreams."

"What particularly?" Brother Nathan inquired.

"It has to do with the two abbots and being cleansed by fire."

"Why does that bother you so much?"

"I don't know," Andrew lied. "Maybe I don't feel clean."

Brother Nathan turned slightly to face him. "Yes, but who of us are?"

Andrew smiled. "I think you are."

"Yeah, right," Brother Nathan replied. He threw back his head and laughed. "I try to be, but I almost always fail."

"I find that hard to believe," Andrew said, with mild surprise.

"But it's true," Brother Nathan insisted.

"Unfortunately, I think people see me as perpetually unclean," Andrew disclosed painfully.

"Why do you say that?" Brother Nathan asked with genuine concern.

Andrew rolled onto his back. His face grew solemn. "You are very kind, Brother Nathan, but I think you know why."

Brother Nathan reacted. "I don't like it when someone says things like that; it's an assumption."

"I'm sorry, but you know . . . I *know* you do. Maybe you just don't want to hear yourself say it."

Brother Nathan made direct eye contact. "Then why am I lying in bed with you?"

Andrew reached up to him. "Maybe this is why," he whispered, as he gently brushed his lips against his. After a slight pause, he opened his eyes and stared into Brother Nathan's eyes and, then, at his full lips. Cautiously, he moved his mouth once again toward Brother Nathan's, hoping desperately that he would not speak or resist. Just at the point of contact, he closed his eyes and met Brother Nathan's open mouth with his when, suddenly, the years of pent-up suppressed sexual energy, buried deep within Brother Nathan, surfaced like an air-trapped barrel.

Amid the flurry of activity that followed, nothing was said. Brother Nathan appeared awkward, yet capable, in the hands of a seasoned sexual savant who knew exactly what would be sensual and, within reason, acceptable. And with time, Andrew had skillfully managed to reassure Brother Nathan that fellatio by another man in the privacy of his darkened cell was not the end of his heterosexual and sacred world. In fact, Brother Nathan realized that it was not only infinitely pleasurable, but also a necessary, willful occurrence waiting to happen.

* * *

At mass, the following morning, Andrew observed Brother Nathan's lack of eye contact and apparent embarrassment, as a result of their earlier encounter. He felt as though it might be beneficial to talk with him, yet he was fearful that Brother Nathan would refuse to talk at all, feeling scandalized by his own permissiveness.

Standing in his room, Andrew removed his habit and hastily decided to knock on Brother Nathan's door to see if the matter could be amicably resolved or, at least, discussed.

Once more, Brother Nathan opened the door quickly. He was obviously perplexed by Andrew's presence.

"Just five minutes," Andrew said, knowing that Brother Nathan was not in the best of spirits.

He stood in silence, questioning Andrew's motives and his own anticipated reaction. "Come in," he said quietly.

Andrew entered the room, closed the door, and stood facing Brother Nathan, who sat at his desk, thumbing through a small notebook.

"I don't have a lot of time," Brother Nathan explained. "I have to help Father Gerald this morning in the infirmary."

"Look. I'm really sorry about last night," Andrew explained. "You were well-intentioned, and I was totally responsible for what happened. I sincerely apologize."

Brother Nathan closed his notebook and looked at Andrew. "It happened because I wanted it to happen," he admitted. "You're not to blame." He ran his hand over his face. "No, I'll just have to live with it because, from a Buddhist point of view, running to confession just doesn't cut it."

Although surprised by Brother Nathan's admission, Andrew was anticipating the possibility of a more cordial resolution. "You probably hate me—and I can't blame you—but is there a chance that we can get beyond this, knowing that it was more or less a mutual occurrence, so that we can continue to be friends without avoiding each other or being embarrassed in each other's company? I don't think any differently of you, and I hope you'll feel the same about me. And by the way, it isn't something I'd ever discuss with anyone, so don't be concerned about that . . . I promise."

Brother Nathan looked relieved. "It had crossed my mind," he said, "so I feel better now that you told me." He managed a slight smile. "I'm going to try to forget it happened. Maybe you can do the same."

Andrew reached out to shake his hand. "I've already forgotten about it, but I'd be less than honest if I didn't admit how grateful I am to have been able to share that particular moment in time with you and to acknowledge my total respect for you."

"Thanks," Brother Nathan said. But before Andrew reached the door, Brother Nathan offered a final comment. "Just so you know . . . it's nothing to do with who you are. You are still my brother, and I will also continue to respect you. Please try to keep me in your prayers."

"I will, as long as you do the same for me."

"I always do," Brother Nathan replied. "Always."

* * *

After a long morning of preparing a hearty vegetable stew, garlic bread, and banana-strawberry-tofu pudding for lunch, Andrew collapsed on his bed for the midday nap. The lack of sun and the constant swirl of snowflakes made it difficult for him to determine the time of day without looking at his watch. Yet it was definitely conducive to crawling under a warm blanket, assuming a fetal position, and drifting off to a deep sleep.

Others may have used this time for a release of sexual energy; in fact, the elders often referred to this hour as "the time of the noonday devil."

But for Andrew, it was a different, more familiar devil that chose to visit him after lunch. It had never before been present at this time, yet his fiery red eyes and hooded head were unmistakable. Andrew could feel his body grow rigid; his hair felt electrified, as if made of metal filings and being pulled out straight by a large magnet.

The dark figure moved closer and hovered over Andrew's face. Once again, it spoke. "I see you have taken another victim. Yes . . . you'll never stop, Andrew, unless you cleanse yourself by fire!"

Andrew felt as if he were choking. "What does that mean?" he barely managed to say.

The figure came even closer and emitted an eerie laugh. "I think you know, don't you?"

Andrew shook his head sideways.

"Fire, my dear boy . . . fire! It will cleanse you. You know what to do. You will be cleansed once and forever!"

"Get the fuck away from me!" Andrew shouted. He swung at the creature and succeeded in waking himself up.

This time, there was no knock on his door—Brother Nathan did not run into his cell. Instead, Andrew sat on the edge of his bed, looked at his watch, and realized it was nearly time for the None prayer service. The grey light outside his window matched his sullen mood, as he thought about the encounter with the creature. 'How did he know?' he wondered. Within seconds, his body was seized with negative emotions and nausea. Blinded by tears, he somehow managed to grab the metal wastebasket before vomiting his lunch.

* * *

The None service was seldom well attended, particularly by the elder members of the community, who would often prefer to extend their afternoon naps. One by one, those who drifted in appeared disheveled with an "I'm-here-because-it's-expected" attitude. And since it was not obligatory to wear a habit at the service, most of the monks arrived in old jeans and flannel shirts, some untucked to hide telltale tumescence.

As if in a nightmare, Andrew looked up and noticed Brother Kevin, yet his entire head had been removed and replaced with that of a grotesque Minotaur. Horrified, he quickly looked down, rubbed his eyes in disbelief, and squinting to blur the image and ease his fear, he again looked up at Brother Kevin who, this time, appeared normal and offered Andrew a brief smile. With a profound sigh of relief, Andrew continued singing the required Gregorian psalms.

Following several readings, a welcomed interval of meditation allowed Andrew to go deep within himself in an atmosphere of complete silence. Moments later, when that silence was shattered by a poorly timed cough, Andrew opened his eyes and glanced upward.

This time, it was Brother Mark who changed—his head resembled that of a large lizard, complete with a long purplish tongue which flicked in and out erratically. Immediately, Andrew shut his eyes and refused to open them. 'Please,' he prayed, 'make it go away.'

When he finally got the courage to open his eyes and look up at Brother Mark, he was overcome with renewed, unspeakable horror. Each member of the community possessed some form of terrifying, gruesome head, either more Minotaurs or lizards or hideously deformed faces resembling devils and tragic birth anomalies.

'This can't be happening,' Andrew thought. 'It must be a dream.' He closed his eyes for a moment and quickly opened them, yet nothing had changed; he was surrounded by ungodly monsters. Unable to remain in the same room, he fled in terror, barely able to refrain from crying out, and returned to his cell.

He quickly locked the door and sat on his bed. Shaking, he pulled his knees up to his chest, leaned back against the wall, and rested his head on his arms. Although he felt sure that the images he saw could not be real, a part of him doubted and, most likely, denied reality. Thoughts raced through his head like a locomotive—'How can this be happening? What if they're real? Should I call Dr. Klein?'

After settling down, he decided, once again, to face his fear by reporting to the library for the afternoon work assignment. The cloisters were empty and typically silent except for the relentless sound of windblown snow against the large arched windows. Drifts had piled up like frozen waves, crisply shaped and unsullied by animal tracks. As he approached the library, Andrew could hear an occasional voice and feel his anxiety level increase. 'Please let them have normal heads,' he thought, 'please . . .' With eyes lowered, he slowly entered the brick room, took a deep breath, and glanced up to see familiar faces rather than what he had feared.

"Brother Andrew," Brother Mark acknowledged. "I wasn't sure you would be here after I saw you leave None in such a hurry. Are you all right?"

"Yes," Andrew nodded. "I . . . needed to use the bathroom."

"Well, we all know what that's like."

Andrew smiled thankfully.

"Let's see. You cooked lunch which, by the way, was absolutely delicious."

Once again, Andrew smiled.

"Are you okay at the eggery as long as you are with someone?"

"Sure, no problem," Andrew said.

"Brother Kevin, I know you have some difficulty in the eggery with the heat. Is it better for you in the winter?"

"I think I'll be fine," Brother Kevin said. "I've done it before." He looked up at Andrew.

"Do you mind helping Brother Andrew?"

"No, not at all. Andrew . . . excuse me, 'Brother' Andrew saved my life down there. I'm sure I'll be fine."

Andrew looked up and smiled. "Just 'Andrew' is okay with me," he quipped.

Brother Mark appeared to frown slightly, as if disregarding the comment. Given even temporary authority, his discrete fondness for power would involuntarily surface and reveal his true ambition.

Andrew chuckled in silence.

"Thanks, everyone," Brother Mark said. "Have a good afternoon."

* * *

Chapter Thirty-Seven

Unexpected Assault

Brother Kevin met Andrew in the boot room where he was pulling rubber overshoes over his sneakers.

"That was interesting," Brother Kevin said sarcastically.

Andrew laughed. "You noticed."

"Someday, I'd like to walk up to him and just call him 'Mark,'" Brother Kevin admitted.

"I think 'shit head' would be more appropriate," Andrew said with a smile.

Brother Kevin laughed heartily. "Oh, that would go over big."

"Yeah, probably get me a free bus ticket out of here." He put on his jacket. "You ready to visit the girls?"

"Not really, but as long as you're with me, I'm sure I'll survive."

Brother Andrew looked back over his shoulder. "You never know," he said quietly.

They trudged through the swirling landscape like two miniature figures in a newly shaken snow globe.

"Think this will ever stop?" Brother Kevin asked, referring to the incessant snow. He opened his mouth to feel a few cold flakes land on his tongue.

"I'd like to see the sun," Andrew replied, "even if for a short time. This unending grey curtain needs to be opened."

"Yeah. It's sort of depressing," Brother Kevin said.

Once inside the eggery, a familiar silence surrounded them with an even more familiar aura of the unnatural. Andrew still found it difficult to look at the canvas covered-candling booth and the poorly disguised renovation of the men's room door and beyond. So when Brother Kevin surprised him by hugging him from behind while he was putting on his apron, Andrew was startled.

"I'm sorry," Brother Kevin said. "I didn't mean to scare you."

"Believe me, it's not you—it's this place."

"Yes, but it's quiet, and we're away from the monastery." He nuzzled the back of Andrew's neck. "Besides, I'd love to feel you inside of me right now." His comment was completely unexpected.

Although he could feel his erection begin to grow, Andrew declined. "This is probably not the best time or place." He kissed Brother Kevin on the forehead. "Let's take care of the girls first, and then we'll see what happens."

"Okay," Brother Kevin said reluctantly.

The heat and stench of the eggery never changed; it was nearly overpowering with thick chicken dander, cloying ammonia urine, and the distinctly rancid odor of maggot-infested chicken dung.

"I think I hate this place," Andrew said, as he collected the eggs to his right.

Brother Kevin stood at the front of the cart and collected the eggs on the opposite side of the aisle.

Every now and then, Andrew would observe his handsome redheaded helper, until, after looking too long, Brother Kevin noticed.

"What . . . ?" Brother Kevin asked with a smile.

Andrew continued to stare at him. "Do you have any idea how attractive you are?"

Brother Kevin's face began to take on the color of his hair. "Not really, but I like it when you say things like that."

"How about this?" Andrew squeezed past the cart, pulled Brother Kevin toward him, and kissed him aggressively.

"Maybe we should take a break," Brother Kevin suggested, still clinging to Andrew.

"I . . . would rather be done with these eggs."

"Great," Brother Kevin said. He separated from Andrew, walked a few yards away, and turned to face him. He then reached down and grabbed his crotch. "How do you expect me to walk with this?"

"I didn't mean to upset you—I just felt like kissing you."

"I'm not upset—I'm horny—and in all honesty, I just feel like fucking you," he said coarsely.

"Well, at least you're not shy," Andrew said with a grin.

Brother Kevin returned to the cart. "So what do you say?"

"Don't get upset," Andrew said quietly. "We don't have much left to do, so let's just finish and get the hell out of this toilet bowl. There will be time after we wash up."

"You sure?" Brother Kevin asked suspiciously.

"Yes, I promise."

Reluctantly, Brother Kevin resumed his task after first making an adjustment in his jeans.

When they finally finished, they rolled the two carts into the cooler and began to carefully stack the flats and date them. When they had only three stacks left to unload, Brother Kevin removed his apron.

"Do you mind if I wash up while you finish the rest of these?" he asked.

"No, go for it," Andrew said. "I'll be through in a few minutes." He continued to stack the eggs on wooden pallets, making sure that each was properly dated, using masking tape and a marker. He hung up his apron, shut the thick metal door, and turned off the light. As he approached the sink, he was presented with an incredibly provocative sight: Brother Kevin was sprawled on his back, completely naked, on top of a stainless steel table, which he had covered with clean towels. In silence, while watching Andrew, he continued to rub his erection, as if blatantly holding Andrew hostage for his earlier promise by making him keep his word.

"I wish I had a fancy camera," Andrew said. "It's a spectacle worthy of immortalization."

"Thanks," Brother Kevin said, "but I'd be happy with intense, temporal pleasure. Now, get out of those clothes."

It was not long before Andrew was washed and naked and hovering over Brother Kevin, a scene reminiscent of a bizarre emergency room where the doctor-patient relationship warped.

The height of the table provided new and interesting positions for both of them—spread eagle, on top, hanging partially off, and other complicated couplings.

At one point, Brother Kevin was on his back at the edge of the table with his legs in the air—supported by Andrew, who was standing on the floor ravaging him, while Brother Kevin masturbated forcefully. Close to having an orgasm, Brother Kevin verbalized intensely sexual commands which further incited Andrew. Rolling his head from side to side, Brother Kevin arched his back, threw back his head, and moaned, as he jettisoned semen onto his chest and face with typical seizurelike shaking.

Stimulated by such an authentic, visceral response, Andrew closed his eyes just prior to ejaculating and exploded inside of him, discharging the final drops with sustained, squeezed thrusts.

Completely exhausted, Andrew's head dropped forward, as he attempted to recover; however, when he slowly opened his eyes and met Brother Kevin's gaze, he recoiled in horror. He saw, instead, the familiar face of a grotesque lizard, staring back at him with glazed, beady eyes and a thin purple tongue darting dangerously close to his face. "Why, why, you fucking lizard!" Andrew screamed, as he struck the lizard's face again and again and again.

A barely audible voice seemed to emanate from its mouth in deep, slurred tones, as if slowed to half speed. "Stop . . . I'm Kevin. Stop. You're killing me. Please . . ."

"I've got to get out of here!" Andrew shouted, his face and arms were spattered with blood. Frantically delusional, he pulled on his jeans and shirt, put on his sneakers, grabbed his jacket, and fled into the early November darkness.

* * *

It was Brother Mark who noticed they were both absent from supper and Compline, an unusual and serious transgression, which demanded follow-up. Halfway into the service, he bowed, left the church, and walked quickly toward their cells. After knocking several times on Andrew's door, he tried the doorknob—the room was unlocked. "Brother Andrew?" He expected that he might be asleep, yet when he got no response, he turned on the light and realized that his cell was vacant.

He immediately went to Brother Kevin's room and repeated the process with the same results. "Something's not right," he said out loud. The sound of his own voice in the darkness startled him.

As he walked through the dimly lit cloister, he was suddenly overcome with more than just concern. An ominous, hollow feeling flooded his head and guts; goose bumps rippled the skin on his arms and neck.

He reentered the church during the meditation service, where hazy incense inundated the occupied chapel. Brother Mark waited near the top of the three steps, until his eyes adjusted to the light. Once he recognized Father Gerald, he immediately walked over to where he was sitting, leaned down, and whispered in his ear. "I apologize, Father Gerald, but we need to talk—it may be an emergency."

He turned to look at Brother Mark. "Find Brother Nathan and meet me in the infirmary." Father Gerald stood and quickly left the church.

Gathered together, they were briefed by Brother Mark and, within minutes, were driving toward the eggery.

With his heart racing, Brother Mark was not surprised to learn that the door to the eggery was unlocked; however, after turning on the lights, the scene before him nearly caused him to faint. Brother Kevin's naked body sprawled unnaturally, with limbs askew, on the concrete floor. His head and matted hair were outlined in a pool of blood which had already begun to coagulate.

Brother Mark was unable to move; he watched the others rush past him.

"Please, God," Father Gerald anguished. "Let him be alive!" He set his medical case on the floor, pulled out his stethoscope, and felt Brother Kevin's throat. "He's breathing, but his pulse is weak."

Brother Nathan removed his jacket and draped it over Brother Kevin. Father Gerald and Brother Mark did the same. "We have no choice—call for an ambulance," Father Gerald said. He looked directly at Brother Mark, who was wide-eyed with terror.

"Do we have to?" Brother Mark stammered.

"Yes, God damn it—do it!"

Father Gerald's demand struck Brother Mark like a slap in the face. He bolted to the office and picked up the phone.

Father Gerald placed his hand on Brother Kevin's head, wanting to make him more comfortable yet afraid to move him without stabilizing his neck. "Brother Kevin," he whispered. "Can you hear me? It's Father Gerald."

His response was delayed. Brother Kevin slowly opened a bruised eye. "My head hurts," he said with a slur, when suddenly, he realized that he was surrounded by blood and lying naked on the floor. "Jesus Christ!" he shouted. He began to cry and attempted to move, as panic overwhelmed him.

"Listen to me," Father Gerald said firmly. "You are going to be all right, but I don't want you to move. Please stay still until the paramedics get here. If anything is fractured, moving may make it worse. Do you understand me?"

Brother Kevin attempted to nod but cried out in pain.

"Keep your head still—just say yes or no."

"I have a headache," Brother Kevin whispered.

"I'm sure you do. I'm going to give you something for pain." He removed a syringe and rubber topped vial from his case, drew the measured dose, and after cleansing an area on Brother Kevin's buttock, he quickly injected him. Brother Kevin barely flinched.

Prior to the arrival of the ambulance, Brother Nathan and Father Gerald did their best to clean open wounds and stanch blood loss with pressure and sterile gauze. "What do we say?" Brother Nathan whispered. His gloved hands were smeared with blood.

"Actually, I'm at a loss. But you're right. I need to think," Father Gerald said.

"Do you think we could get his underwear and pants on?" Brother Nathan hated the question but felt he needed to ask.

Father Gerald was momentarily speechless. Finally, he responded. "What the hell," he said. "Why bother. There will most likely be an investigation, and we would all be forced to lie. Right now, I'm concerned that Brother Kevin survives. Both he and the monastery—with the grace of God—will be forced to deal with the consequences." Once again, he put on his stethoscope, listened, and then took Brother Kevin's pulse. "I hope they get here soon."

Brother Mark drove the van to the front of the monastery where he waited anxiously. Through the darkness, the flashing lights of the ambulance could be seen making a left-hand turn off the main highway and racing down the gravel road. Brother Mark flashed his lights several times, until the ambulance was alongside of him. He rolled down the window. "Follow me," he shouted.

Within minutes, they reached the eggery. Given the nature of their location, the two young paramedics, both males, were more than perplexed by what they saw.

Father Gerald, the only spokesperson, remained truthfully oblique when questioned.

Brother Kevin said very little.

After stabilizing Brother Kevin and getting him safely on the stretcher, one of the paramedics spoke quietly to Father Gerald. "I'm sorry to have to bring this up, but it will be necessary to file a police report. The damage to his face and head is, most likely, inconsistent with a fall from that height. I hope this doesn't present a problem."

"Absolutely not," Father Gerald replied. "Do what's appropriate, but right now, let's get him to the hospital."

"Of course; can you come with us?"

"Yes, I would like to," Father Gerald insisted.

* * *

Cold and incredibly frightened, Andrew watched the flashing lights of the ambulance pass beneath him, as he peered through the open slats from the barn's hayloft. Tears gave way to uncontrolled sobbing and wailing, followed by the inability to breathe and intermittent vomiting. Convinced that he might be dying, Andrew watched involuntarily as snapshots of his life quickly flashed before him, a montage from his childhood to the present, filled with polarities and fueled by emotions, yet it was people who were most prominent—his mother, his aunt, Nick, Sara, Brother Matthew, Brother Kevin, and, of course, Brother Joshua, whom he knew he had neglected since Brother Kevin entered his life. 'I need to see him,' he thought, yet he was sure they would be looking for him. Nevertheless, when he knew that most of the monks would be sleeping, he carefully made his way back to the monastery, across the moderate snow-covered foothills which bordered one side of the property.

Hidden by a large spruce, Andrew could see that the cells were in darkness, except for Brother Nathan's, where a small lamp cast its yellow glow across one side of the draped slider. From the tree to Brother Joshua's window, Andrew was aware that there was nothing to hide behind; the area was completely open. He took a deep breath, walked out from behind the spruce, and moved slowly toward Brother Joshua's room.

Because of the cold temperatures, the snow remained powdery and nearly noiseless as he walked. He approached the glass slider with growing fear, wondering if someone might be sitting in the dark waiting for him. He flattened himself against the building and gently tapped on the glass. Moments later, he saw a corner of the drape rise slightly and then fall back toward the floor. The familiar metallic click meant that the door was being unlocked. With a dull moan, the door opened part way.

"Andrew? Is that you?" Brother Joshua whispered.

"Yes. Please let me in."

Brother Joshua pushed open the slider, until Andrew was able to squeeze past. He held his head down, afraid to look up.

"I can't look at your face," he said. "Tell me honestly that it's really you, that it's really your face."

"Why are you saying this? Of course, it's my face," Brother Joshua stammered. He grabbed Andrew's hand and gently placed it on his cheek. "Feel it. Touch my nose, my eyes, my forehead."

Trembling, Andrew carefully explored Brother Joshua's profile and facial structure. He touched his neck and felt the texture and shape of his hair and head.

"You're beginning to frighten me, Andrew. Tell me what the hell is going on."

Andrew raised his head slightly. "It really is you?"

"Yes. You can't tell?" Brother Joshua said.

"If I open my eyes and run out the door, please don't come after me."

"Look at me," Brother Joshua insisted. "Let me help you."

Andrew moved back cautiously and slowly raised his head while rapidly repeating the same sentence: "Please God, let him be normal. Please God, let him be normal," until he finally made contact with Brother Joshua's eyes.

Even in the darkness, the familiar attractiveness of Brother Joshua's face radiated a passionate concern for the troubled man who stood before him.

"See. I wasn't lying, was I? It's me—Joshua."

Andrew reached out to embrace him. "Thank God," he whispered. He held Brother Joshua tight, afraid to let go. "It's still you, isn't it?" He reached back, once again, to touch his face.

"Yes, it's still me." Brother Joshua separated slowly and looked him in the eye. "Listen to me, Andrew," he said calmly yet firmly. "I need to get you some help. Do you understand me?"

Andrew nodded slowly.

"I think we should contact Dr. Klein. Let him help you."

Andrew raised both hands to his face and began to sob. "I didn't mean to do it . . . I'm sorry. Tell them I'm sorry."

"Do what . . . ? What did you do? Tell me."

At that point, Andrew slowly slumped to the floor, crumpled and crying and barely audible. "His face . . . he changed. Why did it have to change?"

Brother Joshua knelt in front of him and grabbed him by both arms. "Whose face? Who are you talking about?"

"Oh, God!" Andrew moaned. He raked his fingers forcefully across his forehead and down his cheeks and then buried his head against his knees.

It was not until he felt Andrew's blood dripping on his arm that Brother Joshua suddenly realized what had just happened. "Jesus Christ, Andrew! You have to stop this!" He jumped up to get a towel and tried to hold it against the oozing wounds, yet this only caused Andrew to react.

He stood up and slowly backed away, his face striped and smeared with blood. "I know you want to help me . . . but I don't think it's possible."

"Yes, yes it is," Brother Joshua said softly. "Let's both leave now. I can drive you to the clinic. Please . . . let me help you."

Andrew managed a slight, enigmatic smile. "You're a good person, Josh, and you deserve to be happy. I just hope that, despite everything, you'll come to realize how much I've loved you." He turned to look out the window. "I have to go. They'll be looking for me."

"Who? Why?" but before Brother Joshua was able to finish the sentence, Andrew quickly slipped outside where he briefly glanced around and then spoke, softly yet strangely.

"You know... it's a very beautiful night." He immediately disappeared around the building and out of sight.

* * *

Chapter Thirty-Eight

The Cleansing

Totally unfocused and increasingly anomic, Andrew simply placed one foot in front of the other, as he walked toward the barn and the hayloft where he had hidden earlier. Questions, explanations, fears, and outcomes had become secondary to his physical needs; he was aware that he was extremely cold and wanted only to sleep.

Before climbing the steep wooden steps, Andrew pulled an old woolen horse blanket from the side of the nearest stall, held it close to his chest, and struggled up the stairs until he reached his sanctuary. Broken hay bales provided a genuinely monastic level of comfort which, when combined with the scratchy blanket, would have tested even the most profound ascetic. Yet Andrew felt nothing but relief as he wrapped the blanket around himself and collapsed on a cushion of straw.

After only a few hours of deep sleep, he began to toss and turn on the hard surface as indiscriminate bits of dreams manifested themselves as meaningless pictures which quickly faded and were then replaced by more of the same—until the appearance of the black hooded creature was acknowledged.

"Why can't you leave me alone!" Andrew shouted. The wraith hovered above him, undaunted by Andrew's challenge. It appeared to be grinning, determined to convince Andrew of its power. "You pathetic child," it said clearly. "When will you ever learn that I'm only here to help you? You know what you need . . . you must be cleansed. There is no other way."

Andrew thrashed with opposition. "Get the fuck away from me!"

This provoked the creature to come even closer. For the first time, Andrew could see only a moist cavity where its nose should have been.

"Strike out! Try to move!" the creature taunted. "You'll find that you are powerless."

As hard as he struggled, he realized that the creature was telling the truth. He was immobile.

"You see? Now stop your senseless laboring and listen to me. I can help you."

But Andrew refused to listen and struggled even more.

"I watched you destroy your brother's face!" the creature shouted.

Instantaneously, Andrew grew still, as fear ignited every possible nerve in his body. "What did you say?" he whispered.

"Don't be coy. I saw all that you did on that table."

"You're a fucking liar!" Andrew screamed.

Like an instant replay, the creature spoke perfectly in Brother Kevin's voice:

> *"I'm not upset—I'm horny, and in all honesty,*
> *I just feel like fucking you."*

Andrew was beyond terror. Sweat soaked through his clothing and began to freeze.

"I believe you're ready now," the creature commanded softly.

Andrew nodded.

"Don't worry. It will all be over soon. Just do as I say. We need to go downstairs."

Andrew felt himself stand up, and for the first time, he was convinced that this was not a dream. He was completely aware of his surroundings, the smell of the hay, the darkness of the loft, and the smell of his own fear.

The creature, completely three-dimensional, followed him down the narrow stairs, yet the only noise he heard was his own footsteps, as the robed creature appeared to float behind him as if attached to wires.

"You will need that," the creature said. He appeared to be pointing toward a red metal container.

"The gas can?" Andrew asked.

"Yes. Take it with you."

"Where are we going?"

"It doesn't matter," the creature replied. "Just follow me."

The container felt heavy in Andrew's hand. He knew that it was probably full and would be difficult to carry, yet he was unable to resist the will of the demon.

Somehow, the creature remained in front of him in the darkness. Andrew vaguely remembered its black robe blowing in the wind and feeling the cold air rush past his face when suddenly, inexplicably, he was standing outside his cell in the middle of the snow-filled garth. He could not recall walking on the road; he did not remember walking around the back of the monastery, past the large refectory windows, and stopping in the center of such a visible area while carrying the red container. He knew only how we felt—disoriented, hollow, yet unperturbed—even, perhaps, at peace.

"Already you feel it, don't you?" The creature asked.

Andrew nodded, knowing exactly what he meant.

"It's a common story, especially for you, Andrew. The consuming fire Abbot Basil spoke of to Abbot Paul will cleanse you, remove the stain of all your guilt, the agony of those who have hurt you, and those you have hurt. The torments will disappear. Your sleep will be restful, and yes, even I will no longer violate your dreams. Do you understand?"

Once again, Andrew nodded. At that moment, he knew his nemesis had flourished, conquered, and was about to deliver unopposed and willful retribution for which Andrew felt relieved.

"Poor the healing fluid over your entire body," the creature commanded. "You will be rebaptized and born again in Legion's name."

Sinking to his knees, Andrew knelt in the snow and did as he was asked. He felt the liquid permeate his clothing, his face, chest, arms, and legs with only a slightly cool sensation and a strangely familiar, comforting scent, like that of warm nasturtiums. Even the taste of it was similar to the leaf itself—peppery and tangy. When he had emptied the container, Andrew opened his eyes and saw that he was mysteriously clothed in his habit, which appeared to glisten in the waxing light of the moon. He vaguely recalled that it was the first time, in a long time, that the moon was visible, and suddenly, he realized that it had finally stopped snowing.

"Reach into your right pocket," the creature commanded.

Andrew pulled out a small box of wooden matches.

"Now, remove three, strike them on the side of the box, and touch them to your scapular."

As if in slow motion, just before the burning matches fell from his fingers, Andrew was blinded by a multitude of angels, an almost unbearable whiteness within a platinum chamber, as they sang an intoxicating requiem with thundering, harmonic lament, which caused him to smile once more.

* * *

The devastating blaze illuminated the garth, its trees, and the cloister windows with agonizing brightness. Returning to his cell from the infirmary, Brother Nathan was the first to witness the hideous sight, as he raced to reach the far side of the cloister where the only door to the garth existed. His wailing scream of "no!" reverberated throughout the monastery, trailing behind him as he ran and waking even the soundest sleepers. Instinctively, he somehow remembered to enter Andrew's cell, pull the blankets off his bed, and, after crashing through the slider screen, throw them over Andrew's head, as the monks watched in horror.

* * *

As soon as he was notified of the tragedy, Dr. Klein decided that it would be expedient for him to address the members of the community, to provide not only potential support and possible explanations but also serve as grief counselor for those who felt the need to discuss their feelings.

"I'd like to bring two psychologists with me, if that's acceptable," Dr. Klein said as he spoke with Father Gerald by telephone.

"That's fine," Father Gerald said softly. "Does it matter whether they are male or female? You know how rigid this place is."

"I've taken that into consideration—both are males."

"Thanks for doing that."

"What have you heard?" Dr. Klein asked.

Father Gerald took a deep breath before responding. "Well . . . he's still alive, but it doesn't look promising. I just got off the phone with Dr. Bales, head of the burn unit at Creighton City Hospital where Andrew was airlifted. The burns are extensive, from full thickness to sub-dermal, mostly upper body, with 70 percent facial involvement. It looks as though there is significant inhalation injury also. If he makes it, he is going to require a tremendous amount of care and surgery, not to mention prayers and God's grace."

"I am so deeply sorry," Dr. Klein said sadly. "I have the feeling that he completely stopped his medication. And his entire psychological profile will most likely impede his progress. I wish I could have seen this coming."

"Don't berate yourself. We at this monastery could probably be accused of a litany of neglect," Father Gerald admitted.

"It's difficult to predict outcomes. I don't know what to say right now."

"I understand," Father Gerald said.

"May I ask about the other young man who was found that night and taken to the hospital?" Dr. Klein asked.

"Yes, of course," Father Gerald said. "He seems to be stable at Whitehill Medical Center. Apparently, Brother Kevin reported that Brother Andrew suddenly went berserk—something about his face looking different—and then he began to strike Brother Kevin repeatedly. Brother Kevin must have passed out and rolled off the table."

"Andrew was, most likely, experiencing visual hallucinations," Dr. Klein offered.

"It's quite possible. Besides a concussion, Brother Kevin had some facial surgery, but it looks like he's going to be fine—thank God."

"By the way, I've canceled my afternoon appointments for tomorrow. Would that be a good time for us to talk with the monks?"

"The sooner the better," Father Gerald said.

"Fine. And if you can make it, you are welcome to go with me afterwards to visit Andrew. I believe that Creighton is about fifty miles from Bitter Creek."

"Thanks, that's perfect," Father Gerald said. "We can talk more on the way."

* * *

Chapter Thirty-Nine

Hell Materialized

Andrew was contained in a totally sterile environment, surrounded by machines, and covered with bandages. There was very little of him to be seen except for his eyes which, somehow, were still functional. For the moment, he remained unconscious in a drug-induced state, attached to a breathing machine and a barrage of intravenous fluids.

"This is incredibly difficult to see," Father Gerald said. His eyes glazed with emotion.

Dr. Klein remained momentarily speechless. He paced in front of the glass and ran his hand helplessly over his ruddy face. "I've had to experience a variety of suicides in my practice, yet I have to admit, I have tremendous difficulty with immolation attempts, particularly by fire. Those who survive have no idea of the excruciating pain involved."

"And Dr. Bales now seems to think that Andrew may be young enough and strong enough to survive this," Father Gerald added. "I am thankful yet extremely fearful of the suffering he will, most likely, have to endure. May God have mercy on him."

Dr. Klein nodded and stared at the helpless figure beyond the glass. "I am so sorry that it had to come to this."

Within days, Andrew's pain medication was reduced intentionally so that he would be conscious enough to help participate in the debridement process and the cleansing of wounds, yet there was a fine line between maximum pain relief and unconsciousness. Of course, Andrew would have preferred to remain unconscious, most probably, for the rest of his life. His eyes were his main connection to the world around him, and in time, he learned to communicate by blinking—one blink for no, two blinks for yes. His screams were silent, yet his blood pressure and pulse rate would soar and activate a variety of alarms which would send a team of white clad staff into his room to inject various medications and perform other tasks to alleviate his agony. He knew his life was in their hands.

And he quickly learned there was no place for modesty within such a setting. He was often naked or lightly covered with special sheets. Nurses, male and female, tended to all of his bodily functions including the insertion and removal of urethral catheters, bedpans, and urogenital hygiene. He realized that he was charred flesh at the mercy of the well-intentioned. His intention was simply not to be; as much as he wanted to shout out his feelings, it was totally impossible. It was as if he were observing life from a tunnel, experiencing excruciating pain and, for the most part, barely able to move. Tears flowed only from his right eye, and with damaged vocal cords, he was forced to remain completely silent. So when he was asked his favorite question: "Are you in pain?" he would carefully blink twice and watch as another syringe of nepenthe was slowly squeezed into a shunt. Moments later, the fuzzy warmth would flood his body until he felt as if he were floating, and the pain and sorrow eventually dissipated.

Once the medication became effective, Andrew was hydraulically lifted into a whirlpool tub where trained staff would continue with the debridement process by removing loose necrotic skin from his upper body, arms, and neck. Although his thighs were also burned, they escaped the severity of the area above the waist.

Andrew would watch in silent horror as patches of skin were peeled from parts of his body and left to disappear in the swirling medicated waters. He wondered how the therapists, who were wearing swimsuits, could tolerate being in the same tub with him, yet they never evidenced negative feelings; in fact, they were mostly good-natured, compassionate, and very sensitive to his condition. They were constantly asking if he was all right and maintained strong eye contact in anticipation of his blink response.

But he soon learned that the whirlpool baths were simple compared to what would follow. Some of his wounds would harden and require the use of scissors and forceps to remove the eschar, which, when excised, often exposed pockets of pus that needed to be drained. Even with the pain medication, Andrew screamed in total silence, blinking furiously as tears poured from his eye.

* * *

He barely noticed as the days turned into weeks and weeks to months. The dedication of the staff, their relentless pursuit to heal and cleanse, all seemed in vain to Andrew, who lived in constant pain. Relief depended on how quickly he could make eye contact and blink his message. For most, nightmares generally end when one awakes; Andrew's nightmare was permanent, including the return of the hooded creature, who visited him, once again, in the middle of a deep sleep.

"I know what you are thinking," the creature said. "Why am I here after I said I wouldn't bother you?"

Andrew was unable to respond or move, his breathing increased rapidly.

"Well, the answer is simple, you foolish child—you didn't die! One of your victims, Brother Nathan, managed to get to you just a little too soon. What a pity . . . I'm sure you are in agony, but then again, you must be used to it by now."

Andrew tried to lash out with his arms, but this only resulted in extraordinary pain and a guttural sound from his throat. As soon as his pulse elevated, the alarms in the nurse's office were activated and four staff members rushed to his side to administer medication. By then, the creature had departed.

* * *

Chapter Forty

Matthew's Return and Resolution

It was a Sunday afternoon when the nurse approached Andrew's bed. "You have a visitor, Andrew. Now that you are healing, the staff feels there is a reduced risk of infection, so visitors may be allowed. Would you like to see him?"

Andrew stared at her, intentionally not blinking.

The nurse grew puzzled. "Neither yes nor no—you must have a question."

Andrew blinked twice.

"Of course," the nurse said. "You must want to know who it is."

Again Andrew blinked twice.

"He said his name is Matthew and that he used to be in the monastery with you."

Andrew could feel his heart began to race.

"Would you like to see him?"

Andrew turned his head, so that the nurse could barely see his face. If he were able, he would have laughed at her, at first, and then screamed at her for being such a moron. He wondered how she would feel having visitors, after being so horribly burned and disfigured. He turned to face her.

"Is that a yes or a no?" she asked.

Andrew squeezed both eyes shut for a few seconds and then opened them.

"That looks like a no," she said. "Are you absolutely positive that you don't want to see him?"

Andrew blinked twice.

"Okay. I'll tell him."

Just the mention of Matthew's name caused Andrew's head to spin with thoughts, visuals, and auditory messages from the past. He wondered if he brought his wife or, worse yet, his kids, to see the scary monster who used to be his friend when he was in the monastery. Overcome with depression, he closed his eyes to shut out his world, yet the full-sized theater screen in back of his eyes never closed; the projectionist worked twenty-four hours a day. And at that moment, the movie might have been called "Mostly Matthew," since he was featured in nearly every frame, except when there were scenes of the both of them. Until now, Andrew did not recall having dreams or thoughts about sex, yet he could tell by the familiar feeling in his genitals that he was sufficiently aroused.

After the third Sunday of being rejected, Matthew refused to take no for an answer. He graciously thanked the nurse for her efforts, turned to leave, but instead made a hasty entrance into the men's room where he pretended to use the urinal and waited until the room was vacant. Through the partially opened door, Matthew could easily see the nurses' station. He waited until the nurse he had talked with walked away from the desk, carrying a stack of papers. Immediately, he left the men's room and walked quickly, yet casually, past the desk, down the hall toward the glass rooms until he saw the name ANDREW WHITBREAD printed in large black letters on a piece of surgical tape which had been stuck to the corner of the window.

The door opened and closed quietly.

Andrew appeared to be sleeping, his head turned slightly away so that he was unable to see Matthew who sat in the chair next to his bed.

Even now, most of Andrew's face remained bandaged to prevent infection and contain the various ointments which were applied daily, yet for Matthew, it was the same handsome face he had always remembered and loved. He sat in total silence, as if meditating, or mesmerized by the friend before him—a fallen soldier reminiscent, Matthew thought, perhaps, of Alexander the Great, a man too young, too vital, to be so mortally wounded. Overcome with sadness, Matthew refused to let it show in the event that Andrew might wake up and read his face—it was his smile he wanted Andrew to see first.

When he moved slightly in his chair to make himself more comfortable, Matthew noticed that Andrew's right hand was resting on top of the sheet, close to his thigh. Without bandages, he could see where fingers had been fused together, surgically separated, and grafted while numerous scars etched across the back of his hand as raised ridges. As painful as it was to look at, Matthew could only imagine the horror that Andrew must have experienced and the intense pain that the recovery process necessitated. Rather than submit to his sorrow, he was moved by the familiar beauty of that hand, regardless of its flaws. He could have sketched it perfectly from memory—the long, full fingers, which were slightly clubbed at the tips; the structure of the bones and knuckles so proportionally blended; and the prominent vein which fed down from his wrist to his thumb. It was all there—he just had to look a little harder.

But looking was not enough. Without thinking, he saw his own hand reach out and gently grasp Andrew's. Just the feel of its warmth caused Matthew to momentarily lose his breath, as if his heart skipped a beat and doubled up on the next. Yes, it felt somewhat rough but the palm was as soft and familiar as he had remembered. He closed his eyes, and his smile blossomed naturally in the silence.

When he opened them, he saw two dark terrified eyes staring back at him.

"It's only me," Matthew said calmly, despite the fact that Andrew's expression screamed terror in deafening, silent decibels. His breathing became labored and rapid; the exposed skin on his face and neck flushed.

Suddenly, the usual emergency alarms sounded and the room was quickly filled with nurses, orderlies and a physician, who were baffled by Matthew's presence. Once the proper medication was administered, the bedside questioning began.

"I know who you are," the nurse said. "For the past three weeks, I've explained to you that Andrew does not want to see you. You'll have to leave immediately, or we'll call security."

"Wait!" Matthew insisted. "How do you know what he wants? He doesn't speak, does he?"

"Only with his eyes: one blink for no, two blinks for yes. Why are you so persistent?"

"Because," Matthew stammered.

"What kind of answer is that?" the nurse retorted. "What's the reason?"

Matthew inhaled deeply. "Andrew and I were more than good friends in the monastery—he was the person I loved."

Andrew could not believe his ears.

But Matthew did not stop there. "And I still love him now. Isn't that a good enough reason for wanting to see him?"

A palpable level of discomfort filled the room, yet it did not stop the inquisitive nurse. "With all due respect, sir, I noticed that you are wearing a wedding ring."

"That's correct," Matthew admitted, "but not for long. My wife and I are in the process of getting a divorce."

"It has been Andrew's decision not to see you. Shall I ask him again?" she asked.

Matthew ran his hand over his face. "Fine, but let me just say something briefly to him in front of all of you. Then he can make his decision, and I will abide by it." The nurse moved closer to Andrew's bed and made strong eye contact. "Is that all right with you, Andrew?"

Andrew looked briefly at the nurse, gazed quickly at Matthew and then back at the nurse. He carefully blinked twice.

"He said yes."

This time, Matthew approached Andrew's side and began to speak softly. "Thank you. I'm not here to embarrass you or cause you any additional pain or stress, and I'm not here because of any expectations. I'm here because I've always loved you—you know that—and even though I was stupid enough to marry Rebecca, I never stopped thinking of you. I am so sorry for leaving you, but I am not looking for your forgiveness. I understand that you have refused to see all visitors, and if you decide not to see me, it will be very painful, but I will honestly respect your decision."

"When I sat by your bed earlier, you were sleeping. I would guess that you may not feel worthy of being seen, especially by those who represent a part of your monastic life—including myself. But let me tell you what I felt when I sat here watching you sleep. I saw the wonderful handsome man I'd come to know and love—regardless of your bandages and my inexcusable behaviors. Then I saw your hand resting on the sheet. Yes it's scarred but it is still the same strong hand that I've sketched in the past, and I couldn't resist holding that hand and feeling the warmth and softness of your palm. I apologize for waking you so abruptly. I simply want to spend time with you, Andrew, and if you feel—with the staff's consent—that my visits are beneficial, I will see you as often or as little as you wish. You can terminate the visits at anytime. Give me a chance, even though I don't deserve one. Give yourself a chance . . . please."

Once again, Andrew turned away. Tears flowed copiously from his right eye and dripped onto his pillow.

Expecting such a response, the nurse (who also appeared emotional), grabbed a tissue, and gently daubed Andrew's eye.

Matthew turned and walked toward the door. He spoke softly to the doctor. "I'll be in the hallway. You can inform me of his decision."

Moments later, the staff found him sitting in a chair, his head buried in his hands. "Matthew, we asked if he would consider your offer. He said yes."

"Thank God," Matthew replied.

"One thing, keep the visit short today. He's been through a lot. And if he gets upset, his vital signs will set off an alarm. We can't allow that to happen too often."

Matthew reached out to shake the doctor's hand. "Thank you. I can't tell you how much this means to me."

He immediately got up, entered the room, and sat in the same chair next to Andrew's bed. As before, Andrew had his head turned slightly away from his visitor—his right hand remained in the same position.

"Your doctor said it was all right to come back in. Thanks for letting me do this."

There were many pauses in his conversation, since Matthew did not want to overwhelm him on the first visit. He had hoped Andrew would feel comfortable enough to face him, but that too would take additional time. And the choice of subject matter was just as delicate.

"You don't have to look at me," Matthew said softly, "but that means I can't ask you any questions, and that's okay. I just don't want to bring up a subject that might trouble you. Maybe I'll just sit here, quietly, with you for a while before I leave. You might want to get some sleep."

There was absolutely no response from Andrew; Matthew's fallen hero remained motionless.

And then he decided to take a chance—a bold move which completely failed the last time. He carefully rested his hand on Andrew's, so that his fingers were inside of Andrew's palm and his palm rested on the ridges of the back of Andrew's hand.

Initially, he heard Andrew take a deep breath, yet the color of his face and neck remained the same, and apparently, no alarms were activated. He left his hand in that position, neither applying nor relaxing pressure, until suddenly, he could feel Andrew gently squeeze his hand. "I can feel that!" Matthew said excitedly.

At that moment, Andrew turned his head very slowly to observe Matthew; his face appeared masklike, with very little affect.

"I wish you could talk to me," Matthew whispered.

Andrew responded by blinking, slowly, at first, and then more and more rapidly until he seemed exhausted and briefly closed his eyes.

Aware that their conversation was being monitored by the speaker above the bed, Matthew moved closer and whispered. "I'm not exactly sure what that means. I'll watch your eyes. You blink, okay?"

Andrew blinked twice.

"I'll start with the obvious. Do you want me to leave?"

One blink.

"Thank God. You wish you could say something?"

Two blinks.

Matthew felt Andrew's hand slowly move away from his.

"Does my holding your hand upset you?"

One blink.

Matthew watched as Andrew appeared to be staring at the sheet near his hand. "You want me to look where you are looking?"

Two strong blinks.

Matthew looked down at the area that Andrew was looking at, yet nothing appeared unusual, until he saw Andrew attempt to move his fingers. "You want me to look at your hand?"

Again, two strong blinks.

With painstaking effort, Andrew struggled to oppose his index finger against his thumb. He then attempted to move his hand in a slightly circular motion.

"You're drawing!"

One strong blink.

"I'm so stupid!" Matthew confessed. "You want to write, yes?"

Both of Andrew's blinks seemed to signify a major breakthrough, a cathartic, peaceful release, knowing that he was finally understood.

Matthew jumped up excitedly. "Hang on. I'll be right back." He rushed to the nurses' station to share his discovery with the same nurse who was on duty earlier.

"That's great news, Matthew, but Andrew has so many contractures, it will be nearly impossible for him to write."

"I understand," Matthew said, "but let's give him a chance, no matter how long it takes."

The nurse frowned and pursed her lips. "Well, I suppose it can't hurt." She searched the desk for a thick pen and a large white notebook.

"Thanks." Matthew quickly returned to Andrew's side. He placed the pad under his right hand and attempted to position the pen between his fingers; however, as predicted, Andrew had difficulty grasping the pen. Each time he tried, the pen flew out of his hand and landed on the sheet.

Although discouraged, Matthew was persistent; he could only imagine how Andrew felt. "Let's try another way." Matthew found a roll of sterile gauze and tape, wrapped the gauze tightly around the pen, and covered the gauze with the tape to keep it in place and provide a thicker instrument. "Try to grab the pen with your palm and fingers like you are holding a bouquet of flowers." He placed the pen in Andrew's hand where, miraculously, it stayed.

"You've got it!" Matthew shouted. "Now, let's see what you can do." He adjusted the note pad under Andrew's pen. "Can you see it?"

Two blinks.

Andrew barely moved the pen over the white surface—a small black line, more like an extended dot, appeared.

"It's okay," Matthew said. "Take your time." He stood up, realizing that he had already spent more time with Andrew than the staff had suggested. "I'm going to have to leave. You can practice your writing while I'm gone." Matthew leaned forward to kiss him on the forehead but then decided against it. "Oh," he said, turning around. "If you want to write, form a circle with your hand. I'll tell the nurse to leave the pen and notebook by your side, okay?"

Two blinks.

Matthew smiled as bravely as he could. "I'll see you on Sunday, if not before."

* * *

For the next month and a half, Matthew remained true to his word. Even a dangerous spring snowstorm did not prevent him from seeing Andrew, yet it was during that visit when he was called into the staff office and given the tragic news.

Dr. Bales, Chief of the burn unit, sat solemnly at the table. He motioned for Matthew to sit. "I'm sorry to have to tell you this, but both his vision and hearing are rapidly deteriorating."

Matthew remained silent. He watched the doctor's lips move, saw the nurse wipe her eyes with a tissue, but he heard nothing. At first, the room seemed to tip slightly to the left, and then to the right, until the movement became a rapid spin and everything went dark. Unable to breathe, he slipped out of his chair and slumped to the carpet.

Moments later, when he regained consciousness, Matthew found himself on a couch, covered with a blanket and a pillow tucked under his feet.

Both Dr. Bales and a male attendant were present.

"How are you feeling?" Dr. Bales asked.

Matthew nodded.

"You are probably aware that you lost consciousness during our discussion about Andrew. I apologize. I should have been less direct."

"No," Matthew said. "I just didn't expect it."

Dr. Bales smiled. "I can see that now."

Matthew let his feet slide off the pillow and onto the floor, as he attempted to sit up. The attendant was quick to assist him. Acknowledging his despair, he rubbed his face with both hands, unsure of what he should say. "I don't understand," he said softly. "I thought he was doing better, that . . . there was a fragment of hope he might make it."

Dr. Bales sat next to him on the couch. "That hope still exists—he can still survive this, but as you know, his quality of life has taken a turn for the worse."

Matthew quickly left the couch and stood by the window. The snow continued to fall, weighing heavily on the pine boughs. He was reminded of Andrew's affinity for such wintry landscapes, the cold serenity and beauty of the snowy forest or fields or mountain, void of life, permeated with the solitude of self-imposed isolation. 'He'll never see this again,' he thought. 'Never.' It would have been easy for Matthew to simply submit to his emotions, to grieve openly and be consoled; however, he fought desperately to maintain control. He needed to know as much as possible about Andrew's prognosis. He turned to face Dr. Bales.

"You mentioned quality-of-life. What are his chances of living as 'normal' a life as possible?"

It was a question Dr. Bales would have preferred not to answer, at least, not yet. He moved from the couch to the table. "Specifics are more difficult than probabilities—in general, he will face ongoing medical obstacles, as we've already witnessed with his sight and hearing. Depending on his threshold for pain, even with medication, I doubt that he will be completely comfortable or totally pain-free. And it is still too early to predict the extent of his range of motion and ambulation potential."

"It sounds as though he'll be bed ridden." Matthew nearly choked on the word.

"I'm not saying that," Dr. Bales exclaimed. "He may walk—with limitations. It depends largely on Andrew,"

"His motivation?"

"That and the reason he's here. His mental status will also be an important factor."

Matthew shrugged. "You're talking about his psychiatric condition."

Dr. Bales nodded. "Yes. That poses tremendous problems regarding treatment and therapy, particularly now that his sight and hearing are impaired." He stood up and walked toward Matthew. "I'm incredibly sorry to have to share this with you; I wish I had something more positive to say."

Once again, Matthew turned to face the window. With the natural light rapidly fading, he was able to see his own reflection in the glass, a montagelike image intertwined with snow-covered boughs—an anguished composite of the wrong person. He knew that this was Andrew's world.

* * *

Andrew was barely aware that someone had entered the room and stood by his bed. He saw various shades of grey shapes and could still hear, yet he seldom understood an entire sentence or recognized his observer. It wasn't until Matthew gently squeezed his hand when the familiar became obvious. Andrew took a deeper breath than usual and slowly exhaled.

"You're right—it's me," Matthew said. He leaned closer to Andrew's ear. "Can you hear me all right?"

Andrew blinked two quick blinks for yes, paused, and then blinked once for no.

"A yes and a no. Does that mean it's harder to hear me?"

Once again, Andrew blinked twice.

"Then I'll moved even closer," Matthew said. He looked around for Andrew's pad of paper, saw it sticking out from under the sheet, and turned it over. The nurse had thoughtfully attached the pen to the wire binding with string. Just as he had feared, Matthew saw what looked like a second letter "L," scratched painfully after the first. In a period of almost two months, Andrew had nearly completed the word "KILL" in barely decipherable letters.

A conspicuous shudder ravaged Matthew's body. It didn't matter if that was the entire message or only a part of it—it may as well have been written in neon. For Matthew, the message was frighteningly clear. He sat in silence and momentary denial, thinking of possible completions to the sentence. Kill who? Dr. Bales? Kill everyone at the monastery? Kill yourself? He could not tolerate the sentence ending with the word "ME," yet on his next visit, he was painfully aware that Andrew had managed to write what looked like an inverted "V"—one half of the letter "M." His request was impossible to deny, his reason too easily imagined.

Once again, he leaned closer to Andrew, who almost always appeared to be staring straight ahead. "Would it be okay if I asked you about your notepad?"

Andrew blinked twice.

"The word that you are in the process of writing—is it "ME?"

Again, two blinks.

The admission essentially broke Matthew's reserve, as he was overwhelmed with sadness, pain, and the realization that both of them were fully aware of the hopelessness and incessant torture that Andrew would continue to endure. Andrew's hell had, in fact, materialized on earth. Matthew let his head drop next to Andrew's, as tears soaked his pillow—his anguished cries were only partly muffled, his body heaved with total despair.

Moments later, he could feel someone's hand on his shoulder.

"I'm sorry, Matthew, but Andrew's vitals are about to set off the alarm. It would be better if you could give him some space and time to calm down."

He looked up to see the attendant who had helped him earlier when he passed out in Dr. Bales's office. With a slight nod, Matthew slowly backed away and stood up.

"I'm really sorry, man," the attendant repeated.

"I know," Matthew whispered. When he passed the nurses' station, he could sense that he was being observed, yet somehow, he knew that it was with complete absence of malice.

* * *

The single unexpected gunshot shattered bone and silence, spattered the white wall red, and momentarily stunned the staff, who then quickly responded to the grisly scene unfolding before them. Attendants were the first to arrive, followed by numerous professional staff. They watched as Matthew wept, kneeling by Andrew's bed. His back faced them; the gun remained in his right hand, hanging loosely near his thigh. Through his tears, he kept repeating the same phrase, "Oh, God, oh, God!" At the very moment, when Matthew began to slowly raise the weapon, the attendant bolted across the floor, wrestled him from behind, and successfully shook the gun free. Matthew offered no resistance, no denial. He simply collapsed in the attendant's arms.

* * *

Epilogue

The obvious word that comes to mind is despair, an emptiness which galvanized friends, family, and the monastic community into one, as only death can do.

Of course, there was a funeral, after a brief legal battle with Andrew's aunt, Maris, and the powers-to-be at the monastery. She refused to allow Andrew to be simply thrown into a hole, unprotected, with no coffin—and, of course, she won.

It was a humble service, held in Bolton Landing in mid-March. Spring was barely noticeable; most of the Adirondacks were still snow-covered, yet the streams were already swollen with runoff.

Even though they would later have a memorial service of their own, several members of the monastery flew east, including Father Luke, Brother Mark, Brother Nathan, Father Gerald, and even Dr. Klein, who insisted on assuming all financial costs for the trip. Perhaps it was a small gesture to help alleviate some of his self-imposed guilt, which, sadly, continued to trouble him throughout his career.

Although Brother Joshua asked to be able to attend the funeral, the abbot denied his request. Approximately one month later, Brother Joshua decided to leave the monastic life.

Still unsure of his role in life, Brother Kevin recovered completely—except for mild facial scars—and remained at St. Anthony's where he eventually became prior.

Brother Mark died in the monastery at the age of eighty-four.

Brother Nathan asked to visit a Buddhist monastery in Japan and never returned. Instead, he married an exquisitely attractive Japanese woman, settled down in Osaka, and fathered four beautiful children. He continued with his medical studies and became a prominent pediatrician.

Andrew's death was particularly difficult for Father Gerald, who spent many hours with Dr. Klein, less as a colleague than client. He too died in the monastery in his eighties after volunteering many hours at the Halsen Clinic, where he learned to work successfully with young people who demonstrated a high risk of suicide.

Nick and Sara also attended the funeral—separately but together—with Nick's new life mate, Casey, a handsome college student who, most everyone felt, resembled Andrew. Sara finally stopped grieving long enough to marry a wealthy man, twenty years older than she.

And Maris outlived everyone, or so it seemed. Most believed she was totally preserved with Smirnoff's and would never require embalming. She buried Andrew's body on her expansive property overlooking the lake and the Sagamore, knowing how much he loved to play there, swim, and sail the old J-boat, which she left moored just off the dock. In the years that followed, she would make countless visits to Andrew's grave—never empty-handed—usually holding a glass of vodka for herself and a glass of tequila for Andrew, which she poured on the grave in front of the marble headstone. Every spring, the grass immediately yellowed in the same spot, never greening until the following spring, and then, only briefly.

Although tears were copious, Nick managed to lighten everyone's mood by mentioning that Andrew would have insisted on using Connie Francis's version of the song "Where the Boys Are" for the final procession out of the church.

And that leaves Brother Matthew, who was convicted of manslaughter, given a reduced sentence, and sent to a prison for serious offenders where he was brutally gang-raped and beaten. He died in prison, only two months after being admitted, at the age of twenty-six—the same age as Andrew. No one, not even his immediate family, attended the stark prison service.

CPSIA information can be obtained at www.ICGtesting.com
Printed in the USA
LVOW070123271211

261150LV00002B/5/P